MEDITERRANEAN WILDLIFE

D1630986

THE ROUGH GUIDE

THE ROUGH GUIDES

OTHER AVAILABLE ROUGH GUIDES

FRANCE • PARIS • PROVENCE • BRITTANY & NORMANDY
ITALY • VENICE • SICILY • SPAIN • THE PYRENEES
PORTUGAL • HOLLAND, BELGIUM & LUXEMBOURG
AMSTERDAM • IRELAND • WEST GERMANY • BERLIN
SCANDINAVIA • GREECE • CRETE • YUGOSLAVIA • HUNGARY
EASTERN EUROPE • MOROCCO • TUNISIA • KENYA
ZIMBABWE & BOTSWANA • ISRAEL • CHINA • MEXICO
BRAZIL • PERU • GUATEMALA & BELIZE • NEW YORK
CALIFORNIA & WEST COAST USA • WOMEN TRAVEL

FORTHCOMING

WEST AFRICA • TURKEY • EGYPT • NEPAL • HONG KONG

ROUGH GUIDE CREDITS

Series Editor: Mark Ellingham
Editorial: Martin Dunford, John Fisher, Jack Holland, Jonathan Buckley
Production: Susanne Hillen, Kate Berens, Andy Hilliard
Typesetting: Mark Ellingham, Greg Ward, Gail Jammy
Series Design: Andrew Oliver

Many **thanks** for help, advice, manuscript-reading and contributions to:
    Max Gallardo and Jo Weightman (France)
    Mike Smart, Thierry Gaultier, H'maied Kouki and Mike Tulloch (Tunisia)
    Tim Jepson and John Wilson (Italy)
    Alison McNaughton, Alan Ree and Albert Watson (Greece)
    Mark Beaman and Dave Bangs (Turkey)
    Hamish Brown and Neil Williams (Morocco)
    Brian Dudley (Yugoslavia)
and to Joyce Pitt for sharing botanical knowledge, to Mark Ellingham for his encouragment throughout,
and, above all, to Fanny Richmond for her love and support.

The publishers and authors have done their best to ensure the accuracy and currency of all the information in
The Rough Guide: Mediterranean Wildlife; however, they can accept no responsibility for any loss,
injury, or inconvenience sustained by any traveller as a result of information or advice contained in the guide.

Published by Harrap Columbus, Chelsea House, 26 Market Square, Bromley, Kent BR1 1NA

Typeset in Linotron Univers and Century Old Style.
Maps by David Mason and Dominic Beddow of Draughtsman Ltd.
Printed by Cox & Wyman, Reading, Berks

The illustrations for each "Part dividing" page are by Henry Iles; all line drawings by Tessa Lovatt-Smith

384pp
includes place index

British Library Cataloguing in Publication Data
    Raine, Pete
    Mediterranean Wildlife.
    1. Mediterranean region. Organisms 2. Mediterranean region – Visitors' guides
    I. Title II. Series
    574.909822

    ISBN 0-7471-0099-3

MEDITERRANEAN WILDLIFE

THE ROUGH GUIDE

Written and edited by

PETE RAINE

with

Nigel Dudley (Yugoslavia), **Teresa Farino** (Spain),
Chris Gibson (Portugal), **Gerry Matthews** (Yugoslavia),
Chris Overington (Morocco and The Balearics)
and **Mark Walters** (Italy)

Illustrations
TESSA LOVATT-SMITH

Rough Guide editors
MARK ELLINGHAM and JONATHAN BUCKLEY

HARRAP-COLUMBUS ■ LONDON

CONTENTS

INTRODUCTION

T he fertile shores and temperate climate of the **Mediterranean** – the goal of a summer migration of over 100 million visitors – have supported human populations since well before recorded history. Over a rather longer time scale, wildlife has found the area equally attractive, and it flourishes today in a dense, compelling diversity. Strangely shaped orchids and colourful anemones turn the spring hillsides into a riot of colour; prehistoric-looking lizards and tortoises soak up the sun and scuttle around the bushes; millions of birds pass through on their shuttle between Africa and northern Europe; and scarce animals like bears and wolves hang on in the untouched forests of the mountains.

This book aims to bring the humans and wildlife of the Med closer together. As well as pinpointing the locations of the more exotic birds and plants, I have tried to explain the relationships of the whole range of species, both amongst themselves and with humans. The region faces a depressing variety of threats to its nature – from building, intensive agriculture, pollution on sea and land, and hunting pressures from gun-happy local residents – and in our enjoyment of the bird, plant or marine life, in particular, there is no cause for complacency. The more that the Med's visitors and residents appreciate and understand the wildlife, however, the more hope there is that the governments will see the benefits of conservation and ecology.

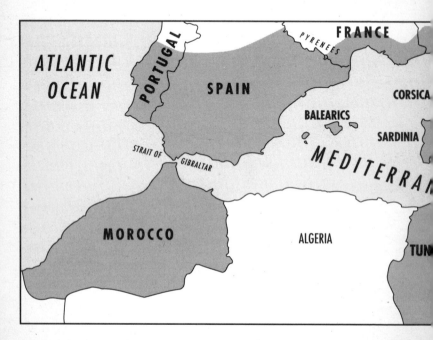

Like many naturalists, my own interest in wildlife began as a kind of "stamp collecting", concerned with what each species was, whether I had seen it before, and whether it was rare so that I could brag about it to my friends. But in thirty years of wildlife-oriented holidays and travels, I have become increasingly interested in the way the whole business hangs together – why a particular species occurs in one place and not in another; where it has come from both in time and space; what it is doing; and how it makes its living – in short, the science of ecology. An ecological perspective, therefore, has found its way into most of the accounts that follow, and I have tried to describe the wildlife in a way that will enable travellers to understand at least the basics of wildlife interaction, as well as providing all the practicalities on the best places for viewing.

The book begins with a guide to the most common groups of species of plants and animals that are likely to be encountered. Even though the Med is a huge area, the whole region is bound by common threads of geology and climate. An iris or a lizard in southern Spain may well be a different species from its counterpart over on the Turkish coast, but it fits into this framework easily enough. Some of these individual sections will be old hat to the experienced birder or naturalist, but as most people are specialists to some extent, I hope there will be something new for most people. The Med is an ideal place to cross boundaries of interest – to look at marine life as well as birds, for instance, or reptiles as well as flowers.

The greater part of the book consists of a country-by-country guide to nine Mediterranean nations, highlighting what to see, where to see it, and how to get to the specific sites. It's written mainly with the independent traveller in mind, but the places covered are usually within reach of mainstream resorts, so the information should be equally useful for anyone roving out from a package holiday.

AREAS COVERED IN THE GUIDE

The area chosen covers, as far as possible, the zone of "Mediterranean vegetation" and is shown on the map on the previous page. The southeast of the region, from Syria around to Libya, has been excluded on ecological grounds, since it is markedly different in flora and fauna, owing more to the desert influences of the Middle East than to the Mediterranean.

Sometimes I have strayed outside my brief. The Alpes Maritimes of France and the deserts of southern Tunisia, for example, are not really Mediterranean, but they are so close that it seems natural to include them; Portugal, too, though an Atlantic nation, shares many features with the Med. Two countries within the chosen zone have been left out for pragmatic reasons: Albania, because of the difficulties of visiting its wildlife sites (at least at present), and Algeria, as it is little visited and wildlife information is sparse. Paradoxically, the isolation of these two countries means that they may hold some of the best wildlife of the entire region; if anyone knows them well, I'd be interested in coverage for forthcoming editions.

Wildlife information on the Med's plants and animals has a long tradition, dating back to Aristotle, who was recording what he saw two thousand years ago. Much of our knowledge, however, is due to the painstaking work done by amateurs over the last couple of centuries, and in particular to such figures as Tony Huxley and the late Oleg Polunin. There is still much to be discovered. If you can record the wildlife you see on your visit, please send it to the relevant conservation organisation in the country concerned, details of which appear at the end of each chapter; only on such knowledge can a realistic conservation strategy be based.

Pete Raine, Spring 1990.

THE NEXT EDITION: UPDATES

We've based this book on a fair few years of wildlife enthusiasm and wandering – and plan to put in a number of fresh research trips for a **new edition** in a couple of years' time. For the preparation of that second (and we hope much-expanded) book, we would enormously appreciate feedback from users. If you spot any errors or omissions, or information which may have changed since publication, please let us know. Any comments you might wish to pass on would also be welcome; I would be interested to know how useful you find certain features, such as the maps and the "Access and Accommodation" details at the end of each section.

All contributions will be credited in print, and a copy of the next edition (or any other Rough Guide if you prefer) is the reward for the best letters. Please write to:

Pete Raine, The Rough Guides, 149 Kennington Lane, London SE11 4EZ.

PART ONE

THE

SPECIES

THE BASICS

Much of the pleasure of observing wildlife comes from understanding its place in the ecology of the area – in other words, what it does and why it's there. This understanding depends on the observer's ability to categorise the plant or animal correctly, and in providing a key to the major wildlife groups of the Med, this section of the guide will make **identification** far easier. The general naturalist does not need to place an exact label on everything seen. Of course, someone doing a scientific study needs to know that the little yellowish bird darting around the tamarisk bushes is a Bonelli's warbler *Phylloscopus bonelli*, but for the lay person it's enough to know that it belongs to the family of leaf warblers, that it migrates from Africa to its breeding grounds in southern Europe, and that it eats insects.

Bonelli's
warbler

Being a generalist has its advantages as well. A winter visit will disappoint a butterfly specialist, but to the generalist every region is fascinating, at every time of the year. A high-summer visit will miss the glorious spring flowers, but it's the best time of the year to see butterflies and marine life. There aren't so many insects in the autumn – but then there's the return migration of birds from northern Europe to Africa. The secret of an enjoyable trip is to **travel light**. If you were to take enough field guides to identify all the animals and plants of the region, you'd use up your baggage allowance with books – it's more of a holiday to relax about identification, and just be able to put a name to a few species, and a general group on the rest.

CLASSIFICATION

To get the most from watching wildlife, a grasp of **classification** is an essential tool, as this framework of species indicates how groups of animals and plants are related to each other, and hence how they have evolved. Living things on this planet are divided into **kingdoms**. There is some disagreement amongst scientists about how to deal with some organisms – are bacteria plants or animals, for instance, and how does one classify a virus? – but as far as the average naturalist is concerned, there are two categories: the **animal kingdom** and the **plant kingdom**. Plants are generally green, don't move around, and tend not to eat other living things. Animals, by contrast, are usually mobile, and do eat other living things – either plants or each other.

Each kingdom comprises a vast number of **species**. No one knows how many species of living things there are in the world – certainly millions, perhaps tens of millions. It's impossible to be precise, anyway, since there is no foolproof definition of the term; living things, by their very nature, resist rigid classification and there is an exception to virtually every rule. As a working generalisation it can be said that a species is a population or set of populations of identifiably similar organisms, which actually or potentially interbreed. Species are often divided into **subspecies**, but here the issue gets hideously complex, and is best left well alone, except to observe that different subspecies are often on the way to becoming so different that they cannot interbreed, and will eventually become a full species – evolution in progress.

Closely related species are grouped into **genera** (singular **genus**); similar genera are grouped together into **families**. Jays and magpies, for instance, belong to the crow family *Corvidae*, and thyme and rosemary are both in the mint family *Labiatae*. Families have common characteristics: all members of the mint family, for example, have lipped flowers, square stems, and leaves which come off the stem in pairs. So a clear description of a plant or animal will often enable you to work out its family, and then its species.

Families in turn are grouped together into **orders**. The crow family belongs to the very large order of perching birds *Passeriformes*, as do warblers, buntings, finches and many other families. The mint family belongs to the dicotyledon order, that is, plants that have two leaves on the initial seedling, along with other plant families such as roses, buttercups and cabbages.

Orders are combined into **classes**. The order of perching birds is lumped in with all the other bird orders to form the class of birds, *Aves*. The dicotyledons join the order of monocotyledons – plants with just one seedling leaf, such as grasses or lilies – to form the class of angiosperms, plants that have seeds enclosed in an ovary.

Classes in the animal kingdom join together to form **phyla** (singular: phylum). Birds have backbones (and hence are called vertebrates) and so

they are combined with all the other vertebrate classes – mammals, reptiles, amphibians – to make the phylum *Chordata*. (Or, to be pedantic, they constitute the subphylum *Vertebrata* which merges with other subphyla to form the phylum *chordata*.) This phylum then joins the other 25 or so animal phyla – sponges, molluscs, segmented worms – to make up the entire animal kingdom.

The conglomerations of plant classes are not actually called phyla, but they are lumped together in much the same way as classes in the animal kingdom. Thus the angiosperms join with the gymnosperms (see "A Botanical Vocabulary", below) to create the seed plants *Spermatophyta*. This guide deals in detail only with these seed plants, although the plant kingdom also includes the ferns *Pteridophyta* and the mosses and liverworts *Bryophyta*.

SCIENTIFIC NAMES

Nearly all birds and mammals have a generally accepted English name, and so their scientific names have been confined to a zoological index on p.369. For other forms of wildlife, however, there is often no alternative to the Latin or Greek terms, as innumerable species have either no common English name or no commonly accepted one. Until recently, naturalists used to invent their own English name if none existed, resulting in endless confusion. If a common English term doesn't exist, we have simply used the scientific name with a descriptive English prefix, for example "a spurge *Euphorbia acanthothamnos*".

Scientific names are not as daunting as they first appear. Invariably they have two parts: the first – the **generic** name – signifies a group of closely related species, and the second – the **specific** name – describes the species. They are useful for two main reasons. Firstly, they give a clear indication of the **relatedness** of species in a way that the common English names don't. For example, the shrubs butcher's broom *Ruscus aculeatus* and Spanish broom *Spartium junceum* are not botanically related, as their scientific names show – they share an English name simply because both were used to make brooms. Conversely, the common names of the blackbird

Turdus merula and song thrush *Turdus philomelos* don't show the closeness of their relationship, whereas their scientific names do. Incidentally, the song thrush is a good example of the descriptive specific name, *philomelos* deriving from the Greek *philos* (lover) and *melos* (song).

The other useful aspect of scientific names is that they are **international**. It is chauvinism in the extreme to expect a Dutch ornithologist to know that the bird that he or she calls a *slechtvalk* happens to be called peregrine falcon in English, but both of you might perhaps know it as *Falco peregrinus*.

An **abbreviation** used throughout is **sp.** (plural: **spp.**) for species. The singular is used for a species that has not been precisely classified, as in "a tiny bellflower *Campanula sp.* grows around here". The plural is used for a group of similar species, either when referring to the group in general or when their precise identity is not established – eg "cuttlefish *Sepia spp.* have 10 tentacles..."

Unfortunately, even scientific names are not infallible. Research is constantly going on, leading to renaming and reclassification. The most recent scientific names have been used, but a few are bound to become out-of-date.

PLANTS

> To talk casually
> About an iris flower
> Is one of the pleasures
> Of the wandering journey.

From *The Records of a Travel-worn Satchel*, by the Japanese poet Basho.

All wildlife starts with plants. They trap the energy of sunlight, converting it into the starches and sugars on which all herbivores – from insects to grazing animals – depend. Occupying the bottom of the food chain, plants make up the vast majority of the **biomass** – the living weight – of the planet. It's a kingdom of such complexity that even the plant life of the Mediterranean is too rich to be fully tabulated. There are, for instance, over 10,000 species of flowering plants in Europe – excluding lower plants such as mosses and ferns – and at least three-quarters of these are found in the Med, a testimony to its variety of habitat and its fertility throughout the ice ages that so affected northern Europe. This section is therefore just an introduction to the diversity of Mediterranean plants, setting up a framework into which individual species can be categorised.

The flowering plants of the Med fall into about 150 families, of which we have concentrated on 25. These have been chosen because they are either typical of the area (like the olive), or conspicuous (like the rockrose), or extremely common (like the daisy), or in some way especially interesting (like the orchid family).

■ Where, when and how to look

Although all habitats have their characteristic plants, some are richer than others. The poorest habitats are those which have been disrupted by humans, through the introduction of agricultural crops or more drastic building developments. Field edges and wasteland can be rewarding botanically, but they have only a limited range of species – generally those annual plants that can exploit a rapidly changing environment.

Because **woodland** takes a long time to develop, it tends to build up a dense assemblage of plants. (This doesn't apply to commercial plantations, since the trees are planted very close together and the soil is disturbed during planting.) However, the foliage of trees excludes light, and so the greatest variety of plants is usually found growing on the periphery or in clearings. **Freshwater wetlands** are another rewarding habitat, owing to their resistance to intensive human use; the few remaining lakes and undrained marshes round the Med are particularly good flower environments. **Mountains** are especially interesting, because their often extreme isolation leads to the development of unique systems of plant life. Lastly, there's the typical Mediterranean landscape of hillside **scrubland**, consisting of areas of dense bush (*maquis*) and sparser zones of scrub, grass and bare soil (*garigue*). Although *maquis* and *garigue* are both products of human interference, the process is so long-established that plants have had time to adapt. The thin limestone soils of these regions is not conducive to vigorous growth, and therefore fosters a large number of species that struggle side by side, rather than just a few dominant species. Anemones, irises, orchids and rockroses make the scrublands a colourful sight in spring, and the bushes of thyme, rosemary and sage give these hot hillsides an equally memorable smell.

Most growth ceases in the hot Mediterranean summer, when plants shut down until the cooler, moister weather of the autumn. Spring and early summer see the peak of the Med flowers; by the end of May, most plants of the seashore and surrounding low hills will have finished flowering, although up on high ground and in the mountains plants carry on until July or even August. A few plants – especially bulbs – flower in autumn, but basically it's best to go between March and May.

How to **observe** a plant might seem self-evident, but it isn't. Identification is not just a matter of what a plant looks like – it can also involve noting what it's doing and where it's doing it. Is it growing by itself or with a mass of other plants of the same species? What sort of soil is it on? Is it putting its energy into a mass of short-lived flowers, or concentrating on a few hardier ones? Even the apparently simple process of recording a plant's appearance is complicated by the fact that some features are variable. Size, for example, changes with the climate and surrounding environment, and leaf shape can be variable too, though it is more reliable. The most consistent guide to identification is the **shape and structure** of the flower, since this is right at the heart of the plant's genetic programme.

BOTANICAL VOCABULARY

Jargon has been minimised in the accounts that follow, but as some is inevitable a brief survey of terms is needed.

Leaves are sometimes all clustered together in a **basal rosette** at the bottom of the plant, but more usually grow off the **stems**. A leaf with an unindented outline is said to be **entire**; otherwise the edges can be **lobed**, **toothed** or **cut**. The leaf shape might consist of a single form arising from the stem of the leaf – a **simple leaf** – or of a number of separate leaflets – a **compound leaf**. Three common compound leaf shapes are: **pinnate**, where leaflets come off the stem at right angles (eg ash); **palmate**, where the leaf is deeply lobed into the shape of a hand (eg horse chestnut); and **dissected**, where the leaf is finely cut in more than one direction (eg parsley).

Flowers are sometimes borne singly, and sometimes in bundles of two or more, called an **inflorescence**. Each flower consists of a central sexual part, and an outer part mostly concerned with protecting the centre and attracting pollinating insects. When the flower is in bud, it is enclosed by the **sepals**; below these, there are sometimes small leaves called **bracts**, which often grow up to surround the flower. After the flower opens, the sepals sit underneath or between the **petals**, which are normally the most colourful part of the flower. The number, shape and colour of the petals and sepals is an important aid to identification. Sepals and petals together are called the **corolla**.

In some plants the male and female **sexual parts** are contained in the same flower, in some they are in separate flowers, and in others (more rarely) they are carried on separate plants. The female **ovary** is protected deep in the heart of the flower, connected to the outside world with a long **style** tipped with a sticky **stigma**. The male pollen is held on **anthers**, which project from the base of the flower on **filaments**. Pollination occurs when pollen from the anthers is transported to the stigma, either by wind or by the agency of an insect. From the fertilised ovary comes the **seed**, which in most plants is protected in a sheath such as a pod, nut or shell; these plants are called **angiosperms**. More primitive plants, such as the coniferous trees and shrubs of the Med, bear their seeds within a cone that doesn't enclose them; these are called **gymnosperms**. The angiosperm/gymnosperm differentiation is one of the great dividing lines of the flowering plants. The other concerns the very first seedling produced by the angiosperms: some have two leaves – the **dicotyledons** – and some have one – the **monocotyledons**. Monocots, such as grasses and lilies, tend to have long linear leaves with longitudinal veins; dicots have more complex leaves and a network of crisscrossed veins.

A few final points. **Pick only the commonest flowers**, and pick the minimum – one flower and one leaf are ample for identification. **Never dig up a plant**, however common it may be. An invaluable piece of equipment is a **hand lens**; magnification to the power of ten will open up a whole new world. And if you intend to do some collecting, a supply of polythene bags will preserve specimens temporarily.

PINES; FAMILY *PINACEAE*

Pines are the most typical Mediterranean conifers, although the native forests have been widely replaced by commercial plantations. All pines have long, stiff needles in bunches of two or three; their cones can remain on the tree for several years before ripening. The **umbrella pine** *Pinus pinea* is a characteristic sight of the western Med in particular, upright when young, but maturing into the spreading shape which gives it its name. The **maritime pine** *P. pinaster* is widespread on acid or sandy soils, and has a reddish bark; the **Aleppo pine** *P. halapensis*, found on limestone soils, is a more slender tree with a silvery bark when young. The last two species have been an important timber source for centuries.

CYPRESSES AND JUNIPERS; FAMILY *CUPRESSACEAE*

Unlike the pines, the cypress and juniper family of evergreen conifers have leaves that are short, single and spiny, or are reduced to scales clasping the stems. The only cypress native to the Med is the **funeral cypress** *Cupressus sempervirens*, with dark green scale-like leaves; it comes in two forms, one spreading and one very thin and upright – the latter is commonly planted in cemeteries, perhaps giving rise to the common name. The cones are covered in five-sided scales, each with a central spine.

Funeral cypress
*Cupressus
sempervirens*

A shrub rather than a tree, juniper is commonly seen in one of three species. The **common juniper** *Juniperus communis* has needle-like leaves and green berries which turn black when ripe; they're used to flavour gin, and their smell when crushed is instantly recognisable. **Prickly juniper** *J. oxycedrus* is even spinier, with berries which turn brown when ripe; it's usually found in *maquis* near the sea. Finally, the **Phoenician juniper** *J. phoenicea* grows higher up on limestone hills, with fruit which turns red when ripe, and scale-like leaves.

BEECHES AND OAKS; FAMILY *FAGACEAE*

The fruit of the beech and oak family takes the form of a nut, usually single, often wholly or partly enclosed in a spiny shell. Catkins are the male flowers (sometimes inconspicuous), and the leaves are always undivided. The **beech** *Fagus sylvatica* is a well-known forest tree, usually growing on inland hills, with a characteristic silvery bark and a small nut enclosed in a bristly shell. In the eastern Med, especially Turkey, it gives way to the **eastern beech** *F. orientalis*, which is almost identical but has more veins on its leaves. The **sweet chestnut** *Castanea sativa*, another member of this family, has very long elliptical leaves with toothed edges, and a soft but very spiny husk around the edible nut. It's frequently planted around villages, but most specimens grow in mountainous forests, where they are felled for timber; chestnut is especially good for fencing, since its wood is durable and splits easily into posts.

Oaks are an essential component of Mediterranean scrub and woodland. The **Turkey oak** *Quercus serris*, a deciduous tree with large leaves of the classic deeply lobed shape, is restricted to the eastern Med. The sandy or acid soils of the western Med enable the **cork oak** *Q. suber* to thrive; its extraordinarily spongy bark – which enables it to withstand forest fires – has provided an economic resource for centuries. Some oaks are smaller than these, such as the **white oak** *Q. pubescens*, which also grows in the west of the region; it is identifiable by the tiny white hairs that cover its leaves. Certain oaks grow large if they have a chance, but will also grow as dense shrubs if grazed by livestock. The **holm oak** *Q. ilex* is one of them, an evergreen tree with leathery dark green leaves, sometimes spiny, more usually with a wavy edge. It's easily confused with the **Kermes oak** *Q. coccifera*, another important feature of the *maquis* scrub, but the latter species has spinier leaves and prickly scales on the acorn cup.

Kermes oak
*Quercus
coccifera*

PINKS; FAMILY *CARYOPHYLLACEAE*

The pinks are a family of mostly **herbaceous plants** – that is, annual or perennial plants without a woody stem. All members of the family have narrow, undivided leaves arranged in pairs on opposite sides of the stem. Typically, they have five pink or white petals, although each petal can itself be forked; the sepals are either fused into a tube below the flower, or come up between the petals, giving the flower a very "starry" appearance.

Over one hundred species of **true pink** *Dianthus spp.* grow around the Med, making precise identification tricky; the ancestors of our garden pinks and carnations, they all have a flat head of five pink or red petals, often fringed at the end. Other well-known members of the family are the chickweeds and campions. One of the most widespread **campions** in the Med is *Silene colorata*, a small plant with bright pink flowers that grows in abundance on cultivated land and especially on sandy soils by the sea. Its five pink petals are each lobed into two, and the whole plant is covered in tiny hairs. The **soapworts** – some species of which produce a lather when crushed in water – are an even brighter pink, often forming sheets of vivid colour in fields and by roadsides; *Saponaria ocymoides* is widespread in the limestone regions of Spain and France, whereas *S. calabrica* is commonly found in *garigue* and by the sea in the eastern Med.

Love in a mist
Nigella damascena

BUTTERCUPS; FAMILY *RANUNCULACEAE*

One of the most primitive plant groups, the buttercup family includes some of the most attractive and conspicuous flowers of the Mediterranean. The leaves are usually dissected, and the petals (normally five) often have a shiny surface, which makes their colour seem even brighter.

Not every member of the family has yellow flowers, and there are even examples of the **buttercup** genus that are not yellow. The **water crowfoot** group, found in still and slow-moving fresh water, generally have small white flowers held above deeply dissected leaves. A buttercup that comes in a range of colours is *Ranunculus asiaticus*, a species that grows in the Dodecanese – where it is bright scarlet – and Crete, where it can be pink, white or yellow. Closely related are the **pheasant's eyes** *Adonis spp.*, which have shining scarlet petals and feathery leaves, and can be found growing on lightly grazed pasture; they often have imperfect flowers, with one petal much smaller than the rest.

Some of the poisonous **hellebores** even have green flowers, a very unusual feature. Typical of the genus is the **Greek hellebore** *Helleborus cyclophyllus*, a large plant with divided flowers and nodding clusters of five-petalled green flowers. Though it's often grown as a garden plant, **love in a mist** *Nigella damascena* is not at all common in the wild, and is generally confined to bare or stony soils; it has blue petals surrounded by a crown of dissected leaves.

Clematis is found in a completely different setting, sprawling amongst the bushes and trees of the woods and *maquis*, especially on limestone soils. *Clematis flammula* is perhaps the most often seen, with very fragrant hanging clusters of white flowers; other species include the beautiful blue **alpine clematis** *Clematis alpina* of mountainous areas, and *Clematis cirrhosa*, whose large hanging white flowers are more commonly seen in the east. All clematis have feathery seedpods, a feature they share with the upland **pasque flowers**; most pasque flowers are deep purple, although some, like *Pulsatilla alpina*, are white.

Two of the most beautiful groups in this family are the columbines and the anemones. **Columbines** *Aquilegia spp.* are familiar from gardens, where they are cultivated in a range of colours; wild columbines are generally dark blue, their hanging petals topped with long spurs from the sepals – in some varieties, however, such as the Yugoslavian *Aquilegia kitaibelii*, the flowers are two-tone blue and white. Columbines tend to grow in woods and mountains, but **anemones** are more truly Mediterranean, and are one of the

Anemone
pavonina

most striking sights of the spring hillsides; look for them in open grassy places amongst the *garigue*, and especially on terraces, olive groves and roadsides. In the eastern Med, the **crown anemone** *Anemone coronaria* is a common sight, usually scarlet but occasionally pink or even white. Its stem leaves are dissected, in contrast to *A. pavonina* which has undivided stem leaves, and comes in a beautiful range of pinks, blues and purples. Both the above species have fewer than ten petals; other species, such as the blue *Anemone blanda* of Greece and Turkey, have up to twice as many.

MUSTARDS; FAMILY *CRUCIFERAE*

As their name suggests, a distinctive common feature of the mustards or crucifers is that their flowers are made up of four petals arranged in the shape of a cross. Beyond that it's a diverse group, including so many species that precise identification requires a specialised field guide and inexhaustible patience.

Two crucifers are particularly common around the whole of the Med seashore. One is **sea stock** *Matthiola tricuspidata*, a plant with grey felted leaves and lilac flowers; the back of beaches is its favoured habitat. In its vicinity you'll often see **Virginia stock** *Malcolmia maritima*, a low-growing annual with flowers in many shades of pink, red and purple, and usually found in a tight mass of plants. Both of these are ancestors of garden plants, as is the other widespread maritime crucifer, **sweet alison** *Lobularia maritima*, which has rounded heads of tightly packed white flowers.

Hills and mountains are the habitat of **burnt candytuft** *Aethionema saxatile*, a low annual whose terminal cluster of pink flowers rises from a blue-grey basal rosette, and *Aubretia deltoidea*, a plant of the mountains of Greece with magnificent large purple flowers.

PEAS; FAMILY *LEGUMINOSAE*

The peaflowers come in a bewildering variety of shapes, sizes and colours, and are one of the most important of all plant families, with hundreds of species in over thirty genera growing round the Med. As with the crucifers, exact identification is hard, but identification of the family is simplified by their distinctively shaped flowers. The peaflower shape is formed by five petals: one upright one at the top (a "standard"), two wings at the sides and two petals at the bottom fused together to form a keel. The fruit is normally the familar pod with seeds down its length.

The **everlasting pea** *Lathyrus latifolius*, with its striking large pink flowers, is scattered throughout the Med in fields, along roadsides and woodland edges. Some of the pea family (or legumes) have clustered heads of tiny pea flowers – the **vetches**, for instance. One of the most attractive vetches is *Vicia villosa*; the colour of its flowers changes as they mature, creating a gradation from blue at the bottom of the cluster through purple in the middle to pale purple in the unopened flowers at the top.

Clovers also have clusters of flowers, usually pink or white, and characteristic three-lobed leaves. The annual **star clover** *Trifolium stellatum*, a common wayside plant throughout the Med, is an unusual case – its flowers are nothing special, but after flowering the sepals turn red and open out in the shape of a star, surrounding a white-haired central fruit.

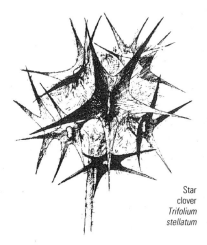

Star
clover
*Trifolium
stellatum*

Clustered flowers are also a feature of the **lupins**; *Lupinus angustifolius*, with its upright pale blue flowers, is a common sight in fields and stony places throughout the region.

Legumes are not all low-growing plants – some develop as shrubs and even trees. The many similar species of yellow-flowered **broom** makes them one of the most confusing groups of shrubs in the Med.

Calicotome
villosa

Calicotome villosa, native to the western Med, has dense clumps of yellow flowers and vicious spines; the **Spanish broom** *Spartium junceum* — found all round the Med, despite its name — is one of the few easily identifiable brooms, with very large pale yellow flowers borne singly on almost leafless green stems.

A dramatic sight in spring on the hills of the eastern Med is the **Judas tree** *Cercis siliquastrum*, its purple/pink flowers often blazing against a background of grey olives. It's so keen to flower that it often puts out flowers from the trunk itself. Legend has it that this is the tree on which Judas Iscariot hanged himself, which is why its flowers blush for shame every Easter. Another leguminous tree of the Med is the **carob** *Ceratonia siliqua*, with large leathery compound leaves and huge brown pods which hang like dried bananas from the branches in spring and summer. Rich in sugar, the seeds themselves are the source of an alternative to chocolate, and were probably the "locusts" that sustained John the Baptist in the desert.

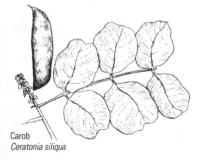

Carob
Ceratonia siliqua

GERANIUMS; FAMILY *GERANIACEAE*

One of the archetypal sights of the Mediterranean village is the house set round with cascading tubs of *Pelargoniums*, a common cultivated member of the geranium family, which flourishes in this largely frost-free climate. Geraniums have a common flower shape — five petals, usually red or pink — and a very distinctive fruit, with the seed pod below a long beak formed from the fused styles. Some geraniums are called storksbills or cranesbills after this feature. Geranium leaves are usually lobed, and often dissected as well.

Many geraniums are small annuals, often found on bare or waste ground. **Herb Robert** *Geranium robertiana* belongs to this category, a sprawl of small pink flowers and dissected leaves that turn bright red. It smells fairly unpleasant, and the story goes that Linnaeus, the great Swedish naturalist who first described it, named the plant after an enemy of his. Much larger geraniums include the **rock cranesbill** *G. macrorrhizum* of the eastern Med, with large blood-red flowers and protruding style and stamens. The storksbills are distinguishable from the cranesbills by their twisted "beaks"; the **common storksbill** *Erodium cicutarium*, which has small pink (sometimes blue) flowers, is a widespread example of the genus, found behind sand dunes and on other sandy soils.

SPURGES; FAMILY *EUPHORBIACEAE*

The spurges are an unmissable feature of the Med seashore and scrub. All have yellowish-green flowers in an umbrella-shaped cluster at the top of the stem, and undivided leaves which grow directly from the upright stem without a stalk. The stems exude a characteristic white sap when broken, evidence of their relationship to the rubber tree *Ficus elasticus*, a tropical member of the same family.

Most noticeable is the **tree spurge** *Euphorbia dendroides*, a woody shrub that reaches a height of two metres; a very rounded bush, it grows among shoreline rocks and on limestone hills, where it can become the dominant shrub. The stems are thick and sometimes reddish, and the whole plant often turns scarlet after flowering in the spring. A smaller but equally widespread plant is the **Mediterranean spurge** *E. characias*, growing to nearly a metre high with hairy, undivided stems and a bundle of green flowers with reddish-brown centres. One of the most attractive spurges is the *Euphorbia acanthathamnos* of the eastern Med; a low creeping plant with many-branched woody stems, it can be seen spilling over rocks in the Greek scrub, protected from browsing goats by its many spines.

CASHEWS; FAMILY *ANACARDIACEAE*

Only a handful of species belonging to the cashew family grow round the Med, but shrubs belonging to it are an important constituent of the *maquis*. One is the **mastic tree** *Pistachia lentiscus*, a dark green shrub with pinnate leaves that lack a terminal leaflet, and dense clusters of tiny reddish flowers. Like most members of this family, its leaves smell strongly, and its name comes from the mastic gum which can be made from the juice of its stems. The **terebinth** *P. terebinthus* looks similar, but has a looser flowerhead and a terminal leaflet; its leaves smell of turpentine, and an aromatic gum is processed from its bark. The edible pistachio nut comes from *Pistachia vera*, a related species from the Middle East, which has been widely planted in the eastern Med.

A third obvious member of the family is the **smoke bush** *Cotinus coggygria*, a low shrub of rocky limestone terrain, with rounded blue-grey leaves that turn a wonderful purple in the autumn. Its name comes from the mass of hairs which surround the tiny and tightly packed fruits; the overall effect resembles puffs of red or grey smoke amongst the foliage.

ROCKROSES; FAMILY *CISTACEAE*

The showy yellow, white or pink flowers of the rockroses are one of the most beautiful and most common sights of the Med. Because of the short lifespan of these flowers – some last just one day – an extraordinarily large number of them are produced, and the shrubby species are often surrounded by a litter of fallen petals. All species in this family have five-petalled flowers, simple leaves, and the fruit is held enclosed in the sepals long after the petals have dropped.

The species belonging to the genus *Cistus* (sometimes confusingly called just "rockrose" in English) are small woody shrubs up to a metre high, with either pink or white flowers. *Cistus salvifolius* is the most widespread, found right round the Med on both alkaline and acid soils; it has white flowers with a yellow centre, and soft

sage-like leaves. The similar *Cistus monspeliensis* is more common in the west of the region, and can be distinguished by its narrow sticky leaves with rolled edges. The pink-flowered species often have large flowers with petals that look as if they're made from crumpled tissue paper. *Cistus incanus*, found in the eastern Med, is typical of this group, with pink flowers and rounded leaves; in the western Med it gives way to *Cistus albidus*, an even more handsome shrub, with the same pink flowers offset against velvety grey leaves.

Cistus incanus

The *Helianthemum* species are best described as woody shrublets, being rarely more than 20cm high. Precise identification can be tricky: the yellow-flowered **common rockrose** *Helianthemum nummularium* is a widespread representative, but there are many similar species with white or yellow flowers. Things get even more confusing in the western Med, where a closely related genus called *Halimium* occurs, also with handsome yellow flowers.

UMBELLIFERS; FAMILY *UMBELLIFERAE*

Umbellifers are so called after their flat umbrella-shaped inflorescence (called an "umbel") – the familiar white flowerheads of cow parsley are a good example. They're not as dominant a family around the Med as they are further north, but still include some impressive plants. One is the **giant fennel** *Ferula communis*, with feathery dark green leaves and a thick stem up to two metres high carrying rounded umbels of yellow flowers.

It's found right round the Med on dry hills and waste land – especially areas that have suffered excessive grazing (it's left well alone by goats and sheep). On a much smaller scale, a white umbellifer common on roadsides and field edges is *Tordylium apulum*. An odd feature of this species is that its white flowerheads are symmetrical although the individual flowers are not: each flower has a mass of small white petals, plus one on the outside which is several times larger than the rest and notched in two. This gives the whole umbel an attractive frothy appearance. Its seed pods are equally distinctive, circular and with a milled edge; at first sight they look like a mass of small caterpillars.

One very untypical plant in this family is **sea holly** *Eryngium maritimum*, which grows on sand dunes and beaches throughout the region. It has beautiful pale blue-grey leaves, curved and spined like huge holly leaves, and the flowerhead is an oval compact mass of tiny blue flowers. Away from the sea, a number of other *Eryngium* species occur on dry or stony ground, with similarly shaped blue or green flowerheads, surrounded by a star of five or more spiny bracts, looking not unlike thistles. The alpine species, in particular, have very elaborate flowerheads and are extremely attractive.

HEATHERS; FAMILY *ERICACEAE*

The smaller heathers are sparse around the Med, but one species is notable – the **tree heather** *Erica arborea*. Growing up to three metres tall with terminal heads of massed tiny white flowers, it is widespread on acid and siliceous soils in the western Med. Each flower is shaped like a bell, a common feature of the family, and one that is shared by the **strawberry tree** *Arbutus unedo*. This is a small tree with large dark green

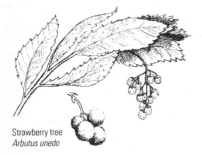

Strawberry tree
Arbutus unedo

oval leaves, and hanging clusters of creamy flowers. Its name comes from its attractive scarlet fruit, which look tempting but don't taste too good; "unedo" means "eat one", seeming to imply that one is enough. In the *maquis* and woods of Greece and Turkey its relative the **eastern strawberry tree** *Arbutus andrachne* is common; a bigger, larger-leaved tree, it often has peeling bark exposing a rose-pink trunk. Both strawberry trees, like the tree heather, are indicators of neutral or slightly acidic soils.

PRIMROSES; FAMILY *PRIMULACEAE*

Most families described so far have a common characteristic that enables a plant to be categorised fairly easily. The primrose family – embracing the primroses, cyclamens and pimpernels – unfortunately has no common denominator apart from the not very useful one that all their flowers have five petals.

True **primroses** *Primula spp.* are limited in the Med principally to wetter areas and higher ground. The "ordinary" yellow primrose *Primula vulgaris* is found region-wide, augmented by many other varieties, mostly with pink but sometimes white flowers. Species are often restricted to a small isolated area, such as *Primula kitaibeliana*, found only in the central Velebit mountains of Yugoslavia.

Of the related but physically dissimilar **pimpernels**, the annual **scarlet pimpernel** *Anagallis arvensis* is as common a wayside weed in the Med as it is in northern Europe, but here it is not exclusively scarlet – it's much more commonly deep blue, though both red and blue forms can be seen growing side by side. Of the same brilliant blue are the much larger flowers (up to 2cm across) of the perennial **shrubby pimpernel** *Anagallis monelli*, a beautiful plant found in the Iberian peninsula and north Africa.

Cyclamens look even less like primroses, with their five petals curiously reflexed in the shape of a nun's headdress. They're a typical plant of the Med spring, growing anywhere from rocky hillsides to pine forests, but usually in shade. Their heart-shaped leaves, sometimes exquisitely mottled, arise from a swollen tuber into which the plant retreats after flowering, which happens either in autumn or spring depending on the species. The pink-flowered *Cyclamen repandum* is a spring-flowering species, widespread in woods from France to

Turkey. *Cyclamen persicum* is the parent of the most of the cultivated varieties; another pink spring-flowering species, it has heart-shaped leaves marked in light green, dark green and cream, and is found in Turkey and the islands of the eastern Aegean. The beauty of cyclamens and the ease of collecting their tubers has led to their economic exploitation, with millions being dug up and exported to garden centres all over Europe. It has been estimated that 20 million have been exported from Turkey alone over the last ten years.

OLIVES; FAMILY *OLEACEAE*

Most of the trees and shrubs in the olive family have flowers in small terminal clusters, but they have two very different leaf shapes – compound in the case of ashes and jasmines, simple in other groups.

The **olive** *Olea europaea* itself is the most characteristic single plant of the entire Mediterranean, where it has been grown for so long that it is unclear whether it's a true native species or was introduced from ancient Persia. The wild and cultivated varieties are quite distinct. The wild olive – found on most Med hillsides – is a low spiny bush with small oval leaves growing from the stem in opposite pairs, and a small black fruit. The cultivated variety is a larger tree, and centuries of plant breeding have produced a heavier crop of larger fruits. Although cheaper vegetable oils have reduced the economic appeal of olive growing, olive oil remains one of the fundamental ingredients of Mediterranean cooking, and is becoming recognised as a healthy oil, with an extremely high proportion of polyunsaturates.

A closely related shrub that grows in the limestone *maquis* is *Phyllerea*, of which there are three very similar species. It's a bit like a small olive, with the same oval leaves, but its flowers and fruit are more tightly packed at the axils of the leaves (where they join the stem). **Jasmine** *Jasminum fruticans* is another small shrub in the same family, with glossy green deciduous leaves, each with three leaflets. It has groups of small yellow tubular flowers, but with only a hint of the heavy, sweet smell for which its tropical relations are famous.

The **ash** *Fraxinus excelsior* is a widespread woodland tree throughout the western Med as far as Yugoslavia, but a more frequent sight in woodlands and hedges is the **flowering ash** *Fraxinus ornus*, especially on limestone. It has the same pinnate leaf as the ash, but has conspicuous white flowers borne in clusters, initially upright but later hanging like pendants. The sweet smell of the blooms is usually undetectable as they hang high in the tree, which can reach twenty metres or so.

BINDWEEDS; FAMILY *CONVOLVULACEAE*

Scrambling across the ground or up trees and walls, most bindweed (or convolvulus) species are flamboyant plants, with large trumpet-shaped flowers in white, pink or blue. Waste ground, field edges and roadsides are their typical habitat – mostly annuals, they are designed for the rapid exploitation of a shifting habitat. The originally tropical *Ipomoea* genus is a good example, some species of which grow widely on the outskirts of towns and villages. **Morning glory** *Ipomoea purpurea*, commonly naturalised in Greece, is the most spectacular one, with huge flowers in deep blue or purple; a similar species grows near the sea in southern Spain.

Of the native species, *Convolvulus altheoides* is common, with triangular leaves and large pale pink flowers veined with darker pink; there are a number of very similar species. *Convolvulus tricolor*, however, has a very different flower, smaller and with a yellow throat to the trumpet, blue margin, and white in between; its beauty has made it popular as a garden plant.

BORAGES; FAMILY *BORAGINACEAE*

The borage family are herbaceous plants with rough and hairy foliage (except in one instance) and five-petalled flowers which often mature from pink to bright blue, though some species have hanging yellow flowers.

Typical of the blue-flowered types is **common borage** *Borago officinalis*, which has a star-shaped flower with protruding darker stamens; it's a tall annual plant of waysides and waste ground, widely cultivated as a herb for cooking. **Large blue alkanet** *Anchusa azurea* grows in the same habitats and is similar in size and shape; its flowers, however, are much smaller and more tubular, with a white throat contrasting with the blue petals. A more developed version of the tubular form is shown by the many species of **bugloss** *Echium spp.* whose trumpet-shaped blue or pink flowers have very conspicuous deep pink stamens. **Viper's bugloss** *Echium vulgare* is a common weed of cultivated or waste ground; very rough and hairy, it grows upright and can reach a metre or more. The blue or pink flowers of the related **forget-me-nots** *Myosotis spp.* are often carried on a curling, one-sided spike; the species range from small waste-ground annuals to larger perennials in the mountains, and it needs a real expert to identify them to species level.

A prevalent yellow-flowered species in Greece and the eastern Med is **golden drop** *Onosma frutescens*, a woody shrub which grows on walls and rocks, with masses of tubular golden flowers hanging down like droplets; related species grow throughout the Med. Unlike every other member of this family, the **honeyworts** *Cerinthe spp.* are almost hairless; found widely on stony field edges, they have rounded blue-green leaves which clasp the stem. *Cerinthe major* is one of the most handsome, the deep brown rim of its tubular yellow flowers making it look as if they have been dipped in melted chocolate.

MINTS; FAMILY *LABIATAE*

As their name suggests, members of this family generally have lipped flowers, but their most useful identifying characteristic is their square stem. Their leaves are in opposite pairs, and are decussate – that is, with successive pairs arranged at right angles to each other. Many are strongly aromatic herbs and shrubs, their essential oils – evolved as a deterrent to grazing animals – being the basis of their culinary value.

A herb of stony hill terrain, **rosemary** *Rosmarinus officinalis* has narrow dark green leaves and masses of small lilac flowers in spring; in the sunny Mediterranean climate it can grow to well over a metre high. **Sage** *Salvia officanlis* is another well-known culinary herb, with its pale grey oval leaves and spikes of blue or pink flowers; there's a mind-blowing variety of very similar species. An attractive annual sage is **red topped sage** *Salvia viridis*, which is widespread in *garigue* and old grassy terraces; it has inconspicuous flowers, but the bracts immediately below them are brilliant pink, red or violet.

Marjoram *Origanum vulgare* is a low plant with branched clusters of white or pink flowers; there are many more members of the genus, more common in the east than the west. Thymes are widespread, growing low on stony ground or in the mountains; the "ordinary" **thyme** *Thymus vulgaris* is a diffuse, very aromatic plant with white or pale pink flowers. Other species are more compact and have larger and brighter flowers, such as *T. granatensis* of the limestone mountains of southern Spain. **Hyssop**, **savory** and **basil** are three more culinary herbs from this family.

The commercial **lavender** used for perfumes is a cultivated derivative of *Lavandula angusitifolia*, with small grey leaves and dense spikes of small purple flowers. It grows throughout the region, as does the more striking **French lavender** *L. stoechas*, which has a tight cylinder of tiny flowers topped with large purple bracts.

French lavender
Lavandula stoechas

Jerusalem sage *Phlomis fruticosa* is a conspicuous shrub from France eastwards, with grey woolly leaves and large lipped yellow flowers held in rounded clusters above the foliage. Widespread on limestone hillsides is **ground pine** *Ajuga chamaepitys*, whose paired yellow flowers have a large lower lip; its narrow leaves do look a bit like pine, but its name comes from the resinous smell it gives off when crushed.

FIGWORTS; FAMILY *SCROPHULARIACEAE*

Like the labiates, many of the plants in the figwort family have two-lipped flowers, but this isn't a reliable distinguishing feature. The flowers of some species are small and inconspicuous, as in the case of the **figworts** *Scrophularia spp.* themselves, whose tiny dull purple flowers look like nodules on the side of a long stem. These nodules gave the plant its name, since they were thought to resemble the swollen glands of a person suffering from scrofula (also called "the king's evil", because the touch of the king was reputed to heal it).

The extended central lobe of the lower lip of the **foxgloves** *Digitalis spp.* is often spotted to attract pollinating insects into the nectaries deep inside the flower. In northern Europe the foxglove is most often pink, but there's a much wider variety round the Med, where brown, yellow and white flowers can be seen as well. **Mulleins** *Verbascum spp.* are as tall or even taller than foxgloves, their flowering spikes rising from a massive basal rosette of usually large grey woolly leaves; the flowers are yellow in most species, much more open and flat than other members of the family. Even so, a close look reveals that the bottom petal is larger than the others – the beginning of the lip that other figworts have.

The flowers of the **speedwells** *Veronica spp.* similarly are open, with an enlarged lower lip; though some speedwells are annuals, most plants are perennials, often with attractive blue flowers. The **spiked speedwell** *Veronica spicata* is a plant of the hills and mountains, with hundreds of tiny blue flowers packed into a dense terminal spike. The best-known flowers in this family, however, are the **snapdragons** *Antirrhinum spp.*; most are restricted to the Iberian peninsula, but the large *Antirrhinum majus*, with its large pink or purple flowers, is more widespread. Native to the western Med, it has become naturalised round the whole area, and is a common sight growing from walls and rock faces.

BELLFLOWERS; FAMILY *CAMPANULACEAE*

Bellflowers *Campanula spp.* are very striking and very common, with well over a hundred species around the Med, most of them endemic. The blue petals are fused together at the base into a corolla tube, flaring at the mouth to give the characteristic belled appearance. They often have a prominent style that protrudes in the centre of the flower, in a contrasting cream or white. They are the ancestors of many garden flowers, including the Canterbury bell.

Some are rock specialists, growing on vertical walls with an amazing density of big blue flowers up to 4cm across – the ancient monumental sites of Greece and Turkey are especially good for them. *Campanula laciniata* of southern Greece is typical of this group. Other species grow in meadows and resemble the harebell of northern Europe, their flowers held on very delicate upright stalks.

More robust types grow in woodlands or scrub – the common **nettle-leaved bellflower** *C. trachelium* for example, a tall plant with pointed and toothed leaves, whose flowers are held in leafy spikes at the top. In complete contrast there's the **annual bellflower** *C. erinus*, rarely more than a few centimetres tall, with tiny flowers only 3mm across. This plant almost needs a microscope, yet its flowers still conform to the perfect bell shape of its larger relatives .

A closely related genus is *Legousia*, to which belongs the **Venus's looking glass** *Legousia speculum-veneris*, a common annual of fields and waste ground. It's a simple upright plant, with shining blue or purple flowers on a slightly branched stem; the five petals are not fused at the base, giving the flower a considerably more open star-shaped appearance than the bellflowers.

DAISIES; FAMILY *COMPOSITAE*

Composites are the largest family of flowering plants in Europe, and well over a thousand species are to be found around the Med. They have a distinctive flowerhead of tightly packed little flowers called **florets**, of which there are two forms: **disc florets**, which are a tiny tube of petals with a fringed edge, and **ray florets**, which end in a long flat flap. Some species have only disc florets (eg thistles), others have only ray florets (eg dandelions), while a third group of composites, such as true daisies, feature both forms – disc florets in the middle and ray florets outside. Most species can be slotted into the family with confidence, although identification down to genus can be tricky, and down to species well-nigh impossible.

FLOWERS WITH DISC AND RAY FLORETS

The familiar **daisy** Bellis perennis flourishes in damp grassy places, and so is not fond of the dry Mediterranean zone. A more typical daisy-type flower of the eastern Med is the **Greek chamomile** Anthemis chia, a low annual with yellow disc florets and white ray florets, and oval leaves which are once or twice cut; this plant can turn the spring fields and olive groves of Greece and Turkey into a sheet of white. The closely related **yellow chamomile** Anthemis tinctoria, a taller perennial with yellow ray florets, is found throughout the Med; as its scientific name suggests, a yellow dye is derived from its flowers.

The **crown daisy** Chrysanthemum coronarium, a handsome tall plant with large yellow

Crown
daisy
Chrysanthemum
coronarium

flowers and feathery leaves, grows by tracksides and on waste ground; one variety has bicoloured petals, pale yellow on the outside, darker yellow in the middle.

This is another plant that can create a blaze of spring colour in fields which have escaped the herbicide spray. The annual **corn marigold** Chrysanthemum segetum is a related species, but much smaller, with leaves that are entire at the top of the stem but toothed at the bottom. Another annual is the orange-flowered **field marigold** Calendula arvensis, very variable in size and with shorter ray florets than the previous species; its characteristic bristly fruit is shaped like a sickle.

The **leopardsbanes** Duronicum spp. are a group of yellow composites that grow in shady spots in the hills and mountains. Mostly tall erect perennials, they have solitary flowers up to 5cm

across and normally have hairless heart-shaped lower leaves.

Typical composite species of the garigue are the **everlasting flowers**; Helichrysum stoechas is the most widespread, growing on rocky sunny places all over the Med. It's a low perennial shrub, much branched, with silver-felted narrow leaves and stems; the flower is yellow, small and rounded, and surrounded by papery bracts which persist long after the flower has died.

FLOWERS WITH DISC FLORETS ONLY

Thistles are the most obvious examples of disc-floret composites, and among the most beautiful specimens are the **carline thistles** Carlina spp., all of which have spiny stems and leaves, and yellow or purple flowers surrounded by two sorts of bract – inner ones that are often woody and closely surround the flower, and outer ones that frame it like a crown. The commonest species is Carlina corymbosa, up to 40cm high and with large yellow flowers surrounded by deeper yellow inner bracts. In the uplands, the **stemless carline thistle** C. acaulis grows on limestone grassland, its pale brown flowers growing directly from the rosette of basal leaves. In parts of France at least, it's commonly collected and mounted over doors as a good-luck charm.

Some Med thistles have large leaves that are heavily veined and blotched with white. Despite its name, the **Syrian thistle** Notobasis syriaca is common throughout the region on waste ground and field edges; each of its small purple flowers is surrounded by very long spiny purple-tinged bracts, and borne in clusters on tall stems that rise above the white veined leaves. The **milk thistle** Silybum marianum has similar leaves, but larger, solitary purple flowers; the young leaves and the leafstems are commonly eaten as a vegetable in north Africa.

FLOWERS WITH RAY FLORETS ONLY

The dandelion-like composites are an especially complex group. There are, for example, hundreds of species of **hardheads** Centurea spp., usually with flat, purple flowerheads and widely spreading outer florets; the brilliant blue flowerheads of the **cornflower** Centaurea cyanea, a common arable weed, make it one of the few readily identifiable ones.

The roots of many of these dandelion-type plants are edible. In fact, the roots of dandelion.

itself can be used as ersatz coffee, and its leaves are often eaten as a salad, although its French name of *piss-en-lit* reflects its diuretic properties. **Chicory** *Cichorium intybus* is another one with edible roots; it's a tall unspined plant of roadsides and waste ground, often growing to over a metre high, and with blue flowers growing all the way up its branched stems. The related **endive** *Cichorium endivia* is commonly cultivated for its tasty young leaves. The thick roots of **salsify** *Tragopogon porrifolius* are eaten as a vegetable; like all species in the genus, it has thin leaves and huge "dandelion clock" seed heads. A related species, **goatsbeard** *Tragopogon pratensis* has yellow flowers which close up in the afternoon; the closed bud is surmounted by a hairy tuft which gives the plant its common name.

LILIES; FAMILY *LILIACEAE*

The lily family, and the families that follow it, are monocotyledons – that is, plants whose first shoot has just one single leaf. All the preceding angiosperm families are dicotyledons, which have two-leaved seedlings. Plants in the lily family have undivided leaves growing from base and sometimes up the stems, and their flowers have three petals surrounded by three sepals, often coloured the same so that they look like six petals; they're all perennials, mostly arising from an underground bulb or corm. They're amongst the most attractive and colourful plants of the Med, well adapted for hot summers when they shrink back into their bulb.

The **asphodel** *Asphodelus aestivus* is a typical Med plant, with tall branched stems up to two metres high, bearing small white flowers streaked with pink. It grows from a large tuber, and is avoided by livestock; often it's the only plant left after everything else has been grazed out, and can therefore be an indicator of impoverished soils. Its smaller relation *Asphodelus fistulosus* grows on stony soils and tracksides, but is a much more delicate plant, growing to no more than 50cm.

Most readily identified by the garlic smell of their crushed leaves, the **onions** *Allium spp.* have white, pink or (more rarely) yellow flowers held in circular bunches at the end of the stem. *Allium triquetrum* is a widespread white-flowered species of the western Med, while the commonest pink variety is the beautiful **rose garlic** *Allium roseum*, which grows on grassland and road verges throughout the region, its flowers varying from pink to deep rose.

True **lilies** *Lilium spp.* are plants of the mountain woodlands and pastures, all with hanging colourful flowers with strongly recurved petals, giving a Turk's-head appearance. **Martagon lily** *Lilium martagon*, its deep pink or purple flowers dotted with black, is the most common.

Tulips *Tulipa spp.* are mostly mountain flowers, though some have adapted to grow as arable weeds. *Tulipa boeotica* is one of the latter, with large crimson petals blotched with yellow and black inside; it's often seen in fields in Greece and Turkey. The mountain species are found right round the Med, often low-growing with yellow or pink flowers; *Tulipa sylvestris* is typical, its yellow petals flushed orange on the outside. **Fritillaries** *Fritillaria spp.*, rather like tulips with hanging heads, are marvellously coloured with a chequering of green, purple or brown; this camouflage, together with their small size, makes them hard to find, but they're well worth searching for amongst the stony *garigue* and up in the hills all over the region. *Fritillaria graeca* is widespread in the eastern Med, but nowhere common; its flower is a mixture of purple, green and black.

Fritillaria graeca

Grape hyacinths *Muscari spp.* are familiar as garden plants, with their dense flower spike of tiny blue bell-shaped flowers. *Muscari neglectum* is the ancestor of the garden forms, found in a variety of stony and rocky habitats. The commonest of the genus, however, is the **tassel hyacinth** *Muscari comosum*, which has a spike of loosely hanging blue or brown fertile flowers topped by an extraordinary plume of brighter blue sterile flowers; look for it on cultivated land as well as stony places.

Smaller members of the lily family include the **stars of Bethlehem** Ornithogalum spp., mostly low-growing plants with clusters of white starry flowers, each petal having a characteristic green streak down the outside. A similar low-growing genus are the Gagea species, also with clusters of starry flowers, but in bright yellow rather than white.

Finally, three plants of this family are extraordinary in that they look nothing like the rest of the group. One is the climber Smilax aspera, twining up through the maquis shrubs with shining heart-shaped leaves, heads of inconspicuous flowers that mature into red berries, and evilly hooked spines on both stems and leaves. The second is **butcher's broom** Ruscus aculeatus, a shrub with small very tough "leaves" which are actually flattened stems, from the centre of each of which grows a single tiny flower. These "leaves" are spiny and robust enough to have been used to scrub down butchers' chopping blocks, hence the name. Lastly there's **spiny asparagus** Asparagus acutifolius, common on rocky limestone hills throughout the Med. The mature plant is a low branched shrub, its leaves reduced to scales and with a formidable combination of spines and stiff branchlets protecting it from grazing; the young shoots betray its origins, looking like long thin spikes of the cultivated asparagus.

DAFFODILS; FAMILY *AMARYLLIDACEAE*

Whereas the buds of lilies appear almost naked, those of the daffodil family are enclosed in a sheath of papery bracts that splits on flowering, and their leaves always grow directly from the basal bulb, never from the stem.

Daffodils and **narcissi**, both belonging to the genus Narcissus, are instantly recognisable, but the individual species are very variable and freely hybridise, making accurate identification almost impossible. **Poet's narcissus** Narcissus poeticus is one of the more straightforward, a widespread plant of damp meadows, flowering in spring with a short central yellow trumpet with red margins, and spreading white outer petals. Of the many species of **daffodil**, Narcissus pseudonarcissus has the familiar long yellow trumpet surrounded by a yellow ring of outer petals, and is also widespread around the Med – native in the west, cultivated and naturalised in the east.

One of the largest and most dramatic members of the genus is the **sea daffodil** Pancratium maritimum, whose huge white flowers blossom on sand dunes in late summer, often growing in large clumps.

The **snowflakes** Leucojum spp. look like large snowdrops, with their hanging white bell-shaped flowers tipped with green. Different species flower at different times – the **summer snowflake** Leucojum aestivum is one of the commonest, found in damp woods and grasslands all over the Med.

IRISES; FAMILY *IRIDACEAE*

Plants of the iris family also have leaves which arise from the base, but these often sheath the stem at the bottom before branching off higher up. The basic shape of the iris flower is complex and beautiful: one group of three petals (the standards) rises upright in the centre of the flower, surrounded by another group of three (the falls) bending outwards and downwards (each sometimes with a beard of hairs in the centre of the petal). To make the flower even more complicated, the styles are large and brightly coloured, and almost look like petals. The rhizomes – underground stems – are swollen and often break through the surface of the earth.

The **yellow flag** Iris pseudacorus is as common by rivers and freshwater marshes round the Med as it is in northern Europe; the tall sword-shaped leaves and yellow flowers are prominent in spring and summer. Of the many species found on dry land, Iris pumila of the eastern Med is one of the most handsome, a low-growing plant with large flowers that are usually purple but can be blue or yellow. The garigue and rocky hillsides of southern Greece, Crete and some of the islands, are the habitat of another large-flowered dwarf iris, Iris unguicularis, with pale blue flowers and a yellow beard in the centre of the falls. In the Iberian peninsula, look for the **Spanish iris** Iris xiphium, also pale blue with yellow beards, and growing to 50cm or more on damp ground in hills and mountains.

The **Barbary nut** Gynandriris sisyrinchium is a close relation of the true irises, and is found on bare and waste ground throughout the region. It tends to grow singly, not in clumps as the true irises do, and it's small, only reaching 25cm. Its flowers are a typical iris shape, ranging from pale blue to deep purple, and with variable amounts of white and yellow on the throat. A peculiarity of the species is the way their flowers open: sit down next to one in the noon sun, and you can actually see the inconspicuous spear-shaped buds opening in jerky movements, the whole process from bud to open flower taking less than an hour.

Not all members of the family have the archetypal iris shape. **Gladioli** are altogether more slender, and have showy pink flowers up their long spike. They are found sparsely in the *maquis* and *garigue*, but do best in cultivated fields, where they can be a serious agricultural nuisance. The flowers – much smaller than the garden varieties – are curving funnels, often with an elongated lower lip that is sometimes streaked with white. *Gladiolus communis* is a common example of the genus, joined by the very similar *G. segetum* in the west.

Gladiolus communis

Other obvious exceptions are the **crocuses**, a genus of mostly mountain bulbs that flower in spring or autumn, often on the edge of melting snowpatches or in Alpine meadows. Some species are narrowly restricted in their range, such as *Crocus nevadensis*, a beautiful pink or lilac species, endemic to the Sierra Nevada area

of southern Spain. Some are more widespread: the yellow *Crocus flavus* and the purple *Crocus veluchensis* are both found in hills and mountains from Yugoslavia to Turkey. On sandy soils by the sea, a crocus relative called *Romulea* can be found, with tiny purple flowers at ground level, surrounded by thin grass-like leaves.

ORCHIDS; FAMILY *ORCHIDACEAE*

Orchids are a large, fascinating and confusing family that contains over twenty-five genera in the Med region alone. They have long leaves (like most monocotyledons), often with longitudinal veins, and their flowers have three outer sepals which enclose the bud and three inner petals. The distinctive feature about orchid flowers is the great enlargement of the lowest of the three petals into a lip, which takes a bizarre variety of shapes and colours.

The growth of the individual orchid is mysterious. Each flower produces huge numbers of seeds too small to store food for the plant's first growth, and so have to extract nutrients from the soil, which they achieve with the help of a fungus of the mycorrhizal type. This fungus invades the seed, living off it while simultaneously providing it with nutrition – a relationship that seesaws back and forth in the fight for survival. Moreover, the seeds' sensitivity to soil conditions means that orchid populations can fluctuate from year to year, appearing and disappearing with bewildering speed. In some cases, the seeds lie dormant in the soil for many years before germination, and even then it can take up to ten years from germination before the first flowers are produced.

The name of the genus comes from the Greek *orchis*, meaning testicle, a reference to the double bulbous roots of some species. The belief that if a plant resembles a part of the human anatomy it must be beneficial for it has led to the orchid's being credited with aphrodisiac properties. You might see huge sacks of orchid tubers being collected in Turkey for this purpose.

What follows is a summary of the seven most obvious Mediterranean genera.

■ Genus *Orchis*

The *Orchis* species all have numerous small flowers packed into a spike, and basal leaves in a rosette at the bottom of the stem; any leaves up the stem sheath it closely. The enlarged lower lip of the flower is sometimes divided into three lobes, and always has a backwards-pointing hollow spike. Containing no nectar, this spike is a contrick for insects, which in probing it become coated with pollen; fortunately for the orchid the insect has no learning capacity, and so it flies off to search the next plant for nectar, and cross-pollinates it in the process. This technique of deluding insects is even more pronounced in the *Ophrys* species (see below).

Orchis is the largest orchid genus in Europe, its members growing throughout the Med in habitats that range from stony *garigue* to mountain woodlands. The **lady orchid** *Orchis purpurea* is typical, a robust plant of limestone soils growing

Lady orchid
Orchis purpurea

up to 80cm, but usually less on grassland and in woodland. Its top petals and sepals form a "bonnet" around the two black eyes of the pollen masses, and the lower lip is divided into two arms and a broad, pale pink skirt dotted with darker pink. The **naked man orchid** *Orchis italica* also lives up to its name, its lower lip deeply dissected to form two arms and two legs with a long central protuberance. It grows on dry stony soils throughout the Med, and is one of the commonest and largest orchids, with a dense cylindrical flower spike up to 10cm long. Most of the genus are pink-flowered like these two species, but some have yellow flowers, of which the **Provence orchid** *Orchis provincialis* is a common and widespread example. The flowers

are pale creamy-yellow, except for the lower lip which has a deep orange central streak with dark dots – a guide path for insects.

■ Genus *Ophrys*

The elusive *Ophrys* genus is the strangest of all the orchids. The slender stem supports just a few flowers, which are peculiarly shaped for a most bizarre reason. Most plants use the lure of nectar to attract the insects they need for pollination; *Ophrys* orchids instead imitate the insect itself, hoping to trick a male into copulating with their flower. They do this both by physical deception and by smell, putting out a scent which resembles the pheromones of many female insects. Having realised his mistake, the insect flies off to repeat his error with another flower, thereby cross-pollinating it. It seems that each species of *Ophrys* attracts only a single species of insect, a truly remarkable process of co-evolution from which the plant gains a lot and the insect nothing at all.

The dry hillsides and *garigue* of the Med are home to the greatest concentration of *Ophrys* in the world, and form a sort of genetic laboratory with species hybridising and changing all the time. A common feature of all *Ophrys* species is an enlarged lower lip, usually hairy, sometimes lobed or divided, and often with a shining blue or purple patch – the speculum — in the middle.

The **bee orchid** *Ophrys apifera* grows to a

Bee orchid
Ophrys apifera

height of 25cm, the number of blooms varying with the species, soil type and especially the weather. After a very dry winter, the plant may not flower at all or produce just one flower; in better conditions, it may produce up to a dozen flowers on each of three or four spikes. A particularly variable species is the **early spider orchid** *Ophrys sphegodes*, which flowers from late

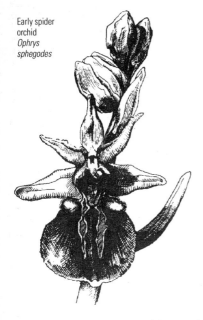

Early spider orchid *Ophrys sphegodes*

March in the south to early May on higher ground in the northern Med; it exists in a dozen named subspecies, which are sometimes regarded as full species. The spreading sepals above the lip are generally green or pink with a central green line, and the two upper petals growing between them are green or more rarely dark pink. The purplish lip is swollen and velvety, and the speculum is often H-shaped or reduced to two shining blue lines.

On the **mirror orchid** *Ophrys speculum* – found throughout the Med except for France – the speculum is fringed with hairs and is large, giving the whole lip a shining metallic blue appearance; it looks like it ought to be pollinated by a large bluebottle fly, but in fact its stooge is a small and obscure wasp. A final example of the genus is the **yellow bee orchid** *Ophrys lutea*, the only one to show much yellow on the flower; its upper petals

and sepals are yellow or green, and the usual blue speculum of the lower lip is joined to a hairy chocolate patch and surrounded by a broad yellow fringe. It's often the commonest *Ophrys*, especially in the eastern Med and north Africa.

■ Other orchid genera

Lacking elaborate flower structures, the genus *Cephalanthera* are amongst the most primitive orchids. The petals and sepals are large with pointed tips, growing in a bell shape. Of the seven or so species in this genus, the **white helleborine** *Cephalanthera damasonium* is perhaps the commonest, with white flowers and broad oval leaves growing off the stem. It grows in shade and woodlands, as does the **red helleborine** *Cephalanthera rubra*, a rarer but very beautiful plant, with bright pink flowers.

Two other orchids look as if they are *Orchis* species but aren't. The **pyramidal orchid** *Anacamptis pyramidalis* is the sole plant in its genus, with a slender stem and a dense pyramidal head of pink flowers, each of which carry a very long thin spur; it's a typical plant of dry limestone grassland throughout the region. The aptly named **giant orchid** *Barlia robertiana*, also the only representative of its genus, grows up to 80cm tall, with a very thick fleshy stem and large broad leaves; the flowers are variable in colour from green to purple, but have the characteristic divided lip with "arms" and "legs".

Some orchids do without photosynthesis, using instead a parasitic relationship with the roots of surrounding plants. The **violet bird's nest orchid** *Limodorum abortivum* – which has a large spike of purple flowers up to 50cm or more, and no green leaves – is a good example. Quite common in Mediterranean woodland, it always grows near pines or oaks, depending on mycorrhiza as its sole means of transporting nutrients from the roots to its own.

The **tongue orchids** *Serapias* spp., commoner round the Med than anywhere else in the world, are named after their lower lip, which protrudes from the cluster of other petals and sepals, and then bends downwards in a triangular tongue shape. This genus ranges in size from the small *Serapias lingua*, with pale purple or pink flowers, to the much larger *Serapias cordigera*, with fat red or purple flowers, each with a broad and very hairy tongue. Both species are widespread on grasslands in the west and central Med – the latter at its best in southern France.

BIRDS

Worldwide, there are around 8500 bird species, classified into some 27 different orders. However, as with most other groups of animals and plants, the majority of these species are concentrated in the biologically diverse tropics; in fact, only about **350 species from 18 orders** are regularly found in the Mediterranean, with an average of **70 species** native to any one area. Even avid "twitchers", charging around in a hired car in a desperate attempt to add just one more tick to their list, would do well to get near to 200 species in a two-week trip.

The birds regularly found in the Med fall into four categories. Obviously enough, **residents** are present all year round and breed in summer; a good example is the ubiquitous Sardinian warbler, found in scrub and open woodland throughout the year.

Sardinian
warbler

Summer visitors come north to breed in the Med from their wintering grounds, often in southern Africa; most summer visitors, like the bee-eater or the familiar swallow, are primarily insectivorous, and are moving around the globe to make the most of the seasonal emergence of their food supply. **Winter visitors** breed in northern Europe and Russia to take advantage of the insects and plants up there in summer, then are driven southwards in winter by the harsh weather. Many of these winter visitors are wading birds like the lapwing, which winters all over southern Europe wherever it can find suitable wetlands. The final category are the **passage migrants**, the great long-distance travellers. Millions of birds winter in Africa south of the equator, but breed in northern Europe and central and northern Russia. Many warbler species such as the willow warbler – the commonest warbler over most of northern Europe – leapfrog the

Sahara and the whole Mediterranean region en route to their breeding grounds. In fact, bird migration is so noticeable in the Mediterranean that it merits a section in its own right.

■ Migration

The extraordinary process of **bird migration** stems from the marked seasonality of the planet's temperate zones and from the fundamental law of ecology that states that if there is a surplus food supply anywhere on the planet, sooner or later it will get eaten by something. In northern latitudes there is an explosion of life in the spring, as the warmth of the sun and the increased length of the days stimulates plant growth, and in turn provides food for insect larvae. These larvae, together with the seeds and berries which have been preserved under the snow over the winter, provide an abundance of food, and the long hours of daylight give lots of time for foraging for it.

This **spare food** is the spur to migration, and the sheer numbers of birds involved gives some idea of how attractive these seasonal food sources are: in 1972 it was estimated that nearly **5000 million** birds cross the Sahara every spring and autumn. Migration strategy is crucial to the bird's survival. A swallow, for example, must leave its wintering grounds to make a 5000-mile journey northwards in time to arrive at the right moment in Europe; if it leaves too early it runs the risk of starving to death because the food supply is not yet in full swing; if it departs too late all the nesting sites will already have been taken and it won't have enough time to complete its breeding cycle, and go through a feather moult, before the cold weather of the northern autumn comes. The actual process of migration is in itself extremely hazardous – storms and predators lie in wait, and the journey crosses the foodless wastes of the Sahara desert, which from nearly all angles is over 1000 miles wide.

Amazingly, most **small birds** fly from the south of the Sahara to north of the Med (and vice versa) in **one flight**, feeding up before they fly to accumulate stores of fat. Studies done on sedge warblers in the Lake Chad area showed they virtually doubled their weight immediately prior to migration. For birds capable of flying these prodigious distances, the Mediterranean Sea poses no real barrier; most of them **cross at night**, flying in a broad front at high altitude. However, adverse winds or harsh weather can check them and bring them down around the Med; on the island of Paxos, off the northwest coast of Greece, thousands of migrating nightingales and blackcaps have been seen in April. Only a tiny percentage of the passage migrants actually stop over, though, and landfalls because of adverse winds are more common in spring than autumn.

Some **larger birds** have evolved a different flight strategy. Storks, pelicans and many of the large birds of prey such as eagles and buzzards depend on **soaring** rather than sustained flight for long distances. They spiral high on rising air currents and then glide to their destination, losing height all the time. This method has one big drawback – rising thermal air currents only occur over land, so water presents a hurdle on any migration route. So, in contrast to the broad-front migration of small birds, the larger species cross where the Med is narrowest, forming a "bottleneck" pattern. Thus there are three migration routes for these broad-winged birds: the **Straits of Gibraltar** for migrants coming into western Europe; the **Bosphorus** for birds coming up the Nile valley and then into central and eastern Europe; and the less-used gap between **Tunisia and Sicily** for birds coming up the middle route into central Europe. These routes are also used for the return autumn migration, which involves greater numbers (adults being joined by offspring) and is spread over a wider period of time (because the time of return is determined by local conditions at the breeding sites). Although smaller species constitute the majority of the passage migrants, the numbers of soaring birds at these bottlenecks can be staggeringly high. Nearly 100,000 honey buzzards passed over Gibraltar during the autumn migration of 1976, and 315,000 white storks passed through the Bosphorus in just six weeks of autumn migration in 1972.

■ Where and how to watch birds

You don't get good birdwatching by simply wandering around aimlessly, however good your eyesight. The first thing to bear in mind is that birds are **most active around dawn** and, to a lesser extent, **dusk**. An early morning walk can produce many more birds – and better views of them – than the same walk taken in the middle of the day. Secondly, the **habitat** is important. Mixed **deciduous woodland** is always good, and so is **fresh water**; **farmland** is very variable – big monocultural arable fields are poor, but small mixed farms, especially if they include pockets of woodland or scrub, can be excellent.

How you watch is important. Birds are easily scared, and you'll get better results if you give them a chance to get used to you, especially in woods or scrubland. When you come to a spot that seems to have plenty of birds, don't just walk through it, but sit down for half an hour – it's surprising how many will return. American birders are particularly keen on a technique called "pishing": you kiss the back of your hand loudly, the sound allegedly being attractive to small birds. It does seem to work sometimes; it can also lead to some strange conversations.

Always take note of what the bird is **doing**. If it's singing a full song from a prominent twig, for instance, it's probably breeding and holding territory. A bird carrying a beakful of food over any distance is almost certainly feeding young in the nest. You need to be aware that the significance of an action changes with its occasion: a bird skulking around the bushes in July making a plaintive noise may be keeping in touch with a family of its fledged young, whereas the same species making the same noise in April or October may just be migrating through. Finally, don't just use your eyes – **use your ears** as well. Even though it takes time and practice to identify birds by song and call notes, a beginner's ears can at least detect activity that's hidden from sight.

Migrating birds of prey

BINOCULARS

Naked-eye birdwatching is perfectly possible, but binoculars add enormously to the pleasure of watching birds. Serious birders come equipped with a whole armoury of binoculars and telescopes that not only cost a fortune but also weigh a ton. Most people don't need such paraphernalia, and modern binoculars can be both light and cheap.

Binoculars are described by the formula "A x B", where A is the magnifying power and B is the diameter of the optic lens in millimetres. An 8 x 40 pair, therefore, magnifies 8 times and has a lens diameter of 40mm. The wider the lens, the wider the field of view and the better the light-gathering power – but the heavier the binoculars. Any **magnification between 7 and 10** is fine, and ideally the ratio between the magnification and

lens diameter should be around 1:4 or upward of that. The *Jenoptem* 8 x 30, made by *Carl Zeiss Jena* (that's the cheap East German *Zeiss*, not the expensive West German outfit), cost around £45 and are fine for most purposes. A recent development are **roof prism binoculars**, which are extremely small, fitting easily into a shirt top pocket. They have a narrow field of view (eg 8 x 20) and aren't cheap, but they are wonderfully convenient.

Binoculars are useful for other wildlife too, especially butterflies and wary animals such as mammals or reptiles. And finally, be extremely cautious of **military zones**; you may know that you're watching birds, but the guards on the Albanian border won't, and they won't wait to hear your explanations before bundling you off in a jeep.

■ The sequence of species

What follows is a brief run-through of the 18 orders of birds you're likely to come across in the Mediterranean region. It should be regarded not as a substitute for a proper field identification guide (see p.367 for details of those), but rather as a key to the features that relate the species of each order. The **sequence** of the orders is the common scientific one, which is based on their evolutionary history. The more primitive birds are at the beginning, but this does not mean that the ones at the end are somehow more "advanced" – it's simply that the birds at the beginning stopped evolving longer ago, presumably because they became perfectly adapted for their particular ecological niche. All good field guides use the same sequence – divers are always at the beginning, perching birds at the end. Some older field guides (and some modern ones) arrange the sequence by habitat or even colour of bird, but since colour is subjective and birds move about a lot, this isn't very satisfactory.

DIVERS; ORDER *GAVIIFORMES*

The divers are large birds, found on the sea in the western Mediterranean in winter (especially a cold winter), having migrated from their breeding grounds in Scotland, northern Scandinavia and Greenland. As their name suggests, they dive for their food underwater. All three Mediterranean species are heavily built and streamlined, and their winter plumage is dark above and light

below. The commonest is the **red-throated diver**, the smallest of the divers; it has a distinctively upturned bill, and a grey head and red throat in summer, the overall plumage changing to grey above and white below in winter.

GREBES; ORDER *PODICEPIFORMES*

Like the previous order, the grebes also dive from the surface of the water, but are smaller, longer necked and dumpier in appearance. The **great crested grebe**, distinguished by the frilly crest of its summer plumage, is still a large bird, though. Resident in Spain, it breeds in small numbers on freshwater from France round to Turkey, moving to the coastal estuaries in winter, along with migrating birds from further north. The other three Med species are all medium size – though they are one of the smallest birds you're likely to see on the water – and only the **little grebe** commonly breeds. Like the divers, they live on freshwater lakes in summer, and concentrate in moderate numbers on the coast in winter.

SHEARWATERS AND PETRELS; ORDER *PROCELLARIIFORMES*

The **shearwaters** are closely related to the albatrosses, which they resemble in their gliding, stiff-winged flight, and in the strange facial feature of the two tubes that lie on top of their bill, enclosing each nostril. They are truly ocean birds, sleeping and feeding exclusively on the water, and only coming ashore to breed and feed their young, usually on remote rocky islands. Two species of shearwater occur in the Med. Commonest is the **Manx shearwater**, a medium-sized bird with a brown back and head contrasting with its grey underparts. **Cory's shearwater** is a larger bird and appears a uniform grey at a distance; it breeds only on rocky islands in the Mediterranean and a few isolated Atlantic islands. As a rule they are most easily spotted from boats out at sea, although huge flocks can sometimes be seen close to land on their way to breeding grounds, as at Cap Bon in Tunisia.

Petrels are also oceanic birds with a "tube nose", but are very much smaller than shearwaters and have a characteristic fluttering flight. Only one species is found in the Med, the **storm petrel**, a small bird that is completely black apart from a conspicuous white rump. It's usually seen in the open sea (it has a convenient habit of following ships), and rarely occurs east of Sicily.

GANNETS, PELICANS AND CORMORANTS; ORDER *PELICANIFORMES*

All the species in this order are large seabirds with webbed feet; they dive to great depths in order to catch fish, sometimes from a great height. The only Mediterranean representative of the family *Sulidae* is the **gannet**, a large white bird with prominent black wingtips and a wingspan approaching 1.5m. It's a spectacular fisher, diving into the sea from a height of up to thirty metres. Breeding in northern Europe, primarily around the British coast, it winters out on the open sea, coming into the Mediterranean as far east as Cap Bon.

Three species of the cormorant family occur in the Med. The **cormorant** and the **shag** are both large diving birds with long necks; shags are smaller, however, and have a crest in breeding plumage, whereas cormorants have an obvious white patch on their throat. Moreover shags are exclusively marine, while cormorants can often be seen on inland freshwater in winter. Both species breed in very small numbers in the Mediterranean, mostly on rocky islands; in winter their numbers are swollen by northern birds coming south from their breeding grounds. Most diving birds have very oily feathers, which prevent the bird from becoming waterlogged. This oil traps a layer of air under the feathers; shags and cormorants, lacking this layer of oil, can dive deeper because they are less buoyant,

but therefore have to spend a lot of time drying their feathers. They can often be seen standing motionless on rocks and posts with outspread wings. The other species in this family is the much scarcer **pygmy cormorant**, a much smaller freshwater bird found on lakes in the eastern Med.

The two Med members of the pelican family are the **Dalmatian pelican** and the **white pelican**. Both are quite unmistakable with their huge size, cumbersome flight and fleshy pouch under the beak; the latter species has whiter plumage than the former, and also has a black trailing edge to its wings in flight. Rare and becoming rarer, both breed on large freshwater lakes and coastal marshes; you're likely to see them only in Greece, Turkey and Yugoslavia. The drop in numbers – caused by drainage, persecution by fishermen, and pesticides – has been dramatic: the Danube delta population, said to number millions in 1873, had dropped to just 60 pairs by 1971.

HERONS AND ASSOCIATED SPECIES; ORDER *CICONIIFORMES*

Birds in this order are all medium to large, long-legged, long-billed and long-necked, catching their prey in shallow water. They tend to be colonial nesters, often settling in trees for safety from foxes and other predators, or in large reed beds.

The herons, bitterns and egrets – *Ardeidae* – constitute one family. There are two **bittern** species in the Med, but both spend most of their time skulking in reed beds and rarely show themselves except in flight. **Herons**, on the other hand, are common to most marshes and freshwater lakes and are frequently seen motionlessly waiting to pounce on a fish or frog, or flying slowly in a characteristic hunched position, with folded neck and trailing legs. The resident **grey heron** – a species distributed throughout Europe – breeds in small numbers in Mediterranean wetlands such as the Camargue and in Andalucia, with the winter population increased by migration from central Europe and Russia. By contrast, the **purple heron** is a trans-Saharan migrant, seen both as a summer visitor and passage migrant; slightly smaller than the grey heron, it is a much darker bird with a purple head and neck. The **great white heron** is a magnificent bird, the size of a grey heron but pure white with black legs; relatively scarce in the region, it breeds on some of the large lakes of Greece and Turkey, but wanders quite widely round the eastern Mediterranean in winter.

Four smaller heron and egret species are to be seen in the Med, though none is common; all are basically trans-Saharan migrants and summer breeders. The **night heron** is distinctively black and white and squat in appearance. Slightly less dumpy are the **squacco heron** and **cattle egret**, both of whose plumage makes them look white in flight but brown when standing; the squacco heron is browner on the head and has a crest of spiky plumes. Finally, the **little egret** is like a smaller version of the great white heron, distinguishable by the incongruous combination of long black legs and bright yellow feet.

Little egret

The **storks** (family *Ciconiidae*) are represented by two species. The rare **black stork** breeds mostly in Russia and is only likely to be seen on passage in the eastern Med, although a small population is resident in central Spain. Much less elusive is the **white stork**, which appears as both a summer breeder (in northern Greece, Turkey and north Africa) and a passage migrant. The huge concentrations of migrating storks at Gibraltar and the Bosphorus are one of the great Mediterranean bird sights (see "Migration", above). A very large bird, dramatically white-bodied with black, trailing wingtips, the white stork flies slowly with its neck extended forwards unlike a heron. Its nest is equally distinctive, since it often builds on top of tall structures such as chimneys or telegraph poles.

The third group in this order are the **ibises** and **spoonbills** (family *Threskiornithidae*). Only one ibis is at all widespread, the **glossy ibis**, a very attractive large bird with a down-curved bill and glossy purple-brown plumage. Nowhere common, it breeds in small numbers around freshwater marshes in the north of the Med and central Europe; the eastern Med is a good place to see it in passage from its winter quarters in east Africa. The other ibis is the **bald ibis**, whose world population of possibly only 200 pairs is now confined to a few isolated colonies in southern Morocco. Small numbers of **spoonbills** – resembling large white herons with an extraordinary black spatulate bill – winter in the eastern Med and north Africa, migrating to Russia and the Danube countries to breed; limited resident populations exist in southern Spain and western Turkey.

The final family, the *Phoenicopteridae*, is represented only by the **greater flamingo**. Impressive enough when dredging their curved bills through the water to sieve out their food, they are transformed into a breathtaking spectacle in flight, necks and legs extended, and wings flashing scarlet and black. They breed in the French Camargue and in two colonies around the Coto Donana of southern Spain, both these areas holding several thousand birds in a good year. In addition they breed sporadically on Tunisian islands and salt lakes, though their noise and visibility make them vulnerable to predation. Outside the breeding season they wander more widely, and in winter their numbers are increased by birds from Russian colonies; look for them on large flat estuaries and saltpans in the south and east of the region.

SWANS, GEESE AND DUCKS; ORDER *ANSERIFORMES*

Represented in the Mediterranean by some 24 regular species from two basic families, these aquatic birds all have long necks and webbed feet, and spend most of their time on or near freshwater. **Swans** and **geese** (family *Anserinae*) are not often seen by the average Mediterranean tourist. There's the odd pair of resident **mute swans** in the eastern Mediterranean and an even smaller population in Provence; its bright orange bill immediately identifies the species. In winter the **whooper swan** comes from its breeding grounds in the far north of Europe and Russia; some 25,000 settle around the Black Sea and the nearby marshes and lakes of Turkey and northern Greece.

With the exception of the semi-wild populations of the **greylag goose**, a species that has got itself thoroughly mixed up with domestic stock, no geese breed in the Med. However, some wild geese from arctic Russia spend their winters in the marshes of Yugoslavia, northern Greece and Turkey; these are predominantly greylags and **white-fronted geese**, but the flocks sometimes include rarer visitors from further east. One of these is the beautiful (and declining) **red-breasted goose**, a small goose with a red chest and throat, divided from the black plumage of its lower body by a neat white line.

Ducks fall into a number of categories (subfamilies) that are based more on behaviour than on strictly scientific grounds. Bridging the gap between ducks and geese are the large **shelducks** (subfamily *Tadorninae*). The **shelduck** itself has a striking black and white body with a dark green head and a chestnut breastband; mostly a northern breeder, it can be found wintering on many Mediterranean estuaries. Its close relation the **ruddy shelduck** is an altogether scarcer bird, breeding in small numbers in Greece and Turkey, and in wet years sometimes seen in Morocco; it has a chestnut body and pale head, with a black ring separating the two.

Some 9 species of **dabbling ducks** (subfamily *Anatinae*) occur in the Med. Although the males are distinguishable by their bright colours, at least in breeding plumage, the females are all an unrelieved brown; look for the coloured panel on the wing in flight – called the speculum, it's a good identifying feature in both sexes. The commonest of the group is the **mallard**, which like all the dabbling ducks feeds by upending itself in shallow water. Most other dabbling species use the region as a wintering area. The majority of the **shovelers** that breed in Britain, for instance, winter on the freshwater lakes and estuaries of the Med. Another relation is the **garganey**, a small duck whose male has a chocolate-brown head with a

white stripe. Unusually for a duck, it is a trans-Saharan migrant, wintering south of the equator but breeding in central and northern Europe and Russia.

One final species to mention in this group is the small **marbled teal**, a shy duck with a very pale speckled brown body; a rare and declining bird, it breeds in reeds and swamps in Spain, Greece, Turkey and (sometimes) Morocco.

In contrast to the dabbling ducks, the **diving ducks** (subfamily *Aythyinae*) entirely submerge themselves to take food, usually jumping off the water to launch into a dive. Most are winter visitors to the region, but the **red-crested pochard** also breeds, especially in the disappearing wetlands around Ciudad Real in central Spain and, to a lesser extent, in the Camargue. The male has a crested red head with a bright crimson bill – unusual and distinctive. **Tufted ducks**, all black with a long crest and white flanks, and **pochard**, chestnut-headed with grey back and black breast, are two common diving ducks which breed in the north but winter in the Mediterranean.

Another diving subfamily are the **sawbills** (*Merginae*), all of which have thin toothed bills for catching fish underwater. Although none breed around the Mediterranean, some come south to winter here; the **red-breasted merganser** is one of them, quite widespread around the coastlines and estuaries of northern Greece and Turkey, with a separate wintering population off the coasts of Spain. It's a long, thin, low-slung species, whose male has a glossy green head, ragged crest, and long red bill, whereas the female is more muted, with a conspicuous chestnut head and upper neck.

The **stifftails** (subfamily *Oxyurinae*) are stubby little diving ducks whose name comes from their manner of swimming with their tail raised stiffly. Only one species is native to Europe, the **white-headed duck**; it's a globally rare bird, with a world population of about 15,000 in 1974, and probably much less by now. The reasons for its decline are that it doesn't fly well (so its escape routes from hunters are limited) and many of its shallow lake habitats have been drained. Some 50 pairs breed around the Mediterranean in Tunisia, Andalucia and central Turkey, but it can be more easily seen in winter, when birds from many breeding populations gather together. Both sexes have a chestnut body, and the male has a white head with a black crown and blue bill.

Garganey

HAWKS, VULTURES AND EAGLES; ORDER *ACCIPITRIFORMES*

The distinguishing characteristic of the 27 species of Mediterranean hawk, vulture and eagle is their **breadth of wing**, an adaptation that permits the bird to locate its prey by soaring without effort at an advantageously high altitude.

These species fall into 2 families. One, the *Pandionidae*, contains just a single and distinctive species, the **osprey**. A large, dramatically black and white bird, it has an obvious kink in its wings in flight; you're most likely to see it on passage through to its wintering grounds in southern Africa, though a few pairs breed on rocky islands in the western Med. As a specialist fish-eater, the osprey is always to be found close to freshwater or on coasts and estuaries.

The other family (*Accipitridae*) contains all the other broad-winged birds of prey. Having dwindled markedly this century, none of the 4 species of Mediterranean **vulture** are common, and they have now become extinct in many countries. Destruction of their habitat and of the birds themselves have been major factors, and the efficiency of modern farming has accelerated their decline by reducing the supply of carrion. The **griffon vulture** is the commonest, with a reasonable population left in Spain and a few scattered colonies elsewhere in the Med. The **Egyptian vulture** is the only summer visitor among the vultures and yet is the most widely distributed of the vulture species, breeding in northern Greece and southern France. Smaller than the other vultures, it's a scruffy yellowish white bird, showing black wingtips and trailing edges in flight. The remaining two species – the **black vulture** and the **lammergeier** – are both very rare.

Although also scavenging birds, **kites** use a different hunting technique from the high-gliding vultures, flying low and slowly over the ground. The **red kite** is easy to pick out, with its very bent wings in flight, and long forked tail; a beautiful cinnamon colour overall, it has grey and black wing patches and a pale head. Human persecution has now confined its population to only a few thousand European pairs; Spain and to a lesser extent southern Italy are its strongholds. The other Mediterranean kite, the **black kite**, is a much commoner bird, often to be seen hunting over fields and by fresh water. A very dark-plumaged bird, with a tail less noticeably forked than the red kite's, it winters mainly in Ethiopia and usually chooses the Gibraltar migration route across the Med; huge numbers can be seen there in autumn and spring – nearly 40,000 were counted in the autumn of 1972.

Harriers operate a similar hunting technique to kites, patrolling the ground on a regular low-altitude beat in search of reptiles, small mammals and birds; the way they hold their wings in flight – sloping sharply upwards from the body – gives them a very bouncy appearance. The **marsh harrier** is probably the commonest, although the drainage of its wetland habitat is reducing its numbers all the time; the female is chocolate brown with a striking cream head, and the male patched in black, grey and brown like a fighter plane. Three other harriers occur in the Med, mostly migratory although there are some breeders; in all 3 species the male is mainly grey and the female brown with a ringed tail and a white rump.

Marsh harrier

Hawks have short rounded wings and long tails, giving them the fast low flight and great agility needed to prey on woodland birds, which they always take in flight. The small **sparrowhawk** is the more common of the two Mediterranean species, although nothing like as common as in the UK and Scandinavia; there's some influx in winter from northern populations. Twice the size of its relation, the **goshawk** is mostly confined to coniferous forests, where it is hard to see except in spring, when it indulges in spectacular high display flights. Unusually, in both species the female is much larger than the male, allowing the pair to hunt a wider range of prey: the male sparrowhawk concentrates mostly on small birds like sparrows and finches, while the female seizes for thrushes and starlings, and can even take prey up to the size of a wood pigeon.

The 12 species of the **eagle** group are all large birds of prey with rounded wings. Colouring isn't much identification help, since these species go through a variety of plumages in the long course of maturation. Largest of the group are the true eagles, of which the **golden eagle** is the most familiar; it's a bird of wild country, mostly but not always mountainous, and just a few breeding pairs are resident round the Med. Even rarer is the **imperial eagle**, an endangered species now reduced to a handful of pairs in southern Spain and the Balkans. All these true eagles have long and broad wings, with widespread primary feathers when soaring. An unusual and distinctive raptor (bird of prey) is the **short-toed eagle**, one of 3 species of smaller eagle that occur round the Med. This is the only large bird of prey that hovers frequently (the white underparts are an aid to identification), and is primarily a snake hunter, showing a healthy preference for non-poisonous species. Normally found in open country, it's a summer visitor that breeds sparsely right round the area, wintering in a belt just south of the Sahara. **Bonelli's eagle**, a resident of low mountains, can be distinguished by the adult bird's diagonal black stripe across the underwing. Open mixed woodland is the habitat of the third of the trio, the smaller **booted eagle**; a summer visitor that preys on small birds and mammals, its most obvious feature is a broad black band on the trailing edge of the wing, which contrasts sharply with the whiteness of the rest of the wing (although confusingly it has two colour phases, and dark-phase birds appear all brown underneath).

Three buzzards complete the eagle group. The **common buzzard** is resident and breeding along the northern coasts of the Med, although nowhere is it as common as in the cooler wetter climates of northwest Europe; very variable in plumage, it's hard to differentiate from a number of similar species. The **long-legged buzzard**, which replaces it in north Africa and Turkey, has an obvious pale ginger tail. Though of similar size and plumage, the **honey buzzard** is a distant relative; it has a distinctive tail pattern of two bars halfway down and a terminal band, and a delicate head with a fine bill. This last feature relates to their specialised diet of wasps, bees and (in their African winter quarters) termites, for which a thin manoeuvrable bill is more suited than a thick strong one. Their spring and autumn crossing of the Med, en route to the breeding grounds of central Europe, is especially concentrated at Gibraltar, where counts of over 10,000 birds a day are not unknown.

FALCONS; ORDER *FALCONIFORMES*

What immediately sets the falcons apart from the hawks and their relatives is that they all have **narrow, pointed wings**, designed for maximum speed rather than soaring ability. This feature, combined with a short, streamlined head and long straight tail, gives them a characteristic anchor-shaped flight silhouette. Their speed of flight makes them one of the most exciting groups of birds to watch, but one of the hardest to identify, since a tantalising glimpse of blurred feather and talons is often all that's seen.

Nine species of falcon are found in the Med. With a body weight of around a kilo, the **peregrine falcon** is typical of the larger species; primarily a winter visitor to the Med, it is an endangered species in some parts of northern Europe, after the drastic decline caused by pesticides, trapping and habitat change in the 1960s. It's a solitary bird, most often seen on estuaries and coastal sites; a few birds actually nest on some of the Med's more inaccessible outcrops and islands. Three other similar species occur, but much more rarely.

The smaller falcons are typified by the **kestrel**, a resident widespread throughout the Med, but nowhere common. Its habit of hovering distinguishes it from all other falcons apart from the lesser kestrel (see below); the male has a grey head and chestnut back with black spots, whereas the female is a more uniform mottled brown. The **lesser kestrel** is at first sight similar (though the male has an unspotted back), but has quite different habits. For a start, it's a summer visitor, wintering in Africa; secondly it's a colonial breeder, nesting in often large and noisy colonies in caves, on cliff faces, and even in buildings; and thirdly, it's mostly insectivorous, so its feeds on the wing and hovers less often. Greece and Spain are two countries where it is widespread.

Two other migratory species are worth mentioning. The **red-footed falcon** is the size of a kestrel, but the male is a beautiful dark grey all over, except for its bright red feet, thighs and undertail. This is a gregarious bird, and flocks on migration will sometimes hunt insects together – a wonderful sight. The entire world population winters in an area centred on Angola and Namibia, crossing the central and eastern Med in late April on the way to the Russian sites where most of them breed; return migration peaks in late September. **Eleonora's falcon** has a different migratory strategy, wintering mostly in Madagascar and moving up to the Med to breed. Again, it's a colonial breeder, this time on rocky sea cliffs and islands, and virtually the whole world population of around 4500 pairs breeds in about 100 colonies in the Med, especially in the Greek islands. Its food is mostly small birds, and so the breeding season is late, timed to coincide food demand from the fledglings with the food supply from migrating species. Midway between kestrel and peregrine in size, it's markedly slender and long-winged and has two colour phases: one all dark grey, the other more like a small peregrine but with darker underparts.

GAME BIRDS; ORDER *GALLIFORMES*

All 8 game bird species found in the Med come from the family *Phasianidae*, which includes pheasants, partridges and quails. Although the natural range of the **pheasant** originally extended no further west than the Caucasus mountains on the Soviet Union/Iran border, it has been widely introduced as a game bird in the woodlands of Spain and France. The very much smaller **partridge** is mostly a bird of the farmlands of central and northern Europe, but is resident on the stony hillsides of various southern parts. The **red-legged partridge** *Alectoris rufa*, the commonest type, provides a textbook example of how distinct populations evolve into separate species. There are now 4 *Alectoris* species in the Med, all with a pale throat and strikingly barred flanks – *A. rufa* in France, Iberia and Corsica, *A. barbara* in north Africa and Sardinia, *A. graeca* in Italy and the Balkans, and *A. chukar* in Crete and Turkey. All are sedentary birds (ie they stay in one place) and here lies the explanation for their development – since there is little or no intermingling of the genes of the individual populations, the differing selection pressures have caused different species to evolve. Only in a small area of the Balkans do the ranges overlap.

The migratory **quail**, only the size of a dumpy, tail-less blackbird, lives especially in cultivated fields and is much more likely to be heard than seen; it has a characteristic "whic, whicwhic" call. Little is known for certain about the habits of this secretive bird, but it seems that most quails winter south of the Sahara, migrating to the northern Med, from Spain to Turkey, for the summer; it's also a common breeder in north Africa, where some birds spend the winter as well.

CRANES, RAILS AND ASSOCIATED SPECIES; ORDER *GRUIIFORMES*

Although 4 families of the *Gruiiformes* order appear in the Med, one of them, the button-quails (family *Turnicidae*), is mostly a family of tropical birds and contains just one Med species, the **Andalucian hemipode**. Another very secretive bird, it bred fairly widely in Spain, north Africa and Sicily in the last century, but is now reduced to a handful of pairs in southern Spain, cut off from the main population in central and southern Africa.

The **rails** and **crakes** (family *Rallidae*) form a strangely mixed family. They are all short-billed, short-winged, long-legged and plump; five species are terrestrial, of which the commonest is the **water rail**, which creeps around in marshes and is therefore rarely seen. It's more frequently heard, having a bizarre call which sounds like a piglet being slowly and nastily put to death. Four other Med species are able to swim, and are therefore less reclusive; notable amongst these are the familiar **moorhen**, a black bird with a red forehead and white undertail, which it constantly flicks when swimming, and the **coot**, again all black but with a noticeable white bill and frontal "shield". Both are freshwater birds and both are resident breeders; they are joined in winter by northern birds migrating south. A beautiful but declining relative is the **purple gallinule**, like a very large purple moorhen with a red bill and "shield"; wetland drainage has reduced its habitat, and it is now resident in only a very few marshes in southern Spain, Tunisia and Sardinia.

The **crane**, the only member of the crane family *Gruidae* regularly seen in the Med, is much the same size as the heron, but with a short bill; the body is mostly grey and black, the head has red and white markings, and a bunch of ostrich-like plumes hang over its tail forming a "skirt". Until recently this graceful species used to breed in western Europe, but drainage and other disturbances have restricted its breeding grounds to the moorlands and marshlands of northeastern Europe and the western Soviet Union. Some of these winter in southern Europe, especially in Spain, while others head for Ethiopia; the migrating flocks fly in a V formation with outstretched necks, but because they have no difficulty crossing open water they don't occur in huge numbers at migratory bottlenecks in the same way that storks do.

Two species of **bustard** (family *Otidae*) occur in the Med, both built rather like a long-legged turkey, with the **great bustard** being a particularly striking bird, the adult males standing up to a metre high and weighing up to 15kg. Hunting and habitat disturbance have much reduced it as a breeding species, although the central plains of the Iberian peninsula still hold a few thousand specimens. The **little bustard** is far smaller, mostly coloured brown, but showing a great deal of black and white on the wings in flight; the male has a smart black and white patterned neck. This species has also declined in the face of land development, and again Spain is its breeding stronghold, with a few pairs scattered in southern France, Sardinia and mainland Italy.

WADERS, GULLS AND TERNS; ORDER *CHARADRIIFORMES*

With some 60 species from 8 families present in the Mediterranean, the waders, gulls and terns are a large and confusing family. Nearly all of them are birds of the sea or the seashore.

■ Waders

Wading birds are exactly what the name suggests – birds adapted to wading in shallow water or paddling around the mud. They feed on small marine organisms in winter, often switching to terrestrial insects in the summer, when they are on their northern breeding grounds. Although they all have long bills and long legs, there is considerable variation from species to species, all having evolved to fill a slightly different feeding or breeding niche. Their winter food tends to be concentrated in small areas of estuaries and mud flats; this is a rather scarce Med habitat, but where it does occur you expect to see quite high numbers of a variety of species.

The **oystercatcher**, the single representative of the family *Haematopididae*, is a striking black and white medium-large wader with a red bill. A few pairs breed around Greece and Turkey, and a small wintering population is concentrated on the Gulf of Gabes in Tunisia.

Two of the most noticeable waders in the Mediterranean are the **avocet** and the **black-winged stilt**, the 2 members of the family *Recurvirostridae*. Both are slim, medium-large black and white birds, and specialists of saline habitats such as saltpans; the stilt is instantly identified by its extraordinarily long pink legs, which enable it to wade in quite deep water and pick its insect food from or near the surface; the avocet feeds by sweeping its characteristically upturned bill from side to side in the water, locating invertebrates by touch. Avocets breed in small colonies around wetlands, especially in Turkey, Spain and southern France; stilts are more common breeders in Spain, but are patchily distributed elsewhere. In winter, the population of both species (avocets in particular) is increased by birds that have bred further north.

Black-winged stilt

The **stone curlew**, sole representative of the family *Burhinidae*, is a medium-sized, heavily built brown bird with yellow legs, a double white wing bar, and large yellow eyes – evidence of its partly nocturnal habits. Stone curlews prefer open habitats such as heathlands or stony fields, relying on camouflage and stealth to protect themselves against predation. Nonetheless, it's an uncommon and declining species through most of Europe, breeding in Spain, north Africa and Turkey, and sparsely from France round the coast to Greece; some northern birds winter on the north African coast, too.

A couple of very untypical waders belong to the family *Glareolidae*: the **cream-coloured courser** and the **collared pratincole**. The former is found only in north Africa, for it is — unbelievably enough — a desert wader, sandy coloured to blend in with its chosen environment. The very short legs and long wings and tail of the pratincole make it look more like a huge swallow than a wader, a resemblance heightened by the fact that it catches its insect prey on the wing; it's a sandy brown colour, with a creamy yellow throat and an obvious chestnut underwing in flight. Wintering south of the Sahara, it is a summer visitor to the Mediterranean, breeding in reasonable numbers in southern Spain, with other small populations in Tunisia, Greece and Turkey.

The **plovers** (family *Charadriidae*) are all dumpy, short-billed waders, identifiable from their jerky run when gathering surface and sub-surface food on mud. Three of the Med species have black and white head patterns. In summer the commonest of these is the **Kentish plover**, which has black legs and an orange crown, and can be seen on mud flats, coastal marshes and saltpans; in winter, its near relation the **ringed plover**, larger and with a prominent black-ringed neck, comes down from northern Europe as a winter visitor and passage migrant. Most familiar of the larger (ie medium-sized) plovers is the **lapwing**, a broad-winged species with a bouncy, flapping flight; its plumage is a striking combination of black, white and iridescent green, and it has a conspicuous head plume. Small numbers stay to breed round the Mediterranean, but most birds seen in winter will be migrating breeders from further north. **Golden plovers** and **grey plovers** are also winter visitors, when their plumage is nondescript; look for them on coastal mud flats and marshes.

Of the 20 or so Mediterranean species of **sandpiper** (family *Scolopacidae*) the largest are the curlews and godwits. The **curlew**, with its distinctive down-curved bill and long legs, is a winter visitor to the region, usually feeding on estuaries and mud flats; its weird bubbling cry is unforgettable, but not heard so often in winter as on its northern breeding grounds. Distinguishable

from the curlew by its straight bill and the black and white patterns visible on its wings and tail in flight, the **black-tailed godwit** is another winter visitor, which can be seen mostly in Greece, Spain and Turkey. In late spring some birds are in full breeding plumage, a glorious chestnut red, but in winter they are a less exciting grey-brown.

Another group of larger sandpipers are the "shanks", the commonest of which is the medium-sized **redshank**, a bird with a thin bill and garish red legs. Over 10,000 of them winter in the Mediterranean — mainly in Tunisia, Turkey and Greece — and some stay on to breed here, especially in southern Spain. The **greenshank** is like a redshank in shape but with dirty green legs and a distinctive triple call note; a trans-Saharan migrant, it winters in southern Africa and breeds in the far north of Scandinavia and arctic Russia. A smaller relative is the **common sandpiper**, mostly a passage migrant and winter visitor, although a few pairs stay on to breed around the northern shores of the Mediterranean. With brown upper parts and white underparts, it's often seen by rivers, bobbing up and down on waterside rocks and flying low across the water with stiff, jerky wing beats.

Two easily identified but very secretive species are the **snipe** and the **woodcock**, both squarely built, short-legged and very long-billed waders. Snipe are winter visitors to the Med, feeding in freshwater marshes and wetlands; they are most frequently sighted as they explode from cover, rising high in a characteristic zigzag flight. The much larger woodcock is the only wader species to live in woodlands, scrub and fields; widespread though nowhere common, it's primarily a winter visitor to the northern Med, though small numbers stay on to breed in suitable terrain.

One of the most exasperating of all bird groups to identify is that of the **small sandpipers**, especially in winter plumage, which is what all eight or so species wear in the Med since they are all winter visitors and passage migrants. American birders call them the "peeps", after their call note. The commonest is the **dunlin**, which feeds in small flocks on estuaries and mud flats, with the biggest concentration of them in Tunisia. They can be told apart (usually) by their wing and tail patterns in flight — but it's not an easy job.

◼ Gulls and terns

The gulls and terns are all fish-eating birds and are mostly marine, although the "marsh terns" are freshwater species and some gulls have adapted to artificial habitats such as ploughed fields and rubbish tips. Most are white underneath, so that fish can't see them against the sky, and many gull species have black wing tips (the black pigment melanin protects feathers from fraying).

Ten or so species of **gull** (family *Laridae*) occur in the Med, but nothing like as commonly as they do in the more productive waters of northern Europe. The 2 largest are the **herring gull**, which has grey wings with black tips, and the **lesser black-backed gull**, whose dark grey back can look almost black. The former species is resident, with breeding colonies scattered round the Med, whereas the latter will only be seen in winter, coming south from its breeding grounds. Next in size is the **black-headed gull**, one of the real opportunists of the bird world; it has increased dramatically throughout northern Europe in the last fifty years, largely by exploiting new feeding sites such as waste dumps. A medium-sized bird, it sports a brown head in summer plumage, and can be confused with the **Mediterranean gull**; the latter does actually have a black head rather than a brown one, and lacks black wing tips. The black-headed gull is commoner, breeding in large colonies often on islands in freshwater lakes and marshes; the stronghold of the Mediterranean gull is around the Black Sea in Russia, from where the population moves to the eastern part of the sea in winter.

Much scarcer is the **slender-billed gull**, a slightly larger bird than the black-headed gull; in summer it has an obvious red bill (yellow in winter), and in breeding plumage its underparts are flushed a beautiful pale pink. There's one sizeable colony in Sardinia and a few scattered ones in France and Spain, but the main breeding populations are in central Turkey and the middle East, so Mediterranean sightings are likeliest off the coasts of Greece, Sicily and Tunisia in winter. Equally rare is **Audouin's gull**, one of only 2 bird species unique to the area (the other being an obscure nuthatch from Corsica). Most of the breeding sites are on remote rocky islands, especially in the Balearics and off the north Moroccan coast, though there's a tiny population in the

Mediterranean gull

eastern Med too; as there are only around 3500 pairs in existence, you'll do well to see one. The black band round its red bill makes the bill look very dark at a distance, and it's the only gull in the Med with dark green legs and feet.

Terns (family *Sternidae*) are like small, graceful gulls. They have long thin wings and forked tails, and often repeatedly patrol a stretch of water with beating wings and down-turned head, catching fish by plunging like a miniature gannet. They are summer visitors and passage migrants, wintering off the coasts of tropical Africa.

All of the 5 species of **marine tern** in the region have a white body with grey back and wings, and a black-capped head. The colour of the bill, their size and their call notes are the best ways of telling them apart. The **common tern**, a medium-sized bird with a black-tipped red bill, is the most widespread marine tern in the Med, breeding in small numbers on northern coasts. Smallest of the group is the **little tern**, which has a prominent white forehead contrasting with its black cap, and a black-tipped yellow bill. The **Caspian tern** is a large, gull-sized species with a massive scarlet bill.

There are 3 Mediterranean species of **marsh tern**, and in breeding plumage they are all three much darker than the sea terns. Mostly they're seen on freshwater lakes and marshes on spring and autumn migration, but there are some breeding colonies, notably in southern Spain and Turkey. The **black tern** has a sooty body relieved by pale underwings in flight – but it can be easily confused with the 2 other (paler) species, especially in winter.

SANDGROUSE; ORDER PTEROCLIDIFORMES

The four **sandgrouse** species found in the region are all from one family, *Pteroclididae*. Resembling slim long-tailed doves (with which they were classified until recently), they are primarily desert and semi-desert birds, living on the ground and relying on their pale sandy plumage to conceal them. The best times to spot them are at dawn and dusk, when they fly in search of water, wheeling and turning in noisy flocks. A unique adaptation to their dry habitat is that the male is able to soak up water in his central belly feathers in order to convey it back to the chicks.

Although the fringes of the Sahara are the main habitat of all four sandgrouse, two species also breed in Europe. The **black-bellied sandgrouse** has an obvious black belly, while the **pintailed sandgrouse** has elongated tail feathers and a white belly. Both are found in desert areas of Spain and Portugal, and small numbers of the latter breed in the Crau, an area of stony semi-desert near the Camargue of southern France.

PIGEONS AND DOVES; ORDER COLUMBIFORMES

Six species of Mediterranean pigeon and dove belong to this one-family order, a category to which the extinct families of the dodo and solitaire used to belong. All species are herbivorous, and most are tree-dwellers and feed their young on "crop milk", a food produced from the cells shed from the crop lining.

The largest pigeon of the region is the **woodpigeon**, which is native to the woodlands of the northern Med, yet is not as common here as in northen Europe, where the combination of arable fields and woodland provide a perfect feeding and breeding habitat. In winter the populations can be considerably increased by migration from further north: It has been estimated that some 3,000,000 birds, mostly from Scandinavia, cross the Pyrenees in October to winter in the Iberian peninsula. Conversely, the smaller **turtle dove** winters south of the Sahara and migrates north to breed in Europe and Russia. A dark brown and pink bird, it gets its name from its slow soothing "turr turr" call. Like the woodpigeon, it is hunted heavily – as many as 100,000 are shot every year in Malta alone.

Two other small doves are notable for the rapid expansion of their range. Until 1930 the **collared dove** was limited to Greece and the Balkans, but in the last sixty years it has progressed so far northwest that it is now found in Iceland. Around the Med, however, the expansion has been less obvious, with lower numbers colonising westwards along the Italian and French coasts. Exactly why it has expanded its range so fast is unclear, but its liking for urban habitats seems a plausible explanation. It's a pale dove, with a black band around the back of the neck and conspicuous white on the tail. The **palm dove** is also fond of urban and suburban environments, and is extending its range in north Africa; it's now very common in many Tunisian towns and oases.

CUCKOOS; ORDER CUCULIFORMES

Both Mediterranean species of the cuckoo order are from the family of parasitic cuckoos (*Cuculinae*). More commonly heard than seen, the **European cuckoo** (or just "cuckoo") is a pale grey bird with bright yellow feet and a long tail, and flies with fluttering wings. They winter in southern Africa and breed in Europe, many of them staying round the Med, laying a single egg in the nest of its chosen host species. It can lay up to 25 eggs (usually about 10) in nests of small birds such as reed warblers, and the young nestling pushes out the original eggs when it is about a day old. Caterpillars are their staple diet, the irritant hairs being removed by the mucous lining of the gizzard and ejected as a pellet. Cuckoos gave the lie to the early theory that young birds are taught migration routes by their parents, for the adult cuckoos leave for the their southward migration a few weeks before the young birds, leaving the young to find their own way.

The similarly long-tailed **great spotted cuckoo** is larger than the European cuckoo and has a white-spotted dark back, cream underparts and a dark crested cap. Another trans-Saharan migrant (though a few birds winter in southern Spain and Morocco), it's a common summer visitor in Spain and Portugal, with small numbers breeding in southern France and Italy as well. Not surprisingly it chooses larger host species than the European cuckoo, generally choosing to evict members of the crow family, especially magpies. And like its relative it feeds on hairy caterpillars, but has a different technique to deal with the hairs, removing them with its beak before swallowing.

OWLS; ORDER *STRIGIFORMES*

Around seven owl species are to be seen around the Med, and they divide into 2 families. The **barn owl**, the only representative of the family *Tytonidae*, has a heart-shaped facial disc and pale plumage that appears almost white in some conditions (although north African varieties are much darker), and hunts by night for small mammals, amphibians and birds. Its old name of "screech owl" comes from the long hissing scream it makes to advertise its presence, but it makes several other strange noises, including a wheezing snore made mostly by the female to the male or young. Although the barn owl is found in the Americas, Africa, Australasia and India as well as Europe, it's becoming a rare bird, declining through most of its European range (especially the eastern Med) through a combination of pesticides, disturbance and loss of nest sites. It's fond of breeding and roosting in quiet rural buildings, hence the name.

The other 6 owl species are all **typical owls** (family *Strigidae*). All are darker than the barn owl, with a round facial disc, and some have ear tufts. Only 3 are likely to be encountered. The **tawny owl** is mostly a bird of lowland deciduous woods, and the species is as scarce round the Med as this type of habitat; its "huhuhuhoooo" call is most often heard in spring and early summer.

The **little owl** is much smaller, rather dumpy, has no ear tufts, flies in a notably undulating line, and is quite active by day. It's not a woodland bird, preferring open countryside and even rocky mountains; all over southern Europe its numbers are declining.

The tiny **Scops owl** – no taller than an adult's hand – is the commonest Mediterranean species. Beautifully camouflaged in grey and brown, it has big yellow eyes and tufted ears. As it hunts by night, feeding on small mammals and night-flying insects, it is almost impossible to see, but it can be heard easily enough: the male makes a rather mournful "tyu" sound, repeated every couple of seconds, seemingly endlessly (one was heard to make 900 calls in 40 minutes). Competing males will call against each other, each bird having a slightly different frequency and pitch. The calling of Scops owls ranks with the trilling of cicadas and the chirping of tree frogs as one of the characteristic sounds of the Mediterranean summer night.

Scops owl

NIGHTJARS; ORDER *CAPRIGULIFORMES*

All three Med species of nightjar fall into the same family (*Caprimulginae*) and look very similar. Since they are active only at dawn and dusk, their call notes rather than their plumage are the best means of identification. Flying insects, especially moths, are their main food, and so in winter they migrate south to avoid starvation.

The most widespread species is the **European nightjar**. A medium-sized bird, it is wonderfully camouflaged in a tapestry of grey, brown and cream, and spends most of its time on the ground, though its long wings and tail give it the agility to take moths and beetles in flight. It's widespread but not common around the Med, found in countryside with no more than a scattering of trees and bushes, which it uses as platforms for singing. The call is a continuous churring with abrupt changes of pitch, like a small, distant, two-geared motorbike.

The other 2 species are much less widespread: the **Egyptian nightjar** is found on the northern edge of the Sahara, while the **red-necked nightjar** is more of a semi-desert species, and extends through north Africa to most of Spain.

SWIFTS; ORDER *APODIFORMES*

There are 5 Mediterranean species of swift, all belonging to the family *Apodidae*. Instantly told from swallows and martins by their thin curving wings and relatively short tails, swifts are the most aerial of all birds, coming to land only for nesting, roosting and mating. Swifts sleep on the wing, ascending to heights of up to 2000 metres in loose flocks and staying there for the night; there have even been sightings of in-flight mating. They feed exclusively on flying insects, usually at low altitude, which they either eat immediately or accumulate into a ball at the back of the throat for feeding to young birds in the nest. The all-black **common swift** is found all round the Med in summer, often nesting in the centre of large towns and flying round the streets at dusk in screaming packs. The **pallid swift** is paler and has a white throat patch, but separation of these 2 species is a job for the expert. The third widely distributed species is the **Alpine swift**, much larger than the previous two, pale brown with white under parts and a brown breast-band. It flies even faster and more dramatically than the other swifts, and breeds on cliffs and buildings around much of the northern Med. All 3 species can be seen on spring and autumn passage as they commute to Europe from southern Africa. The 2 other swift species are only found in north Africa and a small area of southern Spain; hard to tell apart, they are both small and dark with a white rump.

KINGFISHERS AND ASSOCIATED SPECIES; ORDER *CORACIIFORMES*

The *Coraciiformes* order is primarily tropical, but four families stretch up to the Med and beyond; they are amongst the most brilliantly coloured birds of the region.

The **kingfisher**, the only member of the *Alcedinidae* family that's likely to be seen, sports chestnut underparts and dazzling blue upper parts, and can be found by freshwater from Spain to the Balkans – though it's scarce in north Africa, southern Italy and Turkey. Most often sighted streaking along the river in a flash of blue, it also perches on trees and bushes overhanging the water while it spies out its prey. Kingfisher populations have declined throughout Europe and the Med because of drainage and water pollution. Two other kingfisher species occur along the Turkish coast, but in small numbers.

A single species represents each of the next three families. The **bee-eater**, which arrives in April and May from southern Africa, is a medium-sized bird with a long curving beak, projecting central tail feathers and pointed wings, brightly coloured in turquoise, yellow and chestnut. Bee-eaters are sociable birds, their colonies nesting in holes dug in sandy banks; outside the breeding season they stick together, too, and have the endearing habit of roosting in tightly packed lines along a narrow branch. They feed on flying bees and wasps, which they snatch from the air with an audible snap. Open country with a few trees and bushes is their favoured habitat, and they sometimes gather by rivers and ponds, where they hunt dragonflies.

Another gorgeously coloured summer visitor is the **roller**; larger and more stoutly built than the bee eater, it has a chestnut back, black wing tips, and brilliant blue head, underparts and wing patches. Pine and oak forests are its regular habitat (using old trees for nest holes) and it's scattered thinly round the Med, probably being commoner in southern Spain than anywhere else. Its name comes from its spectacular display flights, used both to attract a mate and to drive off rivals, when the bird flies steeply upwards, stalls, and then goes into a rolling dive.

The third family is represented by the **hoopoe**, a strikingly beautiful bird with rounded black and white wings and a bright pink body; the head has a crest of pink feathers tipped with black, which is erected during courtship and when excited or alarmed. Hoopoes are resident in southern Spain and north Africa, whereas the breeding birds of the northern Med are summer visitors that winter in central Africa. A bird of open woodland, orchards and olive groves, it feeds mostly on the ground, probing with its long decurved bill for insect larvae and pupae. Hoopoes are fairly elusive, but their call is strong and distinctive – a liquid "poo–poo–poo" from which both its English and scientific name – *Upapa epops* – are derived.

WOODPECKERS; ORDER *PICIFORMES*

The 8 Mediterranean members of the woodpecker family *Picidae* fall into three distinct categories. Most familiar are the **spotted woodpeckers**, a family of mostly black and white woodpeckers, with variable amounts of red on the head and belly. They are tree-trunk specialists, feeding off insects found under the bark and in rotting wood, and nesting exclusively in holes which they drill into the tree. (These holes are used later by other woodland birds such as the hoopoe.) Spotted woodpeckers are highly sedentary, and this has led to the evolution of a number of similar species. The **great spotted woodpecker** is the commonest species in the western Med, but three other very similar species come in at the eastern end, all with subtle differences of plumage, habitat preference and feeding habits. The much smaller **lesser spotted woodpecker**, only the size of a sparrow, is a rare bird, scattered through old woodlands in the northern Med. As with the hoopoe, you'll hear the spotted woodpecker before you see it: all species drum on side branches during the mating season.

Green woodpeckers use their extraordinarily long tongues to extract ants from their nests, and thus tend to be found in open, grassy woodland. Bigger than the spotted woodpeckers, it has a red crown and moustache-like stripe relieving its otherwise green plumage. Again, separate species have evolved in the eastern Med and north Africa.

Unlike all the other members of the family, the **wryneck** is a migrant around most of the Med, although the north African population is also partly resident. Like the green woodpecker it feeds on ants, and it nests in other woodpecker holes, being unable to excavate its own; its camouflaging grey and brown plumage, its long sinuous shape, and its habit of twisting its head and neck into almost impossible angles combine to make the wryneck look more like a lizard than a bird when it's not in flight. Not a common species, it favours old, open, deciduous woodland, and is most likely to be seen on spring migration.

PERCHING BIRDS; ORDER *PASSERIFORMES*

The final avian order, the perching birds, is easily the largest and most complex, with 160 common species from 22 families – nearly half of the bird species of the region. They don't really have a common distinguishing feature; all of them perch, but then so do many other species. What sets them apart more than anything else is that most of them use **song** for pairing and for settling territorial disputes. Full display song is usually only heard in spring and early summer; the quality and variety of the song conveys to other birds some idea of the experience and physical fitness of the singing bird, which enables disputes to be solved without physical confrontation.

■ Larks; family *Alaudidae*

The 13 Mediterranean species of lark are small, brown and dumpy, with all-purpose bills that enable them to each both seeds and insects. They are mostly ground-dwelling, and run or walk rather than hop. The **skylark**, well-known from northern Europe, is found throughout the region, distinguished by its familiar soaring song flight. But the commonest lark is the **crested lark**; coloured a streaky brown like the skylark, it has a prominent crest on its head, and is an abundant bird of dry, open country and agricultural fields. Another lark of open ground is the **short-toed lark**, a much smaller bird than the previous two species, often to be seen feeding in flocks; whereas most of the other Med larks are resident all round the year, this one is a summer visitor, migrating south across the Sahara in winter. In the north African deserts, a bewildering variety of lark species appear; being omnivorous birds of open country, the desert and semi-desert habitats suit them well.

■ Swallows; family *Hirundidae*

There are 5 Mediterranean swallow species, all relatively easy to identify. The **swallow** itself is a widespread summer visitor, passing over in large numbers in spring and autumn. Look closely, though, at swallows in southern Spain, Greece and Turkey – they may be **red-rumped swallows**, distinguished by the named feature and the chestnut feathers on the back of the head. Both swallows have forked tails with long tail streamers; martins, on the other hand, lack the tail streamers. The **crag martin** doesn't occur further north than southern France; much the same shape as the more familiar **sand martin**, it's a nondescript brown colour, and breeds in ravines, caves and coastal cliffs. Unusually for a member of this family, it tends not to migrate south in the winter.

■ Pipits and wagtails; family *Motacillidae*

Like the larks, the pipits and wagtails are essentially ground-living birds. Unlike larks, however, they are entirely insectivorous, and so have thinner bills; needing great agility to catch flying insects, they are also more slimly built, with longer tails (very long in the case of wagtails). In summer the **tawny pipit** is a typical bird of dry and open Med countryside; it's a uniform pale sandy colour, with long legs that enable it to run at surprising speed. The other 4 pipit species likely to be seen are smaller and darker, but confusingly similar to each other. The wagtails are much more colourful, and live up to their name by constantly bobbing their tails up and down. Two of the three species are essentially residents: the **white wagtail** (actually pied black and white), which lives in a wide range of habitats, including human settlements; and the less common **grey wagtail**, which lives by rivers and streams and is identified by its black bib and contrasting yellow under parts. The **yellow wagtail** is exclusively a summer migrant; especially associated with damp grasslands, it can be told from the others by its shorter tail and lack of black bib (though it is an exceptionally variable bird with at least half a dozen different subspecies).

Bulbuls; family *Pycnonotidae*

Basically a tropical family, distributed through Africa and Asia, the bulbuls have just one species round the Med – the **common bulbul**, which is confined to north Africa. It's a drab bird, looking rather like a blackbird with a dark bill, but it has a mellow and rich song; suburban parks and gardens are good places to spot it.

Shrikes; family *Lanidae*

The shrikes are some of the most typical birds of the region. All 6 species are medium-sized,

Woodchat
shrike

hooked-billed predators, feeding off insects and small birds, onto which they swoop from lookout posts such as telegraph wires; having long tails, short wings and generally monochrome plumage, they look something like small magpies. An alternative name for the family is "butcher birds", after their predilection for storing their prey by impaling it on thorny bushes. The **great grey shrike** is the largest and most striking, with black, white and grey feathers; the smaller **woodchat shrike** is a common summer visitor, with an obvious chestnut crown and nape.

Accentors; family *Prunellidae*

Two species of accentors are found in the region. The **hedgesparrow**, a familiar bird in northern Europe, is mostly a winter visitor to the Mediterranean, although some birds do breed in the north of the area; looking like a slim sparrow, it has a thin bill for eating insects. Its larger relative, the **alpine accentor**, is more colourful, with a black-spotted white throat, and is exclusively found in mountainous regions.

Warblers; family *Sylviidae*

The warbler are a large family, hard to identify down to species level. They're all small insectivores and are mostly migratory, descending on the Med in huge numbers in the summer

The **marsh and swamp warblers** comprise around a dozen species of nondescript brown birds, all of which are associated with reed beds and waterside scrub, have rounded tails, and produce a rather harsh, repetitive song. Typical is the **reed warbler**, a bird with uniform plumage of dark brown above and pale brown below; it spends almost all its time among reeds, where it builds its nest like a sling between stalks. The **great reed warbler** is a giant version of the previous species, almost as big as a thrush, and fairly common around the whole of the Med.

Around eighteen species make up the more brightly coloured **shrub and scrub warblers**; some are birds of the woodland edge, but most are found in the scrubby *maquis* and *garigue* habitats. The **melodious warbler** is a widespread shrub warbler of the western Med, a small bird with bright yellow underparts and eye stripe; in the east it is largely replaced by the pale grey-brown **olivaceous warbler**. About fourteen species of scrub warbler migrate across the Sahara in summer to plunder the Med's insect surplus; the males are brighter than females (in all other warblers, the sexes are similar), and they all have a stepped, tapering tail, often edged with white. Commonest of this group is the resident **Sardinian warbler**; widespread in most scrubby areas, it's sometimes the dominant bird of its area, although like the rest of this group it often lurks invisibly at the bottom of bushes. In spring, however, the males deliver their scratchy song from the tops of shrubs, making them much more visible. The male has a glossy black head, neatly set off by a white bib, and a startling red eye.

The third group, the 4 species of **leaf warblers**, are very small birds, usually green or yellow, which gymnastically forage for insects in trees, often high up in the leaf canopy. The **chiffchaff**, whose name accurately describes its call, crosses the Sahara in early March to breed around the Med and further north. Almost identical is the **willow warbler**, but it has a quite different song, consisting of a liquid cascade of descending notes; more of a northern breeder, it's most likely to be seen as a passage migrant in spring or autumn.

■ Flycatchers; family *Muscicapidae*

The 4 flycatcher species of the region – mostly passage migrants – are best identified by their feeding habits: they catch insects by darting out from a perch, snapping the snack out of the air, and then returning to base to await the next victim. The **pied flycatcher** is a small bird with a striking black and white plumage in the male (the female is pale brown), while the **spotted flycatcher** is a streaky brown all over.

■ Thrushes and chats; family *Turdidae*

The thrushes and chats, with 25 species, are a complicated family, most of which feed off insects and invertebrates on the ground – though the true thrushes will often switch to fruits and berries in the winter. The family can be divided conveniently into six groups.

Blackbirds and **song thrushes** – both **true thrushes** – are basically northern European birds, but are found around the Med wherever there is good cover of deciduous woodland, especially in the mountains. More typical of the rocky and dry Med coasts, however, are the second group, the **rock thrushes**. Two colourful species occur. The **blue rock thrush** is resident on sea cliffs, rocky gorges and in the mountains throughout the region; a slender bird, it's coloured a

gorgeous powder blue. The **rock thrush**, a shy summer visitor found in gorges and mountains, is equally striking, with a red breast, blue head, black wings and a white back.

The smaller **wheatears** are characteristic birds of open and rocky ground; all have white rumps and black-tipped white tails, which are particularly obvious in flight. They have a habit of bobbing up and down on rocks or low walls, rather like wagtails. Eight species occur in the region, though many of these are confined to the north African desert – like larks, wheatears do well in dry semi-deserts. Two species are more widespread, however. The **common wheatear** is a summer visitor that also passes through in large numbers en route to more northern breeding grounds; it has a grey back and head, black cheeks and white underparts. The **black-eared wheatear**, which breeds around the Med, is one of the loveliest of the wheatears – the male has black wings and cheeks, and the rest of the body is a pale buff colour. Look for both species in dry and rocky country, though they use a wider variety of habitats at migration time.

Black-eared
wheatear

Common in bushy rather than open habitats, the 2 species of **chats** are rather like small dumpy wheatears, without the white rump and tail. The male **stonechat** is strikingly coloured, with a black head, orange breast, and white marks on the neck and wings; resident around the Med, it's also a summer visitor to central Europe, so numbers increase at migration time. Perching on the tops of bushes, it flicks its tail and utters a sharp "chack" as its alarm call. The **whinchat** is similar, but is purely a summer visitor, and is visually distinguished by its broad white eye stripe and brown head.

The fifth thrush group are the **redstarts**, with 3 species found in the region. Much the most arboreal of the thrushes, they are mostly hole-nesters and eat mainly insects. All redstarts look like slim elegant robins, and all have a reddish tail – a characteristic shared only by the nightin-gales (see below). The male **redstart** is partic-ularly handsome, with a grey back, black throat and orange breast. The **black redstart**, as its name implies, is basically black but has the same red tail. Often found in cliff faces, the black redstart has adapted well to human settlements, finding nesting sites in stone walls; ancient ruins suit them well, and they're one of the typical birds of Greek and Roman sites.

The final thrush group are a mixed bunch of **miscellaneous small thrushes**. The **robin** is one of them, too well-known to need describing. The **nightingale** is another; a uniform brown colour with a reddish tail, it's a summer visitor and passage migrant around most of the Med. Notwithstanding its name and reputation, you're more likely to hear it by day and especially at dusk; its song is almost impossible to describe – the main feature is the volume and richness of repeated short notes, especially phrases such as "piu piu piu" and "jug jug jug". Also in this mixed group is the **rufous bush chat**; a summer visitor to southern Spain, Greece and north Africa, it's a sort of link between the warblers and thrushes, with a prominent long rufous tail, edged with black and white. The rest of its body is reddish on top and pale below, with an obvious black line through the eye. Look for it in dry, scrubby coun-try and semi-desert, especially around thorn bushes and cactus hedges.

■ Babblers; family *Muscicapidae*

The **fulvous babbler**, sole Mediterranean repre-sentative of its family (as is the case with the next 4 species), is a sort of large pale brown thrush with a long tail, short wings, and a slightly decurved bill. The babblers are basically tropical, but this species reaches up to semi-desert habi-tats in north Africa. They're usually seen in small groups, and always look distinctly dishevelled.

■ Wrens; family *Troglodytidae*

One of the most familiar small birds of northern Europe, the **wren** is unmistakeable because of its tiny size and cocked tail; it breeds as far south as Sicily and northern Spain, and on some of the islands as well. Wrens have an amazingly loud song for such a small bird, but otherwise rarely betray their presence.

■ Dippers; family *Cinclidae*

The **dipper**, which looks not unlike an outsize wren, lives around fast-running mountain streams, and is found in small numbers in the Pyrenees and the French and Italian Alps. Dippers are dark brown with a neat white throat and breast, and their name derives from their habit of standing on a rock near or in the water and constantly "dipping" up and down. They also walk underwater in search of the aquatic inverte-brates on which they feed, facing upstream and using the water pressure on their angled back to hold them on the bottom.

■ Orioles; family *Oriolidae*

Although the male **golden oriole** is one of the most colourful European birds – bright yellow with black wings – it's very shy and thus hard to see. The size of a thrush, it's a woodland bird, and most easily found by its call – a liquid, flute-like "weela-weoow".

■ Parrotbills; family *Pardoxornithidae*

A member of a principally tropical family, the **bearded tit** is a small bird that is thinly scattered in marshland around the northern Med. It has a very long tail, which distinguishes it from any other small bird you're likely to see in reed beds; both sexes are reddish-brown, but the male has a grey head and a black "moustache" running down from the bill.

■ Tits; family *Paridae*

The 9 Mediterranean species of tit are all small insectivorous birds, often brightly coloured, with short bills. The widespread **great tit**, a woodland species, is identifiable by its black and white head and the broad black line down the middle of its yellow breast. Great tits have perhaps the widest call-note range of any bird species, a general birdwatcher's rule being "if in doubt, it's a great tit". The smaller **blue tit** is the only small blue and yellow bird of the region, but comes in different colours as you go further south. Several tit species are less colourful, with plumages simply of black, brown and grey; one of them, the aptly named **sombre tit**, is quite common in woodland in Greece and Turkey. Another notable tit species is the **penduline tit**, usually found in scrub or bushes near to fresh water; it's more populous around the east of the Med, though it seems to be spreading westwards. The plumage of this species is beautiful – pale grey head with a black eye-patch, contrasting with a rich chestnut back – as is the "tisoo" call they make from thick cover. Their bottle-shaped nest is remarkable too, skilfully woven from grasses and suspended from the end of a hanging branch of willow or poplar.

■ Nuthatches; family *Sittidae*

The nuthatches – plump short-tailed birds with a slate grey back and pale or orange underparts – are the only birds which habitually climb down trees as well as up in their search for insects under the bark. They are resident birds that rarely move far, and this has led to the development of six separate species in the region, some in a very limited area. The **Corsican nuthatch**, for example, is found only in pine forests in central Corsica and the **Algerian nuthatch**, discovered just fifteen years ago, is similarly confined to a small mountainous area of eastern Algeria. The **European nuthatch**, however, is widely found in forests and woodland round the whole of the northern Med; it's easily told by its deep orange underparts. In the east, its close relative the **rock nuthatch** lives in rocky terrain, and is a fairly frequent sight amongst the ancient ruins of Greece and Turkey.

The related **wallcreeper** looks quite different, with a thin decurved bill and very striking crimson and black wings, contrasting with its grey body. Wallcreepers are elusive birds, living on cliff faces high in the mountains in the summer, then moving to lower altitudes in winter. Like the nuthatches, **treecreepers** live on tree trunks, but can only climb upwards, and drop down in a spiral flight when they reach the top of the ascent. Mouse-sized, they have a brown back and white belly, and a delicate decurved bill. Although there are actually 2 species around the Med, they are effectively identical in the field except for the slight difference in their calls. Look for them in any woodlands, especially coniferous ones.

■ Crows; family *Corvidae*

The 11 Mediterranean crow species are consistently noisy and conspicuous. The **raven**, for example, is almost as big as a buzzard and has a rasping flight call that sounds almost like an Alsatian's bark; its wedge-shaped tail otherwise marks it out. Ravens are great at aerobatics – in the breeding season, especially, they put on terrific flying displays, tumbling through the air, rolling from side to side, and even flying upside down. They are found in wild country in a variety of habitats from the mountains to sea cliffs. **Crows** and **jackdaws**, both smaller members of the family, are much happier in human company – jackdaws, in particular, will often nest colonially in large ruined buildings. The **chough** is a particularly attractive small crow, with glossy black plumage and bright red legs and bill; like the raven it's a brilliant aerobatic flier. Higher in the mountains its place is taken by the **Alpine chough**, which has a shorter yellow bill and can be very common in some ranges, swooping around in large flocks. Not all crows are black. The **jay** is one of the most brightly coloured birds of the region, its pink, black and white body enlivened by kingfisher-blue wing flashes when it flies. Perhaps the best known of the lot is the **magpie**, with its unconfusable black and white body and long tail.

■ Starlings; family *Sturnidae*

Roosting in noisy chattering flocks and probing for insects in the short grass of parks and fields, **common starlings** are among the most familiar urban birds. The proper collective noun for a flock of them is, appropriately enough, a "murmuration" of starlings. In Iberia and north Africa they are joined by the **spotless starling**, almost identical in looks and behaviour, but the adults are unspotted in breeding plumage, a characteristic apparent only at close range and in good light.

■ Sparrows; family *Ploceidae*

Belonging to a basically tropical family that includes the weaver birds, sparrows are a confusing bunch of species and subspecies. Town sparrows around the Med differ subtly from area to area, and although the "ordinary" **house sparrow** is widespread, it has an Italian subspecies that has a brown head instead of a grey one, not to mention the closely related **Spanish sparrow**, which has a blacker breast and neck. The females of all these are virtually inseparable, even to male sparrows, and much interbreeding takes place, confusing things even more. In dry and rocky mountains, the **rock sparrow** is widely distributed but nowhere common; the adult looks like a female house sparrow, but is more striped and has an almost invisible yellow throat patch.

■ Finches; family *Fringillidae*

Like sparrows, finches are small birds with a stout bill designed for cracking seeds; unlike sparrows, however, they have slightly forked tails and a characteristic undulating flight. The family includes some of the most colourful small birds of the region, as well as good songsters – hence the popularity of canaries, serins and goldfinches as cagebirds throughout the Med. Although they will move around a little according to winter weather conditions and food supplies, they are essentially residents.

Of the 11 finch species found in the region, the **chaffinch** is one of the commonest, present in suburban woods as well as the countryside; the male has a pink breast, blue head and green rump, and both sexes have a distinctive double white wing bar. The **serin** – equally widely distributed in woodlands – is closely related to the wild ancestor of the domestic canary, and coloured a streaked yellowish-green; the male has a yellow head and rump, and delivers his jangling high-pitched song from the tops of trees and bushes.

A bird of brilliant plumage – bright red face surrounded by a white ring, and a brilliant yellow wing-bar – the **goldfinch** is to be seen on wood-land edges and farmland, hanging acrobatically off plants, especially thistles, as it searches for seeds. Other common finches include the **greenfinch**, a large green and yellow finch with a stout bill, and the **linnet**, a frequent bird of heaths and open scrub. The male linnet looks drab at first sight, but closer observation reveals a lovely pink breast and forehead, contrasting with a grey head.

■ Buntings; family *Emberizidae*

The 9 species of bunting are similar to finches in size, general shape and thickness of bill, but belong to a quite different habitat, being almost entirely birds of open country, where they live mainly on the ground.

The largest Med species is the heavily built **corn bunting**; in all other buntings the male is multicoloured, but in this species he's a very plain streaked brown. In spring he endlessly delivers his song from a post or other perch, a recital that sounds exactly like the jangling of keys. The male **rock bunting** – as its name implies, a bird of rocky hillsides and mountains – is picked out by his grey head with striking black stripes. With the **ortolan bunting** – a widespread summer visitor that winters south of the Sahara – the male has a pink belly, yellow throat and green head, though these colours are rather muted.

Breaking the family rule, the **reed bunting** breeds mostly in reed beds by water; the male has a vivid jet-black head, white "moustache" stripe, and brown body. On the grounds of its beauty and its strange migratory habits the **black-headed bunting** deserves a mention, even though it's restricted to the Balkans and Turkey. The male has a pure lemon-yellow breast and throat and a jet-black head, and the species is unusual because rather than following the usual north–south migration pattern they winter in central Asia and fly west to breed.

Goldfinch

MAMMALS

Mammals have a pretty tough time around the Med. For a start, most of them are not well adapted to the hot, dry summers of the region, and human factors such as habitat disturbance and large-scale, long-term hunting have made an already uncongenial environment even worse. Accordingly, mammals are **comparatively scarce** around the Mediterranean, and tend to keep themselves to themselves. The islands, in particular, have a low number of mammal species, owing largely to the inability of mammals to colonise across water.

Before the human population explosion and the development of agriculture, however, it seems that large predators were much more common, which implies that there were more small mammals too. The Caspian tiger vanished from central and eastern Turkey within the last twenty years, for example. Going further back, from the writings of Herodotus and others it would appear that lions and bears were native to Greece 2000 years ago, and some extraordinary species lived round the Med in the preceding millennia. Malta, Sicily and many of the Aegean islands had pygmy hippos and pygmy elephants, but in small populations that were vulnerable to hunting and climatic change, and so became extinct around 8000 years ago.

In general, most extant mammals are animals of the **twilight or night**, either by nature or by force of circumstance. In the daytime look for tracks (especially around freshwater), droppings and other signs such as gnawed bark, nuts or pine cones. **Droppings** of herbivores such as mice and rabbits are usually consistent in shape within each species, and are light and fibrous when dry. Carnivore droppings, by contrast, are long and twisted, irregular in shape, and often go white when dry; feathers, fur, bones or indigestible bits of insects are often embedded in them. Peering closely at animal droppings may be an antisocial pastime, but it can often indicate where their creators might be later, since many mammals are territorial and follow the same route night after night.

There are about 3500 species of mammal in the world, divided into seventeen orders. Of these, around **100 species from nine orders** are found in the Med. Two of these are marine orders (see "Marine Life", p.69), leaving just over 90 species of terrestrial mammals in 7 orders.

HEDGEHOGS, MOLES AND SHREWS; ORDER *INSECTIVORA*

Despite their scientific name, the diet of this order is not limited to insects – they eat earthworms, slugs, snails and more or less any small invertebrates they can get their paws on. Three species of **hedgehog** (family *Erinaceidae*) occur, all nocturnal and similar in appearance; they can often be located by sound as they grunt, snuffle and squeak through ditches and long grass in search of food.

The 3 Mediterranean species of **moles** (family *Talpidae*) are distinguished more by geographical range than by appearance. Exclusively subterranean, they are ill-suited to the stony ground of much of the Med, and molehills are common only in areas of richer and deeper soils. Related to the moles is the bizarre **Pyrenean desman**; mole-sized, with a very long, sensitive snout and webbed hind feet, it lives in streams and other clear waters of the Pyrenees and parts of north-west Spain. It's very much a hangover species from earlier times, and its tiny population is now endangered.

The desman is a sort of intermediary between moles and **shrews** (family *Soricidae*), about a dozen species of which are found round the Med. The size of a mouse or smaller, shrews can always be distinguished by their elongated and hairy snouts, which allow them to hunt by touch and smell at night. Shrews are active by day and night wherever there is thick ground vegetation, emitting a high-pitched squeak as they forage. Identification down to species level is very hard, and often impossible in the field. Some shrews are extremely small, the tiniest being the **pygmy white-toothed shrew** at only 45mm long (not much larger than a big beetle); it's found around much of the Med in lowland habitats. Although most shrews are terrestrial, 2 species of **water shrew** have adapted to a freshwater existence, preying on water animals up to the size of small frogs, which they paralyse with their venomous saliva. They are black above and white below – the same colours, and for the same camouflage reason, as many seabirds.

BATS; ORDER *CHIROPTERA*

With around 28 species from four families around the Med, bats make up about one quarter of the mammal fauna of the region. All Med bats are insectivorous, with one exception – the **Egyptian fruit bat**, which is different in a number of other ways, too. Fruit bats are usually large, have big eyes, and tend not to use echolocation (see below), as typical bats do. It has been suggested that they have evolved along a different route from true bats, and are more closely related to primates than to insectivores – a good example of **convergent evolution**, where a common characteristic (in this case flight) is separately evolved by different species. The Egyptian fruit bat has fairly recently spread into Cyprus and Turkey from the Middle East.

The **typical bats** are small to medium-sized, and almost impossible to tell apart in flight. They're unique in two respects; firstly, they're the **only free-flying mammals**, and secondly they're the only ones to have developed the additional sense of **echolocation**. When bats fly, they continuously emit a squeak that is mainly in the ultrasonic range (ie inaudible to humans); they then monitor the echo from surrounding objects, a process so refined that it enables them to locate insects in flight. They can even step up the frequency of emission as they close in on their prey, in order to gather more precise information on its movements.

Bats can also **migrate** as birds do, and they regularly move their colonial roosting sites over the year, either to exploit another food supply or to find a place that meets their very specific requirements for temperature and humidity – a cave may be fine in March, for instance, but too cool in December. Bat-ringing to track their migratory movements is a much less developed science than bird-ringing, but even so, it's clear that bats may migrate many hundreds of kilometres. Many bat species have declined alarmingly in recent years through the spread of insecticides, the disturbance of caves and felling of large hollow trees, although they have countered this to some extent by colonising roof spaces.

The name of the **horseshoe bat** comes from its strange nose structure, which is used in the transmission and reception of ultrasound. All 5 Med species of horseshoe bat are in decline; the small bat most likely to be seen is the **pipistrelle**, as abundant round the Med as it is in northern Europe. With a body scarcely the size of a mouse's, it forms colonies which in some cave habitats can be several thousand strong.

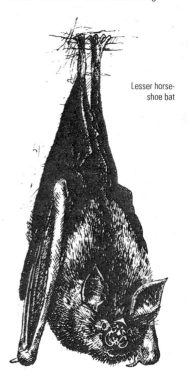

Lesser horseshoe bat

The best places to **watch for bats** are lighted buildings in the countryside, as the lights attract insects and show up the bats themselves. Lakes and waterways are good too, because they have a high insect population.

RABBITS AND HARES; ORDER *LAGOMORPHA*

Two species from the family *Leporidae* are the only representatives of this order in the Med. The common **rabbit** originated in Iberia and northwest Africa; rabbit populations in the rest of Europe are the result of human introductions. Rabbits are colonial, and can be found right round the Med wherever there is sufficient grass and low vegetation for them to browse on. **Hares** are much longer-legged than rabbits, and their long ears are tipped with black; they are solitary except in the breeding season, and live by grazing and browsing, especially in farmland. Rabbits and hares digest their food twice, in order to fully break down the cellulose; rather than regurgitating and re-chewing, like cows, they produce soft faeces which they then immediately eat, digesting it once more and producing the familiar round dry pellets. Another adaptation to grazing is that their teeth are continuously growing.

RODENTS; ORDER *RODENTIA*

Containing all the rats, mice and voles, the rodent order is represented around the Med by at least 26 species from 5 families. Although they vary widely in appearance, they have a common tooth structure, consisting of two large front teeth (for gnawing off plant material) separated by a gap from a row of smaller back teeth (for grinding it up).

The **squirrels** (family *Sciuridae*) are represented only by the **red squirrel**, since the grey squirrel, which has largely replaced it in Britain and Ireland, has never been introduced to mainland Europe. There are two colour phases – the familiar rich red one, which turns a dark brown in winter, and a much darker, almost black, phase. Coniferous forests are their chief habitat, although in parts of the Med they are tame enough to come into gardens and town parks; you can track them down by looking for gnawed pine cones – they always leave a stalk with all the scales nibbled off. **Susliks** are closely related, but live colonially in burrows, especially in open barren land; slightly smaller than the red squirrel, they have less prominent ears and a much smaller tail, but otherwise their body shape is similar. One species occurs in northern Greece and Turkey, and there's another one on the plains of north Africa. **Alpine marmots**, found in many of the Med mountains, are another related ground squirrel.

A single species of **porcupine** (family *Hystricidae*) lives in the region. One of the largest rodents of the Med (up to 70cm long), it bristles with long black and white spines that it employs in combat by reversing into its opponent at high speed. It's fairly common in scrub and woodland in north Africa, and also occurs in southern Italy and Sicily, but its nocturnal habits make it a rare sight. Almost as elusive are the 4 species of

dormouse (family *Gliridae*); they have the squirrel's long bushy tail and arboreal way of life, but are much smaller and nocturnal; one species, the **garden dormouse** is relatively tame and will enter houses on occasions – it's a sandy colour with black facial markings, very big ears, and a black and white tuft at the end of its tail.

The **beavers** (family *Castoridae*) are represented only by the **European beaver**, a very rare animal that survives in parts of France, where it has been successfully reintroduced to some of the rivers in the southern Massif Central.

All other Med rodents belong to the large family *Muridae* – the **voles, mice and rats**. These are by far the commonest rodents, living in most habitats throughout the Med and feeding on seeds, grain and other plant material. They are also one of the most important prey species for predatory birds and mammals. **Voles** are stubby little rodents, with short muzzles, legs and tails; most live underground, although **water voles**, as their name suggests, have adapted to living in freshwater. **Mice** have long thin tails, big ears and eyes, and pointed muzzles; as with all members of this family, identification down to species level is very difficult. **Rats** are simply a bigger version of mice, and there are two widespread Med species: the **ship rat**, which is sometimes black but more often brown with a pale underside, and the larger **common rat**, which is invariably brown. Both frequent human dwellings and are rarely found in undisturbed countryside. In the north African desert, several species of **desert rat** flourish, but they are hard to tell apart.

PRIMATES; ORDER *PRIMATES*

The sole primate species of the Med, the **Barbary ape**, is actually not an ape at all, but a true monkey, related to the African and Asian macaques. Unusually for a monkey, the Barbary ape is tailless, perhaps a response to the relatively cold winters of the region, when a thin heat-losing tail would be a liability. They are now rare animals, confined in the wild to the remnant cedar forests on the Atlas mountains of Morocco and Algeria; the small colony in Gibraltar may have sprung from the now-extinct Andalucian population, but have now been supplemented by north African animals, and can't really be considered as truly wild.

CARNIVORES; ORDER *CARNIVORA*

Although 13 carnivore species from 5 families occur around the Med, they're all **scarce and elusive**, and many are on the edge of extinction. Being at the top of the food chain, carnivores have a low population density in the first place, and human intervention has now greatly disturbed their hunting territories, leading to a drop in numbers; furthermore, carnivores compete with humans for food and so have been hunted throughout the centuries. Only carnivores with non-specialised prey requirements, such as the fox, have been able to adapt.

■ Bears; family *Ursidae*

The brown bear is the largest of all Med mammals, reaching two metres in length and weighing up to 200kg; it's a race of a very wide-spread species, found through north America and much of northern Asia. Strangely for a carnivore, its diet is mostly vegetarian, consisting of roots, berries, nuts and grains, although it will occasionally take fish and domestic animals. These powerful animals are not tolerated close to human settlements for long, and persecution and habitat destruction have driven the bear back to the mountains of Scandinavia, Russia and the Balkans. The Balkan population extends down into Yugoslavia and northern Greece, and some of the wilder national parks in these countries offer the best chance of seeing bears in Europe, with luck and patience. Four other isolated relic populations exist: fewer than 100 individuals hang on in the Cantabrian mountains of northwest Spain, a handful in the Pyrenees, even fewer in the Italian Alps, and some in Abruzzo national park of central Italy. Most of these populations are below critical mass, and only vigorous conservation measures preserve them at all.

■ Foxes and dogs; family *Canidae*

Of the wild species of foxes and dogs, only the **red fox** can be described as at all common. Living originally in woodland but now in a wide range of habitats, it is a very versatile feeder, preying mainly on rats and mice, and foraging for kitchen scraps close to houses. **Jackals**, which resemble large short-tailed foxes, prefer more open country; confined to the Balkans around the northern Med, they are more widespread in north Africa. Bigger still is the **wolf**, another animal to

have suffered greatly from persecution owing to the danger it presents to domestic stock. Extinct in most of Europe, the wolf is still present (though rarely seen) in the Balkans, Iberia and Italy, though this last population is very thin. Contrary to popular belief, wolves do not make unprovoked attacks on people.

■ Weasels and associated species; family *Mustelidae*

Of the 7 Mediterranean species of the family *Mustelidae*, all except badgers are active predators, and all except the weasel are basically nocturnal or twilight animals. The **weasel** is both the smallest and the commonest; around 25cm long, ginger above and white below, it's a formidable predator, hunting primarily rats and mice, and even killing animals up to rabbit size. The **stoat** rarely reaches as far south as the Med lowlands, but there are 2 fairly widespread species of marten, which is basically a large arboreal stoat that lives on birds and small mammals (especially squirrels). The **pine marten** is found in coniferous woods, and the similar **beech marten** in deciduous woods and rocky hillsides, the latter replacing the former in Greece and Iberia; both species are beautiful animals, with glossy dark brown fur and a prominent throat patch – white in the beech marten, yellowish in the pine marten.

The **polecat** is the same size as a marten, but terrestrial, living nocturnally in lowland woods and farmland. The ferrets kept for rabbit-catching in northern Europe are a domestic form of this species; wild polecats are dark brown with white or yellow markings on the face and muzzle. A far larger relative is the **otter**, growing to over a metre overall; it's the only Mediterranean member of this family that lives in water, and has webbed feet and a thick tapering tail, used as a rudder. In spring and summer it stays around freshwater rivers and marshes, where it breeds, but roams widely in winter, often feeding in salt marshes and estuaries. A shy and declining animal, it's present around most of the Med apart from Greece and the islands.

Largest of the family, and unlike the others in shape, is the **badger**, a stocky, short-legged animal with a black and white striped head and immensely powerful forearms, which it uses to dig the huge setts it lives in. Despite its powerful jaws, the badger is less carnivorous than its relatives, often supplementing its diet of worms and soil invertebrates with roots, bulbs and fruits. Its sett has a large oval opening and a prominent mound of earth at the entrance; should you find one of these with fresh prints around it, it is worth hanging around at dusk, especially in spring and early summer, which is when the cubs come out to play. Exclusively nocturnal, badgers rely mostly on smell and hearing, so you should get downwind of the sett and stay very quiet. Look for setts in woodland, especially on sandy soil close to farmland – but they are far less common around the Med than further north.

■ Mongooses and genets; family *Viverridae*

Built like stoats and weasels, the *Viverridae* are basically a tropical family of which 2 species have reached up to the Med. The **Egyptian mongoose** is like a large polecat, but has grey grizzled fur and a distinctively tapering tail; it's a specialist hunter of reptiles, especially snakes, and is found in the rocky scrub of north Africa and southern Spain. The **genet** is a nocturnal tree-dwelling carnivore, like a short-legged cat with an extraordinarily long ringed tail and beautifully spotted coat; it's found in woodlands through north Africa, Iberia and southern France. Both species are native to the southern Med, and were introduced onto the northern shore to help with rodent control.

■ Cats; family *Felidae*

Two rare species of cat occur around the Med. The **wildcat**, one of the many ancestors of the domestic cat, at first sight looks not unlike a domestic tabby; a closer look (if you are so lucky) reveals that it is built more heavily, with a shorter, bushier tail and a wider head. Wildcats are trapped and hunted because of the damage they do to poultry and game, but still seem to be distributed in forests in Iberia, southern Italy, the Balkans and north Africa. Solitary, secretive and nocturnal, the wildcat is an extremely uncommon sight, and the same goes for its larger relative, the **lynx**. This handsome spotted cat, with a short tail and black-tipped pointed ears, grows up to a metre long and stands 70cm high at the shoulder. It preys on mammals up to the size of small deer, as well as rabbits, hares and game birds. (Like the African caracal and serval, it sometimes leaps to catch birds in flight.) Small populations still survive in Greece and Yugoslavia, and the endangered Spanish lynx

(either a subspecies or a full species, depending on your source) is hanging on with perhaps 50 individuals in 2 Andalucian populations.

EVEN-TOED UNGULATES; ORDER *ARTIODACTYLA*

The *Artiodactyla* order includes all the grazing animals with cloven hoofs, and around 9 species from 3 families are found around the Med. They are of particular interest because they include the **wild ancestors** of our most important domestic stock – wild pigs, sheep and goats are still to be found, although with the last two it's hard to say if they are genuinely wild or merely feral reintroductions. The European wild ancestor of domestic cattle was the aurochs, which has been extinct for 300 years or so. These non-domestic populations provide a source of fresh genes to invigorate the domestic stock, which become impoverished by interbreeding, but they are just as attractive to hunters as to farmers, and populations have been hunted to extinction around much of the Med.

Wild boar

Despite hunting, however, the **wild boar** (sole member of the pig family *Suidae*) is still common in many countries with enough deciduous forest to give them cover. Although exclusively vegetarian, they are formidable animals, and the male is especially dangerous, with its two evil-looking curved tusks. Mostly nocturnal, they leave obvious signs in the forest, including muddy wallows and scratching posts; their tracks are usually identifiable by the imprint of the dewclaw behind the cloven hoof.

The large *Bovidae* family includes all cattle, sheep and goats. There are 3 goat species around the Med, one of them the true ancestral **wild goat**; it resembles the domestic goat but has an impressive pair of curved horns that sweep backwards in one plane (domestic goats have twisted or spiral horns). It's confined to Crete and a few nearby islands, and the small Italian island of Montecristo. Many other islands and rocky places support feral populations of escaped domestic goats. The other 2 goat species are the **ibex**, still to be found in mountainous parts of Spain and the Alps, and the **chamois**. The chamois lacks the impressive horns of the other species, and is a specialist mountain dweller; it's still reasonably common though hard to see in mountain ranges from the Pyrenees through the Alps to the Pindos of Greece. The ancestral wild sheep is the **mouflon**, a big-horned wild sheep now restricted mainly to the islands of Corsica, Sardinia and Cyprus, although other populations have been introduced into parts of the Alps.

Whereas bovine animals such as sheep and goats have permanent, unbranched horns that are carried by both sexes, the **deer** (family *Cervidae*) have branched antlers that are grown only on the males and are shed every year. Like sheep and goats, however, deer are grazers and browsers, and have complex stomachs which enable them to chew the cud. The **fallow deer** is probably indigenous to the Med, from where the Romans introduced it to much of northern Europe; a medium-sized deer with a handsome spotted coat and distinctively flattened antlers, it can be found in open woodland in a few places in Spain, France and Italy. The **red deer** is larger and has unflattened antlers; small numbers occur right round the Med and on many of the islands, though the situation has been confused by introductions for hunting; it's basically a woodland animal, living in anything from scrubby *maquis* to mountainous coniferous woodland. The smallest of the three Mediterranean deer is the **roe deer**, which stands only 75cm high at the shoulder and has a short pair of pointed antlers; scarce in the lowlands around the Med, it is more common in woodland and thick scrub further inland, where it lives by browsing off trees and shrubs.

REPTILES

Around 250 million years ago, some of the early amphibians – the first animals to colonise the land – made the great evolutionary step of developing waterproof skins and eggs. The class of animals thus formed, the **reptiles**, was to dominate the planet for millions of years, occupying niches in the sea, land and air. Some even developed feathers and became the ancestors of modern birds. But very suddenly, about 65 million years ago, the great dinosaurs died out – probably because of a climatic cooling – and mammals took over the dominant role on land. The modern reptiles are the descendants of that once supreme class.

Like amphibians and fish, reptiles are **poikilothermic**; that is, their body temperature varies with the ambient temperature, in contrast to the **homothermic** birds and mammals, which generate their heat internally. The advantage of this is that reptiles need to eat much less food – since they are not burning it up to generate heat – and can thus thrive in infertile habitats. The disadvantage is that they can't function in extremely hot or cold temperatures, which is why they tend to become dormant in cold winters (hibernation) or in hot dry summers (aestivation).

All reptiles have dry, scaly skins, and breathe with lungs throughout their lives, dispensing with the gill-breathing stage of amphibian larvae. All produce eggs, and most lay them in clutches, which are buried underground; some, however, internalise the incubation process and produce live young.

The 80 or so reptile species in the Med fall into 3 groups – the tortoises and turtles, the lizards, and the snakes.

TORTOISES AND TURTLES; ORDER CHELONIA

The stout shell carried by the species of this order is a development from the scaly skins of snakes and lizards; the scales are strengthened and enlarged, and reinforced from below by a bony skeleton. Two families of **turtles** are found in the Med, but since they are entirely marine they are covered in the "Marine Life" section. The five remaining species belong to the family *Testudinidae*, the tortoises and terrapins. **Tortoises** are one of the great sights of the Med,

lumbering through the *maquis* and orchards, browsing with surprising delicacy on any vegetation that takes their fancy. They're most active in the morning and the early evening, spending the hottest part of the day asleep under a bush. You can often locate them by the rustling made by their foraging, or by the broad trail of flattened plants they leave in their wake. The precarious mating procedures are hilarious.

Tortoise

Greece is the only country where all three Med species occur, but you'll find tortoises in southern Spain, southern France (if you're lucky), parts of Italy, Turkey and north Africa. Their maximum size is around the 30cm mark. **Hermann's tortoise** *Testudo hermannii* is the most widely distributed, but is now so rare in France that a special "tortoise village" has been set up in the Massif des Maures, their only French habitat. This decline has been partly brought about by the usual pressures of habitat change, but largely by the pet trade; government action has led to a diminution in this traffic, yet over 30,000 Med species were imported into Britain alone in 1983, a senseless business since an average of 60 percent die in their first British winter. The trade has now shifted to tropical species, which are even less happy here.

Terrapins are freshwater tortoises, with longer tails (to act as a rudder) and streamlined flattened shells. Sometimes seen in great numbers in ponds and ditches, they can even on occasion be found wandering some distance from water. Of the 2 species, the **pond terrapin** *Emys orbicularis* is distributed right round the Med, while the **stripe-necked terrapin** *Mauremys caspica* is absent in France, Italy and most of Yugoslavia. The 2 species are similar in size, growing up to 20cm long, but the latter's striped neck makes it distinctive.

LIZARDS; ORDER *LACERTILIA*

Of the six families in the *Lacertilia* order, the **true lizards** (family *Lacertidae*) are the most numerous, with over 30 species. Since lizards have small territories and don't move around much, there is plenty of opportunity for species divergence, and many of the islands have their own endemic species. All species have long fragile tails, which they can discard to escape from a predator, and are agile and diurnal. Most have a body length of less than 8cm, though the tail can treble the total length. Typical of the small lizards is the **common wall lizard** *Podarcis muralis*, a very variable but usually brownish animal, widespread and common through much of the Med; walls, rocks and roadside banks are its usual habitat, and it often lives close to houses. Like all small lacertids, the female is duller than the male, though both are marked with a beautiful combination of spots and stripes; the male often has a coloured underbelly and flanks, usually buff or orange.

The **green lizards** are far larger, brightly coloured lacertids. They tend to live in grassland or scrub wherever there is thick vegetation, and are extremely quick, running on their hind legs from bush to bush. The largest of them is the **ocellated lizard** *Lacerta lepida*, so-called from the "eyes" that pattern the skin of young animals; the adults can grow up to 20cm in body length, and sometimes have blue spots down their otherwise green flanks. This species is only found in Iberia, southern France, and northwest Africa, although smaller green lizards can be seen round the eastern Med too.

Geckoes (family *Gekkonidae*) are basically a tropical lizard family, with 4 species reaching into the Med. They're plump soft-skinned lizards, and do most of their insect-hunting by night, on cliffs, in trees, and increasingly in houses. Large eyes give them excellent vision in the dark, and some species have adhesive pads on their toes that permit extraordinary climbing feats. The pads work a bit like Velcro, having tiny hairs on the underside that stick to the slightest surface roughness on a wall or rock. The most widespread species is the **Moorish gecko** *Taurentola mauritanica*, which has a characteristic ridged skin and prominent toepads; growing to 15cm including its tail, it is distributed right round the Med and is especially common on the Iberian peninsula.

The *Agamidae* family are another group of tropical lizards, of which only one species – the **agama** *Agama stellio* – extends into the eastern Med; there are colonies on some Greek islands, especially the Dodecanese, and it's common in parts of Turkey too. The agama is a large lizard, growing up to 30cm including tail, and its alternative name of "Rhodes dragon" suits it well, for it is noticeably spiny with a well-defined reptilian head; brown or grey in colour, it has a line of paler diamond shaped markings down its back. In Greece they mostly live in walls and rocks, whereas those in Turkey live in trees as well; where it occurs, they can be very common.

The **chameleon** *Chamaeleo chaemeleon*, another representative of a mostly tropical family, is native to Turkey and north Africa, and small populations have spread into southern Spain, the Dodecanese and Crete. With its bulging eyes and prehensile tail it's immediately identifiable, but its flattened leaf-shaped body and ability to change colour makes searching for it among the bushes a frustrating experience. Many other species can change their colour too – including other lizards such as the agama and the geckoes – but none does it so dramatically. Equally astonishing is its sticky tongue, which shoots forward to catch insects from a distance as great as its body length.

Agama
Agama stellio

Thicker bodied than other lizards, the **skinks** (family *Scincidae*) have very large and shiny scales that give them a glistening appearance; they are ground-dwelling, with small legs that in some species have almost vanished. The **ocellated skink** *Chalcides ocellatus* is the largest of the 5 Med species, growing to 30cm; usually sandy coloured with a pattern of dark, pale-centred dots, it lives in sandy places in southern Italy, Greece, and north Africa. Its close relative the **three-toed skink** *Chalcides chalcides* is found round most of the Med; its legs are tiny with three-toed feet, and it behaves more like a snake than a lizard. These 2 skink species are **viviparous** – that is, they give birth to live young, with the female retaining the eggs in her body until hatching.

Some lizards have dispensed with legs altogether. One of these is the **slow worm** *Anguis fragilis*, which occurs through most of Europe except the Iberian peninsula; superficially snake-like, they differ in that they can close their eyes, are slower moving, and look very shiny. They're shy animals, most active after rain has brought out the slugs on which they feed. Unlike other lizards, they prefer to absorb the sun's heat indirectly by lying under a warm object rather than basking directly in the sunshine; sheets of corrugated iron are preferred places. The other Med species of legless lizard is the **European glass snake** *Ophisaurus apodus*, which lives in Greece and the Balkans and looks like a huge slow worm, reaching lengths of over a metre.

Finally, one species of **worm lizard** (family *Amphisbaenidae*) is found in Spain and north Africa, but is rarely seen because it spends most of its life underground; unsurprisingly, it looks like a large plump earthworm.

SNAKES; ORDER *SERPENTES*

Essentially, snakes are legless lizards, and are thought to have evolved from burrowing lizards millions of years ago – some retain skeletal vestiges of legs, such as hip bones. Almost all snakes have enlarged belly scales to assist movement along the ground. Other characteristics can be traced to an earlier evolutionary period of subterranean existence. Thus, they can't close their eyes, their eyelids being fused together to form a transparent covering, and they don't have eardrums; this means they are virtually deaf to sound transmitted through the air, but they make

up for this by being very sensitive to vibrations transmitted through the ground.

Snakes are commonly thought to be slimy, dangerous and capable of wriggling as fast as a man can run. This is largely nonsense. Snakes, like all reptiles, are dry and warm to the touch; they rarely move faster than a swift human walk; they hardly ever attack unprovoked; and, in Med countries at least, only the front-fanged vipers have a dangerous venom that can be injected effectively. That said, people are sometimes bitten by vipers, so it's best to know how to avoid and, if necessary, treat a snakebite.

The Mediterranean has around 30 snake species from 4 families, 2 of them – the **worm snakes** (family *Typllopidae*) and the **sand boas** (family *Boidae*) – represented by a single species. The **worm snake** *Typhlops vermicularis* looks like a dry worm with shiny scales; mostly living underground, it can be found in open habitats in the eastern Med. The **sand boa** *Eryx jaculus* is a small relative of the tropical pythons and boa constrictors, rarely reaching a metre in length. Found in dry sandy habitats of Greece, Turkey and north Africa, it too stays underground much of the time, hunting the rodents that form its staple diet.

The **typical snakes** (family *Colubridae*) constitute much the most numerous category, with nearly 20 species. It's a very diverse family, yet it has some common features: all colubrids have characteristic large scales on top of their heads; all are long (up to 2m) and slender; most have round pupils; and most constrict their prey before swallowing it whole – though three species have poison fangs (situated in the back of the mouth, and therefore virtually harmless to humans). The **grass snake** *Natrix natrix* is a typical colubrid snake, common in northern Europe and widely found around the Med too; colour is variable, but it usually has a yellow collar behind the head. It's a snake of damp places, swimming well, and mostly feeding on amphibians. The similar-looking **Aesculapian snake** *Elaphe longissima*, found everywhere except Iberia and north Africa, reaches a length of two metres and is much more terrestrial than the grass snake, climbing trees with ease and feeding off small mammals and nesting birds. Half a dozen species of **whip snakes** *Coluber spp.* are native to the Med, of which the **western whip snake** *Coluber viridiflavus* is typical; found in France, Italy, Corsica and Sardinia, it is black with variable yellow blotches, and, although not poisonous,

SNAKEBITE

Since **vipers** are the only significantly poisonous snakes in the Med, it's sensible to be able to recognise them. They are all thick-bodied snakes, with a rather short tail and an approximately triangular head. They have prominent brow ridges and vertical eye pupils, and most species have a dark zigzag down the back, though patterns can vary. All seven species found round the Med are venomous to different degrees, and all live typically but by no means exclusively – in dry, rocky and scrubby hillsides.

Most will bite if **disturbed or frightened**. Two pieces of common sense are to wear **shoes and trousers** when walking through likely viper habitats, and to watch where you are putting your **hands and feet**, especially when climbing over walls and rocks. If you do get bitten by a snake, **don't panic**. It may be a non-poisonous snake, in which case shock will be the only symptom; sit quietly and wait to see if a **swelling** develops around the bite – if it doesn't, no poison has been injected. If a swelling does develop, it's important to **minimise blood flow** around the bite to prevent the poison from spreading to the rest of the body; bites are usually on one of the limbs, so keep that limb immobile if you can, and restrict the blood flow by wrapping **a firm but not tight ligature** above the bite. Don't rush or panic, since both will speed up blood flow and spread the poison more quickly. Then get to a doctor or hospital as soon as you can – but bear in mind that even a bad viper bite is unlikely to cause death in less than 24 hours if left untreated. And **don't** try to cut the wound, suck the poison out, or put disinfectants on it – all these things will only make it worse.

is aggressive when handled, biting hard and persistently. Like other whip snakes, its diet includes a high proportion of lizards as well as small mammals, birds, and other snakes.

As stated above, the 7 members of the **viper** family *Viperidae* can usually be identified by their short fat bodies, zigzag markings and well-defined triangular heads. Unlike colubrids, their heads are covered with small scales. Most Med countries have at least one species, although they are absent from some islands, including Corsica, Sardinia, Crete and the Balearics. The poison fangs are connected at the top of the front jaw, and project at right angles when in use; at other times, they are folded back and sheathed along the roof of the mouth. Males sometimes do a "wrestling dance" at mating times, rearing up and intertwining their bodies in an attempt to press the weaker animal to the ground; the loser then retires, leaving the stronger one to mate.

In Iberia and north Africa, **Lataste's viper** *Vipera latasti* is the dominant viper; it grows to 60cm and has a noticeably upturned nose. In France and Italy it is replaced by the **asp viper** *Vipera aspis*, which is very variable in colour; some specimens are even totally black. The commonest viper in the Balkans and eastern Med is the **nose-horned viper** *Vipera ammodytes*, reputedly the most venomous of all European vipers. Don't get too paranoid about them, though – they instinctively avoid contact where possible.

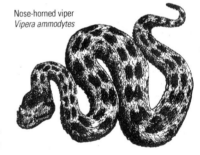

Nose-horned viper
Vipera ammodytes

AMPHIBIANS

Amphibians were the first vertebrates to crawl out of the water into the primeval swamps around 350 million years ago, and they still have several fishy characteristics. Thus they retain a **fully aquatic stage** in their life cycle; the tadpole stage of all amphibians breathes through gills, like fish, and only develops lungs when it leaves the water. An extension of this aquatic way of life is that the skin and eggshells of amphibians are **not watertight**. The importance of this is not that they let water in, but that they leak water out, and so the embryo will dessicate and die unless the eggs are kept moist at all times. Hence, amphibians lay their gelatinous eggs in water, and must themselves keep moist. The final fish-like characteristic retained by amphibians is the thin line of **pressure-sensitive cells** running along the sides of the body; these function as a depth gauge, and also to pick up vibrations in the water caused by other animals.

The 40 or so species of Med amphibians are divided roughly equally into two orders – those with tails (*Urodela*) and those without them (*Anura*).

NEWTS AND SALAMANDERS; ORDER URODELA

Most of the newts and salamanders of the Med are from the family *Salamandridae*. All are essentially carnivores, feeding off small invertebrates. Of the 9 salamander species found round the Med, only one, the **fire salamander** *Salamandra salamandra*, is widespread. This large, black amphibian (up to 25cm long) is brilliantly coloured with yellow or orange blotches and stripes; the pattern varies greatly. Salamanders are mostly terrestrial, and this species spends most of the year in damp

leaf-litter, usually close to a stream. The **sharp-ribbed salamander** *Pleurodeles waltl* spends more time in water, and is found in southern Spain and Portugal, as well as Morocco; another large species, it's an undistinguished grey/green colour, with a row of warty knobs along each flank. All the other 7 salamander species are confined to small areas or islands; Corsica and Sardinia, for instance, each have their own species of **brook salamander** *Euproctus spp.* Salamanders have unusual mating behaviour; the male produces a neat packet of sperm which he lays on the damp ground, and he then picks up the female and deposits her on it – the fertilised eggs are then laid in water.

Newts are more aquatic than salamanders, and generally smaller. You're most likely to see them in water during the breeding season in spring and early summer, when the males develop a flamboyant breeding dress, brightly coloured and with a long crest along the top of the back and tail. The **warty newt** *Triturus cristatus* is dark brown, warty (obviously) and has a bright orange belly; basically a species of north and eastern Europe, its Mediterranean habitats are along the Italian and Adriatic coasts. Over in southwest France and the Iberian peninsula, it is replaced by the similarly sized **marbled newt** *Triturus marmoratus*, which is strikingly blotched green and black. These two are the largest of the 7 newt species of the region, growing to 14cm long. The other 5 species have dark brown dots on a paler background, with red or yellow bellies; the males have breeding crests of various heights.

One of the best ways to watch for newts (and other amphibians for that matter) is to **take a torch** to a pond at night, especially in spring; by the torchlight, you can see newts hanging in the

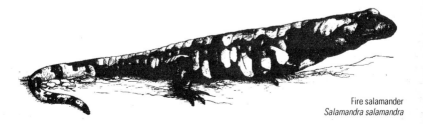

Fire salamander
Salamandra salamandra

water and drifting to the surface for the air. Newts are choosy about where they breed, as not only must there be adequate food in the pond for adults and young, but most species will lay their eggs only on particular plants. Thus all over Europe newts have declined as their breeding ponds have been disturbed, polluted or drained.

Two species of **cave salamander** *Hydromantes spp.* are found, one in northern Italy and the other only on Sardinia. These cave-dwelling salamanders are lungless, absorbing oxygen through their moist skins. All other members of their family (*Plethodontidae*) are American; the nearest relatives of these Med ones are in California, so they have remained unchanged since the time when what is now America was locked snugly around what is now Europe, some 175 million years ago.

Of similar antiquity is the **olm** *Proteus anguinus*, the only European representative of the family *Proteidae*; the other 4 species in the family are native to the eastern USA. Living permanently in the larval state, the olm has external feathery red gills and is almost blind. There's a small colony in Italy, but the largest population lives in caves in Yugoslavia – the amazing limestone karst caves at Postojna near Ljubljana are the best place to see them.

FROGS AND TOADS; ORDER *ANURA*

Frogs and toads differ from the previous order in three obvious ways: they **lack tails**, they have well-developed **back legs**, and they are **extremely noisy**. Otherwise, they have similar habits, needing a moist environment to live in, water in which to lay eggs, and a plentiful supply of invertebrates on which to feed. Again, the best time and place to watch for them is on a warm spring evening, preferably after rain, around a breeding pond or slow-flowing stream.

There are 5 families of frogs and toads around the Med. The first, the predominantly European *Discoglossidae*, includes the **yellow-bellied toad** *Bombina variegata*, a small toad (less than 5cm long) with a brilliant yellow or orange belly; active by day and by night, it will throw itself on its back exposing its belly if alarmed, warning predators that it has an unpleasant taste – black and yellow being universal warning symbols in the animal kingdom. It's a central European species, absent from southern Greece, Iberia and most of the islands. The family also includes the

midwife toad *Alytes obstetricians*, which occurs through southern France and Iberia. As the name suggests, the reproductive cycle of this species is unusual. The female lays a string of eggs in the water in the usual way, but the male then wraps the fertilised string around his hind legs and carries them around with him until they are ready to hatch, dipping them in water if they show signs of drying out; he then takes them to a pool and dangles his legs while the eggs hatch and the tadpoles swim away.

The **spadefoots** (family *Pelobatidae*) are like heavily built toads, from which they are best distinguished by the elongated central toe on their hind feet. They live in burrows in the ground, using their "spade-feet" to excavate them; since they are nocturnal, your best chance of bumping into them is around ponds in the breeding season. Three species of **spadefoot** *Pelobates spp.* occur around the Med, plus the closely related **parsley frog** *Pelodytes punctatus*, found in France and Iberia only.

Three species of **typical toads** (family *Bufonidae*) live round the Med, identifiable by their warty skins, horizontal pupils, and prominent paratoid glands (two long humps behind the eyes). The **common toad** *Bufo bufo* is much the largest frog or toad in the region, with big females growing up to 15cm – comfortably filling an outstretched human hand. At mating time, females emerge from their daytime lairs and make for the nearest water; the much smaller males cling on to the female, sometimes two or three at a time, to make sure they are in position to fertilise her eggs as she lays them. A related species, found in the eastern Med and north Africa, is the **green toad** *Bufo viridis*, smaller than the previous species and beautifully coloured in a tapestry of green and cream.

Although frogs and toads normally live on the ground, there are two Med species of **tree frog** (family *Hylidae*), normally located by their nocturnal call, which sounds like a rapidly quacking duck. The more widespread species has a long brown stripe down its flank, and is usually bright green; however, they can change colour quite quickly to match their surroundings. Representatives of a mostly tropical family, they have round pads on their toes to help them climb; flying insects are their main source of food, skilfully intercepted with their telescopic tongues.

Tree frog

The final family in the order *Anura* are the **typical frogs** (family *Ranidae*), of which some 6 species are found around the Med. They all have horizontal pupils, smooth skins and webbed feet; generally much more active than toads, they move by hopping rather than walking. The brown frogs include 4 very similar species, all about 8cm long, and mostly terrestrial outside the breeding season; the **agile frog** *Rana dalmatina* is probably the most widely distributed in the region, except in the Iberian peninsula. The green frogs are larger and stay in or near to water most of the time; the **marsh frog** *Rana ridibunda* is typical – growing up to 15cm, it is one of the most vocal frogs, making an extraordinary range of grunts and chuckles.

INSECTS

Insects are arguably the most successful animals on earth. They're certainly the most diverse class, with at least a million species and probably many more, making up some **80 percent of all known animals**. They range in size from fleas to moths with wingspans up to 30cm, and some of them have great impact on our lives; modern agriculture, for example, wages a ceaseless war against the depradations of insects, and the *Anopheles* mosquitoes, as vectors of malaria, are responsible for more human deaths than any other animal.

All insects have **tripartite bodies**. The **head** carries a pair of antennae, mostly used for smell and touch, and a pair of compound eyes, which are usually large and conspicuous. These eyes are composed of many individual lenses (up to 300,000 in some dragonflies) – a different system from that of the mammalian eye, which processes light through rods and cones on the back of the eyeball. The insect eye produces a more blurred picture, but can be exceptionally acute at detecting movement. Joined to the head is the **thorax**, which carries three pairs of legs and two pairs of wings. Sometimes only one pair of wings is obvious, the other pair having been reduced to tiny pins called halteres – examine a fly and you'll see them. The hind section is the **abdomen**, made up of ten or eleven fused segments; the ridges between some of these are clearly visible.

Insects are basically held together by their **external skeleton**, made of a substance called chitin, which also protects them and prevents water loss from the body. They don't possess lungs, relying instead on oxygen diffusion through air tubes in the skin; it is this that restricts their body diameter, as the oxygen can only seep in a short distance. Virtually all insects lay **eggs**. In some species, the young insect which emerges from the egg is a tiny replica of the adult, apart from its small wings. As it grows, it splits its skin and expands into the new one underneath, a moulting that can occur up to 50 times (though 10 or fewer is usual). Insects that grow in this way – such as grasshoppers and dragonflies – are called **exopterygota**, because they always have external wings; their young stages are called **nymphs**.

Other insects hatch into an animal that bears no resemblance to the adult – the caterpillars of butterflies, for instance, or the maggots of flies. These insects are called **endopterygota** and the young stages are called **larvae**. The transition from larva to adult is one of the wonders of the living world. Having grown up through various skin-shedding stages in the usual way, the larva then goes through a stage of dramatic transformation called metamorphosis. This occurs inside a protective shell or pupa, within which the larva effectively dissolves itself into a genetic soup, and then reassembles itself into an adult. How this process actually occurs is still poorly understood.

Some 25 insect orders occur around the Med, and of these we shall deal with the 8 most likely to be seen. Of these, the first 4 (dragonflies to bugs) are exopterygotous, and the second 4 (butterflies and moths to beetles) are endopterygotous.

DRAGONFLIES AND DAMSELFLIES; ORDER *ODONATA*

The nymphs of the dragonflies and damselflies live in fresh water, and so ponds, lakes and slow rivers are the best place to look for them; the flying adults, though, can often be seen some distance from the nearest water. Adulthood is no more than a brief flurry in the insect's life – some of the large dragonflies spend four years as an underwater nymph, emerging for only a few months of flying life. The essential purpose of the flight stage is to breed, and dragonflies and damselflies have evolved a unique **mating position** to solve one of the big drawbacks of insect copulation.

The problem is that, as with all insects, the sexual equipment of dragonflies is at the very end of their bodies, so the simplest mating position involves the male and female facing in opposite directions. Since they are brightly coloured, they attract predators such as swallows and other birds, and if they were to be mating at the time, they would only be able to escape by uncoupling, which would mean running the risk of not finding a mate again. The unique solution involves the male transferring sperm to a special pouch underneath the front of his abdomen before mating. He then seeks out a female and grasps her by the back of the neck, in which position the pair fly around quite happily while the female bends her body upwards so that the tip of her abdomen touches the sperm pouch. The eggs are thus fertilised.

Dragonflies are large and often brightly coloured, and always hold their wings outspread when at rest. The largest of them are the *Aeshna* species, which usually have a long thin body up to 8cm long, marked with blue, yellow or green. The *Libellula* species, on the other hand, have a shorter and fatter brown body, and the old adults often develop a powdery blue colour. Finally, *Sympetrum* species are smaller, and have reddish bodies – brilliant red in the case of *Sympetrum sanguineum*.

Dragonfly
Aeshna cyanea

Damselflies are much smaller and more delicate than dragonflies, but have the same metallic blue, red and green colouring. They fly weakly, fluttering over the water like iridescent matchsticks. When at rest, they hold their wings folded down the length of their bodies, unlike dragonflies. One of the most striking of the Med species is *Calopteryx splendens*, with a shimmering blue body and dark blue patches on its wings; look for it by slow-running streams, especially in cooler, hilly countryside.

GRASSHOPPERS AND CRICKETS; ORDER ORTHOPTERA

Any piece of Mediterranean scrub or grassland in summer will be alive with the chirping of male grasshoppers and crickets. Technically called **stridulation**, the noise is made by rubbing a scraper on one wing against a file which is either on the other wing (in crickets) or on the leg (in grasshoppers); each species makes a different

noise, advertising its presence to a potential mate, or sometimes competing with other males for a female.

Although **grasshoppers** (family *Acrididae*) do have wings, these are usually only used to aid the propulsion of their prodigiously developed hind legs, and few grasshoppers can genuinely fly. The **blue-winged grasshopper** *Oedipoda caerulescens* and the **red-winged grasshopper** *Oedipoda germanica* both have coloured wings, making them very obvious in their whirring short flights, although they are inconspicuous on the ground, with camouflaged bodies that blend perfectly with the rocky hillsides. One grasshopper that does fly extremely well is the **migratory locust** *Locusta migratoria*, which looks like a large green grasshopper; they are normally solitary and sedentary, but overpopulation causes them to increase the size of their wings, change colour to brown, and become much more active before moving off in migratory swarms. Such population explosions rarely occur round the Med, though large swarms do form in north Africa and the Middle East, and penetrated as far as northern Tunisia in March 1987, creating concern that they would cross the Straits of Sicily and sweep up through Italy.

Bush crickets (family *Tettigoniidae*) are best distinguished from grasshoppers by their extremely long, swept-back antennae, unlike the short forward-pointing antennae of grasshoppers. As their name suggests, they tend to live in bushes, and they are especially active around dusk, often singing long into the night. The *Ephipigger ephipigger* species is known in France as the *tizi*, which accurately describes its monotonous double chirp; it has a conspicuous "saddle" covering its thorax, and is common in bushes around the Med, especially in high summer. **True crickets** (family *Gryllidae*) are fatter and squatter than grasshoppers, and usually ground-dwelling. Unlike most insects, the widespread **field cricket** *Gryllus campestris* digs itself a sort of burrow, usually on a sunny grassy slope; with a body length of around 2cm, they are all black and bulbous-headed.

MANTISES AND COCKROACHES; ORDER DICTYOPTERA

Cockroaches inhabit many Med buildings, the most familiar being the **American cockroach** *Periplaneta americana* (actually originating from north Africa), which grows to 3cm long and is usually seen at night, scuttling around the floor at great speed. It's distinguished from beetles by the pale brown shield (the pronotum) covering most of its head, and its overlapping wingcases.

The best-known of the mantises is the **praying mantis** *Mantis religiosa*. Reaching a length of 6cm, this green and long-legged insect has front legs modified into spiny pincers with which it captures its prey – mostly smaller insects such as flies and butterflies, although Gerald Durrell tells of one attacking a gecko. Praying mantises stalk their victims through bushes and shrubs,

Praying
mantis
*Mantis
religiosa*

holding their pincers curled in the attitude that has given them their name, and then striking with great speed. There are smaller mantis species round the Med, but beware confusion with the **mantis flies** *Mantispa spp.*, which hunt in a similar fashion and have evolved the same sort of front pincers. Mantis flies, however, are in a quite different order and have large netted wings – true mantises only have short wings, like grasshoppers.

The bugs are an unassuming bunch of generally small insects, easily overlooked despite the fact that they're one of the most numerous orders, with tens of thousands of species worldwide. They have mouth parts adapted for piercing plants or animals and sucking out the juices; many of them are therefore serious agricultural pests, both in their own right (such as aphids) and as vectors of plant disease (such as leaf hoppers).

■ The *Heteroptera*

Bugs divide into two sub-orders. The first, the **Heteroptera**, has two-tone wings (the basal area horny and the tip membranous), which fold over each other at rest, usually creating a characteristic triangle of a different colour at the end of the body. The **shield bugs** are typical of this group. Their bodies are clearly shield-shaped, sometimes green, but often brightly striped in orange and black, perhaps to warn predators that they can give off a foul smell if disturbed – they're also known as stink-bugs. The *Graphosoma italicum* shield bug is handsomely striped in red and black, grows to a centimetre long and is likely to be found in large numbers in umbelliferous flowers such as cow parsley. Unlike shield bugs, which eat plants, **assassin bugs** are predators of other insects, with a beak which can be painful even to a human; *Reduvius personatus* is typical, quite narrow in the body and with relatively long legs. Some bugs have developed the warning red and black coloration as a protective mimicry, even though they themselves are not toxic nor dangerous – *Lygaeus saxatilis* is a very beautiful bug coloured in this way, which can be extremely common throughout the Med, especially in fields and hedges.

Heteropteran bugs are by no means confined to land; many of the commonest water insects belong to this sub-order, such as the **pond skater** *Gerris spp.*, which skates on the surface of freshwater all around the Med, from lakes to puddles. Supported by surface tension, it feeds on the bodies of small insects trapped on the water. Another is the **water boatman** *Corixa punctata*, which swims jerkily below the surface using hairy paddles on its legs. The **backswimmers** *Notanecta spp.* are superficially similar to water boatmen, but swim on their backs, hanging below the surface waiting for their prey; they are fierce predators of other aquatic life, seizing insect larvae and tadpoles and sucking the life out of them.

A final Heteropteran bug is the notorious **bedbug** *Cimex lectularius*. It's a round-bodied, pale brown bug, virtually wingless, and only active at night, when it feeds on the blood of whatever luckless mammal it can find; normally around 5mm long, bedbugs can double their body weight in one good night's feeding.

■ The *Homoptera*

In the other sub-order of bugs, the **Homoptera**, the wings are uniform and do not overlap when at rest, but join up the centre of the back in a distinctive ridge. All Homopterans feed on sap sucked from plants, and they range in size from minute aphids and leaf hoppers to one of the largest and most characteristic of all Mediterranean insects – the **cicada** *Orni*. Although the stout dark body of the cicada can be as much as 5cm long, the insect is hard to locate by sight alone as it sits motionless on the bark of a tree. What makes the cicada so obtrusive is its whirring, relentless song – produced not by stridulation, but by two small vibrating membranes (called tymbals) on each side of the body, amplified by resonating chambers. From the fact that a cicada keeps up its song even when its mate is right alongside, the great nineteenth-century Jean-Henri Fabre deduced that they were deaf, a theory he tested by firing a cannon next to a group of them. The fact that they showed no reaction might seem to prove his point, but it appears that their eardrums are adapted to pick up only the sounds of their own species. The

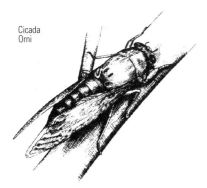

Cicada
Orni

cicada nymph lives for years in a burrow, feeding on sap extracted from the roots of plants, before emerging for its final flying stage.

The sugary diet of plant sap has led to some strange associations between species. **Aphids** and **leaf hoppers** exude a sugary substance called honeydew, which is eagerly seized on by other insects. Ants, in particular, are fond of it and you can often see ants moving around aphid colonies, "milking" them of honeydew by tapping them with their antennae. Like leaf hoppers, **frog hoppers** (family *Cercopidae*) jump extremely well, disappearing into thin air as soon as they are touched. Some frog hopper nymphs spend their time cocooned in a frothy mass of foam on a plant stem, which helps to protect them against drying out; this foam, called "cuckoo spit" in Britain, has given frog hoppers the alternative name of "spittle bugs".

BUTTERFLIES AND MOTHS; ORDER *LEPIDOPTERA*

The characteristic shimmering wing surfaces of the moths and butterflies are created by the **scales** of their wings, which carry pigments and reflect the light at various angles. The only hard and fast rule for distinguishing between the two groups – around Europe and the Med at least – is that butterflies always have clubbed antennae, and moths never do. A guideline only useful under lab conditions is that moths have a **frenulum**, a bristly "zip" that links the fore and hind wings. Less precise distinctions are that most moths fly by night, whereas all butterflies fly by day; most butterflies hold their wings vertically above their body when at rest, while most moths hold them horizontally along the body; and butterflies tend to be more brightly coloured.

In the caterpillar phase, butterflies and moths feed exclusively on plants, and the caterpillar is usually specific to one host species, unable to survive if moved to another plant. As flying adults, both feed on nectar, which they extract from the heart of the flower by means of a **proboscis**, a long sucking tube carried curled up under the head like a watch spring when not in use. (Some hawkmoths, which feed on flowers with a deep flowering tube, have a proboscis longer than their wingspan.)

The life of the adult butterfly or moth revolves around its extremely acute senses of **taste** and **smell**. Red admiral butterflies have been shown to have a sense of taste some 200 times more acute than a human's – presumably to allow them to identify the food plant on which to lay their eggs. Smell plays a vital role in courtship. The female releases substances called **pheromones** to attract a male, who can detect them over enormous distances. In one experiment involving a Chinese silkmoth, males were released 11km from a caged female; a quarter of them successfully located her. Some moths don't feed at all in the adult stage, their antennae being given over entirely to the task of picking up female pheromones. In some cases the interaction works the other way as well: male butterflies of some species carry scent scales on their forewings, and it seems that these are used purely to excite the female once contact has been made.

Lepidoptera is the first order of endopterygotous insects – ie species that have totally different adult and larval phases. Usually, the whole **life cycle** is quite short. A first flight of tortoise-shell butterflies, for instance, are on the wing in the spring, when they mate, produce eggs and die. Caterpillars emerge from these eggs later in the spring, when they feed and pupate. A second flight emerges from the pupae in summer, when they go through the entire breeding cycle again. The last flight emerges in autumn, and of these just a few hibernate to start the process all over again in the spring. Other butterflies may only produce one cycle a year, and some of the larger moths can spend up to three years in the larval stage. The largest moth of the region, the giant peacock, sometimes stays in the pupating phase for two winters.

◼ Butterflies

With about 225 species commonly seen in the region (roughly three times the number in Britain), butterfly identification down to species level can be tricky. Happily, they divide fairly neatly into **8 basic families**, of which 2 are represented by only a single species, and slotting them into the relevant family is usually straightforward.

SWALLOWTAILS; FAMILY PAPILONIDAE

Some of the largest and most striking species belong to the *Papilonidae* group. The **swallowtail** *Papilio machaon*, a magnificent large species with tail streamers, is basically yellow striped with black, with a red and blue "eye" at the back of its hind wing; they fly in late spring and again in high summer. The purpose of these streamers

and eyes is probably to confuse predators: the former imitate antennae while the latter imitate true eyes, and so any passing bird may be fooled into attacking the back end of the butterfly, and only getting a mouthful of wing rather than a fatal lump of the body. Despite its name, the **scarce swallowtail** *Iphiclides podalirius* is common enough, especially around orchards, as the caterpillar feeds on the leaves of fruit trees; it's similar to the swallowtail, but has a cream background and even longer tail streamers. Three species of **festoon** *Zerynthia spp.* and *Allancastria cerisyi* add an almost tropical flavour, with their gaudy zigzags of red, black and yellow; they fly early in the spring. Finally the **Apollo** *Parnassius spp.* is a large white butterfly with red and black spots; found in Alpine meadows at over 700m, it flies in high summer.

Swallowtail
Papilio machaon

WHITES; FAMILY PIERIDAE

Best-known of the whites is the **small white** *Pieris rapae*, a common garden species; the widespread cultivation of the cabbage family – its larval food – has made it so successful that it is now a serious agricultural pest. All members of this family have white or yellow wings, usually with a few black markings, especially on the wing-tips. White and yellow butterflies are particularly easy to spot from a distance; it seems they have little fear of predation, since the chemical that creates their colour is also very distasteful. One of the most attractive of the whites is the **orange tip** *Anthocharis cardamines*, which sports bright orange wing tips and marbled green underwings; in north Africa, it is largely replaced by the **Moroccan orange tip** *Anthocharis belia*, which has bright yellow wings instead of white. Both these butterflies fly early in the spring, often in large numbers. Later in the summer, the larger cleopatra *Gonepteryx cleopatra* becomes obvious; the Mediterranean equivalent of the northern brimstone, it has yellow wings enlivened by a splash of orange on the front ones. The many species of **clouded yellow** *Colias spp.* fly in a succession of broods from April through to the autumn, and are the only yellow butterflies of the region with a complete black wing margin. Clouded yellows are one of the great butterfly migrants, exploding out from their southern European strongholds in search of new territories when their breeding habitats become overcrowded; 1983 was the last "clouded yellow year", when thousands of them reached as far north as Britain.

NETTLE TREE BUTTERFLY; FAMILY LIBYTHEIDAE

The *Libytheidae* are mostly found in the Americas, but one species, the **nettle tree butterfly** *Libythea celtis* is resident around the Med. It's brown with red patches on its front wings, and its larvae feed on the nettle tree *Celtis australis*. It winters as an adult, going into a long hibernation in late summer and emerging to mate the following spring.

THE NYMPHALIDAE

The *Nymphalidae* family is the largest and most varied, containing many of the best-known and most colourful butterflies of the region. The front legs of this group are so reduced in size as to be useless for walking, but obviously this is of limited help as a field characteristic. The **red admiral** *Vanessa atalanta* is a typical nymphalid butterfly, its upper wings of scarlet, black and white making it particularly obvious. Equally conspicuous and widespread are **peacocks** *lanachis io*, with their large iridescent "eyes" on their wings, which they expose if threatened by a predator. Both these butterflies depend on the stinging nettle as their larval food plant, and you'll sometimes see a writhing mass of their black caterpillars on nettle clumps. A closely related species is the **painted lady** *Vanessa cardui*, often the commonest butterfly within the region. Resident throughout the year in north Africa, it migrates across the Med in spring, spreading as far north as Britain; the adults cannot survive the chilly northern winter, however, and either migrate south again or die. Huge numbers of painted ladies can sometimes be seen in around the Med in April and May, as the populations gear up for their northward dispersal. The **two-tailed pasha** *Charaxes jasius* is at the the northernmost limit of its range in the Med, for it is essentially an African species; a large brown butterfly with yellowish wing borders and two tails on the hind wing, it flies in coastal areas of the Med in June and again later in the summer. Like many tropical butterflies it is strongly attracted to moisture, sipping rotten fruit and even drinking sweat from passing humans.

Most of the rest of the *Nymphalidae* species are **fritillaries**, a group with brown upper wings closely patterned with black – perfect for camouflage in sun-dappled woodland. Fritillaries often also have a silvery patch, like mother-of-pearl, on their underwings. The largest of the 25 Med species is the **cardinal** *Pandora pandoriana*; it flies in high summer and is easily told by its large size and pink undersides of the forewings.

BROWNS; FAMILY SATYRIDAE

The browns are a large group of butterflies almost exclusively coloured in well-camouflaged shades of orange, brown and black. All are grassland butterflies, and are most easily recognised by the prominent black eyes on the upper forewing (and sometimes the hindwing too), usually standing out from a pale brown or cream background. The **meadow brown** *Maniola jurtina* is typical of the family, with a prominent eye on the brown forewing, especially in the female; it's widespread around the Med, sometimes being the dominant grassland butterfly from May to September. The **marbled whites** *Melanargia spp.* are the only ones that aren't predominantly brown – they're chequered black and white, but a close examination still reveals the eyes on the forewings. Browns vary in size from the **giant grayling** *Berberia abdelkader* of the north African Atlas, with a wingspan of nearly 7cm, to the widely distributed **small heath** *Coenonympha pamphilus*, with a wingspan of only 3cm.

BLUES, COPPERS AND HAIRSTREAKS; FAMILY LYCAENIDAE

The small butterflies of the *Lycaenidae* include some of the most brilliantly coloured of all insects, the metallic vividness of their colours being due largely to the diffracting effect of tiny corrugations on their wing scales. The **green hairstreak** *Callophrys rubi* has underwings of glistening green; it's common and widely distributed around the Med in March and April, the

Asphodel and hairstreak

adults often feeding on asphodels. The **blues** fly from May and June through the summer, usually over grasslands containing the vetches and trefoils on which their caterpillars mostly feed; their upper wings are usually a shining blue, often with a narrow black and white edge, while their underwings are well camouflaged in pale grey with black and orange dots. Some of the blues have developed an unusual relationship with ants. The caterpillar excretes a sort of honeydew on which the ants feed, thereby gaining the protection of the ant colony against predators – the ants taking the caterpillar underground into their nest, where it continues to provide honeydew. In the case of the rare and declining **large blue** *Maculinea arion*, the ants even feed their guest on their own larvae.

SKIPPERS; FAMILY HESPERIIDAE

With their dowdy colours, weak fluttering flight, and their manner of resting their wings in the horizontal position, the **skippers** resemble moths more closely than their fellow butterflies. The many species are all small, and precise identification needs much practice; they're common in midsummer, over grasslands and rocky Mediterranean hillsides. Many skippers show a dark line across the upper forewing; these are the scent scales, used in courtship to release the aphrodisiac referred to above.

■ Moths

Although there are perhaps a hundred times more species of **moths** than butterflies around the Med, they are much less noticeable since they are largely nocturnal. The easiest way to see moths is to find a white wall near a bright light, preferably out in the countryside or in a large garden; moths are attracted to the light, and will rest in a dazed condition on the wall. Since moths spend the day sleeping, they're an easy target for predators, and so have extremely highly developed camouflage. Of the 40 or so Mediterranean families, the 7 most important and obvious ones are given below.

BURNET MOTHS; FAMILY ZYGAENIDAE

The day-flying **burnet moths** look almost like butterflies, since they have slightly clubbed antennae and are brightly coloured, with a blue-green forewing spotted red or sometimes white, and a plain red or blue hindwing. The adults often feed on the daisy family, and are easy to spot as they drift slowly from one flower to another; there are many different Med species, and limestone hillsides or waste land from May to August are good places to find them. Containing an unpleasant combination of histamine and hydrocyanic acid, they are poisonous to predators, who are warned off by the bright livery.

EMPERORS; FAMILY SATURNIDAE

The **emperors** are large nocturnal moths with a striking eye on each wing, and include the **giant peacock moth** *Saturnia pyri* – the largest moth of the region, with a wingspan of up to 15cm (slightly larger than a pipistrelle bat). Its caterpillar feeds on fruit trees, and so orchards are a good place to look for it; the adults fly in spring and early summer. Emperor moths don't feed at all in the adult phase, and so have no proboscis.

HAWKMOTHS; FAMILY SPHINGIDAE

A group of heavily built, fast-flying and mostly large moths, the **hawk moths** rest with their wings swept back in a characteristic arrowhead. As with other moths, their forewings are mottled to camouflage them by day, but the hindwing sometimes has an eye or a bright colour patch with which to scare predators. The **oleander hawk moth** *Daphnis nerii*, named after its larval food plant, is typical and quite common round the Med; its wings are a wonderful pattern of green, cream and purple, and it has a stout green body with white stripes between each segment. Some hawk moth species feed like hummingbirds, hovering in front of their chosen flower and poking an immensely long proboscis down the flower tube. Three day-flying species that do this are the **hummingbird hawk moth** *Macroglossum stellatarum* and two species of **bee hawk moths** *Hemaris spp.*; the latter have clear wings and a yellow body and do indeed look very like bees, while the hummingbird hawk moth is a small moth with noticeable yellow hindwings.

Hummingbird hawk moth
*Macroglossum
stellatarum*

TIGER MOTHS; FAMILY ARCTIIDAE

Like the burnet moths, the **tiger moths** are brightly coloured to denote the fact that they are poisonous – they tend to have dark forewings and red or orange hindwings, dotted throughout with black and white. The adults fly at night, mostly during July and August; one species, the **Jersey tiger** *Euplagia quadripunctaria*, congregates in vast numbers at roost sites during the day – Petaloudes, the so-called "butterfly valley" in central Rhodes, is the best-known Med site.

PROCESSIONARY MOTHS; FAMILY THAUMETOPOEIDAE

A high-profile moth of the dry pine forests around the Med is the **pine processionary moth** *Thaumetopoea pinivora*, a nondescript specimen in its midsummer flying stage, but a serious forest pest as a caterpillar. They spin themselves a silken nest amongst the pine twigs, marching out head to tail in long lines, mostly at night, to feed on the pine needles. A closely related species lives in oak woodland. The caterpillars have a well-developed defence mechanism against predation, being covered with long poisonous hairs that cause intense irritation if touched. Some European countries even go so far as to erect "Beware of the caterpillars" notices in their forests.

THE NOCTUIDAE

The *Noctuidae* family contains thousands of species, all of them plump-bodied moths that hold their wings almost parallel over their bodies, and have a prominent hairy bulge on top of the thorax. Most noctuid moths have mottled brown or grey forewings, sometimes with brightly coloured hindwings which flash in flight to confuse predators. The **yellow underwings** *Noctua spp.* are typical, with a bright yellow hindwing bordered in black and superbly camouflaged forewings. A larger species, the **red underwing** *Catocala nupta* is one of a group of moths that have the same pattern, but with a red or orange hindwing instead of a yellow one. Some noctuids display metallic colours akin to those of hairstreak butterflies: the **burnished brass** *Diachrisia chrysitis*, for example, has a patch of glistening gold on its forewings. Many caterpillars in this family are agricultural pests; they're usually called cutworms, since they live underground during the day and come out at night to nibble and cut through the stems of growing plants.

GEOMETERS; FAMILY GEOMETRIDAE

The caterpillars of the **geometer** family are most distinctive. Whereas most other caterpillars have pairs of legs right along the body, geometers have them only at the front and back, and so raise the middle section high into the air in order to move – hence their common name of "loopers". If alarmed, they hang on by their rear legs and poke the rest of their body out into space, looking remarkably like a twig. You'll have to look hard to distinguish the flying adults, which are generally small and very variable. **Carpet moths** – so called because they are mottled like a carpet, not because they eat them – hold their wings in a broad arrowhead, whereas the similarly camouflaged **pugs** hold their wings flat out, like a basking butterfly. Some geometers are larger but no more conspicuous: the **emerald moths** *Hemithea aestivara* and other species are bright green, but blend into their leafy background when they settle.

FLIES; ORDER *DIPTERA*

To an extent, flies deserve their bad press. They carry diseases and some of them, especially the mosquitoes, are potentially lethal. But they also perform a useful function. The larvae of most flies feed on rotting material, especially dead flesh and dung, and without them the earth would be littered with animal droppings and decaying corpses. This is not a facile point; when cows were introduced to Australia, there was no local fly that had evolved to eat cowpats, and the heaps of dung posed a serious health hazard until a species of fly was introduced to clear up the mess.

The name of their order – *Diptera* – means **two-winged**, and they are the only insects so equipped apart from mayflies; their second pair of wings are reduced to pins that act as a counterbalance and gyroscope. Flies feed mostly on liquids, and so their mouth parts consist of a sucking tube.

The pupa stage of the **mosquitoes and midges** (family *Culicidae*) is quite unlike the motionless chrysalis of a butterfly or moth: the pupae wriggle around in water like little black commas, and when the time comes for the final emergence the pupa hangs under the surface of the water until the flying adult pops out at amazing speed. In adulthood they survive by sucking blood from large mammals. The malaria parasite is carried in the gut of the female *Anopheles* mosquito, a species that can be identified by the way they rest with their body at an angle to the surface they are on – other mosquitoes rest with their bodies parallel.

Most fly larvae feed on dung and carrion, but some have adapted to become true parasites, feeding on living flesh. Amongst these is the notorious **warble fly** *Hypoderma bovis*; the adult lays eggs on the legs of cattle, and the larvae eat their way under the skin of the beast until they reach the back. There they live in a swelling before emerging to fall on the ground, pupate, and start the whole cycle all over again.

Hoverflies (family *Syrphidae*), by contrast, are thoroughly benign. The adults are nectar feeders, usually striped in yellow and black to imitate wasps and bees; hovering on wings that can beat several hundred times a second, they are especially common on the flat white flowers of umbellifers. The larvae of the many species live widely varying life cycles, but many are very useful as predators of insect pests such as aphids.

WASPS, BEES AND ANTS; ORDER *HYMENOPTERA*

As their name suggests, the *Hymenoptera* all have membranous wings; these are arranged in two pairs, the hind pair often being small and hard to spot. The females of many species have a long ovipositor at the end of their bodies, used to drill a hole into plant or even animal material for egg-laying; sometimes, as in wasps, this has been modified to carry a venomous sting as well.

The sub-order of the **sawflies** (*Symphyta*) get their name from their saw-like ovipositor, used to cut a hole into the stem or leaf of the plant on which the larvae will feed. Sawfly larvae are caterpillar-like, and feed communally, neatly spaced around the outside rim of a leaf; when disturbed, they all raise the ends of their bodies in the air and wriggle about, forming a sort of moving fringe to the leaf. The **woodwasp** *Urocerus gigas* is an alarming though harmless sawfly; the female is 4cm long, broadly striped in yellow and black, and has a very prominent ovipositor. Woodwasp larvae feed on pine and larch, so coniferous plantations are a good place to find them.

All other hymenopterans are in the sub-order *Apocrita*, distinguished by their sharply narrowed "waist" between the abdomen and thorax. Many of them are parasites, either of plants or animals. **Gall wasps** (family *Cynipidae*) lay their eggs in plant tissue, which then swells to produce a cancerous growth called a gall, inside which the larva lives and feeds. Oaks are a particular favourite of gall wasps. The **ichneumon fly** *Rhyssa persuasoria*, one of the largest of the species that parasitises other insects, locates woodwasp larvae by their smell and the vibrations they make, then drills up to 3cm through the wood to lay an egg on the surface of the larvae. After hatching, the ichneumon fly eats its way through the host before pupating, emerging, drilling its way out of the tree and flying free.

The **common wasp** *Vespa vulgaris* is a colonial insect, living in paper nests made from chewed and regurgitated wood; the colonies die out every winter, leaving only a mated female to hibernate over the winter and found a new colony the following spring. Most wasp species, however, are solitary and live in burrows; unlike the common wasp, some are ferocious carnivores, living off other insects and spiders. The **spider hunting wasps** (family *Pompilidae*) are particularly vicious; one species, *Cryptocheilus comparatus*, is over 2cm long and can kill spiders as big as the tarantula.

Bees similarly occur in both social and solitary species. The **honey bee** *Apis melliferae* has the most developed colonial structure, a large colony containing up to 50,000 individuals in high summer; wild colonies are all escapes from domestic bees, since the honey bee is a long established introduction into Europe from southeast Asia. **Bumble bees** form annual colonies in the same way as social wasps, and are easily recognised by their tubby hairy bodies, usually with bright yellow or red stripes on a black background. Like all bees, the adults feed only on nectar and pollen, and are thus of great importance as pollinators. Most other bees are solitary, including the fearsome-looking **carpenter bee**

Carpenter bee
Xylocopa sp.

Xylocopa sp., which nests in dead wood; the largest bee around the Med, it is all black with purple wings, and has a very fast flight.

Ants are exclusively colonial. Like the social wasps and bees, the queen mates only once and then stores sperm in her body, which is then used to produce female offspring; she produces males by laying an unfertilised egg. Ants are great scavengers, but also feed off other insects for protein – the way in which they "milk" certain species has already been described. Only the males and queens have wings, which are used for just one mating flight: the males die straight after mating, while the females retreat underground, where they tear off their redundant wings. **Wood ants** *Formica rufa* are easily located in pine forests by their underground nests, which are always covered by a large mound of pine needles. One nest can contain hundreds of thousands of ants and several queens, and is a highly desirable asset in a managed forest, since ants are very efficient exterminators of insect pests.

BEETLES; ORDER *COLEOPTERA*

Beetles are the most numerous order in the animal kingdom, with over 300,000 species identified worldwide, and doubtless many times that yet to be described. Most spend their lives hidden at ground level, and many are nocturnal, but more visible species like fireflies, glowworms and dung beetles are very much part of the Mediterranean scene.

The beetles' ability to survive in a variety of habitats is partly attributable to the armour-plated adaptation of their front wings, which are called the **elytra**; these fold over the body completely, protecting the delicate rear wings and the rest of the abdomen at the same time. This elytra, meeting neatly down the middle of the back, is a clear aid to identification. The **dung beetles** (families *Geotrupidae* and *Scarabidae*) are stout-bodied, black and shiny,

Dung beetle

and often have horny growths on the head. Having dug an elaborate burrow in the soil, smoothed the sides of the main chamber and laid its eggs, the dung beetle then goes out and collects dung, rolling it into a ball many times its own size and weight. This it rolls to the nest, sometimes with help from its mate, where it provides food for the larvae.

Fireflies *Luciola lusitanica* are an extraordinary dusk and night-time feature of spring and early summer in the central and eastern Med. In order to attract a mate, the male – which looks like a long, thin beetle – uses an enzyme to produce bright and regular flashes of light from the tip of its body; the female watches from the undergrowth, flashing more weakly in reply. **Glow-worms** *Lampyris noctiluca* also produce light, but this time it is the female that does it, making a steady ghostly green glow; unusually for a beetle, the female is wingless, and the males fly around looking for her light. Glow-worm larvae feed on snails, which they apparently entice out by tapping on their shells with their antennae.

Ladybirds (family *Coccinellidae*), perhaps the most familiar of all beetles, are mostly carnivorous, the larvae being particularly good at mopping up aphids. Their bright spotted pattern – more variable than you might think – denotes the fact that they are distasteful, a strategy also employed by the **burying beetles** (family *Silphidae*). These beetles are also called sexton beetles after their habit of burying corpses of small animals; the female then lays eggs next to the corpse, which will provide a ready food supply for the larvae. Burying beetles are usually red and black with sharply clubbed antennae.

Some of the commonest beetles are the numerous species of **longhorns** (family *Cerambicidae*), the adults of which have very long antennae, often longer than their bodies; the adults feed largely on pollen from flowers, but the larvae feed on wood and can be a serious forestry pest. **Weevils** (mostly family *Curculionidae*), a very large group, all have a long snout with elbowed antennae like a TV aerial; some have fused elytra and are therefore flightless.

OTHER LAND INVERTEBRATES

Most other invertebrates are marine creatures, and are covered in the "Marine Life" section following, but some of the essentially aquatic phyla have terrestrial representatives, of which **molluscs** are among the most obvious. **Snails** are widespread in the Med, where the limestone rocks provide plenty of calcium from which to build their shells. The problem of the summer heat is solved by aestivation: they gather in clusters on the stalks of plants (especially thistles), seal up their shells to prevent moisture loss, and wait for the autumn rains. So a crop of motionless snails in high summer are not dead, but simply sitting it out till the cooler weather comes.

Insects are just one class in the phylum *Arthropoda*, the largest phylum of the animal kingdom, which includes all marine crustaceans as well as insects and spiders. The first class in the arthropod phylum are the *Crustacea*, primarily marine with the exception of the woodlice. The **pill woodlouse**, one of the species that can roll its jointed body into an armoured ball when threatened, is common round buildings. But it's in the next class – the arachnids – that the really obvious land arthropods appear.

SPIDERS AND THEIR RELATIVES; CLASS *ARACHNIDA*

The bodies of **arachnids** are divided into two parts. The first part, the "head", has four pairs of legs and two other pairs of appendages, often pincers or fangs for hunting and feeding. The second part is a limbless abdomen. Although there are actually 4 or 5 orders of arachnids, we shall concentrate on just the 2 most noticeable – the scorpions and the spiders.

■ Scorpions; order *Scorpionida*

Instantly identifiable by their large pincers and the curved sting on the elongated tip of their abdomen, the **scorpions** have a formidable but not altogether justified reputation. They are shy and secretive animals, exclusively nocturnal, and you'll only see them in daylight by turning over the stones and rocks under which they hide. Their sophisticated courtship rituals – with pairs promenading claw in claw in the dusk – often lead to the female's killing and eating the male straight after copulation. Despite this unsavoury habit,

the female is an exemplary mother, incubating the eggs inside her body, giving birth to live young, and then carrying the tiny young around on her back until they can fend for themselves – a habit shared by some spider species.

One of the most visible species is the small *Euscorpius italicus*, one of the very few scorpions to commonly come inside buildings. Only 3–4cm long when fully grown, it has a blackish body and is not dangerous to humans. On the other hand, the larger *Buthus occitanus*, which is yellowish brown and grows to 8cm, has a very painful sting. Some of the desert scorpion species in north Africa can be even worse (though not fatal), and walking around at night in bare feet is probably not advisable.

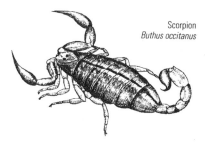

Scorpion
Buthus occitanus

■ Spiders; order *Araneae*

Spiders are widespread in almost every habitat, with hundreds of species found round the Med. One of the best times to look for them is at dawn, especially outside high summer when there may be early morning dew – their webs show up well then, shining in the low sun. All species have silk glands in the abdomen, with which they spin a variety of fibres: sticky ones for ensnaring their prey, strong thick ones for structural web strength, and non-sticky ones that cocoon their eggs and act as a lifeline should they be knocked off their perch.

The **garden spider** *Araneus diadematus* is typical and common; often seen hanging in the middle of its web, it has a dark body relieved with white or cream markings, sometimes in the shape of a cross. Garden spiders, like many other species, will not tackle their large and sometimes dangerous prey until it is safely immobilised; if you're lucky enough to see a fly or a bee caught in a web, you'll see the spider advance cautiously, fling an entangling web of silk around the prey, and then disable it with a bite. Over the next few hours, the spider will suck the fluids out of the alive but anaesthetised victim, and then discard it as a dessicated corpse.

Not all spiders spin webs. Some simply lurk in the foliage, ready to pounce on small insects, while others, such as the **wolf spider**, are basically ground-dwelling, scuttling about in search of prey. Such a mobile lifestyle calls for a mobile nursery, and the female wolf spider encloses her eggs in a silken pouch, which she then carries around with her until they hatch out. Another hunting technique is practised by the **trapdoor spiders**, which dig a shallow silk-lined tunnel in the ground, covered by a closely fitting door; when some unsuspecting beetle or other insect crawls over the top, the spider, alerted by the noise, rushes out to make the kill.

Tarantulas are large powerful spiders which also use this tunnel technique to ambush their prey. Tarantulas are not the hairy monsters of popular fiction, and in fact what are usually described as tarantulas are large tropical species of the family *Theraphosidae*, which can indeed grow to a huge size, but are relatively harmless. Anyway, the true tarantula of the Med – *Lycosa tarantula* – is a large hole-dwelling spider, mostly nocturnal, and found quite widely, especially in Spain and Italy. They can grow to 5cm from leg to leg, and their bite is usually described as no worse than a bee sting. The only spider of the region that is potentially dangerous to humans is the **malmignatte** *Latrodectus tredecimguttatus*, a close relative of the infamous black widow spider. It lives in scrubby bushes, especially in Corsica, and has a body some 7–10mm long, with long legs; it's fairly unmistakeable, having a black body with 13 red spots. The bite is extremely painful, and can cause temporary paralysis.

MARINE LIFE

The marine life of the Med is fascinating and unique for a number of reasons, most of which stem from the sea's **landlocked situation**: the narrowness of the connection to the Atlantic through the Straits of Gibraltar means that the Med is cut off from the currents and tides of the Atlantic, creating a marine environment that is far more stable than the true oceans. This isolation isn't altogether beneficial, however. The Med is extremely vulnerable to **local pollution**, since it doesn't have free access to the cleansing and diluting factors of the wider seas. It is also much less productive. The rising currents that occur in the oceans bring nutrients to the surface, stimulating high populations of algae which in turn produce a knock-on effect all the way up the food-chain. Such currents don't occur to the same extent in the Med, so the sea is relatively impoverished. This, incidentally, is the reason why the Med is so "blue", the clear water indicating its lack of biological productivity more than its purity.

Of the 26 phyla of the animal kingdom, 17 occur in the Mediterranean Sea, as against 5 on the land of the region. This statistic reflects the fact that life began in the sea, and that only a minority of animals made the transition from aquatic life to terrestrial. Many of the animal phyla described below have remained virtually unchanged for hundreds of millions of years. As on land, all animals ultimately depend on the ability of plants to fix the energy of sunlight into the stored sugars that form the basis of the food chain. Hence in this section as in the previous ones, plants are the starting point.

MARINE PLANTS

Most marine plants are **algae** (or phytoplankton), floating in the water and quietly absorbing sunlight. Since they are rarely more than a centimetre long, and usually much less, a microscope is needed to examine them; and as few holiday naturalists carry a microscope around, most algae fall outside the scope of this guide.

However, some algae do grow much larger, notably the **seaweeds**. All seaweeds contains chlorophyll, and can therefore photosynthesise sunlight, but the chemical's colour is only obvious in the **green algae**. These include the **sea lettuce** *Ulva lactuca*, the delicate, semi-transparent leaves of which can often be seen in shallow water. **Ribbonweeds** *Enteromorpha spp.* are more confined to the shore, their very long and thin leaves being found in rock pools in the narrow intertidal zone. **Brown algae** generally prefer cooler water than the Med, so they are relatively uncommon; some have filamentous fronds, whereas others, like *Punctaria latifolia*,

WHERE AND HOW TO WATCH MARINE LIFE

The best places to find marine life in the Med are the **rocky coasts**. Find an unpolluted place where the rocks go steeply down into the sea, and you'll quickly see what a wealth of wildlife there is. Since most of the rocky shores are of soft rock such as limestone or sandstone, crevices and erratic rock formations are common, and these are an ideal habitat for rock-dwelling creatures such as sponges, sea anemones, sea squirts and the like. Gently shelving beaches are far less rewarding, and on sandy beaches there is the added problem of poor visibility caused by suspended sand.

A properly fitting **snorkel and mask** are essential. The way to check the fit is to hold the mask against your face, then breathe in and remove your hands – the external air pressure should hold the mask in place. If it falls off, it'll leak water. Snorkel **diving** is a wonderfully rewarding experience, but it requires some care.

As you approach a depth of five metres or so, an uncomfortable pressure will build up in your ears; don't go any further without **"equalising"**, a technique that involves holding the nose and blowing down it gently until you feel your ears pop – a sign that the pressure inside the ear and nose cavities has become equal to the water pressure outside. Don't get so absorbed in watching the fish that you forget how far you have to go to the surface to get air, and be cautious when diving close to rocks – not only is there the danger of cuts from jagged stone, but nasty things like sea urchins could be lurking in recesses.

For the fortunate few, **scuba** diving offers a real peak experience. Many Med resorts have diving schools that offer tuition, but avoid those that claim to teach you safely in just a few hours. It takes much longer than that to learn, and should involve some pool training as well.

have broad crinkled fronds. One especially obvious brown algae of underwater rock faces is the **peacock's tail** *Padina pavonina*, resembling a small whitish cup-shaped fungus. The **red algae** come in a bewildering and beautiful range of colours from pale pink through to deep purple.

Very few **flowering plants** have adapted to marine life. One exception is the family of **sea-grasses** *Zosteracea*, dense beds of which grow in shallow water on soft mud or sand; their leaves can be up to a metre long, and they provide food and shelter for a wide variety of animal life. One species of sea-grass, *Posidonia oceanica*, has tough fibrous tissue surrounding its base; this is often washed up on beaches, where it is blown and moulded into a soft rounded shape known, not surprisingly, as a "sea ball". Like all aquatic plants, the sea-grasses need clear water, and all over the Med they are slowly being killed as blankets of sediment are laid from disturbed soil on the land.

Sea grass
Posidonia

MARINE ANIMALS

Like the marine plants, many marine animals are too small to see with the naked eye, let alone identify. These minuscule species form the animal constituent of plankton, feeding on the phytoplankton and themselves providing protein for the carnivores higher up the food chain. Some of these animals are small because they are just made that way – **protozoans**, for instance, which are very primitive single-celled animals. Others are small because they are young – for instance, the immature and larval stages of fish, crustaceans and other complex animals.

■ Sponges; Phylum *Porifera*

Sponges are very simple animals, consisting of little more than a soft exterior covering through which water is inhaled into the central body cavity; the exterior is supported by horny fibres called spicules, which are either made of sand or limestone. A familiar species is the **bath sponge** *Spongia officinalis*, large and spherical, usually dark brown or black, and normally found growing on rocks, especially in the eastern Med. (The part used in bathrooms is the skeletal remnant after the outside has been cleaned off.) It has been heavily collected for centuries around certain Greek islands: Symi and Kalimnos in the Dodecanese are particularly famous for their sponge fisheries. Other sponges include ones that form flat encrustations on rocks, such as the **crumb of bread sponge** *Halichondria panicea*, which is green in sunlight and red or cream in shadier and deeper waters.

■ Phylum *Cnidaria*

The *Cnidaria* phylum includes the **sea anemones**, **corals**, and the **jellyfish**, all of which are simple animals, with two layers of cells surrounding a central body cavity. At one end of this cavity is the mouth, which is surrounded with a ring of tentacles carrying stinging cells known as *cnidocytes*, used to capture and immobilise prey. A free-swimming cnidarian (eg jellyfish) is called a **medusa**, while one that stays put (eg sea anemone) is called a polyp, but the issue is complicated by the fact that a polyp's life cycle may involve a medusa stage. Some cnidarians are solitary, while others form themselves into large colonies; coral is an example of a colonial polyp, while some jellyfish are colonial medusae.

SEA ANEMONES

Most familiar of the sea anemones is the red **beadlet anemone** *Actinia equina*, but these animals come in many varied forms. Several species are quite large: the **golden anemone** *Condylactis aurantiaca* reaches a diameter of

7.5cm. All have a mass of waving tentacles, and the polyp base either buries deep into the sand or is modified to a sucker for clinging to rock. Some attach to shells, for example *Calliactis parasitica*, a brown or yellow anemone with vertical stripes that often latches onto hermit crab shells; in this symbiotic arrangement the anemone feeds on scraps of food dropped by the crab, while its stinging cells protect the crab from attack by predators such as the octopus.

JELLYFISH

Cnidarians include 2 different types of jellyfish. The first are the **true jellyfish** or *Scyphozoans*, of which there are around 7 species in the Med. They have a characteristic "umbrella" shape, with tentacles and extended mouthparts suspended underneath. Most have streaks of colour: the **common jellyfish** *Aurelia aurita*, for example, has a transparent umbrella up to 25cm in diameter through which the four purple rings of the reproductive organs can be seen. Most of these true jellyfish don't have a particularly powerful sting; the exception is the **Mediterranean sea wasp** *Charybdea marsupialis*, which has a box-shaped umbrella up to 6cm long trailing four tentacles that can be up to five times that length. Since the sting is alkaline, any acidic substance will alleviate the pain – lemon juice is good, and urine will do if nothing else is handy.

The other cnidarian jellyfishes are the *Siphonophores*. These are free-floating or swimming colonies of medusae, and the twenty or so species in the Med include the formidable **Portuguese man of war** *Physalia physalis*, whose long stinging "tentacles" (up to 30m long) are actually ropes of feeding and reproductive polyps. The floating "body" is blue/purple, and has a conspicuous sail attached. Although this is a very dangerous species, it is mostly found in deep water, but can occasionally be washed inshore by winds.

CORALS

All 3 classes of corals are polyp colonies. **True corals** *Madreporaria* have hard skeletons into which the polyps can withdraw, and some look like sea anemones when the polyps are extended – for example *Astroides calycularis*, whose golden yellow colonies can be found on shady rocks down to 50m. **Soft corals** *Alcyonacea* also have retractable polyps, but their bodies are soft and flexible. Also related are the **sea fans**

Gorgonacea, of which there are around twenty species in the Med, including the **precious coral** *Corallium rubrum*. This species has been collected for centuries, usually in order to make jewellery from its polished skeleton. Polluted water and suspended sediments have reduced its numbers and distribution to the extent that it is listed as "vulnerable" by the *International Union for the Conservation of Nature*; think carefully, therefore, before you buy any form of coral souvenir.

■ Comb jellies; phylum *Ctenophora*

The **comb jellies**, which are closely related to the previous phylum, have non-stinging tentacles with which they lasso their prey. They're colourless animals, moving by means of rows of swimming plates that run down the sides of their bodies. There are about a dozen species in the Med, including the iridescent **sea gooseberry** *Pleurobrachia pileus*, a species found in open water, with a berry-shaped body up to 3cm long.

■ Marine worms

Marine worms are numerous, varied, hard to identify, and come from 3 separate phyla. **Ribbon worms** (phylum *Nemertina*) grow up to 30cm, but since they spend most of their time buried in mud or sand, you're not too likely to see them. **Flatworms** (phylum *Platyhelminthes*), by contrast, are small animals (rarely over 5cm) that glide freely amongst seaweeds and stones; generally leaf-shaped, they have the beginnings of sense organs at one end of the body – two tentacles, and two rudimentary eyes.

Segmented worms (phylum *Annelida*) include the terrestrial earthworms and the largely freshwater leeches, and also a large class of marine worms called **bristle worms** (class *Polychaeta*). Bristle worms come in a great variety of shapes and sizes, but all have a segmented body, each segment having two paddles and a bunch of bristles for propulsion. Some look nothing at all like a worm, such as the **sea mouse** *Aphrodita aculeata*, which lives on soft mud and sands and resembles an elongated hairy pine cone. **Paddle worms** and **ragworms** include some 70 species, often looking at first sight like large and brightly coloured millipedes. Bundles of them can sometimes be seen in seaweed, twined into a fairly unpleasant writhing knot; the bristles on some species can be mildly irritating if touched.

Some bristle worms spend most of their time burrowing in mud, a pile of wormcasts being the only evidence of their presence. Still others have adapted to a sedentary existence, living within a chalky tube and poking their bodies out of the end to feed. Some of these are extremely beautiful, such as the **peacock worm** *Sabella pavonina*, which extends a crown of banded feeding filaments from its tube in the sand. Certain sedentary species lie on the sea floor – around the Turkish coast you can see large numbers of a species called *Hydroides norvegica*, with its long, twisted and chalky-white tube, and its blood-red gills protruding at one end.

■ Molluscs; phylum *Mollusca*

Molluscs are extremely numerous, and are one of the most important phyla in the animal kingdom. Most are marine, although one class, the gastropods, have conquered land as well, in the form of slugs and snails. From the 7 classes of mollusc, we have selected the 4 most conspicuous ones.

CHITONS; CLASS POLYPLACOPHORA

Chitons are also called **coat of mail shells**, because of their armoured mantle of layered chalky plates, which makes them look a bit like a woodlouse. (This existence of overlapping plates in different species – chitons, woodlice, armadillos – is another example of convergent evolution.) Chitons are 2–5cm long, and have a flat foot under the "shell" with which they cling to rocks. They are very hard to identify down to species level.

SNAILS AND SLUGS; CLASS GASTROPODA

The terrestrial **snails and slugs** evolved from marine species and the vast majority of species are still marine. Like their terrestrial descendants, **sea snails** have a foot on which they slide along, and a grazing organ called a radula – a sort of rough tongue, the radula is used chiefly to browse off marine algae. Along with the bivalve molluscs (see below) they produce the shells so frequently found on beaches – and that is all that most people see of them.

Amongst the shells most likely to be found are those of the **limpets**, including the Mediterranean limpet *Patella spp.*, and the **ormers** *Haliotis spp.*, which have large oval shells with a series of holes along the edge and a mother-of-pearl interior. **Topshells** (*Calliostoma* and other species) all have sharply conical shells like the top of a magician's hat; **winkles** (*Monodonta* and other species) are also conical but less sharply pointed. **Periwinkles** are small and black and often found in huge numbers on rocks on the upper and middle shore; they are represented by only one Med species, *Littorina neritoides*. **Cowries** *Cypraea* and other *spp.* look like a grain of barley, with their long ridged slit underneath an oval, polished body. One of the very few free-swimming snails is the **violet sea snail** *Lamnthina communis*, which floats on the surface of deep water, feeding on plankton; its remarkably bright purple shell is often washed up on beaches.

Many of these gastropod shells are very beautiful, and widely collected for sale to tourists. This sometimes involves removing the live animal, an invasive practice that can be discouraged by refusing to buy the shells. Species collected in this way include some of the more dramatic **whelks**, such as *Murex brandaris*, which has distinctive spines around the main part of the shell and a long "tail" (actually the siphonal canal in which it filters its food). This species was the source of imperial purple dye, so highly prized by the Romans for colouring the fringes of their togas. Also collected are the **pelican foot shells** *Aporrhais pes-pelicani* – again a

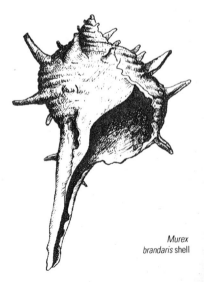

*Murex
brandaris* shell

conical shell with sculptured whorls, and with the margins of the aperture sharply flared to resemble a bird's foot.

As with the land species, **sea slugs** are like shell-less snails. One common group are the **sea hares** *Aplysia spp.*, which have long heads, two tentacles at the "nose" and two ear-like flaps behind the eyes, and can reach a length of 30cm. Others species are similar in shape but brightly coloured – especially **nudibranches**, which have external feathery gills in the centre of the back, and sometimes have groups of defensive tentacles arranged down the sides. They look amazing, but their bright colours often camouflage them amongst sponges, corals and sea anemones.

BIVALVES; CLASS BIVALVIA

The **bivalves** are the other common source of shells. Consisting of a body enclosed by symmetrical shell halves (valves) with a characteristic rounded hump at the hinge, they are usually filter feeders, but can swim by expelling water under force. Many are edible: for example, the **common mussel** *Mytilus edulis*, **scallops** *Chlamys spp.*, the **oyster** *Ostrea edulis*, and the **cockles**, of which there are hundreds of species. **Fan mussels** *Pinna spp.* are very large bivalves (sometimes over 50cm long) that anchor themselves upright in the sand by their long "fan handles". The rockborers or **piddocks** have elongated shells, and are able to bore into soft limestone; another destructive mollusc is the **shipworm** *Teredo navalis*, which drills huge galleries in submerged wood.

OCTOPUS, SQUID AND CUTTLEFISH; CLASS CEPHALOPODA

None of the cephalopods – **squids**, **cuttlefish** and **octopus** – looks remotely like the other molluscs. The shell has been internalised or evolved away altogether, and the foot or radula has been greatly modified to become eight or ten tentacles, each arrayed with suckers. Many cephalopods display an extraordinary ability to change colour – not just for camouflage (which is not uncommon in the animal kingdom) but also with their mood. Octopuses, for instance, go white when they are frightened.

The **octopus** *Octopus vulgaris* is quite common, though hard to see, as it is perfectly camouflaged and lurks in rock crevices. The process of tenderising octopus for eating is a common sight – quaysides all round the Med reverberate to the characteristic and revolting sound of the dead animal being swung like a wet sheet against a convenient wall or rock. Mediterranean **squid**, of which there are two species, have a maximum length of 60cm and usually swim in deep water. Like squid, **cuttlefish** *Sepia spp.* are free-swimming molluscs with ten tentacles surrounding the mouth, of which two are much longer and are used as antennae; its leaf-shaped white internal skeleton, often found on beaches, is commonly fed to cage birds.

■ Crustaceans; phylum *Arthropoda*

As far as marine life is concerned, the phylum *Arthropoda* effectively means crustaceans, a class that is almost entirely aquatic. (The woodlouse is one of the few terrestrial exceptions.) All crustaceans reproduce via an egg stage, and have microscopic larvae that form an important part of zooplankton – the soup of swimming organisms that forms an essential link in the marine food chain. Some crustacean classes remain microscopic through to the adult stage, but two subclasses are commonly seen and widely distributed.

BARNACLES; SUBCLASS CIRREPEDIA

The **barnacles** – represented by about twenty species in the Med – are in appearance nothing like conventional crustaceans, and have only recently been included in the phylum, principally because they show a typical crustacean breeding cycle. After going through immature stages as plankton, they attach themselves to rocks, boats or other shells by their heads, protecting themselves by means of a shell of fused chalky plates. Although most barnacles hug the rock closely in a limpet-like fashion, some have long attaching "stalks". One of these is the **goose barnacle** *Lepas anatifera*, famous in bird folklore as the supposed parent of the migratory barnacle goose: medieval manuscripts show geese emerging from the barnacles – ostensibly an explanation of their sudden reappearance at their breeding grounds in spring. It's equally likely however that the story was concocted in order to allow hungry Christians to reclassify the goose as a fish, and therefore eat it on Fridays and during Lent.

LOBSTERS, PRAWNS AND CRABS; SUBCLASS MALACOSTRACA

The **lobsters**, **prawns** and **crabs** share a basic body composition: a head with compound eyes, two pairs of antennae and a pair of jaws; a thorax with eight pairs of limbs (legs, claws or gills); and an abdomen with six segments, of which the end one is usually modified into a tail fan. The whole body is surrounded by a "shell" – more properly a hard exoskeleton, performing the same function as a vertebrate skeleton, but holding the body together from the outside rather than the inside and providing protection at the same time.

There's a vast variety of Med malacostracans. The ones you're most likely to come across are the **decapods**, which have five pairs of legs on their thoracic appendages (one pair often developed into formidable pincers), and five pairs of abdominal appendages developed into swimmarets, used for swimming and (in the female) for brooding eggs. The two main groups of decapods are the free-swimming prawns and shrimps, and the largely bottom-dwelling crabs and lobsters.

Most of the thirty-odd species of **prawn** live in shallow water, where it's easy to make out the jerky movements of their almost transparent, light-shelled bodies. No less evident are the **true crabs** and **hermit crabs**. The dozen or so species of the latter don't have a shell of their own, and appropriate instead an empty gastropod shell, changing shells as they grow. True crabs include the **common shore crab** Carcinus mediterraneus, a green crab up to 35mm long, often seen scuttling on the edge of the sea in huge numbers, especially at night. The **edible crab** Cancer pagurus has a characteristic pink oval shell with a piecrust edge and grows to 140mm; the biggest crab of the region is the **spiny spider crab** Maia squinado, with a distinctive spiny pink shell. **Lobsters** and **crayfish** need to be searched for – only 5 species are found in the Med, and all are very cautious. The **true lobster** Homarus gammarus is a large, bright blue animal with massive pincers; there are 3 similar crayfish species, all browny red and without the lobster's claws, although one of them, Palinurus elephas, has enormously long antennae. Finally, the **scampi** Nephrops norvegicus is like a miniature slender lobster, but coloured sandy red.

■ Starfish, urchins and related species; phylum Echinodermata

Echinoderms, unusually for animals, are symmetrical around a central point rather than about a line. Most move slowly, and are covered with a "skeleton" of chalky plates of calcium carbonate; in addition, the mouths of most species are located on the lower side of the body, enabling them to graze on dead or decaying matter, though urchins eat algae as well and starfish are usually carnivorous. There are 18 species of **starfish** (class Asteroidea) in the Med, usually scarlet although one – Coscinasterias tenuispina – is variable and can be bright blue. **Brittle stars** (class Ophiuridea) are represented by about twenty separate but similar species – they have thin brittle arms extending from a circular or pentagonal central disc, and come in a wide variety of colours.

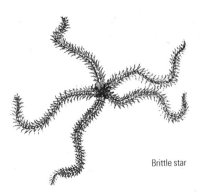

Brittle star

The skeleton of **sea urchins** (class Echinoidea) protrudes through the skin in an armoury of spines; the spines drop off after death, leaving a round "shell" that is a frequent sight on the beach and sea floor. Of the 9 species in the Med, the **black sea urchin** Arbacia lixula is common and widely distributed, clinging to rocks just below the surface, often in large colonies. The spines are a common cause of injury to swimmers and divers: the needles break down in a few days and are expelled from the body, but a dousing with olive oil can ease the pain and speed up the process. The spines of the **long-spined sea urchin** Centrostephanus longispinus can be even more painful if they penetrate the skin; happily, they mostly live in deep water, and are rarely met with except by scuba divers. The **rock urchin** *Paracentrotus lividus* is the *oursin* of French cuisine, and its roe is highly prized all around the Med. **Heart urchins** (or sea potatoes), superficially like a sea urchin, are heart-shaped and have much shorter spines that appear almost like hair. Since they spend most of their time burrowed in the mud or sand you won't easily see one alive, but their hole-patterned shells are often found.

Resembling sparsely spiked sausages up to 30cm long, the thirty or so species of **sea cucumbers** (class *Holothuroidea*) move slowly around on countless tube-feet, sucking up detritus from the sea floor. The mouth is sometimes surrounded by modified tube-feet that act as feeding tentacles.

■ Sea squirts; class *Ascidiacea*, phylum *Urochordata*

The **sea squirts** form an interesting link between invertebrates and vertebrates. Adult sea squirts are filter feeders, and don't have much in common with true vertebrates: living singly or in colonies, often encrusting rock outcrops, they could be mistaken for one of the corals or sponges. However, the larvae – which look like tadpoles – have a primitive backbone called a notochord. They are therefore included in the phylum *Chordata*, which covers everything from sea squirts through to that self-styled pinnacle of evolutionary achievement, *Homo sapiens*.

■ Fishes

Sharks, rays and skates form the first class of fishes, the *Chondrichthyes*, which are distinguished by their **lack of bone** – their skeletons are formed from cartilage. Over seventy species in this class have been recorded in the Med, although swimmers will be relieved to know that the vast majority of the **sharks** are found in deep water, and rarely stray into the coast. Nonetheless, large and dramatic species of shark such as the **blue shark** are found, and can on occasions come in to shallow water. Sharks are easily recognised by their unequal tail lobes, the upper one being longer than the lower one. If you're very lucky, you might see the **basking shark** *Cetorhinus maximus*, which grows to an intimidating fifteen metres – yet it's a peaceful and harmless plankton feeder, which it catches by filtering the sea in the same way as the baleen

whales. Probably the commonest of the shark family are the **dogfishes** *Scyliorhinus spp.* which are usually less than a metre long, and live on the sea bottom in depths up to fifty metres or so.

The flat-bodied **skates and rays** are all bottom dwellers, almost invisible at rest but a tremendous sight when they swim, flying through the water like marine eagles. Usually they move slowly, gliding by barely moving the tips of their "wings", but they can swim extremely fast, and have even been seen to work up such a speed that they break through the water surface. They're all large animals, between one and two metres including the elongated tail. The **common skate** *Raja batis* is typical of the group; up to two metres long with a brown diamond-shaped body, it is widely eaten, as is the **monkfish** *Squatina squatina*, which has well-developed fins along the side of its otherwise ray-shaped body. Two species to avoid close contact with are the **sting ray** *Dasyatis pastinaca*, which carries a poisonous spine instead of a dorsal fin on the top of its tail, and the **electric ray** *Torpedo marmorata*, whose distinctively rounded body can dish out quite powerful electric shocks.

BONY FISHES; CLASS OSTEICHTHYES

All other fish belong to the varied group of bony fishes, of which nearly 500 species are found in the Med. With the exception of the **sturgeons** *Acipenser spp.*, they all have equal tail lobes and can control their buoyancy by an internal organ called a **swim bladder** (which the cartilaginous fishes lack).

Some species swim in large schools, and these are often the most important **commercial fish**. They include the **sardines** *Sardina pilchardus*, **sprats** *Sprattus sprattus* and **anchovies** *Engraulius encrasicolus* – small species that often come close inshore. **Mackerel** *Scomber japonicus* is an important medium-sized fish of open water, which also swims in large schools. Its far larger relative the **tuna fish** *Thunnus thynnus*, which grows to up to three metres, migrates into the Med from the Atlantic in spring and early summer to breed, and is harvested in huge numbers wherever its migratory route takes it into shallow coastal waters, especially off the coasts of Tunisia and Sicily.

Around the rocky shores, most fish tend to swim in smaller groups. Two common species of this habitat are the long and streamlined **grey** mullets *Liza spp.* and *Chelon spp.*, and the **gilt-heads** *Diplodus spp.*, which have deeper bodies, steep foreheads, and often a conspicuous black spot at the base of the tail. In dark crevices among underwater rocks, look for the **cardinal fish** *Apogon imberbis*, a bright red fish up to 15cm long, with very large dark eyes.

An extraordinary and colourful group are the **wrasses**, of which there are some 20 species in the Med; they are hard to identify, partly because they change colour with the time of year, and also with changes in gender – in some species females turn into males. Mostly small fish around 10cm long (although a few species get to 40cm), they spend their time fossicking around rocks and seaweed, swimming in short glides with powerful tail flicks; background colour is generally greenish, dramatically spotted and striped with red, blue or yellow.

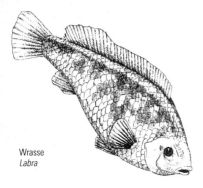

Wrasse
Labra

Among the weed beds lurk **pipefish** *Syngnathus spp.*, marvellously adapted to resemble a strip of weed, with their thin tubular bodies (up to 30cm long) and pointed snouts. The **seahorse** *Hippocampus spp.*, a curled-up version of the pipefish, is uncommon.

On any boat trip, watch out for **flying fish**, of which there are five species in the Med. Growing to a length of 40cm, they are like herrings with enormously enlarged pectoral fins, which can carry them on skimming flights of distances as great as forty metres.

A few poisonous species are native to the Med. The **lesser weever fish** *Echiichthys vipera* is small, brown, and spends much of its time buried in the sand in shallow water; it has upright spines on its back (the first dorsal fin) which can

cause severe pain if trodden on. Equally unpleasant are the **scorpion fishes** *Scorpoena spp.*, a very spiny fish, red-brown in colour, growing to 50cm, and living amongst rocks; the gill covers and dorsal fin of these species bear poisonous spines. Scorpion fish form the basis of a wonderful fish soup in Crete and elsewhere – the spines having been removed first.

Another highly prized delicacy is **red mullet** *Mullus spp.*, which, confusingly, is not at all closely related to the grey mullet. A rock-dweller, it lives in shallow water and can grow up to 40cm, but is usually much smaller; two barbels hanging from its lower jaw help to identify it.

■ Marine reptiles

The only marine reptiles in the Med are the turtles, family *Cheloniidae*. Although 4 of the 7 world species have been recorded in the Med, all are rare, and only one, the **loggerhead turtle** *Caretta caretta*, exists in significant numbers. Loggerheads remain at sea for most of the year, coming ashore only in the summer to breed, when the females crawl onto a sandy beach and bury their egg clutch in the sand. Over the last twenty years, tourist development of their breeding beaches has led to a disastrous decline in numbers, and only two breeding sites of any size remain, on the Greek island of Zakinthos and along the southern coast of Turkey, especially near Dalyan. They can sometimes be spotted from boats as they bask on the surface, or cruising offshore of their breeding beaches.

■ Marine mammals

Two orders of marine mammals occur in the Med. The first are the **seals**, represented by the **Mediterranean·monk seal** *Monachus monachus*, a species endemic to the Med but now on the point of extinction – hunting and disturbance have made it Europe's rarest mammal. Its few breeding sites are centred on remote rocky islands off the Greek and Turkish coasts.

The second order comprises the **whales and dolphins** (order *Cetacea*). All cetaceans give birth to live young in the water, and so are at least immune to the sort of disturbances that have affected seals and turtles, but commercial whaling has seriously reduced their numbers, and the dolphins and porpoises have also been affected by accidental trapping in the nets of fishing vessels.

Baleen whales are so called because instead of teeth they have plates of a horny substance called baleen, used to filter vast volumes of seawater for the plankton on which they live. (Baleen was the "whalebone" used in Victorian corsets.) Only 2 species are at all common in the Med: the **fin whale** *Balaenoptera physalis*, which grows to twenty metres, and the **minke whale** *Balaenoptera acutorostrata*, which grows to just half that size. Both are most likely to be seen in deep water in the western Med, straying through the Straits of Gibraltar from the Atlantic.

The **toothed whales** include the **sperm whale** *Physeter catodon*, probably the commonest large whale in the Med; it grows to eighteen metres in length, and is identifiable by its huge rectangular head and the forward angle of its spout — baleen whales, by contrast, spout vertically.

Although 8 **dolphin** species have been recorded from the Med, only 2 are seen with any frequency. The **common dolphin** *Delphinus delphis* is up to two metres long, with a perfectly streamlined body; its horizontal tail flukes instantly distinguish it from the larger fishes. Black above and white below, it has a complex pattern on its flanks, usually incorporating a large yellow patch. The other common species of the region is the **bottlenosed dolphin** *Tursiops truncatus*, up to four metres long and coloured uniform grey; this is the species generally kept in dolphinaria and zoos. Dolphins are highly sociable, frequently gathering in large schools, and they swim very actively, often leaping clear of the water. The **common porpoise** *Phocoena phocoena*, on the other hand, is a slower swimmer and usually rolls gently through the water, rarely leaping clear of it. Porpoises are smaller than dolphins, and have a blunter head, lacking the dolphin's beak; they also have a smaller and flatter back fin.

PART TWO

THE
SITES

CHAPTER ONE

FRANCE

D espite its long history of development, and particularly its standing as Europe's oldest tourist playground, the Mediterranean coast of France has some wonderful wildlife spots. As is to be expected in such an affluent region, **conservation consciousness** is relatively high and most of these sites are now protected in one way or another by national parks, regional parks, or nature reserves. Areas like the Camargue, the Cevennes and the Alpes Maritimes are quite outstandingly protected and interpreted. Equally predictably, though, all is not entirely rosy. The rate of **building development** on the coast is very high, and although much of this is infill in areas which have already been exploited for tourism, much is not; the new concrete resorts on the Languedoc–Roussillon coast, for instance, have had considerable impact on wildlife habitats through pollution, land drainage, and general disturbance levels.

The whole coast is an extraordinary contrast of high density tourism and genuine wilderness. Mountain regions such as the **Cevennes** and the **Alpes Maritimes** are full of flowers, mountain birds and some spectacular mammals, while the **lower hills of Provence** have long been acclaimed by naturalists for their **spring flowers** and insects, especially **butterflies**. Small **songbirds** still flourish wherever there is traditional agriculture, despite the strong possibility of ending up in an expensive and unnecessary pâté come the hunting season.

Climate and land use

The French section of the Med is no exception to the general climate of cool wet winters and hot dry summers. Summer temperatures – *la grande chaleur* – are consistently high at around 30°C. The region is drier than the Iberian coast but wetter then the eastern Med – Marseille has a rainfall of 55cm a year, roughly halfway between the rainfall in Athens and that in Gibraltar.

Most flat land has been developed for agriculture, and most coastal land for housing, tourism or industry. It is therefore on the mountain slopes and the higher ground that one can find remnants of the natural and semi-natural Med habitats, and since the area is very mountainous, there's a surprising amount left. **Cork oak** forests are found on sandstone hills such as the **foothills of the Pyrenees** and the **Massif des Maures**, while two other oak species, the holm oak *Quercus ilex* and the white oak *Quercus pubescens*, tend to dominate in more alkaline limestone regions. Frequently, this original **forest** cover has been degraded by fire and grazing to form stands of scrubby *maquis*. On the higher ground such as the **Cevennes** or the **Alpes Maritimes**, traditional grazing and mixed farming is still practised, and some of the original deciduous **beech forest** can still be found, giving way to coniferous forest of firs and pines higher up.

French **agriculture** is not all of the traditional nature that tourist posters would have us believe, with large areas of the lowland plains of Roussillon and the

Rhône given over to intensive vineyards, and intensive rice-growing around the Camargue has caused problems with agrochemical runoff. On the bright side, however, it does appear that there has been a recent reduction in pesticide use, resulting in an increase in insects and hence insectivorous birds. **Hunting**, sadly,

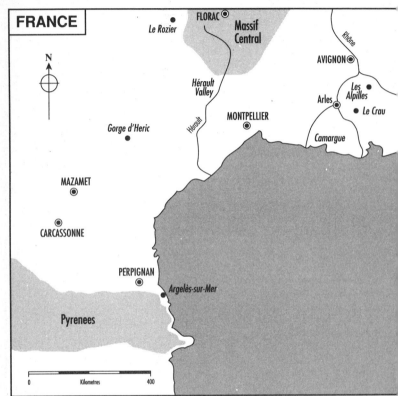

FRANCE

N

Le Rozier
FLORAC
Massif Central
Rhône
AVIGNON
Héault Valley
Les Alpilles
Arles
Le Crau
Hérault
MONTPELLIER
Gorge d'Heric
Camargue
MAZAMET
CARCASSONNE
PERPIGNAN
Argelès-sur-Mer
Pyrenees

0   Kilometres   400

WHEN AND WHERE TO GO

May is the best month to visit, if you can, although April is good on the coast and Alpine flowers up in the mountains keep going until July. The autumn is a good time for bird migration. The whole of the Med coast gets extremely crowded from mid-July to the end of August, the French national holiday season.

Getting around between major towns is simple, with an adequate bus service and one of the best rail networks in Europe. On minor roads and up in the mountains things are a little more difficult, with an uncoordinated and infrequent bus service. Backpacking along one of the GR trails or cycling are two time-honoured French ways of getting around, and ensure you of a welcome; hitching, too, is a lot better on minor roads than major ones.

The main sites described are:

is still a major problem, and most wildlife goes to ground when the season starts in October. Signs saying *Chasse interdit* are vastly outnumbered by ones saying *Chasse privée* or *Chasse gardée*, and stories abound of hunters blasting off at anything that moves, including butterflies and even tortoises.

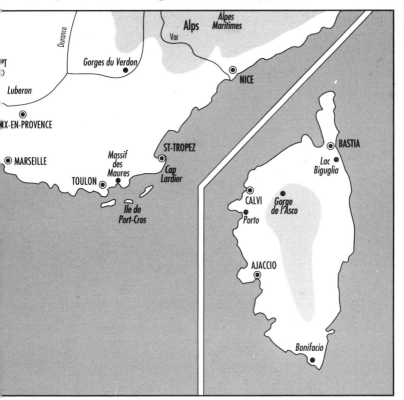

● **ROUSSILLON** In the extreme southwest near the Spanish border, the tourist town of **Argelès-sur-Mer** is a good base for the cork oak forests, for surrounding typical *maquis* scrub, and for some coastal marshes

● **LANGUEDOC REGIONAL PARK** Further north, this park has spectacular scenery and some unspoilt limestone gorges in the **Vallée du Jaur**

● **CEVENNES** This national park has a quite outstanding range of habitats, including deciduous and coniferous forest and the sheep-nibbled plateaux of the Causses, all intersected by massive limestone gorges. It's a superb area for wildlife, including dramatic birds of prey such as the re-introduced Griffon vulture around the town of **Le Rozier**, and the **Hérault valley** runs through the full range of Med habitats

● **RHONE DELTA** Although the **Camargue** is the highlight of the Rhône delta, as one of the best places for wetland birdwatching in Europe, the stony desert of **Le Crau** is also excellent for birds, and the low mountains of **Les Alpilles** are worth visiting for flowers as well as birds.

● **PROVENCE** is typified by the **Luberon**, a Regional Park of limestone hills, interspersed with traditional agriculture and delightful small villages. The butter-flies here are exceptional, but other animals and plants are well represented too. The **Gorge du Verdon** is the most spectacular limestone gorge in Europe, a fine place for seeing the birds and flowers of the mountains.

● **COTE D'AZUR** The **St-Tropez peninsula** and the **Ile de Port-Cros** have both escaped the otherwise continuous development of this coastline, and further inland the **Massif des Maures** deserves Regional Park status for its hills of cork oak forest and typical *maquis*. North of Nice, the **Alpes Maritimes** come close to the sea and are excellent for true Alpine flowers and birds as well as scarce mammals such as chamois and ibex.

● **CORSICA** The wild and mountainous island has superb scenery and dense wood-lands. **Porto** in the northwest is a good base for the coast and forests. **Lake Biguglia** in the northeast is the best spot for wetland birds. The **Gorge de L'Asco** holds rare birds such as the lammergeir and the endemic Corsican nuthatch. In the extreme south, the limestone peninsula of **Bonifacio** has outstanding flowers.

ROUSSILLON

The long coastline of **Roussillon** is far less developed than its counterpart to the east of the Camargue. The plain itself, surrounding the large town of **Perpignan**, is given over largely to vineyards; most of the wildlife interest centres on the coastal lagoons and dunes, and on the extreme southern tip of the region, where the foothills of the Pyrenees rise up to diversify the landscape.

The two sites described are close to the small resort of **Argelès-sur-Mer**; the coastal nature reserve at **Mas Larrieu**, at the mouth of the River Tech, has an intact dune system and good marshes and woodland, and the walk up the road from the town towards **Mas Christine** is an excellent representation of typical Mediterranean cork oak woodland, interspersed with farmland and scrub.

Mas Larrieu

Owned by the Coastal Protection Society, **MAS LARRIEU** covers 145 hectares of seashore, marsh and woodland. Due to its beach, the seashore is too developed for most wildlife, but there are some fine habitats in the dunes and open, sandy ground behind. Among flowers here, look out for the yellow horned poppy *Glaucium flavum*, with big yellow flowers, a long seed pod, and lobed grey leaves. Sea holly *Eryngium maritimum*, with very spiny large blue leaves, grows here too, along with pink-flowered *Convolvulus* and the tiny *Paronychia argentea*, which forms low cushions and has papery bracts surrounding its flowers. The **birds** include wheatears and crested larks, whilst whinchats perch jauntily on top of the bushes. The grasses and vetches also support numerous **butterflies**, especially the brilliantly coloured blues and the more dowdy skippers.

The **marshes** are dominated by the huge giant reed *Arundo donax*, the tallest European grass, and form a home for numerous reed warblers; the saline pools are fringed with tamarix bushes with their feathery foliage, and are especially rich in dragonflies.

Back in the **riverine forest** is a strikingly different habitat – a thick, lush woodland of willow, poplar and alder. It's alive with small birds, especially tits, warblers and the ever-present nightingale, and is one of the last French breeding sites for the **penduline tit** (though only a handful of pairs still survive). Green woodpeckers also breed here, but you're more likely to hear their ringing call than to see them, and the gorgeously coloured **bee-eater** favours the woodland edge and the surrounding sandy soil.

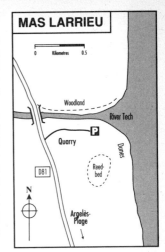

Mas Christine

The walk from Argelès to **MAS CHRISTINE** is typical of the local hillsides, leading through small fields and cork oak forest. The presence of **cork oak** *Quercus suber* with an understorey of tree heath *Erica arborea* signals a soil derived from sedimentary sandstone, in contrast to the limestone of the true Pyrenees.

Although the cork oak dominates the woodland, alder and willow grow too by the streamside. Two of the bushy **rockroses** are very evident: *Cistus albidus*, with pink flowers and downy grey leaves, and *Cistus monspeliensis*, a shrub typical of the region with a profusion of smaller white flowers and narrow, slightly sticky leaves. Beneath these are the tight purple flower spikes of French lavender *Lavendula stoechas* and, twining amongst the trees, honeysuckle and the wickedly-barbed *Smilax aspera* with its shining, heart-shaped evergreen leaves. The unmistakeable Spanish broom *Spartium junceum* is even more obvious, with large yellow pea flowers on almost bare green stems. The widespread Med splurge *Euphorbia characias* grows up to a metre high under the woodlands, and the delicate pink trumpet flowers of *Convolvulus althaeoides* sprawl over the dry ground.

This walk is excellent for **birds**, especially during **spring migration** in May. **Golden orioles** are a highlight, but usually only seen in flight; they have, like parrots, the ability to hide their brilliant yellow and black plumage the moment they go into a tree. The male has a very distinctive call, short but very sweet, usually transcribed as "weela-weeoo". The scrub holds subalpine warblers and blackcaps, while black and white pied flycatchers join with numerous tits and warblers in the cork oaks. Hoopoes feed on open ground but nest in the trees, and the deeply ridged bark of the cork oak makes an ideal habitat for the **treecreeper**, a tiny mouselike bird with a thin decurved bill which creeps up the tree trunks in search of insect food.

Butterflies in this area are dominated predictably by the speckled wood *Pararge aegeria*, a specialist of the woodland edge; its mottled brown wings camouflage it perfectly as it sits on a leaf in dappled sunlight. The Camberwell beauty *Nymphalis antiopa* can be seen in spring as it flies after winter hibernation – it's a large, easily recognisable butterfly, its deep purple wings surrounded by a broad cream border. Marsh frogs *Rana ridibunda* in the river and green lizards *Lacerta viridis* amongst the rocks add further interest along this section.

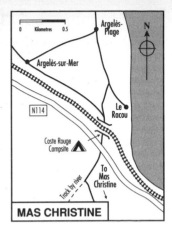

Back at the start of the walk, the woodland and open field opposite the *Coste Rouge* campsite are worth exploring for a similar range of woodland birds and flowers. The field itself, right next to the crossroads, is full of greenwinged orchids *Orchis morio* and tongue orchids *Serapias lingua* in May, and probably other **orchid species** earlier in April.

Other nearby sites

Going up into the hills to the south of Argelès, the wooded valley of the **River Massane** and the **Gorges de Lavall** offer spectacular scenery and a selection of good walks through holm oak *Quercus ilex* forest, rising in a typical Mediterranean succession through sweet chestnut *Castanea sativa* up to beech *fagus sylvaticus* and white oak *Quercus pubescens* at higher altitude, especially around the woodland nature reserve of **Forêt de la Massane**. This reserve is internationally famous for its **insect population**, with the amazing total of 1256 species of beetle alone recorded from fifteen square kilometres.

The SI in Argelès has a useful **guide to the walks** of this region, though transport to the valley (between Argelès and Sorède) is tricky with only one bus a day.

ROUSSILLON: ACCESS AND ACCOMMODATION

Mas Larrieu

Access is from the River Tech bridge, 4km north of ARGELES on the D81 to ST-CYPRIEN. The track past the quarry on the south side of the river leads to the marsh and the better beach; the track to the north side leads to the woodland. On the beach itself, you could be forgiven for confusing nature reserve with naturist reserve. ARGELES PLAGE has plenty of campsites, but no especially cheap hotels.

Mas Christine

The road to MAS CHRISTINE branches off the main N114 coastal highway 2km south of ARGELES, opposite the road down to the beach resort of LE RACOU. Follow the road for a kilometre, and then branch right up a track by the stream. This is a delightful walk for 2km, until it crosses the stream to end in a private vineyard.

ARGELES and LE RACOU both have places to stay; the campsite at the crossroads with the N114, called the *Coste Rouge* (☎68.81.08.94), is very convenient for this area, and has the added bonus of a stunning dawn chorus from the surrounding woodland, including nightingales, hoopoes and golden orioles.

LANGUEDOC

Although the flat plains of Languedoc are for the most part covered in vineyards, they are bounded to the north by the **Parc Regional de Haut-Languedoc**, an area of limestone hills that is reminiscent of the southern Massif Central and effectively forms the border of the Mediterranean vegetation zone. Further to the west, the flat limestone plain at **Conques-sur-Orbiel** is conveniently close to the resort of **Carcassonne**, and is especially rich in flowers.

Vallée du Jaur

The **VALLEE DU JAUR** runs from ST-PONS-DE-THOMMIERES to MONS, where it joins the River Orb for the run down to the sea across the plains and through Beziers. The valley is interesting because it's on the **boundary** of the Mediterranean and Atlantic zones; to the north, the woodland is dominated by beech, sweet chestnut, ash and hazel, and the spring ground flora of violets *Viola spp.*, cowslips *Primula veris* and early purple orchids *Orchis mascula* is reminiscent of northern European woodlands. To the south, true Mediterranean species such as holm oak *Quercus ilex* and white oak *Quercus pubescens* take over.

The **GORGE D'HERIC** runs down to MONS opposite the river Orb. A typical limestone gorge, with dramatic and beautiful scenery, it's at its best in spring; later in the year it's well visited, although a brief walk up the gorge along the obvious path will lose most of your fellow tourists. The **woodlands** on the steep sides are mostly holm oak *Quercus ilex*, with some ash *Fraxinus ornus* and sweet chestnut *Castanea sativa*. Two smaller but typically Mediterranean trees are the Montpelier maple *Acer monspeliensis*, with small three-lobed leaves, and *Amelanchier ovalis* which is covered in white flowers in spring; the flowers consist of five narrow and widely separated white petals. Under the trees and on rocky slopes, the pink flowers of *Cistus albidus* and the blue flowers of French lavender *Lavandula stoechas* continue the Mediterranean theme.

Look out here, and right along the Jaur, for two very characteristic **plants of sunny hills** of the western Med. The first is *Aphyllanthes monspeliensis*, a very unusual member of the lily family which has clumps of leafless stems, making it look like a grass or a rush for much of the year. In spring and early summer, however, a delicate starry blue flower appears on the end of each stem. The second is *Saponaria ocymoides*, a low creeping plant with hairy stems and leaves and a mass of five petalled pink flowers, usually appearing as dense sheets of colour.

Aphyllanthes monspeliensis

The woodlands and scrub along the gorge hold the usual range of small warblers and nightingales, with a few additions of **birds of the gorges**; dippers breed along the stream, unmistakeable with their white breast, dark back, and habit of continually bobbing up and down on a midstream rock; grey wagtails are another typical bird of rocky streams, with a very long tail and undulating flight. Two **birds of the mountain crags** here are the blue rock thrush and the crag martin. Finally, the mouflon *Ovis musimon*, the ancestral wild sheep, is found in small numbers on the mountain of **Le Caroux**, immediately to the east of the gorge; there's a faint chance of seeing them from the gorge itself, although a better option would be the longer walk from the head of the gorge up the GR7 footpath to the refuge on the mountain slopes – a 13-kilometre round trip in all.

Conques-sur-Orbiel

North of **Carcassonne**, the land rises through low hills towards the ridge of **La Montagne Noire**. The road cuts through a large area of degraded heathland which is part of the **FORÊT COMMUNALE DE CONQUES-SUR-ORBIEL**. The area has some similarities to the *Causse* country of the Cevennes, with bare soil and grass amongst a shrubby landscape dominated by box *Buxus sepervirens*, and both pink and white *Cistus*; the white one is *Cistus salvifolius*, which is more tolerant of neutral soils than the narrower leaved *Cistus monspeliensis*. Related, though smaller, rockroses *Helianthemum spp.* grow nearer to the ground, with either yellow or white flowers. The blue flowers of *Aphyllanthes monspeliensis* are especially evident here, and thyme *Thymus vulgaris* carpets the ground.

   Orchids grow wherever there is space amongst the shrubs. The pink spikes of pyramidal orchids *Anacamptis pyramidalis* are obvious, along with some of the insect-imitating species which are harder to spot; several of these grow here, including the yellow *Ophrys lutea*, the mottled brown *O. scolopax*, and rather a boring small form of the early spider orchid, *O. sphegodes litigiosa*. Rustles in the bushes will normally be small brown lizards or the larger green lizard *Lacerta viridis*, but could also be the Montpellier snake *Malpolon monspessulanus*, which is relatively abundant in this habitat; it can grow disconcertingly large – up to 2m long; although venomous, it is only mildly so and back-fanged, so the chances of a bite are remote unless you actually pick one up. The **birds** of this open countryside largely consist of wheatears, larks and stonechats, while the black kite finds this a good hunting habitat, quartering the ground on its long thin wings.

LANGUEDOC: ACCESS AND ACCOMMODATION

Vallée du Jaur
Getting around the valley of the Jaur is relatively easy, with both a main road and the railway between Mazamet and Bédarieux. ST-PONS-DE-THOMMIERES is a good base, with the very friendly headquarters of the regional park up behind the cathedral; there's a campsite, and you might find cheap rooms by asking at the restaurant *La Croix Blanche*, which also serves delicious food.

   Another alternative is OLARGUES, further east and only 6km from the Gorge d'Heric; it has a campsite and is an old town with a wonderful bridge arching over the river. Both towns have **museums** which provide useful background to the wildlife of the park – prehistory at St-Pons, geology at Olargues.

Conques-sur-Orbiel
The plain is some 10km north of CARCASSONNE on the main RN118 road to Mazamet, which is well served with buses. The centre of it is 1km south of the minor D411 turn to SALSIGNE. Carcassonne itself is the obvious place to stay, with plenty of cheap hotels and places to eat in the lower town.

THE CEVENNES

The **Cevennes** is a mountainous region forming the southern portion of the Massif Central, the ancient rocky core of southern and central France. Its wildlife is exceptionally rich, partly through the protection afforded by its National Park status, and partly due to geological diversity. **Mont Aigoual** and **Mont Lingas**, the two highest peaks in the southern Med, are granite and schist, while, surrounding the mountains, the rocks are mostly sedimentary limestone. A feature of the latter is the **Causse Méjean**, part of the *Grands Causses* system of high limestone plateaux intersected by riverine gorges. This geological diversity is compounded by the position of the Cevennes on the Mediterranean/Atlantic watershed. While the rivers Tarn and Jonte eventually flow into the Atlantic, the Hérault, just the other side of Mont Aigoual, flows into the Mediterranean.

The two base areas featured here are highly worthwhile for all kinds of wildlife. **Le Rozier** stands at the intersection of the gorges of the Tarn and the Jonte, which also gives easy access up onto Causse Méjean. And on the southern side of the Cevennes, the valley of the **River Hérault** crosses a fascinating succession of different habitats from its source down to its entry to the flat plains.

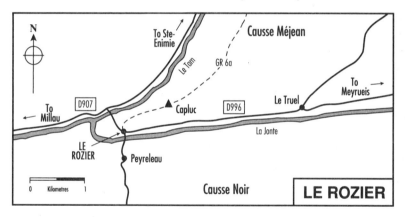

Le Rozier

LE ROZIER is the best base for both the **Gorge du Tarn** and the **Gorge de la Jonte**. Although the former is the most famous of the limestone gorges of the Cevennes, the latter is almost as spectacular – and far less crowded. One special feature of this area are the breeding **Griffon vultures**, whose return from extinction is a major conservation success story (see opposite). **Other big raptors** around here include the snake-eating short-toed eagle and the magnificent golden eagle – though this is now a rare bird, with only four or five pairs left in the park.

Other **birds of the gorges**, easily seen by the river or on any of the short walks from Le Rozier, include dippers and grey wagtails on the river, and blue rock thrushes on the surrounding crags. Black redstarts are common breeders in the town and on the cliffs, and choughs wheel around the rocks, distinguished from the crows and ravens by their higher-pitched call and red bill and legs. Look out too for the rare and spectacular **eagle owl**, as large as a small eagle; a few pairs breed in the limestone cliffs, and a walk along the bottom of the gorge at dusk may just turn up one as it emerges to hunt hares and rabbits.

Surrounding walks

Many **trails and walks** radiate out from Le Rozier. The main GR6a, one of the *grand randonnée* series of long-distance footpaths, passes just behind the church at Le Rozier and continues up to **Capluc**, a rocky outcrop overlooking the village and crowned with a large cross. This is an easy stroll until the final section up to the cross itself, which is reached by vertical iron ladders set in the rock – not for the vertigo prone. Crag martins wheel around the rock itself, joined by choughs and the occasional vulture. From the top, there's a wonderful view along the Jonte to the *Corniches de Méjean*, a series of white limestone pinnacles standing out amongst the dark green pine forests.

THE RETURN OF THE VULTURES

Griffon vultures are huge and spectacular birds; the sight of them wheeling over the white cliffs that line the gorges is truly magnificent. Until the 1930s they were a relatively common sight here and elsewhere in France, but extinction came rapidly and tragically. *Les Bouldras*, as they are locally known, feed largely on **carrion** – mostly dead sheep, since the main agricultural activity on the limestone plateaux is the raising of sheep for meat, wool and especially cheese – and their extinction was mainly due to hunting pressure and the use of poison bait to eradicate foxes and other farm vermin.

There the matter would have stayed but for the determination of a handful of local activists, well supported by the Park authority, who were determined to see the birds in the Cevennes once more. A stock of live birds was obtained from all over Europe from zoos, from injured wild birds, and from birds which were confiscated after illegal capture. A breeding centre was set up in the Gorge de la Jonte near the village of LE TRUEL, where more birds were bred in captivity during the 1970s, and between 1981 and 1985 they were released into the wild to fend for themselves. There's now a healthy and self-sustaining population of around **seventy birds**, with nearly thirty pairs regularly breeding. The birds are fully protected, and the use of poison bait forbidden in the central park zone.

The vultures are usually seen soaring in the distance in search of carrion, but even then their huge size is evident. They have enormously broad wings, perfectly designed for circling on rising air currents, and a full grown adult can have a wingspan of up to 2.8 metres; they're essentially living hang-gliders.

The easiest place to see the vultures is around the village of **LE TRUEL**, 3km up the Jonte from Le Rozier, where it's not unusual to see twenty birds in the air at one time. They nest on the steep cliffs next to the village, but they can usually be seen from **LE ROZIER** as well, especially in the late afternoon and evening.

Continuing along the GR6, beyond Capluc, the track cuts through some marvellous **abandoned terraces** near where a path marked *J.Brunet* branches off. These terraces are fabulous for plants and butterflies. The blue starry flowers of *Aphyllanthes monspeliensis* (see Languedoc) combine with the yellows of vetches and rockroses *Helianthemum spp.* and the white of ox-eye daisies *Leucanthemum vulgare*. Against this spectacular backdrop up to a dozen species of orchid can be found flowering in May, dominated by the lady orchid *Orchis purpurea* and monkey orchids *O. simia*, both very striking plants with tall spikes of pink flowers. The man orchid *Aceras anthropophorum* grows here too, with its thin spikes of yellow and brown flowers, each looking like a hanged man.

On sunny days, this wealth of nectar-bearing flowers attracts **butterflies** in their hundreds. Many of these are blues, which depend on vetches as larval food plants. At least three species fly in early summer, including the spectacular Adonis blue *Lysandra bellargus*; the male is a pure shining sky blue, edged with a white fringe which is cut through with black veins. Familiar species such as the yellow brimstone *Gonepteryx cleopatra* and the scarce swallowtail *Iphiclides podalirius* fly with less familiar ones such as the fritillaries; these are a group of confusingly similar butterflies, all with a beautifully marbled colour of brown, black and yellow.

The **green lizard** *Lacerta viridis* is common in this region, as elsewhere in France, but the ones around here seem to be particularly brightly coloured – the male has a psychedelic body of mottled black and brilliant green, along with blue on the cheeks and throat, sometimes extending to the whole head; but despite these colours, it's still a hard species to spot as it scurries away from the paths. Higher up the path, the track winds steeply up amongst pine forest with an understorey of box *Buxus sempervirens*; on the rocky outcrops, dwarf alpine flowers flourish in the cracks, including the blue flowers of *Globularia sp.*, looking like round buttons, and the big deep yellow flowers of a flax, *Linum campanulatum*.

Causse Méjean

The final habitat close to Le Rozier is **Causse Méjean**, a high limestone plateau at around 1000m, nibbled by innumerable sheep, and studded with occasional pine plantations and rounded shrubs of box and the white-flowered *Amelanchier ovalis*; the Causse is very rich botanically, with some 900 species recorded. The best area is some way from Le Rozier, around the centre of the plateau at the aerodrome of Florac-St-Enemie, but a reasonable idea of this strange region can be had from the small road leading from Le Truel to LA PARADE.

The River Hérault

The **RIVER HERAULT** rises high on the southern slopes of Mont Aigoual near L'ESPEROU and immediately plunges down a series of waterfalls. The vegetation round here is almost alpine, clinging to the granite outcrops, but soon turns into the highest of the wooded zones of the region – **beech forest**. The beech trees here are superb, often rising from coppiced stools, and interspersed with damp meadows used for summer sheep grazing. These meadows are rich in plants such as cowslips *Primula veris*; the large purple spikes of the **marsh orchid** *Dactylorhiza majalis* are common, with the more delicate yellow flowers of *Orchis provincialis* growing amongst them. In spring, drifts of *Narcissus poeticus* are widespread, its pale cream petals surrounding a deep yellow central tube. In the **forest** itself, the dense shade cast by the trees inhibits plant growth, but meadow saxifrage *Saxifraga granulata* and wood anemone *Anemone nemorosa* are two dominant white-flowered plants of the forest floor. These beech forests are also home to one of Europe's rarest and most beautiful beetles, a **longhorn beetle** *Rosalia alpina*. The adult can, with luck, be seen from June to September, and has a blue body variably patterned with large black spots, and enormously long blue antennae.

Dropping down the valley towards VALLERAUGUE, the river passes briefly through a zone of sweet chestnut before the dark green of holm oak becomes dominant. This is especially striking round Valleraugue itself, with the evergreen foliage of the oak forming a noticeable boundary with the paler green of the beech and sweet chestnut. A minor road follows the river along from Le Gasquet to PONT D'HERAULT, and the vegetation changes again with the geological transition from schist to limestone; *Cistus salvifolius* makes its first appearance, signalling the start of typical Mediterranean *maquis* scrub, and the river becomes wide enough to have the occasional orchard growing alongside it. False acacia *Robinia pseudacacia* is widely planted around here, with pinnate leaves similar to the ash, and abundant hanging strings of white pea-shaped flowers in April and May.

From Pont d'Hérault to the town of GANGES the river runs alongside the main D999 road. The woodlands of the valley sides are mixed, with white oak *Quercus pubescens*, ash and alder joining the holm oak, and with a rich understorey of box, elder *Sambucus sp.* and butchers broom *Ruscus aculaeatus*. Ivy and clematis grow through the trees, and the ferns underfoot complete an impression of lushness.

The woodland around ST-JULIAN-DE-LA-NEF is typical of this habitat, and is especially rich in **woodland birds**, including the rather scarce lesser spotted woodpecker as well as the usual range of warblers, tits, finches and abundant nightingales. Dippers and grey wagtails breed on the river itself – any bridge is a good place to watch from – while buzzards hunt small mammals in the clearings. These clearings are also rich in flowers in early summer; the spiked star of Bethlehem *Ornithogalum narbonse* is a common sight, with a loose spike of white starry flowers, each with a characteristic green stripe on the underside of the petals. Orchids of the clearings include monkey orchid *Orchis simia*, burnt tip orchid *Orchis ustulata* and the widespread pyramidal orchid *Anacamptis pyramidalis*.

The next stretch of the river is different again – though the plains around BRISSAC are an altogether less exciting region. The Hérault flows quietly through willows, before **rocky limestone hills** take over again on the run down through a very bleak and deserted region of *maquis* scrub to the village and monastery of ST-GUILHEM-LE-DESERT. The holm oak is joined by typical Med shrubs such as *Pistachia terebinthus* and rockroses, as well as the yellow sweet-smelling jasmine *Jasmine fruticans*; the grey bushes of the everlasting flower *Helichrysum stoechas* are a common sight, and the woodland birds of the higher reaches are replaced by scrub warblers such as Sardinian and subalpine warbler. At St-Guilhem itself, the river is about halfway down its 150-km journey to the sea, but after the next village of St-Jean-de-Fos, the **endless plains** of Béziers appear, and the river rapidly loses much of its wildlife interest. It flows tamely amongst vineyards and orchards from Gignac to Agde until finally, encased in concrete, bridged by motorways and surrounded by holiday villages, it slips quietly into the Med at LE GRAU D'AGDE. It's rather an anti-climactic end to a river whose higher reaches are so varied and exciting.

CEVENNES: ACCESS AND ACCOMMODATION

Le Rozier

LE ROZIER lies on the main road along the Gorges du Tarn, and is easily reached by bus from either MILLAU at the west end or ST-ENIMIE at the east. It's actually two towns – the suburb of Peyreleau is on the other side of the Jonte – and has three campsites, a *gîte d'étape* and several hotels. It's a seasonal place – some of the campsites and hotels are only open Easter to September – and booking would be a wise idea in high summer. Try the *Camping Municipal* (☎65.62.63.98) or the *gîte d'étape* at Peyreleau (☎65.62.62.98), both convenient for the middle of the town.

For **walks** around the area, the SI at Le Rozier has maps showing the main trails; the central area of the park is a remote and thinly inhabited region (600 inhabitants in over 90,000 hectares) and so walkers should take sensible precautions.

The **National Park Office** in the old château at FLORAC is the best source of information about the Cevennes, with a good range of displays and a stock of free leaflets; in summer, a number of other temporary offices are open around the park.

River Hérault

The public transport situation is a bit tricky for the upper reaches of the Hérault. A daily bus runs between ESPEROU and GANGES in summer, but only three times a week for the rest of the year. There seem to be no buses at all between GANGES and ST-GUILHEM – but hitching is fairly easy.

Campsites are at ESPEROU, VALLERAUGUE (a lovely old town with the river running through the middle of it), and – plentiful – between PONT D'HERAULT and GANGES; *Camping Isis* at ST-JULIEN-DE-LA-NEF makes a good base for the woods in this area. The stretch between Ganges and St-Guilhem has few places to stay – it's probably easier to push on to GIGNAC, the first town after the river meets the plains.

THE CAMARGUE AND AROUND

The **Camargue** is probably the best known place in Europe for birdwatching and ranks with the Guadalquivir estuary in Spain and the delta of the Danube as one of the three greatest European wetlands. Experienced birders bemoan its recent popularity as a tourist resort, although frankly the 900,000 annual tourists seem to have had little impact on the wildlife; flamingoes, waders, ducks and terns all feed and breed unconcernedly despite horseback safaris trotting past and countless expensive pairs of binoculars focussed on them. Parts of the Camargue are still a genuine wilderness of saltpans, marshes and reed beds, and offer extraordinary opportunities for seeing a wide variety of bird species.

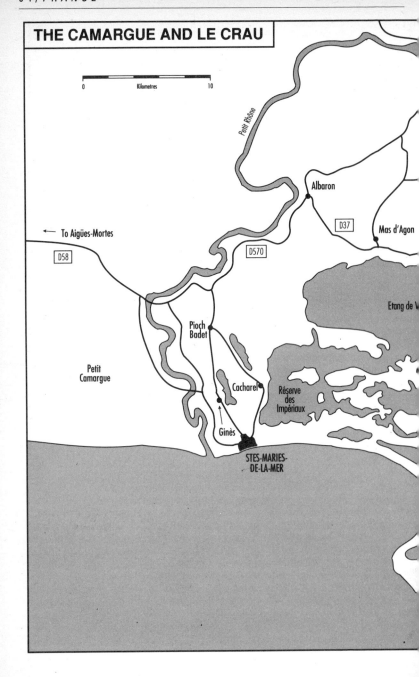

THE CAMARGUE AND LE CRAU

Kilometres
0 — 10

Petit Rhône

Albaron

D37

Mas d'Agon

← To Aigües-Mortes

D58

D570

Etang de V

Pioch
Badet

Petit
Camargue

Cacharel

Réserve
des
Impériaux

Ginès

STES-MARIES-
DE-LA-MER

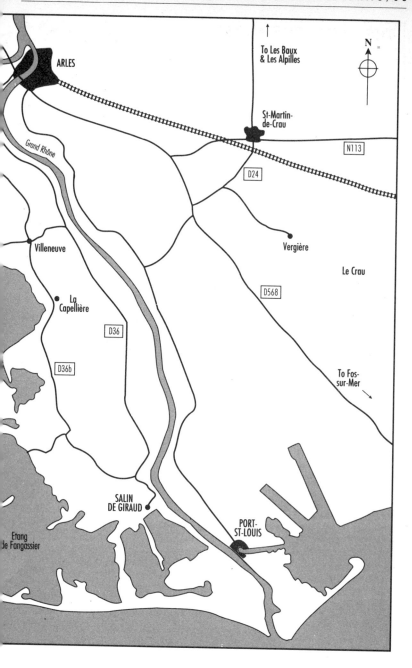

ARLES

To Les Baux
& Les Alpilles

N

St-Martin-
de-Crau

N113

Grand Rhône

D24

Vergière

Villeneuve

Le Crau

La
Capellière

D568

D36

D36b

To Fos-
sur-Mer

SALIN
DE GIRAUD

PORT-
ST-LOUIS

Etang
le Fangassier

Also included in this section are two other classic, nearby spots: **Les Alpilles**, a range of limestone hills running to the east of Arles, with exciting birds and flowers, and **Le Crau**, a diminishing and threatened area of stone desert that is a remnant of the estuary of the Durance.

The Camargue Regional Park

The **CAMARGUE REGIONAL PARK** covers some 850 square kilometres in a triangle south of ARLES, formed by the two arms of the Rhône as they run down to the Med. Inland of the narrow shingle coastline, huge shallow saline lakes called *étangs* dominate the scene; the nearer the sea, the saltier they are, and there is a sizeable salt extraction industry centred around the town of SALIN-DE-GIRAUD in the southeastern corner of the Park. Further from the sea, the freshwater influence of the Rhône takes over, leading to a patchwork habitat of reeds, marshes, and agricultural land now largely given over to rice-growing. At the heart of the park, the National Reserve of the **Etang du Vaccarés** and the local **Reserve des Impériaux** form a protected area into which there is no public access, but in fact the excellent network of paths and tracks around the outskirts makes observation easy enough.

With such a huge area, it's impossible to describe it all. I've chosen three areas: **Les Saintes-Maries-de-la-Mer**, the tourist centre of the Camargue in the southwest; the marshes around **Mas d'Agon** in the north; and the eastern fringes south of **La Capellière**, a difficult but rewarding area to explore.

Climate – and mosquitoes

The Camargue is at its best from April to mid-June, when the breeding birds are all very evident. Earlier, you'll catch the spring migration, and in September and October the return migration. In winter, the water level rises and the whole region becomes an internationally important wintering ground for wildfowl from breeding grounds in northern Europe.

The only time to avoid is July and August, when the park becomes very crowded and the **mosquitoes** are at their worst. And don't take the Camargue mosquitoes lightly – they are mean little animals, and have reduced me to wearing a beekeeper's veil before now. The only thing that keeps them away is **wind**, which in itself is formidable enough – either the *mistral* from the northwest or the *vente d'est* – both of which can blow unremittingly for days and make cycling a frustrating experience.

Les Stes-Maries

Well geared up for tourists with hotels and campsites, **LES STES-MARIES** is much the easiest place to stay in the Camargue – although wilderness it certainly isn't. However, from here, you can explore the marshes in an organised way in a jeep or on horseback, or more independently by foot or hired bike. The latter is probably the best way of getting around, though exhausting if the wind is up.

Right next to the northern edge of the town, the **Etang des Launes** and the **Etang de Gines** are both good places to start. Both have the typical birds of saline marshes; flamingoes feed here, along with avocets and black-winged stilts, two very typical saltmarsh waders. Common **terns** and the much smaller little tern both nest here, bringing fish in from the sea; the beach either side of the town is a good place to watch them fishing, beating over the water and then plunging vertically in to emerge with a fish. Wherever there are exposed mudflats **waders** can be seen – redshank are very common – and lurking on the edge of the reed beds are grey herons and little egrets.

Further north, on the most easterly of the three roads leaving the town, is **Cacharel**, a good place to watch out over the Reserve des Impériaux; the birds are similar, but there are many more of them, with feeding flamingoes building up to the thousands. Marsh harriers and black kites are commonly seen here (as elsewhere in the Camargue), the former gliding over the reed beds on raised wings. The **vegetation** surrounding the *étangs* typically consists of shrubby salt- tolerant plants with fleshy stems and minute flowers that scarcely protrude from the stem; called glassworts *Salicornia* and *Arthrocnemum spp.*, they dominate vast areas and are a favourite habitat for yellow wagtails, crested larks and spectacled warblers, a shy bird rather like a whitethroat. North of Cacharel, a track up the side of the *étang* is well worth exploring by foot or bike; cars are technically forbidden.

Mas d'Agon

The isolated farm and woodland at **MAS D'AGON**, on the northern edge of the Etang de Vaccarés, is a good example of freshwater marshes, dykes and agriculture. The main attraction here is the **heron roost**; just north of the farm, a woodland on the east of the track is used by many little egrets as a night roost and by the largely nocturnal night heron as a day roost. Watch from the road at dusk and you should see the two species crossing over; night herons are normally secretive and hard to see, and look small and dumpy in flight. The reeds and ditches around Mas d'Agon are also frequented by great reed warblers, a very large pale brown warbler with a conspicuous eyestripe and a loud repetitive song. In winter, the grazing fields are flooded and are excellent for **wildfowl**; even in the summer, they're full of ducks and waders, including the uncommon pratincole, a short-billed wader that looks more like an outsize swallow.

Another attraction of this area are the tropically coloured **bee-eaters** that breed in the sandy fields to the south of the road that skirts the *étang*; although they are a widely spread summer visitor throughout the Camargue, they're nowhere common, and so the colony of twenty or so pairs here is a real bonus. They can be easily seen from the road just to the east of the Mas d'Agon turn, so there is no need to disturb them.

La Capellière and the east

Although the east of the Camargue has a similar habitat range to the west, there's no major town and the so the impact of tourism is far less. The series of lagoons surrounded by bushes and small woodland pockets south from **LA CAPELLIERE** to Salin de Badon offer an outstanding range of habitats; flamingoes and avocets come over from the saltpans, ducks and waders breed, and there are several heronries in the woods, especially over towards the Grand Rhône; these woods are also used by scarcer birds of prey, including red kite and hobby. Frogs are not only common in the ditches; the tree frog *Hyla arborea* can be found by diligent searching in the bushes, especially at night, though it's hard to spot because of its small size and and variable skin colour. At La Capellière itself, there's another **Park Information Centre**, as well as a signed nature trail through the surrounding woods and marshes.

On the **saltpans** further to the south, a network of tracks leads along the dyke tops out towards the lighthouse of Phare de la Gochelle; the flamingo numbers round here increase dramatically, for the main **breeding colony** is in the centre of Etang de Fangassier. It can only be seen from a distance, but even so the sight of some 10,000 pairs of flamingoes crammed onto a small island in a shimmering haze of pink is an unforgettable one. There's the usual range of waders too, as well as breeding terns and gulls. From the lighthouse, a track open only to walkers and cyclists leads along the Digue de la Mer to Les Stes Maries, some 6km to the west.

Flamingo

Le Crau

At the beginning of the sixteenth century, **LE CRAU** covered over 600 square kilometres to the east of ARLES; now, it has been reduced to only 110, and has been split up into fragments. It is a habitat, however, that is unique in France, a **flat stony desert** that finds its nearest counterpart in the *hammada* deserts of the northern Sahara. The stones that carpet the ground are up to the size of a human fist, with low vegetation growing between them, closely cropped by traditional sheep grazing; thyme *Thymus officinalis*, various *Euphorbia* species and the graceful little asphodel *Asphodelus fistulosus* make a colourful show, although there are rarer plants too, including a species of germander *Teucrium sp.* that is found nowhere else. The thyme, in particular, is a popular nectar source for **butterflies**; in spring, the marbled white *Melanargia* is present in huge numbers.

Le Crau is best known, though, for its **birds**, and especially for the **pintailed sandgrouse**; the entire French population of this bird breeds in Le Crau – only about 200 pairs in all. They fly around in small flocks in the early morning and evening but are hard to see for the rest of the day since they are well camouflaged and spend their time sitting and feeding close to the ground. The **stone curlew** is a similarly well camouflaged bird, but much larger; mostly ground dwelling, it shows a double white wingbar on a brown background in flight. The little **bustard** is another specialist bird of this habitat, looking similar to a stone curlew but more heavily built and showing much more white on the wing in flight. The male has rather a natty black and white neck in breeding plumage, and with 600 pairs, Le Crau is a major French stronghold for it.

Two other birds have adapted well to Le Crau, since both are natives of the **unimproved plains**, a habitat that has largely disappeared to the plough throughout Europe. The first is the brilliantly coloured **roller**, a crow-like bird with a plumage of turquoise, chestnut and black. The French population has declined dramatically over the last fifty years, to the extent that only 140 pairs remain in the country; half of them live in Le Crau. The second species is the **lesser grey shrike**, similar to the far commoner great grey shrike but smaller and with pink-tinged underparts; it's fond of sitting on the cairns of stones that dot Le Crau, searching for the large beetles and small lizards on which it feeds. Only ten pairs are left in Le Crau, representing a third of the French population.

Les Alpilles

The white limestone hills of **Les Alpilles** are easily visible from the Camargue on a clear day; rising to 350 metres, they form the northern boundary of the eastern half of the Rhône delta, straddling the gap between the Grand Rhône itself and the valley of the Durance. Much of their area has been planted with pines, but the rocky hillsides between the plantations are rich in typical Mediterranean flowers and insects, and the windblown tops offer marvellous, if windy, ridge walks and spectacular views.

The medieval hilltop town of **LES BAUX** is a tourist centre, perched on the col above St-Remy, and as artificial as Carcassonne in its single-minded pursuit of daytripper enterprise. Alpine swifts wheel and dive around the Roman ruins on the hilltop, while blue rock thrushes live amongst the jumbled rocks. A better place to see Les Alpilles is the hilltop of **La Caume**, a lonely peak northeast of Les Baux, dominated by a huge radiocommunications tower. The track to it winds through coniferous forest, and the roadsides are bright with the shrubs of *Cistus albidus* and clumps of the blue *Aphyllanthes monspeliensis*; open sunny spaces attract butterflies including blues, fritillaries and marbled whites.

The main bird attraction at the top is the chance of seeing large **birds of prey** which are becoming scarce elsewhere in France. This is one of the last breeding sites for the black and white **Egyptian vulture**; **Bonelli's eagle** and short-toed eagle are regularly seen; and **eagle owls** breed in some of the rocky ravines. All these rare birds are carefully guarded by the *Fonds d'intervention pour les rapaces (FIR)* who, in cooperation with *Garrigues*, maintain a small information centre (April to mid-July daily 10am–6pm) at the top. Other birds of the windblown scrub of the hilltop include Dartford warblers and subalpine warblers, while the inevitable nightingales sing from the bushes and Alpine swifts dive around the rockfaces.

Egyptian vulture

The **maquis and garigue vegetation** includes two species of juniper, rockroses *Cistus albidus*, box *Buxus sempervirens* and large bushes of rosemary *Rosmarinus officinalis*, along with some woodland thickets of holm oak *Quercus ilex*. Lower plants growing amongst and below the bushes include the white-flowered rockrose

Helianthemum appeninum, other yellow-flowered species of *Helianthemum*, and the wonderful striking blue flowers of the flax *Linum narbonse*. The information centre has laid out a short botanical trail around the hilltop, but for longer ridge walks, you can use the GR6 long-distance path which runs past the summit.

Other nearby sites

Almost any of the minor roads that wind through the mountains from LES BAUX along to EYGUIERES in the east are worthy of exploration. The **pine forests**, especially where they are broken up by roads, clearings or firebreaks are very rich in flowers. The flax *Linum narbonse* grows here, as at La Caume, but is taller and more sprawling than on the windy mountain top; it's joined by its close relative *Linum campanulatum* with handsome deep yellow flowers.

Orchids are also prominent: lady orchids *Orchis purpurea* grow in clumps amongst the shrubs, some of their purple spikes reaching to 75cm high, and two species of white helleborine occur – *Cephalanthera longifolium*, with narrow leaves and pure white flowers, and *C. damasonium* with broader leaves and cream flowers. In grazed clearings, the rare *Ophrys bertolonii* can sometimes be seen, along with the extremely variable *Ophrys arachnitiformis*. But the most striking orchid of the pine forests is undoubtedly *Limodorum abortivum*; it's a parasite on pine roots and therefore has no green leaves, sending up a tall naked purple stem on which large purple flowers are widely spaced. April and May are, as usual, the best months for seeing these flowers.

CAMARGUE AND AROUND: ACCESS AND ACCOMMODATION

The Camargue
Les Stes-Maries has two large campsites, numerous hotels and a few rooms to rent. The tourist office in av van Gogh on the seafront has very complete lists. The youth hostel at **Pioch Badet**, 9km to the north, is ideally placed for exploring some of the freshwater marshes; booking is essential (☎97.91.72). To the north of Les Stes-Maries, many rural farms offer accommodation, but they too get booked up quickly; alternatively, bus services provide a link to ARLES (5 daily, more in summer, less in winter) and AIGUES MORTES (2 daily). Bike hire costs around 60F per day from numerous outlets in town; horse riding stables on the outskirts charge from 60F per hour for a trek on one of the famous white Camargue horses. There's a Park Information Centre at GINES, 4km north on the main Arles road, with a good range of standing exhibitions and a variety of leaflets.

Mas d'Agon is to the north of the D37, halfway between ALABARON and VILLENEUVE; since it's well off the tourist route there's no public transport. There is an expensive *gîte rurale* at Mas de l'Ange, the neighbouring farm, but at over 200F a night, most travellers will choose to stay in Albaron or even Arles, which is only 10km away.

La Capellière and the east has more difficult access, unless you have a hired car or are prepared to cycle long distances. A bus service connects SALIN DE GIRAUD to ARLES, but it goes along the main D36, some way from the D36b which skirts the reserve. The only town of any size is SALIN DE GIRAUD, with two hotels; the cheaper is *Hotel des Saladelles* at 90F a room. There are no official campsites, but it's worth asking at farms; the farm at St-Bertrand, near to Etang du Fangassier, is said to allow camping.

Le Crau and Les Alpilles
The best remaining fragment of **Le Crau** lies to the west of the military aerodrome at ISTRES, and can be reached by a network of tracks running northeast off the main N568, the bus route between Arles and Fos-sur-Mer. Alternatively, from ST-MARTIN-DE-CRAU, follow the D24 south signposted *Dynamite*, and turn left to the château at Vergière; Le Crau is just east of the château.

ARLES is a convenient base for Le Crau and for the next area, Les Alpilles, with plenty of hotels and campsites. For closer access, stay at ST-MARTIN-DE-CRAU, which has its only campsite at the *Hôtel Restaurant de la Crau*, and the added attraction of the excellent exhibition of the *Ecomusée de la Crau* in the centre of town. The museum is run by a local conservation group called *Garrigues*, a mine of information for local conservation issues in general and Le Crau in particular; it's open daily April to September, Wednesdays and weekends the rest of the year.

In **Les Alpilles**, LES BAUX is easily reached by public transport from Arles or St-Remy. LE CAUME is a bit more difficult. The road to the summit leaves the main D5 4km south of St-Remy just south of the col on the way to Maussane-les-Alpilles. From here, walk or hitch the remaining 2km up to the radio mast. Arles or St-Martin-de-Crau are both good places to stay.

PROVENCE

East of the Rhône delta, the hills of Provence extend in a line parallel to the sea, mostly new-fold limestone hills formed by the same collision pressure that created the Alps and the Pyrenees. The lower hills are a mosaic of woodland, scrubby hillsides and narrow gorges – a classic Provençal landscape immortalised by Van Gogh and typified by the Regional Park of the **Luberon**. In some places, great rivers such as the Durance and the Verdon have carved deep gorges amongst the limestone – the most spectacular of these is the **Gorge du Verdon**.

Luberon

The 1300-square-kilometre **LUBERON REGIONAL PARK** describes an oval shape, with CAVAILLON at the western tip, MANOSQUE at the eastern, and with the River Durance making up the southern boundary. The main mountain ridge runs through the southern section of the park, bisected by the valley of the River Aigue Brun into **Petit Luberon**, rising to 700m in the west, and **Grand Luberon** at over 1100m to the east. Much of this core mountainous section is banned to cars in summer, mostly for fire protection, and so there's something of a wilderness feeling to the remote walks.

Such a large and varied area is predictably rich in wildlife. There are over 1000 species of flowering plants, and half of the 260 breeding birds of France have been recorded nesting within the park.

Gorge de Regalon

The **Gorge de Regalon** is a varied walk on the southern side of Petit Luberon and gives a good introduction to the Luberon's wildlife. The gorge itself is quite extraordinary – a cut through the limestone so narrow that it becomes genuinely subterranean at times, and is so dark that little grows apart from huge climbing ivies up the rocks. At the top, however, it passes through a tangled jungle of woodland, mostly of box *Buxus sempervirens* growing very unusually to 10m or more. Above this woodland zone the landscape opens out into a typical *maquis* habitat and the box is joined by bushes of Kermes oak *Quercus coccifera*, holm oak *Q. ilex* and rosemary *Rosmarinus officinalis*. In the more open and sunny patches **butterflies** are abundant, including the handsome black and white southern White Admiral *Limenitis reducta*, and many species of fritillary including the Provençal fritillary *Mellicta deione*. The Moroccan orange tip *Anthocharis belia* flies here from May to July – a small yellow butterfly with deep orange wingtips, widely distributed around the western Med.

Butterflies are not the only insects to look out for in the Luberon. **Grasshoppers and crickets** are, as always, abundant in the dry grassland and low bushes, but one rare species which stands out is *Saga pedo*. It's remarkable partly because it is carnivorous, mostly eating other crickets; partly because only females have ever been recorded; but mostly because of its sheer size – at 10cm long it is one of Europe's largest insects. The *garigue* habitat above the Gorge de Regalon is one of its known haunts, although it's a rare species and only to be seen between July and September. Earlier in the summer, a strange relative of the antlions called *Libelloides* is widespread; it's shaped like a short plump dragonfly but has a ragged yellow patch at the base of its otherwise transparent wings. In flight only this yellow patch can be seen, giving it an oddly dishevelled appearance.

Lizards and snakes also like this open sunny habitat, among them the ocellated lizard *Lacerta lepida*, the largest in Europe at 20cm – excluding its very long tail. Short-toed eagles come over from the hilltops of Petit Luberon to hunt these reptiles but large raptor numbers have declined in the Luberon, as much of the *garigue* and other open hunting grounds have been lost to coniferous afforestation. The scrub is full of Dartford warblers, while the wooded slopes lower down the valley have other warblers and inevitable nightingales. Limestone rockfaces add another dimension to the bird population with breeding crag martins and blue rock thrushes.

Combe de Lourmarin

The **Combe de Lourmarin** bisects the park, running from the delightful town of LOURMARIN up to the town of APT – although the *combe* proper only runs through the southern section. The limestone rocks flanking the road are clothed in holm oak scrub, and any small clearings or glades are worth exploring; as in the Cevennes, the blue stars of *Aphyllanthes monspeliensis* and the pink sheets of *Saponaria ocymoides* are a characteristic sight, and lady orchids *Orchis purpurea* are abundant in May.

Halfway between Lourmarin and Apt, the tiny village of **BUOUX** lies at the centre of some dramatic and beautiful scenery, with dense woods of white oak *Quercus pubescens* interspersed with small farms and rocky limestone cliffs; a wide range of **woodland and scrub birds** are to be found here, as well as abundant **butterflies**. In addition to those already mentioned, notable species include the large yellow brimstone *Gonepteryx cleopatra*, and marbled white *Melanarga sp.*, plus a host of blues, whites and fritillaries. At night the mournful calls of Scops owls combine with the croaks of frogs and the song of nightingales to create the perfect background music for a Provençal night.

THE BEAVERS OF THE DURANCE

The River Durance is one of the last refuges of the **beaver**, although they have been reintroduced in southern Germany and other parts of France. They're not easily seen, being entirely nocturnal, and here they live in unobtrusive riverside burrows rather than the more usual dams and lodges. But it's good to know that they're still around; widespread in Europe until the twelfth century, they declined rapidly with the clearance of riverside woodlands, the artificial damming of rivers, and above all because of hunting for fur. The European population is now over 50,000, but these are mostly in Scandinavia and Russia and some are the result of introductions of the closely related American species *Castor canadensis*; the animals on the Durance are a precious remnant of the original European population.

Gorges du Verdon

Seventy kilometres east of the the Luberon, the **GORGES DU VERDON** are hailed as the Grand Canyon of Europe, which isn't altogether fair since it sets up unrealisable expectations in the average visitor's mind. All the same, with a vertical drop approaching 500 metres and an overall length of twenty kilometres, the gorge is quite a sight. The white limestone of the cliff faces contrasts strongly with the river at the bottom, coloured a deep green from fluorine washed from the higher rocks near the river's source at Col d'Allos, 70km north in the Alps.

The western approach to the gorge is guarded by MOUSTIERS-STE-MARIE, a pleasant agricultural town which is now something of a tourist spot. The fields around Moustiers, especially up on the alluvial plateaux, are largely given over to **lavender**, destined for the perfume factories of Grasse. The fields are a splendid sight, with the purple of the lavender relieved by the pink of sainfoin *Onobrychis sativa*, which is cultivated as a green manure and fodder crop to rejuvenate the fields after the four-year lavender cycle is finished. Sadly, competition from artificially synthesised lavender has recently threatened the viability of this traditional crop. Another, less endangered, tradition around Moustiers is hunting for **truffles**; many oak groves have been specially planted to provide a habitat for this delicacy, which can fetch up to 3000F a kilo. Apparently, the largest one collected in the area weighed a mighty 450 grammes.

From Moustiers, **the gorge** can be seen by climbing the road up the north bank (the *Route des Crêtes*) or the south bank (the *Corniche sublime*); both offer stunning views. The *Route des Crêtes* is more open and gives an opportunity to explore into the hinterland around the village of LA PALUD-SUR-VERDON; the *Corniche sublime* is more wooded but bordered to the south by the huge military camp of Canjuers, into which entry is forbidden. Both routes are crowded with cars in high summer; the *Route des Crêtes* is better for public transport with an irregular bus route linking to CASTELLANE at the other end of the gorge.

The **birds of the gorge** include specialist cliff dwellers such as blue rock thrush, crag martin and alpine swift, and there's a chance, too, of seeing such rare raptors as short-toed and golden eagles and peregrine falcons. In winter, the cliffs are used by the wallcreeper, a grey rock-dwelling bird like a large nuthatch but with bright pink rounded wings that make it look like a huge butterfly in flight; by April it has left for its breeding quarters higher up in the Alps. Down by the river itself, dippers and grey wagtails breed along the base of the gorge.

On the **Corniche sublime** the road winds through a full succession of habitats, starting with low scrub with a ground flora of thyme and moving on to woodland. The lower woodland is dominated by species such as white oak *Quercus pubescens* with an understorey of juniper *Juniperus communis*, box *Buxus sempervirens* and various yellow-flowered brooms *Genista spp*. At the highest point of the road, around Le Marges at 800m, the oaks give way to beech *Fagus sylvaticans*.

The interface between the two habitats is exceptionally rich in **woodland flowers** in early summer, but any woodland clearing or roadside verge is worth examining. In these clearings huge plants of a pink-flowered paeony *Paeonia officinalis* can occasionally be found, while under the trees grows a blue anemone *Hepatica nobilis* with kidney-shaped leaves (hence the scientific name), along with Solomon's seal *Polygonatum sp.*, looking like a tall curving lily-of-the-valley. Lady orchids *Orchis pupurea* and military orchids *O. militaris* grow together under the oaks – often confusingly hybridised – while the yellow *Orchis provincialis* takes over on more open verges. Some of these verges, especially near the café at Les Chevaliers, have subalpine flowers such as the little yellow tulip *Tulipa saxatilis* along with more widespread species like grape hyacinths *Muscari spp.*, rockroses *Helianthemum spp.*, and dense blue patches of milkwort *Polygola spp.*

PROVENCE: ACCESS AND ACCOMMODATION

Luberon

The bottom of the **Gorge de Regalon** is reached from a marked turn to the car park off the D973, 13km east of CAVAILLON. The walk up the gorge itself takes a leisurely hour but can be extended by taking a circuit via the farm at Les Mayorques and down through pine woodland in the next valley to the west. The Park Office at Place Jean Jaurès in APT has a good range of booklets about walks in Luberon, including this one; the SI in Cavaillon or Manosque will also have details. The nearest campsite is just across the River Durance at MALLEMORT.

For the **Combe de Lourmarin** and the centre of the park, APT is a convenient base for those who prefer towns, with the excellent and informative Park Office in the centre. There are numerous restaurants and three campsites. The SI has a list of rural *gîtes d'étapes* if you want to get away from it all, though public transport is non-existent off the main roads. One place I can recommend is the *gîte* at BUOUX called *La Sparagoule*; the village is too small even to have a bar, but the surrounding countryside is wonderful. Max Gallardo, who runs *La Sparagoule* with his wife, is a zoologist employed by the Park and is a mine of useful wildlife information. The *gîte* at LOURMARIN would be worth investigating too, but phone in advance (☎90.68.11.10) since the town is very popular in the tourist season.

Gorge du Verdon

MOUSTIERS and CASTELLANE are both served by buses, the latter more so since it is on the N85 from Grasse to Digne. As mentioned above, access between the two is harder; the very fit may want to cycle up to either the *Corniche sublime* or *Routes des Crêtes*, or use the GR4 footpath which runs between Castellane and La Palud, and traverses the base of the gorge along the *Sentier Martel* path.

There are campsites at both Moustiers and Castellane, as well as at LA PALUD, which also has a **youth hostel** (booking essential in summer; ☎74.68.72) and is fast becoming the outdoor pursuits centre of the region. At Moustiers, the bar and restaurant at *Le Relais* in the middle of the town is a lively and friendly place to go; it has reasonably priced rooms.

THE COTE D'AZUR

At first sight, the **Côte d'Azur** looks more like the *Côte concret*, with wall to wall development, beaches full of gently browning tourists, a crowded system of coastal motorways and major roads, and seemingly little room for wildlife. But there are some gems nestling amongst the concrete, especially just inland from the coast and to the west of the Côte d'Azur.

On the coast itself, the **St-Tropez peninsula** is surprisingly unspoilt, with a well preserved wooded headland at Cap Lardier, while, offshore of Le Lavandou, the **Ile de Port-Cros** is protected as a National Park. Inland of this stretch of coast, the **Massif des Maures** is a range of densely wooded low mountains, excellent for all forms of wildlife. Further to the east, the coast from Cannes to Nice and the Italian border has virtually no wild spaces, but there are some wonderful areas close inland, like the **Alpes Maritimes**, a genuinely Alpine region less than 50km north of Nice.

St-Tropez Peninsula

The southern tip of the **ST-TROPEZ PENINSULA** is a complex of reserves owned by the *Conservatoire du Littoral*, stretching from Gigaro round past Cap Lardier to Cap Camarat. Covering some 3.2 square kilometres of wild coastline and forest, it's an unspoilt remnant of the original coastal vegetation. A coastal footpath runs the 12km from Gigaro to Cap Camarat.

The area has the best concentration of **semi-natural forest** on the Côte d'Azur, dominated by the aptly-named umbrella pines *Pinus pinea*. This is a sandstone coastline and so the understorey is made up of shrubs that like neutral to acid soils: tree heath *Erica arborea*, strawberry tree *Arbutus unedo* and myrtle *Myrtus communis* are all much in evidence. The strawberry tree is the larval food plant of one of the most dramatic and beautiful butterflies of the Med, the **two-tailed pasha** *Charaxes jasius*; it's large, and flies extremely fast amongst the woodlands in June. Behind the rocky coast and shingle beaches, plants that can tolerate salt grow well; prominent amongst them are the yellow horned poppy *Glaucum flavium* and silver ragwort *Senecio cineraria*, a shrubby plant with white furry leaves and branches and flat yellow flowers. Thrift *Armeria maritima* grows here too. Another striking plant is the tree spurge *Euphorbia dendroides*, which grows abundantly on the rocks around Cap Lardier. In high summer it reacts to the heat by shedding all its leaves and remaining a bare skeleton, but it produces its yellow flowers in early spring, and by early summer its leaves turn bright scarlet, making the rocks look red from a distance.

Two-tailed pasha *Charaxes jasius*

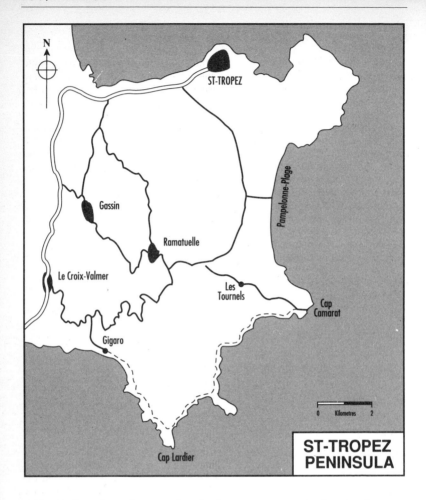

N

ST-TROPEZ

Pampelonne-Plage

Gassin

Ramatuelle

Le Croix-Valmer

Les
Tournels

Cap
Camarat

Gigaro

Kilometres
0   2

Cap Lardier

**ST-TROPEZ
PENINSULA**

The further along the coastal path, the more remote the beaches become, although in July and August everything will be crowded. Round tennis balls of brown fibre washed up on the beach are made from the fibrous roots of sea grass *Posidonia*, which grows in beds offshore and is a rich habitat for all forms of marine life. **Snorkelling** in this area, especially where the coastline is rocky, can be very rewarding.

Birds here include the usual nightingales and scrub warblers, while the graceful and long-winged Eleonora's falcon can sometimes be seen here as a passage migrant, especially in May when it has just made the long haul to its Mediterranean breeding grounds from its winter quarters in Madagascar.

The headlands of **Cap Lardier** and **Cap Camarat** are fine vantage spots for watching out for passing **dolphins and porpoises** throughout the year, and (in winter only) there's a faint chance of seeing one of the larger **whales**.

Ile de Port-Cros

ILE DE PORT-CROS, the smallest of the three **Iles d'Hyères**, has a quite exceptional range of wildlife – partly because of its dense forest cover and mountainous terrain, and partly because its marine life has flourished under protection since it was declared a National Park in 1963. The **dense woodland** that covers most of its area is dominated by Aleppo pine *Pinus halapensis* and holm oak *Quercus ilex*, while the understorey shrubs are similar to those of Cap Lardier, including wild olive *Olea europaea*. The woodland is so thick that it shades out the ground vegetation, and so the coastal fringes are the best places to explore. Here, specialist salt-tolerant plants include lavender *Limonium spp.* and sea samphire *Crithmum maritimum*, a fleshy yellow-flowered umbellifer.

As is to be expected on an offshore island, the **bird life** is less varied, though there is a good range of passage migrants in spring and autumn. **Seabirds** are a particular attraction, with nesting herring gulls and Manx shearwaters, and the sea cliffs support a few pairs of rare raptors such as peregrine falcon and **Eleonora's falcon**, the latter making a welcome recent return to the islands after an absence of some 200 years. Port-Cros is also home to two species of **gecko**, one of them the European leaf-toed gecko *Phyllodactylus europeaus*, a small nocturnal reptile found elsewhere only in Corsica, Sardinia and a few places in northwest Italy. The Tyrrhenian painted frog *Discoglossus sardus* has a similarly restricted distribution; you might with luck sight it around the small dammed reservoir near the port.

A visit in summer is the best time to see **marine life**, although in July and August the island gets a staggering 2000 visitors a day. Most of the bays have good snorkelling, and the bay of LA PALUD even has an underwater nature trail. La Palud is in fact the most accessible bay for marine life – other bays further to the north of the island involve long hikes through the forest. As in Cap Lardier, it is the underwater forests of sea grass *Posidonia oceanica* which are the richest in marine life; they survive more or less intact, unlike many other sections of the Med. If you don't fancy snorkelling, some idea of the wealth of marine life can be had from the *Aquascope*, a semi-submersible boat which leaves every hour from the port of Port-Cros, though less often in winter. It's not cheap at 50FF per person, nor is it as immediate as snorkelling – but it's good when the sea is cold.

The Park's **Information Centre** is at *La Pointe Nord* on the quayside in the little port which is the only village on the island. It's friendly, helpful and informative, with excellent literature and maps for sale. Treat the English translations with some caution; you'll be pleased to know that the field rat is "the most diffused mammifer on the island. Ribbled pin appel kernels attest his presence". The other literature (in French) is great, however.

Iles de Porquerolles and Levant

Of the two other Iles d'Hyères, **Ile de Porquerolles**, the largest and most densely populated, has good forest cover – most of it is a forest park – and some wildlife interest, including an interesting botanical exhibition at Le Hameau Agricole, just outside the port on the way to La Plage d'Argent.

Ile de Levant, to the east of Port-Cros, doubtless has wonderful wildlife – but it is hard to see since the majority of the island is a military zone, apart from a tiny bit round the port which is a nudist colony.

Massif des Maures

The low hills of the **MASSIF DES MAURES** run just inland from the coast between TOULON and FREJUS. Their underlying rock is ancient and metamorphic, quite unlike the more recent limestone of most of this region, and the forests and *maquis* that covers most of the hills have been much influenced by **fire** (see box opposite) for thousands of years.

The **forest** consists mainly of cork oak *Quercus suber*, interspersed with some sweet chestnut *Castanea sativa*, white oak *Quercus pubescens* and scattered pines. Underneath, bracken *Pteridium aquilinum*, strawberry tree *Arbutus unedo* and heathers *Erica arborea* and *E. scoporia*, are all indicators of a soil which is neutral or even acidic. A feature of the woodland is the abundant growth of the **red helleborine** *Cephalanthera rubra*, one of Europe's loveliest orchids with bright pink bell-shaped flowers in early summer. Open clearings and roadsides are, as always, worth stopping for; colourful *garigue* plants include French lavender *Lavandula stoechas*, the white-flowered bushy rockrose *Cistus salvifolius*, a smaller rockrose with pure lemon flowers *Tuberaria lignosa*, and a variety of blue and purple thistles, scabious and hardheads.

These flat purple flowers are attractive to **insects** for two reasons: firstly, the flat shape makes the nectar easily accessible, and secondly, all insects are preferentially attracted to the ultra-violet end of the spectrum. Notable **butterflies** include the black-veined white *Aporia crataegi*, a large white species with conspicuous black veins, as well as the usual variety of blues and fritillaries.

Almost any walk through the Massif is of interest; the **GR9 footpath** runs for 20km along one of the most spectacular ridges from PIGNANS in the west to LA GARDE-FREINET in the east; take supplies – there's nowhere to stay en route. Good access to the ridge can be had by walking up the twisting roads from Gonfaron or Les Mayons in the north, or Collobrières in the centre. There's very little public transport on these minor roads, and many of them are closed to cars in summer because of fire risks.

North of the Massif, roughly in a triangle between Gonfaron, La Garde-Freinet and Le Luc, is a large flat **plain**; regular fires have reduced it to open cork oak forest – cork oaks can resist fire because of their thick protective bark – with a lower layer of heathers, rockroses and other shrubs. Effectively, this is **Mediterranean heathland**, a very scarce and unusual habitat,

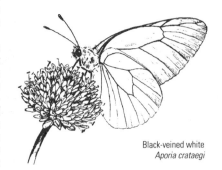

Black-veined white
Aporia crataegi

and in need of some protection. Current threats to this particular area include proposals for golf courses and a Michelin test track, and a main road has just been completed across the middle of it.

The open woodland is good for birds such as golden orioles and rollers, and nuthatches and tree creepers are both common in the cork oaks. The heathland habitat is also ideal for woodchat shrikes; unmistakeable with their chestnut crown and black and white plumage, they perch menacingly on telegraph wires

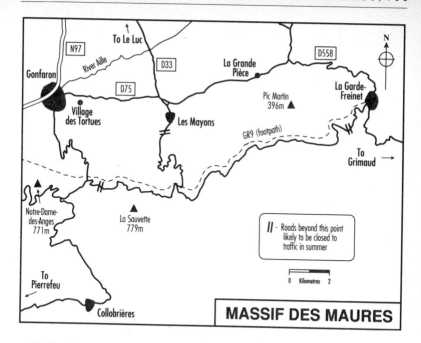

MASSIF DES MAURES

and isolated trees, seeking out the insects and small reptiles on which they feed. Bee-eaters nest in the open sandy fields, too.

In open spaces, and especially by the roadsides in the plain, **flowers** include the pink spikes of *Gladiolus segetum* and the white spikes of St Bernard's lily *Anthericum liliago*, but it is the profusion of **orchids** which makes the area exceptional. In May, a dozen different species can easily be found flowering together, including some huge specimens of the tongue orchids *Serapias spp.*, as well as relatively uncommon species such as the bug orchid *Orchis coriophora*. This latter species is reputed to smell like "squashed bed bugs", but it's too many years since I last squashed one for me to be able to substantiate this!

The plain is a large area, and would take a long time to explore thoroughly. Three areas worth exploring are the roadsides of the D33 to LE LUC, just north of the **crossroads north of Les Mayons**, a promising area for orchids; open heathland around **La Grand Pièce**, near the mines 4km east of LES MAYONS, which is good for bee-eaters, ortolan buntings and rollers as well as orchids and other flowers; and the **River Aille**, with its fringing alder woodlands which are full of nightingales, small warblers, and an impressive density of golden orioles.

The Tortoise Village

Another attraction in the Massif des Maures is the **VILLAGE DES TORTUES**, a unique centre just outside Gonfaron on the road to Les Mayons. It was started in 1981, and as the name suggests, it aims to safeguard the future of tortoises – or, to be precise, Hermann's tortoise *Testudo hermanni*, probably the most endangered reptile in France. Although the mass collection and export of this animal

FOREST FIRES ON THE FRENCH MED

1989 was a bad year for **forest fires** on the French Mediterranean. On May 25, following a very dry spring, eight square kilometres of forest between Le Rayol and Le Lavandou went up in flames. Although this was the biggest single fire for two years, far worse was to follow. On August 2, thousands of hectares of forest burnt in dozens of separate fires, affecting the woodland behind Toulon, Marseille and Hyères, and stretching as far north as Pertuis on the edge of Luberon. The Corsican *maquis* was worst hit of the lot, especially in the north of the island. M. Hubert Fournier, director general of civil security for the region, estimated that 350 square kilometres burnt on *mardi rouge*. Apart from the impact on people, with thousands of holidaymakers evacuated and some homes burnt, the forest itself was widely reported as being "totally destroyed".

Paradoxically, this may not be the case. Fires have been a regular part of the Med's **woodland cycle** since Neolithic times, 10,000 years ago, when people began to use fire to clear woodland in order to open up space for grazing and agriculture. Most of the coastal woodlands in this part of France are secondary regrowth on woodland sites which have been cleared or burnt; some tree species, such as cork oak, are resistant to fire and form the basis of the secondary woodland, and some of the undershrubs, especially the heathers, have seeds whose germination is stimulated by fire. So, in many cases, fire actually produces the patchwork of forest, *maquis* and open space which is the preferred habitat of many Med plants and animals.

The problem now is the **frequency of fires**, caused partly by exceptionally dry summers, and partly by increasing use of the forest both for recreation and for housing development. As the tourist resorts, always short of land, expand up into the hills, so the pressure on the forest inevitably increases. Once the fires have started they are very hard to bring under control because of the steepness of the terrain and because sparks are flung forward to start another fire downwind; most fires are driven by either the *mistral* or the *vente d'est*.

An effective system of firebreaks may be one answer – the regional government is already encouraging houseowners to cut down the scrub around their houses – but the use of **fire to fight fire** may be another. In the USA and Australia, preventive burning is widely used to reduce the flammable understorey and therefore make the forest less vulnerable. Providing this deliberate burning is well controlled and done in the autumn to minimise wildlife damage, it could effectively limit the frequency and extent of accidental spring and summer fires.

More obviously, caveats have to be issued about visits. **Don't smoke anywhere in the forest**, and don't drop **glass bottles**, which can reflect enough sunlight to ignite the grass. These are two major fire causes, although fires are also perennially caused by idiots having barbecues – and by lunatics who start fires deliberately. Into the latter category come would-be **property developers** who, finding their building plans turned down because of the woodland growing on the site, resort to a box of matches to solve their problem.

has now been stopped, it is still threatened by habitat change and building and road developments and the Massif des Maures is now its only refuge in France.

The village acts as a collection centre for tortoises which have been injured or whose habitat is threatened; it then breeds them in pens (achieving a much higher success rate than in the wild) and releases them when they are three or four years old and past the stage of being vulnerable to predators. The village is open to the public all year, and has been very successful as a tourist attraction, with visitor numbers currently running at 30,000 a year. It's a well interpreted and fascinating place, and worthy of a few hours of anyone's time, as well as a few francs of anyone's money, since it relies on public donations to keep going.

The Alpes Maritimes

The **ALPES MARITIMES** are so close to the coast that it's impossible to ignore them in this book, even though their wildlife is utterly different from the true Mediterranean region. The range is protected within the Parc National du Mercantour, one of the six French National Parks; the central zone, covering nearly 700 square kilometres, is a remote and wild region, populated by just a scattering of hamlets where shepherds stay with their flocks in summer.

Apart from the scenery, which is magnificent with mountain peaks rising to over 3000 metres on the Italian border, the main wildlife attractions are alpine flowers and large mammals. **Alpine flowers** are famous for their beauty, basically because the harsh conditions and short summer force plants to make the high investment of developing a colourful flower to attract pollinating insects; when this flower is set against the plant itself, which is often dwarfed to withstand the snow and high winds, the effect can be stunning. **Large mammals** have survived in the Alpine zones simply because of its remoteness, although the presence now of ibex, mouflon and chamois is largely due to protection and hunting regulation.

Refuge de la Cougourde

A rewarding Alpes Maritimes walk, very good for these large mammals, is the path from BOREON, 15km north of the town of ST-MARTIN-DE-VESUBIE, to the **Refuge de la Cougourde**. Allow about four hours for the trip, which climbs a total of 500 metres.

Setting out, it's best to drive or hitch as far as the **Vachérie de Boréon**, where the track starts. The intial stretch from here is through fir forest, but the path soon breaks out into more open country, with scattered pines and larches amongst the grassland meadows. Typical alpine shrubs dot the grasslands – bilberry *Vaccinium myrtillus* is evident, but higher up there is much alpenrose *Rhododendron ferrugineum*, with shining dark green leaves and deep pink bell-shaped flowers in June and July. Juniper *Juniperus communis* mingles with *Daphne mezereum*, a small shrub which produces pale pink flowers on bare wood, followed by the pale green leaves. Amongst the grassland, crocus flowers earlier in the spring, followed by the very large deep blue flowers of the trumpet gentian *Gentiana acaulis*; violets are much in evidence, especially the big

Trumpet gentian *Gentiana acaulis*

yellow flowers of *Viola lutea*, and the delicate fringed purple flowers of the Alpine snowbell *Soldanella alpina* are widespread. Look at the rock faces by the path and by the stream; a splash of pink may be *Primula integrifolia* or one of its close relatives, with a clustered head of pink or purple flowers and untoothed deep green leaves.

All three specialist large mammals can be seen here in summer. **Ibex** are like a stoutly built goat with (in the male) long swept-back horns; females have much smaller horns. They can sometimes be seen grazing apparently bare rock, but in fact they live partly on lichen, which they scrape off with their abrasive tongue. **Mouflon** have been re-introduced here over the last twenty years, and a small population of around 300 in the park is doing well; only the male has the huge curling horns, and the female looks like an ordinary sheep – not surprisingly, since the mouflon is the ancestor of most of our modern domestic stock. Finally, the **chamois** is now relatively common; slimmer than the ibex, they have distinctive thin erect horns which curve backwards at the tip, and the adults have a black and white head.

All these three mammals can be seen on rocks amongst scattered trees, as well as on the rock faces higher up the mountain. For most of the year, the males are solitary while the females and young live in small groups. A final mammal to watch for is the **Alpine marmot**, a ground squirrel about twice the size of the familiar grey. They live in burrows on Alpine meadows and are most active early in the day, feeding in groups on grasses and sedges, often sitting upright to look out for danger, and giving a sharp penetrating whistle when alarmed.

The **birds** of this Alpine region include choughs and ravens, and occasionally a larger predator such as one of the thirty or so pairs of **golden eagles** that breed in the park. Notable birds of the pine woods include crested tits – tiny birds with a mottled black and white crest; scarcer species such as the nutcracker or the black woodpecker need great luck or perseverance for a sighting.

Le Madone de Fenestre

The tiny hamlet of **LE MADONE DE FENESTRE** consists of a large church and a mountain refuge, accessible by road from St-Martin-de-Vésubie. No real walking is needed to get into the **Alpine meadows** which surround the church and the flowers are similar to those mentioned above, but even more profuse; additional species include the small blue gentian *Gentiana verna* as well as masses of the Alpine pasque flower *Pulsatilla alpina*, with large white flowers and feathery seed pods. The elder-flowered orchid *Dactylorhiza sambucina* grows in abundance on the grassy slopes, its clustered flower spike in both pink and yellow colour forms.

Below the church a **stream** flows past the car park. Don't miss this area, for as well as all the above plants, its wet margins hold a wonderful variety of species, from the marsh marigold *Caltha palustris* to the tiny **butterwort** *Pinguicula spp.*, which has a single spurred purple flower held above its slightly sticky leaves. The leaves are sticky with good reason, for this is a carnivorous plant, trapping insects on its leaves and digesting them with a secreted fluid. False helleborine *Veratrum album* grows here, with broad pleated leaves sheathing its stem, topped with a tall spike of greenish yellow flowers in summer. A final delight are the hanging blue bells of *Clematis alpina*, to be found sprawling amongst the rocks by the stream.

Above the church, a network of tracks lead over the **scree slopes** towards the mountains. **Chamois** are common, especially on the edges of the pine woods, whilst the bright pink primrose *Primula integrifolia* brightens up the rock faces.

COTE D'AZUR: ACCESS AND ACCOMMODATION

St-Tropez peninsula

The path around **Cap Lardier** starts at GIGARO in the west, which is close to the town of LE CROIX VALMER, on the main coastal bus and train route. However, Le Croix Valmer has no campsite and precious few cheap hotels. An alternative is to start from **Cap Camaral** at the eastern end, which is close to several campsites south of RAMATUELLE, the hilltop town which dominates the centre of the peninsula. *Camping Les Tournels* is the closest campsite, but access to it by public transport is a bit complex; no buses run along the twisting road between Le Croix Valmer and Ramatuelle, although buses do run from St-Tropez to Ramatuelle. Hitching is probably the best bet. The rewards of the peninsula, apart from the wildlife, include the superb beach of Pampelonne and excellent wine from the vineyards around Les Tournels. If you like quiet, give the area a miss in high summer.

Ile de Port-Cros

There's only one hotel on the island, and at 500–600F a night it's beyond the means of most people. There's a frequent **ferry service** from LE LAVANDOU, with six or seven boats a day in high summer, dropping down to only four a week in winter. Some boats also call in at CAVALAIRE, further east towards Le Croix Valmer.

There's no vehicular transport on the island, so a fair bit of walking is called for. It's sensible, therefore, to catch the earliest boat possible to give maximum time on the island. It's a good place to give up smoking, which is banned on the island outside the port for fire reasons.

Massif des Maures

The towns of GONFARON and LA GARDE-FREINET are both on public transport routes and have hotels; La Garde-Freinet also has a youth hostel and campsite. COLLOBRIERES is a good base for the mountains of the Massif, and has a municipal campsite. For the plain north of Les Mayons, *Camping Les Bruyères*, 5km south of LE LUC, is convenient, and the campsite itself is good for orchids and many of the heathland birds mentioned above.

Refuge de la Cougourde and La Madone de Fenestre

Both sites are accessible by road (no buses) from ST-MARTIN-DE-VESUBIE, 2hr north of NICE and connected to it by a twice daily bus. St-Martin has only expensive hotels, but there's both a campsite and a *gîte d'étape* at *Camping du Touron*, just south of the town. Book first in high summer (☎93.03.21.32). There's both an SI and a Park Office in the main square. Alternatively and more adventurously, walk along the well marked trails and stay in the *mountain refuges*. Call at any of the Park offices to find out about these; if you're passing through NICE, a visit to the main Park Office at 23 rue d'Italie can save a lot of time later on.

Although the whole park is well used by tourists, obvious precautions are necessary if walking high – the weather can change very quickly, so good waterproofs are sensible. A good **map** is essential; the IGN have recently brought out a series of 1:25,000 maps, *Promenades et Randonées Balisées*, well worth the steep 50F price tag. All the trails are well marked, and each signpost is numbered, making it (almost) impossible to get lost.

CORSICA

Corsica is an extremely rugged island, with long mountain ridges rising to well over 2500 metres, a rocky coastline (still undeveloped in places), and tangled forests and *maquis*. Most of the island is granite, although in the extreme south this is replaced by the more usual Med limestone.

In the north of the island, **Lake Biguglia** shelters numerous wetland birds, especially at migration time, while the **Gorge de l'Asco** has rich woodlands. Over to the east, the resort of **Porto** is within easy reach of the coastal nature reserve of **Scandola**, more forests at the **Foret d'Aitone**, and yet another gorge at **Spelunca**. Finally, the region around **Bonifacio** down on the southern tip is the place to go for limestone hills with their attendant flowers.

Lake Biguglia

LAKE BIGUGLIA is the largest lake on the island, right next to the airport for BASTIA. Although fed with freshwater by several rivers, notably the Bevinco, it has a saline influence from the narrow connection to the sea at its northern end. The **reed beds** that fringe it are rich in **breeding warblers** in summer, especially at the southern end where the water is freshest, with summer migrants such as reed and great reed warblers joining the resident Cetti's warblers. The latter bird lurks around the bases of bushes; it is hard to spot but has a distinctive, loud and repetitive song.

Larger birds in the reeds include purple herons and the secretive water rail, while, as in the Camargue, marsh harriers float over the reeds in search of prey. A breeding speciality here is the **red-crested pochard**, a rare duck frequently kept in ornamental waterfowl collections in northern Europe. The handsome male has a red bill as well as a rounded red head – it has red feet too, though these are not a particularly useful identification feature since it's mostly seen paddling in the water. Predictably, the lake is a magnet for migrating birds in **April** and **September**, and always worth a visit at these times.

Gorge de l'Asco

The **RIVER ASCO** starts high up on the edge of **Mount Cinto**, the granite mountain which is Corsica's highest point at 2710 metres. For the first 10km of its course, up until the village of ASCO, the river runs through a landscape dominated by pine forests, and this is one of the best areas on the island for large **birds of prey** such as golden eagles and lammergeirs. Keen birders will want to search these forests for the endemic **Corsican nuthatch**; like other nuthatches, it's an active bird, running both up and down tree trunks, but the male has a black crown and rather a neat white eyestripe. It's smaller than its relative on the mainland, too.

Below the village, the river has carved out a spectacular **gorge** through the surrounding granite massif. Crag martins and blue rock thrushes are likely here, along with choughs nesting high up on the rocky crags. The **wallcreeper**, one of the more sought after bird species, breeds on the cliff faces as well.

Porto

The resort and fishing village of **PORTO** gets crowded in summer, but for most of the year it is a quiet place, and a fine base for the delightful small village of PIANA, 10km out on the road south to Ajaccio. The roadsides around Piana are rich in wild flowers, and orchids are there for the finding on the surrounding hillsides in spring. But the highlights are the gargoyles of **Les Calanches**, where the red granite is eroded into fantastic shapes. Along the cliffs, tree spurge *Euphorbia dendroides* defies gravity as it clings to the rocks; and there is a rare, endemic stonecrop *Sedum caerulea*, a low fleshy plant with a stunning combination of red leaves and bright blue flowers.

Further on from Piana, a minor road leads over the headland of CAPO ROSSO and down to a beautiful sandy beach at ARONE. This is another interesting stretch for flowers, with wayside species such as grape hyacinths *Muscari spp.* and the spotted rockrose *Tuberaria guttata* producing a riot of colour. As elsewhere along this coast, the variety and abundance of the various **tongue orchids** *Serapias spp.* is extraordinary. Down on the beach, sea holly *Eryngium maritimum* grows on the sand, and the round fibrous balls of sea grass *Posidonia spp.* indicate a rich marine life; snorkelling in summer would be worthwhile, too.

Around Porto: the Spelunca Gorge and Forêt d'Aitone

Inland from Porto, the **SPELUNCA GORGE** is not to be missed, with granite peaks crowning the *maquis*-clad slopes leading down to the gorge and the River Porto itself. The *maquis* is typical of neutral soils derived from granite, with holm oak *Quercus ilex* and strawberry tree *Arbutus unedo* dominant; the understorey consists mostly of tree heath *Erica arborea* and the abundant white rockrose *Cistus monspeliensis*. In the valley bottom, box *Buxus sempervirens* takes over as the dominant species. Two plants to note are the snowflake *Leucojum longifolium*, growing like a huge snowdrop on damp shady rocks, and the charming small cyclamen *Cyclamen repandum*, which grows literally in sheets under the taller shrubs and on the edge of clearings.

Higher up the gorge, beyond the village of EVISA, the River Porto runs through pine forest in the **FORÊT D'AITONE**. This is another site for the endemic nuthatch, as well as breeding sparrowhawks and goshawks, two specialist woodland predators. The latter species is hard to spot except in spring, when they indulge in soaring display flights over the pines.

Along the coast: Scandola

The whole of the Porto region is protected by Corsica's Regional Park – which covers nearly half of the island. The park's outstanding feature is the nature reserve of **SCANDOLA**, covering nearly ten square kilometres of coastal headland north of PORTO, and about the same area underwater. It amply repays the considerable effort needed to get to it, with **superb snorkelling** possibilities, since stringent restrictions on underwater fishing have led to a resurgence of marine life around the rocks and seaweed beds.

The undisturbed coast and the abundant fish have also led to good colonies of gulls, while a few pairs of **ospreys**, a fish-eating bird of prey very rare in the Med, nest on the cliffs. Peregrine falcons nest here too, stooping down on the rock doves which form their main prey. On the land, a dense scrub of myrtle *Myrtus communis* and the mastic tree *Pistachia lentiscus* stretch almost to the coast; among plants just behind the shore are the sea daffodil *Pancratium maritimus* (autumn flowering) and *Senecio cineraria* with its conspicuous furry silver leaves.

Bonifacio

Around **BONIFACIO**, the granite mountains that cover the rest of the island suddenly give way to lower limestone hills. **Orchids** are prominent here in spring, with numerous of the insect-imitating *Ophrys* species to be found including *Ophrys tenthredenifera*, a magnificent flower with a prominent yellow fringe to its purple and blue lip. With luck, Alpine swifts and blue rock thrushes can be seen round the cliffs between the village and the lighthouse. A notable seabird, usually to be seen, is **Cory's shearwater**, a large petrel which comes ashore to its nest at night; they breed in burrows at the back of the beaches and cliffs, and an evening stroll down towards the lighthouse may be rewarding for them.

CORSICA: ACCESS AND ACCOMMODATION

Unlike mainland France, Corsica is not well served with trains, with only one line linking the three main towns of AJACCIO, BASTIA and CALVI. Buses are good between main centres, but infrequent elsewhere when hitching may be the only option. A hire car would be an expensive but rewarding investment for the centre of the island. Even more rewarding for those with time would be to walk part (or even all, if you have the strength) of the 160-kilometre GR20 from CONCA to CALENZANA, one of the most demanding and dramatic of all the French long-distance footpaths.

Lake Biguglia
The lake is within easy reach of BASTIA, with the best access and views down the coastal road towards LA CANONICA, which itself has a campsite and would be a good base for the southern end of the lake.

Gorge de l'Asco
The D147 road runs up the gorge and through ASCO to the forests beyond. ASCO has a campsite and is infrequently linked by bus to PONTE LECCHIA.

Porto
PORTO has plenty of cheap hotels and two campsites, and is the obvious base for the region. PIANA and the gorge of SPELUNCA can be reached on foot from Porto; for the Forêt d'Aitone, it might be better to move up the gorge to EVISA, which also has a campsite. The nature reserve at SCANDOLA is only reachable by boat (trips operate from PORTO), and only for the day since camping is forbidden.

Bonifacio
BONIFACIO is a good base for the southern tip of Corsica, with campsites and bus services linking it to PROPRIANO on the Ajaccio road, and PORTO-VECCHIO on the BASTIA road.

information and publications

In most towns you'll find a tourist office, either called the *Office du Tourisme* or the *Syndicat d'Initiatif*. These will often have a simple leaflet about local nature reserves. Many of the sites in this book are part of a protected area – either a *Parc National*, a *Parc Regional Naturel*, or a privately owned reserve from one of a variety of voluntary organisations. The first two of these categories always have a head office in a nearby big town, and usually a series of information points scattered throughout the park, sometimes open only in summer. Whatever the case, they're always a good source of information about where to go and what to see.

MAPS
The whole French coast is well covered with maps. For general orientation, and for finding all the places mentioned, the 1:100,000 maps of the *Institut Géographique National* are fine. In a few places, and especially where walks are planned in the wild or mountainous areas, it may be worth splashing out on the IGN 1:25,000 series. Michelin have begun to bring out a 1:100,000 series as well, but they don't have contour lines and are in general inferior to the IGN series.

FOOTPATHS
France has one of the best networks of **long-distance footpaths** in Europe. Called *Sentiers de Grande Randonnée* or GR for short, they are usually well marked, and often link in with a series of *gîte d'étapes* for overnight accommodation. The main GRs in the Med region are the GR4 (Mediterranean to Atlantic), GR6 (Alps to Atlantic) and GR7 (Loire to Pyrenees). Annotated **route maps** – *topo guides* – are available for all GR's; get them locally, or in advance from the *Comité National des Sentiers de Grande Randonnée*, at 8 Avenue Marceau, Paris.

GUIDES
Provence and the Côte d'Azur: The Rough Guide (Harrap Columbus) is ideal for Mediterranean France – strong on landscapes and countryside, as well as practicallties.

BOOKS
Apart from the general texts, there are two more detailed floras available in English. One is *The Alpine Flowers of Britain and Europe* by Grey-Wilson and Blamey (Collins, London; £7.95) which is worthwhile only if you go to the regions over 1000 metres, such as the Alpes Maritimes, the Cevennes or the Provençal Alps. It's a companion volume to the *Wild Flowers of Britain and Northern Europe*, brilliantly illustrated and very easy to use. The other flora is more weighty – *The Flowers of Southwest Europe* by Oleg Polunin and Brian Smythies (OUP, Oxford; £9.95). It's a detailed and excellent flora for the more serious botanist, covering the Iberian peninsula and southern France as far east as the Rhône delta.

Two older books to read before you go are H. Thompson's classic 1920s book *The Flowering Plants of the Riviera* (out of print, try a library) and anything by the great French entomologist Jean Henri Fabre, to absorb the insect background of Provence.

CHAPTER TWO

GREECE

The **flowers** alone would put Greece high on the list of the Med's wildlife attractions; with some 6000 species (four times that of the UK), their variety and colour is staggering in spring and early summer. This richness is due largely to Greece's long physical **isolation** from the rest of Europe, surrounded as it is by sea on three sides and high mountains to the north. Its **climatic stability**, unaffected by the ice ages, has combined with the isolation to give perfect opportunities for plants to develop into new species, especially on the islands and mountain ranges. Most **Greek forest** was affected by humans in classical times, with clearance for agriculture as well as construction, fuel and shipbuilding. This created a familiar mosaic of arable crops on the rich soils, pasture on poorer soils, and *maquis* and *garigue* (called *phrygana* in Greece) scrub vegetation. Extensive forests really only remain in the mountains. However, Greece's relatively sparse population of ten million has meant that, outside the cities, the impact of development and pollution has been less than in other Mediterranean countries.

Greece's wildlife highlights stem from this sheer range of habitats, most of which have survived relatively unspoilt. Mountains like Olympus and Parnassos have an outstanding range of mountain flowers as well as large birds of prey, and the lower limestone hillsides that ring the coast have a richness of flowers equal to anything around the Med. A spring day on a warm hillside, surrounded by orchids, anemones and aromatic shrubby herbs with their attendant insects, is quite unforgettable. Bird migration is another highlight, since Greece's position puts it on a major flyway between Africa and Eastern Europe. Finally, the seventy-odd visitable islands add a special dimension, from the green fertility of the Ionian to the Asian influences of the Dodecanese; and Crete, the largest island, well known to visiting naturalists, almost merits a chapter of its own.

An awareness of **conservation** started only recently, but voluntary bodies like the Hellenic Society for the Protection of Nature have done an outstanding job in raising public and governmental awareness. Many problems still exist, particularly with drainage, overgrazing and pollution; however, there is now a good and extensive network of national parks, with more in the pipeline.

Climate and land use

Greece, as an eastern Med country, has colder winters and hotter, drier summers than those at the western end. The mountains in the north are influenced by the central European weather system, where summers can be quite wet, but the majority of Greece is under typical Mediterranean influence. In summer, a north-erly wind – the *meltémi* – often blows down the Aegean, while the west coast is more affected by moist westerly winds.

Land use is almost entirely agricultural outside the cities, although much of the soil is virtually bare limestone, incapable of supporting anything apart from a few goats. The main monocultures are cereal crops on the plains, and olive groves on the lower hills. Outside the cereal fields, Greek agriculture is relatively free from chemicals; hay crops and field margins have noticeably more flowers than richer countries which have sprayed poisons around with greater abandon. **Goats and sheep** are very evident on scrubby hillsides and on the mountains, although Greece is less intensively grazed than nearby Turkey.

Eastern festoon

WHEN AND WHERE TO GO

Flowers have quite a long season if you move around the regions to find them: they're at their best in Crete in March, in the high mountains in July; April and May are probably the best general months, and April also sees the peak of the **bird migration**. September sees the return bird migration, and October is good for autumn flowers such as crocus.

Buses are the best way of getting around, supplemented by ferries where necessary and, on the islands, scooter or moped hire. Internal flights can be useful if time is short and money isn't, and at about three times the cost of the bus they are relatively good value. Trains are slow but cheap.

The main sites described are:

The Mainland

● **ATHENS AND AROUND** The capital is ringed by three mountains of which **Párnitha** is typical; wetland birds are to be found in the **Marathon marshes**; and typical Med spring flowers at **Cape Sounion**.

● **CENTRAL GREECE** This very varied area is again surrounded by mountains. **Mount Olympus** and **Delphi and Mount Parnassus** are both outstanding, while **Mount Pílion** is a delightful microcosm of Med habitats, and **Metéora** has birds of prey as well as pinnacled monasteries.

● **EPIRUS AND THE WEST** The most accessible sites here are **Ioánnina** and its lake. Moving into the mountains around, there is the flower-rich and remote archaeological site of **Dodona**, as well as upland meadows around **Métsovo** and some of the country's wildest mountains and gorges in the **Zagóri**.

● **THE NORTH** The provinces of Macedonia and Thrace have some of the Med's best wetlands, with outstanding sites around **Thessaloníki** and in the **Évros delta**. The **Prespa lakes** are a breeding ground for pelicans and other water birds.

● **THE PELOPONNESE**
This beautiful, southern peninsula has dramatic mountains for flowers at **Mount Helmós** and around the Byzantine city of **Mystra**, while the ancient amphitheatre and sanctuary at **Epidavros** is good for flowers too.

The Islands

● **IONIAN ISLANDS** A lush and green archipelago with heavy autumn rainfall. **Corfu** and **Zákinthos** both retain excellent wildlife, despite their tourist development.

● **CRETE** The largest Greek island is more like a country in itself, with a whole range of Med habitat features. Highlights include the **Samarian Gorge** in the west and the **Lasíthi Plateau** in the east, both with excellent flowers and mountain birds, and the **Gulf of Messará** on the south coast, with its typical Med coastline and hillsides.

● **EASTERN AEGEAN** This group of islands show a definite Turkish flavour in their fauna and flora; **Rhodes** (Rhódos), **Kós** and **Lésvos** are all large enough to have varied wildlife habitats.

● **CYCLADES** The "scattered isles" are mostly small, heavily visited and desiccated in summer; **Ándhros** and **Náxos** are green and hilly exceptions.

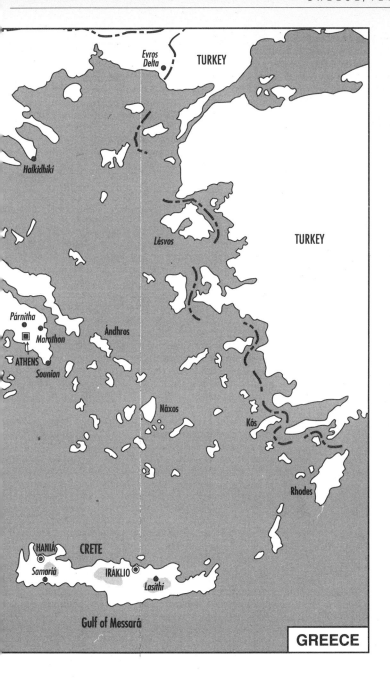

GREECE

ATHENS AND AROUND

Despite its crowds, traffic and horrendous air pollution, **Athens** is surrounded by surprisingly rewarding spots for wildlife. Chief amongst these are the three mountains that poke up from the plains of Attica; **Párnitha**, the most northerly, is perhaps the best for wild flowers, including genuine Alpine species. Also to the north of the city, the complex of lakes, reed beds and marshes around **Marathon** are excellent for birds of all sorts, and, away to the south, the much-visited headland of **Sounion** has superb flowers on its limestone outcrops and headlands. All three sites are less than two hours by local bus from central Athens.

Cape Sounion

The headland of **SOUNION** (Soúnio) is protected as a national park, due to the presence of the fifth-century Temple to Poseidon which stands imposingly on the tip. This has, sadly, been thoughtfully sprayed with herbicides and so has little botanical interest, but the surrounding *phrygana* is rich in flowers, especially around the ruined smaller temple to Athena.

The typical **colourful shrubs** of spring grow here – Jerusalem sage *Phlomis fruticosa* with its whorls of large yellow flowers, yellow brooms *Calicotome spp.* and both white and pink rockroses *Cistus spp.* Amongst them, scarlet anemones *Anemone coronarium* are prominent, as are the tassel hyacinths *Muscari comosum* and the large and very variable flowers of *Iris pumila*, its almost stalkless solitary flowers ranging from yellow through to blue or purple. A closer look is

Jerusalem sage *Phlomis fruticosa*

needed to spot the various **orchids**. Notable amongst them are small populations of the pink butterfly orchid *Orchis papilionacea* and the large *Ophrys tenthredenifera*, but the real highlight is the horseshoe orchid *Ophrys ferrumequinum*, which has large insect-imitating flowers, each marked with a metallic blue horseshoe on a velvety purple lip. Further towards the cliffs, the small campion *Silene colorata*, a widespread Med seaside species, grows in sheets of pink. Later in the year, various pink *Convolvulus* species flower in June, along with scarlet poppies; after the heat of the summer, the site is well known for its **autumn bulbs** – crocus relatives such as the purple *Colchicum autumnale* and the yellow *Sternbergia lutea*, as well as pink-flowered autumn cyclamens.

Birds at Sounion include the ubiquitous Sardinian warbler, chattering from the tops of the bushes, while rock nuthatches hunt amongst the ruins. Blue rock thrushes haunt the cliffs, and kestrels hunt above; there's a chance of rarer falcons during spring migration, including the red-footed falcon and Eleonora's falcon. Like all sunny ruins, the hot stones are favoured by basking **lizards** – small brown wall lizards and the larger green lizard *Lacerta viridis*.

Marathon marshes

Marshes cover a large area south of the village of **MARATHON** (MARATHÓNAS) and behind the beach resorts which line Marathon bay. **Wetland birds** are the main attraction here, with purple herons and little egrets feeding in the reed beds and on the shallow lakes, while hunting marsh harriers drift overhead. In spring and autumn, **migrating waders** stop over to refuel on the plentiful insects in and around the water – ruffs, stints and sandpipers have all been seen in good numbers, along with much scarcer birds such as the glossy ibis. In summer, the reed beds are full of breeding warblers, including the large and noisy great reed warbler. A visit in autumn or winter would doubtless turn up wintering **ducks** as well as waders.

Keen birders may want to stalk the **crakes** which are found here; at least two species can be seen – Baillon's crake and little crake – and they're both like small brown moorhens. They're one of the hardest of all birds to see well, since they spend their lives lurking at the bottom of reed beds, but at Marathon they feed in the vegetation-fringed dykes; a slow and cautious approach might be rewarded by the sight of them feeding in the open.

The **surrounding damp fields** are also rich in birds. In spring, migrating yellow wagtails move through in large numbers, including the handsome black-headed race which breeds around the Black Sea. Tawny pipits, a long-legged sandy bird, and short-toed larks like the open land as well, and brightly coloured rollers flash overhead. Predictably, the marshes are full of **reptiles and amphibians**, a food source for some of the larger birds, and in summer the beauty of the dragonflies outweighs the more dubious attraction of mosquitoes and midges.

Mount Párnitha

Rising to 1400 metres, **MOUNT PÁRNITHA** is the highest of the three Attican mountains, although by no means the only one worth a visit. Most of the flowers and other wildlife described are also to be found on **Imitós** (Hymettus) and **Pendhéli**, to the east of the city.

The lower slopes of Párnitha, above the suburb of THRAKOMEDHÓNES, have a typical *maquis* vegetation of bushy shrubs – mostly rockroses *Cistus spp.*, brooms of many species, and the lower aromatic plants of rosemary *Rosmarinus officinalis* and sage *Salvia officinalis*. *Officinalis*, incidentally, means "of the shop", since these are the herbs which are commonly used in cooking and herbal medicine. In openings amongst the shrubs, many of the colourful plants of the Med spring flourish on the bare limestone soil – anemones, tassel hyacinths and irises, along with a dozen or so orchid species; the horseshoe orchid *Ophrys ferrumequinum* is obvious, and so is the shining blue lip of *Ophrys speculum*. The south-facing slopes are sunny, and so are beloved of **reptiles**; along with lizards and the occasional snake, **tortoises** can be found lumbering amongst the shrubs, usually located first by the rustling noise they make. Greece is the only Med country to have all three European species of tortoise, but the one most likely to be seen is Hermann's tortoise *Testudo hermanni*.

Higher up the path, the scrub vegetation gives way to **coniferous forest** – Párnitha is the only Attican mountain to retain its forests at the top. The tree that dominates these woodlands is the Greek fir *Abies cephalonica*; like all firs, it has short leaves which come singly off the twigs (pines are in bunches of two), and upright cones. Truly natural forests of this fir are now very rare, since the trees have been heavily used since classical times for construction and shipbuilding; this particular one is planted.

In bare patches amongst the firs, the land is high enough for genuinely **Alpine plants** to thrive. One highlight is the bright purple *Aubretia deltoidea*, far more beautiful in its wild state than growing in the usual clichéd combination with yellow *Alyssum* in a cultivated rock garden. Another outstanding rock plant is a species of candytuft *Aethionema saxatile*, with a rounded head of pink flowers rising from a tight basal rosette of grey leaves. Amongst the firs in spring grows *Anemone blanda*, with its many-petalled flower of brilliant blue; the handsome leopardsbane *Doronicum caucasicum*, another familiar garden plant with large yellow flowers, grows here too. In early spring and in the autumn, **bulbs** come into their own; cyclamens *Cyclamen graecum* and *C. hederifolium* flower in the autumn along with *Scilla autumnalis*, carrying delicate blue flowers on its slender stems. In spring, its equivalent is *Scilla bifolia* with dark blue flowers, along with the spring-flowering purple *Crocus seiberi*; both these flower very early, often right on the edge of melting snow patches.

AROUND ATHENS: ACCESS AND ACCOMMODATION

All three sites described are easily accessible by bus from the centre of Athens.

Sounion
The bus to SOUNION leaves regularly from the KTEL terminal at Mavromatéon street, just south of Aréos Park. The journey, along a pretty nasty coastal strip of beach resorts, takes around 2hr. There are a couple of campsites within easy reach of Sounion itself, but hotels in the area are understandably pricey.

Marathon marshes
Buses to MARATHON leave from the same KTEL terminal and go via the port of RAFÍNA. Rafína, incidentally, is a good spot to stay, with notable seafood restaurants, cheap hotels, and thousands of Manx and Cory's shearwaters cruising offshore down the narrow strait separating it from the long island peninsula of ÉVVIA.

To get to the marshes, follow signs towards the airport off the main road between MARATHÓNAS and NÉA MAKRÍ – final access is possible only on foot along tracks running into the fields from the surrounding roads. Although Marathon itself doesn't offer much in the way of accommodation, there's a campsite at SKHINÍAS, a beach resort at the north end of the bay.

Párnitha
The mountain (often referred to as PARNES) is most easily reached by foot from the suburb of THRAKOMEDHÓNES, although a road goes all the way to the top if you lack the energy to walk. Get there by catching a bus #726 from Platía Váthi, just north of Omónia, and change at MENÍDHI; the trip takes an hour or so, depending on connections.

There is a good network of trails on the mountain, usually marked with red dots of paint; for further details, call in on the office of the *Hellenic Alpine Society* (*EOS*), who can also tell you about staying in the mountain refuge at the top.

CENTRAL GREECE

Central Greece is dominated by the flat plains of Thessaly, where the wildlife is as poor as the agriculture is rich. But things are very different around the edges of the region. **Mount Olympus** on the northwest corner is simply outstanding for its mountain flowers and scenery; the peninsula of **Mount Pílion** on the east coast is lush and hilly, and offers a microcosm of typical Greek habitats. To the south, **Delphi**, the most beautiful ancient site in Greece, lies in the shadow of **Mount Parnassus** and within easy reach of some unspoilt coastline. Finally, **Meteora**, on the eastern slopes of the Pindus mountains, is well known for its birds of prey.

Mount Olympus

MOUNT OLYMPUS (Óros Ólimbos) is an extraordinary mountain, its height – at 2917m it's the highest in Greece – accentuated by the fact that it rises almost directly out of the sea. This, together with its position at the crossroads of Mediterranean and central European floras, makes it one of the **best botanical sites** in the whole of the Med. Over 1500 plant species have been recorded from the mountain, including around twenty which are found nowhere else

Botanically, the mountain falls into three distinct zones. At the **lower levels**, up to 700 metres or so, the slopes are covered with typical *maquis* and *phrygana* vegetation, at their best in April and May; between this and 2000m, there's a **forested zone**, largely of pine species, Greek fir *Abies cephalonica* and beech *Fagus sylvatica*; **above the treeline**, the vegetation gives way to lower shrubs and finally to a true Alpine zone, with a sparse growth of low plants reduced to cushions by the harsh elements; at the top, plants can still be in full flower throughout July and even into August.

Equipped with decent boots and warm clothing, no special expertise is necessary to get to the top of the mountain in summertime (mid-June to October), though it's a long pull, requiring a good deal of stamina. Winter climbs, of course, are another matter, and at any time of year Olympus is a mountain to be treated with respect; its weather is notoriously fickle and it does claim lives. If you are not a confident hiker, best follow one of the published guides to the area.

The lower levels

The well developed **shrub** layer can easily be explored just north of the main base of LITÓHORO, on the road to the smaller village of PRIÓNIA. Leave Litóhoro, cross the gorge, and strike out left on a track through the *maquis* uphill of the road. The evergreen shrubs are dominated by the Kermes oak *Quercus coccifera* with its spiny, holly-like leaves, joined by other species such as the strawberry tree *Arbutus unedo*. Deciduous shrubs include the smoke bush *Cotinus coggygria* and the hop hornbeam *Ostrya carpinifolia* with (unsurprisingly) a toothed leaf like a hornbeam and a nut enclosed in scales like a hop.

A range of orchids and other typical *maquis* plants grow amongst the shrubs, and **birds** include the usual nightingales, whitethroats and Sardinian warblers, as well as scarcer species such as the cirl bunting. **Swifts** are numerous in the air above, with the pallid swift outnumbering the ordinary swift, though they're notoriously hard to tell apart.

Tracks loop through the shrubs and back to the **Enipévs gorge**, which runs from Litóhoro towards the heart of the mountain. The gorge itself is filled with massive pollarded plane trees *Platanus orientalis*, and willows hang over the river. The wet conditions here are ideal for mosses and ferns, including the feathery maidenhair fern *Adiantum capillus-veneris*; butterworts *Pinguicula hirtiflora* cling to the mossy rocks, with pale purple flowers and rosettes of sticky leaves in which they trap and digest insects. The **birds of the gorge** include river specialists such as grey wagtails, while blue rock thrushes and crag martins can be seen up on the rockfaces. Glistening green damselflies *Calopteryx virgo* haunt the streams and pools, and a diligent search might turn up a yellow-bellied toad *Bombina variegata*, a small toad, rather unassuming at first sight but with an amazing bright yellow belly.

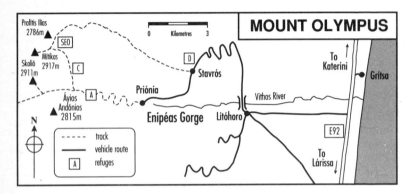

The forests

The village of PRIÓNIA is a good starting point for this zone, since the track from here up to Refuge A passes through excellent woodland. The native **pine forests** are good for birds, with crossbills, firecrests, and many tit species including the crested tit, which can be very confiding. Under the pines, the parasitic orchid *Limodorum abortivum* flowers in early summer, while the nearby beech forests are richer in plants, with such delights as the red helleborine *Cephalanthera rubra*. It's not all forest, though; there are numerous **gorges and waterfalls** too, and a few isolated **subalpine meadows**.

The **waterfall** near Priónia is worth visiting, for it has many plants of shady rocks as well as a spectacular flow of water. High on the rocks are a few plants of Olympus's most famous plant, the endemic *Jankaea heldreichii*. This plant has all three features of being rare, beautiful and interesting. It's interesting because it's one of only five European members of the largely tropical **Gloxinia** family, and it's only here at all because it got stranded on high ground at the end of the Tertiary period over two million years ago. It's beautiful, looking rather like an African violet (to which it is related), with clusters of purple flowers rising from a silvery rosette of basal leaves. The gorges round here have a similar range of birds to the lower gorge above Litóhoro, plus **peregrine falcons** which are regularly seen. Rock buntings, a bird of wild rocky country, can also be found here.

Between Priónia and Refuge A the path passes a number of grassy clearings. In sunny weather, these are exceptionally rich in **butterflies**, especially in June and July. Large colourful species such as the Camberwell beauty *Nymphalis antiopa* can be abundant, along with many fritillaries and browns. The plants of these woodland clearings include several species of *Geranium* and *Campanula*, but one to look for is the very striking scarlet martagon lily *Lilium chalcedonicum*, each plant with up to a dozen hanging bright red flowers with protruding red anthers and reflexed petals.

Peregrine falcon

Above the treeline

Refuge A, at just over 2000 metres, is the obvious starting point for any walk above the treeline, and is also the start of a number of trails to the summit. The forest is soon left behind, and an altogether barer landscape appears, with the white limestone crags of the summit ridges dominating the scene. Large **birds of prey**, including golden eagles, hunt these slopes and there's always a chance of a small group of chamois clambering amongst the rockfaces.

The vegetation is much sparser than lower down, not surprisingly in view of the wintry conditions that grip the mountain for much of the year. However, it can be rich in summer, when late melting snow patches disappear to expose fresh green grass, which is soon nibbled down by grazing sheep. Late July and early August is the best time, with colourful plants appearing on the exposed rockfaces as well as the grassy areas; saxifrages are very characteristic of this area, especially *Saxifraga sempervivum*, with nodding purple flowers above cushions of leaves, usually stiff and encrusted with lime. Another plant of the high screes is *Omphalodes luciliae*, a member of the borage family with clear blue flowers like large forget-me-nots and glossy blue-green leaves.

Other nearby sites

The sites described above cover only the most obvious and easily accessible parts of the mountain. For those with time (and money, for a taxi or a hired car is necessary), two of the best gorges for flowers and birds are on the northern slopes of the mountain; they are called **Pápa Réma** and **Xerolákki Réma**. Both are accessible via the village of VRÓNDHO.

Don't ignore the coast hereabouts, either. The **beaches and sand dunes** around GRÍTSA are within easy reach of Litóhoro, and have typical sand dune plants such as sea holly *Eryngium maritimum*, and many of the sand traps of the large ant-lion *Palpares libelluloides*. The open land behind the dunes is full of birds such as larks, pipits, wheatears and rollers, while gulls and terns can be watched offshore.

Mount Pílion

MOUNT PÍLION (or Pelion) is part of the same limestone mountain range as Olympus, but further south, and lower, at only 1650m. It's a lush and wooded peninsula, rather like the lower slopes of Olympus writ small, and with similar vegetation, too, with scrubby *maquis* giving way to forests of beech at the top around the ski resort of HÁNIA.

For the lower habitats, the village of MAKRINÍTSA is a good starting place, surrounded by olive groves, small terraces, and scrubby hillsides. Here in spring all the typical *maquis* and *phrygana* plants can be found, with orchids, anemones and irises galore. Of the latter, the snakes head iris *Hermodactylus tuberosus* is conspicuous, its pretty yellow flowers tipped with chocolate. The terraces below the olives are good for butterflies and tortoises in spring and summer, and the martagon lily *Lilium chalcedonium* can sometimes be found here.

On the other side of the peninsula, the slopes above the fine beach at MILOPÓTAMOS also have a rich vegetation, including the huge blue bells of the bellflower *Campanula incurva*. The late Oleg Polunin, who ought to know, called this the "finest of all Balkan campanulas . . . domes of glorious pale blue-violet flowers, sometimes a metre across, with several hundred large bells opening to the sun at the same time, grow on the rocky hillside".

Higher up, **woodland** appears, mostly regularly coppiced sweet chestnut and beech, but also with some plane. The higher village of TSANGARÁDHA is a good base for this zone, worth a stop if only for the enormous **plane tree** – reputedly one of the oldest in Greece – that shades its main square. The woodland is rich in small birds, especially nightingales which nest in the dense coppice regrowth; two notable plants are the St John's wort *Hypericum olympicum*, with very large yellow flowers on low woody stalks, and the spurge *Euphorbia characias wulfenii*, a very large variety of the usual Med species.

At the top, around the resort of HÁNIA, the snow melts late, and a visit in April can be rewarded with the sight of the pale purple *Crocus veluchensis* flowering in quantity; later in the year, these upland meadows are good for butterflies, and the tall pink spikes of the orchid *Dactylorhiza saccifera* are very evident.

Delphi

DELPHI is as rich in wildlife as it is in history. The archaeological site itself is worthy of naturalist exploration, for rock nuthatches are common around the ruins, and the green lizards *Lacerta viridis* which bask on the rocks have become used to the thousands of tourists and are remarkably tame. On the ancient walls, one of the many blue bellflowers *Campanula rupestris* produces striking purple flowers in April and May, and golden drop *Onosma frutescens* blooms in a mass of hanging yellow tubes. It's worth keeping an eye on the sky, for at any time a golden eagle may glide across from the cliffs of Mount Parnassus, and the swifts and swallows are always worth checking out; some of the swallows will be red rumped ones, Alpine swifts are regular residents, and crag martins nest on the nearby cliffs.

From a wildlife point of view, the best part of the archaeological site is up the hill at the **stadium**, which can be full of wild flowers and attendant insects in spring; orchids are plentiful, with the early spider orchid *Ophrys sphegodes* very common, and many plants of *Ophrys speculum*. From here, there is a marvellous view over the site down to the sea of olives inland of the port of Itéa. Above the stadium, the **ruined walls** are home to yet more lizards, and the scrubby growth around them develops into a good *maquis* habitat, with all the usual spiny and aromatic bushes. With luck, some of the small warblers darting from bush to bush will turn out to be Ruppell's warblers, and blue rock thrushes and black-headed buntings have both been seen. Eventually, the goat tracks lead up into the pines that fringe the bottom of the cliffs; look for sombre tits in these pines, a largely eastern species that looks like a great tit filmed in black and white.

April and May are as always the best months for flowers, and the time when the breeding birds are arriving and displaying. Whatever you do, **arrive early in the day**. Any chance of peaceful wildlife spotting is hopeless once the tour buses have arrived, though this applies mainly to the lower part of the site; even the short walk up to the stadium discourages most of them, and on the tracks above the stadium you'll have the hillside to yourself.

Green lizard
Lacerta viridis

Mount Parnassus

Above Delphi, **MOUNT PARNASSUS** (Óros Parnassós) shows a familiar habitat succession through forests of Greek fir *Abies cephalonica* to the barer limestone outcrops towards the summit at nearly 2500m. Birds of prey on the mountain are often impressive, with golden eagle, short-toed eagle and peregrine falcon regularly seen, and there's always a chance of the rare lammergeir.

As the snow melts in June above the treeline, spring bulbs of *Crocus* and *Scilla* appear, followed by a rich flora which soon becomes grazed by the summer flocks. Shore larks breed on the upland plateaux, the male with a black and yellow head pattern and two conspicuous "horns", and scarce woodpeckers such as the black woodpecker and the white-backed woodpecker are present but hard to find in the fir forests.

The mountain can be **walked**, but this is not to taken lightly – the distances are long, the weather changeable, and water infrequent in summer. The two main routes are from the villages of DELPHI, to the south of the mountain, and from ÁNO TITHORÉA to the north. The northern route is easier and shorter.

For those with a **car**, this is one of the most accessible Alpine zones in Greece. The summit region has been developed for skiing, and a road from ARÁHOVA and GRAVÍA goes almost to the top.

The Metéora

The limestone pinnacles of **METÉORA** rise out of the edge of the plain of Thessaly, overlooking the floodplain of the River Piniós. Capped by Byzantine monasteries, they are one of the most dramatic tourist destinations in Greece; although much visited, they are also a fine spot for wildlife – and primarily birds.

Alpine swifts nest in their hundreds on the pinnacles and, unusually, can be viewed from above from the monasteries. The biggest swift in Europe, they are perfectly adapted for their almost exclusively aerial existence, with scythed wings and aerodynamically inset eyes. Being on the eastern fringes of the Píndhos mountains, Metéora gets its fair share of **birds of prey** coming over to hunt the valleys; peregrines, golden eagles and Bonelli's eagles are all possible sightings, and Egyptian vultures more than likely. The latter vulture is handsome enough in flight, soaring on its black and white wings, but distinctly scruffy on the ground. **White storks** often soar above the pinnacles; in spring and autumn, some will be on the way to their northern breeding grounds, but in summer they'll be local breeders. The rare black stork has been seen here, too.

The Meteorite **plant life** isn't startling, but many of the common spring and summer shrubs flower by the roadsides: the rockrose *Cistus incanus*, with large pink flowers looking as if they're made from crumpled tissue paper, and a variety of yellow brooms. The huge purple spikes of the dragon arum *Dracunculus vulgaris* are common, and so are the pale blue flowers of love-in-a-mist *Nigella arvensis*.

CENTRAL GREECE: ACCESS AND ACCOMMODATION

Mount Olympus

LITÓHORO is easily reached by bus or train, since it's on the main coastal road. Access up the mountain by car is possible as far as PRIÓNA, where the track stops; hire a taxi or hitch a lift to save yourself a rather sweaty 18km grind up there. The walk from PRIÓNA to Refuge A (aka *Spílios Agapitós*) takes around 3hr; double that if you stop to take in the wildlife wonders on the way. From Refuge A to the top takes a further three. The mountain often clouds over at midday.

All this means that you'd be very wise to plan an overnight stop at Refuge A (☎0352.81.800) to give time for a leisurely exploration at the best time of the day. For the lower reaches, LITÓHORO is as good a place to stay as any other, with a youth hostel and a couple of hotels. For an alternative, the *Stavros refuge*, halfway between Litóhoro and Prióna may have basic accommodation, and certainly serves wonderful bean soup. There are campsites down by the beach at GRÍTSA.

Pílion

The most attractive option for the peninsula is to stay in one of villages such as TSANGARÁDHA or MAKRINÍTSA, where there are hotels; the EOT also run a series of lodges. This isn't especially cheap, but it's convenient. Alternatively, stay in VÓLOS, which no one could pretend is the most beautiful Greek city, but does have cheap hotels, outstanding seafood in some of the cheap *ouzeria*, and excellent bouzouki music.

Either way, you're stuck with a bus service linking Vólos with the villages, which exists but is neither frequent nor fast.

Delphi
Access to Delphi is straightforward, either directly by bus or by a combination of bus and train via LIVÁDHIA. For those without transport, it's best to stay in the village of DELPHI itself, although the port of ITÉA is a reasonable alternative; if you do the latter, access to the site is possible along the ancient and somewhat over-grown track through the olive groves.

Nearby ARÁHOVA is some way from the ancient site, but is a good base for the mountain trails. On the coast to the west is GALAXÍDHI, a quiet and unspoilt village which is surrounded by low headlands; these are excellent for spring flow-ers. Galaxídhi also has a number of hotels, including the wonderful *Pension Ganymede* (0265.41.328), with a fine garden and superb breakfasts and liqueurs.

Metéora
The main base is the town of KALAMBÁKA, accessible by bus from IOÁNNINA in the west and by both bus and train from TRÍKALA in the east. Hotels and rooms are plentiful, both in KALAMBÁKA and in the village of KASTRÁKI, right at the foot of the monasteries. The cheap *Kastraki Hotel* (☎0342.22.286) is recommended.

The circuit of the monasteries has a few buses serving it; far better to walk at least some of the way – a 10-kilometre loop from KASTRÁKI covers all of the main monasteries except for the more remote Ayios Stéfanos.

EPIRUS AND THE WEST

Epirus, dominated by the northern Píndhos mountains, is wild and rugged, and one of the least visited parts of Greece. The best timing for this part of Greece is **early summer** – May through to July depending on height; it can be distinctly cold and snowy earlier in the year in the mountains.

Ioánnina is a fine base, with good wildlife in its own right on Lake Pamvótis. Three places can be easily reached from there. To the south, the remote and flower-rich amphitheatre at **Dodona**; to the north, the extraordinary mountain villages and gorges of the **Zagorí**; and to the east, the upland meadows surround-ing the village of **Métsovo**.

Ioánnina

White storks are a common sight throughout Epirus, and even in the centre of IOÁNNINA they nest on top of roofs, chimneys and telegraph poles. It's not just these nest sites that bring them here every summer, however, but the plentiful fish and frog population of **Lake Pamvótis**, on whose shores the town stands.

Large freshwater lakes are uncommon in Greece, and this one has many of the **waterplants** familiar from lakes further north. In summer, look for the flowering rush *Butomus umbellatus*, a waterside plant with a lovely rounded flowerhead of pink three-petalled flowers. Much of the lake is fringed with dense beds of reed *Phragmites australis*, which makes viewing the open water frustratingly difficult; they're full of purple herons as well as storks, feeding on the abundant marsh frogs *Rana ridibunda*, which are collected for local consumption in restaurants. The lake, predictably, has many aquatic reptiles, especially the European pond terrapin *Emys orbicularis* and many dice snakes *Natrix tessalata*, a non-poisonous relation of the grass snake. In summer, the reeds hold numerous nesting reed warblers and great reed warblers, and are a reliable spot for sighting the elusive **little bittern**, the smallest European member of the heron family.

On the water, summer breeding birds include mute swans, mallard and moorhen, but the spring and autumn **migration** can bring almost anything; terns, waders and ducks regularly call in here. It should be excellent for wintering waterfowl, too.

The easiest way to see the lake is on one of the regular ferries out to the island of NISSÍ, also known as Ali Pasha's island. For a good view of the reed beds, walk or drive south of the town as close to the lake as possible (start on Garivaldi street); after a few kilometres, a series of tracks lead off to the southwestern shores of the lake.

Dodona

The isolated site of **DODONA** is best visited in May or early June for its flowers. Although nothing spectacularly rare is to be found, the density and colour of flowers around the site are exceptional. One of the tallest orchids grows here – the lizard orchid *Himatoglossum hircinum*, so called because each of the green/white flowers bears a long twisting tail like that of a lizard. Another striking plant is the Madonna lily *Lilium candicum*, with large pure white funnel-shaped flowers; for centuries it has been the symbol of purity and innocence, figuring as such in Minoan art and carried to this day by Greek brides.

On the scrubby slopes around the site, **breeding warblers** include lesser whitethroats and subalpine warblers, the latter with a handsome cinammon breast and grey back. The wealth of flowers pulls in butterflies for their nectar – especially scarce swallowtails – and, as in all ancient sites, lizards are common. **Snakes** are too, including the large whip snake *Coluber jugularis*. Adults are coloured pale brown with a yellowish belly, and can grow to a heart-stopping two metres long; although they're non-poisonous, they can bite fiercely if handled.

The Zagóri

The **ZAGÓRI** is a large and mountainous region northeast of Ioánnina. It is scarcely Mediterranean in habitat type – the deep gorges, mountain massifs and pine forests owe more to the central Balkans – but is rich in wildlife and, agriculturally, relatively undeveloped, due to its thin soils.

The valleys

The bottoms of the **river valleys** that dissect the region are lush and green. That of the **River Aóos**, close to the village of ARÍSTI, is typical. A mosaic of riverside walks, it is interspersed with deciduous woodland and small meadows, and in early June it is terrific for all forms of wildlife. Orchids grow on the barer ground, with pyramidal orchids *Anacamptis pyramidalis* as well as the *Ophrys* insect-imitating species. Amongst the latter is *Ophrys sphegodes hellenae*, a rather rare variety with a velvety lip of unrelieved deep maroon; it grows around the car park by the river on the road down from Arísti. Dippers and grey wagtails both breed by the river itself, and on some of the shady rocks by the path a few plants of the rare *Ramonda serbica* grow. Related to *Jankaea heldreichii* of Mount Olympus, it has dark green hairy leaves and purple flowers.

The more open meadows are excellent for **butterflies**. In late May, a variety of whites, fritillaries and blues dance amongst the flowers. A special species is the **nettle-tree** butterfly *Libythea celtis*, the only European representative of its genus. The butterfly is dark brown with orange patches and a noticeably ragged wing outline. Not surprisingly, its caterpillars feed on the nettle tree *Celtis australis*, a slender tree with very toothed leaves. It is attracted, like many tropical butterflies, to urine, and there are records of hundreds coming to urine-soaked sand by the river here in June. This is an experiment any naturalist can try! Other butterflies of the woodland edge here are commas *Polygonia egea*, Camberwell beauties *Nymphalis antiopa* and southern white admirals *Limenitis reducta*, the latter handsomely patterned with black and white uppersides and brown, white and mother-of-pearl undersides.

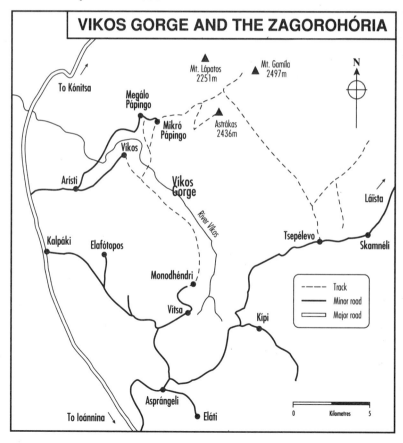

VIKOS GORGE AND THE ZAGOROHÓRIA

The Víkos Gorge

Most people come to MONODHÉNDRI to look at or walk the **VÍKOS GORGE**. This is a rival to the more famous Samarian gorge on Crete: a grand chasm, over twenty kilometres from end to end and up to 1000m deep as it cuts through the limestone plateaux of the Mount Gamíla complex.

One of the best views of the gorge is from the monastery of **Áyia Paraskeví**, perched on the very edge of the cliffs. This is a good place to sit and search the sky for passing **predators**; Egyptian vultures are commonplace, golden and short-toed eagles regular, and the huge wingspan of the Griffon vulture not unknown. Alpine swifts and crag martins wheel around the rockfaces, which are hung with white saxifrages, the bright pink soapwort *Saponaria calabrica*, and most memorably of all, great sheets of purple *Aubretia deltoidea*.

The very steep walk down to the gorge from Monodhéndri passes through **mixed woodland** including hornbeam *Carpinus betulus*, sycamore *Acer pseudoplatanus* and linden *Tilia tomentosa*, before it ends up by the river, which is overhung with alders *Alnus glutinosa*, various willows, and plane trees *Platanus orientalis*. The flowers at the bottom are similar to those by the river at Arísti, but with more species of the cliffs and ledges; amongst the woodland, Madonna lilies *Lilium candicum* grow, along with the magnificent white-flowered foxglove *Digitalis lanata*, with a protruding and reflexed lip. The Greek hellebore *Helleborus cyclophyllus* is evident too, with large divided leaves and pale green hanging flowers. A striking blood-red geranium growing on the rocks in the gorge will probably be *Geranium macrorrhizum*, with projecting stamens. Birders should keep an eye on the cliff faces as they walk down for the beautiful and elusive **wallcreeper** which has been seen here.

The full **gorge walk** takes at least six hours from Monodhéndri to the village of Víkos, along the river towards ARÍSTI. Most is well marked with splashes of red paint, but it commands respect with steep climbs, slippery boulders and rushing water. At the northern end of the gorge, a more ambitious hiking choice is to bypass Víkos and push on up a long steep climb to the two PÁPINGO villages.

The higher ground

Above the gorges and valleys, things are much barer, with a **subalpine flora** growing on rockfaces and amongst the scree slopes. There's the occasional Alpine meadow, too – at their best in June and into July. **Birds** of the tops are limited but unusual; Alpine accentors occur, like a large hedge sparrow with chestnut flanks and a white throat spotted with black. An even more specialist bird of the tops is the snow finch, which is actually an alpine sparrow; it has black and white wings and tail, most apparent in flight. Shore larks breed on these upland plateaux and Cretzschmar's bunting is a fairly common summer visitor.

Any **hiking across the tops** is an arduous business, but there are two good starting places. The first is the village of TSEPÉLOVO, wonderfully situated at the head of a valley clothed in beech and chestnut forests; a good track leads on up to the next village, SKAMNÉLI, and then into excellent wild flower meadows with mountainous cliffs and gullies on either side. Many of the plants up here will be familiar from rock gardens at home; low, cushioned and colourful, they include species of *Aubretia*, *Potentilla*, *Campanula* and *Veronica*, as well as a bewildering variety of saxifrages. Pick of the bunch of the latter is *Saxifraga marginata*, which clings to the vertical cliffs in huge clumps of lime-encrusted leaves, bearing large white flowers in early spring. Wallcreepers breed in some of the higher gorges.

Other useful starting points are the two villages of PÁPINGO; you don't have to walk to them from the Víkos gorge, since a road links them to Arísti. Here again there are flower meadows, while the twin peaks of Astrákas tower above.

Métsovo

MÉTSOVO is largely on the tourist circuit as the capital of the Vlachs, and is heavily visited in high summer for that reason. In winter, it's a growing ski resort. In between, and especially in May and June, it is outstanding for its **Alpine meadows** with flowers and butterflies; and it's always a dramatic place, perched at 1700 metres on the Katára pass over the Pindhós ridge.

The meadows lie between the beech woods that surround the village; good ones are either side of the road a few kilometres out on the Ioánnina road. Too early a visit, even in April, can be rewarded by nothing but snow, but a little later spring bulbs bloom in their thousands, and *Crocus veluchensis* and *Crocus flavus* cover the fields in purple and yellow. Later, in May, the sweet-smelling *Narcissus poeticus* takes over, growing in clumps; between them orchids such as *Dactylorhiza sambucina* grow – with two colour varieties of pink and yellow, this species is more usually associated with the Alps proper. Violets, bellflowers and primroses complete a colourful picture – though a short-lived one, for the summers are dry and the pressure of grazing flocks intense.

As well as the large eagles and vultures, **smaller raptors** can be found around Métsovo. Sparrowhawks nest in the beech woods, buzzards search the open slopes, and red-backed shrikes are particularly common, hunting for large insects and small reptiles. **Butterflies** are at their best in June, with spring species such as the orange tip *Anthocharis cardamines* joined by the early summer browns and fritillaries; of the latter, the pearl-bordered fritillary *Clossiana euphrosyne* is abundant, searching for the violets on which it lays its eggs.

EPIRUS: ACCESS AND ACCOMMODATON

Ioánnina

Access and accommodation are both simple in this major town. There are also a couple of inns on the island of NISSÍ, a pleasant but popular alternative; in summer, it's wise to book ahead.

Ioánnina has two bus stations; the one on Zozimádhou is the largest and serves routes north (including the Zagorohória) and east to Metsovó and Kalambáka. The other bus station is just south of Platía Pirroú; it serves the south, including Dodóna.

Dodóna

Twice daily buses run to the site from IOÁNNINA (see above). The adjacent village of DODHÓNI has a pension, a taverna, and plenty of room to camp.

The Zagóri

Access is inevitably by bus or car from IOÁNNINA. Buses serve most of the larger villages, but are daily or even less; a hired car would be a good investment, but you'll still need to walk to most of the really good wildlife areas.

Accommodation can be found in most of the villages of the Zagóri (collectively called the **Zagorohória**). Ones with a good range of rooms, hotels and tavernas are ARÍSTI, MONODHÉNDRI, MEGÁLO PÁPINGO and TSEPÉLAVO. At the latter, Alekós Gouris, who runs the main taverna in the village square, has guided many hunters through the mountains and forests and is knowledgeable about both walks and wildlife; he speaks English, too.

Métsovo

Access is easy, since the village is on the main road across the Pindhós from TRÍKALA and KALAMBÁKA to IOÁNNINA. So is accommodation, with hotels at all price ranges; the *Acropolis* (☎0656.41.672) is said to be cheap and excellent. The meadows are an easy walk out of the village on the road west.

THE NORTH:
MACEDONIA AND THRACE

Northern Greece is known primarily for its **wetlands**, some of which are of outstanding importance for birds. In 1975, Greece ratified the Ramsar Convention, an international agreement for wetland protection; as a result, eleven sites have been designated as Wetlands of International Importance – seven of them along the coast of Thrace. The largest and most important is the **Évros delta**, though this is also the hardest to get to; others are more easily accessible from the northern capital of Thessaloníki.

Traditional Med habitats can be found along the coast, and the three-fingered peninsula of **Halkidhikí** is no exception. Inland on the Albanian and Yugoslavian borders, the National Park and Ramsar site at the **Prespa lakes** is exceptional for its breeding water birds, including both pelican species, while the ancient Rhodope Massif, which forms the Bulgarian border, is a remote, forested region, home to small and largely invisible populations of wolf, lynx and brown bear.

Sites around Thessaloníki

Three worthwhile sites lie close to Thessaloníki: the inland **Lake Korónia**, the coastal marshes of the **Aliákmon delta** (a Ramsar site) and the saltpans at **Angelohóri**. Using the city as a base, they are each easy enough day trips.

Lake Korónia

LAKE KORÓNIA (sometimes called Lake Vasílios) is a large, reed-fringed and very shallow lake, 10km east of Thessaloníki. Storks, herons and egrets all nest here, while the reed beds and open land are hunted over by marsh harriers and

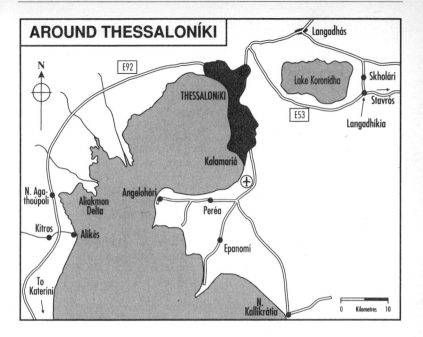

AROUND THESSALONÍKI

N

E92

Langadhás

Lake Koronídha

Skholári

THESSALONíKI

Stavrós

E53

Langadhíkia

Kalamariá

N. Aga-
thoúpoli

Aliakmon
Delta

Angelohóri

Peréa

Kítros

Alikés

Epanomí

To
Kateríni

N.
Kallikrátia

0   Kilometres   10

black kites. Within the reeds themselves, nightingales and reed warblers breed, and the surrounding scrub is also rewarding for other small warblers, including penduline tits. In spring and autumn, numbers are greatly swelled by **migration**, with pelicans, terns and many waders calling in to break their journey.

At the eastern end of the lake, between the villages of LANGADHÍKIA and SCHOLÁRI, is an area of low-lying fields intersected with **drainage channels**. As well as the bird interest, these are full of dice snakes *Natrix tessallata* and marsh frogs *Rana ridibunda*, and terrapins; grey herons also breed communally in two enormous plane trees near Scholári. Rough tracks lead across the fields to give good views of the lake, which can alternatively be viewed easily from the main road that skirts its southern shore. On stony soils, look for the **European susliks** – they resemble a small short-tailed squirrel and can be often seen squatting on their hind legs to look out for danger.

The northern road back to Thessaloníki leads through LANGADHÁS; a **fire-walking ritual** is held here on May 21, which is a couple of weeks too late for the peak bird migration, but a good time to visit all the same.

Angelohóri

ANGELOHÓRI is more of a promontory than a village, although there is a small taverna at the end of the road, overlooking the straits leading into the bay of Thessaloníki. A series of **saltpans and a large lagoon** are attractive to water birds; avocets and black-winged stilts, the two specialists of saline habitats, can easily be seen.

Avocet

Around the lagoon, glossy ibis and spoonbills, two globally scarce birds, are present throughout the summer, though they don't breed. On the barer stony soils surrounding the site, stone curlews breed – large brown birds with a distinctive white wingbar, they have incongruously large yellow eyes.

Predictably, things are more exciting at migration time, when a variety of **waders** call in. Most of them will be migrating across western Russia to and from breeding grounds in northern Russia and Lapland, and some of them, like the marsh sandpiper and Terek sandpiper, are rarely seen further west than northern Greece. Other waders like turnstones and little stints are far more familiar to western European birders. A special bird at Angelohóri is the **slender-billed curlew**, one of the world's rarest waders, which breeds on the Russian steppes. It is regularly seen in winter and on passage; northern Morocco is the only other reliable Med area for this bird. Positive identification is a bit tricky – look for a small curlew, without any head stripes and with large dark spots on its flanks; the latter feature is not as obvious as field guides would have us believe.

Smaller birds are plentiful at migration time, too, and the **flowers** of the beach include the yellow horned poppy *Glaucum flavum*, with large yellow flowers and greatly elongated seed pods. Later in the year, sea holly *Eryngium maritimum* blooms, and the autumn brings the white flowers of the sea daffodil *Pancratium maritimum*.

The Aliakmon Delta

Directly opposite to Angelohóri, the **Aliakmon Delta** has much the same range of birds, but more of them. It's the least developed of the four river deltas west of Thessaloníki, and has many breeding Mediterranean gulls as well as a few pairs of the rarer slender-billed gull. It's said to be full of wintering wildfowl in winter, and flamingoes are frequently seen. All these birds are bound to attract the odd **bird of prey**; notable amongst these is the **white-tailed eagle**, a very large eagle with a square wing outline in flight, reminiscent of the broad wings of a vulture.

The delta is best viewed from the south, from the village of NÉA AGATHOÚPOLIS which is on the main coastal road, some 45km south of Thessaloníki. Another 12km further south on the same road there are excellent saltpans at ALÍKI.

Halkidhikí

The three fingers of the **HALKIDHIKÍ** are at their best in May, when the spring flowers and bird migration are at their peak and the resorts on the two westerly peninsulas – **Kassándhra** and **Sithonía** – relatively empty. Kassándhra and Sithonía each have a variety of habitats; their alternately rocky and sandy coastline gives way to ranges of low hills covered in *maquis* scrub and forests of Aleppo pine *Pinus halapensis*; flat land tends to be agricultural, with many olive groves, while the river valleys often have attractive fringing woodland, largely of plane trees *Platanus orientalis*. The most easterly finger, the monastic peninsula of **Mount Áthos**, has an equally excellent mountain flora, but it is open only to male visitors, and even then only after considerable bureaucracy.

Polichróno

The resort of **POLICHRÓNO**, just south of KALLITHÉA on Kassándhra, is typical of the Halkidhikí. On the shoreline and the sand dunes there are specialist maritime plants such as cottonweed *Otanthus maritimus*, with its unmistakeable silver felted leaves and heads of small yellow flowers; one of the sea stocks *Matthiola tricuspidata* is another common species. Behind the dunes, the land rises to sparse pine woods, and the shrub layer includes the rockrose *Cistus parviflora*, covered with small pink flowers against its slightly grey foliage in spring. Fighting through this scrub can be fraught; Christ's thorn *Paliurus spinus-christi*, an exceptionally spiny bush, often bars your way, as does the climber *Smilax aspera*, with glossy heart-shaped leaves and wicked barbs. This defence mechanism, originally developed to ward off browsing animals, serves just as well to deter frail humans. Orchids, irises and anemones are the flowers of early spring; later, in May and June, the tall spikes of bear's breeches *Acanthus spinosus* are evident.

The peninsula's **birds** include the familiar nightingales and warblers of the Med scrub, with black-headed buntings arriving later in the spring to breed. Look for hoopoes amongst the olive groves, and the brilliantly coloured roller on more open, sandy or stony habitats. Shrikes are widespread, with a fair chance of the **masked shrike**, a more eastern species, as well as woodchat shrikes perched on telegraph wires.

Holomón Mountains

North of Halkidhikí, the **Holomón Mountains** rise only to 1000 metres or so, but are densely wooded with oaks, chestnut and hornbeam. There is straightforward road access to the range between GALATISTA and ARNAEA.

Woodland clearings in the hills are excellent for butterflies and should include the largest of the fritillaries, the cardinal *Pandora pandoriana*, in June; look for the strawberry bush *Arbutus unedo* – with luck you may find the two-tailed pasha butterfly *Charaxes jasius* flying around it. Mammals, as always, are hard to spot but the beech marten has been seen in this woodland. Under the trees, woodland flowers include the red helleborine *Cephalanthera rubra* and the Greek hellebore *Helleborus cyclophyllus*, unrelated despite their similar common names. The fact that four woodpecker species have been seen here indicates the richness of the bird population.

The Préspa lakes

Over in the north of Macedonia, the two **PRÉSPA LAKES** – Megáli (which straggles the Yugoslav and Albanian borders) and Mikrí (which lies entirely in Greece) – have been a National Park since 1971. **Mikrí Préspa** is important for birdlife, partly due to its remotenesss, and partly because surrounding lakes in Albania have been drained. Both **pelican** species breed at Préspa and the colony of the **Dalmatian pelican** is one of the few in Europe; the species is listed as "vulnerable" by the International Council for Bird Preservation. Pygmy cormorants nest by the lake as well, yet another species listed as vulnerable, and one which is in steady decline throughout its range.

Dalmatian pelican

Rarities apart, Préspa is a marvellous place to see large colonies of **breeding herons**, **spoonbills** and **egrets**, and is even better at migration time, when its wide waters are a magnet for passing water birds and waders. Although the "core area" of the National Park covers just five square kilometres of the lake and shore, the "peripheral area" of woods and hills covers a further sixteen square kilometres, holding such exciting large mammals as **wolves**, **bears** and **jackals**, and birds such as breeding golden, Imperial and lesser spotted eagles, and goshawks. Needless to say, these are hard to see, and particularly so as access into the surrounding hills is difficult; to the south and west of the lake considerable caution is needed as the Albanian border guards do not fully understand the fascination of wildlife for visiting tourists.

There are two easy access points to the lake; the first is the **causeway** that separates Mikri Préspa from Megali Préspa. There are watchtowers here, and it's close to the pelican colonies. The second spot is halfway down the eastern shore of the lake, near the settlement of **Mikrolimni**, where there is a hide and a series of tracks lead through the reed beds along the lake shore. Two hills on this eastern shore give good general views over the lake, and are fine places to scan the reed beds for harriers and the sky for passing eagles.

The Évros Delta and Ávas Gorge

In its time, the **ÉVROS DELTA** has ranked alongside the Camargue and the Danube for its **breeding birds**, and especially for its wintering ducks and geese, said to number up to 100,000. Sadly, the area has shrunk substantially as land has been drained for agriculture, but it remains nonetheless an outstanding bird site.

For any naturalist, the sight of numerous birds in one place is inspiring, especially when they include large and charismatic species such as storks, herons, ducks and waders; for the confirmed birder, the site is attractive because it holds eastern species on the very edge of their range – spur-winged plover, sociable

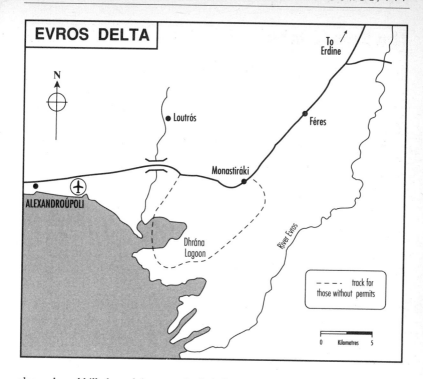

plover, broad-billed sandpiper, masked shrike and Isabelline wheatear are just a few from a long list that is mouthwatering to birdwatchers. Such a concentration of wildfowl brings predatory birds in its wake, from the inevitable marsh harriers that cruise the reed beds to sometimes numerous formations of migrating buzzards and eagles, the westerly tip of the main passage that has crossed into Europe via the Bosphorus.

But the **importance of the delta** is far greater than just the presence of a few unusual birds. It is a vital breeding ground and migration staging post, and its decline over the last twenty years brings into sharp focus the conflict between agricultural production and wildlife conservation. This is a problem far from unique to Greece; in fact, richer countries such as Britain and France have drained many more wetlands over the years, and are more to blame for that reason. International pressure and cooperation is one way; creative tourism is another, where visiting naturalists can put their money where their mouth is and show local people that nature reserves can be a source of revenue to balance any potential loss of agricultural production.

The Ávas Gorge

While in Alexandhroúpoli, it's worth a visit to the **ÁVAS GORGE**, a few kilometres north of the town. Head towards ÁVAS and turn left just before it up a track. Higher up the gorge there's a chance of sighting the impressive eagle owl at dawn and dusk, as well as other large birds of prey.

MACEDONIA AND THRACE: ACCESS AND ACCOMMODATION

Around Thessaloníki

Heading for LAKE KORÓNIA by public transport, catch a bus to STAVRÓS and get off at the village of LANGADHÍKIA (not be confused with LANGÁDHAS to the north of the lake). From here explore on foot amongst the fields and the lake edge to the west of the minor road to SKHOLÁRI; then to return, catch a bus back to Thessaloníki round the north of the lake. A hired car makes things a lot simpler.

For ANGELOHÓRI, leave Thessaloníki on the southern road past the airport, and branch westwards through the village of PERÉA; keep straight on, and the road ends at the saltpans. Buses are uncertain towards the end of this road.

The ALIAKMON DELTA is less easy to reach, unless you have a car. For the delta itself, get off the Lárissa bus at NÉA AGATHOÚPOLIS, and explore northwards into the delta by foot; for the saltpans, get off the bus on the main road crossroads near KITRÓS, and walk the 4km down to ALÍKI. Both these sites are on the main road between Thessaloníki and Mount Olympus; it could be sensible to visit them en route, perhaps staying overnight at KATERÍNI.

Halkidhikí

Access to the peninsulas of Kassándhra and Sithonía is straightforward from Thessaloníki, with regular buses from the terminal at Karakássi 68 (some way out from the centre: take local bus #10 to the Bótsari stop). On the peninsulas there's plenty of accommodation at the various coastal resorts, though these are crowded enough in summer for a reservation in advance to be sensible.

The HOLOMÓN MOUNTAINS are accessible by bus from Thessaloníki, but a hired car would make sense here, or perhaps a hired moped from one of the Halkidhikí resorts.

Préspa Lakes

The best base is the small town of FLORÍNA, 25km to the east of the lakes, where hotels and pensions are in good supply. There is an irregular bus service from the town to the lake, winding up at PSARÁDHES, over the causeway and hard against the Albanian border, where you can alternatively find accommodation at the taverna. FLORÍNA itself is a good place to rest up for a couple of days. The surrounding hills and woods are excellent for flowers, butterflies and woodland birds.

KASTORIA to the south is another option for accommodation; it's further from Préspa, but is set on its own lake, which is worth a trip in its own right, especially for spring bird migration.

Évros Delta

The delta is large and a car is essential for a thorough look. Access is via ALEXANDHROÚPOLI, which is also the best place to stay.

A large part of the south of the delta is a military zone, since it lies on the Turkish border, and it's necessary to obtain permits. You can get them from the police or the military headquarters, near the lighthouse in the town. No permits are needed for a limited circuit of the area, going no further than the village of MONASTIRAKI and the Drana lagoon (which has recently been drained but may yet be reflooded).

Despite all the hassles, this is genuinely one of the last wilderness areas in Europe and well worth the effort.

THE PELOPONNESE

The huge, southern peninsula of the **Peloponnese** is surprisingly ignored by visiting naturalists, although it offers (in addition to ancient sites such as Olympia and Mycenae) a complete range of Greek habitats. *Maquis* and *phrygana* are to be found on the coastal hills, there are rolling hills and flat plains, and genuinely high mountains rising to nearly 2500 metres.

Of the three sites described, **Epidaurus** is a perfect ancient amphitheatre set amongst scrub-covered hillsides rich in spring flowers; the Byzantine city of **Mystra** is another flowery site, with the mountain of **Taíyettos** conveniently close for its mountain flowers and birds. In the north of the peninsula, **Mount Helmós** is another mountain site with exceptional plant life.

Epidaurus

The low hills that frame the amphitheatre and Asclepion sanctuary at **EPIDAURUS** (EPÍDHAVROS) are covered mostly by olive groves, but interspersed in spring with the the pink flowers of wild almond trees and the darker pink of the Judas tree *Cercis siliquastrum*. Many typically Greek wayside flowers grow on the roadsides and on the grassy banks surrounding the theatre – especially the large white daisy flowers of the Greek chamomile *Anthemis chia*, which grows in sheets. The scarlet of *Anemone coronaria* and the blue of the tassel hyacinth *Muscari comosum* stand out against this background, as does the delicate white umbellifer *Tordylium apulum*, with its asymmetrical individual flowers.

The theatre itself is kept spotlessly clear of vegetation but the other ruins on the site are overhung by flowers of blue *Campanula*, and you might catch sight of rock nuthatches hunting amongst the rocks for insects. In scrubby *maquis* in the patches amongst the olives, nightingales and Sardinian warblers are plentiful, tortoises lumber through the vegetation, and orchids grow in the barer soils; the yellow insect-imitating species *Ophrys lutea* is perhaps the commonest, but the much rarer *Ophrys argolica* is also to be found here; it has pink sepals and two white-edged blue eyes on its lip, though, like all *Ophrys* species, it's variable and hybridises easily and confusingly.

Mystra (Mistrás)

Perched on a steep hillside below the mountains, the ruined Byzantine city of **MYSTRA** (MISTRÁS) has flowers both in its old walls and ruins, and on the mountains above. The site is formed from the whole city, rather than one focal point, and this perhaps explains why herbicide sprays have not been used – hence the richness of the flora.

On the **walls**, yellow alyssum *Alyssum saxatile*, more familiar as a garden plant, is common, alongside golden drop *Onosma frutescens* with its hanging yellow trumpets. As at Epidaurus, pink Judas trees stand out against the olives on the plain below, and the bushy shrubs of Jerusalem sage *Phlomis fruticosa* are widespread. On patches of wasteland *Chrysanthemum coronarium* flourishes, along with poppies, pink mallows, and (later in the year) a host of scarlet poppies.

Anemones, tassel hyacinths and the occasional wild *Gladiolus segetum* complete the colourful spring picture, and in rock crevices the small arum lily *Arisarum vulgare* pushes up its strange brown and white striped flower; not for nothing is it called friar's cowl. **Orchids** are plentiful on the site, especially *Ophrys sphegodes* and two closely related species *Ophrys spruneri* and *Ophrys argolica*; purists will have fun sorting out the different species, while ordinary mortals can simply enjoy the variety of combinations of pink sepals, purple lips and blue lip markings.

Butterflies are plentiful amid this wealth of nectar bearing plants. Swallowtails *Papilio machaon* and scarce swallowtails *Iphiclides podalirius* both glide around, joined in spring by the yellow brimstone *Gonepteryx cleopatra*, orange tips *Anthocharis cardamines* and green hairstreaks *Callophrys rubi*, the latter often feeding on the flowers of the tall pink asphodel *Asphodelus aestivus*.

Within easy walking distance of the ruins is the **Parori Gorge**, described as "one of the most flower-filled places we have seen" by Paul and Jenne Davies, authors of the best book on European orchids. Praise indeed. The familiar anemones combine with *Cyclamen repandum*, whilst saxifrages, *Aubretia deltoidea* and *Campanula* species brighten up the rocks. The **Langádha Gorge**, above the nearby village of TRÍPI, is said to be even better.

Scarce swallowtail
Iphiclides podalirius

Mount Profítis Ilias

The summit of **Mount Profítis Ilias**, the highest mountain of the Taíyettos range, can be reached from near Mystra, although it's not an easy trek; walkers would do well to contact the Alpine Hellenic Society (EOS) office in SPÁRTI (Kéntriki Platía) for information before setting out.

Late June is the best time to make the ascent for the mountain flowers; the path starts at the tiny village of POLIÁNA, itself 10km up a dirt track above the village of PALIOPANAYÍA. The **track** starts amid orchards, continues through forests of black pine *Pinus nigra* and Greek fir *Abies cephalonica*, and eventually comes out above the tree line into an open landscape of upland meadows, scree slopes and limestone cliffs. Allow eight hours for the ascent if you start from Paliopanayía, around six hours if you can hitch or drive up to Poliána. There's a refuge, operated by the Spárti EOS, two and a half hours below the summit.

Mount Helmós

Just south of the Gulf of Corinth **MOUNT HELMÓS** (also known as Mount Aroánia) is a continuation of the long range of mountains that were last seen at Parnassus before dipping into the gulf. Like Taíyettos, the mountain holds superb Alpine flowers including, even by Greek standards, an unusually high proportion of endemic species. There's a good range of **mountain birds**, too, from the relatively common crag martin and Alpine chough through to large birds of prey such as golden eagle, griffon vulture and Bonelli's eagle.

There are two bases from which to explore the mountain. The first is the town of KALÁVRITA to the west of the mountain; a clear track winds up to the top, some five hours away at 2341m. The other base is the small and more remote village of SÓLOS, on the east of the mountain, a good place to start from for the valley of the **Styx**, the legendary river flowing through Hades.

This latter walk passes through woodlands with masses of flowers in the clearings before arriving, five to six hours later, above Solós, at the **Mavronéri waterfall**, where the Styx pours over into a ravine. Special plants here include a beautiful blue and white columbine *Aquilegia ottonis* – found only here and in Sicily – in the cave behind the waterfall. Another endemic that grows on the limestone crags above the ravine is *Macrotomia densiflora*, whose nearest site is 500km away in Turkey and hangs on here as a remnant from a time when the Med was lower and the plant had a wider range. It's a plant of the borage family, with a dense head of tubular yellow flowers held above its lance-shaped leaves.

Although the most unusual flowers are towards the highest parts of the mountain, even a **gentle stroll** from either base will be rewarding in May, when the woodland clearings are rich in flowers and insects.

PELOPONNESE: ACCESS AND ACCOMMODATION

Epidaurus

The site is firmly on the tourist route and buses run from Athens, Korinthós (Corinth) and Náfplio, from any of which you could make a day trip. Many paths lead up into the surrounding hillsides. The nearest place to stay is the village of LIGOÚRIO, 5km north of the site.

Mystra

SPÁRTI is the nearest town and the transport base for PALEOPANAYÍA (for the walk to Profitías Ilías) and the village of TRÍPI (for the Langádha gorge). Nearer Mystra, there is a hotel (the *Byzantion*, ☎0731.93.309) and rooms in the village of NÉA MISTRÁS, plus campsites on the Spárti-Mystra road.

Mount Helmós

KALÁVRITA has a few cheap hotels, and is linked to the coast at DIAKÓFTO by a memorable rack and pinion railway which runs through the Vouraikós gorge. Halfway along is the village of ZÁHLOROU, the most attractive local base. There are buses along the gorge, too – but they're a pale alternative to the railway.

For the eastern side of the mountain, above SÓLOS, camping is the best option. Buses to SÓLOS run three times a week from AKRÁTA, directly north on the coast; there are campsites there, too.

IONIAN ISLANDS

Since westerly winds bring rain to this part of the Med, the **Ionian islands** are amongst the lushest and greenest of the Greek islands. All of them are good for wildlife in spring and autumn, and better than much of the rest of Greece even in high summer because of their relatively wet climate. **Corfu** is a popular and well known tourist destination, especially for British tourists, and is big enough to have a good range of habitats; **Zákinthos**, the other island described in detail, is another major tourist destination, notable for its breeding **loggerhead turtles**.

Corfu

I have a soft spot for **CORFU**, partly because it was the first Greek island I visited, and partly because, like many other childhood naturalists, I was inspired by Gerald Durrell's classic book *My Family and Other Animals*. Durrell's purple prose is sometimes over the top – though anyone who can cover five pages with a fight between a mantis and a gecko deserves a medal for persistence – and much of the island way of life he describes is now long gone. But the general wildlife that he described is still very much in evidence.

The north of the island holds most of the trump cards. For a start, there's the mountain of **Pantokrátor**, rising to nearly 1000m. Around the lower slopes, and especially the villages of SGOURÁDHES and SPARTÍLAS, the small terraced olive groves are the domain of tortoises and lizards, while spring flowers include a profusion of *Anemone coronaria* in shades of red and purple, sheets of the small blue iris *Gynandriris sisyrinchium*, and many orchids. Higher up the road up the mountain, the village of STRINÍLAS is surrounded by barer habitat, but orchids still grow in the scrub by the road-side, including many man orchids *Aceras anthropophorum*, the yellow flowers of *Orchis provincialis*, and the huge spikes of the giant orchid, *Barlia robertiana*. Other notable flowers include the elusive hanging greenish bells of the fritillary *Fritillaria graeca*, and the many-petalled blue flowers of *Anemone blanda*. At the top of the mountain, crowned by the inevitable radio installation, the rocks are almost bare, but are worth searching for Cretzschmar's bunting which is here on the westernmost edge of its breeding range. Large birds of prey including lammergeir have been recorded, drifting across the strait from the Albanian mountains – but don't count on a sighting.

Anemone blanda

On the coast north of Pantokrátor is **Lake Antionóti,** a saltwater lagoon next to Corfu's most northerly point, Cape Áyias Ekateríni. The lake has reed beds with hunting marsh harriers and you can spot – with patience and luck – breeding little bittern, a tiny heron the size of a jay. This is a good spot, too, for migrating birds in spring and autumn, with egrets, spoonbills and even glossy ibis dropping in from time to time. It's also a worthwhile site for orchids, especially in the fringing woodland to the south of the lake; amongst many others, there are varieties of the tongue orchids *Serapias spp.*, a delicate form of the woodcock orchid *Ophrys scolopax cornuta* with long horns at either side of its lip, and the pink-flowered butterfly orchid *Orchis papilionacea*. North of the lake, the dune slacks at the back of the sand dunes are worth investigating for flowers in spring, and the wonderful *Pancratium maritimum*, looking like a huge white daffodil, flowers here in profusion in the autumn. My only encounter with the highly venomous nose-horned viper *Vipera ammodytes* was here: it was (characteristically) more interested in escape than aggression.

Further west, a series of hill villages lie behind the coastal resort of **Arílas.** This region is marginally damper than the rest of the island, since it faces the moist northwesterly winds, and plants such as bracken *Pteridium aquilinum* grow under the olive groves, creating an odd mix of habitats. This is the classic Corfiot landscape of low hills, small fields, rolling silver-green olive groves, with the tall dark green fingers of the funeral cypress *Cupressus sempervirens* pointing skywards. Look out for hoopoes, especially in the older olive groves, while in spring the whole area is rich in migrating small warblers, nightingales and flycatchers. Evenings can be exciting, for apart from the usual Scops owls, crickets and frogs, the open fields are used by displaying **fireflies** *Luciola lusitanica*, the males steadily flashing as they cruise above the long grass.

Other sites on Corfu

The south and centre of the island should by no means be ignored. For those with time, the following are worth exploring: the lower mountain of **Ayíi Dhéka**, which has similar flowers to Pantokrátor and dense *maquis* and woodland on the slopes leading up to it, behind the coastal resort of BENÍTSES; the saltpans at **Alíkes** near the town of LEFKÍMI in the extreme southeast, good for migrating waders and terns in spring and autumn; and two stretches of **rugged coastline** on the west coast, one south of LIAPÁDHES and one west of ÁYIOS MATTÉOS. In **Corfu Town**, the British cemetery is renowned for its orchids.

Zákinthos

At the southern end of the Ionian archipelago, **ZÁKINTHOS** is a lush island, much reputed for its spring flowers. Most of the western side of the island is rocky, its forest reduced to a few pine plantations and *phrygana* scrub; the middle of the island is productive agricultural land, with olives, vineyards and orchards, while tourist development is concentrated on the south and east coasts.

Developments aside, it is on the south coast that some of the best wildlife is to be seen, notably around **Lagánas**, where the most popular tourist beaches on the island coincide with the most important single Mediterranean site for the endangered **loggerhead turtle** *Caretta caretta*.

TURTLES ON ZÁKINTHOS

The **conflict between tourism and turtles** is no accident; turtles need a sheltered warm and sandy beach on which to lay their eggs for their two-month incubation period, and tourists need the same for holiday play. It just happens that people generate money, and turtles don't. On Zákinthos, they co-exist somewhat uneasily, and turtles have now more or less deserted the main beach at LAGANÁS, moving to smaller beaches further east, notably YÉRAKAS.

Turtles face a formidable gamut of problems when their **breeding season** starts in June. As they approach the beach in the late afternoon, powerboats and jetskis frighten them and in some cases cut them to pieces. By nightfall, any lights or movement on the beach will stop them from hauling themselves ashore to lay their eggs in a nest under the warm sand. The eggs remain there for nearly two months, probably the safest part of the breeding cycle though a beach umbrella can easily spike through the nest. Finally, the tiny hatchlings have to crawl down to the water, a time of extreme danger from predation, and a time when they can easily become disorientated by bright lights from discos and the like. As if this wasn't enough, polythene bags floating in the water can be mistaken for jellyfish and eaten, with fatal results.

There are recent, hopeful signs for the turtles' protection, mostly due to the efforts of the *Sea Turtle Protection Society of Greece* (PO Box 511, 54 Kifissia, 14510 Greece). During the summer they run a **Turtle Information Centre** on the beach and organise volunteers to guard the nests and the beaches at critical times. The more supported they are by tourists, the more effective they will be; and if tourists can resist the temptation to use jetskis, drive motorbikes on the sand or hold loud discos then there is a chance that turtles and people can live side by side. The breeding population is currently around 800 females, half of what it was in 1973, but still a sizeable chunk of the Med population. Access to the beach is forbidden at night, but turtles can be seen swimming offshore, especially in the late afternoon. As well as acting sensitively on Zákinthos itself, visitors can support turtle conservation by **joining the Society** at the above address – membership is currently 2000dr, for which you receive a regular newsletter.

Turtles aside, the south coast of the island has other good wildlife sites. Behind LAGANÁS beach, an extensive **dune system** stretches back to the airport. Typical plants include the marram grass *Arenaria ammophila*, which is the primary dune builder throughout Europe, accumulating sand around its base and so stabilising the whole system. The very prickly sea holly *Eryngium maritimum* and the silvery foliage and yellow flowers of cotton weed *Otanthus maritima* are two other seaside plants, and in spring there's a small member of the pink family *Petrorhagia prolifera*, with tightly packed heads of bright pink flowers. Stable sand dunes are often a good place for butterflies in high summer, and other interesting insects here include the **mole cricket** *Gryllotalpa gryllotalpa*, an extraordinary burrowing insect with a furry body and strong forelegs well adapted to digging.

Still on the south coast, the marshland at LÍMNI KERIOÚ has extensive reed beds alive with with the ringing calls of marsh frogs *Rana ridibunda* and the splashes of diving stripe-necked terrapins *Mauremys caspica*. And a **boat cruise** around the headland at KÉRI on the southern tip of the island may turn up a monk seal, the rarest mammal in the Med, as well as a chance of shearwaters, porpoises and flying fish.

In the rest of the island, **birds** are best during migration time, but Cretzschmar's bunting breeds in rocky places, and the beautiful black-headed bunting in scrub and olive groves; the male of the latter species has a pure black head contrasting with a brilliant yellow breast – it's a late summer visitor, not arriving before mid-May. Around the olive groves, both olivaceous warblers and olive-tree warblers breed – but both are pretty dull and boring, and only serious birders will have the patience to search for the latter, which is decidedly secretive. Lanner falcons have been seen along the west coast – looking like a slender brown peregrine, they're nowhere common.

Other islands in the Ionian

PAXÍ, just south of Corfu, is a tiny island full of olive groves, but with some delightful walks along green lanes between them. It has excellent spring flowers, and stunning views along the cliffs of the west coast.

LEFKÁDHA and KEFALLONIÁ have been omitted simply for lack of space; all evidence suggests that they are just as rich in wildlife as Corfu and Zákinthos. Kefalloniá is particularly worthy of a visit, with the **National Park of Mount Aínos** on its southeastern tip; the park was originally established to protect the Greek fir *Abies cephalonica*, but it's a wild and rocky area with some large birds of prey and good early summer flowers on the limestone outcrops around the mountain. The village of PÓROS is the best base for the National Park, and a very pleasant place in its own right.

IONIAN ISLANDS: ACCESS AND ACCOMMODATION

Corfu

Corfu is well served with hourly ferries from the port of IGOUMENITSA over on the mainland. There are also direct flights from Britain – a useful way to avoid the hassle of Athens airport if you're planning a trip to the Ionian or to Epirus. On the island, buses travel the coastal road, but are less reliable inland around Pantokrátor or the small villages; failing a car, a hired bicycle or moped is a good alternative.

Out of season, most of the north and west coasts (with the major exception of PALEOKASTRÍTSA) are peaceful and there's little problem finding somewhere to stay. In high summer, the whole island is overcrowded, though the north coast still remains reasonably quiet by comparison with the east coast resorts.

Zákinthos

Frequent ferries link the island to KILLÍNI on the Peloponnese, and there are regular flights to CORFU and ATHENS, plus charters direct from Britain. A bus service links the island's south coast to the main town and port of ZÁKINTHOS (or ZANTE), and continues up the east coast to the tourist resort of ALÍKES.

Although LAGANÁS is attractive enough out of season, it's packed with tour companies in the summer. YERAKÁS on the southeastern tip of the island, is (slightly) quieter, and the villages up the east coast north of Zákinthos Town are quieter still, though they probably won't stay that way for long.

THE CYCLADES

The scattered and often tiny islands of the **Cyclades** are formed by the tips of long drowned volcanoes and other mountains. Though beautiful holiday destinations, they aren't the best group of Greek islands for wildlife: most are too small to have a wide habitat range, many are short of water, and some such as Míkonos and Íos have become real tourist honeypots. But amid the group, there are some islands which still retain their tree cover, unspoilt habitats and good animals and plants. Chief amongst these are the islands of **Ándhros** and **Náxos**.

Ándhros

A long and hilly island, **ÁNDHROS** lies off the southern coast of Évvia, at the northern edge of the Cyclades. The interior rises to just over 1000m at Mount Petalón, and its green valleys still have abundant **woodlands**, mostly of sweet chestnut *Castanea sativa* and plane trees *Platanus orientalis*; in spring there is a rich flora under and amongst the trees.

Two rewarding areas to explore are both within easy reach of the main town, HÓRA. The first is the walk up to the ridge around the village of VOURKOTI, 10km northwest of Hóra, which used to be inaccessible to vehicles but has now been linked by a new road; tracks lead up to the monastery of Áyios Nikólaos, and the whole region is very attractive, with mountain streams, woodland, and green terraces around the villages. This variety of habitat makes for good wildlife; most of the usual bird species are here, with Sardinian and a few Ruppell's warblers amongst the low scrub, hoopoes in the woodland, and crested larks and wheatears in open, barer ground.

South of Hóra, the road snakes past the eastern edge of Mount Yerákonas on its way to the beach village of KORTHÍ. The village of FALLIKÁ and the monastery of PANÁHRANDOU both lie on a track which loops off the road – most of it is marked with red dots. The pastures around the villages are full of spring wildflowers, and there are spectacular views up to the ridge of the mountain at 760m, and down the valley to Hóra.

Náxos

The largest of the Cyclades, **NÁXOS** is fertile enough to treat tourists as a luxury rather than a necessity. Its rich soil, especially in the valley bottoms, supports a flourishing agriculture, although the windswept and rugged coastline is in stark contrast to the fertile centre of the island.

The central mountain of Mount Zás is the highest point of the island at 1000m, and the village of FILÓTI lies only an hour's walk from the summit. Wheatears, larks and Cretzschmar's buntings are all typical birds of the hilltops, while the fertile fields below are best in spring when wild flowers such as anemones, poppies and some orchids flourish on the field edges and in the scrubby *phrygana* of poorer soils.

The **coastline** is less accessible, certainly in the south, but a new road should be in place now linking APÓLLON, the most northerly town, with the capital,

HÓRA. This is a jagged and spectacular coast, worth exploring for rocky coves offering good snorkelling in summer. Keep an eye open for **seabirds** such as Cory's shearwaters, and even the very rare Audouin's gull, which is regularly seen in small numbers around the Cyclades – endemic to the Med, it's the only medium-sized gull with a white head that you're likely to encounter; its more specific, close range features are a black ring round its red bill, and green legs .

CYCLADES: ACCESS AND ACCOMMODATION

Ándhros

ÁNDHROS TOWN (HÓRA) or the southerly resort of KORTHÍ are both good bases for the two walks described, although the island is small enough to use almost any of the villages. The main resort of BATSÍ is well placed for inland walks around villages such as KATÁKILOS and ARNÍ, both on the road back to Hóra. Buses exist between the major towns on the island, but they're not frequent; a hired bike makes much the best form of transport. Although this is the second largest of the Cyclades, distances are still small; from the port of GÁVRIO in the north down to KORTHÍ in the south is less than 20km.

Náxos

Most people stay on the coast, either in NÁXOS TOWN itself, or on the beaches to the south. Buses run frequently from the town up to the centre of the island. For staying in the centre of the island, FILÓTI is the best bet, with plenty of rooms and tavernas. For the north, APÓLLON is the obvious choice, although there are small tavernas with rooms to let dotted along the coast. There's a reasonable bus service, especially from the main town.

CRETE

Crete is an isolated island, but its sheer size ensures that it carries a full range of wildlife species; and its ten-million-year isolation from the mainland has meant that plants here have evolved into their own separate species. These **endemics** make up around ten percent of the 2000 or so flowering species on the island. Animals do not evolve into separate species so readily – but the Cretan spiny mouse is at least one species to have done so.

Deforestation, started by the Minoans 4000 years ago and continuing since, has led to a lack of woodlands, but much of the island is covered by *maquis* and *phrigana*, and the high **mountain ranges** hold Alpine plants well into summer, as well as scarce birds of prey. The **Omalós Plateau** and the **Samaria Gorge**, in the east of the island, are outstanding for flowers, while their western counterparts, **Mount Dhíkti** and the **Lasíthi Plateau**, hold the promise of birds of prey as well as rich spring flowers. The **Gulf of Messará** on the south coast contains a variety of different habitats within a small area.

Paeonia clusii

Omalós and the Samarian Gorge

The **OMALÓS PLATEAU** is a fertile upland plain, tucked in at 1000m on the northwestern corner of the White Mountains. The base of the plain is mostly given over to agriculture, used mainly for summer pasturage and cereal production, and it's on the **limestone slopes** surrounding the plateau that the real wildlife interest begins.

Here, May or June are the best months for **flowers,** with the two-tone pink and yellow flowers of the shrub *Daphne sericea* dotted amongst the boulders. Cretan dittany *Orignanum dictamnus* grows in the same place, a low shrub with furry rounded leaves and purple flowers. Nestling amongst the rock crevices, the endemic tiny white cyclamen *Cyclamen creticum* can be seen, while there are occasional clumps of the splendid large white-flowered paeony *Paeonia clusii*, found only on Crete and Kárpathos. Yet another endemic plant is the Cretan alkanet *Anchusa caespitosa*, a member of the borage family, with deep blue flowers amongst a low basal rosette of bristly leaves. **Orchids** of the plateau include the yellow spikes of *Orchis provincialis*, and the fritillary *Fritillaria messanensis*, its nodding head a chequered mixture of brown, purple and green. Higher up the slopes, on the edges of the snowpatches that persist well into the summer, small **bulbs** are evident, including the pink *Crocus seiberi* and the delicate blue stars of *Chionodoxa cretica*, one of the few species from this mostly Asian genus to creep into Europe.

The plateau is good for **birds** too, if you can turn your head upwards from the flowers. Lammergeirs are perhaps commoner here than anywhere else in Europe, and there's a chance of other dramatic birds of prey such as Bonelli's eagle and peregrine falcon.

The two most rewarding areas for plants and birds are at either end of the plateau: the **hillsides to the north**, near where the main road from Haniá drops over a col and down into the plateau, are excellent for plants, and the slopes above the **tourist pavilion** at the head of the Samarian gorge are similarly rewarding, as well as having the odd remnant patch of forest, especially the cypress *Cupressus sempervirens*.

The Samarian Gorge

The **SAMARIAN GORGE** drops down from the Omalós Plateau to the sea at ÁYIA ROÚMELI, a distance of some sixteen kilometres. A fairly leisurely five- or six-hour walk, it gets very crowded in high summer, and is at its best in April and May; however, high spring rainfall in the mountains can make it impassable at this time, since the water can fairly roar through the narrow gaps at the bottom. In the winter, it's closed for the same reason. In summer, it's best to start as early as possible to avoid the crowds and to give time to do it justice.

The best section, in all senses, is the **top of the gorge**; wreathed in early morning mists, clothed in forests and dominated by high white peaks, the views from the steep wooden staircase here – the *Xiloscalon* – are magnificent. You can search the sky for soaring raptors, and the trees for **woodland birds** including crossbills and the yellow and green citril finch. On the steep rockfaces by the path are colourful plants, especially the bright purple of *Aubretia deltoidea* and the deep yellow flowers of a flax, *Linum arboreum*. Two endemic species to note

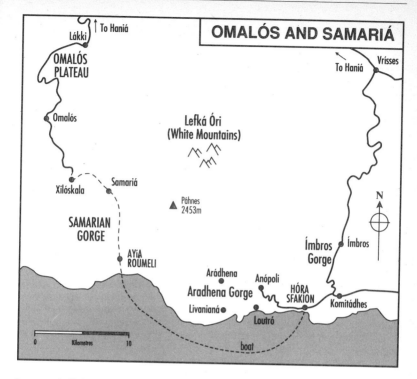

here, and all the way down the gorge, are *Ebenus cretica*, a silver-grey low shrub with masses of spikes of pink pea-shaped flowers, and the Cretan wall lettuce *Petromarula pinnata*; confusingly, this isn't a lettuce at all but is a member of the bellflower family, and has long spikes of blue flowers.

The mountains around the side of the gorge are the home of the **Cretan wild goat**, known locally as the *kri-kri*, the ancestor of the domestic goat and a rare beast; its existence here was a main reason for the gorge being declared a National Park. Always elusive and shy, the males have huge horns, curving backwards in one long sweep. They're evidently hard to photograph – some of the tourist booklets on sale at the top of the gorge have had to resort to rather hysterical photos of stuffed goats posed unrealistically amongst the rocks.

In clearings by the path, the ground can be full of orchids, cyclamens, anemones and fritillaries. The ruined chapel 3km down has great clumps of the **white paeony**, and the few grassy meadows round the deserted village of SAMARIÁ are a mass of wild flowers and butterflies in spring and early summer.

Blue rock thrushes can be seen throughout the gorge, but the real cliff experts are the **crag martins**, which career past the cliffs at great speed on the way to their nests, perched on the vertical rock. Below the village, the cliffs tower high which makes plant-spotting a frustrating experience, and by the time the "iron gates" at the bottom have been passed, the walk degrades into a dull slog across the boulder-strewn river bed down to the sea.

Other nearby sites

The standard route down the Samarian gorge starts with an early bus from HANIÁ, then zips across the plateau, down the gorge, on a boat to HÓRA SFAKÍON, and back to Haniá on the evening bus. This is a very convenient tour but misses out on some good possibilities on the way. The northern fringe of the White Mountains can be explored from the village of LÁKKI, or from OMALÓS itself, which has a few rooms available. To explore the gorge thoroughly, you could try staying in the **tourist lodge** at the top (☎93.237), though it's not cheap.

Samariá is by no means the only gorge in the region – around a dozen come down from the mountains hereabouts to the sea. Two worthwhile extras or high summer alternatives are the **Imbrós Gorge**, which runs from KOMITÁDHES, some 5km east of HÓRA SFAKÍON, to the village of IMBRÓS itself. It has most of the wildlife of Samariá, and though the views are less exciting (since the track goes along the bottom), there are infinitely less people. Even less visited is the **Arádhena Gorge**, which starts near the small village of ANÓPOLI, 12km north-west of HÓRA SFAKÍON and linked to it by two buses a day. The path down into the Arádhena Gorge from the village is a rather hair-raising mule track down the almost sheer rock face.

Lasíthi and Mount Dhíkti

Away at the other end of the island, the **LASÍTHI PLATEAU** is another upland plain like Omalós, but lower, more fertile from the rich soil washed down from its surrounding mountain ring, and hence more heavily cultivated. Tourist buses regularly climb up the hill from ÁYIOS NIKÓLAOS to see the windmills, though they've now almost entirely been replaced by diesel or electric pumps.

The peak of the **wild flowers** on the plateau comes a little earlier – late April or May are the best times. The field edges are rich in colourful species such as the widespread tassel hyacinth *Muscari comosum*, and undisturbed land will have *Anemone coronoria* in a variety of colour forms from white through pink to purple. Look closely at these anemones, though, for some of them will turn out to be large **buttercups** *Ranunculus asiaticus*, an Asian species which (in Crete) comes in white, yellow or pink. The petals of buttercups always have green sepals underneath, the remains of the flower bud; the petals of anemones are not really petals at all and rise nakedly from the stem without any sepals below them. Other typical plants of the field edges include wild gladiolus *Gladiolus segetum* with its delicate spikes of pink flowers, poppies and chrysanthemums. Corn buntings are abundant around the fields, and quail call incessantly from the arable crops.

At the sides of the plateau, the **foothills** of the mountains come down in a jumble of limestone rocks and shrubby *maquis*. The sides of the well trodden path up to the Dhiktean cave from the village of PSIHRÓ have many of the plants of rougher, thinner soils, including *Iris unguicularis*, an iris with solitary large purple flowers, each with a yellow and white centre. Orchids are here in abundance, especially the large flowers of *Ophrys tenthredenifera* and the broad pink lips of *Orchis papilionacea*. All the usual scrub warblers such as Sardinian warbler are here, along with hoopoes and woodchat shrikes. The Dhiktean cave is on the northern flank of Mount Dhíkti itself, so large birds of prey will occasionally drift across; both griffon vultures and Lammergeirs can be seen, plus the odd eagle.

Climbing **MOUNT DHÍKTI** is not for the fainthearted or those without a strong sense of direction. Marc Dubin in *Greece on Foot* says that he "spent a day being buzzed by flies, ripped by thorns and branches, being impaled by jagged limestone, tripping and falling on smooth limestone, and panting from thirst". And he's not normally one to complain. The highest point of Dhíkti is variously described as Psári Mádara, Aféndi Hristós or Mt Dhíkti, depending on which map you look at; the only thing that doesn't change is its height, which is 2148m. The rewards of the climb in spring are many of the **Alpine flowers** described above the Omalós Plateau, including crocus, paeony and cyclamens, and the wild rocky country holds vultures, eagles and other specialist mountain birds such as Alpine chough. You don't need to go all the way to the top to find all of these; one of the best-described tracks heads south from the Lasíthi village of ÁYIOS KONSTANTÍNOS. Carry water with you, and be prepared for changeable weather in spring and autumn.

Lató, Mália and Mount Youktas

On the road from Lasíthi to ÁYIOS NIKÓLAOS, the ancient site of **LATÓ** is renowned as one of the most flower-filled in all of Greece. There's a mass of colour in spring and notable species include the Cretan wall lettuce, growing on the rocky heights above the site, and the four-spotted orchid *Orchis quadripunctata*, never a common species, which has delicate pink flowers appropriately spotted on the lip.

MÁLIA, back along the north coast towards IRÁKLION, is sandwiched between mountains and the shore; the coast itself is good for spring flowers, and a small and rapidly disappearing marshland between the Minoan site and the modern town of the same name is rewarding for **birds**. There's a chance of unusual species such as pratincole, purple heron and fan-tailed warbler here; it's one of the last freshwater marshes on the island.

Nearly a quarter of the world population of **Eleonora's falcons** breed on islands off the northern coast of Crete; the coast around **SITIA** is a well-known place for seeing them, often hunting in flocks in the early evening. **MOUNT YOUKTAS**, south of IRÁKLION, is another excellent spot, like Samariá and Lasíthi, for mountain plants and birds of prey.

The Gulf of Messará

The ancient Minoan site of **Phaestos** (Festós) is a real naturalist highlight of this central part of the southern coast, along with the whole coastline and surrounding *maquis* and *phrygana* scrub from AYÍA GALÍNI west to MONÍ PREVELÍ. Visit early in the year if you can; the spring comes in March to this coast and things are pretty burnt out by June. The summer is horrendously crowded, too.

PHAESTOS has almost everything for the naturalist in spring, and its largely unrestored Minoan ruins are magnificently set, dominating the plains below. Its position is ideal for watching **bird migration** in spring, with marsh harriers moving through as well as perching birds such as flycatchers, wheatears and pipits. The low hills around the site, and especially between it and the neighbouring site of Áyia Triádha, are superb for **spring flowers**. The endemic Cretan orchid *Ophrys cretica*, with two white marks on its purple lip, grows here, along with a host of other orchid species under and amongst the fragrant herbs of thyme, sage and rosemary. The striking blue flowers of love-in-a-mist *Nigella spp.*, more familiar as a garden plant, are worth searching for; once the flower is over, the plant develops an extraordinary inflated fruit surrounded by a crown of deeply dissected bracts. The yellow pea flowers of brooms and the pink and white of *Cistus* species make this an exceptionally colourful place, whilst butterflies such as the scarce swallowtail *Iphiclides podalirius* and the green hairstreak *Callophrys rubi* drift from flower to flower.

The River Geros runs past the nearby site of **ÁYIA TRIÁDHA**, and although the marshes have been recently reduced by drainage, this area is still a magnet for birds. Herons, terns and waders can be seen on the river at migration time, the bushes are alive with warblers, and with luck **penduline tits** can be seen building their flask-shaped nests amongst the waterside shrubs.

ÁYIA GALÍNI, for all its summer crowds, is set amongst low headlands of coastal *phrygana*, and is well placed for access to small fields and olive groves to the north of the town. There's a particularly good walk over the coastal hills to the west, towards the little beach at ÁYIOS YIÓRYIOS, with rampant spring flowers including the giant orchid *Barlia robertiana*, and the local Cretan form of the late spider orchid *Ophrys fuciflora maxima*, a large plant with beautiful lip markings. The huge yellow umbels of giant fennel *Ferula communis* are very evident, and so are the downy yellow-flowered shrubs of the Jerusalem sage *Phlomis fruticosa*. **Scrub warblers** thrive in this habitat; most are Sardinian warblers, but the rare and localised Ruppell's warbler is relatively common here, its black cap offset by rather a natty white moustache.

Spider orchid
Ophrys fuciflora maxima

To the east of ÁYIA GALÍNI, the river flows in past a series of caves high in the cliffs. Lesser kestrels and Alpine swifts both breed here, nightingales thrive in the marshy shrubs, and hoopoes can be seen flashing through the olive groves like huge pink, black and white butterflies. The surrounding hills are also good for anemones, irises, orchids and other spring flowers.

Some way along the gulf to the west, the monastery at **MÓNI PREVÉLI** has less visitors, and the added bonus of nearby seacliffs on which blue rock thrushes live. This whole area between the monastery and nearby PLÁKIAS has a good variety of habitats, and is less developed than Áyia Galíni; the vegetation of the *phrygana* is similar to that described above; Ruppell's warblers are numerous in the scrub, along with nightingales and the occasional golden oriole in taller trees, and the gorge of Kotsifoú on the approach road to Plákias has a chance of large birds of prey.

CRETE: ACCESS AND ACCOMMODATION

Buses are the main form of rural transport in Crete, reliable and cheap; getting off the beaten track, it's worth hiring a moped or scooter – and walking, too.

Omalós and Samariá

For a day trip to the gorge, HANIÁ is the obvious base, with lots of rooms to rent and the first bus out to Omalós and the gorge at around 6am. For a more leisurely circuit, the village of LÁKKI, north of Omalós, or the Tourist Lodge at the top of the gorge have already been mentioned. HÓRA SFAKÍON is a good place to stay if you don't want to flog straight back to Haniá after walking the gorge, and is also the best base for the Imbrós and Arádhena gorges. There's no shortage of rooms and some reasonable restaurants along the seafront.

Lasíthi and Mount Dhíkti

Most visitors to Lasíthi come by bus from the resorts of the north coast around MÁLIA and ÁYIOS NIKÓLAOS. For a more leisurely exploration of the plateau, stay in one of the villages up there such as TZERMIÁDHO or ÁYIOS YIÓRYIOS; most of the plateau villages have rooms or even hotels.

For the ancient site of LÁTO, the choice is either to brave the crowds of ÁYIOS NIKÓLAOS or to stay in nearby KRITSA, which is wonderful out of season.

Gulf of Messará

There's a string of places to stay along the coast, from ÁYIA GALÍNI itself to smaller and less crowded resorts such as PLÁKIAS to the west. Transport between the two detours inland via SPÍLI, a mountain village on the way to Rethímnon; staying here would be a good move in early summer, for the flowers are later here than on the coast and there are good birds in the hills above.

For PHAESTOS, the choice is to stay in ÁYIA GALÍNI again, or on the coast further south; the plain to the north is dominated by the agricultural town of TIMBÁKI and appears to consist solely of polytunnels growing tomatoes, aubergines and the like. South of Phaestos, resorts such as MÁTALA and KALAMÁKI are convenient, though the caves of the former have long since ceased to be the legendary retreat for resting travellers.

THE EASTERN AEGEAN

The **EASTERN AEGEAN** islands hug the Turkish coast and so show a peculiarly Asian influence in their wildlife. From the yellow azaleas of Lésvos and the blue hyacinths of Samos, down to the turban buttercups and agamas of Rhodes, the islands are full of species which just creep over the water.

As with all islands, the bigger the land mass the greater the range of species, and the three islands picked here are all large ones. **Rhodes** and **Kós** both have long mountainous spines, and are good for a visit out of season; in the crowded summer they become very dried up anyway. **Lésvos** has been considerably less developed for tourism, and with its southern mountain rising to nearly 1000m, has a good range of habitats; it's good for migratory birds, and features a number of Asian bird species.

Rhodes

Although most of the northern tip of **RHODES** (RÓDHOS), and especially
RHODES TOWN, has been mercilessly developed, good wildlife awaits in the
mountainous interior and the south. The so-called Butterfly Valley at
PETALOÚDHES (see below) is a good place to start exploring the wooded and
rugged interior of the island, though the scenery gets even better around the
villages of ELEOÚSSA at the foot of **Mount Profitis Ilías** and EMBÓNAS, near
to **Mount Atáviros**.

The lower reaches of both these mountains are wooded with pines and some
dense *maquis* scrub, and in spring a special prize is the endemic Rhodes paeony
Paeonia rhodia, with a small white flower. Under these woods in spring *Cyclamen
persicum* is to be found – one of the finest of all the **cyclamens** with its large,
veined leaves and delicate flowers of white or pale pink. Orchids of the pine
woods include *Limodorum abortivum*, a handsome purple plant which has no
leaves, gathering its energy by parasitising the roots of the pine trees. On the
edges of the woodland, the more open scrub and roadside verges are good for
anemones and yet more orchids; amongst the commoner **butterflies**, look out
for a scarcer one – the **southern festoon** *Zerynthis polyxena* which flies in April
and May, resembling a small tailless swallowtail, to which it is related. Near
EMBÓNAS, a forest of ancient and almost pure **cypress** *Cupressus sempervirens*
is important enough to have been declared a "protected national monument".

The hillsides around LÍNDHOS, the island's major resort, have abundant wild
flowers in spring, when the rocky gullies are particularly worth investigating for
rockroses *Cistus spp.*, brooms and all the aromatic plants of the Greek *phrygana*.
In summer, however, the area is overrun with coachloads from Rhodes Town.
Things are more peaceful further south, where the seaside village of YENÁDHI
makes a good base. The surrounding landscape is a lovely mix of small fields and
olive groves, interspersed with flowery *phrygana* and tall cypresses *Cupressus
sempervirens*. As elsewhere on the island, the turban buttercup *Ranunculus asiaticus* grows on the field margins and roadsides; an Asian species, it's found in
yellow or white on Crete, but on Rhodes is a quite astonishing scarlet.

Inland from Yenádhi, towards the village of PROFÍLIA, anemones, irises, and
yet more **orchids** are common, and the ground rises so that a visit as late as May
could still be profitable for flowers. The orchids include the uncommon *Ophrys*

BUTTERFLY VALLEY

One of the outstanding wildlife features of Rhodes is now a major tourist attraction
– the so-called "Butterfly Valley" of **Petaloúdhes**. Strictly speaking, this should be
called "Moth Valley" (though the tourist packaging is understandable), as each
summer it is used as a gathering place by literally millions of a brightly coloured
moth, the Jersey tiger *Euplagia quadripunctaria*.

They gather here because the valley has a permanent spring and is therefore the
coolest and moistest place in high summer on an island which is otherwise dry and
arid. From all over the island, and perhaps from Turkey too, the moths fly to roost
on the damp rock faces, where they stay in huddled in **aestivation** (the summer
equivalent of hibernation) until autumn; then they mate, fly out, lay their eggs, and
finally die. July and August are the best months to see this, one of the most extraordinary wildlife sights of the Med. Unfortunately, everybody else goes there too.

rheinholdii, with a maroon and white lip, as well as more frequent species such as *Ophrys lutea* and *Ophrys speculum*.

Dragon arum
Drancunculus vulgaris

Another plant of the roadsides is the striking dragon arum *Drancunculus vulgaris*, a tall plant with a spotted stem and a typical arum lily flower, a huge purple "petal" encircling a central spike. This plant is pollinated by flies, and lures them by its foul scent which resembles rotting meat; attractive no doubt to flies, but repellent to humans. YENÁDHI also seems to have abundant **tree frogs** *Hyla arborea*, their night-time croaks blending with the calls of Scops owls, which are also common around the village. The **agama** *Agama stellio* is to be seen, too, a lizard with a distinctly prehistoric look about it, grey and spiny with a series of pale diamonds down its back; it's relatively common in the Dodecanese, but is found nowhere else in Europe, hence its alternative name of Rhodes dragon. Look for it on any dry walls and old stone ruins.

Further south still, the remote village of PLIMÍRI at the tip of the island is surrounded by more open country, hunted over by marsh harriers and buzzards, the latter in their confusing pale ginger plumage typical of the eastern race. There is (or at least was) a wonderful and isolated fish restaurant here. Right round on the western coast of the island, MONOLITHOS is impressive, too, with high cliffs and clear water below. Blue rock thrushes breed here, and it's a good spot in late spring and summer to watch out for the **Eleonora's falcons** that breed on the small islands offshore.

Kós

Kós is like a smaller version of Rhodes: its capital, KÓS TOWN is the crowded equivalent of Rhodes Town, and the east coast resort of KARDHÁMENA is just as packed out in summer as Líndhos, although far less beautiful. As on Rhodes, the central mountain spine and the less developed south of the island are the places to go to seek out wildlife.

A good place to start is the village of PILÍ, high on the western slopes of pine-covered Mount Dhíkeas, and surrounded by terraced fields and olive groves. Tortoises are common here, the grassy verges are rich in anemones *Anemone coronoria* in shades of red, pink and blue, and most of the common orchids of the eastern Med can be found, especially the very tall spikes of *Orchis italica*, with a dense flowerhead of pale pink flowers. The scrub and woodlands are well used by migratory and some resident birds; **nightingales** and **whitethroats** pass through in large numbers in spring, while the woods are home to hoopoes and orioles, as well as a few pairs of Ruppell's warbler. Any trip to Pilí could well end up in one of the tavernas in the old (higher) village of ZÍA, looking across to the island of Kalímnos; the sunsets are stunning.

On the coast below Pilí are the **saltpans and marshes** between TIGÁKI and MASTHÁRI. This is a damp and soggy area, and access to it involves a certain amount of creative trespass, but the rewards are there at the right time of year. **Flamingoes** winter here in small numbers, and non-breeding birds linger on until the early summer; other specialist saltmarsh waders such as avocets and black-winged stilts can be seen, along with herons and marsh harriers. Since Kós is on the main flyway up the Turkish coast, spring and autumn passage can turn up anything, and with luck **white storks** and **pelicans** may drop in on their way up to their breeding grounds in northern Turkey and eastern Europe. Between the saltpans and the sea, low-lying grassy areas are rich in flowers, including (unusually) orchids growing right down to the back of the sand dunes.

Aptly named KÉFALOS is at the "head" of the leaping dolphin shape of the island, down on the southwestern tip. The ruined basilica overlooking the beach at ÁYIOS STÉFANOS has plentiful agamas *Agama stellio* and the smaller Erhard's wall lizard *Podarcis erhardii*. South of Kéfalos a rough road leads down over the mountainous tip of the island, where *maquis* and *phrygana* habitats are full of colour in spring; there are huge plants of the mirror orchid *Ophrys speculum*, and flowery meadows with oxeye daisies *Chrysanthemeum leucanthemum* and the small scarlet flowers of pheasants eye *Adonis annua*, a relation of the buttercups. Blue rock thrushes are common around these cliffs and hillsides, and it's always worth watching the sea, especially in the late afternoon, for passing Cory's shearwaters; Eleonora's falcons have been seen here, too.

Lésvos

Lésvos is the third largest of all the Greek islands, and at first sight seems to consist entirely of olive groves. Further investigation, however, reveals some rocky volcanic gullies and hills, a couple of sizeable mountains, and saltpans at the head of the gulf of Kallóni.

The highest of these mountains, **Mount Olympus** (Óros Ólimbos) rises to 950m, and its pine-clad slopes are rewarding for both birds and flowers. The place to make for is the village of AYIÁSSOS, on its northern slopes; cyclamens and fritillaries can be found under the pines above the village, especially *Fritillaria pontica*, a plant with green and brown flowers and no trace of the chequered markings found on most other fritillaries. There's a second chance at the flowers in the **autumn**, for this area is rich in late-flowering cyclamens and the autumn crocus *Colchicum variegatum*, which pushes its pink flowers up until December. Spring orchids on the edge of the pines include *Orchis anatolica*, a predominantly Asian species, a variety of *Ophrys* species including *O. rheinholdii* and, with extreme good fortune in early summer, the very rare *Comperia comperiana* at one of its few known sites. The **bird** to look out for here is **Kruper's nuthatch**, which lives primarily in the pine forests of Turkey but has made it across to the island; a small nuthatch with a black and white head, it has a distinctive brown smudge on its breast.

On the lowlands of the island the olive rules supreme; the soil under them is dry and bare by summer, but carpeted with anemones and arable weeds in spring. At the head of the **Gulf of Kallóni**, just south of the town of the same name, a complex of **saltpans** is worthwhile for waterside birds including both black and white storks, avocets, and black-winged stilts; the handsome ruddy shelduck, a large and scarce ginger coloured duck, has been regularly spotted. Amongst the coastal marshes, along with the usual profusion of frogs, toads and terrapins, the very large yellow and white flowers of *Iris spuria* can be seen.

Rocky volcanic hillsides are a feature of the island; some of the best are around the village of E**ressós**, at the remote western end of the island. The bare hills above the village hold cinereous bunting, an Asian species which keen birders will doubtless wish to search for; other birds of this habitat include larks, wheatears, Cretzschmar's bunting and rock nuthatch, the latter usually seen fossicking noisily around broken cliffs and ruined buildings. Lanner falcons, looking like a small brown peregrine, hunt the hillside, feeding mostly off chukars, species of partridge. Gullies running up into the hills are usually greener and hold denser vegetation; the fragrant yellow azalea *Rhododendron lutea* is found on these stream beds; Lésvos is its only European site.

Other Aegean islands

The island of **SÁMOS** is just as close to Turkey as Lésvos for its Asian specialities and even more mountainous and lush; it's particularly noted for its spring flowers, especially in the undeveloped western end of the island around Mount Kérkis.

Many other of the smaller islands are too dry to have really varied wildlife, but **KÁLIMNOS**, just off the north coast of Kós, has some good rocky hillsides and a large colony of Eleonora's falcons on its nearby islet of **Télendhos**.

EASTERN AEGEAN ISLANDS: ACCESS AND ACCOMMODATION

On all these islands, a **hired moped, car or motorbike** is a real bonus for exploring off the beaten track – bus services tend to be skeletal away from main tourist routes.

Rhodes
Buses are good and reliable on the routes from RHODES TOWN to LÍNDHOS and MONÓLITHOS, the service comes to grinding halt in the south and centre of the island. Hitching is possible, though limited by infrequent traffic. Of the smaller villages mentioned, EMBÓNAS and YENÁDHI both have rooms and tavernas.

Kós
KARDHÁMENA is a good base for the east coast, but only outside peak season. PILÍ, up in the hills, has rooms and tavernas. For the south end of the island, the beach resort of KAMÁRI has plenty of rooms, while the town of KÉFALOS offers a less touristed base.

Lésvos
The sheer size of the island, and the indifference of some of its roads, make for slow travelling, although regular buses link the main centres. AYIÁSSOS is easily reached by bus from MITILÍNI, and the saltpans on the GULF OF KALLÓNI are just off the main road from Kallóni to Mitilíni. ERESSÓS is accessible by bus from Kallóni, and is on the road down to the fast developing resort of SKÁLA ERESSOÚ, where there is plenty of accommodation.

---

information and publications

For general information, the *National Tourist Organisation of Greece (EOT)* is the obvious first step; there are offices overseas (in Britain: 195 Regent St, London W1; ☎071/734 5997) and in major Greek towns and resorts. In smaller Greek towns, you can get information from the local Tourist Police. For more detailed information on walking in the mountains, contact the *Hellenic Alpine Club (EOS)*; they have offices in many of the "trailhead" towns for the mountain ranges, can provide good information about routes and refuges, and can sometimes help with maps. Their head office is in Athens at 7 Karayíoryi Servías.

For specific wildlife information, the *Hellenic Society for the Protection of Nature* (24 Nikis St, Athens, 10557 Greece) is an active group. The bird angle is covered by the *Hellenic Ornithological Society* (PO Box 64052, 157 01 Greece). Both these groups are voluntary, and welcome donations; they would also be glad of any records of wildlife after your trip.

MAPS

The best general maps are published by **Freytag and Berndt**, with a road map of the whole country at 1:650,000 and a dozen more detailed maps

of selected areas at anything from 1:100,000 to 1:300,000. They're widely available outside Greece.

More detailed maps are hard to get hold of because of military restrictions; the mountaineering magazine **Korfes** has produced a series of maps for some of the alpine areas at 1:50,000; try their office at Platía Ayíou Vlassíou 16, Aharnés, Athens.

BOOKS

Flowers The best introductory guide is *Flowers of Greece and the Aegean* by Huxley and Taylor (Chatto & Windus, 1977). For more detailed coverage, *Flowers of Greece and the Balkans* by Oleg Polunin (OUP, 1987) is excellent but heavier in both senses.

Birds Use general guides for identification. For Crete, *Easter birdwatching in Crete* is a useful pamphlet by Stephanie Coghlan (25 Thorpe Lane, Almondbury, Huddersfield, HD5 8TA). *Let's Look at Northeast Greece* is another useful booklet for Thessaloníki and the north by Michael Shepherd (*Ornitholidays*, 1/3 Victoria Drive, Bognor Regis, Sussex).

Walking There are two excellent English books, both by *Rough Guide* authors: *The Mountains of Greece* by Tim Salmon (Cicerone Press) and *Greece on Foot* by Marc Dubin (Cordee Press).

CHAPTER THREE

ITALY

Nowhere in Italy is very far from a range of hills or mountains. The **Apennine** chain is the main feature of the mainland, forming the backbone of the peninsula and providing a scenic backdrop to many coastal areas. Heights hover around 1200m for the most part, rising in the bigger massifs – the Gran Sasso and Maiella – to 2500m and above. Most of the country's population live in towns and cities outside the upland areas, leaving large virtually uninhabited tracts of land in between. The biggest of these are in the Abruzzo – the mountainous heartland of central Italy – and in the deep south, for centuries the poorest and most neglected part of the country. Between the extremes of mountains and coast lies a patchwork of habitats – perhaps some of the most varied landscapes in Europe.

Virtually all of the Italian countryside, however, has been much changed over the last two thousand years. **Drainage** of swampy areas such as the Pontine marshes south of Rome and the Po Delta began in Roman times and peaked under Mussolini; the **ship building** of city-states such as Genoa stripped the Ligurian Alps of much of their forests; **marble quarrying** over the centuries has remodelled parts of the Apuan Alps behind Pisa; and finally, **forest fires** have taken a heavy tolls of the coastal *maquis* vegetation in recent years.

For all this wear and tear, however, Italy has preserved numerous unspoilt habitats. Upland areas everywhere are particularly good for **wild flowers**, mingling Ice Age relics, stray alpines, trans-Adriatic specimens, and a host of rarities and endemics. Mammals thrive also – despite the attention of hunters – most notably the **bears** and **wolves** of the central Apennines. And **birdlife**, both indigenous and migratory, is excellent, particularly on the coastal marshes and lagoons, with **birds of prey** – though in decline – numerous and varied.

Climate and land use

Italy has a typical Med climate of dry summers and cool winters, with most rain falling in winter, often in intense bursts. August temperatures can be cruel – anything up to 40°C in Sicily and the southern plains. Drought is an ever-increasing problem in such areas – parts of Sicily have seen no rain now for two years – and virtually all of the south sports a parched appearance for much of the summer. Elsewhere, the Po valley and the Venetian lagoon are peculiarly prone to fog and drizzle. In winter, snow lies on the Apennines – and sometimes on coastal areas – often lingering as late as June and reappearing at the end of October. Though milder, the lowlands are occasionally prone to debilitating winds – either the icy blast of the *tramontana* from the north, or the scorching heat of the sirocco from North Africa. For all these extremes, spring – and to a lesser extent autumn – have almost perfect climates, spurs to butterflies, insects and an incredible profusion of wild flowers.

Land use on **the coast** has been dominated by tourism, an activity which in thirty years has seen virtually all of Italy's once pristine coastline lost to property speculators. The sea has suffered in tandem, pollution and crowds having driven shy animals like the monk seal to the more inaccessible parts of Sardinia. **Low fertile areas**, intensively farmed for centuries, now endure the widespread use of chemical fertilisers and pesticides – leading to bumper crops, massive surpluses and appallingly polluted rivers. On the **higher ground**, in addition to grazing and forestry, **hunting** is a major activity, involving about two million Italians – five times as many as all the members of environmental groups put together.

WHEN AND WHERE TO GO

Although most sites hold something of interest throughout the year, April to June is the best period for wildlife. August is hot, crowded and expensive. The mountains are most accessible from May to October, but the weather can always turn nasty, and the Apennines have a reputation for sudden storms. Another hazard is the army of hunters who take to the country in full force between August 17 and March 11; nature rambling outside designated reserves in this period is often frustrating and at times dangerous. Tuesdays and Fridays are officially non-hunting days, throughout the year; Sundays are especially awful, with the combination of picnickers and hordes of hunters.

Public transport in Italy is cheap, if not always frequent or reliable. A good rail network connects the main urban centres; less frequent services run to more isolated towns. Buses go to most country sites, but a hired car is an asset in remote spots such as the interior of Sardinia. For hitching, minor roads are generally easier than major ones.

The main sites described are:

● **LIGURIA** A thin coastal strip sandwiched between the Maritime Alps and the sea. **Portofino** offers superb walks through a variety of habitats from *maquis* scrub to beech and chestnut forest.

● **TUSCANY** A very productive region, with a high mammal population in the **Maremma** and rich bird life in the lagoons of **Orbetello** and **Lake Massaciuccoli**. At **Orecchiella**, up in the Apennines, there are excellent flowers and first-class hiking country.

● **PO DELTA** The delta itself offers excellent bird-watching all year round, and there's a terrific swamp forest at the WWF reserve of **Punte Alberete**.

● **ROME AND AROUND** There are forests around the volcanic **Lake Vico**, and the **Abruzzo National Park** has abundant wildlife, including wolves and bears. The **Circeo National Park** includes the island of Zannone and packs in a great variety of habitats.

● **BAY OF NAPLES Capri** is an important stop-over for migrating birds, and the old lava fields of **Vesuvius** are surprisingly rich in both flowers and birds.

● **GARGANO** This limestone peninsula juts out into the Adriatic, and has a staggering variety of plant life; the coastal marshes just to the south have abundant bird life, especially in spring.

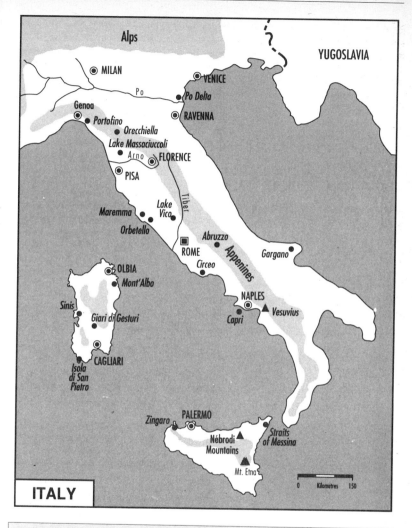

ITALY

● **SICILY** There is impressive though inadequately protected bird migration across the **Straits of Messina**; **Mount Etna**, a proposed national park, has a bizarre lanscape and vast variety of flora – plus birds of prey; the heavily forested **Madonie and Nebrodi Mountains** are again impressive for birds of prey; and the **Zingaro reserve** is one of the few unspoilt parts of the scenic northern coastline.

● **SARDINIA**. The saltpans and coastal lagoons of **Cagliari** and the **Sinis peninsula** have a fine range of birds including flamingoes. **Mont'Albo** and the **Isola di San Pietro** are both outstanding for birds of prey, and the cork oak forest of **Giara di Gesturi** provides a lovely setting for its wild horses.

LIGURIA

The coastal strip of **Liguria** offers typical Mediterranean habitats plus the montane landscapes of the Ligurian Alps, which are traversed by a fine long-distance footpath, the Alta Via del Monti Liguri. The natural highlight of these generally overlooked mountains is the proposed regional park north of Genoa, the Parco delle Capanne di Marcarolo; a vast plateau of lakes and forests of oak and beech, it has fairly widespread foxes, badgers, hares and wild boars. East of Genoa, the coast is dominated by the *autostrada*, but the little promontory of **Portofino** stands out with its woodlands, scrubby hillsides and rocky coastline. The headland lies on an important migration route, and is the chief point of respite for migrating birds between the urban desolation of Genoa and La Spezia.

Portofino and around

Few visitors to the bay at **PORTOFINO** realise that there is a fascinating nature reserve stretching all the way over the headland and down to CAMOGLI on the other side. The area has many signposted walks, and is accessible by both sea and land. Starting from Camogli, walk or take the bus up to SAN ROCCO, where the almost tropical gardens – a riot of colour with palms, bougainvillea, hibiscus and the blue trumpets of morning glory *Ipomoea* – give way to woodlands of sweet chestnut *Castanea sativa* and, at the top of the hill, beech *Fagus sylvaticus*.

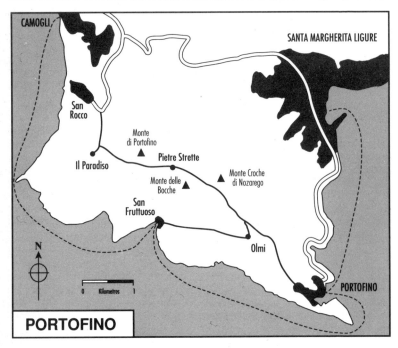

A good path leads up the hillside to IL PARADISO, on the western edge of the ridge that runs towards Portofino. Shortly after this, the path opens up with magnificent views down to the sea. The numerous springs on the hillside should save the bother of carrying heavy water bottles. The woods are rich in **mammals**, although some early-morning patience is needed to see them well. Foxes are common, while up in the trees there are both red squirrels and beech martens. **Bird life** is interesting without being spectacular: hobbies, looking like small peregrine falcons with smart orange thighs, hunt the headlands, and wrynecks are to be seen in the woods.

The path continues along the ridge at around 500m, past the picnic site at Pietre Strette, and then begins to head downhill towards Portofino. If you feel in need of refreshment, stop at the *Trattoria Olmi*, which does good food at less than Portofino average prices. At this stage you're presented with the choice of descending through olive groves to Portofino, or crossing the low south-facing *maquis* to the delightful fishing hamlet of SAN FRUTTUOSO, from where boats depart to Camogli and Portofino.

The **flowers** on the headland deserve special mention, since this area lies on the meeting point of the Mediterranean and Alpine ecosystems. Despite forest fires that have killed off many of the pines *Pinus pinaster*, there are some 700 plant species in the woodland and on the lower *maquis* hillsides, including some impressive specimens of the tongue orchid *Serapias cordigera*, flowering in May amongst the aromatic shrubs.

Tongue orchid
Serapias cordigera

Cinque Terre

South of Portofino, virtually on the northern outskirts of La Spezia, is the **Cinque Terre** (Five Lands), another lovely stretch of coastline broken by five popular but still charming villages. Cliffs and ancient terracing fall to the sea, best seen on the marked path between the villages – a twelve-hour trek easily broken down into short stages.

The vegetation here is as luxurious as at Portofino, and the local micro-climates support fauna as specialised as the flora. You might find the rare river crab *Potoman edule* and the Hydromantes *italicus* newt, both species confined solely to the Cinque Terre's coastline.

LIGURIA: ACCESS AND ACCOMMODATION

The headland can be explored from either PORTOFINO itself or, as described, from CAMOGLI. Camogli is on the rail line down from GENOA, and both are accessible by boat. This is a well-touristed area, and prices in and around Portofino are somewhat above average.

TUSCANY

Everyone is aware of the cultural diversity of **Tuscany**, but few people know it as a region with much to offer in the way of wildlife. In the hills north of Pisa, however, the natural park at **Orecchiella** has upland forests and mountains; the extensive reed beds of **Lake Massaciuccoli**, near Pisa, are excellent for birds, while further south are two more sites for birds, at the **Maremma** regional park and the WWF reserve at **Orbetello**.

Orecchiella

Many of the mountains in the Apuan Alps north of Pisa and Lucca have been irreversibly altered by centuries of marble quarrying. Further inland, however, is the little-known park of **ORECCHIELLA**, in a relatively unspoilt part of the Apennines just north of an area called the Garfagnana.

Tracks and paths radiate out from CORFINO, a village at the base of some impressively craggy mountains about 15km north of CASTELNUOVO DI GARFAGNANA. **Three walks** laid out in 1985 with the aid of the wildlife magazine *Airone* are clearly signposted. Walk no. 1 is a five-hour circular trek from Corfino, linking to the visitors' centre 10km on; the park's resident pair of golden eagles can often be seen early in the morning on this walk, especially near PANIA DI CORFINO. The other two walks both start from the centre itself. Not-so-early risers may find walk no. 2 more amenable; it passes through forests of oak and beech and ends with a stroll down through grassy meadows into the river valley. Walk no. 3 is longer and goes through more remote country; there's a chance of seeing some really spectacular mammals on this one – including red deer, mouflon and wolves – but it's best taken as a two-day trek with an overnight stop at one of the mountain refuges. Apart from the eagles, native **birds of prey** include kestrels, buzzards and sparrowhawks, and honey buzzards pass through on spring and autumn migration. The smaller birds provide few surprises, although the colourful wallcreeper can occasionally be seen on the crags.

The **flowers** are spectacular throughout, at their best in late spring and early summer. A trek up the mountain isn't strictly necessary; the grassy slopes around the visitors' centre are rich in colourful orchids and forget-me-nots. Walk no. 2 is notable for the red paeonies *Paeonia mascula* on the slopes of La Ripa, with the martagon lily *Lilium martagon* lower down; on the rocks lining the river valley there's the endemic *Globularia incanescens*, a low matted plant with rounded blue flowerheads. **Fungi** are a special feature of the park; Italians, like all Europeans apart from the British, are well aware of the tastier varieties, and it's worth sampling some of the more unusual mushrooms in local restaurants.

Lake Massaciuccoli

LAKE MASSACIUCCOLI, part of the Natural Park of Migliarino and San Rossore, is one of Italy's best-known birding sites, with outstanding reed-bed and open-water habitats. The Italian bird protection society LIPU has built hides at the end of raised walkways crossing the reed beds, making it easy to get good views.

Over 250 bird species have been recorded around the lake, of which about 50 stay on to breed. **Kingfishers** are fond of perching on the walkway rails, the stunning blue of their back feathers only exposed as they fly away. The reed beds hold the shy crakes and rails, as well as almost the entire range of the confusingly similar *Acrocephalus* warblers – Cetti's, Savi's, reed, sedge and the rarer moustached warbler. Several tern species are attracted to the lake, and duck numbers build up in the winter, when the lake is also used by marsh harriers.

Sadly, the local population are still used to looking at birds down the barrel of a gun, and have been slow to appreciate the lake's wildlife significance. In the village bar, a focal point for the local hunters, a pair of binoculars might attract hostile glances. Early in 1989 a LIPU information hut was burned down, and several of the hides have also gone up in flames. All that visitors can do is to bring home the lake's economic potential by staying and spending money in the immediate surroundings.

The Maremma

The **MAREMMA REGIONAL PARK** consists of a fertile river valley with marshes to the north, a central chain of hills – the **Monti dell'Uccellina** – and 15km of unspoilt coast to the south, one of the very few stretches of Tuscan coastline to have escaped development. Controlled agriculture is permitted within the park: olives are widely grown, along with fruit and vegetables on the flatter fields to the east, and long-horned cattle graze on the hillsides.

ALBERESE, the best base for the park, is the centre for a number of excursions. The **Itinerario Faunistico**, a gentle amble round the surrounding hillsides, is one of the least demanding. It starts through grassy pastures with occasional oak trees, a landscape reminiscent of English parkland, and favoured by fallow deer. Birds of this habitat include hoopoes and green woodpeckers, and butterflies of summer include the great banded grayling *Brintesia*

Hoopoe

circe, a startlingly large species marked in black, grey and cream, which gives it good camouflage against the tree trunks on which it frequently rests.

Another excursion, possibly only open on Wednesdays and weekends, involves a special **bus ride** from the Information Centre in Alberese into the heart of the park (last bus 3.30pm). Visitors are dropped in the thick of the *maquis*, from where there is a 45-minute walk down to the beach, and a selection of short walks into the hills. **Short-toed eagles** breed on the low hills, conspicuous by their almost pure white underparts and their habit of hovering as they search for snakes and lizards. As well as these reptiles, numerous tortoises *Testudo hermanni* rustle around the bushes of rosemary and other aromatic herbs.

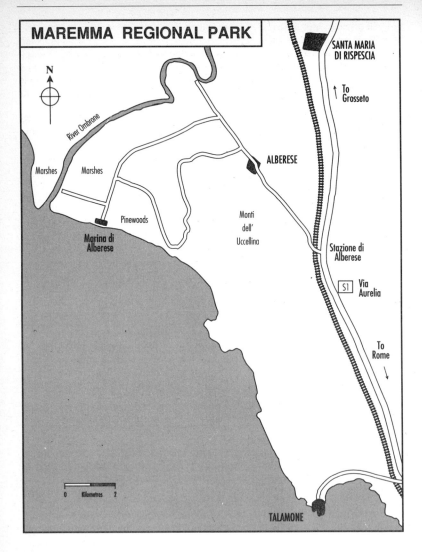

MAREMMA REGIONAL PARK

N

SANTA MARIA
DI RISPESCIA

To
Grosseto

River Ombrone

ALBERESE

Marshes

Marshes

Monti
dell'
Uccellina

Pinewoods

Marina di
Alberese

Stazione di
Alberese

S1 Via
Aurelia

To
Rome

0   Kilometres   2

TALAMONE

Further towards the sea, the sandy soil is suited to the umbrella pine *Pinus pinea* with its unmistakeable spreading canopy. Although it's thought of as a symbol of the Italian countryside, it was almost certainly imported from Spain by the Etruscans or Romans.

Another Roman introduction to these hills is the **crested porcupine** *Hystrix cristata*, which north of the Med is found only in Italy, although it's common enough in north Africa. It's a nocturnal animal, and your best chance of seeing one is on an evening stroll across rocky hillsides or open woodland. Since they have no natural predators in this part of the world, they're not easily frightened, and will often go into a **threat display** if disturbed. They turn their back on the intruder, stamp their feet, and rattle the hollow spines on their tail; in an extreme case, they'll even rush backwards and try to lodge their spines in their opponent's skin. Since an adult porcupine can grow to a metre long and weigh as much as 20kg, this can be an alarming and possibly painful experience. An evening walk could also turn up badgers or wild boar, both of which are relatively common in the Maremma.

At the other end of the park are the pinewoods and marshes at the **Ombrone Delta**. The best way to visit this is undoubtedly by bicycle, firstly because this approach doesn't scare the birds and secondly because a bicycle can outpace the unpleasant minuscule flies of the genus *Micterotypus*, which appear to be immune to normal insect repellants.

The long straight road down to MARINA DI ALBERESE, just south of the river, is flanked by umbrella pines and is good for **birds**. Roadside perches are occupied by **shrikes**, of which three species are common here: the woodchat shrike, the lesser grey shrike, and the red-backed shrike. All three are predatory, feeding on anything from beetles to small birds, and have clawed feet and viciously hooked bills. Rollers are fond of the open spaces amongst the pines, and the reed beds have the noisy great reed warbler as well as the resident Cetti's warbler, with its loud staccato song.

The road ends up on the shore near some caravans selling drinks. From here, retrace your steps back to a tarmac road leading north to the **Ombrone River**. The beautiful and spectacular bee-eater breeds in low sandy fields around the river in summer, and migration time produces an exciting assortment of waders, ducks, herons and egrets, with even a passing flamingo or two.

On the coast **north of the Maremma** is the WWF reserve at BOLGHERI – the first to be created in Italy. The animals here are now so used to humans that there are few places in the country where it is so easy to see fauna in their native habitat. Expect to see boar, roe deer, and a wealth of aquatic birds – including rarities like the bluethroat and Blyth's warbler.

Orbetello

Fifteen kilometres south of the Maremma, the WWF reserve at **ORBETELLO** is one of two lagoons between the rocky promontory of MONTE ARGENTARIO and the mainland. The reserve proper is open only on Thursdays and Sundays (September to April inclusive), in order to ensure some peace for the nesting birds, especially black-winged stilts, stone curlews, bee-eaters and Montagu's harriers. This protection from disturbance, combined with the banning of hunting from the reserve, has turned Orbetello into a very significant bird site.

Outside the visiting season, the lagoons can be seen fairly well from the roads that cross from the main road to Orbetello, and there's a delightful nature trail at the village of PATANELLA which has all the representative plants of the Med *maquis* amongst forests of cork oak *Quercus suber*. There is also plenty of cover in which to steal up to the lakeside. Patanella is unspoilt simply because it is a very well-kept secret; it doesn't figure prominently in the WWF literature, and at dusk and early morning you can expect to have the site to yourself.

The **reserve** is reached down a dirt track near Patanella. The warden, Luigi Calchetti, is there during opening hours to sell tickets and guide visitors around the series of nine observation hides that look out over the brackish waters of the lagoon. The bird life, especially during migration, is breathtaking, with large numbers of familiar species such as grey herons and little egrets, plus a smattering of much less common ones. Glossy ibis are regular, and so are cranes on their long journey from northern Europe to Africa. Ospreys hunt over the lagoons, black terns and white-winged black terns dance over the water, and the occasional eastern wader such as marsh sandpiper may drop in. The lagoons also hold flamingoes, and non-breeding birds sometimes stay for the summer.

TUSCANY: ACCESS AND ACCOMMODATION

Orecchiella

Like many mountain sites, Orecchiella is not easy to get to. A train runs from LUCCA up the scenic valley of the River Serchio to CASTELNUOVO DI GARFAGNANA, where a bus leaves twice a day for the village of CORFINO. Corfino has hotels, but it's better to hitch or drive the 10km further to the park visitor's centre and stay at the *Albergo Miramonti* (☎0583/619.012/619.005). The owner, Signor Bolognini, is a mine of information and can advise on local treks, which can also be done on horseback.

Lake Massaciuccoli

The nearest town is LUCCA, 15km away. Although there's no direct bus link to the lake, a train goes to MASSAROSSA, where buses leave regularly for the village of Massaciuccoli (except on Sundays, when there is no service). At the village, look for a road leading down to the lake, signed towards the *Ristorante Oliva*.

The Maremma

ALBERESE is the best base for the park, reached by a reasonably regular morning bus service from the railway station at GROSSETO – except on Sundays, when you may need to hitch. Ask in the bar in Alberese about local accommodation with families in the village, and cycle hire.

Orbetello

ALBINIA, which has a small mainline station on the Rome/Livorno coastal line, is the nearest town, and the nearest hotel to the reserve is *Albergo Fagiano* on Via Aurelia Sud (☎0564/870.191). There are also camping facilities along the road from Albinia to Porto San Stefano.

THE PO DELTA

The **Po Delta** lies within easy reach of VENICE and RAVENNA – a good wildlife interlude for those suffering from a surfeit of culture. A proposed National Park, the area's 300 square kilometres of lagoons, swamps and mud flats are considered Italy's premier birdwatching area, and are known (without exaggeration) as the Italian Camargue. The lagoons closest to Venice have been overtaken by tourism, development and pollution, although they are still attractive to visiting birds – the delta being a key stepping stone on northern migration routes. Further south, the reserve of **Punte Alberete** is a marvellous swamp forest, and the nearby town of **Comacchio** a fine centre for the least disturbed marshes and lakes.

Punte Alberete

The WWF reserve at **PUNTE ALBERETE** (open daily all year) encompasses a **flooded forest**, one of the last of its kind in Italy and the only surviving example on the Adriatic coast. Most of the rest of the delta has been drained for intensive agriculture, and Punte Alberete would have gone the same way had it not been for the activities of local wildlife organisations in the 1960s.

The forest is a mixture of ash *Fraxinus excelsior*, poplar *Populus alba* and willow *Salix alba*. In early summer, the marshes beneath them are yellow with flag iris *Iris pseudacorus* and white with floating water lilies *Nymphaea alba*. The area is a paradise for **herons** and **egrets**, since the shallow pools support abundant food and the trees provide space for nesting. From April on, three heron species – the familiar grey, the slightly slimmer purple, and the night heron, a squatter bird with black and white plumage – fly overhead at the rate of one a second, making it hard to decide where to point your binoculars. They're joined by large numbers of little egrets, and the occasional rarer species such as the glossy ibis.

THE ADRIATIC ALGAE

The northern Adriatic has never had a reputation for crystal-clear waters; as far back as 1729 there are accounts of "unspecified substances" preventing fishermen from hauling in their nets. But in 1988 and 1989, the problem took on a different dimension. Vast stretches of the sea from the Po Delta to the Marche – 180km south – were covered in a thick mat of **mucillagine**, a jelly-like substance produced by various types of micro-algae. In July 1989, Alberto Bernstein, in charge of "Operation Algae" declared " . . . almost the entire lagoon, two hundred square miles, is covered."

In **small quantities**, algae is fine – in fact, it's an important food source for tiny animal plankton, which itself feeds fish and other larger sea animals. But when the waters are over-enriched with thousands of tons of phosphates washed from intensive agriculture upstream, and further contaminated by the sewage and other wastes of the million people living in the Venice region, the whole situation gets quite alarmingly out of hand.

What seems to happen is this. As phosphates and nitrates enrich the water – a process called **eutrophication** – the algae grows at a faster and faster rate until it forms a scum. The plants buried underneath this layer die, and the rotting plants **consume oxygen**; furthermore, the scum reduces wave action, which would normally add oxygen to the water. Without oxygen, the water becomes a death-trap for the marine animals which would otherwise feed off the algae. They die, adding to the pollution by their own decay – so there's even more enrichment, a thicker scum, more dead algae, less oxygen, more dead fish, more enrichment . . .

It's a vicious circle which can only be reversed by halting the pollution. So far, only the symptoms of the problem have been dealt with. A dozen dredgers have been hauling out 500 tons of algae a day from Venice's lagoons; a grandiose scheme has been proposed by the Po Delta Consortium to filter the water before it gets to the lagoons and the sea; tourists wear surgical masks to shut out the stench; and airports have been shut down because pilots can't see the runways for the clouds of gnats and midges.

Something similar happened to Lake Erie in the 1950s and 1960s; stringent pollution regulations applied from the mid-1970s has returned the lake to something like normality. Hopefully, the same will happen in the northern Adriatic.

It's worth shinning up the banks of the River Lamone to look over the **reed beds**. Gliding marsh harriers and little bittern may be the reward, along with bearded tits – one of the few birds able to digest the seeds of the reed *Phragmites australis*, off which they feed in the winter. In summer, the **butterflies** are impressive, with the large copper *Lycaena dispar* having pride of place; a specialist of marshland, its caterpillars feed on water docks.

Comacchio

To see the heart of the Po Delta, it's best to head a little further north to the attractive canal town of **COMACCHIO**, close to a series of excellent bird sites. The saline lagoon of **Valli di Comacchio** lies just south of the town, ringed by roads from which viewing is fairly simple. The best place to watch from is the promontory of **Boscoforte**, near the village of SANT'ALBERTO at the extreme south of the lake. The salty water suits wading birds such as avocets and black-winged stilts, and attracts numerous terns – including the Caspian with its huge red bill – and gulls. Bushes of *Tamarix* densely cover the fringes of the lake with their feathery green foliage and pale pink plumes of tiny flowers, and various species of glasswort *Salicornia spp.* blanket the ground. This is a rewarding area for small birds, and even the rare pratincole is an occasional breeder. Equally scarce is the otter, a mammal which is all but extinct in the rest of Italy.

Further north from Comacchio is another lake, the **Valli Bertuzzi**. More of the same can be seen here, and there's a useful observation platform on the road running to its east. On both lakes, **wintering ducks** concentrate in good numbers, including species such as pochard, wigeon, teal, garganey and gadwall. At migration time **waders** gather on the surrounding mud flats, sometimes including eastern species such as Terek and marsh sandpipers. Further north again, the **Forest of Mesola** – the last of the Delta's relic woodlands – provides a refreshing change from the surrounding marshes, with its woodlands of holm oak *Quercus ilex*, elm *Ulmus carpinifolia* and ash *Fraxinus excelsior*. Some 250 **fallow deer** roam the woods, alongside about 150 red deer – both species easy to see, though their grazing has perhaps made the flowers less interesting.

PO DELTA: ACCESS AND ACCOMMODATION

Punte Alberete

Buses run to Punte Alberete every four hours from RAVENNA, 13km south. Alternatively, stay in COMACCHIO and head south down the coastal N309. Best access to the reserve is from the bridge on the main road over the Lamone; from there either head north for the observation platform, or take the path on the south side of the river, skirting the woodland. Don't be put off by *Divieto di Accesso* signs; if you read the small print underneath, this is one part of the reserve you *can* visit.

Comacchio

The town itself is easily reached by bus from VENICE to the north and RAVENNA to the south. There's plenty of accommodation, including the recommended *Hotel La Pace* (☎0533/81.285), on the canal, just two doors away from a bike hire and repair shop. (Bicycle is one of the best ways of exploring the marshes and lakes.) Campsites are dotted around all of the nearby coastal towns.

AROUND ROME

Three very different sites lie in a ring around **Rome**. In the hills to the northwest, the reserve of **Lake Vico** is the smallest but best of the three volcanic crater lakes of the region. To the east, up in the Apennines, the **Abruzzo National Park** is famous for its bears and wolves. Finally, on the coast to the south of Rome, **Circeo National Park** has woodlands and coastal marshes, as well as the little-visited island of Zannone.

Lake Vico

The reserve of **LAKE VICO** covers the lake itself, the marshes and farmland around it, and the wooded slopes of the crater on all but the southern side. The lake itself creates a microclimate of high humidity that nurtures a dense **beech forest** on the surrounding slopes. Walks through the forest are easy, especially along the nature trail at **Monte Venere**, where well-marked paths follow the gentle slopes. It appears that wolves might have returned to the lake, but you're extremely unlikely to encounter one. Butcher's broom *Ruscus aculeatus* grows between the trees; its strange spiky foliage makes it a popular ornamental shrub in Italy. The blue wood anemone *Anemone appenina* and the Alpine squill *Scilla bifolia* brighten up the path edges and clearings in spring and early summer.

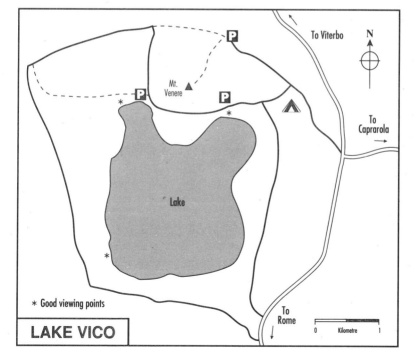

The **woodland birds** are similar to those of northern Europe, and you'll hear the familiar songs of robins, chiffchaffs and chaffinches, as well as the ringing whistles of nuthatches as they forage around the beech trees. In the evening, this is a good place for tawny owls (not a common bird round the Med), as well as the **fat dormouse**. In summer this species builds a nest high in the trees and comes down to the woodland floor at night to search for nuts and seeds, making a range of grunts and squeaks that sound like a mobile lover's lane; like all dormice it hibernates through the winter. Other nocturnal mammals in the reserve include wild cats and crested porcupines, and wild boars have become common enough to be considered something of an agricultural nuisance.

The main interest of Lake Vico, though, is the **bird life** on the lake itself. In winter, thousands of coots, pochards, wigeons and tufted ducks settle here, while water rails lurk in the reeds and marsh harriers hunt above. Things are quieter in the summer, but there's much of interest during spring and autumn migration.

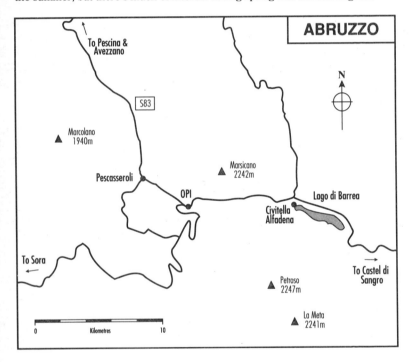

Abruzzo National Park

No casual visit can do justice to the **ABRUZZO NATIONAL PARK**. With an area of 400 square kilometres and an altitude range from 700m to 2247m, it presents an astonishing variety of landscapes from rocky gorges and lowland beech forests to limestone crags and upland pines – a physical backdrop to an equally rewarding variety of wildlife. Within the park, there are a total of 1200 species of plant, 40 species of mammals, 30 types of reptile, 300 different birds and 267 various *funghi* or mushrooms. To get the most from the area involves a fair amount of walking, best done from May to October; even in summer the weather can be changeable.

The park headquarters are at PESCASSERÔLI, but the best base is further east along the valley of the River Sangro at CIVITELLA ALFADENA. A small enclosure here holds some of the last specimens of the endangered Apennine subspecies of **wolf**, kept for study and breeding purposes; despite complete protection since 1977 the wild population is down to fewer than 50, partly owing to cross-breeding with domestic dogs. Along the **Sangro** river from Civitella there's typical riverine woodland of poplars and willows; a little higher, the woods are dominated by the turkey oak *Quercus cerris*, looming over Montpelier maples *Acer monspessulanum*, whose three-lobed leaves turn an attractive golden colour in autumn.

A path up the **Valle di Rose** towards the imposing peak of **Monte Caprara** starts in Civitella, winding through rocky grazing land towards the beech forests. Banks of the early purple orchid *Orchis mascula* grow here in spring, with their tall spikes of deep purple flowers and characteristic spotted leaves. After about an hour's climbing, **chamois** begin to appear; the isolated population in the park is doing well, and is more approachable than its counterparts in the Alps. In the beech forests, there's a faint chance of seeing the white-backed woodpecker, one of the rarest birds of the park; one of the confusingly similar spotted woodpeckers, it has mostly black and white plumage with a completely red crown. Higher up, through the pine zone, some of the truly **Alpine birds** appear, including Alpine accentors, Alpine and common choughs (one of the few areas where the two species overlap), occasional wallcreepers on the crags and snowfinches on the summits. With luck, one of the three pairs of golden eagles that breed in the park might soar over the uplands.

The Abruzzo is especially famous for its **bears** – which are descended from alpine ancestors, but over the centuries have developed enough indigenous features to be named after the area, *Ursus arctos marsicanus*. The park, support-ing a population of around a hundred animals, is one of the best places to see them in Europe. They are shy animals, and are most likely to be observed at berry time in autumn, when they forage amongst the woodlands in search of the vast quantities of vegetable matter they need to sustain them through their winter hibernation.

The bare ground above the tree line is excellent in May and June for **Alpine flowers**, showing a colourful array of violets, gentians, and the white flowers of the Alpine pasqueflower *Pulsatilla alpina*. The rare Apennine edelweiss thrives here too. In spring crocuses bloom on the edge of the melting snow, and in summer the scarlet hanging flowers of the **Martagon lily** *Lilium martagon* are a highlight of the mountain woods. Recently discovered is an endemic iris *Iris marsica*. Other notables include the Venus slipper orchid – a splendid yellow black colour, and endemic gentians, columbines and *Botton d'Oro*.

Martagon lily
Lilium martagon

Circeo National Park

The Pontine marshes defied all efforts to drain them from Roman times until 1918, when an energetic programme was started; just before Mussolini threatened to complete the job, a fragment was saved by the creation of the **CIRCEO NATIONAL PARK** in 1934. At 114 square kilometres, it's the smallest of Italy's five National Parks, and also one of the most visited, situated as it is roughly halfway betwen ROME and NAPLES. All the same, it has some fine coastal marshland, a small rocky promontory at Monte Circeo, thirty square kilometres of woodland to the east (added to the park in 1974), and the island of ZANNONE, added in 1979. The town of SABAUDIA is the most obvious base for visiting the whole range of Circeo's habitats.

At all times of the year, the **lakes and marshes** have plenty of birds. The most southerly one, Lago di Sabaudia, is too disturbed by visitors for good wildlife, but the ones further north are still excellent. Simply follow the coastal road to **Lago di Caprolace**, find a bank overlooking the lake, and watch. White storks breed in the park and feed here from spring to autumn, and spoonbills regularly call on migration. The lakes are the most important Italian wintering ground for **cormorants**, and their slightly saline conditions also attract migrating flamingoes.

The limestone promontory of **Monte Circeo** at the southern edge of the park has woodlands of holm oak *Quercus ilex* on its northern flanks and typical *garigue* and *maquis* habitats on the sunnier southern side. An April visit here will be rewarded with many orchids and irises, along with lizards, butterflies, and migrating birds – quail, turtle doves, cuckoos and nightingales. Amongst the shrubs, look out for the Sardinian warbler and the subalpine warbler, two of the most widespread scrub birds of the region. Later in the summer, the two-tailed pasha butterfly *Charaxes jasius*, one of the most splendid in the Med, can be found flying around the *maquis*, especially near strawberry trees *Arbutus unedo*.

In the **woodlands** of Selva del Circeo, the green foliage of the various oak species creates a quite different atmosphere; holm oak *Quercus ilex*, turkey oak *Q. cerris* and white oak *Quercus pubescens* all grow here, some to great size. Spring butterflies such as orange tips *Anthocaris cardamines* and speckled woods *Pararge aegeria* flit around the clearings. Cyclamens *Cyclamen hederifolium* carpet the ground under the trees with their large variegated leaves, but you have to wait till autumn to see their pink flowers. Numerous tranquil trails thread through the woods; some of them are open to bikes – on hire in Sabaudia – and all are marked on the detailed map available from the Park headquarters.

Zannone

The little island of **Zannone** can be reached by fishing boat from the nearby island of PONZA; in theory, a permit is needed, but in true Italian fashion the local fishermen have come to a tacit agreement with the wardens, and such formalities can be sidestepped.

The island is a significant staging post for **migrating birds** – 200 species have been recorded – and peregrine falcons breed in the summer near the aptly named Monte Pellegrino. It is also a good place to get a close-up view of the **mouflon**, introduced in the 1920s, and several trails are mapped out through the holm oak forests in the north and the lower *maquis* of rockroses *Cistus spp.* in the south. Finally, Zannone offers brilliant snorkelling, with a rocky coastline, clear and unpolluted water, and large offshore beds of the seagrass *Posidonia*.

AROUND ROME: ACCESS AND ACCOMMODATION

Lake Vico

The reserve is 50km from ROME, off the bus route to VITERBO. Although the bus runs along the top of the crater, it turns off at one point down to CAPRAROLA; get off at the crossroads, and walk down towards the lake, passing the campsite on the way. For an alternative to the humidity of the lakeside, the *Albergo Farnese* (☎0761/646.384) on the road down to Caprarola is reasonably priced. Most of the hotels are well stocked with maps of the reserve and information about the Monte Venere nature trail; the **Park Office** in Caprarola has even more information, including species lists.

Abruzzo

Access to the park is by train from ROME to AVEZZANO, from where the regular bus service to CASTEL DI SANGRO runs right through the centre of the park. Although PESCASSEROLI has the most hotels, owing to its development as a winter ski resort, there's a good one-star at OPI, *La Genziane* (☎0863/912.158); Opi also has a superb campsite – *Campeggio dell'Orso*, right by the river. There's a cheapish hostel in CIVITELLA ALFEDENA (☎0864/89.166).

Circeo

To get to SABAUDIA, where there is a visitors' centre and reasonably priced accommodation, take a train from ROME to LATINA; buses connect Latina with SAN FELICE CIRCEO every 45min, and stop right outside the centre, on the outskirts of Sabaudia. There is accommodation in San Felice Circeo as well; it's a far more attractive town than Sabaudia, but more expensive and further away from the park.

THE BAY OF NAPLES

Unless you count its estimated six million rats, **Naples** is pretty much devoid of wildlife. However, outside the city, it is long enough since the last eruption of **Mount Vesuvius** for the lava fields to have developed a dense flora and fauna, well worth a short detour. The **Isle of Capri**, for all its summer crowds, has some pleasant walks, too, while the **Lattari Peninsula**, west of Salerno, features limestone hillsides of classic Med spring flowers.

Vesuvius

Of the thousands of people who climb the 1277-metre, conical peak of **VESUVIUS** in the course of each year, few go on to explore the nearby Valley of the Giants. This area can be a blaze of colour in early summer, with vivid flowers of red valerian *Centranthus ruber* at ground level, surmounted by the yellow of the Mount Etna broom *Genista aetnensis*, a shrub of almost tree-like dimensions. In all, there are over a thousand species of flora, the most interesting of which are the pioneering varieties – notably the endemic, ash-coloured lichen *Stereocaulon vesuvianum*; often overlooked are the forests on the southern slopes, comprising mainly oak, chestnut and even birch – a rarity in Italy.

From the main car park on the north side of the volcano, walk back down the road to the first bend, and take a small path off to the right. (Ignore the *Divieto di Accesso* signs, which are designed to stop coachloads of visitors from picnicking in this unspoilt area.) The path stays on a level plane, joining up after about half an hour with one of the old approach roads to the volcano.

Bird life is varied but not always easy to identify; whitethroats perch conspicuously on bushes and telegraph wires to sing their scratchy song, but other warblers, such as Sardinian and subalpine, are less obliging and spend most of their time at the bottom of bushes. **Rock thrushes** can be seen above the tree line, the male's blue head, reddish orange belly and white back making it one of the most striking of all mountain birds. Raptors are not uncommon – buzzards, merlins and sparrowhawks.

Mammals are rare up here; foxes, despite their assistance in keeping down the rat population, are keenly hunted. **Insects** are prolific, however, with butterflies such as the painted lady *Vanessa cardui*, clouded yellow *Colias spp.* and various blues all in large numbers. A wasp-like insect of the genus *Scolia* buzzes around here in high summer; mostly black with two yellow bands on its abdomen, it can reach a length of 4cm, but despite its formidable appearance is harmless enough.

Capri

Opposite Vesuvius, out in the Bay of Naples, lies the island of **CAPRI**. Birdwatching starts on the ferry from Naples, as Manx and Cory's shearwaters are both to be seen as skimming over the waves. Leaving Naples in early summer, keep an eye out for swifts circling over the Castel Nuovo – amongst them are Alpine swifts, distinguished by their larger size and white bellies.

On the island itself, some good walks cross the slopes of **Monte Solaro**, the highest point on the island at 589m. One of the paths starts in ANACAPRI close to the villa of San Michele, once owned by the Swedish doctor and nature-lover Axel Munthe and now open, with its well-kept gardens, to the public. All round this area serins can be heard jingling away at the tops of pine trees, joined in spring and summer by the more melodious songs of blackcaps and nightingales. In spring, migrating bee-eaters and golden orioles are present as well. The spring **flowers** are full of colour, especially the yellow Spanish broom *Spartium junceum* and the crumpled reddish purple flowers of the rockrose *Cistus crispus*. Orchids are here too, notably the large and crowded pale pink spikes of *Orchis italica*.

Further up the track more open land produces abundant **butterflies**, including many yellow cleopatras *Gonepteryx cleopatra* and swallowtails *Papilio machaon*. Eventually the path divides, one branch carrying on up to Monte Solaro, the other going down to a hermitage, which looks back on the cliffs – with their resident peregrine falcons – above the marina.

The Lattari Peninsula

West of SALERNO, the **LATTARI PENINSULA** pokes out towards Capri and forms the southern edge of the Bay of Naples. It's a marvellous tract of limestone hills, mostly covered in *garigue* scrub but also cultivated with olive groves. This is primarily a botanist's haunt, although the open hillsides offer good walking, with lovely views down to the sea, and the abundance of wild flowers means that insects do well. The flowers are at their best from mid-March to early May.

The **shrubby hillsides** are perfect *garigue* habitat, dominated by the bushy rockroses, both the pink-flowered *Cistus incanus* and the white *C. salvifolius*. Amongst them grow French lavender *Lavandula stoechas*, the rounded blue heads of *Globularia vulgaris*, and a variety of plants in the labiate family, including the woolly *Ballota acetabulosa*, with tiny purple flowers nestling at the base of its silvery hairy leaves. Outstanding on a long list of orchids are the pink butterfly orchid *Orchis papilionacea* and a local brown and green form of the late spider orchid *Ophrys fuciflora ssp. oxyrrhynchos*; asphodels and irises are widespread too, pursuing a similar strategy to the orchids by withdrawing into their bulbous roots to survive the baking summer heat.

Field margins and **olive groves** abound with a blaze of "weeds" such as poppies, the pink *Dianthus plumarius*, pheasant's eye *Adonis annua* and its larger relation *Adonis aestivalis*, and both red and blue varieties of the anemone *Anemone coronaria*; as if this wasn't enough, orchids such as the green winged orchid *Orchis morio* grow in their thousands. This latter species has a typical pale purple orchid flower, but the two sepals that point sideways above the lip are tinged and veined with green.

Any patches of **rough grassland** support yet more flowers, including the pea *Tetragonolobus purpureus*, a beautiful low plant with dark red pea-like flowers. It's called by a variety of English names: **winged pea** because the small pea pods have ridges up the sides, **asparagus pea** because they taste a bit like asparagus when cooked – true enough – it briefly became a trendy vegetable in the 1980s) and, best of all, **dragon's teeth**. It's easy to imagine the red curved flowers as the teeth sown by Jason in his mythological quest for the golden fleece.

If you haven't got much time, the finest and most interesting floral enclave is the **VALLONE DELLE FERRIERE** reserve, a craggy valley rising on the south of the peninsula above AMALFI. This has extraordinary microclimates, resulting in plants normally confined to Africa and South America. Notable rarities include the orchid-like *Arisarum proboscideum*, and the fern *Woodwardia radicans* – of which there are just ten known examples.

BAY OF NAPLES: ACCESS AND ACCOMMODATION

Vesuvius
NAPLES is the obvious place to stay. Circumvesuviana trains run regularly from Naples to ERCOLANO, from where buses run up the mountain every two hours from 7.30am to 1.30pm.

Capri
Ferries leave from NAPLES (Molo Beverello) and from SORRENTO. Accommodation on the island is pricey to say the least.

Lattari Peninsula
A twisting road runs right round the peninsula, taking in the resorts of AMALFI and SORRENTO. There are several places along this coast route where you can stop to look at the marvellous flowers, but it's even better to explore the tracks and village roads into the interior. Resorts with accommodation are to be found on the south side of the peninsula.

GARGANO

The **Gargano Peninsula**, a limestone massif jutting out into the Adriatic halfway down the Italian coast, forms the spur to the boot of Italy. Because of its isolation and relative lack of disturbance, its plant life is exceptionally interesting. Outside the peninsula proper, the **Manfredonia marshes** to the south and the **lakes of Varano and Lesina** to the north are both good bird sites.

The Gargano Peninsula

The southern slopes of the **GARGANO PENINSULA** are scrubby limestone hills, replaced towards the higher ground by forests of beech and oak centred around the **Foresta di Umbra**, a woodland reserve at the heart of the peninsula.

The village of MONTE SANT'ANGELO makes a good base for the stony hillsides; the main road down to MANFREDONIA has lots of opportunities for rambling off along paths that reveal a quite unbelievable variety of **orchids**. There are numerous endemic species and local varieties, some of which are a headache to sort out: academic taxonomists have a field day here, trying to compartmentalise every species, though what is on the ground is often a continuous phase of intermediate and hybridised forms. Among the twenty or so species that can be found in a single trip, the lady orchid *Orchis purpurea* is particularly attractive, its robust tall spikes rising up from the roadsides and on the woodland edges; each flower looks remarkably like a woman in a flounced pink dress and dark purple mob cap, with two dark eyes formed by the pollinia (the orchid equivalent of an anther). In addition to the orchids, these lower slopes offer yellow and blue irises, the yellow flax *Linum flavum*, pinks *Dianthus spp.*, poppies and anemones, all flowering in a mass of colour on the terraces and roadsides.

Of the familiar scrub **birds**, the black-eared wheatear stands out – a relatively common bird of stony and rocky slopes in this part of Italy – whilst predators such as long-legged buzzards, short-toed eagles and even Egyptian vultures hunt over the slopes.

Up in the **forests** the scene changes dramatically, sunny slopes giving way to cool woodland. Yet more orchids grow amongst the trees, including a whole hillside of one of the strangest and most elusive of all European species, the **ghost orchid** *Epipogium aphyllum*. This orchid flowers only sporadically, with up to ten years between flowering, and has a white flower and stem and no green leaves; it grows here at the southern limit of its range. More familiar plants under the woods include wild garlic or ransoms *Allium ursinum*, and the lovely columbine *Aquilegia vulgaris*; the deep blue flowers of the latter showing up the multicoloured garden varieties for the vulgar cousins they are. The list goes on and on – over **two thousand plant species** have been recorded on Gargano, nearly as many as in the whole of Britain.

Most **birds** in the woodland are familiar ones such as tits, treecreepers, and nuthatches – the last extremely tame, with a habit of foraging in litter bins. Real specialities like the black woodpecker and the white-backed woodpeckers need some patience and luck to find. On the woodland edges, especially on the roads down from the reserve to VIESTE and PESCHICI, a dawn or dusk walk might turn up one of the area's two hundred or so **roe deer**, a species about the size of a large Alsatian dog.

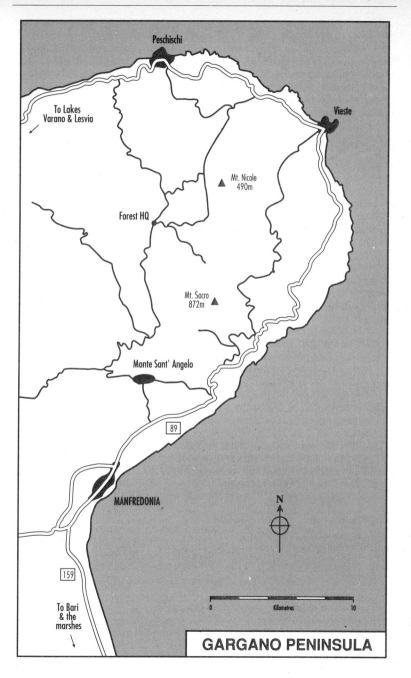

GARGANO PENINSULA

Lakes Varano and Lesina

The two lagoons of **VARANO** and **LESINA**, on the northern shoulder of the peninsula, both merit a trip for their birds, although weekends in the hunting season should be avoided. Of the two, Lesina is easier to observe from the road that skirts its southern edge. At their best in winter, when the wildfowl population includes white-fronted and bean geese as well as ducks, they have reed beds that hold breeding bitterns, feeding herons, and perhaps the odd marsh harrier.

The Manfredonia Marshes and Cesine

The whole coastline south of **MANFREDONIA** down to the saltpans at ZAPPONETA and MARGHARITA is the edge of a floodplain, once a wilderness of marshes and lakes but long since drained for agriculture. A few fragments remain, including the WWF reserve at FRATTAROLO, about 9km south of Manfredonia on the coast road. If it's wet, this reserve holds a good variety of herons, egrets and other water birds, while great reed warblers sing loudly from the reed beds and penduline tits busy themselves in the surrounding shrubs. Spoonbills and glossy ibis are regularly seen on passage at the end of April.

Some way to the south lies the only other protected area on this coast, the **CESINE** lakes, a state nature reserve with added WWF protection since 1979. These glittering lagoons are a stepping stone on the Adriatic migration route for huge numbers of birds. At the same time, the shelter of trees and conservation has allowed the proliferation of 320 species of plants and shrubs. Wild orchids have a notable presence, and amongst the trees there are rarities like Canary pine, locust tree and the oak *Quercia spinosa*.

GARGANO: ACCESS AND ACCOMMODATION

Gargano
The reserve of the Foresta di Umbra is on the inland bus route from MANFREDONIA to PESCHICI, but there are only two buses a day and it's easy to get stranded in the reserve with no transport out. Either of the above two towns are good places to stay on the coast; just north of Manfredonia, the village of MONTE SANT'ANGELO is a more convenient base, with a reasonably priced pension at *Albergo Moderno* (☎0884/61.331). Manfredonia itself is the centre of communications for the peninsula, but is not an attractive town, housing a huge and ugly chemical plant.

Lakes Varano and Lesina
Both lakes are so large that a car is almost essential to do them thoroughly. They are skirted by the main road running along the northern edge of the peninsula from RODI GARGANICO to the main E2 *autostrada*.

Manfredonia Marshes
The bus from Manfredonia to BARI passes next to the WWF reserve of Frattarolo, although getting the bus driver to stop at the right place can be tricky. The spot to get off is 9km south of Manfredonia, just by the *Bagni Romana* immediately after a river bridge; the WWF reserve is 400m north.

SICILY

Although much of **Sicily** is baked by the sun and grazed by multitudes of goats, it is by no means a wasteland for the naturalist. The **Straits of Messina** are a passageway for migrating birds of prey, which run the gauntlet of the massed guns of the Italian hunting fraternity every spring. Along to the west of the island, the **Zingaro Nature Reserve** near Castellammare is a rare stretch of virgin coastline. Mountains occupy the northern edge – the **Madonie** and **Nebrodi** ranges both designated nature reserves – crowned in the east with the huge bulk of **Mount Etna** (3323m), Europe's highest volcano, an extraordinary natural wilderness recently proposed as Sicily's only National Park.

The Straits of Messina

Most broad-winged birds of prey crossing the Med go through the Bosphorus or the Straits of Gibraltar; any bird flying the middle route, however, passes over northern Tunisia into Sicily, and then is funnelled into the narrow **STRAITS OF MESSINA**, separating the island from mainland Italy.

Honey buzzard

However, this mass migration is often not so much a wildlife spectacle as a grand skirmish on both sides of the Straits between local hunters and heavily outnumbered environmentalists. The unfortunate **honey buzzard** – the species that uses the Straits most heavily – has the hardest time reaching its destination. Calabrian superstition holds that males will be cuckolded unless they shoot one down – a stunning example of the machismo of hunting.

On the Sicilian side, the best vantage point is **Monte Ciccia**, on the outskirts of MESSINA. The peak spring migration is from mid-April to mid-May, with a multitude of honey buzzards coming over around the end of the first week in May.

Mount Etna

One of the Mediterranean's most imposing landforms, **MOUNT ETNA** completely dominates the northeast of the island. Bubbling and spluttering almost constantly, the volcano is a major tourist attraction, and this has slightly spoilt what otherwise would be a natural enclave almost without parallel. The WWF and Italia Nostra consider it the most important wilderness in Italy still lacking environmental protection.

The most straightforward access is from the *Rifugio Sapienza*, reached by road from Catania and the south (and by a daily bus service from Catania first thing in the morning). Jeeps and minibuses run to the main crater between April and October (L30,000 return). The walk is long and difficult (3hr) – and not to be taken lightly – but the rewards are enormous. Vegetation is extraordinary, changing as you climb from a tropical profusion low down to lichens and rare mosses on the apparently denuded deserts of the upper slopes. Coastal macchia gives way to vines and citrus – nutured by fertile volcanic soils and then to huge forests of oak and chesnut. An endemic broom provides the dominant cover, its yellow flowers offset by the pink of *Astragalus siculis*, another extensive endemic also known as *spino santo*, or 'holy thorn'. Wild flowers generally are breathtaking, with spring displays – especially of violets – which flourish as high as 3,000m.

Most interesting botanical rarities are the *Bagolaro di Tournefort* – known locally as the "rockbreaker", its roots able to penetrate the coarsest lava – and *Stereocaulon vesuvium*, a lichen able to thrive even on lava which is still warm. For all the lushness of ground cover, however, and the huge variety of habitats, Etna's fauna is relatively humble. You may see martens and porcupines – perhaps the odd wild cat – but most animals have been hunted to the edge of extinction. Birds have had a happier time of it, and the woods teem with rock thrush, rock partridge, green woodpeckers and many more.

Nebrodi and Madonie Mountains

The **Madonie and Nebrodi ranges** form an unbroken mountain wall separating Sicily's northern coast from the barrenness of the interior plains and plateaus.

The Nebrodi

The more easterly **NEBRODI** are one of the few areas to retain the island's primal appearance – high, rounded slopes covered in dense forests of oak beech – a habitat decimated elsewhere by centuries of clearance and overgrazing. Most of the woodlands are centuries old, most notably those at Pumeri and on Monte Soro. In all some 140,000 hectares are designated as a *Parco Naturale*, which would make the region the largest protected area in Italy. A large variety of animals roams the forest floor, foxes and wild cats in particular, and there are pairs of grifons, golden eagles and Egyptian vultures – all under constant LIPU surveillance. Unusually for Sicily there are also several lakes, all spring resting sites for migrating birds. Biggest is the man-made reservoir at Ancipa in the south, with a smaller natural lake at Biviere di Cesaro near Monte Soro.

The Madonie

The **Madonie** to the west – Sicily's highest mountains after Etna - suffer from their proximity to Palermo, scarred by new roads and ski resorts. Dense forests of beech and chestnut, however, still gild their slopes – most notably at Piana Battaglia and Monte Quacella. Amongst them are just 25 examples of a rare endemic fir — uniquely adapted to heat and aridity and concentrated in the Madonna degli Angeli valley near Polizzi Generosa. As in the Nebrodi, hunters have wiped out all but the smallest mammals; though birds thrive, and there's a good chance of seeing birds of prey – Egyptian vultures in particular. The planned natural park for the Madonie will cover 25,000 hectares, considerably more than the existing reserves – at Monte Quacella (1900ha) and Faggeta Madonie (3000ha) – both largely mixed woodland habitats

Zingaro

West of PALERMO, near the small village of SCOPELLO, the **ZINGARO NATURE RESERVE** occupies virtually the only unspoilt stretch of coastline in the area. The reserve, the first in the whole of Sicily, was set up in 1980 in response to pressure from local people and wildlife organisations. Building contractors were blocked, and seven kilometres of coast were saved.

Scopello itself is the best base for the park, and also holds the informative and welcoming **visitors' centre**. From the village, a track leads across open fields and meets up with the lower road to the car park. Fan-tailed warblers are much in evidence, bobbing across the sky with their monotonous "zit" call, and cirl buntings can be seen in the scrubby vegetation as well. Inside the reserve, an immaculately kept path weaves amongst the clumps of a grass *Ampelodesma mauritanica*, with patches of the European fan palm *Chaemerops humilis*, a low-growing species that is one of only two native palm species in Europe. The path leads along the coast, with wonderful views down to the sea.

Branches lead off this main path up the hill towards **Monte Speziale**. A spring visit will find these full of flowers of the *garigue*, including many specimens of the so-called naked man orchid *Orchis italica*. Foxes and rabbits are both easy to spot, while higher up a single pair of Bonelli's eagles is resident – one of the last pairs of this declining bird of prey in all of Sicily.

SICILY: ACCESS AND ACCOMMODATION

Straits of Messina

MESSINA is the obvious base on the Sicilian side. Monte Ciccia is just north of the city, and a bus from the town train station stops at the bottom of it.

Mount Etna

Easiest access is from CATANIA (see text).

The closest shelter to the summit is the SAPIENZA REFUGE (☎095/911.062). There are plenty of hotels in CATANIA (probably the best base), RANDAZZO, LINGUAGLOSSA and TAORMINA. There is an all-year round campsite at MILO, the Miraneve (☎095/951.396).

Madonie and Nebrodi

Access is straightforward from CEFALÙ and other towns along the northern coast. The SS120 takes in much of the Nebrodi.

There are numerous forest refuges in the Nebrodi (contact the Forest Rangers' Office – where you can also stay – at RANDOZZO; ☎095/921.124). In the Madonie, the best bases are the villages of PETRALIA SOTTANA, POLIZZI GENEROSA and PIANO ZUCCHI, all of which have hotels.

Zingaro

SCOPELLO is reached by bus from the nearest large town, CASTELLAMMARE, itself served by regular buses from PALERMO. The last bus into Scopello leaves Castellammare at 2pm. The visitors' centre has a good selection of maps and other information. If the *Pensione Torre Benistra* (☎0924/596.003) is full, try asking around in local shops for rooms elsewhere.

SARDINIA

Sardinia is so large and varied an island that there's something of interest even in the torrid heat of midsummer; it's hard to prune down a list of interesting wildlife sites. In the south, the town of **Cagliari** has a wetland of international importance for birds, right within the city boundary, while the **Isola di San Pietro** has Italy's biggest colony of Eleonora's falcon. Up the west coast, the **Sinis Peninsula** is a rewarding complex of lakes and marshes, and inland from it lies the weird upland plateau of the **Giara di Gesturi**. Finally, **Mont'Albo** in the north is the best place on the island for birds of prey.

Cagliari

CAGLIARI is a bustling port and industrial centre, which makes the presence of **Lake Molentargius** just to the east of the city rather a surprise. The five-square-kilometre lake is protected from hunting, and has consequently developed a full breeding and migrating bird population. The lake is rather inaccessible by foot, which is possibly a good thing; rare birds such as glossy ibis have bred here in the past, and need all the protection from disturbance they can get. An easy way to get an eagle's eye view of the lake (preferably with binoculars) is to go up the belvedere on **Monte Urpino**, within walking distance of the city centre.

Observation of the **saltpans** that surround the city is more straightforward. One complex lies to the east between the suburb of QUARTU and the beach, the other a few kilometres along the main road west to PULA. On any of these salt pans **flamingoes** are likely throughout the year, often in several hundreds; little egrets are common, as are Kentish plovers, a small wader with a chestnut and brown cap that runs around as if on clockwork legs. Black-winged stilts and avocets are both to be seen, and the gulls are worth a second glance, as the

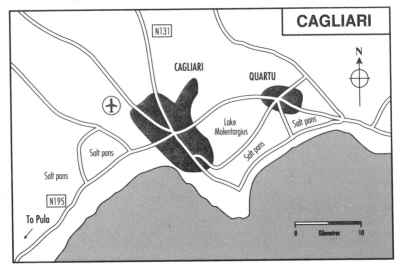

uncommon slender-billed gull breeds around here. None of these birds seems to be concerned by the traffic thundering past and the industrial background of pipelines, pylons and factories. The saltpans may not be the most beautiful places to watch birds in the Med, but they are amongst the most accessible.

L'Isola di San Pietro

The bird highlight of the island of **SAN PIETRO** is the colony of Eleonora's falcons at **Capo Sandalo**, with a hundred pairs at a recent conservative estimate, efficiently guarded by volunteers from the local branch of LIPU. The birds arrive from their Madagascar winter quarters in April, and time the fledging of their young for September, nicely coinciding with the peak autumn passage of the small birds – especially swallows – on which they feed. Late afternoon and early evening are the best times to see them, with **Cala Fico** just north of Capo Sandolo being particularly spectacular.

Other **birds of prey** on the island include peregrine falcons and Bonelli's eagles, and the dense *maquis* that covers much of the land is rewarding for flowers in early spring. Many of the typical Med birds such as Alpine swift, Scops owl and woodchat shrike breed on the island, along with scarcer ones such as Marmora's warbler. There's a good **reptile** population too, with the fearsome but harmless western whip snake *Coluber viridiflavus* commonly seen. Growing to one-and-a-half metres, it feeds on small mammals, amphibians, and especially the local wall lizard. In sandy places the ocellated skink *Chalcides ocellatus* can sometimes be seen; looking like a shiny thick-bodied lizard, it's usually seen from the rear as it buries itself in the sand.

The Sinis Peninsula

The **SINIS PENINSULA**, on the west coast of the island near ORISTANO, used to be an important source of grain for the Roman Empire, and cornfields are still an obvious feature of the landscape. Between them are vast tracts of uninhabited *maquis* and lakes of varying degrees of salinity. The coastline alternates between impressive sea cliffs and superb beaches of white crystalline sand. New roads built to serve the coast's tourist sites provide easy access to the sea, but a place to avoid in July and August is the ugly development around PUTZU IDU in the north, where building seems to be totally uncontrolled.

Lake Cabras is the largest lake, with good views possible from the minor road that loops round to the west of NURACHI. Avocets and stilts breed in good numbers, and the duck population includes the **red-crested pochard**, a rare species for which this is the major Italian breeding site. Two even rarer birds that breed here from time to time are the **purple gallinule** and the endangered **white-headed duck**. But rarities apart, the lake is a splendid place to see commoner species such as herons and egrets, and it has an excellent variety of species on migration.

Most of the land around Lake Cabras has been reclaimed for agriculture or planted with eucalyptus trees – productive enough in forestry terms, though certainly not good for wildlife. To see the best of the local **flowers** stick to the **coast**; late summer is the time to see the handsome white flowers of the sea daffodil *Pancratium maritimum*, which grows behind the sand dunes, while spring, as always, is best for the *maquis* of the clifftops. Further south from Lake Cabras, **Lake Mistras** is another saline lagoon that attracts flamingoes on passage as well as large numbers of wintering ducks. When you've had your fill of marshes, lagoons and cliffs, go down to **Tharros** at the south of Sinis. The clear waters and superb backdrop of Graeco-Roman ruins make this a perfect snorkelling place.

The Giara di Gesturi

An hour's drive inland of ORISTANO is the volcanic plateau of the **GIARA DI GESTURI**, a startling contrast to the coast. It's a flat expanse of boulders and cork oak forest, totally uninhabited and of quite haunting beauty. To experience the morning and evening colours at their best you'll have to **camp overnight** on the plateau, as there is no alternative accommodation.

The area is managed by a young cooperative who keep the forest in immaculate condition. They are particularly proud of the flora: the Giara sustains 16 of Sardinia's 22 orchid species, and *Narcissus* species grow in the damper fields around the plateau's lakes. Local cutters look after the cork oaks, carefully stripping the bark every nine years; this is a high-precision job, because the tree's growth will be stunted if it is cut too deeply.

The **bird life** of the plateau includes woodchat shrikes, common here as they are all over Sardinia, with colourful summer visitors such as hoopoes and bee-eaters. The **lakes**, dried out in summer, are worth checking out during spring and autumn migrations for herons, egrets and glossy ibis. Buzzards and goshawks are the main birds of prey. Pride of place in the forest goes to the 200 or so **wild horses**. Their genetic line has been adulterated by cross-breeding and the introduction of domestic horses earlier this century; every year there is an attempt to round them up and brand them, after which they are returned to the wild if they conform to the original stock. The owners get handsome subsidies from the EC and the regional authorities – a source of some discontent with those who don't own horses, who complain that people should not be paid for doing so little. Goats and cattle graze widely on the Giara, making horseflies and ticks an occupational hazard for the camper.

The Giara is not a reserve, and **hunters** use it heavily, especially on Sundays in season, with as many as a couple of hundred firing away at thrushes and other legal "game". Most of the other days of the week are rest days for hunters and hunted alike, and the forest becomes an oasis of peace and quiet.

Mont'Albo

Situated a little above the midpoint of the eastern coast, **MONT'ALBO** has superb limestone landscape of gorges, grottos and cliffs, as well as forests of holm oak and extensive areas of *maquis*. The rivers are lined with bushes of oleander *Nerium oleander*, a fine sight when they flower in summer and very typical of Sardinia. The wildness of this region makes it ideal for large **birds of prey**, which are best seen around the rocky heights of the 1000-metre **Punta Cupetti**.

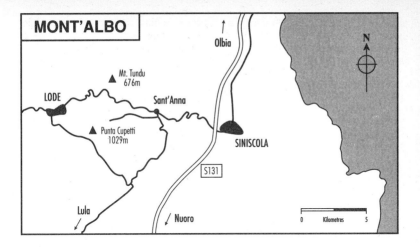

Punta Cupetti can be watched either from the top, near the radio mast, or from above the village of CANTIERA DI SANTA ANNA at the bottom. The cliffs are patrolled by buzzards, kestrels and peregrine falcons, with a good chance of **golden eagles** as well, especially early in the morning. **Griffon vultures** are said to be resident along the mountain ridge – one is said to have died in June 1989 from overeating on a dead cow, a rather unlikely fate for a vulture. Ravens swoop amongst the birds of prey, making a welcome change from the hooded crows found almost everywhere else on the island, while choughs swarm acrobatically round the peaks.

Other **bird life** in the area includes Marmora's warblers, lurking around bushes at the foot of the cliffs, and crag martins, which swoop to their nests high up on the rock faces. Bee-eaters, hoopoes and the inevitable woodchat shrikes are common in the rest of the area. **Mouflon** live on the rocks, but a sighting of a head poking over the rocks is more likely to be one of the abundant goats.

SARDINIA: ACCESS AND ACCOMMODATION

Cagliari

As the biggest town in Sardinia, CAGLIARI has simple access and plentiful accommodation. For the QUARTU saltpans take a bus or walk along Quartu beach (but it's a long way); if you're taking the bus, get off at the intersection for Quartu itself. For PULA take a bus along state highway 195, which runs past the saltpans after 15min.

L'Isola di San Pietro

The island is served by a regular bus/ferry link from CAGLIARI (via PORTOVESME or CALASETTA). Accommodation is fairly easy outside high summer; the main town of CARLOFORTE is the best base. A bus from here runs the 14km to Capo Sandalo, although the independently minded may prefer to check out the bike hire facilities near the town's information centre.

information and publications

Two active wildlife organisations are the WWF (Via Salaria 290, 00199 Roma) and the Italian bird protection society LIPU (*Lega Italiana per la Protezione degli Uccelli, Vicolo San Tiburzio 5, 43100 Parma*). There are WWF and LIPU branches in virtually every major town; most offer courses, nature walks or the chance to do voluntary work in local reserves.

MAPS

The northern mountain areas – the Alps, Dolomites, the Apuan Alps – and one-offs like the Sibillini, Chianti and Siena hills are covered by Kompass and Tabacco maps, and the Italian *IGM* 1:50,000 maps cover many popular scenic areas. The IGM 1:25,000 sheets cover the whole country, but most of them date from the Forties. The Touring Club Italiano 1:200,000 regional maps are generally reliable.

GUIDES

By far the most exhaustive and practical guide book to the country as a whole is *Italy: The Rough Guide* (Harrap Columbus, £8.95). Walkers may want to look at some of the Cicerone Press guides to the Dolomites, etc.

BOOKS

There are virtually no books in English on Italian wildlife, bar Tim Jepson's excellent *Wild Italy* (George Philip, 1991). Plenty of Italian publications are in print though, both for specific areas and for birds, snakes, mammals and so forth.

MAGAZINES

Airone is the market leader among the magazines, with good articles on current environmental issues, and often features on the country's wildlife reserves. *Oasis* is popular with wildlife photo enthusiasts.

CHAPTER FOUR

MOROCCO

F ew countries match the variety and quality of Morocco's wildlife habitats. The great Atlas mountain ranges have allowed some of the more elusive Med **mammals** to evade extinction – Barbary ape is relatively easily seen, and scarcer mammals like lynx, genet and even leopard are possible; while the Saharan fringes hold more mammals in the shape of desert foxes, rodents and occasionally gazelle, as well as providing an ideal environment for cold blooded **reptiles** with a wide variety of snakes and lizards. The Atlas also have some stunning **flowers** and butterflies, the combination of traditional land use and remnants of the original cedar forest suiting them both well.

Birds in Morocco are well known and well studied, and the country is quite exceptional in terms of both resident and migratory species. The coastal wetlands, especially south of Agadir, are internationally significant migration and wintering sites, and the Sahara offers a range of true desert species. In spring and autumn, birds from all over Africa funnel through Morocco to and from the Straits of Gibraltar, the major migration bottleneck in the western Med.

Climate and Land Use

Sadly, many important habitats are under threat. The progress of **desertification** through intensive agricultural land practices, is advancing at an alarming rate, and the effects of **overgrazing** have caused irreparable damage to soils and vegetation alike. However, the government has undertaken some impressive afforestation and reclamation schemes. And by Mediterranean standards, direct persecution of wildlife is limited, though the market places of Marrakesh hold their share of unfortunate chameleons, ground squirrels, goldfinches and Barbary apes imprisoned for entertainment purposes, while bustard hunting continues in the South.

There is better news, on the whole, on **wetlands**, through the combined efforts of the *International Committee for Bird Preservation* and the *Eaux de Fôret* of the Agriculture Ministry. Certain sites are at last receiving the protection they deserve, including study centres at Merdja Zerga and Sidi Bourhaba.

Prickly pear

Morocco's **climate** and vegetation falls into several distinct zones. It is warm and humid along the coastal zones, cooler at altitude within the Atlas ranges and distinctly hotter and drier south of the High Atlas, where midday temperatures often exceed 40°C in summer. Not suprisingly, the plant and animal life in Morocco is accordingly **parochial**, species distributions being closely tied to the habitat and climate type to which they are specifically adapted.

There are three main **vegetation zones**. In the northwest it is typically **Mediterranean**, with semi-arid pastoral land of olive groves and cultivated fields; further inland lie the **Atlas mountains**, where the montane flora of the Middle Atlas range is dominated by cedar forest which forms a unique mosaic of forest and grassland; finally the most southerly zone is the desert fringe or **Sahel**, a harsh environment characterised by tussock grass and the occasional acacia tree. The **soils** are similarly variable. The Atlantic coastal **dune systems** are composed of *rmels* – thin, moveable soils; either *dehs* (which are silty) or *harrouchas* (which are pebbly). The Atlas ranges are predominantly **limestone** and have suffered considerable water erosion. Conversely, the underlying **clay soils** of the lower-lying plains and valleys form good arable land with available water, often appearing as green ribbons through the wilderness. These blackened clay soils cover the regions of Zaer, Chaouia, Abda, Ghaib and Doukkala and, despite their calcium deficiency, provide good cereal crops during the wetter years. The Meknes plateau is however composed of light, red **silicate soils** which are rich in lime and phosphate but are prone to rapid drying.

The **coastal zones** enjoy a more humid atmosphere with frequent morning sea mists and include some of Morocco's most fertile agricultural land, used predominantly in cereal production.

The extensive Atlas zone is dominated by three main mountain ranges: **the Rif** extends along the length of the Mediterranean coast for over 300km from Ceuta to Mellila, reaching an altitude of 2500m. The **Middle Atlas** range lies beyond the Fes plain, rising up from the southwest to the northeast and covered by

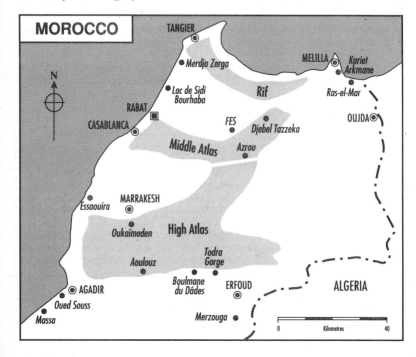

extensive cedar forest. The **High Atlas** range is the highest in Morocco, rising to 4167m in Djebel Toubkal.

Further south on the fringes of the Sahara lies the **Sahel** with its austere landscape; "true" sand dunes, called *ergs*, occupy only twenty percent of the area and of the many types, the mobile crescents known as *barchans* are the most common. Most of the area is covered in a pebbled plateau, known as *hamada*; where these pebbles have become eroded over time to form fine gravels they are known as *reg*, and it is the integrated make-up of these landscape types that creates the unique appearance of the region.

WHEN AND WHERE TO GO

Spring comes surprisingly late in Morocco. April and May are the best overall months for wildlife, though flowers can still be flourishing up in the mountains into July. Bird migration returns through September and October, and these can also be rewarding months for insects, though most of the flowers are pretty burnt-out by then. A winter trip to the south is a good idea, too.

Buses are the standard form of travel and go virtually everywhere, supplementing the limited **train service** along the coast and major city routes. A faster, often less frustrating, alternative is to use **grands taxis** – usually big, old Mercedes – which run along regular routes, carrying up to six passengers; they can be chartered if you want to make more obscure journeys. Car hire is useful, but expensive.

The main sites described are:

● **MEDITERRANEAN COAST** The Moroccan Med has many coastal saltpans and mud flats, and their exceptional accessibility and proximity for **birdwatching** forms a major wildlife attraction. Three of the best sites are clustered around the town of Nador – **Kariet Arkmane**, **Ras-el-Mar** and **Oued Moulouya**.

● **ATLANTIC COAST** The Atlantic is obviously more exposed and its tidal influence leads to a more resilient flora and areas of abundant seabird passage. **Lac de Sidi Bourhaba** and **Merdja Zerga** are two excellent coastal wetlands between Tangier and Rabat, while **Essaouira**, further south, has estuaries and the bird reserve of the **Isle of Mogador** within easy reach.

● **RIF AND MIDDLE ATLAS RANGES** These ranges hold a wide variety of habitats. Near Taza, **Djebel Tazzeka** is a largely commercial forest at the junction of the Rif and the Middle Atlas. Around **Azrou** there are superb cedar forests as well as the lake of **Aguelmame Azigza** and its nearby waterfalls. **Marrakesh** has the remarkable **Jardin Majorelle**, while the Toubkal National Park at **OUKAÏMEDEN** offers outstanding mountain scenery and wildlife.

● **LOWLANDS** Areas such as the plain of Fes have a lower altitude and milder climate, making for vigorous plant growth. Surrounding lakes such as **Lac Douyèt** and **Dayet Aoua** are important as feeding grounds for wintering waders and wildfowl.

● **THE SOUTH** This is in no way a Mediterranean habitat but six of its best wildlife sites have been outlined briefly and include the mountain passes of the **High Atlas** with their superb variety of **raptors**, the stony *hamada* with its collection of **reptiles** and the sand **desert** in the far south and its **oasis** wildlife havens.

THE MEDITERRANEAN COAST

One of the best ways of entering Morocco is via the Spanish enclave of **Melilla**, which is connected by ferry with the Spanish mainland ports of Malaga and Almeria. Once through the administrative muddle at the border, it is a straight run (frequent buses) to the town of **Nador**, which, if lacking the most salubrious accommodation in Morocco, does form a good centre for sites along the Mediterranean coast. Two within easy reach are the salt marshes of **Kariet Arkmane** and the beach of **Ras-el-Mar**. To the east, heading towards the Algerian border, is the freshwater estuary of **Oued Moulouya**.

Kariet Arkmane

KARIET ARKMANE is an excellent site, with easy access and three good viewing points over saltpans and salt marsh. Just outside the town, on the Nador road, it is possible to walk down to the coast (map point 1). The sewage outfall here isn't exactly aesthetic or aromatic but the resulting lack of disturbance allows good views of several **wading birds**. These include both ringed and Kentish plovers, which scamper along the water's edge in their incessant search for food, and the ubiquitous little egret, distinguished from its larger relative, the cattle egret, by its smaller size, black bill and diagnostic yellow feet.

Passing through the town, with the sole mosque and minaret on your left, a track leads out onto the coastal causeway which isolates the lagoon of MAR CHICA. This track then runs past a pumping station and **saltpans** on the right (map point 2). These pans may well hold other waders when not being worked but patience is required. An easier alternative is to continue along the causeway into the **salt marsh itself** (map point 3). The area is covered by the green, fleshy-stemmed shrubby glasswort *Anthrocnemun fructicosum*, whose ability to survive in this most saline of environments is achieved by the use of glands which are capable of salt excretion. This tolerance, making it a characteristic "salt plant" or **halophyte**, allows it to dominate the entire area without competition from other plant species.

The **insect** population of the area is conspicuous and diverse, with a variety of brightly-coloured grasshoppers including the red-winged *Oedipoda germanica*, dragonflies and sand ants *Camponotus vagus*. The **birds** are similarly abundant; positioned comfortably amongst the glasswort, there are good views both across the salt marsh and out to sea, with the species on view including black-winged stilts and greater flamingoes. Out to sea large flocks of coot and great crested grebe can be seen feeding amongst the variety of gulls and terns which pass overhead.

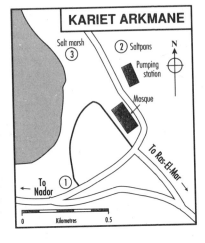

KARIET ARKMANE

Salt marsh ③
② Saltpans N
Pumping station
Mosque
To Ras-El-Mar
To Nador ① ←
0   Kilometres   0.5

Ras-el-Mar

RAS-EL-MAR is a sandy beach resort much frequented by Moroccan holiday-makers. However, past the town and beyond the array of sun-shades, lean-tos and "home tent kits", the beach stretches away uninhabited for miles east towards the Algerian border.

The beach offers a virtually undisturbed **dune system**, colonised by the local plant community. This process of sequential colonisation of an area or habitat by a series of plants is known as **succession** and can be seen in a variety of natural and man-induced situations. First into the sand are the **primary colonisers**, notably the grasses such as marram grass *Ammophila arenaria* and sand couch *Agropyron junceiforme*. Their roots have a binding effect on the sand and the nutrients from their dead leaves enrich the terrain, allowing other species to colonise in their wake. At Ras-el-Mar, examples of these secondary colonisers include sea holly *Eryngium maritimum* and sea spurge *Euphorbia paralias*, which are followed by the larger woody-stemmed species such as mastic tree or lentisc *Pistacia lentiscus*, prickly juniper *Juniperus oxycedrus*, sarsparilla *Smilax aspera* and narrow-leaved cistus *Cistus monspeliensis*. The sequential change as one moves away from the water's edge is particularly noticeable and provides an instantaneous "snapshot" of a continuous and dynamic process.

The passage **seabirds** are dominated by gulls and terns, including that Med speciality Audouin's gull, which breeds offshore on the adjacent CHAFARINAS ISLANDS. Amongst the **waders** found along the shoreline are Kentish plover, dunlin and the now rare slender-billed curlew. This bird strongly resembles its cousin, the curlew, but is smaller (more whimbrel-sized), has a shorter decurved bill and characteristic heart-shaped dappling along its flanks. It is primarily a winter visitor to Morocco but can be seen along the Med coast from late summer onwards. A more familiar wader along the shore is the oystercatcher – unmistakeable in its contrasting black and white plumage with long orange-red bill and bright pink legs. Most interesting of all amongst this variety of waders is the obvious difference in bill lengths which allows **differentiation** in feeding depths. This ensures that the various birds can co-exist with a sufficient food supply without ever being in direct **competition** for the same food source.

One of the most enjoyable aspects of the walk from Ras-el-Mar is the beauty of the sand dunes themselves; and, at the end of the day, there is always the inviting Mediterranean for a quick dip before the return walk.

Oued Moulouya

Further along the coast, almost at the Algerian border, lies the mouth of the **OUED MOULOUYA**. This river (*oued*) runs into a series of freshwater **lagoons**, surrounded by common reed *Phragmites communis* and separated from the Mediterranean by a sand bar only 50m wide at its narrowest point. Such a remarkable division retains the freshwater character of the lagoons while attracting a variety of birds quite distinct from the saline species of Kariet Arkmane.

The lagoons offer a perfect habitat for several of the larger aquatic species such as grey herons and white storks. The herons hunt around the edge of the **reed beds** using stealth and a quicksilver stab to catch their prey of abundant small fish and marsh frogs *Rana ridibunda*. Storks can be distinguished from herons in flight by their extended neck – clearly visible in silhouette – as they soar or fly, often at great height, with outstretched wings or characteristic languid wing beat. The storks are especially obvious during spring and autumn **migration**, when they gather in flocks several hundred strong, flying in oddly shapeless groups.

The site is again readily accessible and offers excellent views of the mixed wader flocks which congregate on the lagoons. These contain large numbers of black-winged stilt, black-tailed godwit, redshank and spotted redshank. The latter bird shows a distinct **seasonality** in its plumage; in winter it has a pale plumage, with a white patch extending up its back, whereas in summer it takes on a much darker (sooty-black) appearance and can be distinguished from the closely-related redshank by its lack of white wingbars.

Black terns and kingfishers demonstrate contrasting **feeding techniques** at Oued Moulouya. The black tern is an expert aviator, skimming over the water surface looking for small fish which it seizes from the water with apparent nonchalance. It is easily distinguished from other terns by its darker upper wings and black body (at least in summer). The kingfisher uses a different technique; its stocky form can be seen hovering over the water until the appropriate moment when it plunges beak-first into the water, more often than not returning to the surface with its unfortunate prey tightly clasped in its bill. The iridescence of the kingfisher is unmistakeable, with a mix of blue and turquoise upper parts, white throat and neck, and chestnut cheeks and underparts. Smaller insect-eating birds in the reeds include fan-tailed and Cetti's warblers.

This Mediterranean coastal strip also holds the remaining spur-thighed **tortoises** *Testudo graeca* to be seen in Morocco, but their numbers are few and sadly declining.

MEDITERRANEAN COAST: ACCESS AND ACCOMMODATION

Kariet Arkmane and Ras-el-Mar

A daily bus from NADOR runs through KARIET ARKMANE on its way to RAS-EL-MAR, returning from the latter around 5.30pm. NADOR is the nearest town for all three featured sites and has a good range of accommodation, from the basic but comfortable *Hotel Marrakech* (Avenue des F.A.R./Omar Al Khiyam 69) to the *Hotel Halid* (two blocks along on the same street), which is a bit pricey but one of the few Moroccan hotels (and restaurants) where you can pay in plastic!

NADOR also provides the additional spectacle of small **bats** hunting for moths around the lamps along the main street. The overhead view from hotel balconies allows a real opportunity to appreciate the skills of echo-location and radar-assisted flight in the half light at dusk.

Oued Moulouya

Personal transport to OUED MOULOUYA is unfortunately a necessity, either by car or chartered taxi (or thumb!). Leaving RAS-EL-MAR on the BERKANE road, follow signs to ZAIO until the left turning which crosses the Oued itself (after about 13km). Then follow the signs to BERKANE until the T-junction where the left turn is sign-posted to EN MOULOUYA (a further 15km). This road eventually comes out onto the beach; the lagoons are clearly visible on the left along the last 3km of the road.

THE ATLANTIC COAST

Morocco's **Atlantic coast** is long and sandy, and broken by occasional river estuaries. Two of these – **Merdja Zerga** and **Lac de Sidi Bourhaba** – are sited between TANGIER and RABAT, and are amongst the best (and certainly most accessible) birdwatching spots in the country. Further south, the delightful coastal town of **Essaouira** has dunes and estuaries, as well as a strong colony of Eleonora's falcons on the offshore **Isle of Mogador**.

Merdja Zerga

MERDJA ZERGA (MERDJA LERGA on some maps) is a large coastal wetland area, close to the town and small summer resort of MOULAY BOUSSELHAM. The site combines deep and shallow water areas, an extensive grassy island, and sand banks – ideal conditions for a variety of terns and gulls.

The surrounding areas typify the Atlantic and Mediterranean coastal belts, with rich agriculture because of their milder **climate**. The relatively humid atmosphere and frequent morning sea mists reduce the extremity of the Moroccan climate, leading to a typical Mediterranean arable landscape of cereal crops (with their spring magenta hue of wild gladioli *Gladiolus segetum*) and groves of olives *Olea europaea*. The roads are lined with a mix of dwarf fan palm *Chamaerops humilis*, the giant succulent century plant *Agave americana*, an introduced species from Mexico whose flowering spike can exceed 10m in height, and especially the **prickly pear** *Opuntia ficus-indica*, introduced it is said by Columbus to the Med and producing red fruits which are edible (and excellent for stomach upsets). These areas are interspersed with open, more barren regions which are used by the large nomadic herds of goats, sheep and cattle as seasonal grazing areas.

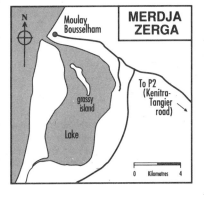

The deeper water areas hold good numbers of **flamingoes** during the autumn and winter, and the shallows teem with mixed **wader flocks** of little ringed plover, black-winged stilt, redshank and black-tailed godwit. Hidden amongst the surrounding vegetation are the ubiquitous grey heron and cattle egret. It is however the **gulls and terns** on the central island which are worthy of the closest inspection, as the large flocks of black terns and lesser black-backed gulls can hold some rarer varieties such as Caspian tern, distinguished by its larger size and huge red bill. The grassy area north of the lake has small numbers of African marsh owl and the site is frequented in winter by slender-billed curlew, another Moroccan rarity.

The size and **habitat diversity** of the site ensure high numbers of birds at any time of year but they also reduce accessibility so that views are often distant and indistinct. It's probably a site for the more dedicated (and equipped) observer with sufficient time to do the site justice. Encouragingly, the Merja Zerga has recently achieved protected status and a warden, Hassan Kachich, is in residence. Another ICBP and *Eaux de Fôret* venture, an Education Centre in MOULAY BOUSSELHAM, is planned for the future.

Lac de Sidi Bourhaba

LAC DE SIDI BOURHABA is an excellent freshwater site with good access, campsite facilities and, since its designation as a nature reserve in 1987, an Education Centre and a resident (and English-speaking) warden, Mustapha El Hanzaoui. The **Education Centre**, on the eastern edge of the lake over the central causeway, is part of a project joint-funded by the International Committee for Bird Protection (ICBP) and the *Eaux de Fôret* of the Agriculture Ministry and provides interpretive material about the site.

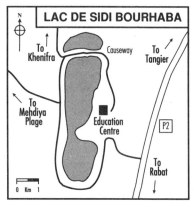

The best viewing points of the lake are from the causeway and from the roadside at the southern tip. The larger **southern section** of the lake has substantial reed beds of *Phragmites communis* and a variety of edge species, such as the brightly-coloured oleander bush *Nerium oleander* and eucalyptus groves (most commonly of the blue gum variety *Eucalyptus globulus* – a local favourite in the Kenitra area) on the slopes. This section holds the deeper waters and attracts numerous crested coot in spring and marbled teal in autumn and winter. The reed bed areas are frequented by little egrets and the melodious warbler whose green and yellow plumage aids its identification. This is also an ideal habitat for a variety of **damselflies** and the western marsh frog *Rana ridibunda*, famed for its spring chorus. Sharing the habitat, in the marshier **northern section**, is the common toad *Bufo bufo*, another nocturnal baritone eager to advertise its presence.

Marsh harriers are often seen circling over the lake, whilst another predator, more frequently seen over the scrubby areas, is the **black-shouldered kite**, with long wings and a shortish forked tail. The bird can easily be identified by its whitish head, pale blue-grey upper parts with white tail and diagnostic "black shoulders", or its distinctive flight pattern, which includes sporadic slow hovering and rapid glides on pointed wings. It is a fascinating bird to watch hunting for mice and large insects at dusk. Another bird to watch for at dusk over the northern section of the lake is the **African marsh owl**, whose contrasting pale face and chocolate "eyes" make it quite unmistakeable. It's confined to Africa, having, strangely, never made it across the Straits of Gibraltar into Iberia.

The site and Centre are well worth a visit if only to encourage the continuation of such ventures through the interest of visitors, both local and tourist. Any such small action which enhances the status of wildlife in Morocco and shows its economic value definitely needs support.

Essaouira

South of the picturesque town of **ESSAOURIA**, an extensive **sandy beach** stretches away, backed by a dune system with a spartan covering of marram grass *Ammophila arenaria*. About 2km south of the town are the remains of an old royal pavilion, half-submerged in the sand. Looking out to sea, the ISLE OF MOGADOR – a protected reserve – is clearly visible, whilst inland an open river course (*wadi*) flows off in the direction of the main ESSAOURIA–AGADIR road (the P8). This **wadi** combines both open water and muddy edges, encouraging a variety of waders and egrets, among their number Kentish plover and cattle egret. The area also has a large contingent of gulls and terns, worthy of close inspection as it often contains unusual varieties such as gull-billed tern and Mediterranean gull.

In summer and autumn, a walk back to the town in the half light will almost certainly produce a sighting of the **Eleanora'a falcons** which breed on the Isle of Mogador (its only non-Mediterranean breeding site) as they come inland to hawk for insects at dusk. They make a breath-taking sight, gliding in low over the sea with their characteristic slow wing-beat, and the short return walk can produce as many as two or three dozen of these magnificent birds.

Finally, look out for **arboreal goats** as you travel around the neighbouring countryside; the ones in this part of Morocco have become adept at climbing to the argan trees in their search for fodder, making a very bizarre sight.

ATLANTIC COAST: ACCESS AND ACCOMMODATION

Merdja Zerga

MOULAY BOUSSELHAM can be reached by bus from SOUK EL ARBA DU RHARB on the main Tangier to Rabat road (P2) and railway. The road south from the town has a right turn (towards Kenitra), leading to a smaller village on the right-hand side; passing through this, a track leads to the southern side of the lagoon and a good though distant viewpoint of the whole area.

Accommodation is limited in MOULAY BOUSSELHAM; there is one hotel, the three-star *Le Lagon*, which also has the only bar in the town. Camping facilities are also available, however, in an attractive setting alongside the lagoon.

Lac de Sidi Bourhaba

LAC DE SIDI BOURHABA is located close to the town of MEHDIYA PLAGE and is easily reached by travelling north from Rabat (on the P2) until, after about 25km, you reach a left turn signposted MEHDIYA PLAGE. This leads directly to the lake and eventually the Education Centre. There are camping facilities along the edge of the lake; closest accommodation otherwise is at RABAT (30km) or KENITRA (12km).

Essaouira

The town is regularly served by bus from Marrakesh or Casablanca. Among many hotels, the *Remparts* (18 Rue Ibn Rochd) is welcoming and economical; there is a campsite east along the beach towards Diabat.

The port at Essaouira is a fascinating morning sight – and stalls serve brilliant fresh sardines on scrubbed tables just outside the harbour.

THE RIF AND ATLAS RANGES

The **Rif**, the the lowest of Morocco's three main mountain ranges, rises just inland of the Mediterranean coast. It's a typically Med habitat, with cork oak forest and a few truly mountainous outcrops – such as the featured 2000-metre **Djebel Tazzeka**.

Further south are the ranges of the Middle and High Atlas. **Fes** – Morocco's most fascinating medieval city – is the gateway city for the **Middle Atlas**, and a good base to see the wildlife of the **lowlands** of the country. The city itself is full of roosting and nesting birds at night, while the nearby "Middle Atlas lakes" – **Douyèt** and **Aaoua** – are excellent for waterfowl and waders. Into the Middle Atlas proper, the cedar forests around **Azrou** are amongst the last remnants of this habitat type, which once surrounded much of the Med, and the lake at **Aguelmame Azigza** adds further interest to the area.

Approaching the High Atlas, you will almost certainly travel via Marrakesh, which has wildlife interest in its oliveries, and in the beautiful Jardin Majorelle, created by the French artist. Heading into the hills, the easiest and most rewarding access to the High Atlas is the National Park at **OUKAÏMEDEN** .

The Rif: Djebel Tazzeka

The National Park at **DJEBEL TAZZEKA** (1980m) provides a fascinating insight into the status of "protected areas" within Morocco. Located at the point where the Rif merges with the Middle Atlas, the park is managed predominantly for **forestry** purposes, although in terms of wildlife the 76-km loop from TAZA contains several other points of interest. The main timber crop is **cork oak** *Quercus suber*, which is stripped of its bark up to a height of approximately three metres, apparently as a function of the curvature of the bark itself; younger trees of smaller diameters remain untouched. Making up the rest of the forest flora are holm oak *Quercus ilex* and grey-leaved cistus *Cistus albidus*, whose bright pink flowers add a welcome splash of colour to the forest, and the commonplace bracken *Pteridium aquilinum*.

The National Park has several open plains, flatter areas whose sparsely vegetated landscapes provide perfect habitat for hunting **shrikes and rollers**. The telegraph lines are the place to search for these sharp-eyed predators. Amongst the more obvious ground-living species are tawny pipits and crested or thekla larks. These two larks are virtually indistinguishable in the field unless seen together; for identification connoisseurs, the thekla lark is slightly smaller with paler underparts, the bill is shorter and less pointed, and the erected crest is more fan-like than the tall spike associated with the crested lark.

Cork oak
Quercus suber

There are many familiar north European species, too, amongst the woodland birds, such as the wood pigeon, nuthatch, short-toed treecreeper and various titmice. The woodland floor also provides ideal conditions for a variety of **butterflies**; from June onwards the glades and forest margins provide shelter for dark green fritillaries *Mesoacidalia aglaja*, and the more open flowery fields for knapweed fritillaries *Melitaea phoebe*, large grizzled skippers *Pyrgus alveus* and Barbary skippers *Muschampia mohammed*. Another frequenter of this forest floor is the magnificent **hoopoe**; impossible to mistake, with its cinnamon plumage barred with black and white, it nests in holes in the older cork oaks.

Fes and the "Middle Atlas Lakes"

No matter how dedicated a naturalist one may be, time should be found on every schedule to appreciate something of the atmosphere of **FES**. The so-called "artisan centre" of Morocco, the whole town is a protected UNESCO site as the most complete medieval Arab city in the world, and despite the huge influx of tourists, it still merits the designation. While taking in these ancient characteristics of the city, spare a thought for the **pollution** caused by the various craft activities. The river bubbles in at the top of the old city in a relatively clean state, but by the time it has flowed past the tanneries at the bottom of the hill it has become turgid and foul; although traditional dyeing techniques remain in use – the dyeing pits look like something out of Hieronymus Bosch – chemical dyes have mostly been substituted for vegetable ones, and the resultant mix is truly unpleasant.

Pollution aside, there are few cities to compete with Fes for the quality of its **evening bird roost** – and if you're lucky enough to find a room in the *Hotel du Commerce* in Fes el Djedid you can enjoy it from the windows, which overlook the gardens of the **Royal Palace**. The frenzied activities of the resident starlings are soon overshadowed as dozens of **little egrets** fly over the city to their nocturnal roost sites in the Middle Atlas lakes and environs. Their yellow feet, barely visible in the half light, are diagnostic but one soon becomes accustomed to their languid, graceful flight and the long, slender silhouette. However the stars of the show must be the hordes of

Alpine swift

Alpine swifts which gather at dusk before returning to their nests in the old city. The number of swifts may well exceed ten thousand and they make an exhilarating spectacle as they wheel through the skies in their characteristic crescent-shape, hunting for insects. Their shrill calls, reminiscent of a small falcon, make a resounding chorus in the evening sky.

Finally, as the light begins to fade, cast your eyes along the rooftops and you may be able to make out the angular profiles of **white storks** on their nests atop the buildings that line the perimeter of FES EL DJEDID. Even when their unmistakeable pied plumage is no longer discernible in the fading light, the unique shape of body and bill adds a final memorable touch to the end of the day.

Lake Douyèt

LAKE DOUYÈT is one of the series of "Middle Atlas Lakes" which lie to the south and west of Fes. Access to the lake is straightforward enough though there was some objection to my entering the area at the western edge of the lake – over the fairly obvious field boundary – so it may be as well to restrict any visit to the eastern side of the lake, which anyway allows adequate views over the water.

The **surrounding vegetation** is fairly sparse by summer, the ground flora consisting of sporadic clumps of spiny asparagus *Asparagus acutifolius* and European sarsparilla *Smilax aspera*, although the wetter lake margins still have reed beds. Doubtless the flora is richer in the wetter months of spring. However, even in the summer drought the lake retains excellent **wader and wildfowl** numbers. The deeper waters are frequented by ruddy shelduck, gadwall and Cape shoveler; the former is resplendent in its orange-chestnut plumage with distinctive pale head, black bill and legs, black tail, and obvious green speculum on the wing in flight; the Cape shoveler is a vagrant to Morocco and closely resembles its more familiar relative, the shoveler, but has a smaller head which accentuates the length of the bill.

The margins of the lake form an ideal feeding place for a variety of **waders**, including black-winged stilts, Kentish plover, green sandpiper, dunlin, redshank and avocet, another distinctive wader with its black and white plumage, long lead-blue legs and diagnostic long slender upcurved bill. This most elegant of waders is fascinating to watch as it feeds in the shallows with its characteristic sideways-sifting motion of the head. The swallow-like collared pratincole is another typical summer species of the lake.

Amongst all the activity on and around the water, it is easy to forget to glance skywards for circling **raptors** but the occasional check can produce dividends. This is a fine site for harriers and a particularly frequent visitor is the **Montague's harrier**. About the size of the more familiar hen harrier, Montague's can be distinguished from the hen by the reduced band of white on the rump and a more buoyant flight.

Dayet Aaoua

Keen birders with time and a vehicle will want to check out each of the main Middle Atlas Lakes between Fes and Azrou – Dayet Ifrah, Dayet Hachlaf and Dayet Aaoua. If time is limited, though, **DAYET AAOUA**, just off the road to the south of IMMOUZER, is the most convenient and offers a fine mix of habitats, with extensive shallows at its eastern end, a deep central zone and a reed bed fringe at the western end which leads into an area of mud flats.

The **deep water areas** hold large numbers of **grebes** (great-crested, black-necked and little) and two species of **coot**. The more familiar common coot has a white facial shield and bill contrasting sharply with its black plumage; it's joined in spring and summer by its rarer and more showy relative, the crested coot. Slightly larger in size, the crested coot can be distinguished by its blue-grey bill and, during the breeding season, a pair of bright red knobs on either side of the facial shield. The **shallows** are stalked incessantly by grey herons and cattle egrets, the latter using its diagnostic yellow bill to spear the abundant **marsh frogs**. The cattle egret derives its name from its feeding strategy of walking behind grazing livestock and feeding on the trail of insects that are disturbed in their wake; bolder individuals have been known to hitch a ride on the backs of the horses and cattle. In late summer, the shallows hold large numbers of **green frog** *Rana ridibunda perezi*, who lie immersed in their watery sanctuary and are particularly vocal during the night and early morning. One of the few remaining species of **amphibians** to be found in Morocco, they are relics of a bygone, more fertile era and are now restricted to marshlands and oases.

Also abundant in spring and summer are brightly coloured **dragonflies** and **damselflies**, including the large red damselfly *Pyrrhosoma nymphula* and the blue species *Enallagma cyathigerum*; in their iridescent reds, blues and greens, they form a brilliant spectacle whirring over the water. The **reed beds** ring with the sound of migrating reed and fan-tailed warblers and glimpses of flitting grey and yellow wagtails are frequent. In the summer the skies are full of hirundines, predominantly swallows and sand martins, the latter with their contrasting brown upper parts, white underparts and brown breast-band.

The variety of wildlife provides an irresistible magnet to resident and migrant **birds of prey**, one of the most common being the red kite. A true master of the skies, it can be identified by its long deeply-forked chestnut tail and narrow, strongly-angled wings, as it soars effortlessly in its search for carrion or live prey, such as rabbits and small birds. The local individuals seem to have learnt that there is an abundant source of carrion readily available along the lengths of nearby roadsides, casualties which provide a supplement to their natural diet.

Azrou

The **Atlas cedar** *Cedrus atlantica* forests of **AZROU** are a unique habitat in Morocco, and one well worthy of extensive exploration; their verdant atmosphere contrasts starkly with the bleakness of the surrounding Middle Atlas range. As you travel south from Azrou, the landscape becomes progressively dominated by extensive kermes oak *Quercus coccifera*, manna or flowering ash *Fraxinus ornus*, Atlas cedar and juniper *Juniperus communis* forest. Watered by the depressions that sweep across from the Atlantic, these slopes are ablaze with colour during the spring months; the deep blue of mountain germander *Teucrium montanum* and claret of thyme *Thymus vulgaris* intermingle to form a resplendent carpet over the forest floor.

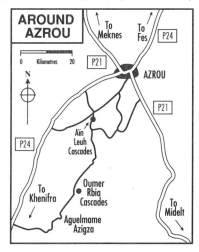

Amongst the glades beneath the giant cedars there's a rewarding flora, dominated by the vibrant pink **paeony** *Paeonia officinalis*. Other species which form this carpet are the bright red pheasant's eye *Adonis annua*, mountain cranesbill *Geranium pyrenaicum*, alkanet *Anchusa officinalis*, narrow-leaved bellflower *Campanula persicifolia*, the tiny, scarlet Deptford pink *Dianthus armeria* and a wealth of golden composites and orchids. These forested slopes are also frequented by the Moroccan **rock lizard** *Lacerta perspicillata* and the Mediterranean chameleon *Chamaeleo chamaeleon*; the former uses its size and agility to capture its prey whereas the latter relies on the more subtle strategy of colour coordination, stealth and a quicksilver tongue.

Insect life is widespread throughout Morocco and most colourful of all are the **butterflies**, of which over one hundred species have been recorded, primarily within the Middle and High Atlas ranges. The more obvious varieties, which can be seen from April onwards, are generally larger and more brightly coloured, such as the brilliant sulphur Cleopatra *Gonepteryx cleopatra*, large tortoiseshell *Nymphalis polychloros* and the cardinal *Pandoriana pandora*. Flying on the grassy slopes within the ranges are less conspicuous varieties such as the hermit *Chazara briseis*, Spanish marbled white *Melanargia ines* and blues, including the small Lorquin's *Cupido lorquinii* and false baton *Philotes abencerragus*.

These grassy slopes also offer the best opportunities for observing one of Morocco's most famous inhabitants, the **Barbary ape** (this is in fact not an ape at all but rather a macaque without a tail). The apes can be seen foraging for food on the ground beneath the cedars, often at the forest edge. The troupes are however relatively shy and any excessive intrusion is likely to be met with a rapid retreat to the nearby invisible sanctuary of the treetops. Other, more elusive, inhabitants of the cedar forest include wild boar and red fox.

The **birdlife** of the cedar forest is just as exciting. It includes a variety of finches and titmice, and this is one of the few places in Morocco where both resident species of **woodpecker** may be seen; the great spotted and Levaillant's green. The former is a familiar resident of north European woodlands, instantly identifiable by its pied plumage and red crown and rump, but the latter is singularly north African, separated geographically from its more familiar European cousin, the green woodpecker. **Booted eagles** are also to be seen cruising over the forests in their search for prey down below, often closely pursued by the mobbing ravens.

Aguelmame Azigza and Oum er Rbia

Further into the cedar forests lie the large lake of **AGUELMAME AZIGZA** and the spectacular **waterfalls of Oum er Rbia**. The lake is large and frequently used by Moroccans for camping and picnicking. The steep-sided slopes which lead into the cedar forest form an ideal habitat for many forms of **insect** life. One of the more common groups are the grasshoppers, crickets and locusts; a particularly noticeable one is the red and black *Eugaster spinulosus*, whose bright colouration acts as a warning to would-be predators about its use of a foul-smelling liquid as the ultimate deterrent. Another common group are the **beetles**, which generally avoid the heat of the day by remaining underground in burrows, emerging at night to feed. The darkling beetles (part of the family of beetles known as the *Tenebrionids*) are particularly abundant and voracious scavengers. A common, carnivorous species is the white-spotted *Anthia venator*, whose colour pattern acts as an aid to heat reflection. Finally there are numerous **butterflies** adorning the slopes; particularly attractive is the Amanda's blue *Plebicula amanda*, which can be found at altitudes in excess of 600m through till midsummer, if nectar remains available.

The deep waters of the **lake itself** provide perfect feeding grounds for water-birds. Grebes and coot are abundant, and in winter the lake is an important refuge for marbled teal, a rather rare duck, recognisable by its light and dark brown "marbled" plumage and dark smudge through the eye. Amongst the woodland birds, it is possible to come across the elusive **hawfinch**, whose huge bill, short white-tipped tail and bold white patches high on blue-black wings make it one of the most attractive of the finches.

Around 18km north are the **cascades** of OUM ER RBIA, which are a fascinating contrast to the tranquillity of AGUELMAME. There are over forty waterfalls which fall dramatically from the huge limestone cliff, making an exhilarating spectacle. Back alongside the car park area, there is also a small lagoon, again with cascades, which allows good views of wagtails and warblers.

Marrakesh – the Majorelle Gardens

Any visit to the **High Atlas** will take in a trip to **MARRAKESH**, still a distinctive and vibrant city despite the infamous tourist hassle, especially around the Place Djemaa el Fna. When you have bustled your way through the story-tellers, snake charmers, dancers, acrobats, stall holders, souvenir sellers, musicians and water-peddlars of the Place (and if you have any dirhams left!), you may well benefit from a retreat to the peaceful haven of one of the many **ornamental gardens** which can be found in the city.

One of the most fascinating of these is the **Jardin Majorelle** (or BOU SAF SAF), created by the French painter Louis Majorelle. It's a mere ten minutes by taxi (at a negotiable fare) from the centre of the medina and its green tranquillity contrasts starkly with the surrounding marketplaces. Its collection of rubber trees *Ficus elastica*, dwarf fan palms *Chamaerops humilis* and century plants *Agave americana* create a distinctly subtropical feeling. The many pools are covered with white waterlilies *Nymphaea alba* and provide drinking and bathing water for the resident turtle doves and house buntings. Turtle doves can be identified by their sandy-rufous upper parts and well-graduated black tail with white edges, whilst the contrasting chestnut body plumage and ashen head of the house bunting make it instantly recognisable. The overriding sound of the gardens however is the constant chatter of the **common bulbuls** amongst the upper leaves of the date palms *Phoenix dactylifera*. The bulbul resembles a dark, long-tailed thrush with brown upper parts and a rounded, sooty head, but it is its perky and voluble behaviour which most characterises this African speciality.

At the end of the day as you overlook the Place Djemaa el Fna, you may notice the thousands of **little swifts** (distinguishable by their white rumps) which wheel overhead in the half light.

Oukaïmeden and Toubkal National Park

South of MARRAKESH the extensive **TOUBKAL NATIONAL PARK** forms the heart of High Atlas hiking territory, with North Africa's highest peak, the Djebel Toubkal at 4167m. In addition to walking, the range offers another unique collection of flora and fauna. A good base to use, at the eastern end of the park, is the winter ski resort of **OUKAÏMEDEN**.

The National Park boasts many **endemic plants** which have become isolated over the centuries. Thyme *Thymus vulgaris* and thorny caper *Capparis spinosa* are interspersed with the blue-mauve pitch trefoil *Psoralea bituminosa*, pink mallow-leaved bindweed *Convolvulus althaeoides*, everlasting pinks *Xeranthemum annuum*, cupidone *Catananche coerulea*, rock phagnalon *Phagnalon rupestre* and golden spreads of broom *Cytisus scoparius*. At their highest altitudes, the limestone slopes of the Atlas offer a bleak environment, either covered by winter snows or scorched by the summer sun. However some species are capable of surviving even under these conditions, for example the widespread purple tussocks of the hedgehog broom *Erinacea anthyllis*.

Moorish gecko
Tarcentola mauritanica

Some Moroccan **amphibians** are also capable of survival at these altitudes. The painted frog *Discoglossus pictus* is a frequent contributor to the chorus of the High Atlas *oueds*, whilst the whistle of the north African race of the green toad *Bufo viridis*, famed for its ability to change its body colour to blend in with the surrounding environment, can be heard at altitudes over 2000m. Several species of **reptile** have adapted to the specific environment of the stony walls that form the towns and villages. The Spanish wall lizard *Podarcis hispanica* is a common basker on domestic walls, as is the Moorish gecko *Tarcentola mauritanica* which feeds, by day and night, on the abundant spiders.

TOUBKAL's rocky slopes are home to butterflies such as the Moroccan copper *Thersamonia phoebus*, whereas in the higher gorges (1700m) the desert orange tip *Colotis evagore* is prevalent, being found on its larval food plant, the thorny caper. Praying mantises may also be seen, such as *Eremiaphila* and *Rivetina baetica* whose brown colouration provides excellent camouflage in these stony parts. Amongst the rocky outcrops you might also catch a fleeting glimpse of the black and white tail of a foraging **ground squirrel**, quite common in this area.

The **birds** of Oukaïmeden are similarly distinct from those of the lower ranges. The beautifully coloured **Moussier's redstart** lives in the scrubby bushes and the **crimson-winged finch** often feeds in flocks on the grassy slopes around the village. Both these species are found only in the north African mountains; the latter is a rather thick-billed finch, with mottled brown plumage and pink wings, tail and cheeks. Dippers are common along the riverbeds and, in the rocky crevices above, both species of chough – the mountain dwellers of the Corvid family – can be seen.

It is also possible to see the resident booted eagles or lanner falcons wheeling in the skies, or even a flock of brilliant **bee-eaters** with their multi-coloured plumage, long curved bill and projecting middle-tail feathers, making their characteristic "prruip" call as they glide gracefully above.

RIF AND ATLAS RANGES: ACCESS AND ACCOMMODATION

Djebel Tazzeka

There is no public transport to the park, but the road is signposted from TAZA or from the main FES-TAZA road (P1). If all else fails, ask locally for directions. TAZA is the obvious base for the region; the *Grand Hotel du Dauphine* (Place de L'Independence, Taza) is superb value, or there's a campsite.

Fes

FES is the easiest base for Douyèt and Aaoua lakes. A good base in the city is the *Hotel du Commerce* (Place des Alaouites), in the Fes El Djedid quarter. For an absolute blow-out on couscous and tagine, try the *Roi De La Biere* restaurant (Av. Med. V.); and for the best view of the old town from an atmosphere of total decadence have at least a drink at the *Palais Jamai* hotel above the old town walls.

Lake Douyèt

The lake is only 20km from the centre of FES on the MEKNES road (P1); get off the bus (or hitch) at DOUYÈT and it is 2–3km west along the P3 on the right-hand side. It does not feature on the main road maps of the country.

Dayet Aaoua

Aaoua is about 8km south of IMOUZZER on the main FES–AZROU road (P24). The turning is to the east, signposted DAYET AAOUA, and the lake lies a further 1–2km along this road on the right. AZROU is a reasonable alternative base to FES (see below).

Azrou

The cedar forests are extensive, but a rewarding loop follows the P21 MIDELT road to the TOUMLILINE turning (right) through the forest to the S303 junction; from here turn left to AÏN LEUH or right to TICURIRINE and back to AZROU. The road is good but narrow, and hitching (over any part of the way) is a distinct possibility. The OUM ER RBIA CASCADES are also accessible from AZROU, where a daily bus runs as far as AÏN LEUH (which has its own, smaller falls); from here Oum er Rbia is 35km south, with no public transport and uncertain hitching. AGUELMAME AZIGZA is another 18km on the main road towards KHENIFRA.

For the cedar forets, AZROU is the best base, with the good and cheap *Hotel Restaurant Bar des Cedres* (Place Mohamed V) amongst other hotels. For the cascades and the lake, KHENIFRA is an alternative but less attractive base.

Marrakesh

The city offers a wide variety of accommodation (and associated price range); try to persuade the hassle merchants to take you to the *Hotel CTM*, next to the old bus station on Place Djemaa El Fna, which has been the best cheap hotel in Marrakesh for the last ten years – and has a roof terrace overlooking the Place.

Oukaïmeden

As a winter ski centre, OUKAÏMEDEN has plenty of accommodation, including the recommended *Chez Juju, Hotel de L'Angour*, which provides dinner, bed and breakfast for under £10. Access from MARRAKESH is by *grand taxi* (less frequent outside the skiing season) or by negotiating a fare with an ordinary taxi. TOUBKAL can also be reached from ASNI and IMLIL, to the west.

THE SOUTH

The south of Morocco is scarcely a Mediterranean habitat, but with its terrific desert scenery and splendid wildlife, it seems perverse to exclude it from this account. The sites chosen, **Oued Sous** and especially **Oued Massa**, both close to AGADIR, are primarily for water birds; the gorge at **Aoulouz** has birds of prey and spectacular scenery; while the **Todhra Gorge** and the area around **Boulmane du Dâdes** give an excellent picture of the rocky steppes on the desert edge. For true sand desert landscape, **Merzouga** is the easiest spot to get to.

Around Agadir: Sous and Massa rivers

OUED SOUS, ten minutes by car or taxi from the resort of AGADIR, could not be more conveniently situated. Once there, a walk along the northern bank of the river gives good close views of a variety of **waders and wildfowl**. Most common are the greater flamingo, spoonbill, ruddy shelduck, avocet, greenshank, curlew, bar-tailed godwit and black-winged stilt – a real feast of size, shape and colour. Amongst the large numbers of less conspicuous gulls and terns, there are sandwich terns and slender-billed gulls. Even the scrubby banks, where they merge into the expanse of marsh glasswort or samphire *Salicornia herbacea*, hold good numbers of migrant warblers and Barbary partridge.

Oued Massa

OUED MASSA is a little further south from AGADIR – and takes some effort to reach if you don't have transport. However, the inaccessibility of this superb site is balanced by the quality of its wildlife. Oued Massa is a large inland lagoon, separated from the Atlantic by a narrow sand bar, only 50m wide.

The habitat mix is as good as anywhere in Morocco: the northern **sand bars** hold good flocks of sandgrouse (black-bellied and spotted varieties) in the early morning; the various **pools and reed fringes** along the eastern edge have a variety of waders, including black-tailed godwit, turnstone, dunlin, snipe and little crake; whilst the **deeper waters** teem with greater flamingo, spoonbill, white stork and black-winged stilt. Look out also for the **glossy ibis** – never common, it has a curlew-like decurved bill and is coloured an iridescent purple – and, overhead, for the marsh harrier, Bonelli's eagle, and that most accomplished of anglers, the osprey.

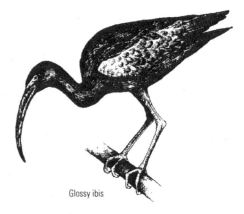
Glossy ibis

A special bird of this part of the coast is the **bald ibis**, whose world population is now down to well less than 100 pairs, almost all breeding in remote gorges in southern Morocco. It's a strange-looking bird, all glossy black apart from a bald red face surrounded by a shaggy ruff of spiky feathers, making it look like a cross between a glossy ibis and a turkey. Oued Massa is as good a place as any for seeing feeding flocks of them.

The surrounding scrubby areas are frequented by black-headed bush shrike and a variety of mammals such as Egyptian mongoose, Cape hare and jackal.

The Dâdes Steppe and the Todra Gorge

The Dâdes, rambling east from Ouarzazate, is the harshest and most desolate of the southern valleys – the river, for much of its length, barely visible above ground. However, a route along the valley provides a fine diversion in the loop of the Dâdes and, to the east, Todra gorges. And there is excellent opportunity to observe some of the Moroccan desert edge, or steppe, wildlife

The **steppe wildlife** is easily accessible. A good point to start from is **BOUMALNE**, from where a 7-kilometre dirt track leads to the village of TAGDILT. The skyline is broken only by the occasional acacia or wattle trees *Acacia pycnantha* or date palm *Phoenix dactylifera* and expanses of esparto grass *Stipa tenacissima*, although rocky outcrops do have flowering broom *Cytisus scoparius* in May and large pink cistus *Cistus icanus* and Southern corn marigold *Crystanthemum myconis*, which break up the monotony of the landscape.

These drier, *hamada* plains provide an ideal habitat for some of Morocco's larger **snakes**, the horseshoe whip snake *Colouber hippocrepis*, which can exceed 2m in length, and the Montpelier snake *Malpolon monspessulanus*. Also found in this harsh environment are the Atlas agama *Agama stellio* and the spiny-footed lizard *Acanthodactylus erythurus*. Amongst the insect life hidden during the heat of the day under any available shelter, such as rocks or boulders (or rucksacks or shoes!) are **spiders, scorpions and camel spiders**. Only six species of scorpion that are found in Morocco are actually poisonous, although the dark-brown *Androctonus australis* is particularly venomous. The camel-spiders catch their prey with the use of their (relatively) huge jaws rather than a poisonous sting; one of the most abundant varieties is *Galeoides granti*, whose rapid movement and small size make close observation almost impossible.

Water conservation is the major problem for larger animals and birds in this arid environment; the edmi gazelle and the smaller, rarer addax antelope obtain their moisture from the thorn bushes and dried grasses. The **bird species** are quite different to those in the cooler and wetter north, with specialists of the steppes such as cream-coloured courser, thick-billed lark, tawny pipit and mourning and red-rumped wheatear. The skies are patrolled by long-legged buzzard and lanner falcon, and sightings of houbara bustard have been recorded.

The Todra Gorge

The **TODRA GORGE**, stretching into the High Atlas north of Tinerhir, offers the rare combination of convenient access and accommodation, whilst managing to retain a feeling of isolation and abandon. And the wildlife is good, too!

Walking from the hotels, which lie within the "outer" part of the gorge, you soon get a superb view of the gorge walls, rising at points to 100m. The river has fine resident populations of marsh frog and green toad *Bufo viridis*, and the lower slopes hold numbers of scampering ground squirrel. Crossing the **ford** (only knee-deep in late summer), you enter the inner part of the gorge, whose steep-sided slopes make a breathtaking sight. The scrubby areas have common bulbul, olivaceous and Cetti's warbler and the rocky slopes ring with the songs of black wheatear, blue rock thrush and rock dove. Overhead wheel numbers of pale crag martins, while Bonelli's eagles soar over the gorge crests from their nearby eyries.

Merzouga

The village of **MERZOUGA** stands adjacent to the biggest sand dune system in Morocco, **Erg Chebbi**, and offers fascinating views of Morocco's true **"desert" wildlife**. Within these desert areas, plants must survive on the short-lived spring bloom strategy whilst conditions are favourable; such strategists include dwarf varieties of pink asphodels *Asphodelus aestivus* and *A. fistulosus* and yellow crown daisies *Crysanthemum coronarium* which are literally here one day and gone the next! Even under the stones of the broken *hamada*, colonies of **lichens** and microscopic algae eke out an existence, their shade-tolerance and ability to obtain water from condensation allowing them to survive in this harshest of environments.

Of the **reptiles**, the desert is the home of many colourful variations of the spiny-tailed lizard *Uromastyx acanthinurus* and three-toed skink *Chalcides chalcides*, commonly known as "sand fish" because of their apparent ability to "swim" through the sand. Typical desert **mammals** adopt a nocturnal lifestyle to avoid the heat of the day and include the desert hedgehog, numerous rodents such as the jerboa (or kangaroo rat) and predators such as the fennec fox, whose characteristic large ears serve two purposes, used both in directional hearing (invaluable for nocturnal hunting) and heat radiation to aid body cooling.

For obvious reasons, these mammals (and some reptiles) are most active at night. Short of walking out into the desert with a torch – an exciting experience, but *be sure to wear boots* – some idea of the night-time activity can be had by looking for **tracks and trails** in the sand, early the next morning. Lizards plough a furrow with their tail with dots either side from their feet; most rats and gerbils hop, leaving a row of double dots; snakes leave a long bed or a series of S-shapes; and foxes and jackals leave footprints. Even beetles leave a distinctive trail. All good stuff for the aspiring nature detective.

The **birdlife** of the area is also distinct from that found throughout the rest of Morocco; the oases form sanctuaries for fulvous babblers, blue-cheeked bee-eaters and the elusive, and rare, desert sparrow, whilst the open areas occasionally hold Arabian bustard, desert warbler and hoopoe lark.

Merzouga is well and truly on the "birding circuit". John Gooders' *Where to Watch Birds in Britain and Europe* – essential reading for any self-respecting birder – says that the first café on the track from Erfoud to Merzouga has a birders' log which is a "gripping read". Certainly, the diversity of desert larks and wheatears around here can have even the expert reaching for a field guide.

THE SOUTH: ACCESS AND ACCOMMODATION

Oued Sous

The site is easily reached from the main AGADIR–INEZGANE road (P8) where there is a right turn, signposted *Hotel Pyramid/Hotel Hacienda*, 2km beyond the airport. Where the road turns right again (another 2km) to the Royal Palace, a track leads straight to the Oued banks. AGADIR, only 14km north, is the obvious place to stay.

Oued Massa

For a prolonged visit to **OUED MASSA**, the camping and chalet complex (☎08) at SIDI R'BAT is ideal. It is an attractive place, popular with birders, and extremely well run by the affable Marcel Hamelle (who speaks good English). The complex also has a good but slightly expensive (licensed) restaurant – and it holds interesting populations of Mauritian toad *Bufo Mauritanica* in the shower block at night! The café terrace makes a luxurious viewing platform, too: one which provided me with the magnificent sight of an overhead flock of eight bald ibis on my first afternoon; birdwatching the easy way!

Getting to the complex is not easy without your own transport. SIDI R'BAT is signposted from the AGADIR–TIZNIT road (P30) at TIFERHAL, and the complex is further signposted (right) beyond MASSA, as a sandy track takes over for the final 8–9km. Without a car, your best bet is to take a bus from AGADIR to MASSA, then hitch or walk. Once at Sidi R'bat the lagoons are right next door along a well-marked trail; access to the dunes is prohibited since the site has recently achieved protected status.

Boumalne du Dâdes

The town is on the main OUAZARZATE–ER RACHIDIA road. Travelling east from the town, the track to TAGDILT lies on the right-hand side just beyond a garage on the opposite side of the road. The track crosses a dry river bed (*wadi*) after about 3km and most of the species described can be seen from here onwards. Accommodation adjacent to the site is available in BOUMALNE, with two recommended hotels along the track that leads north from the roadside service station.

Todra gorge

The Todra Gorge is located north of TINERHIR (53km east of BOUMALNE DU DÂDES on the P32). It's on the tourist circuit, so there are shared taxis available. There are campsites on the approach and three small hotels at the gorge mouth.

Merzouga

Access to MERZOUGA is obtained via a series of ill-marked tracks over the *hamada* either from ERFOUD (about 50km), which is a worse track but follows (approximately) the line of telegraph poles to Merzouga, or from RISSANI (about 30km), which is a slightly better track but virtually unmarked. Good orienteering skills or preferably a guide (readily available from Erfoud or Rissani) are recommended, as is a reliable form of transport.

The hotel in Merzouga, just outside the village alongside ERG CHEBBI, is excellent value and an experience in its own right. From here you can simply walk out into the dunes, and find a comfortable resting place; after watching the sun set over the dunes, sit back and appreciate the formation of a perfect night sky over the lightless desert. The hassles of the journey are soon forgotten!

information and publications

General information is available from local tourist board (*ONMT*) offices or *Syndicats d'Initiatives* which can be found in most major capitals as well as in Morocco.

National conservation issues are the responsibility of the *Eaux de Fôret* of the Ministère de L'Agriculture.

MAPS
The best available are published by Michelin (1:1,000,000; sheet 169 and generally the most accurate), Kummerley and Frey (1:1,000,000) and Hildebrand (1:900 000; updated and clear).

More detailed — though semi-restricted — **Moroccan Survey sheets** are printed in French in scales of 1:50,000 and 1:100,000. These can sometimes be obtained in Britain from the map shops listed on p.368.

GUIDES
Morocco: The Rough Guide (Harrap Columbus) is a bit of a classic. If you're exploring the Atlas, supplement it with the walkers' guides on the area published by Collomb or Cicerone.

BOOKS
There are few books written in English specifically about Moroccan wildlife but much of the country is covered by the general guides listed on p.367. For birds, try the excellent ***A Birdwatcher's Guide to Morocco*** by P and F Bergier (Prion Press, 1990), the *Ornitholidays'* guide ***Let's Look at Southern Morocco*** (c/o 1/ 3 Victoria Drive, Bognor Regis, Sussex), and Hollom, Porter, Christensen and Willis's ***Birds of the Middle East and North Africa*** (T & AD Poyser, 1988).

CHAPTER FIVE

PORTUGAL

S trictly speaking, Portugal is an Atlantic country, but in climatic and botanical terms it is allied equally firmly to the Mediterranean. The interior shares many wildlife characteristics with central Spain and even north Africa, though its plants and animals are modified to varying extents by the Atlantic influence. It is a more wooded country than Spain, with trees covering thirty percent of the land area – a reflection of the moister climate. Similarly, large tracts are relatively fertile and suitable for agriculture, especially north of the **Rio Tejo**, which runs west to Lisbon and delimits the main transition from western European to Mediterranean vegetation. South of the Tejo, dry rolling plains and heathland are more typical. A number of mountain ranges (*serras*) add diversity to the landscape, containing large areas of forest and uncultivated land. In the extreme south lies the **Algarve**, a region of tourism, sun and sand, with well-developed, if diminishing, coastal habitats of mud flats, salt marshes, dunes and saltpans (*salinas*).

Wildlife cannot, of course, be considered in isolation from social and historical factors. Nowhere is this more apparent than in Portugal, especially the south coast, where in many places most of the more obvious plants are **alien species** from South Africa, America and elsewhere. Portugal has long been a great seafaring and exploring nation, providing a **rich source of potential colonisers**, many of which were able to gain a foothold in the open habitats, degraded through centuries of overgrazing. The tree-clad *serras* and limestone outcrops are particularly rich in flowers and insects, while at least four of Portugal's coastal wetlands are internationally important for their waders and wildfowl. Bird highlights include the resident azure-winged magpie and black-shouldered kite, both scarce birds with their only European base in western Iberia.

Climate and Land Use

Portugal's proximity to the ocean produces **rainfall** – particularly in winter – and **reduces extremes in temperature**. Even in midwinter, the daily maximum in the Algarve rarely falls below 14°C. This of course has profound effects on the wildlife, which thinks it is spring all winter long. Flowers bloom in profusion from December, butterflies and other insects are always active, and many normally migrant birds remain throughout the year. By May, however, the sun has begun to burn off the vegetation in all but the mountain areas.

The Atlantic's **greater tidal range** gives rise to more extensive intertidal zones than on the Med. Many coastal marshes have been modified into *salinas* and rice fields, or converted into marinas, golf courses and hotels. For example, **Vale de Parra**, on the Algarve, was a prime site for water birds until 1988, when it was drained to create a golf course; important breeding populations of black-winged stilt, collared pratincole, spoonbill and purple heron, amongst others, were lost. Even the more intact estuaries fail to achieve their full potential, owing to intensive **hunting**. Every Thursday and Sunday morning in winter, out go the hunters and away go the birds. The contrast between the few sanctuary areas – eg the Ria Formosa – and the hunted areas – eg Quinta da Rocha – is remarkable.

Arable and stock farming occupy much of the fertile terrain of northern Portugal; further south, relatively barren soils and hotter summers restrict agriculture to **drought-resistant crops** such as cork oak and olives, often underplanted with secondary crops and interspersed with extensive grazing land. As in most Mediterranean countries, soil erosion and general impoverishment caused by overgrazing has resulted in the development of *maquis* and *garrigue* habitats. Recently, **agricultural intensification** promoted by the EC Common Agricultural Policy has seen the advent of vast wheat fields, replacing the previous mosaic of uses and reducing the value of such areas to wildlife.

Large tracts of the uplands are unsuitable for agriculture, and **forestry** is one of the primary land uses. In most places the native broad-leaved forests have been felled and replanted with other species. Cork oak plantations are fairly rich, being sufficiently similar to the native forests to support much of the original flora and fauna. Not so, unfortunately, with **eucalyptus plantations**: they provide a regular rotational crop of timber and pulpwood, but their dense canopy excludes ground flora, and chemicals in their leaves acidify and pollute water courses.

WHEN AND WHERE TO GO

Plants and birds are good in the **winter** in the Algarve; best timing for a spring visit ranges from February in the south to May further up in the northern hills. Peak bird migration is in April and September, although southern Portugal has bird interest right through the year.

The international **airport** at Faro in the Algarve is conveniently placed for the majority of the sites covered. A **rail network** links most of the Algarve with Lisbon, although buses are in general quicker. Off the beaten track, buses are less regular but hitching is possible, though often time consuming. Most of the sites selected here are in the **Algarve**, which is by far the most "Mediterranean" coastline; a few further north have been described to complete the range of Portuguese habitats.

● **WESTERN ALGARVE** Includes the unique heathland habitat of **Cabo de São Vicente** and **Ponta de Sagres**, while the towns of **Luz and Lagos** are close to good sea cliffs, limestone outcrops and marshes. **Quinta da Rocha** is a varied mixture of wetland habitats.

● **EASTERN ALGARVE** Extensive wetlands at **Castro Marim** and **Rio Formosa**, and diminishing areas of coastal pine forests.

● **INLAND ALGARVE** Limestone hills at **Bensafrim** and the damp and lush mountains of the **Serra de Monchique**.

● **ALENTEJO** This vast lowland plain has been described generally rather than by concentrating on specific sites.

● **LISBON AND BEYOND** The capital is within easy reach of the internationally important wetlands of the **Rio Tejo** as well as the coastline and low hills of the **Serra da Arrábida**. Much further inland, the **Serra da Estrêla** is the richest site in Portugal for mountain wildlife.

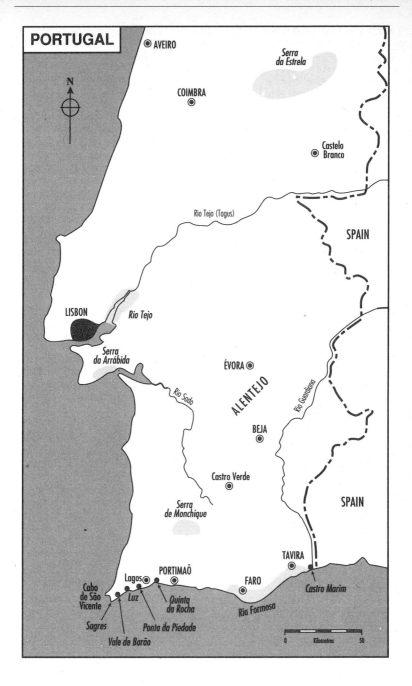

PORTUGAL

N

AVEIRO

Serra
da Estrela

COIMBRA

Castelo
Branco

Rio Tejo (Tagus)

SPAIN

LISBON

Rio Tejo

Serra
da Arrábida

Rio Sado

ÉVORA

ALENTEJO

Rio Guadiana

BEJA

Castro Verde

Serra
de Monchique

SPAIN

TAVIRA

PORTIMAÕ

FARO

Castro Marim

Lagos

Cabo
de São
Vicente

Luz

Quinta
da Rocha

Ria Formosa

Sagres

Ponta da Piedade

Vale de Barão

0   Kilometres   50

WESTERN ALGARVE

The outstanding site of the **Western Algarve** is the promontory of **Cabo de São Vicente** and **Ponta de Sagres**, westernmost point of continental Europe. Along the coast, the developing resort of **Luz** is an excellent centre for coastal cliffs, limestone outcrops and the unspoilt **Vale de Barão**, while the more established port at **Lagos** is close to seabird breeding colonies. Finally, **Quinta da Rocha** is on a river delta with great wildlife value, and is a handy base for the whole region.

Cabo de São Vicente and Ponta de Sagres

Forming the southwestern extremity of mainland Europe, the twin headlands of **CABO DE SÃO VICENTE** (Cape St Vincent) and **PONTA DE SAGRES** are a classic tourist site, and unique for their wildlife. Here the Atlantic influence is

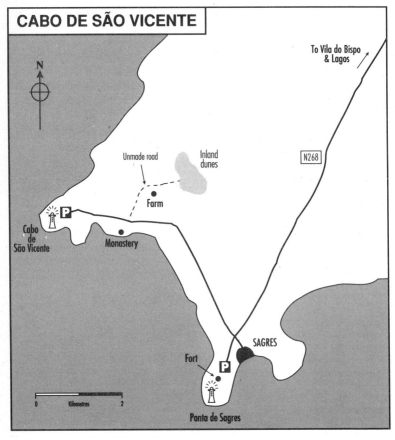

CABO DE SÃO VICENTE

To Vila do Bispo
& Lagos

N

Unmade road

Inland
dunes

N268

Farm

P

Cabo
de
São Vicente

Monastery

SAGRES

Fort

P

0   Kilometros   2

Ponta de Sagres

greatest, and despite floral similarities with the Mediterranean the overall feel is like that of other Atlantic extremes, such as Brittany or southwest Ireland. The whole area has recently been afforded statutory protection as a Natural Park.

The windswept, salt-sprayed rocks cannot support trees, and so a **heathland** has developed on the calcareous plateau. Several **endemic plant species** and subspecies grow here, most obviously the dominant rockrose *Cistus palinhae*, a low shrub with extremely sticky leaves and large white flowers. It is especially well developed on the less trampled Cabo de São Vicente. Other fascinating plants include a form of honeywort *Cerinthe major* lacking purple bracts, a shrubby sea pink *Armeria pungens*, the pimpernel *Anagallis monelli* and *Antirrhinum majus spp. linkianum* – a variety of the common snapdragon that has developed tendrils to raise itself on the surrounding shrubs. One of the more conspicuous plants to anyone wearing sandals is *Astragalus massiliensis*, accurately described as a "vegetable hedgehog".

Although the cliffs do not have vast colonies of breeding birds (they are disturbed by anglers), **seabirds** are plentiful offshore, and in rough weather there can be major passages of gulls, skuas, auks, gannets, shearwaters and petrels. Even in calm conditions – if this exposed area can ever be called calm – you might see vast flocks of Cory's shearwater feeding and resting on the sea. Birdwatchers on late summer boat trips off the cape have found numerous rare wanderers, including Wilson's petrel, Madeiran petrel, sooty shearwater and Sabine's gull; with perseverance and appropriate weather, any of these could be seen from the land.

Blue rock thrushes and peregrine falcons breed on the cliffs, while spectacled warblers breed in the scrub. This is also a prime site for **migrating passerines** and **large raptors**. In winter, the cape has a small and elusive population of Alpine accentor, presumably from the mountains of central Spain, as there are none in Portugal. The Thekla lark, similar in appearance to the more widespread crested lark, makes itself known with its fluid song, full of mimicry. Black redstarts are common, too, around these sites – the species may be familiar to British birdwatchers, but the northern birds do not compare with the smart black and abundantly white Iberian race.

To the north of the road between the two headlands lies an open, rolling area of **sandy plains**, covered in grasses, heathers, arable fields and conifer plantations. In spring, the meadows sparkle with the star-like flowers of *Romulea bulbocodium* and an endemic squill *Scilla vincentina*. A careful search in the *Cistus* heath may reveal the strange, red, hemispherical flower clusters of *Cytinus hypocistus*. This is one of only two European members of the largely tropical *Rafflesiaceae*, reminiscent of fungi by virtue of their parasitic lifestyle and lack of leaves and stems. Another distinctive plant is lavender *Lavandula stoechas*, a widespread Mediterranean plant, but here in its striking Iberian

Cytinus hypocistus

form (*pedunculatus spp.*) with very elongated purple bracts. Its smell is also rather different, something like Oxo cubes.

Choughs, which breed on the nearby cliffs, forage for insects on the grassy heaths; different species are typical of sandy plains – for example tawny pipits in summer, and little bustards and raptors in winter.

Lagos and Luz

The town of **LAGOS** is still a relatively unspoilt fishing port, and a visit to its fish market is a fine crash-course in local marine life. The harbour is always thick with **gulls** (including the Mediterranean gull in winter), and seabirds such as Leach's petrel can be seen offshore in rough weather. The other natural attraction is a tall chimney by the eastern approaches to the town, now home to a pair of **white storks**. When the old factory was being pulled down, the intervention of the mayor saved the chimney for the storks, and they have now become a tourist feature, especially welcome now that the stork population in the western Algarve has dropped to just a handful of pairs.

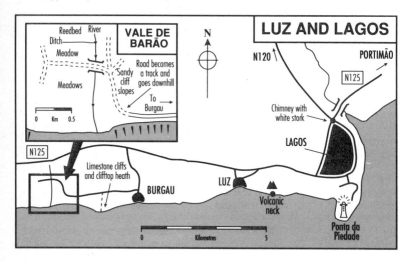

To the south of the town lies **Ponta da Piedade**, a rocky headland jutting into the Atlantic, where gulls sit side by side with several hundred pairs of both little and cattle egrets. The Mediterranean flora of the cliff top is supplemented by showy aliens, including the invasive Hottentot figs *Carpobrotus spp.*. Despite the heavy public use, subalpine and Sardinian warblers skulk amongst the scrub.

A developing tourist area is centred around the town of **LUZ**, but its valley situation has prevented excessive encroachment. The **cliff slopes** rise steeply, particularly to the east, and their typical Mediterranean flora is dominated by *Cistus spp.* and Jerusalem sage *Phlomis purpurea*. The scrub is relieved by a fine display of orchids, vetches and other low plants such as *Asteriscus maritimus*, but they tend to dry out rapidly, and an **early spring** visit is advisable.

To the west, beyond the village of BURGAU, orchids are a feature of the limestone flora, including the tongue orchid *Serapias parviflora*. Of the range of bulbous plants, the beautiful little *Tulipa australis* is one of the most obvious. The shrubby plants show an Atlantic influence, with Mediterranean *Cistus* and *Rosmarinus officinalis* mixing with the more western hairy greenweed *Genista pilosa* and the endemic *Thymus cephalotus*. Breeding ravens and kestrels inhabit the cliffs; to the birding world this site is known for lesser kestrels, but the majority of birds seem to be common kestrels.

Still further west, the cliffs drop down into the lovely, broad **Vale de Barão**; the valley floor has been reclaimed for agriculture, but it is now largely neglected, and an extensive **reed bed** has developed. Reed warblers and Cetti's warblers are present in good numbers, their songs mingling with those of thousands of marsh frogs. The river and ditches contain numerous European pond terrapins *Emys orbicularis*, which can be observed basking at the water's edge if approached with care. Vale de Barão has not been well worked by naturalists, but repays a closer look: spotted crake, mongoose, viperine snake *Natrix maura* and Montpellier snake *Malpolon monspessulanus* have all been reported. The south coast is believed to support a healthy population of **otters** *Lutra lutra*, and it is likely that they too occur here.

Quinta da Rocha

Between the mouths of the **rivers Alvor and Odiáxere** lies a peninsula known as the **QUINTA DA ROCHA**, an area whose **diversity of habitats** nurtures a vast range of plants and animals. It's easily accessible and an ideal centre from which to explore southern Portugal.

Moves are afoot to have the Quinta declared a nature reserve, and this is probably the most intensively studied part of the Algarve, being the Portuguese base of a Christian environmental group *A Rocha*, which operates from a field centre called *Cruzinha*, on the peninsula. The warden, Peter Harris, is an experienced birder, and he, his wife and staff are a valuable and welcoming source of information. Set amidst one of the few substantial wooded areas on the peninsula – a magnet for migrant birds – the field centre operates an intensive ringing programme.

An especially lively resident bird is the **waxbill**, a tiny, busy, pink-flushed species introduced from Africa. A couple of **garden ponds** harbour a strong population of marsh frogs *Rana ridibunda*. Dusk can be almost deafening, with the frog chorus supplemented by churring mole-crickets *Gryllotalpa gryllotalpa* and trilling Italian crickets *Oecanthus pellucens*.

Much of the Quinta is devoted to agriculture, especially fruit crops. In contrast to the agricultural prairies of British intensive farms, these cultivated areas support a range of wildlife: quails calling from every field, woodchat shrikes on the fence posts, fan-tailed warblers in every bush, and little owls everywhere at night. The orange and almond groves are much frequented by **migrant birds**, in the absence of more natural cover. **Winter** is as rewarding as other times of the year, bringing swarms of chiffchaffs, blackcaps and other northern warblers. Hoopoes (the emblem of *A Rocha*) are abundant here even in winter, despite being primarily a summer visitor to Europe.

Except during the dry summer period, the groves are rich in **flowers**. Throughout the winter, the attractive yellow Bermuda buttercup *Oxalis pescaprae* (an introduced species) is interspersed with white *Lobularia maritima*. Come spring, many bulbous plants appear: *Narcissus papyraceus* and *Asphodelus aestivus* are two of the most obvious, set among carpets of the pink catchfly *Silene colorata* and set off by the dramatic blue of *Anchusa azurea* and borage *Borago officinalis*. Even orchids grow as "weeds of cultivation", especially *Ophrys lutea*, *O. speculum* and *O. bombyliflora*.

Several areas have remained as grassland, and these are filled with many commoner plants. Look especially for showy legumes such as *Scorpiurus vermiculatus* (with its abnormal lanceolate leaves), the tiny bird's-foots, yellow *Ornithopus compressus* and pink *O. sativus*, and the gorgeous blue lupin *Lupinus microphyllus*. Of the many butterflies in these pastures, the most dramatic are swallowtails *Papilio machaon* and scarce swallowtails *P. alexanor*. With every footfall, grasshoppers leap to safety, including the large sandy Egyptian locust *Anacridium aegyptium*. The migratory locust *Locusta migratoria* also occurs here: the striped eyes of *Anacridium* are the key to identification. Along the rocky field margins, there are clumps of one of the two native European palms, dwarf fanpalm *Chamaerops humilis*, an indication of a north African element in the flora.

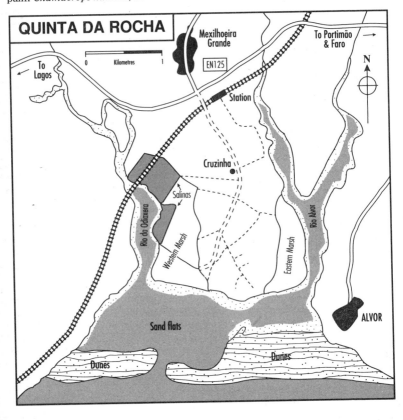

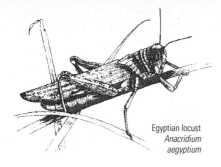

Egyptian locust
*Anacridium
aegyptium*

At the end of the peninsula, the groves give way to **umbrella pine** woodland and **Mediterranean scrub habitats**. The pines attract good numbers of migrant birds, and breeding bee-eaters reside in the low, inland sandy cliffs; from May onwards it's possible to hear red-necked nightjars on their dusk flights. In the clearings grow brown bluebell and *Cerinthe major*, its tubular yellow flowers surrounded by large purple bracts.

The rocky areas sloping down to the sea are dominated by *Cistus* species: deep red *C. crispus*, paler *C. albicans*, and white *C. salvifolius*, together with their close relatives, yellow *Halimium commutatum* and yellow-with-black-spots *Tuberaria guttata*. It's worth getting on your hands and knees to look for and examine the intricate beauty of the delicate endemic toadflax *Linaria algarviana*. Of course, there are also birds here, especially the ubiquitous Sardinian warblers, which proclaim their presence seemingly from every bush. Ocellated lizards *Lacerta lepida* can be found amongst the bushes and trees; green with blue spots, these large species pose none of the identification problems of the smaller wall lizards.

The Marshes and Estuary

The Quinta is fringed by saline and brackish **marshes**, enclosed by a sea wall. One of the most obvious plants is sharp rush *Juncus acutus*, growing in large tussocks around the pools; beware of getting too close, as its spine-tipped leaves can inflict a painful wound. In spring, the marshes turn golden with the flowers of the introduced buttonweed *Cotula coronopifolia*. Waders and wildfowl abound on the marshes and lagoons, including breeding black-winged stilt, Kentish plover and collared pratincole, and there is also a small but regular wintering group of stone curlew. Wintering crag martins hunt insects over the water, occasionally joined by Alpine swifts and red-rumped swallows. One of the most attractive summer birds is the distinctive Iberian race of yellow wagtail, with its grey head, almost black ear coverts, and white throat and eye stripe.

The **sea wall** itself is fringed with shrubby salt marsh plants such as *Atriplex halimus* and *Limoniastrum monopetalum*, which are the favoured location for a small wintering population of bluethroats. These are birds of the white-spotted race, and a proportion retain traces of their breeding plumage throughout the winter. In spring the yellow, waxy broomrape *Cistanche phelypaea* appears on the sea wall – one of the few parasitic plants that can tolerate saline conditions.

Outside the sea wall, the rivers open out into a broad **sandy estuary**, with a good range of northern waders in winter. Though the total number of birds – around 1000 – is relatively small and is surpassed by six or seven other sites in Portugal, the number of wader species (up to 22) is the highest of any estuary in the country. At low tide, the inner flats are covered with fiddler crabs, which look like stones until they are disturbed and they raise their defensive pincers ready for action.

Finally, enclosing the mouth of the estuary, two **sand dune systems** provide another interesting habitat. Marram *Ammophila arenaria* is, as always, the primary dune builder, allowing colonisation by other drought-resistant plants, such as cottonweed *Otanthus maritimus*, *Lotus creticus*, and *Medicago marina*. Bird life is restricted – mostly crested larks, with occasional gannets, Cory's shearwaters and petrels out to sea.

WESTERN ALGARVE: ACCESS AND ACCOMMODATION

Cabo de São Vicente

On the approach to the village of SAGRES along the coast road (N268), there is a roundabout. Left leads to Sagres; straight on is Ponta de Sagres; right to CABO DE SÃO VICENTE. Ponta de Sagres is the better site for sea-watching as the cliffs are lower, though there is better shelter around the lighthouse at the cape. Just before the monastery near the cape, a good unmade track cuts northeast across an expanse of heath and inland dunes.

SAGRES has several small hotels, a state *pousada* and a youth hostel. Sea trips are bookable through the hotels, or you could negotiate directly for a trip on a shark-fishing boat. An alternative base for Sagres is LAGOS, 40km away and connected regularly by bus.

Lagos and Luz

LAGOS is on the main coast road (N120) and at the end of the rail line from FARO. The harbour and market are in the centre of the sea front, and Ponta da Piedade is just 1km to the south of the town. There is ample parking for the latter site next to the lighthouse. PONTA DA PIEDADE has a campsite, and there are numerous hotels in Lagos.

LUZ, BURGAU and the VALE DE BARÃO are linked by a well-trodden clifftop path that starts at Lagos. Both Luz and Burgau are signposted off the main coast road, and both are on a regular bus route from Lagos. At Burgau, a road runs west just before the main part of the village, about 100m from the cliff edge, until it descends into Vale de Barão some 3km further on. Holiday rooms are available in Luz and Burgau, but scarce in the summer. There is also a campsite at Luz.

Quinta da Rocha

An unmade road leads directly to the Quinta from the main coast road (N125), opposite a junction signposted to MEXILHOEIRA GRANDE, the nearest village. Mexilhoeira Grande railway station is also situated here, and the slow but frequent train from FARO and PORTIMÃO is one of the best ways to take in the contrast between the developed and undeveloped Algarve.

Once on the Quinta, numerous tracks lead in all directions, and access is generally permitted throughout. Good paths follow the sea walls, although visitors are requested not to use them at high tide, when the birds are most vulnerable to disturbance. Cars may be parked at the very end of the peninsula, near a derelict bus that serves as a hide during inclement weather, or at the **Cruzinha field centre**, if you're visiting it. Peter Harris holds open house every Thursday lunchtime – recommended as a source of local information.

Cruzinha is fully equipped with shared-room accommodation and study facilities; the price is very reasonable and the traditional food outstanding. However, as the main aims of *A Rocha* are to increase the awareness in Portugal of Christianity and the environment, precedence is given to Portuguese visitors. Alternatives are the campsites and tourist accommodation across the estuary at ALVOR, within very easy reach of the eastern sand dune system.

EASTERN ALGARVE

The **Eastern Algarve**, a coastline of sand and lagoons, is more clearly under Mediterranean influence than the rocky coast to the west of Faro, which is wilder and damper from the Atlantic gales. Right next to the airport at Faro, the **Ria Formosa** includes a remnant of the umbrella pine forests that used to cloak much of the Algarve coast, along with one of the best marshy areas in the country. Further east, on the Spanish border, are the estuary and saltpans of the Rio Guadiana at **Castro Marim**.

Ria Formosa

A daytime flight into Faro airport gives an unrivalled opportunity to view the complex of wetlands that make up the **RIA FORMOSA**, a vast estuary enclosed by a sand and shingle spit. More than 100 square kilometres of this area is now protected as a nature reserve, an uneasy companion to the burgeoning tourist developments. Nowhere is the tension betwen the two more pronounced than in the immediate surrounds of the airport, where the sand spit is all but obliterated by bars and restaurants. On the plus side, however, this does allow naturalists some degree of access to the area.

Immediately to the northwest of the airport stands a remnant of **umbrella pine** *Pinus pinea* forest, its extent diminishing each year as sand extraction, refuse disposal and housing developments take their toll. The thick canopy and deep layer of fallen needles tend to restrict the ground flora, but a number of sand-loving species can be found in clearings. In spring, members of the sun-rose family *Cistaceae* are obvious, especially gum cistus *Cistus ladanifer* and two species of yellow sun-rose *Halimium commutatum* and *H. halimifolium*, the latter with dark blotches at the base of its petals. Added splashes of colour are given by small-flowered catchfly *Silene gallica* and hoop-petticoat daffodil *Narcissus bulbocodium*. Brown bluebell *Dipcadi serotinum* is remarkable for its drabness, especially when nestled under fronds of bracken *Pteridium aquilinum*.

In common with the rest of the Algarve, one of the commonest **song birds** is the serin, its delightful tinkling call filling the air (when you can hear it over the roar of jet engines). The pines also support coal tits, short-toed treecreepers and azure-winged magpies, with woodchat shrikes and black-eared wheatears in the clearings. One butterfly worth looking for is the beautiful yellow and orange Moroccan orange-tip *Anthocharis belia*, more usually a mountain species.

A little to the west lie **Ludo Marshes**, a complex of lagoons, reed beds and grazing marsh. In the birding world, this is renowned as the only locality for **purple gallinule** in Portugal; according to the latest information, however, the species might no longer be found there. It does hold substantial winter populations of **waders and wildfowl**, including black-tailed godwit, avocet, wigeon and pintail, as well as breeding black-winged stilts. Authorised access can be difficult, and most of the birds may be seen elsewhere in the Algarve.

For those with time to kill, a small section of the **lagoons** can be seen from the beach road, and the reed bed in that area may produce penduline tits. Equally, the **tidal flats** on each side of the causeway hold waders when the flats are not disturbed, together with Caspian and Sandwich terns and little egrets.

Castro Marim

In terms of habitats, the mouth of the **Rio Guadiana** at **CASTRO MARIM** is similar to the Ria Formosa, and it has many of the same birds. Being close to Spain, though, it benefits from the regular appearance of slender-billed gull and greater flamingo, the latter often in flocks of several hundred.

Other **Spanish specialities** that occur with less regularity include white-headed duck and crested coot. Griffon and black vultures have been seen overhead – again, these may be wanderers from across the border. Castro Marim nature reserve includes marshes and *salinas* that have the largest Portuguese breeding colony of black-winged stilts, and Mediterranean chameleon *Chamaeleo chamaeleon* (always elusive) and western spadefoot toad *Pelobates cultripes* have been noted too.

Mediterranean chameleon
Chamaeleo chamaeleon

EASTERN ALGARVE: ACCESS AND ACCOMMODATION

Ria Formosa

Just outside the airport, to the left, a road signposted for Praia de Faro skirts the pine forest and the eastern edge of Ludo Marshes. It then continues as a causeway across to the overdeveloped sand bar. All these sites can be reached on foot from the airport in 15min. The eastern end of the reserve can be explored from TAVIRA. For permits to visit LUDO, and general information, try the **reserve office** in Rua Teofilio Braga, FARO (☎089/27514).

The outskirts of FARO have many small hotels and rooms for rent, especially outside the main tourist season, but this site is probably best seen as a stop on the way to or from the airport. There is a campsite on the Praia de Faro.

Castro Marim

The mouth of the river can be viewed from VILA REAL, and the main road to the west skirts the northern edge of a fine umbrella pine forest. The road to CASTRO MARIM runs between the two main *salinas*, which can be reached by a number of (occasionally) marked tracks. The whole site is within easy walking distance of the railway station at Vila Real.

Tourist accommodation is seemingly plentiful in MONTE GORDO, but availability is a problem in high season. Nearby campsites, or the small hotels and youth hostel in VILA REAL are the only summer option. It is in the extreme east of the country, and consequently rather off-centre for general exploration. However, a regular ferry from Vila Real to SPAIN would allow day trips by car to, for example, the Coto Doñana, some 120km distant. The ferry crossing takes only about 20min, but be prepared for long delays on busy days.

INLAND ALGARVE

Areas of the grey and white limestone rocks of **inland Algarve** form a distinctive habitat known as the *barrocal*, where the rich flora is interspersed by valleys of olive, fig and almond groves. A north-facing scarp near **Bensafrim** is one of the best examples of this environment, and the **Serra de Monchique** is a more extensive area of higher limestone.

Bensafrim

Much of the *barrocal* is now heavily grazed or under crops, and the natural vegetation of holm oak *Quercus ilex* has mostly disappeared. The grazed areas nevertheless support fascinating flora, a wonderful example of which can be seen near **BENSAFRIM**, on a scarp slope whose northern orientation – protected from the fierce summer sun – greatly prolongs its flowering season. Spring is the time to visit, before the succulent new growth gets nibbled back by goats. Limestone terraces down the slope are like a natural rock garden, full of orchids, *Tulipa australis*, *Narcissus bulbocodium* and *Astragalus lusitanicus*, set off perfectly by the intensely blue *Lithospermum diffusum*. *Anemone palmata* grows here too, in both its white and yellow colour forms. Patches of scrub are dominated by **Kermes oak** *Quercus coccifera*; its spiny leaves and red berries could lead you to mistake it for holly, but a close look reveals that the berries are in fact galls caused by a tiny wasp.

Just a couple of hundred metres further along the road are clearings filled with *Orchis italica*, a close relation of the northern monkey orchid. One of the most dramatic Iberian plants is *Scilla peruviana*, which also grows by the road here: 50cm tall, it is topped by a spherical cluster of small deep blue flowers.

The Serra de Monchique is fairly close, and wandering raptors are reasonably frequent – you may well get stunning views of short-toed eagles sailing past on the up-draughts. Looking across to the *serra*, there is an obvious contrast between the calcareous limestone and the acid shales and sandstones. On the acidic rocks the vegetation is much less diverse, largely dominated by gum cistus; the scent from its leaves, borne on a gentle northerly breeze, is an unforgettable experience. Unfortunately, this site will not be intact for too much longer, as it's being sold off to create a housing estate. Thankfully, though, there are no plans as yet to develop the scarp, so perhaps one green hill will remain.

Serra de Monchique

The **SERRA DE MONCHIQUE** is a range of small mountains in the north Algarve, culminating in the twin peaks of Foia (902m) and Picota (773m); the whole area is a proposed nature reserve. The summit of **Foia** is now devoid of trees, and scarred by radio masts and other developments, including stalls selling often much-needed knitwear. One can, however, drive to the top to experience the **sub-montane habitats** and enjoy splendid views down to the Algarve coast when the mountain is not shrouded in cloud. This, unfortunately, is rather uncommon, especially in winter, in an area with around 100cm of rain annually.

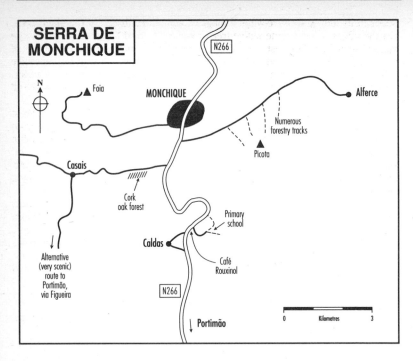

SERRA DE MONCHIQUE

The **mountaintop heath** of Foia is dominated by the heathers *Erica lusitanica*, *E. australis* and the white rockrose *Cistus salvifolius*, interspersed with grassy areas and abundant drifts of the little bulb *Romulea bulbocodium*, its low flower of six pale purple petals veined with a darker purple and nestling amongst thin, grass-like leaves. Blue rock thrush and rock bunting are found amongst the outcrops, and Dartford warblers are common in the scrub during summer.

Picota is altogether more lush, with a fairly complete forest cover on the slopes. Originally this would have been oak forest of two Iberian species, *Quercus canariensis* and *Q. faginea*, which would have supported a luxuriant flora and fauna; sadly, this has now been replaced with commercial plantations of *Eucalyptus spp. Acacia melanoxylon* and *Pinus pinaster*, of far less interest to wildlife. Some natural understorey plants remain, notably enormous tree heaths *Erica arborea*, more than 4m tall in sheltered places. Strawberry tree *Arbutus unedo* is also abundant; a local brandy called *medronho* is distilled from its "berries" – as with all local firewaters, it looks innocuous, tastes disgusting, and leaves a desperate hangover. One special, and protected, plant of the forests is *Rhododendron ponticum*, all too familiar in many British woods, but here in an isolated western population – apart from these few plants here and elsewhere in western Iberia, the nearest native populations are in northern Turkey and southern Bulgaria.

Not many birds use the dense **eucalyptus plantations**, as they support just a small number of insects. Siskin is one of the few birds to include the eucalyptus seeds in its diet, and azure-winged magpies sometimes breed in the plantations. On the edges, where some native trees remain, the bird life is richer and more varied, including firecrest (in winter), crested tit and the Iberian race of chiffchaff. This looks and acts like the northern species, but its repetitive "chiff-chaff" call ends with a liquid cadence, similar to that of a willow warbler. Large raptors are scarce, but golden, imperial, booted and Bonelli's eagles are all possible.

Cork oak *Quercus suber* plantations are another extensive managed forest type on the *serra*; a good and accessible example is situated next to the road from Monchique to Casais. Unnatural though these pure stands are, they still maintain a variety of wildlife. Small birds such as warblers, short-toed treecreepers and woodpeckers abound, and the woodland flora is diverse. One of the most distinctive plants is *Scilla monophyllus*, its powder-blue spike of flowers subtended by a single, broad basal leaf.

Another site worth visiting is near **Caldas**, which has a well-developed *maquis*, with *Cistus spp.*, *Daphne gnidium* and *Juniperus phoenicea*. *Freesia refracta*, from South Africa, is naturalised here, its scent putting that of native species to shame. *Orobanche ramosa*, a parasitic broomrape with a delicate violet tinge, is common, and the unspectacular two-leaved scrub-orchid *Gennaria diphylla* – a species first recorded in the Algarve in 1984 – can be found under bushes. This is also reputed to be a good site for cirl buntings, but they tend to be elusive.

One final requirement of a visit to the Serra de Monchique is to taste the water that issues from springs throughout the year: rich in dissolved salts, it tastes delicious. And while you are taking the waters, keep an eye open for fire salamanders *Salamandra salamandra* in the pools and damp areas.

INLAND ALGARVE: ACCESS AND ACCOMMODATION

Bensafrim

In ODIÁXERE, take the right turn off the main road, to BARRAGEM. After 5km, a sharp left junction leads up the scarp. Once at the top, the main part of the site is on the down slope to the right. Alternatively, a right turn off the N120, 7km out of LAGOS, leads to the same spot. The round trip is ideal by bike, and a taxi from Lagos would not be too expensive. Best base for accommodation is LAGOS.

Serra de Monchique

A good road and regular bus route runs from PORTIMÃO to MONCHIQUE. Six kilometres before Monchique lies the picturesque village of CALDAS, an old Roman spa. Almost opposite the road down to the village, next to the *Café Rouxinol*, a minor road leads uphill to a primary school. From there it is possible to explore the hill slopes and walk down the valley to the village.

Approaching Monchique, the road to ALFERCE runs along the northwestern flanks of Picota. Numerous tracks lead from this road up towards the summit: take pot luck. Finally, in Monchique itself, a signposted and steep road runs up to the summit of Foia, where there is a large car park. This can be a hair-raising drive, especially in low cloud and rain, but there is no public transport.

Monchique has a range of hotels, as do Caldas and Alferce – Caldas is the better bet for cheaper accommodation.

THE ALENTEJO

The **ALENTEJO** is a vast lowland plateau in eastern Portugal, contiguous with the plains of central Spain. It is dominated by agriculture, producing one third of the world's supply of cork, but because of the infertile sandy soils, agriculture is generally of low intensity. Sparse olive and cork oak plantations stretch for miles, sometimes with an understorey of gum cistus, in other places underplanted with lupins or grain crops. There are also more open areas, for the extensive grazing of cattle and sheep. The human population is concentrated in numerous widely spaced market towns and regional centres, such as Mértola, Beja, Serpa, Évora and Estremoz. In so large an area it is difficult to pinpoint prime sites, as many of the specialities can be wide-ranging.

In floral terms, the Alentejo has limited interest, although some of the **road verges** produce delightful displays of commoner spring flowers, including *Iris sisyrinchium*, *Onobrychis peduncularis*, *Echium plantagineum* and *Chrysanthemum coronarium*. In the grazed olive and oak groves, the unpalatable *Asphodelus aestivus* is often a significant feature, and in March and April large areas are turned red by the flowers of a small sorrel *Rumex bucephalophorus*. At the same time, many of the grove edges blaze with yellow *Calicotome villosa* and *Coronilla emerus*, and white *Lygos monosperma* – all shrubby members of the pea family.

Black-shouldered kite

But it is for **birds** that the Alentejo is most renowned. Every roadside perch and post seems to have its corn bunting, stonechat, great grey shrike or spotless starling. **Raptors** course the field margins: you could see Montagu's harriers, booted eagles, red kites, black kites and, with luck, **black-shouldered kites**. The last is a beautiful small species, pale grey with black "shoulders"; in Europe it's confined to southern Portugal and a couple of Spanish sites, and is never easy to find. Its preferred habitat seems to be cork oaks underplanted with wheat, and the triangle defined by Serpa, Brinches and Pias is reputedly a fine site.

The Alentejo is also one of the best breeding areas in Portugal for great spotted cuckoos. Other avian specialities require long and detailed scanning over the plains. Whereas little bustards are reasonably abundant, the extraordinary **great bustard** is never easy to find, despite the fact that the male is almost the size of a turkey; the areas around Castro Verde and east of Évora are said to be good. Searching for them can be quite effective from a car window, but black-bellied sandgrouse usually require walking. In tracking them down, you are also likely to come upon Calandra lark and other ground-dwelling passerines.

The Alentejo can produce all or none of these birds, according to luck, skill, perseverance and season; either way, it is a very atmospheric part of the country, and worth a visit simply for the expansive views and rural way of life.

THE ALENTEJO: ACCESS AND ACCOMMODATION

Because of its vast area, to explore the Alentejo properly needs a car; otherwise, it could be an interesting cycling tour for those not committed to hills or coast, and certain areas could be explored on foot from the main towns.

Most of the towns mentioned in the text have hotels, but there could be some difficulty finding rooms outside the tourist season. SERPA, ÉVORA and ESTREMOZ each have a *pousada*, reliable but expensive, and there are campsites at BEJA and ÉVORA.

LISBON AND THE NORTH

Lisbon itself is right next to the estuary of the **Rio Tejo**, with excellent bird-watching at all times of the year but especially in winter, when huge numbers of waders congregate. Just south of the city, the limestone mountains of the **Serra da Arrábida** have a typically Mediterranean *maquis* vegetation, strange for a site on the Atlantic coast. Away to the northeast, the **Serra da Estrêla** is scarcely a Med habitat, but it is the best mountain range for wildlife in Portugal.

Rio Tejo

The **RIO TEJO** (River Tagus), is one of the great natural features of Portugal, crossing the country from east to west in a deep valley. At its seaward end it opens out into a broad estuary, of which over 200 square kilometres are protected as a **nature reserve**. This is considered to be one of the **most important wetlands in Europe**, in winter holding around 40,000 waders, most of them concentrated on the mud flats and *salinas*. Six species are present in force: grey plover, ringed plover, redshank, bar-tailed godwit, black-tailed godwit (in excess of 5000 birds) and over 10,000 avocet – making it the most important wintering site in Europe for this species. In addition, there are regular occurrences of more southern species, such as spoonbill and greater flamingo. The extensive **salt marshes and dunes** have a similar flora to those on the south coast, although less rich in Mediterranean species. At the head of the estuary, there are also large areas of **reclaimed marsh**, much of it now converted to arable land, but still of importance for harriers and egrets. Black kites and great grey shrikes hunt here, too, and the colourful roller finds the open land to its liking.

Serra da Arrábida

The **SERRA DA ARRÁBIDA** is an area of low, rugged limestone mountains that forms the southern part of the Setúbal peninsula, between the mouths of the Rio Tejo and Rio Sado. The whole of the range, some 108 square kilometres, is designated a Natural Park.

Rising to just over 500m, the mountains still retain extensive **natural forests**, largely of Portuguese oak *Quercus faginea*. The ground flora is dense and varied, as is typical of limestone areas, and includes such specialities as western paeony

Paeonia broteroi. The lower slopes are clothed in characteristic Mediterranean **maquis**, reputably the best example of this habitat in Portugal. In many ways the flora resembles that of the *barrocal*, with, for example *Fritillaria lusitanica*, *Astragalus lusitanicus* and a range of commoner orchids, including a robust variety of mirror orchid *Ophrys speculum*. The scrub holds a number of *Sylvia* warblers, including the fairly scarce Orphean warbler.

On the south coast, the mountains tumble dramatically in to the sea, providing cliff nesting sites for guillemot and peregrine falcon.

Serra da Estrêla

The northern and very rainy **SERRA DA ESTRÊLA** displays a Mediterranean character only at low levels, where there are areas of *Cistus* scrub. It's briefly mentioned here because it contains the best series of montane habitats in the country.

The middle altitudes are clothed in **deciduous forest**, mainly pedunculate oak *Quercus robur* and sweet chestnut *Castanea sativa*, but with patches of Pyrenean oak *Q. pyrenaica*. Above the tree line, forests give way to spiny **dwarf shrub** communities and extensive **grasslands** of mat-grass *Nardus stricta*. About half a dozen endemic plants are found in the Serra, mostly at the higher levels. Previously, they were endangered by grazing, but this threat has now subsided with the controlling of the goat population. Perhaps the greatest threat now is from the development of tourist and ski facilities.

LISBON AND THE NORTH: ACCESS AND ACCOMMODATION

Rio Tejo
The north shore can be viewed from the main road (N1) to LISBON; the south shore and marshland from minor roads off the N10, east of VILA FRANCA. The ferry-train across the estuary gives a less land-based perspective.

LISBON, on the north bank of the estuary, is the obvious base, with all the facilities of a capital city – including an airport.

Serra da Arrábida
There are no restrictions on access within the park, which is traversed by a number of roads. The coast road west out of SETÚBAL is particularly scenic. From ARRÁBIDA it is only a short distance to both the Sado and the Tejo rivers.

SETÚBAL is a major town, with a range of hotels and other facilities. In addition, there's a *pousada* at PALMELA in the east of the park, and a campsite at SESIMBRA, to the west.

Serra da Estrêla
The Serra is a Natural Park with unrestricted access; several mountain roads cross the range. The *pousada* at MONTEIGAS in the centre of the park is an ideal, but expensive, place to stay. Rather cheaper is the youth hostel at PENHAS DA SAÚDE. At the eastern end of the park, GUARDA – self-designated "highest city in Europe" – has numerous hotels and a campsite.

information and publications

The primary voluntary conservation body in Portugal is the *Liga para a Protecçâo de Natureza*; it is not an information service, but since its work is dependent on detailed knowledge, it can use any records, species lists etc. compiled by naturalists. Information about Natural Parks and nature reserves can be obtained from the *Serviço Nacional de Parques, Reservas e Património Paisagístico, Rua da Lapa 73, 1200 Lisbon or Rua Justino Cumaro 4, 8000 Faro.*

As already mentioned, Peter Harris and the staff of *A Rocha* are valuable contacts, especially for the western Algarve but also more generally. They can be found at *Cruzinha, Mexilhoeira Grande, 8500 Portimão, Algarve (☎082/96117).*

The *Portuguese National Tourist Board* (1-5 New Bond St, London W1) have some literature on wildlife available.

MAPS
Michelin map 437 covers Portugal at 1:400,000, and 990 covers Spain and Portugal at 1:1,000,000. Larger scale tourist maps of the Algarve, often showing limited detail, can be purchased at many places in the region.

GUIDES
The best guide book for self-sufficient travellers in Portugal is **Portugal: The Rough Guide** (Harrap Columbus, £5.95)

BOOKS AND REPORTS
There are few readily available books about Portuguese wildlife. Two privately published booklets that detail some of the common and special plants of the Algarve are **Wild Flowers of the Algarve** and **More Wild Flowers of the Algarve**, both by Marie McMurtrie and widely available in local tourist shops. You may also come across **Birds of Southern Portugal** by Randolph Carey, though it's of little help for details of sites, and gives some misleading and out-of-date information. Standard field guides are much more useful.

A Rocha have produced a number of useful reports. In particular, they issue an annual bird report for the Quinta da Rocha, which also contains papers of more general interest. Their **Atlas of Wintering Birds in the Western Algarve** by Mark Bolton is invaluable to the winter birder, and of interest to the summer visitor. Details of all *A Rocha* publications can be obtained from their Portuguese address (above), or from their British office at 13 West Drive, Upton, Wirral, Merseyside.

For those with a more detailed conservation leaning, Dr Bob Pullan, a trustee of *A Rocha*, has produced a report entitled **A Survey of the Past and Present Wetlands of the Western Algarve** (University of Liverpool Papers in Geography no. 2). This detailed work is of immense value in stating the case for conserving those wetlands that remain. A similar report is expected shortly on the *barrocal*.

CHAPTER SIX

SPAIN

S pain occupies something of a no-man's land in the Med – isolated from Europe by the almost impenetrable mountain barrier of the Pyrenees and cut off from Africa by the Straits of Gibraltar. But these barriers were not always in existence. In ancient times plants and animals typical both of the colder north and warmer south were able to enter the country with ease, so that Spanish wildlife became a unique mixture of tundra and tropical species. Once **geographically isolated**, however, there proved to be no escape for those species unable to cross mountains and oceans and gradual "inbreeding" was initiated. Today Spain is one of the richest of all European countries in terms of **endemic species**, boasting plants, invertebrates, reptiles and amphibians which are found nowhere else in the world.

No one country can claim to be the "best" for Mediterranean wildlife, but if there has to be one, then Spain is it. This is mostly because the Mediterranean zone covers the majority of the country, including the **mountains** and flat **tablelands** of the centre as well as the coast – and the Balearic Islands add another dimension. The country is outstanding for large birds of prey, whilst **wetlands** such as the **Coto Doñana** are amongst Europe's finest for birds. Inland, mountain ranges from the **Sierra Nevada** in the south to the **Pyrenees** in the north are simply superb for flowers. All wildlife has suffered to some extent from building development and intensive agriculture, but Spain's sheer size has meant that many areas are untouched by such so-called progress, and plants and animals thrive.

The diversity is heightened by the presence of the Balearic Islands, which include many **endemic plant** species, cliff-nesting Cory's shearwater and Eleanora's falcon and several interesting species of **reptile and amphibian** such as Hermann's tortoise, the Mallorcan midwife toad and Lilford's wall lizard.

Climate and land use

Central Spain – dominated by the flat, treeless tableland of the *meseta* – has an almost continental climate, with freezing winters, scorching summers and rainfall confined to short bursts in spring and autumn. The east and south of the country, however, are for the most part typically **Mediterranean**, with mild winters and hot summers, and a higher level of rainfall; exceptions include parts of Almería, in the southeast, which have so little rainfall that Europe's only true desert is found there. Towards the west the river valleys allow **Atlantic systems** to penetrate the *meseta* and again rainfall is more prolific. And all around the plains, the **high mountains** (Spain is the most mountainous country in Europe after Switzerland) experience almost Arctic conditions in the peaks, with permanent snow in the Pyrenees and for much of the year in the Sierra Nevada.

The long history of mankind in the western Med has left Spain almost denuded of its original forest cover and only about ten percent of the country is today natural woodland. The remainder, however, is not the bleak agricultural desert you might expect. Much of the *meseta* is set aside for cultivation but the use of pesticides and fertilisers is not yet widespread and Spanish cereal fields remain a refuge for many of Europe's rare and decreasing arable weeds and also provide valuable feeding areas for wintering wildfowl.

Elsewhere such cultivations have long since turned out to be unprofitable. Their abandonment has made way for a uniquely Iberian shrub community known as *matorral*, dominated by hardy evergreen species and especially rich in wildflowers. Much of southwestern Spain was never completely deforested, but instead given over to *dehesa* – a parklike landscape of sparse evergreen oaks and herb-rich pastures, managed in the same way for centuries.

WHEN AND WHERE TO GO

Spain is big enough for wildlife to be good at almost any time of the year, from March on the south coast to the high summer in the mountains. Wintering birds are excellent from October to March on the coastal wetlands. Getting around is straightforward, with good bus and rail networks and Europe's cheapest car hire.

The following sites have been described:

● **MADRID AND AROUND** The parks of **Caso de Campo** and **El Monte del Pardo** lie within Madrid itself, while the nearby hills of **Sierra de Guadarrama** are easily accessible as day trips.

● **CENTRAL SPAIN** Highlights include the wetlands of **Laguna de Gallocanta** and **Las Tablas de Daimiel**, and the outstanding inland mountain range of the **Sierra de Gredos**. Over to the west, the open landscape of **Monfragüe** is particularly rewarding for its birds.

● **THE PYRENEES** This rich mountain habitat is represented by the two national parks at **Ordesa** and **Aigües Tortes**.

● **EAST COAST** Amid the developments, there are surprisingly good bird sites in the rice paddies and marshes of the **Aiguamolls de L'Empordà**, the **Ebro delta** and **La Albufera de Valencia**.

● **ANDALUCÍA** This huge southern province has a wide contrast of Mediterranean sites, from the peaks of the **Sierra Nevada** to the inland salt lake of **Fuente de Piedra**, as well as the inland hills of **Sierra de Grazalema**, **El Torcal de Antequera** and the **Sierras de Cazorla y Segura**. Along its Atlantic coast, west of the British enclave of **Gibraltar** with its apes, there are the windswept low marshes of the **Coto Doñana** – one of the great European wetlands – and **Las Marismas del Odiel**, rich in all wildlife but especially noted for birds.

● **BALEARIC ISLANDS Mallorca** features a rich variety of habitats: well preserved coastal flora on the **Formentor peninsula**; a bottleneck for migrating bird in the **Boquer valley**; internationally significant marshes at **Albufera** for wading birds; genuine Alpine flowers as well as rare birds of prey on the mountain of **Puig Tomir**; and numerous migrating birds at the saltpans at **Salinas de Levante**.

Of the **other Balearic islands**, **Menorca** is notable for its limestone cliffs, **Ibiza** for its woodlands, and **Cabrera** for its lack of disturbance.

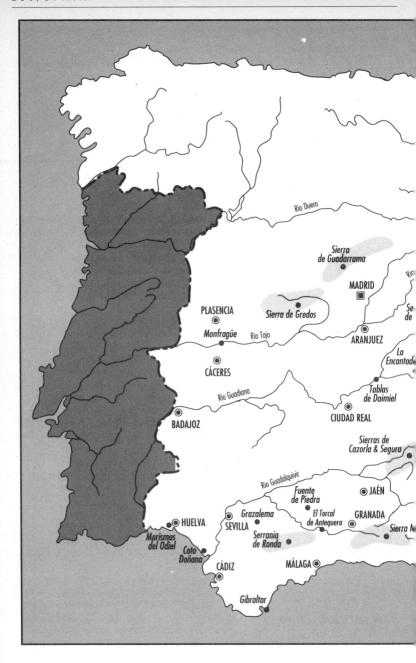

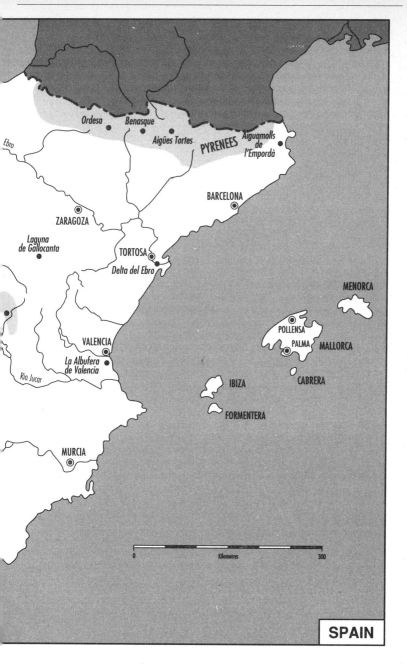

Ordesa
Benasque
Aigües Tortes
PYRENEES
Aiguamolls de l'Empordà
Ebro
BARCELONA
ZARAGOZA
Laguna de Gallocanta
TORTOSA
Delta del Ebro
MENORCA
POLLENSA
PALMA
MALLORCA
VALENCIA
La Albufera de Valencia
Rio Jucar
IBIZA
CABRERA
FORMENTERA
MURCIA

0   Kilometres   300

SPAIN

MADRID AND AROUND

The immediate environs of Spain's capital city shelter an unusual multitude of sites of considerable wildlife interest. Within Madrid itself, the parks at **Casa de Campo** and **El Monte del Pardo** are excellent introductions to Spanish species. Further out, the **Sierra de Guadarrama** is a low range of hills covered in dense, scrubby *matorral* and some woodland, linked to Madrid by the green corridor of the **Cuenca Alta del Manzanares**.

Casa de Campo, El Pardo and Manzanares

Within the city boundaries, and accessible either on foot or via cable car from Paseo Rosales, lie the 17 square kilometres of the **CASA DE CAMPO**, once the royal hunting grounds of Philip II. Although the grasslands are parched and dry in summer, the shady holm oaks provide cover for colourful birds such as hoopoes and woodchat shrikes, and the maze of paths between the trees allow hares and other small mammals to coexist with joggers and picnickers.

El Monte del Pardo

Once part of the same estate as Caso de Campo, but now separated from it by the multi-carriageway of the N6, **EL MONTE DEL PARDO** is located on the north-west borders of Madrid. Its circuit of walls enclose some 150 square kilometres of evergreen oak woods, though only a fraction of this area is freely open to the public: mainly around the villages of EL PARDO and LA QUINTA, accessible from the C602 ringroad to MINGORRUBIO on the shores of the *embalse*, or reservoir.

Within this former hunting preserve are good opportunities to see red and fallow deer and wild boar at close quarters; indeed, their numbers have escalated in recent years, so much so that the native vegetation is now severely overgrazed. The woodlands support wildcats and badgers, too, while foxes are very much in evidence. Raptors also abound, including about ten percent of the world population of **Spanish imperial eagles**. In 1986 a census revealed just 104 pairs of this magnificent, white-shouldered race, which only occurs in Iberia, although the population is thought to be recovering.

The **EL PARDO RESERVOIR**, on the upper reaches of the Río Manzanares, is an important pre-migration congregation point for **black storks** before they head south to Africa for the winter. Less than 100 breeding pairs remain in Spain – the most important population in western Europe – so if you are in the capital in autumn, then this wetland, with its water bird community, is a must.

Cuenca Alta del Manzanares

The upper reaches of the Río Manzanares (which goes on to flow through central Madrid) have been declared a *parque natural*, the **CUENCA ALTA DEL MANZANARES**. It encompasses the granite enclave of **La Pedriza**, a magnificent landscape of Dartmoor-like tors – a favoured destination of picnicking *Madrileños*. The lower slopes are clothed in stunted holm oaks *Quercus ilex*, and higher up by junipers *Juniperus spp.*, holly *Ilex aquifolium* and plantations of pines *Pinus sp*. The main escarpment is known as *Las Buitreras*, "the vultures", and superb views of **griffon vultures** are possible.

Sierra de Guadarrama

The **SIERRA DE GUADARRAMA**, the "gable of Madrid", is a mass of holm oak woodland, accompanied by cork oaks *Quercus suber* and strawberry trees *Arbutus unedo*, and dotted with small patches of native conifers, including Spanish juniper *Juniperus thurifera* and stone pines *Pinus pinea*. Much of this native Mediterranean woodland was cleared early in the history of man to make way for cultivated land and dry pastures, but later abandoned due to the poor quality of the soil. As a result the lower slopes of the Guadarrama are today clothed in dense, aromatic *matorral* – essentially scrub vegetation – containing cistuses *Cistus spp.*, brooms *Cytisus spp.*, retama *Lygos sphaerocarpa*, round-headed thyme *Thymus mastichina*, rosemary *Rosmarinus officinalis*, purple-flowered French lavenders *Lavandula sp.* and the enormous steppe grass *Stipa gigantea*.

Deciduous woodlands and extensive plantations of *Pinus uncinata* form a belt above the drought-resistant evergreen oak forests. **Montejo de la Sierra** houses the southernmost beechwood *Fagus sylvatica* in Europe, the smooth, grey-barked boles mixed with the gnarled trunks of sessile oaks *Quercus petraea*. Higher still, at 1400–1900m, lie the dark, cool **forests of Scots pine** *Pinus sylvestris* – Guadarrama's most characteristic tree. The shrub layer contains common juniper *Juniperus communis*, bearberry *Arctyostaphylos uva-ursi*, tree heath *Erica arborea* and a shrubby Mediterranean legume *Adenocarpus telonensis*, distinguished by its yellow flowers growing in flat-topped clusters. The clearings and forest tracks are ablaze with yellow brooms *Genista florida, Cytisus purgans* and *C. hispanica*. And keep an eye out along the edges of the tracks for the unmistakable red-purple or white long-spurred flowers of the toadflax *Linaria triornithophora*.

The regular influx of humanity into the Sierra de Guadarrama has undoubtedly had an adverse effect on the fauna; the only **large mammals** which can be seen with regularity are wild boar and roe deer, although small populations of red and fallow deer persist. Smaller herbivores include arboreal creatures such as red squirrels and oak dormice. The bizarre and rare Pyrenean desman, now confined to a few mountain ranges in northern Iberia, still occurs where the mountain streams are unpolluted and undisturbed, and it is possible that a few otters are hanging on in the same habitats. **Small carnivores** such as wildcats and polecats are found in the more remote forests, although rarely seen, and American mink have been accidentally introduced.

White storks start breeding here in early February, constructing untidy stick nests on any prominent point, especially church spires. **Raptors** are particularly varied, including red and black kites, sparrowhawks, goshawks, booted eagles and peregrine falcons. A wealth of **small forest birds** such as woodlarks, nightingales, crested tits, short-toed treecreepers and nuthatches delight both ear and eye. The *matorral* is populated with bee-eaters, hoopoes, ortolan buntings, quail, great grey shrikes and golden orioles.

The sunnier **lower levels** of the Sierra de Guadarrama support plenty of **reptiles**, including Schreiber's green lizards *Lacerta schreiberi* – females brown but males large and green with characteristic brown heads and black-speckled backs; small brown scuttling lizards of rocky terrain are likely to be Iberian wall lizards *Podarcis hispanica*, common wall lizards *P. muralis* or the large psammodromus *Psammodromus algirus*, the latter identified by its extraordinarily long tail. Water-loving viperine snakes *Natrix maura* and the larger Montpellier snake *Malopon monspessulanus* are also common.

Above the tree line the **acid pastures**, with their scattered boulders and faulted slabs of granite, are dominated by mat-grass *Nardus stricta* studded with clumps of the red-flowered thrift *Armeria splendens*, spring anemones *Pulsatilla vernalis* and dense tussocks of the pink *Dianthus subacaulis*, found only in the mountains of southwest Europe. Local rarities include the hawkweed *Hieracium castellanum* and a fleshy-leaved relative of the stonecrops *Pistorinia hispanica*, both endemic to Iberia. The upland region known as **Siete Picos** (2138m) is the Spanish stronghold for the daffodil *Narcissus rupicola* and the pink-lilac spring-flowering crocuses *Crocus carpetanus*, which is restricted to Spain's central sierras and some Portuguese highlands.

The alpine zone of the Guadarrama is home to the Iberian rock lizard *Lacerta monticola*, the males often with a turquoise flush, which occurs only in the northern and central mountain ranges of the peninsula, a distribution shared by the endemic Iberian frog *Rana iberica*. Fire salamanders *Salamandra salamandra*, natterjack toads *Bufo calamita* and smooth snakes *Coronella austriaca* all take advantage of the wetter, cooler climate of the higher reaches. Wheatears and rock buntings are the commonest **small birds** of these uplands, while the skies are again the undisputed realm of the griffon vulture.

Guadarrama's **butterfly and moth** fauna is also outstanding – some species are so large that they are almost impossible to miss. Apollo butterflies *Parnassius apollo* are everywhere in the mountains in late summer but the most interesting is undoubtedly the Spanish moon moth *Graellsia isabellae*, which is found only in the mountains of Spain and parts of the French Alps. Found from March to July in pine woods, they can't possibly be confused with anything else: large, pale green silk-moths with an orange eye on each wing and long "tails", most pronounced in the male.

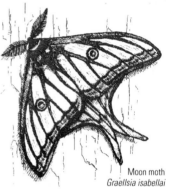

Moon moth
Graellsia isabellai

AROUND MADRID: ACCESS AND ACCOMMODATION

Madrid

For the parks of **Casa de Campo** and **El Monte del Pardo**, MADRID itself is the best base. Casa de Campo is easily accessible from the suburb of ROSALES; for El Monte, catch a bus to the villages of EL PARDO or LA QUINTA.

For the higher reaches of the **Río Manzanares**, there are campsites at the village of LA PEDRIZA and at MANZANARES EL REAL, as well as a basic camping ground on the northern shores of the Embalse de Santillana on the M612.

Sierra de Guadarrama

The main access points are the passes of SOMOSIERRA (NI; 1444m), NAVACERRADA (N601; 1860m) and GUADARRAMA (NVI/A6; 1511m) from east to west. To get a good idea of the variety of habitats present on the south flank take the C604, which links Navacerrada to the NI in the eastern part of range, following the course of the Río Lozoya and passing close to the highest point of the range: PEÑALARA, at 2429 metres. By public transport, buses go to the main ski resort of NAVACERRADA, and nearby CERCADILLA is on the railway line.

Free camping is available at LA ACABEDA just west of the Somosierra pass, and in the western part of the range to the south of PUERTO DE FUENFRÍA. Mountain refuges exist at Puertos de Navafría (1778m), Navacerrada and Fuenfría, all of which lie on the Madrid/Segovia provincial borders, and to the south of Peñalara. I would recommend NAVAFRÍA as a good place from which to begin your exploration of this mountain ridge.

CENTRAL SPAIN

Although **central Spain** is dominated by the flat tablelands or *mesetas*, there are outstanding sites within easy reach of Madrid. The **Sierra de Gredos** has the full transition from lowland woodlands to bare mountain tops, while, over to the west, the national park of **Monfragüe** is a superb spot – especially for the birds of the *dehesa* landscape. The remaining wetlands in the plains include the **Laguna de Gallocanta** and the declining but still excellent **Tablas de Daimiel**.

Sierra de Gredos

Northeast from Monfragüe is the granite and gneiss bulk of the **SIERRA DE GREDOS**, separated from the Sierra de Guadarrama by the swinging reaches of the Río Alberche. The chain of peaks extends over 5000 square kilometres and culminates in the 2592-metre pinnacle of Pico Almanzor. It is bounded to the south by a vertiginous valley housing the Río Tiétar but the north flank slopes gently up from the *meseta*. Extensive glaciations during the Quaternary left a legacy of spectacular cirques with jagged margins and idyllic glacial lakes often trailing like rosary beads across the moraine.

Pico Almanzor and its surrounds are best approached via the track that cuts across the massif from CANDELEDA north to HOYOS DEL ESPINO. This wilderness, the **Reserva Nacional de Gredos**, contains several mountain refuges and discreet freelance camping is no problem. Almost without stirring from the tent you can see **griffon and black vultures**, while rock buntings will unashamedly approach the camp.

The southern reaches of Gredos are warm and very humid, affected by moist winds from the Atlantic. Here the natural vegetation of the lower slopes is **Mediterranean woodland**, dominated by evergreen oaks with aromatic shrubs in the understorey, though the habitat is fragmented and degraded, due to centuries-old cultivations of citrus fruits and tobacco. Above this man-influenced landscape lies a belt of Pyrenean oaks *Quercus pyrenaica*, easily distinguished by their felted leaves and the fact that they are the last of all deciduous oaks to break into leaf in the spring.

The cold, dry **north face**, by contrast, is clothed in extensive Scots pine forests which, although not native, are of considerable age and support an interesting shrub and herb community. At Hoyocasero, for example, pale yellow alpine pasque-flowers *Pulsatilla alpina ssp. apiifolia*, St Bernard's lilies *Anthericum lili-*

ago, martagon lilies *Lilium martagon* and carmine peonies *Paeonia sp.* grow in the shady pinewoods. Two of the more special Gredos plants are the endemic snapdragon *Antirrhinum grossii* and the weld *Reseda gredensis*, which occurs elsewhere only in Portugal's Serra da Estrêla.

Between 1600 and 2000 metres lies the **broom and juniper zone** that is most characteristic of the sierra, the yellow-flowered *Genista florida* and *Cytisus striatus* contrasting with the white blooms of *C. multiflorus*. Above this, ancient boulder-studded pastures support a specialised herb flora including *Dianthus laricifolius*, a pink endemic to the central ranges, *Aquilegia dichroa*, a columbine distinguished by its white-tipped inner petals, and *Erodium carvifolium*, a striking crimson-flowered storksbill with two of the five petals enlarged and decorated with eyelike dark blotches.

About 130 **birds** have been recorded from Gredos, the more interesting among them including **black-shouldered kites** and **azure-winged magpies**. The kites, which here nest in the Tiétar valley, were only discovered to be breeding in Spain as recently as the 1970s, and the magpies occur in two widely-separated areas in the world – Iberia and the Orient, and may well have been introduced in ancient times to their European locality. The **pine**

Azure-winged magpie

forests are home to firecrests, at only nine centimetres long, one of Europe's smallest birds, and crossbills, the adults characterised by their distinctive crossed mandibles with which they prise seeds from the cones of pines and firs, although the young hatch with straight beaks. Birds of the heathlike habitats which are so typical of the Gredos include bluethroats, this population isolated from the main breeding grounds in central and eastern Europe, black-eared wheatears, stone curlews and Thekla larks, confined to southern Iberia but difficult to tell from crested larks in the field. The **high rocky zones** are the domain of alpine accentors, choughs and both the rock thrush and the blue rock thrush. Descending sharply into the Tiétar valley the presence of the river and its associated vegetation attracts Cetti's, melodious, Orphean, Dartford and fan-tailed warblers as well as golden orioles, hoopoes, white storks and bee-eaters. True riverine species, dependent on the water for their food, include kingfishers and dippers, an extraordinary dumpy brown bird which literally "flies" underwater as it picks small invertebrates from the river bed.

The true forte of Gredos, however, is that it is exceptionally rich in **reptiles and amphibians**, both of which are represented by more than half of the total Spanish faunas. Although you are not likely to come across more than a fraction of this immense diversity, the huge ocellated **lizards** *Lacerta lepida* are easy to see (and, better still, to identify), while overturning a slab of rock will often reveal a slow-worm *Anguis fragilis*. A smaller green lizard in the rock-strewn uplands may be the male of an endemic race of the Iberian rock lizard *Lacerta monticola ssp. cyreru* which is also found in the nearby Sierras de Peña de Francia and Guadarrama.

There's a chance, too, of seeing up to eight kinds of **snake**, including horse-shoe whipsnakes *Coluber hippocrepis* and Lataste's vipers *Vipera lastati*, some-times found basking in the sun to increase their internal temperature and thus metabolic rate so as to be able to hunt more effectively. Lataste's vipers are found only in Iberia and northwest Africa and are distinguished from other European vipers by the distinct upturned nose-horn; they are distinctly poisonous. Both stripe-necked and European pond terrapins *Mauremys caspica* and *Emys orbicu-laris* inhabit the freshwater lakes, which are also home to an endemic race of fire salamander *Salamandra salamandra ssp. almanzoris,* as well as the Gredos toad *Bufo bufo ssp. gredosicola*, a smaller, greener version of the common toad with lighter-coloured warts.

A total of 35 **mammals** occur, most conspicuously the magnificent **ibex** *Capra pyrenaica spp. victoriae*, a race endemic to these mountains. Although almost extinct at the beginning of the century there are now an estimated 4000 of these mountain goats in the high Gredos, the males endowed with massive, lyre-shaped horns. The uplands are inhabited by the snow vole, here represented by a race not found outside these mountains: *Microtus nivalis ssp. abulensis.* These small, pale rodents are most common above the tree line, where conditions are so harsh that survival seems almost impossible; on sunny days they can be seen warming themselves on tussocks.

The upper reaches of the streams and rivers, where unpolluted and undis-turbed, still host small populations of **Pyrenean desmans**, although sightings of this long-nosed, bewhiskered relative of the mole are usually only granted to those who spend long periods motionless on the riverbank. The woodlands shel-ter a far greater diversity of mammals than the high mountains, including roe deer and wild boar, as well as smaller, arboreal species such as oak dormice and red squirrels and their predators: beech martens and genets.

Monfragüe

One of Spain's best-known wildlife reserves is the **PARQUE NATURAL DE MONFRAGÜE**, which extends over more than 175 square kilometres in the province of Extremadura. Monfragüe provides three interesting habitats: the **reservoirs** created from the dammed Tajo and Tiétar rivers, the ancient **Mediterranean forests** on the steeper slopes and the *dehesa* (see box), for which the park is renowned.

One of the most worthwhile trips in the park is down to **Puente Cardenal**, a vey ancient crossing point of the Tajo, used by the merino sheep travelling from their winter grazing lands in Extremadura to summer pastures in the Cordillera Cantábrica in northern Spain. Close to the bridge stands a great crag known as **Peñafalcón** which houses a large colony of **griffon vultures**, the chicks easily visible from the road with the aid of binoculars. The skies are always dotted with the massive silhouettes of these birds as they go about their business, but a closer look is quite likely to reveal a black vulture in their midst or the long-legged profile of a **black stork**, one of the Spain's rarest birds; six or seven pairs regularly breed at Monfragüe.

The path up to the **Castillo y Ermita de Monfragüe** on the quartzite ridge of the Sierra de las Corchuelas passes through typical **Mediterranean woodland**, with its canopy of evergreen oaks, stone pines and other drought-resistant shrubs and trees, most of which have leathery, inrolled leaves. Mastic trees *Pistacia lentiscus*, and the related turpentine trees *Pterebinthus* are both among the most typical *matorral* shrubs in southwest Europe, here growing with wild olives, laurustinus *Viburnum tinus* and strawberry trees. The shrub layer contains grey-leaved *Cistus albidus*, poplar-leaved *C. populifolius* and sage-leaved *C. salvifolius*, as well as Spanish heath *Erica australis*, French lavender *Lavandula stoechas*, retama and bladder senna *Colutea arborescens*. Excellent views of Monfragüe's extensive *dehesa* and the reservoirs are to be had from the ruins of the *castillo*.

Black stork

All in all Monfragüe boasts a total of 218 breeding vertebrates, about twenty percent of which are **raptors**, among them a substantial proportion of the world populations of black vultures and Spanish imperial eagles, both of which nest in the tops of ancient evergreen oaks in undisturbed forest regions. Other striking birds of prey are the black-shouldered kites, usually seen hovering near water at

---

DEHESA: A UNIQUE LANDSCAPE

Dehesa is an agricultural habitat restricted to Iberia and northwest Africa. Sparse plantations of **evergreen oaks** – usually cork oak and holm oak – provide acorns, traditionally used as fodder for the black pigs of the region, as well as fuelwood, charcoal and, of course, cork. Beneath the trees lies high quality **pastureland**, protected from the worst ravages of the elements by the shade-giving trees, often cultivated with cereals on a ten-year rotation to prevent the invasion of shrub species, especially gum cistus *Cistus ladanifer*.

If I had to choose just one Spanish habitat to visit early in the year I would go for the *dehesa* every time. At Monfragüe there is nothing in the world to rival a **spring dawn**: the scent of dew-drenched flowers underfoot, the gradually intensifying hum of thousands of insects, a colony of bee-eaters spreading their iridescent wings to catch the first warming rays of the sun on a gnarled and ancient evergreen oak. At this time of year the floor of the *dehesa* is a blaze of colour with striking plants such as rose-pink gladioli *Gladiolus spp.*, huge, trident-shaped asphodels *Asphodelus aestivus*, the deep-blue flowers of narrow-leaved lupins *Lupinus angustifolius* and *Dipcardi serotinum*, which resemble brown-flowered bluebells.

Centuries of **traditional management** have produced a plant and animal community that is uniquely adapted to the *dehesa*. Throughout the day the senses are bombarded with a wealth of colourful **birds**, their calls often as distinctive as their plumage, none more so than the soft, monotonous notes of the hoopoe and the fluting song of the male golden oriole. Every bird that flits to the next tree at your approach merits a look, since such brightly-coloured species as woodchat shrikes, azure-winged magpies and black-eared wheatears are common here. Rollers too are abundant: crow-sized blue and brown birds which get their name from their habit of somersaulting during courtship flights.

dusk, as well as more common species such as goshawks, booted, short-toed, Bonelli's and golden **eagles** and Egyptian vultures. The **reservoirs** provide a focal point for alpine swifts and collared pratincoles in summer. Collared pratincoles, almost the whole western European population of which breeds in Spain, are elegant birds with long forked tails and black-bordered bibs, that nest in noisy colonies. Winter visitors include spoonbills, cattle egrets and night herons.

Mammals are more difficult to see, mainly because they are more active at night. Although Spanish lynx are reputed to live in the park you are unlikely to catch even a glimpse of this magnificent feline amongst the dense *matorral*, but red and fallow deer, wild boar and wildcats are less retiring. Smaller carnivores such as genets, beech martens and polecats are all abundant forest-dwellers, otters are not uncommon in the quiet tributaries feeding the reservoirs, and careful surveillance of a dry, rocky hillside may reward you with a sighting of a slender but ferocious Egyptian mongoose.

Nineteen **reptiles** have been recorded from the park, including the bizarre Moorish gecko *Tarentola mauritanica* as well as the wormlike lizard known as the amphisbaenian *Blanus cinereus* which is confined to Iberia. The most interesting of a variety of **amphibians** is the huge sharp-ribbed salamander *Pleurodeles waltl*, one of Europe's largest at 30 centimetres, with commoner species including western spadefoots *Pelobates cultripes* and Iberian midwife toads *Alytes cisternasii*, painted frogs *Discoglossus pictus* and parsley frogs *Pelodytes punctatus*.

Laguna de Gallocanta

Approached from the south, **LAGUNA DE GALLOCANTA** is invisible, marked only by an increase of birdlife in the plains around. From the north, however, driving in over the Puerto de Santed (1153m) from DAROCA, you get a view of the lagoon's true conformation. The whole area has a half-abandoned look, its tumbledown lakeside villages testifying to increased agricultural mechanisation and the defection of the rural population to the cities.

Except in high summer the well-marked track down to the lake and observatory from Tornos may be impassable by car; a quiet spring or early summer walk will in any case give opportunity to explore the margins of the **cereal fields**. Violet, white and blue delphiniums *Delphinium spp.*, flixweed *Descurania sophia*, one of the more easily identified crucifers, with greyish, pinnate leaves and drooping yellow flowerheads, pheasant's-eye *Adonis annua*, with red-petalled, sooty-centred flowers and long spiky seedheads, candelabra-like asphodels *Asphodelus fistulosus* and two members of the poppy family – the purple-flowered *Roemeria hybrida* and the curious flattened yellow blooms of *Hypecoum imberbe*: all these are in places more abundant than the crop plants themselves.

Gallocanta is in fact the least degraded and largest continuous natural waterbody of inland Spain. At almost 1000m above sea level it can dry out almost completely at the height of summer and expand to cover 40 square kilometres with the winter floods. It is rarely, though, more than 1.5m deep, the clear waters supporting prolific meadows of stoneworts *Chara sp.* and *Lamprothamnion sp.*, which provide fodder for diving ducks and coots. Other aquatic plants such as pondweeds *Potamogeton spp.*, tiny floating duckweeds *Lemna sp.* and watermilfoils *Myriophyllum sp.* support surface-feeding ducks and moorhens.

The lagoon was declared a *Refugio Nacional de Caza* in 1978 and has increased in ornithological importance since, as surrounding sites have succumbed to drainage and coastal wetlands been disturbed and polluted. In addition, the surrounding croplands provide winter feeding areas for large numbers of water birds, about half of which are **diving ducks**, especially pochard and red-crested pochard. Small nuclei of shelduck, ferruginous duck (also known as white-eyed pochard on account of the prominent pale eye-ring of the male) and more than 100 greylag geese also winter here with regularity. **Surface-feeding ducks** such as gadwall, teal, shoveller and wigeon, the latter bird often pursuing diving ducks until they drop their catch, account for less than ten percent of the total. The star attractions of Gallocanta, however, are undoubtedly the 3000 or so **common cranes** which settle here every winter to feed in the fields and roost by the lake; around sixty percent of Iberian cranes spend the winter here. They are best seen in March when they congregate by the lake before heading north to their breeding grounds: an unforgettable sight.

Apart from the wealth of waterfowl, Gallocanta provides an oasis for the typical birds of the surrounding agricultural land and **dry steppes**, including both great and little bustards, stone curlews, quail, sandgrouse, corn buntings and larks. Sandgrouse congregate in large flocks and to see them on the wing is to witness a remarkable display of aerial acrobatics in which each bird closely follows those around it, rather like a shoal of fish.

When the weather is bad the rain sweeps across the exposed lakeside in horizontal sheets – which might not be a bad time to go and visit the **bird museum** in Gallocanta, right on the northern shores of the lake.

Serranía de Cuenca and Ciudad Encantada

South of the Laguna de Gallocanta, roughly at the junction of the provinces of Teruel, Cuenca and Guadalajara, lies a complicated series of mountain ridges known as the **SERRANÍA DE CUENCA**. Here Jurassic and Cretaceous limestones mingle with sporadic sandstone, shale and schist outcrops, providing refuge for both calcicolous (lime-loving) and calcifugous (lime-hating) plants. Botanical diversity is, therefore, extremely high within a very restricted area. **Orchids** are a particular speciality of the Serranía, including marsh helleborines *Epipactis palustris* in the damp flushes and red helleborines *Cephalanthera rubra* in the limestone woodlands. A galaxy of other orchids on the site includes woodcock *Ophrys scolopax*, late spider *O. fuciflora*, frog *Coeloglossum viride*, burnt-tip *Orchis ustulata* and violet bird's-nest *Limodorum abortivum*.

Ciudad Encantada

The nearby **CIUDAD ENCANTADA** is a sort of geological "zoo", famous for its eroded limestone sculptures that cover some 20 square kilometres. It is an impressive place, but also a popular one, with picnicking Madrileños descending en masse at weekends. Then, and high summer, are best avoided if you want to see much of the wildife.

Two interesting plants, growing apparently straight from the rock, are *Sarcocapnos enneaphyllea*, a creeping member of the poppy family with pealike flowers and glaucous pinnate leaves, and the pale-yellow snapdragon *Antirrhinum pulverulentum*. Both are typical montane species of southwest Europe.

La Encantada

If you're motivated by the search for botanical rarities, then a visit to the ten-hectare *ADENA/WWF* reserve of **LA ENCANTADA** should prove worthwhile. Situated a few kilometres south of VILLARROBLEDO, just off the N301 from MADRID to ALBACETE, this site comprises cereal fields around a rocky limestone knoll, covered with sparse holm oaks and *matorral* containing kermes oak *Quercus coccifera*, prickly juniper, Mediterranean mezereon *Daphne gnidium* and the steppe grass *Stipa tenacissima*: vegetation typical of the southern *meseta*.

The best time to visit the reserve is in May and early June, with access from the road which links SOCUÉLLAMOS and SOTUÉLAMOS. The cereal fields are not intensively cultivated, thus supporting a variety of **arable weeds**, most of them annuals: corn poppies *Papaver rhoeas*, *Biscutella auriculata*, one of the most distinctive crucifers, with pale yellow flowers and broad, flattened seeds, corn cleavers *Galium tricornutum*, now very rare over much of Europe, and annual scorpion-vetch *Coronilla scorpioides*, a glaucous, yellow-flowered legume with long, narrow pods curved like the scorpion's tail from which it derives its name. Colourful herbs such as annual bellflower *Campanula erinus*, distinguished by its pale rose-violet flowers and calyx which becomes star-shaped in fruit, a tiny, pink-flowered annual valerian *Centranthus calcitrapae* and small toadflax *Chaenorhinum minus*, with spurred blue-purple flowers and lower leaves which are reddish beneath, line the edges of the tracks.

A search among the *matorral* on the knoll will reveal the handsome, blue-flowered flax *Linum narbonense*, the dwarf shrub *Teucrium gnaphaloides* with white-woolly leaves and purple flowers, a white-flowered thyme *Thymus zygis*, and *Sisymbrium cavanillesianum*, a crucifer restricted to this and a very few localities around Madrid. Several other **endemic species** of the Iberian peninsula are to be seen, too, including the toadflax *Linaria glauca*, the candytuft *Iberis crenata*, with comb-like leaves and 3.5-cm white flowers, and the aromatic labiate *Ziziphora acinoides*.

Las Tablas de Daimiel

Almost due south of MADRID, the national park of **LAS TABLAS DE DAIMIEL** was once one of Spain's most important wetlands for breeding and wintering ducks. Today, sadly, it is a shadow of its former self, due to the exhaustion of the aquifer – which for centuries maintained the high water table – and drainage of the fertile floodplain marshes for agriculture.

The park, nonetheless, encloses an interesting maze of freshwater lakes and pools, 1–2m deep, though shallower and more saline in the summer. Arrive early in the day and you will have the place almost to yourself; later on, in summer especially, and at weekends, local picnickers take over.

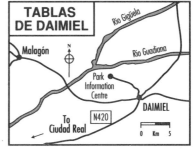

An early morning stroll through the **marshes and groves of tamarisk** *Tamarix gallica* – Daimiel's most characteristic tree, salt-tolerant and used by nesting herons and passerines – is an opportunity to see linnets, stonechats, tree sparrows, hoopoes, bearded tits and a multitude of warblers. The **freshwater lakes**, meanwhile, support meadows of stoneworts together with rigid hornwort *Ceratophyllum demersum* and lesser bladderwort *Utricularia minor*, an aquatic carnivorous plant which traps small waterborne invertebrates in air-filled bladders for extra sustenance.

The surrounding vegetation is worth examining for the presence of common tree frogs *Hyla arborea*, which cling to their perches by means of suckers on the tips of their fingers and toes, or it may reveal a sleepy oak dormouse. Stripe-necked terrapins may be spotted basking in the sun or slipping quietly into the water at your approach. The inaccessible interior of the park is still dominated by large stretches of reeds *Phragmites communis* with greater reedmace *Typha latifolia*, true bulrushes *Scirpus lacustris*, and possibly the largest extent of saw-sedge *Cladium mariscus* in western Europe. Good views of airborne purple herons and marsh harriers are to be had from the bird observatory on the Isla del Pan.

Giant fennel
Ferula communis

Don't overlook the **dry, grassy hummocks** adjacent to the centre of the park as they contain the silver-leaved pink bindweed *Convolvulus lineatus* and giant fennel *Ferula communis*, a plant which can attain five metres. Also abundant here are field eryngo *Eryngium campestre*, a spiky umbellifer of disturbed ground, and two large composites: the wing-stemmed cotton thistle *Onopordum sp.*, sometimes taller than a man, and holy-thistle *Silybum marianum*, distinguished by its white-veined leaves and deflexed spines below the flowerheads.

An interesting bird which is still thought to nest in Daimiel's drying marshes is the **night heron**, which produces a harsh croaking call similar to that of the raven; a small colony may persist on the Isla de Martinete – *martinete* being the Spanish name of this bird. The smallest of all Spanish herons, the little bittern, may also still breed here, but its larger relative, the bittern, located more often by its booming call than by sight, probably no longer uses this site. Water rails and little crakes, the latter a rare occurrence in central Spain, are also rumoured to be hanging on. Black-winged stilts and avocets still nest in large colonies on the more inaccessible islands and can be seen feeding around the edges of the shallower lagoons, while little, whiskered and gull-billed terns are a common sight.

The **best time to visit** Daimiel is between April and July for breeding water birds and flora, while September sees the first flush in incoming wildfowl, peaking in December.

CENTRAL SPAIN: ACCESS AND ACCOMMODATION

Sierra de Gredos

There are several points at which the Sierra de Gredos can be crossed. To the west, the Puerto de Piornal (1269m) is at the top of a narrow winding road near JARANDILLA DE LA VERA, which has both a *parador* (one of a chain of state-owned luxury hotels) and two campsites. From Jarandilla, tracks lead north into the mountains, one of which terminates at the mountain refuge of Nuestra Señora de las Nieves, also accessible from the pass of Tornavacas on the N110.

Some 50km further east lies the focal point for visits to the Gredos, just north of ARENAS DE SAN GREDOS. A network of mountain roads radiates from here, many of which have excellent viewpoints, or *miradores*, and camping is available near GUISANDO. Access to the numerous mountain huts in the *Reserva Nacional de Gredos* is possible either from here, or from the northern side of the ridge, via a track which is a continuation of the AV931 from HOYOS DE ESPINOI on the C500. There are also several crossing points further east in the range.

Monfragüe

Monfragüe is one of the least accessible Spanish national parks, although the town of PLASENCIA, some 20km north of the heart of Monfragüe, is served by sporadic trains from MADRID and CÁCERES. Buses are perhaps a better bet, with five services daily from Madrid.

Once in Plasencia the park is accessible only by occasional local buses along the C524 towards TRUJILLO. A sensible disembarkation point is the tiny village of VILLAREAL DE SAN CARLOS where the park's information centre is located. Camping is possible here, and officials can let you know about other designated areas within the park. There is fairly liberal access throughout the park, the only prohibited zone being the *reserva integral*. The exact location of this reserve-within-a-reserve is not public knowledge but it goes without saying that fences and signs requesting you to steer clear of an area are to be respected.

Apart from camping, the nearest towns for accommodation are TRUJILLO or PLASENCIA.

Gallocanta

The lake is 100km southwest of ZARAGOSA, just off the N330. There are no camp-sites in the immediate vicinity, but the walled town of DAROCA to the north has plenty of cheap *fondas* and *pensiones*.

Daimiel

About 120km south of MADRID, and slightly northeast of CIUDAD REAL, Las Tablas de Daimiel lies at the confluence of the rivers Guadiana and Cigüela. There is public transport to the reserve, but it's simple and cheap enough to travel the 11km from the town of DAIMIEL by taxi. There is access to the park from 9am to 8pm during the summer, and the information centre is open from 11am. The main nature trail starts at the centre and runs westwards to the Isla del Pan; there is also a less unpublicised route to the Laguna Permanente, starting just outside the car park.

Campsites are few and far between in the area, the closest being near CONSUEGRA some 20km to the north. DAIMIEL and MANZANARES both have a limited selection of accommodation, with more variety available at CIUDAD REAL, the provincial capital.

THE PYRENEES

The dividing line between Spain and the rest of Europe coincides with the 500-km mountain chain of the **Pyrenees**, the longest range in the Iberian peninsula. The central axis of the Pyrenees is composed of ancient granitic and slaty rocks more than two hundred million years old, flanked by younger limestone deposits to both north and south. Evidence of Quaternary glaciation is everywhere, with stunning cirques and ice-smoothed, U-shaped valleys. **Ordesa** and **Aigües Tortes**, the two national parks, are both quite exceptional for scenery, mountain flowers and other wildlife.

Ordesa

The **PARQUE NACIONAL DE ORDESA** covers some 150 square kilometres. It includes the valleys of Añisclo, Pineta and Gargantas de Escuaín as well as that of Ordesa itself, which houses the Arazas river. The park borders the infamous Cirque de Gavarnie to the north, where it abuts the French frontier, and at its heart is the 3355-metre peak of **Monte Perdido** ("lost mountain"). Geologically Ordesa is composed largely of limestone, creating thin, dry soils and a haven for calcicolous plants – those that grow especially well on base-rich soils.

Above 1200m the valley slopes are flanked with Scots pine, beech and firs, but the most hardy and most **typical tree** of the Pyrenees is the pine *Pinus uncinata*, a relatively recent coloniser that came south with the ice sheets of the last Ice Ages and stayed in the high mountains when the glaciers retreated. Today it is the highest-growing tree in Spain, found at 2700m at Els Encantats in the Catalan Pyrenees. It is also one of the longest-lived of Spanish trees, with individual trees frequently reaching 600 years old. The upper limit of the *Pinus uncinata* forests coincides with the tree line, above which are **alpine meadows**, rich in orchids, sky-blue gentians, creeping azaleas *Azalea procumbens* and alpenrose *Rhododendron ferrugineum*, both of which produce a magnificent pink-crimson floral display in early summer. The best-known mountain plant in the world grows here too – the **edelweiss** *Leontopodium alpinum* – its false white-woolly petals surrounding the flowers to protect the buds against the extreme cold and desiccation experienced at such high altitudes.

The **highest points of the park**, close to **Gavarnie**, are dominated by sheer walls of rock. Look out for the rare carnivorous butterwort *Pinguicula longifolia*, with bright yellow-green, strap-shaped leaves with glandular hairs for trapping unwary insects, and deep purple flowers more than 4cm in diameter. Other plants on the rock walls include *Dioscorea pyrenaica*, an ancient relic of the tropical yam family with separate male and female flowers, which grows only in the Pyrenees, and the attractive endemic *Ramonda myconi*, reminiscent of an African violet, which is also one of the last European representatives of a tropical family.

For **summer mountain flora**, the **Pineta valley** is the place to visit. Species here include two easily identifiable umbellifers: Pyrenean eryngo *Eryngium pyrenaicum*, with grey-green leaves boldly veined in white and spiky steel-blue bracts around the flowers, and masterwort *Astrantia major*, with drooping silvery inflorescences. Look out, too, for English irises *Iris xiphium*, identified by their robust flowers and leaves which are semicircular in section, and the Pyrenean bellflower *Campanula speciosa*, with its pyramidal spikes of large, blue-pink flowers.

The Pyrenees as a whole support more than 60 species of **plants found nowhere else in the world**, including the unmistakable Pyrenean saxifrage *Saxifraga longifolia*, with its enormous, cylindrical flowering spikes, Pyrenean columbine *Aquilegia pyrenaica*, and Pyrenean beaked milk-vetch *Oxytropis pyrenaica*, with globular heads of blue-purple flowers. An attractive, but more widespread species is the rush-leaved jonquil *Narcissus requienii*, with slender leaves and golden-yellow trumpets.

Of the park's mammals, **chamois**, here called *sarrio*, have recuperated from very low numbers to a stable population today, but the **ibex** are confined to the higher levels of the Ordesa valley. With less than thirty now left in existence the population is probably incapable of maintaining itself, and this magnificent mountain goat, known locally as *bucardo*, is one of Spain's most endangered species.

Another highly endangered species is the bearded vulture, or **lammergeier**, of which some forty pairs were identified in the Pyrenees in 1986; their only other Spanish locality are the Sierras de Cazorla y Segura in Andalucía, where a single pair is hanging on. In the Pyrenees, two distinct groups of lammergeiers can be distinguished – those which frequent the high mountains, feeding mainly on the carcases of wild herbivores, and those which prefer the peripheral sierras, relying on the domestic livestock. The lammergeier is known as *quebrantahuesos*, or "bone-breaker", referring to its habit of dropping large animal bones from a great height to smash on the rocks below, after which the vulture can easily extract the tasty marrow. Ordesa is one of the strongholds for these birds, so with any large, soaring raptor look for the characteristic diamond-shaped tail, dark wings and pale head and belly.

Other typical birds of Ordesa include the **capercaillie**, a turkey-like species, clumsy in flight, and more often seen than heard, especially in spring when the handsome black males – weighing up to 5kg – display in clearings deep in the forest to attract females. The presence of an isolated population of these birds here, and also to the west in the beech forests of the Cordillera Cantábrica, is probably due to their being marooned in the high mountains by the retreating ice and warming of the lowlands. This is certainly the case for the **ptarmigan**, again isolated from the main population in northern Europe. These small game birds are perfectly adapted to life above the tree line, changing their plumage from mottled brown to pure white in the winter for camouflage, and excavating hollows in the snow for shelter during poor weather.

Spanish ibex

Benasque and Vall d'Aran

Between Ordesa and its fellow national park, Aigües Tortes, to the east, lie two very famous Pyrenean valleys.

Benasque, overshadowed by the enormous turrets of Pico de la Maladeta (3308m) and Pico Aneto (3408m) on the left-hand flank, has the typical north–south orientation of the Pyrenean chain. The lush meadows support radish-leaved bittercress *Cardamine raphanifolia*, globe-flower *Trollius europaeus* and alpine cotton-grass *Eriophorum alpinum*.

Further north is the **Vall d'Aran**, a good place to see eye-catching displays of alpine pasque-flowers *Pulsatilla alpina*, pale Lent lilies *Narcissus pallidiflorus* and pheasant's-eye narcissi *N. poeticus* in the upland pastures in spring. Pyrenean fritillaries *Fritillaria pyrenaica* also occur here, although their inconspicuous purplish bells, chequered on the inside, require more diligent searching among the rougher grazing lands.

Aigües Tortes

The second Pyrenean national park – **AIGUES TORTES Y LAGO DE SAN MAURICIO** – covers some 100 square kilometres and takes the form of two east–west valleys divided by the watershed of the Sierra de Crabes. It is essentially a mountain park, with no point within its boundaries lower than 1620m, ascending to the 2982m peak of Peguero. The main physical features are the peripheral ring of amazing **glacial cirques** which more or less coincide with the boundary, and the **glacial lake of San Mauricio**. Access to the park is primarily along the river valleys – Sant Nicolau to the west and Escrita to the east – from where routes exist to practically every cirque. The park itself is crisscrossed with paths and tracks in almost every direction.

The east–west orientation of the **Sant Nicolau valley** has a marked effect on the vegetation of the opposing slopes, with the lower regions of the south-facing flank supporting a flora dominated by **sun-loving Mediterranean plants** such as box, the broom *Genista scorpius*, a spiny shrub with small orange-yellow flowers and barely visible leaves, savory *Satureja montana*, Montpellier milk-vetch *Astragalus monspessulanus*, identified by its oval clusters of large, pink-purple flowers, and wall germander *Teucrium chamaedrys*. Conifers play an important role in the landscape, especially Scots pine in the lower reaches and *Pinus uncinata* above 1800m, forming large, virtually unadulterated stands. On the shadier, north-facing slopes, silver fir *Abies alba* forms mixed stands with the pines, aspen *Populus tremula* and willows.

The **scrub formation** which accompanies these pine forests comprises common juniper *Juniperus communis* at the lower levels with dwarf juniper *J. communis ssp. nana*, bilberry and alpenrose ascending to the tree line. Interesting herbs which thrive in the shrubby understorey include lesser twayblade *Listera cordata*, an inconspicuous, green-flowered orchid, typical of coniferous woodlands and bogs, and several more primitive vascular plants, including alpine clubmoss *Lycopodium alpinum* and lesser clubmoss *Selaginella selaginoides*. Colour is provided by the pale-violet flowers of alpine coltsfoot *Homogyne alpina*, alpine leek *Allium victorialis*, with spherical heads of off-white flowers, and pink bird's-eye primroses *Primula farinosa*.

At the top of the valley, by the lake known as **Estany Llong**, at 1896m, look out for such delightful alpine plants as edelweiss and alpine snowbell *Soldanella alpina*, with nodding, deeply fringed blue-violet flowers and dark, kidney-shaped leaves, growing in the alpine pastures on the lake shore. Up here amongst the cirques and jagged peaks there is a fair chance of seeing **chamois**, which live in small, female-dominated herds while nursing their young, usually one or two per female. Both sexes have small, backward curved horns piaced very close together between the ears. Stoats are not uncommon among the rocky uplands, although their white winter coats, highly valued as ermine, make them difficult to pick out when snow is on the ground.

Lower down in the woodlands, agile **red squirrels** are frequently seen leaping from branch to branch in search of pine cones and other seeds. Unfortunately these endearing, red-coated acrobats are the main source of food for **pine martens**, much persecuted in the past but now increasing in the park. These lithe, nocturnal predators are most often seen at dusk. They have an amazingly long gestation period for such a small animal – 270–285 days – with litters varying from two to seven young. Pine martens are so agile that, during a reintroduction programme in the USSR, one is said to have jumped from the aeroplane and was recaptured months later! **Beech martens** are also found, differing from the pine marten only in the white throat triangle (this is yellow in the pine marten). They are much more likely to approach settlements, and in central Europe motorists have reported considerable damage to parked cars since the females have taken to using the engine area as creches for their young, which try out their teeth on everything!

Beech marten

The upland lakes are poor in nutrients and thus do not attract much in the way of water birds, but **raptors** are a distinctive feature of the park. A good place to start looking is the Amitges track, which gives views over all the peaks above the Ratera lake, or the area around Estany Llong. **Griffon vultures**, which are known to travel up to 70 kilometres from their roosts/nest sites in search of animal carcasses, soar over the peaks on wings with a span of nearly three metres. A smaller bird of prey could be a **golden eagle**, of which only 800–900 pairs remain in Spain, mostly in mountainous regions. Unlike the sociable griffon vultures these eagles are highly territorial, each pair defending a range of some 25 square kilometres of open mountain. They nest on inaccessible scarps, or less frequently in the tops of Scots pines. Other cliff-nesters include peregrine falcons, which mate for life and return to the same nest year after year. A peregrine descending on its prey – usually a pigeon or similar-sized bird in flight – can reach speeds of more than 375km per hour.

Although the larger elements of the wildlife at Aigües Tortes are fascinating, don't overlook the **invertebrates**. Large, brightly-coloured butterflies such as cleopatras *Gonepteryx cleopatra*, scarce swallowtails *Iphiclides podalarius* and apollos are common in meadows and flower-strewn woodland clearings. Keep an eye out, too, for the clouded apollo *Apollo mnemosyne*, which differs from the apollo by having yellowish eyespots rather than red ones, and is confined in Spain to the Pyrenees.

Nearby sites: Sierra de Cadì and Montserrat

The **Sierra de Cadì**, nearby Aigües Tortes, has probably the richest alpine flora in the eastern Pyrenees, with upland pastures full of Southern and Pyrenean gentians *Gentiana alpina* and *G. pyrenaica* as well as the golden, twelve-petalled flowers of Pyrenean pheasant's-eye *Adonis pyrenaica*, some of them up to 7cm in diameter. The rocky regions support pink-studded pincushions of moss campion *Silene acaulis* and the pink-flushed buttercup *Ranunculus parnassifolius*, while the Puerto de Tossa is a mass of alpine Lent lilies *Narcissus alpestris* in spring.

Between BARCELONA and the main chain of the Pyrenees lie several smaller, coastal *sierras*, all easily accessible from the Catalan capital. The most dramatic is the **Sierra de Montserrat**, especially if you view its smooth-sided pillars and pinnacles of conglomerate rock from the IGUALADA–MANRESA road (C241). It is worth exploring for the commoner **tree and shrub species** of this corner of the Med. Laurustinus *Viburnum tinus*, scorpion senna *Coronilla emerus*, the pink flowered *Cistus albidus*, Mediterranean spurge *Euphorbia characias*, mezereon *Daphne gnidium*, shrubby hare's ear *Bupleurum fruitcosum*, strawberry tree *Arbutus unedo*, Phoenician juniper and the glossy-leaved and evil-thorned climber *Smilax aspera* – all these grow in profusion.

Herbs which flourish along the margins of this dense woodland include martagon lilies *Lilium martagon*, grape hyacinths *Muscari neglectum*, tufts of the woolly-leaved, white-flowered bindweed *Convolvulus lanuginosus*, and the blue stars of *Aphyllanthes monspeliensis*. A wide variety of **orchids** includes violet bird's-nest orchid *Limodorum abortivum* under the trees, while the grassy clearings hold others including man orchid *Aceras anthropophorum*, *Ophrys fusca* and early purple orchids *Orchis mascula*.

PYRENEES: ACCESS AND ACCOMMODATION

Ordesa

By car, an exciting route is to follow the Río Aso up the Garganta de Añisclo, due north from the HU631 road which links ESCALONA to the villages of Fanio, Nerín and Buerba. Alternatively, take the continuation of the HU630 from TORLA, which leads almost to the foot of Monte Perdido and a handy mountain refuge. By bus, go from SABIÑÁNIGO to TORLA, where there is an information centre (ask here about camping and mountain refuges), and accommodation.

Aigües Tortes

Public transport into the region is best by bus from BARCELONA to POBLA DE SEGUR, whence buses run to LES (close to the French border on the N230) via LA GUINGETA, an ideal jumping-off point for exploring the eastern side of the park. The western part of the park can also be reached from Pobla de Segur by hopping on a bus to VIELHA; get off at PONT DE SUERT for the Sant Nicolau valley. Pobla de Segur is accessible by train from Barcelona and Lérida.

There is no shortage of places to stay in the area, with plenty of campsites around the fringes of the park, including one at ESPOT, where there is a park information centre. There are *pensiones* at ESPOT to the east of the park, at BOI (another information centre here) and at BARRUERA on the west. Within the park itself, a rudimentary campsite is located near Pic de las Agudes (2762m), on the northeastern boundary. All are open throughout the summer, from June to September.

The best **mountain refuges** are at AMITGES (2400m), where half of the 50-person capacity is set aside for members of the *Centro Excursionista de Cataluña*, the remainder to anyone. (Access is via the track from the Lago de San Mauricio in the north of the park.) On the other side of park there is an unconditional refuge at BARRACÓN (1988m), near Estany Llong.

THE EAST COAST

From the Pyrenees south along the **shores of the Mediterranean** to MURCIA is a coastline characterised by great beauty, a wonderful climate, and some of the nastiest excesses of tourism. The presence of millions of sun-seekers flocking to the coast every summer would be sufficient to put the fear of God into the local wildlife, but it is the spin-offs of the industry which have been most damaging. The "concrete wall" of hotels has completely isolated inland regions from the shore, and the scale of destruction of native habitats, especially coastal marshes, in the name of development is beyond belief.

And yet there are oases along this beleaguered shore, among them some of Europe's most important ornithological refuges. The **Aiguamolls de Empordà**, up by the French border, and the **Delta del Ebro** are both wetlands of the first rank, while **La Albufera** has survived right on the outskirts of VALENCIA.

Aiguamolls de L'Empordà

After the Delta del Ebro, the **PARQUE NATURAL DE AIGUAMOLLS DE L'EMPORDÀ** is the most important wetland in Catalunya. Based around the Fluvia and Muga rivers, a good number of the 294 birds (90 breeding) observed here can be seen even in high summer, although a trip timed to coincide with the **spring or autumn migration** is best of all, when an average pair of binoculars can spot over 100 species in a day. A good place to start is the **Information Centre** at EL CORTALET, off the coast road linking CASTELLÓ D'EMPÚRIES and SANT PERE PESCADOR, where detailed maps of the park can be obtained.

From the centre a nature trail leads off into the wilderness of salt marshes, brackish pastures and rice fields. It is popular with local people and tourists alike, so the weekend is best avoided if you want to get undisturbed wildlife. The damp woodland fringes of the first part of the nature trail provide cover for many **small birds**, the most audible of which are Cetti's warblers, with their piercing calls, as well as reed warblers, great reed warblers and nightingales. The calls of some of these warblers can be confused with the croaks and chirrups of the marsh frogs *Rana ridibunda* which inhabit the adjacent ditches and ponds, but careful pursuit of the noise should soon show up the differences.

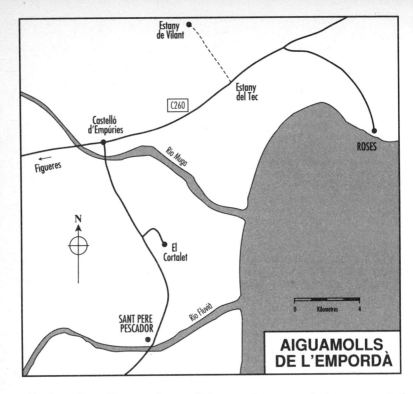

In places the **saline marshes** are little more than a succulent green carpet of marsh samphire *Arthrocnemum spp.*, replaced in drier areas by the plantain *Plantago crassifolia*, typical of brackish regions on the shores of the Med, growing together with the slender lilac-coloured flag *Iris spuria*, sea lavender *Limonium sp.* and a local race of sea wormwood *Artemisia caerulescens sp. gallica*. Further on, **hides** have been constructed at strategic points overlooking the salt marshes and reedbeds, from which marsh harriers and purple herons can be spotted hunting and returning to their nests. With great good luck, a **bittern** might be spotted soaring low over the reeds; it looks rather like a huge owl with its long neck hunched up but the trailing legs giving it away as a heron. Bitterns are now classified as an endangered species in Spain, having been practically exterminated as a breeding bird.

The **shallow pools** in front of the hide are appreciated as breeding and feeding grounds by an abundance of little egrets and black-winged stilts. Examine the fringing vegetation of the slightly deeper pools for small, dabbling ducks with a blue wing panel and (in the male) a handsome striped head; these are **garganey**, which are the symbol of Aiguamolls de L'Empordà since the park is their only regular breeding site in Spain. In winter these lagoons become the haunt of hen harriers and short-eared owls, while hoards of waders – including golden plover, lapwings and snipe – arrive to probe the mud and stalk the shallows in their search for food.

The trail ends up on the beach, which, although adjacent to a large municipal campsite, supports a surprisingly rich **dune flora**, with sea daffodils *Pancratium maritimum*, sea holly *Eryngium maritimum*, sea bindweed *Calystegia soldanella* and sea rocket *Cakile maritima*. The dunes are very low here – largely due to the effect of the *tramontana*, the Spanish equivalent of the *mistral* – stabilised by marram grass *Ammophila arenaria* and sand couch-grass *Agropyron junceiforme*.

The marshes and grasslands

The **freshwater marshes** are totally separate from the salt marsh site and are reached by taking the ROSES road from CASTELLÓ D'EMPÚRIES. Parking is by the side of the road, and a signposted track leads across a mixture of limestone outcrops and abandoned cultivations to the **Estany de Vilaüt**, where a hide gives good views of marsh birds. The ditches and margins of the lake are choked with dense masses of water plants, the yellow iris *Iris pseudacorus* and purple loosestrife *Lythrum salicaria* standing out against a green background of reeds and bulrushes.

Aiguamolls de l'Empordà is possibly the only place in Spain where all three species of **marsh tern** can be seen. White-winged black terns pass through on spring migration, despite the fact that their nearest breeding ground is Yugoslavia. Black terns also call in on passage, and may possibly breed in Spain, and whiskered terns certainly do on the Ebro delta, although the Guadalquivir population has crashed in recent years, possibly because of the indiscriminate use of pesticides and herbicides.

Botanically, the **dry limestone grasslands** are the most interesting part of the freshwater reserve, with a fantastic showing of *Orchis lactea* in early April, followed shortly by tassel hyacinths *Muscari comosum*. The ex-cultivated areas are thick with yellow corn marigolds *Chrysanthemum segetum* and blue borage *Borago officinalis*, with an occasional clump of the highly poisonous henbane *Hyoscyamus niger*. Stonechats and corn buntings are typical birds of these open fields.

A trip through the traditional agricultural land along one of the many tracks that dissect the area will certainly reveal some of the more **unusual birds of the reserve**, including small groups of stone curlew, of which Spain has the most important population in Europe, lesser grey shrikes, a rare bird in Spain since they are at the southern limit of their western European range, and moustached warblers, which resemble sedge warblers but have a distinctive habit of cocking the tail like a wren when perched. Colourful denizens of this open land include great spotted cuckoos, rollers and bee-eaters.

Aiguamolls de L'Empordà is not wonderful for **mammals**, owing mainly to the lack of cover and high human profile, but polecats are said to be common in the marshes, as are water voles. A reintroduction programme for fallow deer is currently underway and the enclosure lies a short distance from the visitor centre. **Reptiles** are a little easier to see, with burrowing three-toed skinks *Chalcides chalcides* characteristic of the dunes, large, venomous Montpellier snakes in the drier salt marshes and woodland fringes, and spiny-footed lizards *Acanthodactylus erythrurus* in the rocky limestone outcrops.

The raptor which is considered to have declined most in Europe recently – **Montagu's harrier** – is known to breed at Aiguamolls de L'Empordà. Although Spain supports only a few hundred pairs of this small bird of prey, mostly in the southwest, this population is probably the most important in the world. Male Montagu's harriers differ from the commoner, and larger, marsh harriers in the lack of brown across the back and upper wings, and the females lack the distinctive white head and shoulders of the latter species.

The best **time to visit** Aiguamolls de l'Empordà is from March to May and August to October for the birds, but the plants are definitely at their finest in April and May. Insect repellant is a must for a trip to the freshwater marshes, since mosquitos have not yet been completely eradicated here.

The Delta del Ebro

The **DELTA DEL EBRO**, 70km southwest of TARRAGONA, sprawls across some 320 square kilometres of alluvial plains, lagoons and dunes. The landward parts are divided into small strips of land dedicated to **agriculture** – orchards of oranges, lemons and peaches, rows of tomatoes and artichokes – but travelling east you soon reach the extensive **rice fields** which have dominated the landscape of the delta for many centuries.

In the spring, when the rice has just been planted and the fields flooded, it's impossible to pass a single paddy without several **black-winged stilts** and at least one off-white **cattle egret** stalking through the shallow water or standing motionless in the lee of a bank. Here on the Delta, cattle egrets far outnumber their snow-white relatives, the little egrets – a situation reversed in the majority of Spanish wetlands. Cattle egrets are distinguished from little egrets by their buff-coloured breeding plumes on head and breast, which gives them a "dirty" appearance, as well as by their reddish legs and short yellow beak.

Sandwich terns are a common sight hawking over the rice fields, identified by their heavy flight, slender, yellow-tipped bills and prominent crest on the back of the head, although this is rarely evident in flight. The Delta del Ebro supports the only breeding colony of Sandwich terns in Spain, which numbered about 350 pairs in 1985 and appears to be on the increase. Later in the year the rice paddies produce a rich harvest of **water plants**, including white water lilies *Nymphaea alba*, pondweeds *Potamogeton spp.*, duckweeds *Lemna spp.*, bladderworts *Utricularia sp.* and stonewort meadows *Chara sp.* All these plants help to support the breeding duck population, which descends on the flooded fields at night to feed, often causing considerable damage.

The Delta is slowly pushing out into the Mediterranean. Silt deposited by the river is responsible for the build up of the alluvial plain, whilst sands tossed onto the shore by the occasional storm-driven sea have produced a rim of **sand bars and dunes** around the outer margins of the Delta. Spiny-footed lizards and large psammodromi are common among the dunes, taking cover amid such typical beach vegetation as sea spurge *Euphorbia paralias*, sea daffodils, large yellow restharrow *Ononis natrix*, with yellow flowers prominently marked with red or violet veins and glandular-sticky, egg-shaped leaves, shrubby seablite *Suaeda fruticosa* and the rare *Limoniastrum monopetalum*, a distinctive silvery shrub with bright pink flowers and narrow fleshy leaves.

The innumerable **ditches and dykes** of the Delta are lined with tamarisk and oleander *Nerium oleander*, as well as reed-type vegetation. The Ebro itself has a better-developed **riverine woodland** along its banks, with white and black poplars *Populus alba* and *P. nigra*, alders *Alnus glutinosa*, white willows *Salix alba*, and a black-fruited climbing honeysuckle *Lonicera biflora*; the latter, only recently discovered here, makes its northernmost appearance in Spain.

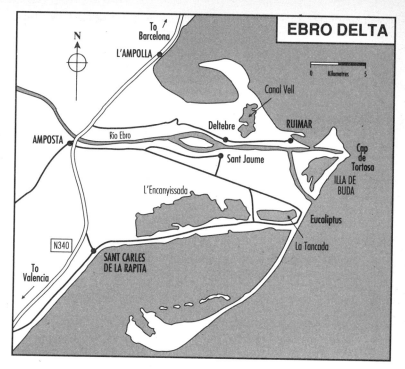

In these freshwater habitats **aquatic reptiles and amphibians** are abundant, especially grass snakes *Natrix natrix* and viperine snakes *N. maura*, as are stripe-necked terrapins, although the European pond terrapin population is declining. Marsh frogs are extremely common, advertising their presence with loud calls both day and night; western spadefoots *Pelobates cultripes* and painted frogs *Discoglossus pictus* are less in evidence. Large mammals are almost nonexistent in this highly humanised environment; only the birds can exploit this fertile alluvial plain, with its rice fields, lagoons and coastal habitats, to the full.

And the range of **bird life** on the Delta is phenomenal, some 300 species – sixty percent of Europe's total – having been recorded here. Especially important localities are the southern lagoons of **L'Encanyissada** and **La Tancada**, together with the **Illa de Buda**, a 1300-hectare island at the extreme tip of the Delta, and **El Canal Vell**, a lagoon on the north side. All of these are within the Parc Natural del Delta de l'Ebre, declared by the Catalan government in 1983.

After the rice harvest the fields are full of birds, with an autumn average of 53,000 **duck** – mostly mallard, shoveller and wigeon, with lesser numbers of shelduck, gadwall, teal and pochard – and 13,000 coot, with about half this number staying for the winter; a figure which represents some ten percent of Iberia's wintering wildfowl. The **wader population** during the winter months is one of the highest of any Mediterranean site, standing at around 20,000 birds, though few stay on to breed; among them are avocets, collared pratincoles, black-winged stilts and oystercatchers.

The bulk of the **breeding ducks** on the Delta are also mallard, the second most numerous species, interestingly enough, being the **red-crested pochard**. Not a common breeding species in Europe as a whole, the majority – up to 6000 pairs – are resident in Spain and almost ten percent of this number choose to breed on the lagoons of the Delta del Ebro.

But the most important family of all to utilise the Delta resources are the **herons**, with almost 1500 pairs of 8 species breeding here regularly. Some 250 of these are purple herons, of which there are now less than 1000 reproductive pairs in Spain following an alarming decrease in recent years due to the widespread use of pesticides in aquatic agriculture.

La Albufera de Valencia

LA ALBUFERA DE VALENCIA, known as *S'Albufera* in the local dialect, is a remarkable place in that it is considered to be of international ornithological importance as a wetland and yet it grazes Valencia's capital city at one end and the holiday mecca of CULLERA at the other. Most of the land between the rivers Túria and Júcar, stretching inland as far as the N332, was in 1986 declared a *parque natural* by the Valencian authorities; some 200 square kilometres of rice fields, saltings, fresh, brackish and saltwater lagoons and pine-clad dunes.

La Albufera itself is a huge **freshwater lake** – one of Spain's largest – and separated from the Mediterranean only by a thin sand bar covered with pine woodland, La Dehesa de Saler. The lake once covered the whole of the area which now lies within the park but it has been whittled away over the centuries to create the extensive **rice fields and saltings** which cover most of the region today. Although the present area of open water is less than 30 square kilometres, it is of immense value to birds because it is only about one metre deep, fringed with dense reedbeds, has several small islands and is largely inaccessible, despite its proximity both to the city and tourist resorts.

The main value of La Albufera is as a refuge for **wintering birds**, particularly mallard, wigeon, teal, pintail, shoveller, red-crested pochard and pochard, the numbers of which oscillate between 50,000 and 100,000; at times more than seventy-five percent of the European population of red-crested pochard are congregated here. Some of these ducks stay on to breed, including 200–400 pairs of red-crested pochard. Although the very rare **ferruginous duck** is now considered extinct as a breeding bird in Spain, La Albufera was one its former haunts, and fair numbers pass through on migration each year, so it is possible that the odd pair nests from time to time.

The rice fields are an essential part of the success of La Albufera in hosting such large numbers of wildfowl during the winter since they provide nocturnal feeding and roosting areas. **Waders** are also abundant in these deliberately flooded fields during the winter, and an estimated 1000 **grey herons** are in residence at this time. All told more than 250 birds have been recorded here, at least 90 of which breed, often in large numbers. For example it is estimated that more than 2500 herons' nests are occupied every year, including purple, night and squacco herons and little and cattle egrets. Bearded tits and reed warblers breed in the reedbeds which surround the lake and great crested grebes construct their floating nests in their shelter. Colonies of black-winged stilts and common terns also utilise the islands.

EAST COAST: ACCESS AND ACCOMMODATION

Aiguamolls de l'Empordá

There are five campsites in and around the park, and both CASTELLÓ D'EMPÚRIES and SANT PERE PESCADOR have hotels. Trains run regularly between BARCELONA and GERONA – get off at FIGUERES and bus from there to Castelló d'Empúries. Alternatively, the coastal bus *Lancha Littoral* northbound from Barcelona goes past the park, stopping at most of the beaches on the way.

Delta del Ebro

The Delta backs onto the N340 VALENCIA to BARCELONA road, along which buses run between the two cities, as well as trains serving L'ALDEA-AMPOST, L'AMPOLLA and CAMARLES, making access superlatively simple. An **Information Centre** is located in Deltebre, on the north side of the park; it is open daily except Monday: 10am–2pm and 4–8pm in July and August, 9am–2pm the rest of the year.

Although the Delta is crisscrossed with dykes and neatly bisected by the Río Ebro itself, getting around is remarkably easy. A comprehensive network of metalled roads serves the rice fields, with tracks giving access to most of the seaward regions of the Delta. A flat-bed barge ferries vehicles across the Ebro from SANT JAUME D'ENVEJA to DELTEBRE; a private boat operates to the **Illa de Buda**; and sightseeing tours are available to the mouth of the river from AMPOSTA. Local buses serve the delta villages.

There are two campsites on the Delta itself, both well-positioned for birdwatching. One is at RUIMAR, between Illa de Buda and El Canal Vell, with the other on the south side of the delta at EUCALIPTUS, close to La Tancada. Both are highly exposed to the *tramontana* in spring, and a well-anchored tent is a must. Additional zones may also be set aside for camping in the peak tourist season. Other accommodation is easily found, with *pensiones* and *fondas* in most of the delta villages.

Mosquito repellent is essential for much of the year, and wellington boots advisable; leeches were once so common in the rice fields that hundreds of thousands were exported every year for medicinal use.

La Albufera de Valencia

Access to the rice fields is straightforward, with small roads linking the N332 with the coast road, and tracks dividing each paddy from the next. There is an **information centre** in EL PERELLONET, one of the coastal villages. Typical Mediterranean resort campsites are available all along the coast, while the city of VALENCIA itself is just up the road on the main road and rail route.

ANDALUCÍA

Despite the concrete jungles of its Costa del Sol, the southern province of Andalucía has an extraordinary variety of habitats. Limestone ranges such as the **Sierra de Grazalema** and **El Torcal de Antequera** contrast with the inland salt lake of **Fuente de Piedra**, long famous for its breeding flamingoes. The truly alpine heights of peninsular Spain's highest peak – Mulhacén (3482m) – in the **Sierra Nevada** is right adjacent to **Las Alpujarras**, a totally different and more cultivated mountain range; while the valley of the Guadalquivir, north of Sevilla, contains the largest national park in Spain – the **Sierras de Cazorla y Segura**.

Once past Gibraltar, the coastline is technically **Atlantic** rather than Mediterranean, though the transition is scarcely obvious. The coastline is notable for its marshes – those at **Odiel** and **Doñana** are outstanding for their wetland birds – and the rock of **Gibraltar** is worth a visit for its apes and bird migration.

Sierra de Grazalema

The rugged **SIERRA DE GRAZALEMA**, in the heart of hot, dry Andalucía, holds the record for the rainiest place in Spain. A line was drawn around some 470 square kilometres of this fascinating **mountain region** in 1984, declaring it a *parque natural*. The designated area lies roughly between the town of UBRIQUE and the C339, which links ALGODONALES with RONDA; the most enjoyable (and picturesque) base is the old wool trade town of GRAZALEMA.

For a quick but rewarding **botanical excursion**, take the road from Grazalema towards UBRIQUE (C3331) and stop a few kilometres after the junction with the C344 in a flat region of open, unfenced scrubby pastures which graduate into woodland as they ascend into the hills. Among the plants to be found here are *Scilla peruviana*, with stunning 15-cm umbels of deep-violet bluebell-type flowers; look for it in the shady, wetter areas in the lee of banks or ditches. Slender gladioli *Gladiolus spp.*, Spanish irises *Iris xiphium* and stars-of-Bethlehem *Ornithogalum spp.* dot the pastures, together with *Anthericum baeticum*, a similar plant to the *scilla* but with pure white flowers and long yellowish stamens.

The shorter, drier areas of **pasture** are worth examining for the bindweed *Convolvulus meonanthus* with small multicoloured flowers – orange-yellow at the centre, then white and finally lilac-blue around the margin of each bell. An attractive labiate is the low-growing relative of self-heal called *Cleonia lusiatanica*, which has long-tubed lilac flowers emerging from a series of overlapping,

Pyramidal orchid *Anacamptis pyramidalis*

trident-shaped bracts. **Orchids** are also abundant, including woodcock *Ophrys scolopax*, pyramidal *Anacamptis pyramidalis*, early purple *Orchis mascula* and sawfly *Ophrys tenthredinifera* – the latter with almost luminous pink outer perianth segments – all still in flower at the end of May, long after their season outside the rain-washed sierras.

The crevice and fissure plants of Grazalema's **limestone outcrops** are legendary, with such bizarre species as *Rupicapnos africana*, a fleshy-leaved member of the poppy family with large pink flowers, found only in southern Spain, and the yellow-flowered, woolly-leaved knapweed *Centaurea clementei*. Three species with very localised distributions are the brick-red **poppy** *Papaver rupifragum*, endemic to Grazalema and the Serranía de Ronda; a yellow-flowered **toadflax** *Linaria platycalyx*, easily identified by the broad oval leaves which clasp the stem in whorls of three; and *Thymus granatensis*, the most exceptional **thyme** species I have ever seen, with large, reddish-purple bracts in a terminal, egg-shaped cluster, from which emerge tiny pink flowers.

Although there is so much wilderness to explore here it would be unforgivable to visit Grazalema and not pay your respects to one of the **last Spanish fir forests** *Abies pinsapo* in existence. These firs are the descendants of those pushed south by successive glaciations during the Ice Ages, becoming isolated in only a few southern Spanish sierras when the ice retreated; they are found nowhere else in the world today owing to their high rainfall requirements and inability to withstand winter frosts. Their principal locality is the nearby Serranía de Ronda, and to a lesser degree the Sierra Bermeja (which spans the coast behind ESTEPONA and MÁLAGA and so is less well preserved). At Grazalema the firs are to be found on the northern slopes of the **Sierra del Pinar** which towers above the village. Owing to the extreme rarity of this tree, you cannot visit the forest without a permit; ask at the *Tajo Rodillo* campsite for details.

Apart from being a botanical paradise, Grazalema, like most Spanish mountain ranges, is also excellent for **birds**. The limestone crags are the principal breeding area of **griffon vultures** in Europe, with around 500–600 pairs distributed across forty *buitreras*, or colonies – about twenty percent of the total Spanish population. If you can tear your eyes away from the dazzling array of plants you should manage to see Egyptian vultures, booted and Bonelli's eagles, kites and peregrine falcons, and with luck one of Spain's last few **black vultures** might put in an appearance; a 1986 census revealed the presence of only 365 pairs of this magnificent bird on the peninsula. A trip to the **Embalse de los Hurones** to the west of the park should be rewarded with views of the pair of ospreys which breed and fish there.

Some forty **mammals** have been recorded in the park. Strangely enough, wild boar are absent, despite seemingly perfect conditions, and other large mammals such as roe deer and ibex have only recently arrived from ranges further south. But there are stable populations of ibex in the Sierra de Líbar – in the south of the park – and Sierra del Pinar, where they find shelter in the fir forest. Foxes, genets and mongooses are also common in this undisturbed *pinsapar*.

El Torcal de Antequera

Only a few kilometres south of the town of ANTEQUERA, an extraordinary lime-stone outcrop, **El Torcal de Antequera**, has been sculpted into a landscape of vertiginous columns and obelisks by millions of years of geological weathering. Assuming the hills aren't in thick mist, as unfortunately is quite often the case in this part of Spain, the 15-kilometre approach to El Torcal is breathtaking, the narrow road winding up the south flank between **flower-filled meadows** from which rise the bizarre, pale grey columns of limestone.

Interesting plants to watch out for in the roadside verges are the southern Iberian bugloss *Echium boissieri*, with salmon-pink-flowered spikes up to 2.5 metres high, and a catmint *Nepeta tuberosa*, easily distinguished by the paired leaves which cling vertically to the stem and a dense spike of purple flowers protected by large, reddish bracts. Equally striking, but more widespread, plants include large Mediterranean spurge *Euphorbia characias*, the tall, furry-leaved labiate *Phlomis purpurea* and mallow-leaved bindweed *Convolvulus althaeoides*, identified by its large pink flowers and dissected triangular leaves.

The calcareous nature of Torcal's rock and the thinness of the soils gives rise to an enormous diversity of plants; no one species can become dominant because of the scarcity of available nutrients such as nitrates. A five-minute wander from the car park at the top of the road reveals jagged **limestone pavement**. Paving-stone-like slabs are known as clints and the deep fissures which divide them as grykes, where windblown debris accumulates, soils form and plant life flourishes. Here the spring-flowering yellow violet *Viola demetria* can be found, along with a saxifrage which is endemic to Spain's southern sierras: *Saxifraga biternata*. Another interesting rock-dwelling species is the toadflax *Linaria anticaria*, which as its name suggests, is a speciality of Antequera, and in fact has its centre of distribution here. Look out too for brown-bee orchids *Ophrys fusca*, and the superb tongue orchid *Serapias cordigera*.

The best course for exploration is to follow the **"yellow" route** from the car park. The loop is only three kilometres long but of such interest that you can happily take a half-day over it, scrambling through the beautiful **limestone karst** area. Features to look out for include dozens of sawfly orchids on the margins of the car park, and the May display of paeonies and deep purple irises *Iris subbiflora* among the stunted hawthorns. Choughs wheel around the peaks, curiously incongruous so far from their northern mountain fastnesses, and views of the striking black and white Egyptian vultures are likely, often so close that you can see their yellow beaks even without binoculars.

El Torcal de Antequera was declared a *parque natural* in 1978, and a newly-furbished information centre adjoining the car park is likely to open shortly. Avoid visiting over the weekend or at the height of summer as it is, understandably, extremely popular with locals.

Fuente de Piedra

Close to El Torcal is a completely contrasting habitat: **FUENTE DE PIEDRA**, a shallow **inland salt lake** fed by runoff from the surrounding hills and by the most extensive lagoon in Andalucía. Apart from the Camargue, it is the only place where the **greater flamingo** breeds regularly in the western Mediterranean and is worth a visit if only for this reason.

The habitat has been declared a *reserva integral* by the Andalucían government, and as such there is no access to the central breeding colony. However, from the end of the rough track that leads down to the lake from the nearby village of FUENTE DE PIEDRA, it is usually possible to get good views of the **flamingoes** nesting on a low island called La Colonia, sometimes in such numbers that their nests are less than one metre apart. Each pair incubates a single egg, which usually hatches in May.

In 1988 12,000 pairs of these elegant birds bred at Fuente de Piedra and raised over 9000 chicks between them, the immense colony a little piece of Africa in the centre of Spain and a truly breathtaking sight. In 1989, though, the failure of the winter rains meant that the lake shrunk to its smallest for years (its average extent is 14 square kilometres), and the flamingoes were almost invisible amid the

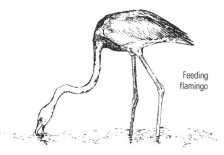

Feeding flamingo

haze rising from the crystallised salt in the dried-out lagoon. A warden from the village told me that less than a thousand flamingoes had taken up residence that year and that even by May there were no signs of nest-building. Those present were so far away that even with binoculars it was difficult to pick them out.

Other **breeding birds** on the lake include colonies of black-winged stilts, avocets and gull-billed terns which also vary according to annual fluctuations in water level, as well as Kentish plovers. In **winter** Fuente de Piedra usually expands to cover over 30 square kilometes with its shallow waters, supporting up to 50,000 duck, about a third of them pochards, together with shelduck, pintail and wigeon. Spoonbills, egrets, herons and storks drop in on migration.

The diversity of the area is increased by the presence of a small **freshwater lagoon** on the north side of the main lake, which provides feeding grounds for the gull-billed terns and black-winged stilts in times of drought as well as black terns. It is fringed with rushes *Juncus spp.*, club-rushes *Scirpus sp.* and galingales *Cyperus spp.*, mixed with tall stands of reedmace *Typha sp.*. There are plans afoot for the province to purchase this small wetland, but even at present there is free access through the cereal fields, provided you stick to the edges of the crops.

Sierra Nevada and Las Alpujarras

Behind Spain's legendary Costa del Sol runs what is probably the most impressive mountain range on the peninsula, with no less than ten peaks exceeding the 3000-metre mark. Foremost among these is **Mulhacén** (3481m), the highest point in mainland Spain, though also one of the most accessible since it lies less than a kilometre from the mountain track linking the villages of **LAS ALPUJARRAS** with the ski resorts on the north-facing slope of the **SIERRA NEVADA** above GRANADA.

The approach: Las Alpujarras

The best **route** onto the ridge, which separates the *meseta* from the almost tropical coastal plain, is to wind through the **LAS ALPUJARRAS** on the southern flank. Little remains of the original vegetation which once clothed these rounded forerunners to the dark, forbidding mountains behind, since the amiable climate meant money to the original farmers of this land and the trend continues today. Terraces of olives, almonds and oranges dominate the lower slopes, with rocky suntraps sprouting succulent figs and prickly pears *Opuntia ficus-indica*.

Retama *Lygos sphaerocarpa* and large yellow restharrow *Ononis natrix* create a blaze of gold along the side of the road, which ascends in a series of hairpin bends from ORGIVA to CAPILEIRA. Look out also for *Antirrhinum barrelieri*, a rose-flowered snapdragon, and Spanish rusty foxglove, both typical of southern Iberia. In the warmth of this man-made landscape flourish such exotic-looking birds as azure-winged magpies, rollers, black wheatears, hoopoes and woodchat shrikes.

Capileira to Pico Veleta: the Sierra Nevada

Above Capileira the road becomes little more than a track. Take heed of signs warning that the pass is closed by snow; the foot of Mulhacén is usually clear by the end of May, but the final, crucial kilometres to the **Pico Veleta** (3398m) are normally snowbound until midsummer. Even at the height of summer it's unwise to drive this trans-Nevada route without a four-wheel drive vehicle.

From Capileira the first section of track passes through **pine plantations**. Because the trees are still quite young plenty of light penetrates to the forest floor and plants flourish, including species such as tassel hyacinths *Muscari comosum* and the pink form of white rockrose *Helianthemeum apenninum var. roseum* which is particularly prevalent in Spain. Climbing higher, the pines are left behind and the landscape opens out to windswept **mountain pastures**. In spring the melting snow reveals carpets of the tiny, white-flowered buttercup *Ranunculus acetosellifolius*, endemic to the Sierra Nevada and one of the easiest of all montane species to identify, even when not in bloom, by its arrow-shaped leaves, the "barbs" of which are often divided into several filaments.

The scenery at this point is reminiscent of Dartmoor, with its grim grey-green slopes and swirling mists; there are even a few **granite tors** thrown in for good measure. The crystalline rock of the main ridge is very resistant so the range is not broken up into distinct peaks, as in a limestone landscape, but presents one daunting, snow-capped mass which never seems to get any nearer, always assuming you can see it through the low-lying cloud. Wheatears, rock thrushes and rock buntings are your only companions, and yet this seemingly barren wilderness is one of the **botanical jewels** of Europe, with more than 1725 species of vascular plant identified to date, of which sixty-odd are found nowhere else in the world.

Two reasons for this **richness and specialisation** are that the Sierra Nevada was little affected by the Ice Ages, providing a refuge for plants driven relentlessly south by the advancing ice, and that these mountains were once linked with those of Africa when the Mediterranean sea was a closed lagoon, providing a similar escape route for tropical species forced north by the spreading Sahara.

The highest degree of endemism is found above the 2500m level among the **snow-tolerant herbs**, some forty of which are unique to this range. Look out for the bizarre spiky umbellifer known as glacier eryngo *Eryngium glaciale* and the snow-star *Plantago talackeri*, both of which grow in the same "tundra" zone as *Ranunculus acetosellifolius* but require a little more application in searching them out. The snow poppy *Papaver suaveolens*, also found in the Spanish Pyrenees, is another species of this montane wilderness.

Typical high altitude herbs often adopt a **cushion-like growth habit** to maintain the internal temperature, such as several of the Sierra Nevada's best-known endemic species: the pink-flowered violet *Viola crassiuscula* found in screes above 2500m, *Saxifraga nevadensis*, and the wormwood *Artemisia granatensis*, also found in nearby ranges. *Linaria glacialis*, with its glaucous leaves and lilac-veined, pale yellow flowers, and the insectivorous butterwort *Pinguicula nevadensis* are also found here. Away from the main Capileira-Veleta track there are still isolated areas where one of the Sierra Nevada's most attractive endemic plants, *Narcissus nevadensis*, has managed to escape the hands of irresponsible visitors.

Among animals, the **ibex**, which almost became extinct here in the 1930s, is today thriving and starting to reoccupy some of its old haunts. As with the flora, the ibex is here considered to belong to a subspecies endemic to the Sierra Nevada. Golden eagles are among the commonest **large birds of prey**, and sharp eyes should spot peregrines on the bare slopes and sparrowhawks patrolling the pine woodlands lower down. Both griffon and Egyptian vultures thrive on the leftovers of the traditional livestock-rearing activities of the region, and choughs and lesser kestrels, once common raptors which have been decreasing over the past two decades, nest in noisy colonies in undisturbed rocky terrain.

Sierras de Cazorla y Segura

The **SIERRAS DE CAZORLA Y SEGURA** are parallel limestone ridges on either side of the infant Río Guadalquivir – the watercourse which is eventually responsible for the famed Doñana marshes. In 1986, 214 square kilometres were declared a *parque natural*, the largest protected area of this kind in Spain, and encompassing the former *Coto Nacional de Cazorla*: a centre for the breeding of large game species.

The **Tranco gorge**, along which the Guadalquivir flows as it exits the Cazorla-Segura valley, is indeed impressive, with limestone walls clothed with beech woodland looming over coniferous forests on either side of the road (which seems to have the highest density of potholes of any in Spain). The canopy of pines shelters a wide range of Mediterranean **shrub species**, including grey-leaved cistus, lentisc and its close relative, the turpentine tree, and the golden-flowered *Halimium atriplicifolium*, a typical pine forest species of southern and central Spain. Look out for the bright-blue flowers and rushlike leaves of *Aphyllanthes monspeliensis* among the more colourful herbs lining the roadside banks, as well as the tall, rose-pink "bunny-rabbits" of the snapdragon *Antirrhinum majus*.

Just south of the town of CAZORLA it's worth taking a detour via the village of TISCAR, which is perched on a steep slope beneath a row of magnificent **jagged limestone peaks**. From from the 1183m heights of the **Puerto de Tiscar** the road winds back down to the olive groves of the *meseta*, the verges a riot of colour: the composite known as cupidone *Catananche caerulea*, with papery bracts and blue-lilac strap-shaped petals, the yellow labiate *Phlomis lychnitis*, *Echium boissieri* and *Moricandia arvensis*, a strange violet-flowered crucifer with smooth, glaucous leaves clamped tightly around the stem.

In Cazorla take the road signposted to the *parador* (but turn off before reaching it) for access to the **Guadalquivir valley** which dominates the centre of the park. Having negotiated the hairpin bends of Puerto de las Palomas (1290m) you descend alongside the young Guadalquivir through pine forests where it is impossible to miss the small groups of red and fallow deer – a legacy of the breeding programme of the *Coto Nacional* – at semi-liberty in the woodlands.

The **route down the Guadalquivir** from Palomas is excellent for seeing the altitude-dependent **woodland types** present within the park. The only native pine is black pine *Pinus nigra ssp. salzmanii*, which forms forests together with the junipers *Juniperus sabina* and *J. communis*, yew *Taxus baccata* and holly *Ilex aquifolium* above 1200m. *Echinospartum boissieri*, a limestone-loving shrubby legume of south and southeast Spain, the barbary *Berberis hispanica*, typical of the same region, *Lonicera arborea*, a honeysuckle distinguished by its yellowish berries, and St Lucie's cherry *Prunus mahaleb* are among the more interesting elements of the shrub layer.

Moving **down the valley** there's a maritime pine *Pinus pinaster* zone which has replaced the native evergreen oak woodlands, although pockets of *Quercus rotundifolia*, Lusitanian oak *Q. faginea* and the southern Spanish maple *Acer granatense* occur here and there. The understorey is also different, with strawberry tree *Arbutus unedo*, the honeysuckles *Lonicera splendida* (endemic to the mountains of southern Spain) and *L. etrusca*, laurustinus *Viburnum tinus* and prickly juniper *Juniperus oxycedrus* being more abundant here. The 600–850m range is occupied mainly by plantations of Aleppo pine *Pinus halapensis*, again a later substitute for the original Mediterranean woodland.

Some 1300 vascular plants have been recorded from the sierras, which are of great significance as a last refuge of several **alpine species** stranded by the retreating ice, 24 of which are endemic to the Cazorla-Segura ranges. Foremost among these are the insectivorous butterwort *Pinguicula valisneriifolia*, only discovered in 1851 and then not seen again until the beginning of this century, the pale-blue columbine *Aquilegia cazorlensis*, the carmine-flowered violet *Viola cazorlensis*, and the cranesbill *Geranium cazorlense*, all of which are plants most at home on limestone outcrops at high altitude.

The peak of **Cabañas** (2036m), easily accessible via a track leading up from Puente de las Herrerías at the south end of the park, is a good place for serious botanising. *Viola cazorlensis* is also found around the *parador* but the butterwort is more elusive. A denizen of damp, shady cliff-faces and limestone caves, it flowers only for a few days in mid-June and only then if the weather is sufficiently wet.

Over 140 species of **birds** have been recorded in the sierras of Cazorla and Segura, the most distinguished residents being the lone pair of **lammergeiers** – which testify to the former wide range of this magnificent vulture. Golden and booted eagles are the commonest eagles here, and choughs, ravens and jackdaws populate the rocky uplands. The introduced mouflon, while providing plenty of food for the lammergeiers, griffon and few pairs of Egyptian vultures, have largely displaced the native race of ibex, which are now to be found only in the highest peaks.

The woodlands are the haunt of **owls**, from the tiny Scops owl to the huge eagle owl, along with other predatory birds such as goshawks, hobbies and sparrowhawks. **Small mammalian carnivores** are present, too, including wildcats, genets and beech martens. Their prey consists largely of mice and shrews, but the pine forests of the Sierra de Segura are also home to an endemic race of red squirrel. Thirty-six mammalian species in all have been recorded within the boundaries of the *parque natural*, along with 16 **reptiles**, including horseshoe whipsnakes, Lataste's viper, ladder snakes *Elaphe scalaris* and southern smooth snakes *Coronella girondica*. The most notable reptile, however, is the Spanish algyroides *Algyroides marchi*, a small, white-throated lizard that is probably endemic to the mature pine forests of these mountains.

Las Marismas del Odiel

Situated in the extreme southwestern corner of Spain and abutting the city of HUELVA, **LAS MARISMAS DEL ODIEL** comprise a large area of tidal salt marshes and creeks. The area includes operative saltpans, mature sand dunes now supporting umbrella pines and Mediterranean shrubs, and young shoreline dunes where the Río Odiel discharges into the Atlantic. Most of this zone has been declared a *parque natural de intere's nacional* by the Andalucían government on account of its superb coastal flora and ornithological interest.

Just over the river from Huelva are **saltpans**, initially new ones, though traditional workings are soon reached, distinguished by their small size, well-vegetated banks and their **bird life**: black-winged stilts, avocets and spoonbills during the long summer days and wintering wildfowl at night. Just before a small suspension bridge there is a car park on the right.

The drier marshes bordering the river provide an opportunity to get to know some of the **cistus species** typical of Mediterranean Spain, always assuming you're there at the right time of year – mid-May is the optimum flowering season. Of the **white-flowered** species, the largest blooms, often with dark blotches at the centre, belong to gum cistus *Cistus ladanifer*. Shrubs with smaller flowers are more difficult to separate, but those with long, thin, shiny leaves are probably narrow-leaved cistus *C. monspeliensis*, whilst those with rounder, rougher leaves are sage-leaved cistus *C. salvifolius*. *Cistus psilosepalus* is very similar to sage-leaved cistus, but has stalkless leaves and long bristly hairs on the sepals. Even though it has white flowers similar in size to gum cistus, there is no mistaking the poplar-leaved species *Cistus populifolius*, which can be identified even when it is not in flower by its large, heart-shaped leaves. Of the two **pink-flowered** species found here, grey-leaved cistus *Cistus albidus* has larger, paler flowers and grey-green velvety leaves, while *C. crispus* is distinguished by its crumpled, deep crimson flowers and wavy-edged, three-veined leaves; it is also a much lower-growing shrub.

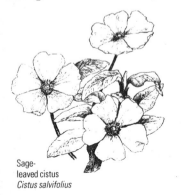

Sage-leaved cistus
Cistus salvifolius

From the suspension bridge, look over to the right to **La Isla de Enmedio,** an island set aside as a *reserva integral*, with access prohibited. You'll need binoculars, but here is one of the star attractions at Odiel – a large **spoonbill colony** of around 300 pairs, remarkable for the fact that here they nest on the ground, amid tussocks of the wiry grass *Spartina densiflora*, rather than in trees as at their more famous locality at Doñana further east. Mixed in with the spoonbills are around 80 pairs of nesting grey herons and a large colony of little egrets, both of which do perfectly well on this treeless island.

On the far side of the suspension bridge there's the diverse world of **Mediterranean coastal shrubs and herbs**. Among the more striking species are *Limoniastrum monopetalum*, a silvery bush with narrow fleshy leaves, covered with lilac-pink flowers, and sea heath *Frankenia spp.*, another pink-flowered woody plant, but with reddish stems which creep along the ground and tiny leaves like those of heather. The high proportion of bare sand in this zone makes it a favourite basking place for **reptiles** and if you have exceptionally sharp eyesight you might spot one of a thriving population of Mediterranean **chameleons** *Chamaeleo chamaeleon*, released here following their reprieve from illegal trading.

To the west of the road the salt-tolerant shrubs are backed by a belt of **Mediterranean forest** of stone pines *Pinus pinea*, junipers *Juniperus sp.* and holm oak *Quercus ilex*, with an understorey of turpentine tree *Pistacia terebinthus*, wild olive *Olea europaea* and myrtle *Myrtus communis*. Growing in amongst these shrubs is the rue *Ruta chalepensis*, the most nauseatingly pungent plant I have ever come across and unmistakable since each petal is fringed with long teeth giving the bright yellow flowers a ragged look. This narrow strip of forest is a good place to see **rollers and golden orioles,** too.

Further towards the river mouth, where the salt marshes abut the road, grows one of Odiel's most spectacular plants. Half-metre high spikes of a golden-yellow-flowered relative of the **broomrapes** known as *Cistanche phelypaea* stand out from the dull greys and greens of the marsh like candles on a birthday cake. Like all broomrapes *Cistanche* doesn't possess chlorophyll and thus has no green leaves; it obtains all of its nourishment by parasitising other plants, especially sea purslane *Halimione portulacoides*. It grows only in southern Iberia, north Africa, Crete and Arabia.

All in all **280 birds** have been recorded at Odiel, largely because the marshes lie on one of the most heavily used **migration routes** between Europe and Africa: in fact, the narrowest point between the two continents in western Europe. Ospreys drop in regularly, and the park officials have erected a nesting platform, similar to that at Loch Garten in Scotland, to encourage this raptor to breed; it is considered endangered in Spanish territory, with only four pairs known to breed on the mainland, and a further twenty or so in the Balearic Islands.

With the splendid habitat provided by the traditional *salinas* it is a bit of a mystery as to why Odiel's **greater flamingoes** prefer the new commercial salt-pans. In spring 1989 the team of wardens constructed 65 conical mud nests in an effort to encourage these magnificent birds to breed, and while I was there, in mid-May, there were encouraging signs of courtship display. Although they have never before bred at Odiel, it seems possible that a colony may become established, especially as the more famous colony at Fuente de Piedra is in decline, perhaps because of successive droughts. Views of the flamingoes are not possible without first obtaining a permit.

Las Marismas and the Coto Doñana

It is highly likely that the vast extent of *marismas*, or marshes, which surrounds the Río Guadalquivir where it discharges into the sea represents the largest intact natural ecosystem in southwest Europe today. The only problem is that the **PARQUE NACIONAL DE DOÑANA**, which covers the best part of the marshland, plus extensive areas of coastal dunes and pine forests, is harder for the average wildlife enthusiast to get into than Alcatraz was to escape from!

There is no access to the national park except for a limited **tour** in an all-terrain vehicle; these depart from El Acebuche reception centre just to the north of the resort of MATALASCAÑAS. A little further up the H312 towards ALAMONTE, however, is a second centre, La Rocina, from which a two-kilometre **nature trail** heads away from the park; there is a further route of a little over a kilometre commencing from the Acebrón museum to the west. **Observatories** have been constructed along both routes.

For more **informal birdwatching**, especially on foot, many of Doñana's commoner species can be seen without resorting to such organised ornithology.

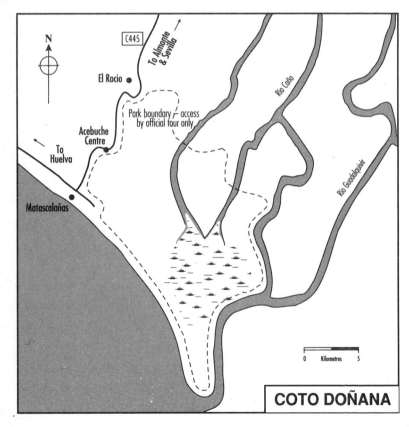

The best option is to head out of SEVILLA on the SE660 for CORIA DEL RÍO and LA PUEBLO DEL RÍO. This road goes into the very heart of the Guadalquivir marshes ending at **Villafranco del Guadalquivir**, from where tracks radiate out in all directions. Not surprisingly there is no public transport available along this route.

Birds of the Doñana

There is no doubt that the national park is of phenomenal ecological interest, with well over 200 birds, about thirty mammals and the same number of reptiles and amphibians having been recorded here.

Among the **water birds** of particular interest are marbled teal, whose only breeding sites on Spanish soil are in Andalucía, and purple gallinules, like large, violet-tinged moorhens with stout red bills, which if disturbed will "run" across the water surface; their national stronghold is here in the Guadalquivir marshes. Crested coots, very similar to the common coot, but distinguished by the presence of two small red knobs on the forehead and the lack of a white wing-bar in flight, have only recently started to breed again in Spain after an absence of many years – at Guadalquivir and some of the Lagunas de Cádiz.

Important colonies of grey and night herons, cattle and little egrets, spoonbills and white storks breed every year in the evergreen oak and *Halimium* thickets which dominate the plains around the freshwater lagoons. The number of **wintering wildfowl** is almost unbelievable, with over 100,000 coot, around 20,000 shoveller, 60,000 wigeon, over 30,000 teal and 20,000–30,000 greylag geese flocking to these rich marshes and lagoons every year.

Other **birds of interest** in the Guadalquivir marshes are the dozen or so pairs of **Spanish imperial eagles** which nest in the evergreen oak forests, and the quail-like **Andalusian hemipode**. Although this bird is believed to be extinct both in Iberia and Europe as a breeding bird, several are caught every spring in the lower marshes of the Guadalquivir and it is possible that a few clandestine pairs manage to raise their young here. Slender-billed gulls, identified by their pinkish chests in the breeding season, nest only at the Delta del Ebro, Fuente de Piedra and here at Doñana. **Pin-tailed sandgrouse** can be seen in the drier scrubby areas of Doñana, their needle-like tail feathers trailing characteristically in flight; in Europe, sandgrouse are only found in Spain and at La Crau in France. Pallid swifts are a common sight hawking over the marshes, as are red-rumped swallows (with a broad orange-red band across the base of the tail), which build the mud nests typical of all hirundines but with long entrance tunnels.

Other animals

The most exceptional mammal at Doñana is one which, quite frankly, there is almost no chance of seeing – the **pardel lynx**. Although once widespread across the peninsula, lynxes are now restricted to the southwestern quarter. They are specialist rabbit-feeders, about eighty percent of their diet being accounted for in this way, although deer may also be taken; from this habit the lynx derives one of its local names of *lobo cerval,* or "deer-wolf".

You've more chance of seeing some of the unusual **reptiles** for which the Guadalquivir marshes are renowned. Among these is the rare spur-thighed **tortoise** *Testudo graeca*, so called because of the pointed protruberances on the hind legs. Although drastically over-collected for the pet trade over the past few decades, especially along the east coast, the population here at Doñana appears to be stable. False **smooth snakes** *Macroprotodon cucullatus*, distinguished by the flattened head, blackish collar and stripe beneath the eye following the line of the jaw, are found only in the southern half of Iberia and the Balearic Islands in Europe, although also distributed across northern Africa as far east as Israel.

Bedriaga's **skink** *Chalcides bedriagai*, confined to the Iberian peninsula, is a small, sandy-coloured, blunt-nosed lizard which can burrow very quickly into the sand at the slightest hint of danger. In a subterranean lifestyle, legs are superfluous and most skinks have greatly reduced limbs – the legless **amphisbaenian**, also found here, is the extreme example of this evolutionary process.

Gibraltar

GIBRALTAR is one of the less attractive resorts of the Mediterranean, packed out with day-trippers since the border reopened in 1988. However, its wildlife – like its history and physical appearance – has a distinct curiosity value.

It is not immediately obvious that any **wild plant** exists on "The Rock", since the roadside flora consists almost entirely of introduced species such as agaves, aloes, geraniums and palm trees. But a climb to the top of its sheer limestone bulk reveals a **stunted forest** of wind-pruned wild olives, lentisc *Pistacia lentiscus* and Mediterranean buckthorn *Rhamnus alaternus*, punctuated by tall aleppo pines *Pinus halepensis*. Two yellow-flowered leguminous shrubs, spiny broom *Calicotome villosa* and shrubby scorpion vetch *Coronilla valentina*, brighten up the understorey. Spring flowers in these upper regions of the Rock are mainly tuberous plants, capable of withstanding the withering summers, including hollow-stemmed asphodel *Asphodelus fistulosus*, rose garlic *Allium roseum* and the barbary nut *Iris sisyrinchium*.

The top of the Rock is best-known and most-visited for the **apes**, in fact a type of macaque *Macaca sylvanus*, introduced more than 240 years ago by the Moors and

maintained by periodic infusions of new blood from Africa. There is a modern legend recounting that the British will only surrender Gibraltar when the last ape leaves; not leaving anything to chance, Winston Churchill ordered the importation of several dozen more during the Second World War! There are only about forty apes left on the Rock today, in two troops, one at Queen's Gate – the Apes' Den, which attracts more than two million visitors a year – and one at Middle Hill – Rooke Battery.

The cliffs have been more successful at resisting the invasion of alien plants. Indigenous species include the Gibraltar candytuft *Iberis gibraltarica*, a north African species which testifies to the ancient link between this limestone outcrop and Mount Abyla on

Alyssum maritimum

the southern side of the Straits of Gibraltar. The splash zone at the base of the cliffs is an ideal·habitat for the white rounded heads of *Alyssum maritimum* and the dunes behind the sandy beaches of CATALAN BAY on the eastern side of the Rock are dotted with the slender wiry leaves of *Romulea clusiana* in spring, within which nestle large, orange-centred violet bells. Later in the year, the tall leafless spikes of sea squill *Urginea maritima* take over; friar's cowl *Arisarum vulgare*, with its flask-shaped flowers, and paper-white daffodils *Narcissus papyraceus* can still be found in flower even at Christmas.

As the shortest sea crossing between Europe and Africa in the western Mediterranean, Gibraltar sees the coming and going of innumerable birds on **spring and autumn migration**. A September visit will coincide with a flush of honey buzzards and kites moving south for the winter, followed by booted eagles and marsh harriers in October and passerines and terns in November. A total of over 200 bird species have been noted here, although of these only fifteen can find a suitable breeding niche on the Rock itself; the rest are just passing through. Breeders include cliff-nesting peregrine falcons and blue rock thrushes in the dry rocky uplands, but the most distinctive resident is the Barbary partridge, probably introduced by the Moors since Gibraltar is its only known locality outside Africa.

ANDALUCÍA: ACCESS AND ACCOMMODATION

Sierra de Grazalema

Easiest access is on the bus from RONDA to UBRIQUE, which passes through the old village of GRAZALEMA. Both Ubrique and Grazalema have places to stay, and at the latter an excellent campsite, *Tajo Rodillo*, is carved into terraces; here mountain and wildlife guides can be hired and information about the park is available (☎956/137316). More remote camping options include *Los Linares* at Benamahoma, *El Moralejo* at Benaocaz or *Las Cobatillas* near Zahara de la Sierra.

Fuente de Piedra

Turn off the N334 just a few miles northwest of ANTEQUERA, through the unprepossessing village of FUENTE DE PIEDRA on the MA454 to Sierra de Yeguas. The village is on the MALAGA/SEVILLA bus route, as well as on the railway line. An extremely rough track on the left, signposted *Reserva Integral de Fuente de Piedra*, leads down to the edge of the lake where an information centre is currently under construction. As with El Torcal de Antequera, there are no campsites for many kilometres: an indication of the "untouristy" nature of the surrounding countryside.

Sierra Nevada and Las Alpujarras

On foot the CAPILEIRA–VELETA route is a long haul and the scenery doesn't change very much, so if you plan a walking holiday in the Sierra Nevada your best approach is to ascend the north face. Buses run from GRANADA almost to the foot of Veleta, taking in the ski resort of SOLYNIEVE en route, leaving the city at 9am daily and returning each afternoon.

From the top you can head west, hiking between the mountain huts (run by the Spanish Mountaineering Federation) at Laguna de las Yeguas and Elorrieta (3200m) and on to Cerro del Caballo at 2850m, or follow the track on up to Mulhacén to the east before dropping down into the sun-warmed Alpujarras. Many of the villages boast *fondas* and campsites.

Sierras de Cazorla y Segura

Several roads lead into the Guadalquivir valley around which the park is centred. My own favourites are the one along the gorge from VILLANUEVA DEL ARZOBISPO on the N322 to the dam at TRANCO (which is responsible for the reservoir at the heart of the park) and the winding road from CAZORLA. Access by bus is from JAEN via UBEDA to Cazorla, which is also a sensible place to stay if not camping. Buses within villages in the park are infrequent.

There are information centres at CAZORLA and another at the northern end of the park at SILES, but should these be closed you can get leaflets showing the locations of the free campsites (camping outside of which is prohibited) at the manned barrier which marks the start of the park. There is also an interpretation centre in the park at Torre del Vinagre, at around km18 on the Cazorla–Tranco road, which is open 11am–2pm and 5–8pm (closed Mon).

Las Marismas del Odiel

Approaching **Odiel** from HUELVA follow signs to PUNTA UMBRIA but, after crossing the river, turn immediately left down a small road which leads to the *Monumento a Colón*; the *paraje* may be signposted at this point, but on my last visit the board had been vandalised. A permit allows free access to any part of the *paraje* – except of course the *reservas integrales* – and must be obtained from the *Agencia de Medio Ambiente* (c/Sanlúcar de Barrameda 3, Huelva); they are granted on the spot, but normal Spanish opening hours apply! Without this permit you'll have to keep to the access road and its immediate environs.

The permit also enables visitors to drop in on the freshwater lagoons of **La Gravera**, where hides have been erected for excellent views of feeding spoonbills and hunting peregrines. The hides are replicas of the first houses built by Huelvan marsh-dwelling peoples, all materials derived from the *marismas* themselves.

There are several campsites in the area, all rather tourist-oriented. The best of these, *Las Vegas* at ALJARQUE, makes amends for this by being located in the pine-clad dunes alongside the Huelva–Punta Umbria road, bordering the western margin of the *paraje*. There's also accommodation in HUELVA, a largely industrial town, or at the resort of PUNTA UMBRIA. The information centre within the *paraje* is situated at LA BACUTA, a small group of huts by the side of the main access road.

Coto Doñana

The Doñana reserve lies southwest of SEVILLA and is accessible from there or from HUELVA at the western end. MATALASCAÑAS is the best bet for local accommodation, although it's a fairly standard concrete resort.

For the official tour of the reserve, there are two departures per day, at 8.30am and 5pm, each of which takes four hours, costs 1750 pesetas (almost £9), and must be booked days in advance (telephone the reception centre at El Acebuche on ☎955/430432). At almost any time of year you will share the experience with a horde of Spanish sightseers and their children; visitors midweek in midwinter should be a little luckier with the crowds. For more leisurely exploration around the outskirts of the reserve, a lot can be seen on foot, although a hired car is a real bonus.

Gibraltar

Staying on the Rock is expensive (UK prices). For those staying in Spain and coming over a for a day visit, it's definitely best to leave the car outside and walk in (there is no public transport between the two countries), since the perimeter road is chock-a-block with cars and parking is a nightmare.

THE BALEARIC ISLANDS

The **Balearic Islands** lie to the east of the Spanish mainland, at distances varying from 80 to 300km. In all, there are some fifteen islands, though only four – Mallorca, Menorca, Ibiza and Formentera – are populated. Tourism determines much of the character of these islands, though even on Mallorca, the most developed, there are large expanses of unspoilt wilderness which offer an abundance of wildlife to the visiting naturalist.

Mallorca

The mountains of **MALLORCA** are thought to be a natural extension of the Spanish mainland ranges. The range along the northwest coast is very narrow and forms precipitous cliffs which fall dramatically to the sea. To the east lies a second, almost parallel, **mountain range**, which extends to the inhospitable limestone headlands beyond Arta in the north and includes fascinating submarine caves of Karstian origin. South of this second range are the **coastal bays** which first attracted the tourist industry to the Balearics. The narrow inlets which ring this coast are remnants of ancient river valleys, formed when sea-levels were considerably lower.

The package tourist market has concentrated almost entirely on the south and east coasts. No surprise, therefore, that four of the five selected sites are in the north of the island, which has remained remarkably undeveloped.

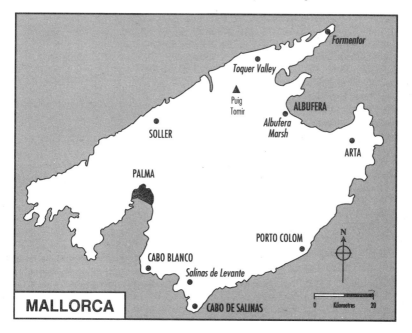

The Formentor Peninsula

The **FORMENTOR PENINSULA** is the northern tip of Mallorca, an exposed, finger-like projection with a very restricted flora. However, further inland, on the PUERTO POLLENSA road, you pass through the tunnel which overlooks, at the south end, the turquoise waters of CALA FIGUERA. The scrubby areas which lie at this **tunnel entrance** hold several of the species of plant which are endemic to the Balearic Islands, and some which are found solely on Mallorca.

These plants include the brilliant **peaonies** *Paeonia cambessedessi*, bright red, in colour during its all-too-brief flowering period in April. Also, along the walls which line the right-hand side of the road, careful inspection may reveal either *Senecio rodriguezii* or *Erodium reichardii*; both have small white flowers but the

Dwarf fan palm
Chamaerops humilis

former is distinguished by its dark pink centres and purple underside of the leaves, whereas the latter has a violet-coloured centre vein on each petal and large, lobed leaves. Higher up on the slopes, there's the diminutive endemic foxglove *Digitalis dubia* with its pink and purple-spotted thimble-shaped flowers, and occasional melanic form. The road-sides which line the route north to the lighthouse are rich in a mixture of **white asphodels** (*Asphodelus albus* and *A. aestivus*), **dwarf fan palm** *Chamaerops humilis* and the mastic tree or lentisk *Pistacia lentiscus*, whose sparse coverings typify this windswept peninsula.

This scrub holds good numbers of wheatears, whinchats and stonechats and the more patient observer may catch a sight of the more elusive **Marmora's warbler**, never a common bird and now declining throughout the Mediterranean. And the rocky slopes which fall away from around the **lighthouse** form an ideal habitat for a variety of small birds and lizards. More obvious residents include the blue rock thrush, blackbird-like in profile but a deep royal blue in colour, and rock doves, displaying their white rumps in flight. Wheeling overhead there may be ravens, crag martins and possibly pallid swifts. The peninsula is also a good vantage point for passage **birds of prey** and spring and autumn can produce spectacular overhead flocks of black kite and honey buzzard.

From April to October, the **eastern cliff faces** are occupied by nesting colonies of **Eleanora's falcons**, which feed on the abundant insects on the nearby marshlands, before making their long return journeys to Madagascar for the winter. They are true masters of flight and a delight to watch gliding over the cliff tops. Formentor also offers excellent views of passage **seabirds**. Following the path down the northern cliff face beyond the car park, it is possible (with care!) to descend 100m or so onto a rocky platform from which one can look out to sea. Both the yellow-billed Cory's and Manx **shearwaters** (the latter of which is a distinct Balearic race) pass in high numbers and gannet and Arctic skua have been recorded. At the base of the cliffs there are colonies of nesting shags and, if extremely fortunate, you can occasionally see schools of **dolphins** performing their underwater acrobatics as they pass the headland.

The Boquer valley

The **BOQUER VALLEY** lies to the north of PUERTO POLLENSA and cuts across the Formentor peninsula. The valley reaches the sea after about 4km making an easy day's round trip on foot (or a brisk half day!).

The lower slopes of the valley are sparsely vegetated with **matorral** which forms in response to grazing pressure. The dominant species are grey-leaved and narrow-leaved cistus (*Cistus albidus* and *C. monspliensis*) and the mastic tree *Pistacia lentiscus*. Other intermingling species include the pink-flowered bush-heather *Erica multiflora*, the endemic St. John's wort *Hypericum balearicum* – characterised by its crimped and leathery leaves – and *Osyris alba*, a member of the sandalwood family with yellow-green branches. The coastal reaches hold areas of Mediterranean buckthorn *Rhamnus alaternus*, the endemic broom *Genista lucida* and the archetypal *matorral* plant, the labiate *Teucrium subspinosum*, one of the "hedgehog shrubs" which appear more twigs than foliage and have small pink flowers. This scrub combination provides excellent cover for a variety of **warblers and small songbirds** such as Sardinian, Marmora's and Dartford warblers and nightingales.

The adjacent open fields require closer inspection as they provide feeding grounds for a variety of summer migrants such as black-eared wheatear, black redstart, rock thrush, wryneck and rock sparrow. Further along the valley the rocky slopes are home to the resident blue rock thrush and red-legged partridge. However it is the overhead **passage of raptors** which is most memorable here. Resident species include **peregrine**, **kestrel**, **raven** and the occasional **black vulture**, and during the spring and autumn migration periods these are joined by passage species such as booted eagle, osprey, Egyptian vulture and various kites and buzzards. During the summer, the valley also provides a convenient corridor for hunting Eleanora's falcons returning to their nest sites on the Formentor peninsula.

At the end of the valley, a short detour to the left of the beach leads to perfect picnic (and swimming) conditions before the stroll back along the valley.

Albufera marsh

The **ALBUFERA MARSH** derives its name from the Arabic *Al-Buhayra*, which means a lake or lagoon. Under threat from development, a large section of the marsh was purchased and designated as a Nature Reserve in 1986. There is a reception centre, Sa Roca, a short walk or drive from the main road, where the free permits are issued. Access beyond this point is restricted to footpaths only, which lead to the interior and viewing hide.

The open mounds abound with **orchids** during April and May, especially the insect-imitating bumble-bee *Ophrys bombyliflora* and sawfly *O. tenthredinifera* species, as well as the tongue orchid *Serapias lingua*. The adjacent wooded areas are also filled with flowers in spring, with sawfly orchids and tassel hyacinths *Muscari comosum* being particularly prevalent. These **wooded areas** hold many of the smaller bird species such as serins and crossbills, which are most commonly located in the upper branches of the trees.

The marshy areas are best approached via the path which leads from the main coast road, just south of the Hotel Esperanza. This crosses the so-called English bridge and runs alongside the main canal, over the cross bridge and eventually reaches the double bridge. The walk gives fine views over the marshy areas where a wide variety of birds may be seen; the canals themselves have been known to house the occasional **terrapin** and snakes are not an uncommon sight.

It is, however, for its **birds** that Albufera is famed. The area has many moorhen, coot and Baillon's crakes amongst the shorter grasses, while hidden within the reedbeds are most of the **herons and egrets** of the Med. Look overhead, too, and you should spot black terns, pallid and Alpine swifts, bee-eaters and red-rumped swallows. Far less visible in the reeds, and more easily identified by song than sight, are moustached, great reed, fan-tailed and Cetti's **warblers**, nightingale and reed bunting. The **raptors** in the area are correspondingly outstanding and include osprey (most often found perched on the pylons), marsh and Montagu's harrier and lesser kestrel. The mid-spring period of April and May is, as always, a particularly rewarding time to visit.

Salinas de Levante

The **SALINAS DE LEVANTE** are just north of COLONIA DE SAN JORDI in the south of the island. They are also known locally as *Salobra de Campos* – which may come in useful if asking for directions – and are open to the public every day except Saturday, Sunday and Fiesta days (if access to this private property is to continue, it is essential that visitors respect the owner's wishes and avoid the Salinas on these days).

The **saltpans**, or evaporation beds, are surrounded by expanses of shrubby glasswort *Salicornia fructicosa*, whose monotonous landscape is punctuated only by the occasional dead tamarisk tree, *Tamarix canariensis*, the predominant variety on the south of the island. The few scrubby areas that remain hold Sardinian, fan-tailed and Cetti's warblers, woodchat shrike and, in the damper places, bluethroat. However, it is the saltpans themselves which attract large numbers of **waders and terns** each year. Regular visitors include avocet, black and whiskered tern, little egret, black-tailed godwit, collared pratincole and Temminck stint. Rarer individuals are flamingo and Caspian and gull-billed tern.

The **salt marshes** hold large numbers of waders such as sandpipers, redshank, grey and purple heron and several hundred pairs of black-winged stilt which arrive to breed in April before returning south in early September. This abundance of prey attracts many **raptors** including marsh harrier and osprey as well as the occasional migratory booted eagle. The **cultivated fields** northwest of the Salinas are also worth close inspection as they regularly shelter hoopoe, corn bunting, wheatears and turtle dove. Rarer birds include bee-eater (up until the end of August), short-toed lark and the resident stone curlew.

Puig Tomir and the northern mountains

The 60-km road from PUERTO SOLLER to PUERTO POLLENSA passes through the high Mallorcan Sierras which run along the length of the northern coastline. This route covers many aspects of wildlife interest and offers, in particular, an opportunity to observe that most regal of birds, the **black vulture**.

PUIG TOMIR, at 1200m, provides a challenging and rewarding investigation. The walk from the nearest parking area is demanding, but not dangerous, and the views from the summit of what is Mallorca's **third highest mountain** are quite breathtaking. The mountain slopes are sparsely covered above the tree line of Aleppo pine *Pinus halapensis* and holm oak *Quercus ilex*, by hardy, low-growing shrubs such as wild rosemary *Rosmarinus officinalis* and the rarer endemic *Thymus richardii sp. richardii*, which are resistant to the **grazing** of the ever present mountain goats and sheep. Amongst the crevices, you might also find another of the Balearic endemics, *Cyclamen balearicum*. Nearby **Puig Mayor**, the island's highest peak, is even richer in unusual and endemic plants, but access is more difficult and walkers banned from the summit.

The **birds** which can be seen vary as one climbs higher up the mountain slopes. The **lower wooded slopes** are frequented by crossbill, firecrest, blackbird, blue tit, wood pigeon and the occasional elusive wren. On the more exposed **rocky slopes**, a local speciality from November to March is the Alpine accentor, easily distinguished by its reddish flanks and throat details. For most birders, it is the **raptors** which are the most outstanding feature of the climb up Puig Tomir. Overhead it is possible to see Eleanora's falcon, peregrine and black vulture, as well as passage booted eagle and osprey. The **black vulture** is a particular feature of these northern mountains; the number of birds fell to fifteen according to the G.O.B. census of 1978 and, despite numerous efforts to encourage a recovery, breeding pairs remain notoriously susceptible to disturbance. With a wingspan in excess of 3 metres, it is no wonder that these magnificent birds have been referred to as "flying bedsteads"!

THE MALLORCAN MIDWIFE TOAD

The northern mountains provide the final refuge for what is probably the rarest amphibian in Europe, the **Mallorcan midwife toad**. First identified in 1980, it differs from its mainland relatives in its reduced fecundity (producing only a quarter of the number of eggs) – possibly as an evolutionary response to the absence of natural predators – and the lack of poison glands in the skin. This distinction almost led to its extinction following the introduction of the viperine snake onto the island, and has led to its retreat to the permanent pools of the higher sierras where the snakes do not venture. There are probably less than 500 pairs left in the world.

Menorca

Although **MENORCA** lacks the variety of endemic plant species to be found on Mallorca, it does have several species without a close relative anywhere else in the world. These include the dwarf shrub *Daphne rodriquezii*, a purple-flowered evergreen found on the siliceous cliffs of the northeast coast, where the average of 165 days of *tramontana* each year create a more humid climate. Other species which benefit from this moisture are *Hypericum balearicum* and the loosestrife *Lysimachia minoricensis*, with its unusual pink flowers.

Menorca's **mountains**, like those of Mallorca, are thought to be a continuation of the ranges of Andalucía; primarily Tertiary Miocene limestones, except those in the north which contain the more durable Devonian strata. The island centre also contains a **low plateau**, focused on Mount Toro (375m). The durable rocks produce poor soils characterised by sparse populations and rugged coastlines but, to the south, stone removal still produces extensive fertile farmlands. The coastal **limestone cliffs** have a flora uniquely adapted to the combination of lime-rich yet saline soils. Aromatic inula *Inula viscosa*, a shrubby perennial with sticky leaves and clusters of yellow flowers, can be found growing alongside *Bellium belloides*, a daisy-like plant adapted to stony areas alongside the sea. Also abundant are the caper *Capparis spinosa* with its red seed pods and purple seeds and the yellow stars of *Astericus maritimus*, with its folded leaves and spiny swelling below the flowerhead. Menorca also has abundant areas of coastal marshland which attract many of the migrant bird species seen on Mallorca.

But it is the **reptiles** which are the outstanding wildlife feature of the island. Of the four species of lizard which inhabit the Balearics, Menorca boasts populations of three. Lilford's wall lizard *Podarcis lilfordi*, typically green and blue with black and blue underparts, is characterised by its "turnip-shaped" tail. The Moroccan rock lizard *Lacerta perspicillata*, only found on Menorca outside Africa, was introduced onto the island and has a bronzed, olive skin or reticulated blue-green colouration. Another diagnostic feature is the transparent "window" in its lower eyelid. The third Menorcan lacertid is the Italian wall lizard *Podarcis sicula*, resembling the Corsican and Sardinian populations with its highly reticulate dorsal pattern of black on vivid olive green, and with a black vertebral stripe.

Italian wall lizard
Podarcis sicula

Ibiza

In ancient times, **IBIZA** was the predominant member of the *Pityussae* (or pine-clad islands) which included Formentera and Espalmador to the south, Tagomago to the east and Vedra and Conejera to the west. The island is predominantly composed of **secondary limestones**, folded and eroded into a series of hills, the highpoint of which is Atalayasa at 475m. It is far more **heavily forested** than Menorca; the main species being Aleppo pine *Pinus halipensis* in the higher areas. The lower slopes are dominated by *Cistus* scrub, with Phoenician juniper *Juniperus phoenicea* and the large yellow restharrow *Ononis natrix* comprising the understorey layers.

Other widespread **shrub components** include the dwarf fan palm *Chamaerops humilis*, the only palm native to Europe, which is found in dry, sandy stretches along the Mediterranean coast and provides invaluable cover for a variety of birds and reptiles. You will find, too, shrubs such as *Cistus clusii* with its small white flowers and evergreen leaves and *Cneorum tricoccon*, a native of shady areas, with a characteristic slender evergreen foliage and small yellow flowers. The chaste tree *Vitex agnus-castus* is most commonly found in river estuaries along the Mediterranean coast and can be identified by its palmate, grey-felted leaves and lilac-pink flower spikes.

Herbs of interest include the bright-pink-flowered catchfly *Silene littorea* and red stonecrop *Sedum rubens*, both of which occur locally on sandy areas, and the spectacular orchid *Ophrys bertolonii*, whose furry, brown-orange flowers are crowned by three slender pale-pink perianth segments. However, the most characteristic plant of the island is the **oleander** *Nerium oleander* which blossoms along the dried riverbeds in midsummer. Its grey leathery leaves are arranged in whorls of three and the plant is topped with huge pink blooms, often over 5cm in diameter. It is frequently associated with myrtle *Myrtus communis* whose fragrant white flowers and aromatic foliage create a tantalising combination for eye and nose alike.

Among fauna, the island is home to the **Ibiza wall lizard** *Podarcis pityusensis*, endemic to the Balearic islands (but particularly common on Ibiza and Formentera; it has been introduced relatively recently to Mallorca). The Ibiza form is robust and short-headed, with a vivid green back and spotted underparts. It is most commonly found in barren, scrubby areas. Equally interesting perhaps is the **Ibiza hound** known locally as *ca ervissenc*, reputedly introduced by the Egyptians or Carthaginians many centuries ago. It is still possible, despite centuries of domestication, to find individuals of almost pure bloodline – typically tall, loose-limbed beasts, often fawn in colour, and probable descendants of the world's original hunting dog.

Cabrera

CABRERA is one of the smaller Balearic islands, and conservationists have long argued for its designation as a *parque nacional*. It is currently, along with its islets such as Conejera, a military zone, inhabited only by a lighthouse keeper and a garrison of about a dozen soldiers, who use the island as an artillery firing range!

The vegetation is very similar to that on southern Mallorca, but its small population and lack of tourist development have maintained its potential as a **refuge** for several species of plant, bird and reptile, and a wide variety of marine life. The Cabrera sub-species of the Lilford's wall lizard is particularly abundant and forthcoming individuals can be enticed to feed from one's hand! The lack of disturbance also encourages the presence of marine mammals such as **whales, seals and dolphins,** which can be seen occasionally from the coast, and **snorkelling** off the rocky coastline is excellent.

The island has no tourist facilities whatsoever and whilst it is possible to explore the interior with the benefit of a **permit** (obtainable in advance in Palma), overnight stays are not permitted.

BALEARIC ISLANDS: ACCESS AND ACCOMMODATION

Access by air or ferry from the mainland is mostly to Mallorca, which has regular links with the other islands. Once on the islands, you'll have a lot more flexibility with a hired car (or bike); buses can be infrequent.

Mallorca

Formentor

The peninsula is clearly signposted on the road east of PUERTO POLLENSA.

Albufera

The reserve lies on the main ARTA road, south of PUERTO POLLENSA; heading south, the entrance to the marsh lies over the "English bridge", on the right-hand side, just past the *Esperanza Hotel*.

Puig Tomir

The site is to the west of PUERTO POLLENSA on the SOLLER road. The sideroad which leads to the track is about 17km from Puerto Pollensa and enters through a gate marked *"Ministerio Agricultura. Jefetura Provincial Icona. Vivero Central de Manut"*. Take the left-hand of the two gates and follow the path until you reach the water bottling plant (after 3km), where the path leads up from the right-hand side of the works boundary fence.

PUERTO POLLENSA is the best base for all four of the above sites, and is an attractive place in its own right, with several good value *hostales* along the seafront. For car hire try the reliable *Motor Formentor*.

Salinas de Levante

Leaving the nearby town of CAMPOS on the road signposted COLONIA SAN JORDI, take the right fork at the *velodrome* (it looks like a bullring), until you reach the right-hand turn which forms the entrance to the saltworks themselves.

The other islands

Menorca

The island bus service is restricted to the road between MAHON and CIUDADELA, so hire of a bike or car is invaluable. Wide range of accommodation in main towns and resort.

Ibiza

Ibiza has its own airport, and, on the island, a bus service which is both comprehensive and reliable. Again, a wide range of accommodation.

Cabrera

Only day visits are possible, by boat from COLONIA SANT JORDI, in the south of MALLORCA. Permits are available from the tourist office in PALMA.

Boquer valley

Heading east from PUERTO POLLENSA, take the first track on the left which reaches a large house with farm buildings after about ten minutes; the attached gate leads into the valley itself and eventually to the sea.

information and publications

Most *parques naturales* have their own information centres, always an excellent first port of call. Tourist offices will only be able to answer basic questions. The national body for wildlife conservation is *ICONA* (*Instituto Nacional para la Conservación de la Naturaleza*), with a central office in Madrid at Gran Vía de San Francisco 35. *ICONA* has regional offices in Cuenca, Avila and Huelva, amongst other cities. In addition, some of the autonomous communities have their own conservation agency; in Andalucía this is the *Agencia del Medio Ambiente* with offices in Huelva and Malaga.

The national bird society is *Sociedad Espanola de Ornithologica*, Faculdad de Biologica Planta 9, Cuidad Universitaria, 28040 Madrid. Within the islands, the local and very active bird society is the *Grupo Ornithologia Balear*, Calle Veri 1–3 2a, Palma da Mallorca.

MAPS

Free ones from the tourist offices are good; those from the Catalan *parques naturales* excellent. The standard survey maps of the country are at 1:50,000 and produced by the *SGE*, and are widely available both in Spain and at good map shops in Britain.

GUIDES

For general information, **Spain: The Rough Guide** (Harrap Columbus) is as good as they come. There's more area detail in the new **Pyrenees *Rough Guide***, while walkers may find Marc Dubin's **Trekking in Spain** (Lonely Planet) a useful supplement.

BOOKS

For plants, Polunin and Smythie's **Flowers of Southwest Europe** (OUP, 1988) is far and away the best serious book. For birds, apart from the usual general field guides, Andy Paterson's **Birdwatching in Southern Spain** (Golf Area SA, Torremolinos, 1987) is good. Generally, Frederick Grunfeld's **Wild Spain** (Ebury Press, 1988) is a worthwhile travelling companion.

The bird sites on Mallorca are well covered in **A Guide to Bird-watching in Mallorca** E. Watkinson (Alderney Printers Ltd, 1986). For local botanical information, try **Plants of the Balearic Islands** by A. Bonner (Editorial Moll, Palma de Mallorca, 1985).

CHAPTER SEVEN

TUNISIA

For a country a mere 800km long by 250km wide, Tunisia packs in an amazing **variety of habitats**. Although the north of the country will be familiar to anyone who knows the north of the Mediterranean – a combination of limestone and sandstone hills, pine and cork oak forest, and agricultural land – as soon as you get south of the great Dorsale ridge of mountains that split the country, it's something totally different; north of Chott Djerid the country is made up of **flat steppes**, degraded by grazing and vegetation clearance, while south of the Chott is **true desert**, either of sand dunes or, more usually, of stone *hammada*.

The highlights of **the north** include its beautiful rocky coast, backed by flower-rich hillsides wherever towns and tourism have not encroached. The easterly tip of **Cap Bon** has the added pull of bird migration; a little to the west, **Lac Ichkeul** is arguably the finest lake for **birds** in north Africa; and still further towards Algeria, the **cork oak forests** of the Khroumerie are damp and hilly, offering a strikingly different range of wildlife.

The coastal **mudflats and wetlands** of the **Gulf of Gabes** are another high spot, mostly for their wintering birds, including exceptionally high numbers of flamingoes; slightly inland from the coast, the **saltpans** around **Sfax** and **Sousse** are accessible and equally rewarding.

In common with the rest of north Africa, **desert** dominates the **south** of the country, with plants and animals found nowhere else around the Med. The steppes are punctuated by one of Tunisia's most unusual habitats, *sebkhets* or **salt lakes**, often huge areas of salt-encrusted mud which occasionally flood in wet winters. **Chott Djerid** is the biggest and best known, though there are many smaller ones. The **true desert** has a bewildering variety of small birds such as larks and wheatears, birds of prey in the rugged desert gorges, and specialised and elusive mammals and reptiles. The **oases** that break the desert up are amongst the country's most exciting habitats.

Climate and land use

Climate, as always, plays a major role in determining the distribution of plants and animals. Any visitor from northern Europe has to keep the **lack of water** firmly in mind – it is the dominant factor. Although Tunisia includes one of the wettest places in north Africa – the cork oak forests around Aïn Draham on the Algerian border – large areas of the south have an average rainfall of under 5cm. And average rainfalls are highly misleading, both in the south and north of the country; often there is no rain at all for years, then a sudden deluge.

All of which is confusing for the average naturalist. It means that animals and plants have adapted to be highly flexible and unpredictable in their appearances. Whereas in Britain you can go to a wood and see the same orchids flowering year after year, assuming some lunatic hasn't dug them up, you can't always do that in

Tunisia. After a **very wet year**, parts of the desert will bloom in a blaze of colour, the *sebkhets* will flood and suddenly support huge populations of wintering birds – and roads and houses may have been washed away. After a **very dry winter**, annual plants may simply not germinate, some perennials will retreat down into their bulbs or roots and not even bother to flower, and the desert will remain dry and devoid of vegetation.

Parallel with climate, **agriculture** is the other hugely important factor. The fertile north of the country has been used as an intensive agricultural belt from the first century BC right through to the French colonial period, and agricultural pressures are no less now with Tunisia's population growing at two-and-a-half percent per annum. This has meant that the original forests have long since been cleared, and much of the scrubby Mediterranean hillsides have been converted to arable land or greatly modified by grazing pressure.

Grazing pressure accounts for changes to the dry south, too, with the familiar pattern of desertification caused by a combination of overgrazing and climatic change. Many people who live in the south depend on wood for their cooking and heating; combine this with over seven million grazing animals, and this is a powerful force for the degradation of forests to scrubland and thence to desert.

WHEN AND WHERE TO GO

Spring comes early in Tunisia – March sees the **flowers** of the north at their peak, while further south flowering depends on rainfall rather than on the season. **April** is the peak **bird migration** month, and things go very quiet in the summer heat from June to September. After the return bird migration, the **winter** is an excellent time for **waders** in the Gulf of Gabes or wildfowl on Lac Ichkeul, though the weather can be surprisingly cold and wet, especially in the north and west.

Getting around on public transport is almost invariably by bus or *louages*, the long-distance taxis that run between most towns of any size. Trains, apart from the ones around and between Tunis and Sousse, are excruciatingly slow. Car hire is most useful for exploring the (in summer, exhausting) south.

The main sites described are:

● **TUNIS AND AROUND** Right in the centre of the city, the **Lac de Tunis** has exciting birds, and **Carthage** and the mountain of **Bou Kornine** are both worth a trip. Further out, the mountain (and alpine town) of **Zaghouan** is worthwhile for its Med flowers and birds of prey.

● **NORTH COAST** Cap Bon is a promising site for its bird migration and agricultural fields; inland from BIZERTE is the internationally important wetland of **Lac Ichkeul**; and flanking **Tabarca** are extensive cork oak forests.

● **EAST COAST** This is mostly shallow and sandy – a most unusual Med habitat. The resultant mudflats and saltpans at **Sousse** and **Sfax** are both extremely rich in birds.

● **STEPPES AND DESERT** These habitats each show distinctly different characteristics, though as wildlife tends to be thinly and equally distributed, few specific sites have been chosen.

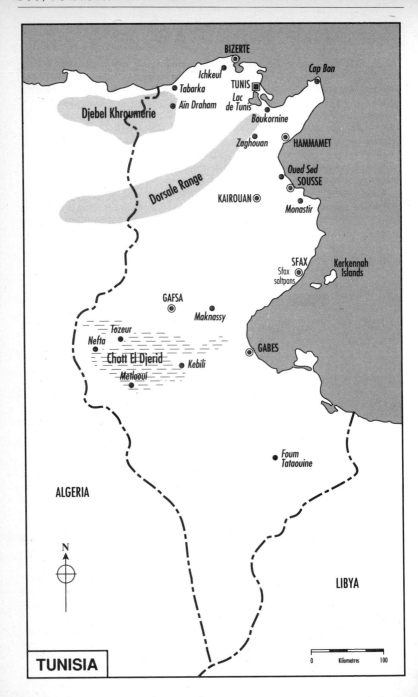

TUNISIA

TUNIS AND AROUND

The suburbs of **Tunis** sprawl in all directions but enclose a number of worthwhile sites, primarily for birds; for flowers, there are promising sites at the opulent suburb of **Carthage**. Further out, the National Park at **Bou Kornine** is a conveniently accessible introduction to country's wildlife, as is the mountain of **Zaghouan**, at the eastern edge of the long range of the Dorsale mountains.

Tunis

Even in the city of **TUNIS** there's a bit to see. The **Belvedere Park** has quite a range of small birds, and you can't miss the huge sparrow roost in the trees of Ave. Habib Bourguiba – barn owls sometimes come to hunt here at night. Just along the road, the **Cathedral** has breeding pallid and common swifts (which are hard to tell apart) and a colony of the rarer little swift, which is much smaller with a white rump.

It's the **Lac de Tunis**, though, that is the main pull – offering the chance of sighting some of Tunisia's more exciting birds. Forget the northern half of the lake, the edges of which are now being reclaimed for hotel and other developments, and head instead for the southern half, which attracts flamingoes, wading birds, gulls and terns. Although it's best in the winter, when flamingo numbers can build up as high as 10,000, and with comparable numbers of other waders, there are still good birds present in spring and autumn (swollen by migration), and it's worth a look even in high summer.

Carthage and Sidi Bou Said

If you're short of time, **CARTHAGE** and its environs can produce interesting (and typically Tunisian) birds and flowers. Some of the fields between Carthage and Sidi Bou Said have a good display of the typical agricultural "weeds" in spring; look for yellow chrysanthemums, scarlet poppies, blue borage and bugloss, and pink catchflies and campions.

The neighbouring beach suburb of **SIDI BOU SAID** is worthwhile, too. It retains its charm despite an abundance of tourists and many of the gullies leading down to the sea from the clifftops are rewarding for wildlife. One of the easiest to find leads off the end of Rue du Front de Mer, near the police station just next to where the train stops.

Down at Carthage and Sidi Bou Said are many of the **imported plant species** that dominate much of the country – such as the prickly pear *Opuntia ficus-indica*, century plant *Agave americana*, and the Australian mimosas and eucalypts. Serins and goldfinches are the two commonest finches, while Sardinian warblers scold from any suitable bush. **Butterflies** include swallowtails *Papilio machaon* – unmistakable with their long "tails" and yellow and black wings – as well as the Moroccan orange tip *Anthocharis belia*, a small butterfly with yellow wings with brilliant orange tips. Down by the sea, Sandwich and gull-billed terns patrol offshore, and, in spring, hundreds of migrating painted lady butterflies *Vanessa cardui* feed on the sea stocks *Matthiola sinuata* at the back of the beach.

Bou Kornine

The imposing mountain of **BOU KORNINE** on the southern shores of the Gulf of Tunis is a National Park, heavily forested at the bottom, but with a more open *maquis* vegetation at the top.

In the open spaces **amongst the pines** you find the typical Med shrubs – rosemary *Rosmarinus officinalis*, pink and white rockroses *Cistus spp.*, and orchids especially the yellow *Ophrys lutea*. The whole place is carpeted with a delightful small pink cyclamen *Cyclamen persicaria* in spring. Later in the summer, a large yellow-flowered *Sedum* is common, with fleshy leaves and flat yellow flowerheads. The **birds of the pines** are mostly chaffinches, linnets and serins, but higher up there are hoopoes amongst isolated trees and ravens circling overhead.

Moussier's redstart

At the top, the pines give way to scrubbier, more open vegetation, whose birds include **Moussier's redstart**, one of Tunisia's specialities and a very beautiful one at that. Look closely at the swifts screaming overhead – alpine swifts are found here, much larger than the common swift, and with an obvious white belly and throat. A large eagle with a black band across its underwing is likely to be **Bonelli's eagle** – a pair breeds here regularly on the inaccessible mountain crags.

Bou Kornine is also a good place to watch for spring migration – and the view over the Gulf of Tunis up to Sidi Bou Said is terrific!

Zaghouan

DJEBEL ZAGHOUAN, rising 1300m above the surrounding plains, is the most typical of the long limestone ridge of mountains that form the "backbone" of Tunisia, from Djebel Chambi on the Algerian border to Bou Kornine near Tunis. Its **limestone rocks and crags** make it a superb site for flowers, while it's also perhaps the easiest place in Tunisia to get good views of large and spectacular **birds of prey**. Added to all this, the views are magnificent, the town of ZAGHOUAN is delightful, and the site is very easily accessible from Tunis.

From the bus and *louage* station near the Roman arch in Zaghouan, walk through the stairways and steps of the town up onto the main ridge, from which the road drops down through the outskirts. It doesn't much matter how you approach the mountain from here, though the **Roman ruins at Nymphaeum**, about thirty minutes' walk away, is as good a starting point as any. If you're in a car, a road snakes its way up the 16km to the television relay station, from which there are superb views over the countryside and circling eagles and vultures.

The **walking** is straightforward until the mountain starts to climb steeply, and then becomes very hard. The combination of limestone crags and very prickly bushes is not much fun; don't wear shorts, if you value your legs, and be aware that it's classic legbreaking country. Having said that, the closer you can get to the rock faces, the better your views of the birds of prey.

It is these **birds of prey** that are the highlight of Zaghouan. It is possible to see up to a dozen species in a day, including golden eagle, Bonelli's eagle, booted eagle, Egyptian vulture, black kite and peregrine falcon. Most of these nest on the mountain, and they're a superb sight wheeling around their nest sites, or soaring hundreds of metres before they glide out over the plains in search of food. The birds are active most of the day, but **early morning and early evening** are the best times to watch. The identification of birds of prey in distant flight is notoriously difficult, and a good field guide and binoculars are essential. Size, wing angle, and the pattern on the underside of the wing are the things to watch for. For example, Bonelli's eagle has a broad black stripe running down the front of the wing, whereas booted eagle has white underwings with a black trailing edge; or, at least, the pale phase does – there is also a dark phase which is a much less identifiable brown colour.

With such a concentration of predatory birds, there's bound to be a high degree of territorial dispute over the nesting season, and one of the most exciting things to watch are the **aerial dogfights** over the mountain. The peregrines (possibly Barbary falcons, for ornithological pedants) in particular are aggressive to any other species that approaches their territory, and they climb high up in the sky before falling on the often larger intruder in a breathtaking power dive. Ravens breed on the mountain, too, and they also will not hesitate to take on the smaller eagles and buzzards, usually with two ravens "mobbing" the intruder until it gets tired and retreats.

Although the birds of prey are the big attraction, don't ignore the **smaller birds**. Blue rock thrushes – like blackbirds but in a beautiful shade of powder blue – are common. Hoopoes continually make the call after which they are named, a ringing "poo poo poo". Moussier's redstarts breed amongst the scrubby bushes, wrens on the rocks, and a variety of small warblers as well.

The **flowers** on the mountain are typical of Mediterranean limestone hills. Most of the trees are planted pines, but on the slopes to the mountain you'll find the holm oak *Quercus coccifera*, brooms *Genista spp.*, olive *Olea europea*, and mastic tree *Pistachia lentiscus* – all short and scrubby, rarely growing above head height, and forming an impenetrable *maquis* scrub. One very striking and characteristic species, particularly abundant here, is the tree spurge *Euphorbia dendroides*; it forms very rounded bushes, with yellow flowers in the spring and early summer. Another common shrub is *Globularia alypum*, a low compact shrub with attractive rounded blue flowerheads; it's a poisonous plant, incidentally, and a violent purgative – so don't try chewing it!

Below the shrub layer, the **ground flora** includes many orchid species, as well as aromatic herbs such as thyme and rosemary. A very handsome black-centred dandelion flowers here in the spring, and a yellow flowered tulip – probably *Tulipa sylvestris* – grows in the rock crevices. Further up, yellow asphodel *Asphodeline lutea* is abundant, with striking yellow bell-shaped flowers on top of a narrow-leaved stem.

All in all, it's a fine site, rewarding at any time of year for birds of prey, but best of all in the spring and early summer for flowers. It is also a cool and refreshing place; even in the exceptionally dry winter of 1987–88, when northern Tunisia had a semi-drought, water was still overflowing from the taps and basins at the street corners in the town.

TUNIS AND AROUND: ACCESS AND ACCOMMODATION

Tunis

For LAC DE TUNIS, the best place to watch birds is the southeastern corner; take the train from Place Barcelone along the southern shore of the lake, get off at RADES, and walk up towards the old port of LA GOULETTE. For CARTHAGE and SIDI BOU SAID, the TGM train across the lake is the best access – look out for flamingo flocks as you go across the causeway.

Making for BOU KORNINE, take the train as above for Rades, but stay on until HAMMAM-LIF; from the railway station, walk south to the main road, turn right, and then left up Rue Essoudess near the *Chalet Vert* sign. From here, a succession of winding tracks lead you up the mountain through pine forests.

TUNIS is the easiest base for all of these sites, with plentiful accommodation.

Zaghouan

Access is simple from TUNIS; a *louage* from the Bab Alleoua takes about 45min and follows the line of the **Roman aqueduct**, which used to take water the 70km from Zaghouan to Carthage. Approaching from other directions, from SOUSSE via ENFIDA for example, is more difficult and may involve a combination of bus and *louage*.

The *Hotel des Nymphes*, the only hotel in Zaghouan, is ideally placed for early morning birdwatching at the Roman ruins.

THE NORTH COAST

Tunisia's **north coast** is rugged and rocky – and nowhere more so than around the headland of **Cap Bon**, famed for its bird migration. Inland, the national park of **Ichkeul** contains a large and important lake for wildfowl and a limestone mountain rich in flowers as well. And over to the east at **Tabarka**, close to the Algerian border, the coast is backed by the Khroumerie, an extensive area of mountains and cork oak forests, rewarding for both birds and flowers.

Cap Bon

Although the whole peninsula of **CAP BON** is of interest, with its green fields and rocky coastline, the northern tip is the highlight. The village of EL HAOUARIA is the place to head for – regular *louages* and somewhat less regular buses run up the east coast through KORBA and KELIBIA.

KORBA itself is worth a stop in passing. It has very interesting lagoons and salt marsh just to the north which hold flamingoes, spoonbills and avocets in the spring, and a good range of migrants – especially pratincoles – in spring and autumn. There are wintering ducks, too. The town doesn't have a great deal else of interest apart from an expensive Club Med.

The actual **headland** of Cap Bon is special because it is the last jumping off point for **migrating birds of prey** before they cross the Med to Sicily, and they concentrate into a narrow funnel at the northern tip. The migration of tens of thousands of birds of prey here every year has been much studied by ornithologists; **April and May** are the peak spring passage months, with lesser numbers coming back each autumn. It is not uncommon to see over 1000 migrating birds of prey in one day, far less than at the main bottlenecks at Gibraltar and the Bosporus but impressive all the same. Honey buzzards are the dominant species, although black kites, marsh harriers and common buzzards also occur in good numbers, together with a variety of migrating eagles, sparrowhawks and hobbies. Hobbies are small, rather dashing falcons, midway in size between kestrel and peregrine; since they prey mostly on swallows and the like, they simply follow the migrating swallow flocks up from Africa, catching a snack on the wing.

The best place for **viewing the migration** is the top of **Djebel Abiod**, the last rocky outcrop of Cap Bon. This needs a **permit** during the migration season: write in advance to the *Direction des Fôrets*, 30 rue Alain Savary, Tunis. Just north of El Haouaria, about 500m out of the village on the road to the Ghar el Kebir caves, there's an **information centre** about wildlife in general and birds of prey in particular. It's run by the *Cellule Nature et Oiseaux*, and they're extremely helpful and informative to visiting naturalists. The building is called the "Aquilaria", after the Latin for "eagle"; El Haouaria is supposed to be a corruption of the same root word.

El Haouaria hosts a big **falconry festival** most years in mid-June. Two species are involved: sparrowhawks, which are trapped in nets on the mountain as they migrate, and peregrine falcons, which are taken as young from the nests on the rocky cliffs. The number of birds each falconer can catch is strictly limited, they may not be sold, and the sparrowhawks are later returned to the wild .

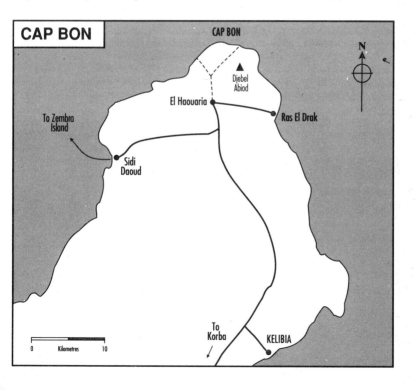

The rocky hillsides around the mountain are rich in **flowers**, and so is the walk to the beautiful beach at RAS ED DRAK. All the common flowers of field edges grow here, including a large blue pimpernel *Anagallis monellii*. Look out for asparagus pea *Tetragonolobus purpureus*, too – a low growing pea with bright red flowers tinged with purple. The fields and field edges have abundant bird life, with many finches, buntings and warblers, along with stonechats – their black-headed males perching prominently on bushes and telegraph wires.

Once on the beach, head for the **steep hillside** at the end, habitat for many white rockroses, the dwarf fan palm *Chamaerops humilis*, and familiar species like white alyssum *Alyssum maritimum* and Virginia stocks *Malcolmia maritima*. The back of the beach is carpeted with a tiny purple flower – *Romulea*, a spring flowering bulb found all along the north coast. The scrub is full of migrating small birds, with blue rock thrushes and Moussier's redstarts both relatively common residents. I was also told that there are "many serpents" here in the summer!

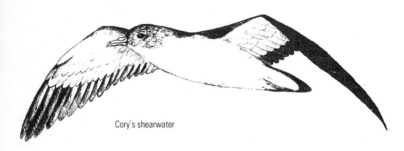
Cory's shearwater

The **sea** is worth watching, too. Some 150,000 pairs of **Cory's shearwater** – a big seabird with a characteristic stiff-winged flight skimming the waves – breed on Zembra Island, off Cap Bon, and they can often be seen flying past in huge numbers. I estimated some 25,000 birds an hour coming past one afternoon in late March, together with several thousand of the smaller, black and white Mediterranean race of the Manx shearwater. The area is good for gulls and terns, with several tern species including gull-billed and Sandwich terns occurring as winter visitors and passage migrants.

Finally, if you can get out to **Zembra Island**, do so. It's a National Park and you may need a permit (from the *Direction des Fôrets*, address above). The only way to get there is to take a fishing boat from SIDI DAOUD, and there's nowhere to stay, but it's a stunning day trip, with beautiful scenery, lots of seabirds, and excellent snorkelling in summer (too chilly the rest of the year).

Lac Ichkeul

LAC ICHKEUL, the best known of Tunisia's National Parks, is an extraordinary spot – internationally significant for its winter wildfowl populations, and with a superb limestone mountain, Djebel Ichkeul, rising directly from the southern edge of the lake. The site also illustrates the conflicting demands of conservation and agriculture for its water, with two dams already constructed on its feed rivers, and a further four planned before the end of the century.

The **pressures on the lake** stem partly from simple grazing pressure which reduces the plant interest, but mostly from a shortage of fresh water in the feed rivers, both from lack of rain and from upstream dams. The less water there is, the lower the level drops and the more saline the lake becomes, as salt water from Lac Bizerte flows back into it, and from evaporation. This salinity kills off the water plants and in turn the wintering wildfowl run short of food and move elsewhere, or may even decline in numbers if alternative sites aren't available. This conflict boils down to the relative value of providing water for human beings or for wildlife. Increased tourism to the lake, bringing money with it, may convince the authorities that there is an economic argument for maintaining the right water levels to ensure the lake's survival as an internationally important site.

Waterfowl are the highspot of Ichkeul. The lake has extensive beds of pond-weed, on which ducks feed, and of a club rush *Scirpus maritimus*, which supports greylag geese. These plants, together with the sheer size of the lake (12km by 6km), make it the major wildfowl wintering ground in north Africa. Some of the numbers recorded are genuinely staggering: 112,000 wigeon in November 1973, 120,000 pochard in October 1971, 188,000 coot in November 1973, and 20,000 greylag geese in December 1984 – the last figure representing almost the entire breeding population of greylag in central Europe. These are peak counts, and the number of birds the lake supports depends on its water level and salinity, and on the climate of competing wetlands in Algeria and north of the Med. More recent figures suggest that the lake carries around 150,000 birds at its winter peak.

Although these **huge flocks** are only present between October and February, ducks remain in good numbers until the spring, with a few staying on and occa-sionally breeding over the summer. The birds move around the lake depending on the distribution of their food plants, but in general the best **viewpoints** are

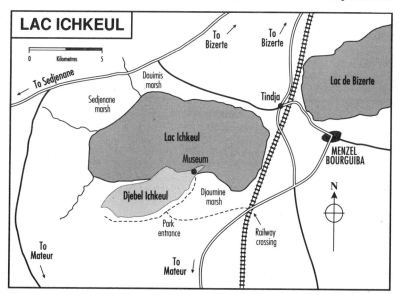

from the coast north of the **mountain** (there's a good track along it starting from the museum), or from the **Douimis and Sedjenane marshes**. The latter marsh requires a walk along the river from the road, but that's no great hardship since the bushes that line the river are rich in small birds, especially during the spring migration months of April and early May. However, because the lake is so large, it's not the easiest place to get close to birds.

As well as ducks and geese, the lake supports a variety of **wading birds** around its fringes. If the water level is high enough, both the Douimis and Sedjenane marshes are good year-round for waders, with sizeable populations of avocets, blackwinged stilts and Kentish plovers. These are augmented in winter by black-tailed godwits, redshanks and the smaller sandpipers. If wet, the edge of the Djoumine marsh closest to the level crossing is a great spot to watch waders but beware of the evil dogs around here! Herons and egrets breed amongst the reeds, with grey heron as a resident and purple heron as a summer visitor; there is sometimes a colony of night herons in the reeds at the north edge of the mountain. Although white storks don't breed in the park, they nest close by and they often feed around the lake edges, unmistakable because of their sheer size.

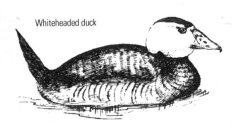
Whiteheaded duck

Three of the lake's **speciality birds** are the purple gallinule, a rare bird rather like a huge redbilled coot; marbled teal, a small and shy duck with a mottled brown plumage; and white headed duck, a globally rare bird which winters in small numbers on a few Tunisian lakes, including Ichkeul.

With all these waterbirds about, as well as small mammals and reptiles, the lake also attracts **birds of prey**. Marsh harriers are the most dominant species, identifiable by their upturned wings as they drift over the reedbeds and surrounding fields in search of small prey. The male and female are quite different – the female a dark chocolate brown with a pale golden head and the male a patchwork of grey, brown and black, camouflaged like a fighter plane. Of the falcons, peregrine, lanner and kestrel all breed on the mountain; Bonelli's and short-toed eagle wheel high in the sky, and long-legged buzzard breeds here too.

Don't ignore the **smaller birds**, either. Reed warblers and great reed warblers visit in summer to breed in the reedbeds, nightingales are common, and bee-eaters breed in the river banks and spoil heaps. Quail, the smallest game bird, breed in the park too; listen for their "whic whic" call from the surrounding fields in spring – they're notoriously hard to spot. Moussier's redstarts are common amongst the scrub on the mountain, and Sardinian warblers are everywhere. Woodchat shrikes perch on telegraph wires and lone trees in summer, and a related and very rare species, the blackheaded bush shrike, breeds here in very small numbers. Bulbuls are here, too; primarily Asian and African birds, they reach the most northerly part of their range in Tunisia. Boring to look at – a bit like a drab blackbird – they have a loud and rich song.

The mountain and the lake have a high **mammal population**, too, though as elusive and shy as ever. There are wild boar and jackals on the mountain as well as porcupines, a locally high population of mongooses, and otter; and a small herd of **water buffalo**, descended, so it is said, from a gift of a pair from the king of Sicily to the Bey of Tunis in 1729. The lake also abounds in **frogs and toads**, including a very handsome and vocal species with green stripes down the back, and there are **tortoises** amongst the scrub on the mountain, and **terrapins** in the lake – the Sedjenane marsh is a good place for the latter.

For **flowers**, the mountain is the place to go. Remember that flowers, like everything else in Tunisia, are utterly dependent on the **winter rains**. I walked up the mountain in April 1980, after reasonable winter rains, and found it a riot of colour – like walking through a huge rock garden. There were wild gladioli, love-in-a-mist, narcissus and shrubby rock roses, as well as over ten species of orchid including the lovely *Ophrys speculum* with a metallic blue lip. I did the same walk in April 1988, and saw almost no plants at all; this was after an exceptionally dry winter, which not only desiccated the plants, but also forced the grazing herds off the dried out marshes and onto the mountain. This combination of drought and grazing won't kill the plants – unless it happens year after year – it simply means that the perennials don't have enough energy to put up a flowering spike. As well as the mountain, interesting flowers grow around the rivers feeding the lake – around the Douimis river, for instance, you'll find a white star of Bethlehem *Ornithogalum sp.*, and a delightful tiny wild narcissus – *Narcissus serotimus*.

The **agricultural weeds** are spectacular even in a dry year, since many of the fields to the north of the lake are irrigated. Look out for fields ablaze with poppies and wild chrysanthemums, and for various colourful convolvulus species around the edges, including the aptly named *Convolvulus tricolor* – blue round the outside, yellow in the middle, and white in between. Honeywort *Cerinthe major*, with its strange pendulous yellow and brown flowers, is also common by the roadside, and there's a shocking pink soapwort *Saponaria sp.* in the fields.

Tabarka and Aïn Draham

This region is one of the richest wildlife habitats in Tunisia, with the interface between the **cork oak forests** around Aïn Draham dropping down to the so-called **"coral coast"** around Tabarka. The coral is Mediterranean coral, a species which has been collected for jewellery use for centuries, with the result that it is now fast declining and has been listed as an internationally endangered species – think twice, therefore, before buying a coral souvenir in one of the many shops in Tabarka and throughout northern Tunisia. The presence of the coral does, however, make for some of the best snorkelling in the Med. The **Isle de la Galite**, though remote, also offers great snorkelling in summer, and is the only place in the country where you could hope for a glimpse of the endangered Mediterranean monk seal.

TABARKA is a convenient base for the area, since it has plenty of hotels, some good walks from the town, a fairly regular bus service up the hill to Aïn Draham and excellent fish restaurants if you're into seafood. It's also a pleasant and fairly uncrowded seaside resort, except in high summer when the combination of the cool climate and a large cultural festival packs the town out.

For a good walk to the **west of the town**, go up Rue Farhat Hached from Rue Habib Bourguiba, and then take a track off to the right which scrambles up to the road by the army camp. Turn left along this road, and follow it as it winds up through shrub-covered hillsides. The sandy rock doesn't support a great variety of flowers, but there are some unusual species; the Mediterranean medlar tree *Crataegus azarolus*, a species of hawthorn, just creeps into Tunisia across the Algerian border, and the scrub on the hillsides is mostly heavily grazed mastic tree *Pistachia lentiscus* and Kermes oak *Quercus coccifera*. Turn right off the road and head towards the coast; look closely under the white-flowered rockroses on the hill and you will find the extraordinary parasitic plant *Cytinus hypocistus*; with red and yellow waxy flowers, it has no green leaves, getting its energy from its host plant, and it is particularly common around here. In between the shrubs is *Romulea*, an abundant and very beautiful tiny purple crocus relative. You can then return along the cliffs to Tabarka, passing above Les Aiguilles. Blue rock thrushes are common on this stretch of cliffs.

A longer but more varied walk is up the hill to the **east of the town**, at the other end of the beach. Check out the Oued el Kebir river as you cross it – it's full of small birds at migration time, and marsh harriers are usually wheeling their way over the marshy river valley. Nightingales sing from the riverside shrubs, and the "tsip tsip" of fan-tailed warblers is constantly heard. The **sand dunes** to the back of the beach are covered in pines and windblown junipers; stone curlews are found here, and there are often terns passing along the coast. Lesser kestrels breed in the old Genoese fort, and can be seen patrolling the sand dunes for small mammals. Very similar to the common kestrel, they breed communally and are much noisier, and the male has an unspotted chestnut back.

Fork left after the road to the modern *Hotel Morjane*, and a firebreak up the hill from the pines makes an easy walk to the **top of the ridge**. The pines, junipers and cypress trees at the bottom soon give way to a typical *garigue* vegetation of sandy soils – cork oak *Quercus suber* and Kermes oak above a shrub layer including tree heath *Erica aborea*, strawberry bush *Arbutus unedo* and mastic tree *Pistachia lentiscus*. The tree heath and strawberry tree are both in the heather family, with bell-shaped white flowers, but it is the fruit of the strawberry tree that gives it its name. They look good, but don't taste so wonderful! The **ground flora** includes lots of French lavender *Lavandula stoechas* – its purple flowerheads make it one of the most conspicuous small shrubs of the region. At the bottom of the firebreak there is the inevitable rubbish dump – not a pleasant place, but attractive to ravens; I found an extraordinary flock of over fifty one April.

Aïn Draham

The third direction to go from Tabarka is inland, up the mountain to **AÏN DRAHAM** in the Khroumerie. Bus is the easiest way to get there from Tabarka, via BABOUCH. Both villages are surrounded by **cork oak forests**, an important local crop. Almost any walk from either of the villages will lead you through the oak forests, with plantations of pine; the valley leading from BABOUCH towards HAMMAM BOURGUIBA is one especially beautiful and rewarding area.

As this is the only large **deciduous forest** in Tunisia, the wildlife is distinctive. One thing to look for is the way that individual **woodland birds**, familiar from northern Europe, are developing differences that will in a few thousand years lead them to be classed as separate species – evolution in progress. The blue tit here has a black head – ours is blue; the chaffinch is paler, without a red breast; the green woodpecker (already regarded by some as a separate species) is greyer and lacks the red "moustache"; and the jay is quite different, with a red, black and white head. The birdsong in spring is uncannily similar to an English woodland, with blackbirds, great tits (a rare bird in Tunisia), robins and cuckoos.

NORTH COAST: ACCESS AND ACCOMMODATION

Cap Bon

Buses and *louages* run regularly from TUNIS (Bab Alleoua) to KELIBIA, and some go further on up the coast to EL HAOUARIA. Local buses and *louages* connect Kelibia with El Haouaria, which has a small pension and a number of places to eat – the *Restaurant Fruits des Mers* has good food. KELIBIA has a much wider range of hotels and restaurants, and the fish at *Hotel Florida* is not to be missed.

Lac Ichkeul

Getting to the National Park is not easy by public transport. From BIZERTE, the bus or *louage* to MATEUR passes the southeastern corner of the lake; get off at the level crossing and hitch or walk past the southern end of the Djoumine marsh. A turn to the right then takes you through the park gates and a track leads along the southern edge of the mountain to its northeastern tip, where a small museum and interpretation centre should now be open. Alternatively, for viewing the northern shore of the lake, the bus from BIZERTE to SEDJENANE passes along the water edge, passing both the Douimis and Sedjenane marshes.

The nearest hotel is *Hotel Younes* in GUENGLA, 3km north of MENZEL BOURGUIBA; this is ideally placed for exploring Oued Tindja, the river that connects Lac Ickheul with Lac Bizerte, and a local bus goes from there to TINDJA: hitch from there either along the north or (more promising) south side of the lake.

Tabarka and Aïn Draham

Access is simplest by bus direct from TUNIS (Gare du Nord), although there is a tortuous *louage* route via BEJA and DJENDOUBA. On the coast road through Sedjenane in spring or summer, look out for white storks – they nest on some of the roofs. TABARKA has a wide range of hotels, although these tend to get booked up in the crowded summer months. The same is true of the only two hotels in AÏN DRAHAM, which are both fairly expensive. Tabarka is certainly a good base, if you are prepared to be patient getting a bus up the hill to Aïn Draham.

THE EAST COAST

The East Coast resorts of Sousse, Hammamet and Djerba have seen the bulk of Tunisia's tourist development, centred largely on their broad sandy beaches. This feature makes the region good for birds as well, and the low coastline offers some of the most extensive mudflats of the whole of the Med in the **Gulf of Gabes** around Sfax. Further north, **Sousse** has nearby saltpans and wetlands.

Wetlands around Sousse

SOUSSE and MONASTIR are both heavily visited tourist areas, but nonetheless have a good range of wildlife sites around them.

Monastir's saltpans

One of the most accessible is the **saltpans of Monastir**. Since they are simple saltpans, without extensive marshes, they are not as interesting as the marshes of

Sfax further to the south, but they still hold a good bird population. The complex lies around the airport at SKANES, between Sousse and Monastir and easily accessible by road or by train (get off at SAHLINE and walk down to the airport station). **Flamingoes** are usually present, along with smaller waders such as black-tailed godwits, avocets, blackwinged stilts, redshanks, and Kentish plovers. It's a good spot for pratincoles, too, and marsh sandpipers, a bird that breeds in Russia, make this their most westerly wintering ground.

Oued Sed

Some 20km north of Sousse, another wetland complex lies around the **Oued Sed**, a freshwater and reedbed area; the river flows under the main road and eventually ends up in **Sebkhet Halk el Menzel**, a salt lake close to the sea. As always, freshwater is a magnet for birds; if there is enough water in the river and the salt lake, it's well worth a trip, with all the usual wading and waterside birds plus a chance of breeding purple gallinule and marbled teal. Peregrine falcons and marsh harriers hunt over the area – the latter feeding off the abundant frog population. Flamingoes are present on the *sebkhet* whenever there is enough water, and I have seen large flocks of migrating cranes there, too.

Sebkha Kelbia

The final wetland worth mentioning is **Sebkha Kelbia**, a huge salt lake lying inland of Sousse towards Kairouan. In the past, it has been of international significance for its wintering wildfowl and waders, and many books still refer to it. But beware – dams have been built on its feed rivers, and it has been completely dry since 1982. If there happens to be a very wet winter, though, it would certainly be an outstanding site.

The fields around Kelbia are rich in gypsum, and hold a very colourful and characteristic spring flora. The lake itself, in common with all other Tunisian salt lakes, is dominated by shrubby species of glasswort *Arthrocnemum spp.* which, as the only plants able to withstand high salinity, dominate vast areas. Tamarisk bushes form a shrubby fringe, and are worth scouring for small warblers. The lake can be best explored from the village of DAR EL OUESSEF at the northern tip where the Oued Sed flows out, or (with a bit of a walk) from the village of BIR DJEDID at the southwestern corner.

Gulf of Gabes

The **GULF OF GABES**, running from SFAX in the north to DJERBA in the south, is the single most important Mediterranean site for **wintering waders**. These birds – primarily small waders such as dunlin, little stint, redshank, plovers and sandpipers – breed in northern Europe and Asia, and a Dutch study in 1984 found an estimated population of 332,000 wintering waders in the gulf, almost exactly half of the total Mediterranean wintering population.

The region is attractive to wading birds due to the combination of a shallow coast and a tidal range of one to two metres, an extremely unusual feature in this largely tideless sea. This exposes huge areas of **mudflats** at low tide, rich in the molluscs and invertebrates which form the bulk of a wading bird's winter diet. In addition, the area supports high winter populations of flamingoes (up to 14,000), spoonbills (up to 2500), and a variety of herons, egrets, gulls and terns.

Flamingoes are surely the most extraordinary flying machines invented. Over four feet high (for these are greater flamingoes, not the smaller lesser flamingoes that breed in their millions south of the Sahara), their wings flash in scarlet and black as they fly in honking flocks.

Most of the wintering birds here come from breeding colonies in the Camargue in southern France and in southern Spain, although ringed birds have also been traced to colonies at Lake Tengiz in central Kasakhstan, nearly 5000km east of Gabes. Their variation in colour, from dirty white to deep pink, is caused partly by age but partly by their staple diet, the brine shrimp *Artemisia sp.*. Flamingoes are present most of the year at Sfax – in summer, non-breeding birds stay behind – but it is in winter that numbers peak, reaching several thousand on occasions.

Although the highest numbers are recorded in **winter** from November to the end of February, birds are still present through to April, and many species such as avocet, blackwinged stilt and redshank stay on to breed in the coastal salt marshes surrounding the mudflats. The bulk of the winter flocks seem to be centred around Kneiss island, halfway between Sfax and Gabes, but that area is difficult to get to and the birds are hard to see because the area is so huge. I have chosen two more accessible sites to describe in detail – the marshes and **saltpans** just south of Sfax, and the **Kerkenna Isles**, a short ferry ride from Sfax harbour.

The saltpans of Sfax

The **saltpans of Sfax** stretch almost continuously from SFAX to THYNA, and although they often attract big concentrations of wading birds, especially at high tide, the mudflats beyond the saltpans are the actual reason why the birds are there. The whole area offers **exceptional birdwatching**, partly because of the sheer numbers and range of species, but mostly because the birds have become used to human disturbance from the saltpan workers and from shell fishers. This has made them very approachable.

Take a look at the little **inlet closest to Sfax** first; it's heavily used by flamingoes, spoonbills, egrets and herons. For aesthetic reasons alone, the sight of hundreds of wading birds amongst the shell fishers in the early morning sunlight is magical. The birds will be found on the mudflats at low tide, and just a chosen few of the saltpans, depending on their salinity. There are 1500 hectares of saltpans (producing around 300,000 tonnes of high quality sea salt a year), so it may take a bit of time to find where the birds are.

A few hours watching the mudflats gives a fascinating insight into the degree of **feeding specialisation** of these wading birds. Flamingoes hunt by sieving their huge bill from side to side in the shallow water, and avocets use a similar technique with their upturned bill. Spoonbills, a rare bird globally, use the same method but have a bill which ends in a rounded "spoon". Blackwinged stilts, which have extrordinarily long legs, wade out into the water and delicately pick out individual prey items one by one. Herons and egrets stand poised on the water's edge, ready to pounce on small fishes. Most of the true waders probe in the mud, but at different depths and for different prey; the short-billed stints and dunlins can only reach a few centimetres, while the longer-billed curlews and godwits can go much deeper.

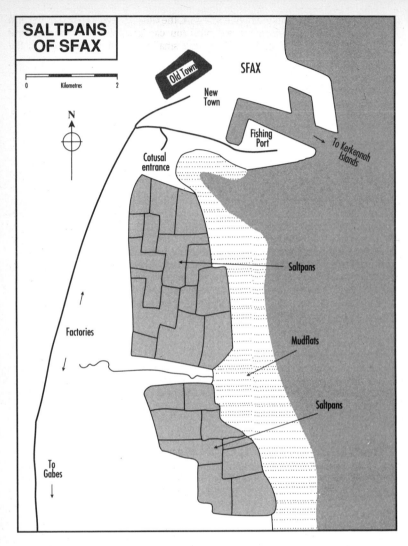

These wintering waders go **north to breed**; some as near as central Europe (dunlin and redshank, for instance) but most further up towards Lapland, and arctic Russia. Others migrate further east; the marsh sandpiper, like a miniature greenshank but with a needle-thin bill, breeds in the steppes of central Russia, and Tunisia is the most westerly point of its wintering range. The Gulf is also the most southerly part of the breeding range for some of the species, like redshank, which stay on to nest over the summer.

As well as wading birds, Sfax is a good place to watch for **seabirds** such as gulls and terns. Slender-billed gulls and black-headed gulls are common, along with a variety of terns, including the region's largest, the Caspian tern – almost as big as a herring gull with an enormous red bill. You can also see, in winter, several hundred **black-necked grebes**; like a very small round duck, they bob on the surface of the water.

The Kerkennah Isles

The **KERKENNAH ISLES** lie a short ferry ride off SFAX. The same wading species (but less of them) occur on the mudflats around the islands in winter and spring, especially between the causeway and village of OULED YANEG. **Spoonbills** in particular occur in high numbers in winter – 400 have been seen.

The islands are flat and are dominated by date palms but have interesting flowers. Two species that occur, here and also on the mainland, are a smaller asphodel *Asphodelus fistulosus*, much more delicate than its larger relative, and *Fagonia*, a low plant with sprawling thin leaves and a beautiful five-petalled flat purple flower. Other common seaside plants include a yellow dandelion *Cladanthus arabicus* and cottonweed *Otanthus*, with yellow "everlasting" flowerheads and covered with fine silvery hairs. Both of these species combine with the pale blue sea lavender *Limonium* to form a fine carpet of colour at the edges of the beaches and rocks.

Land birds are a bit thin on the ground, predictably with such sparse cover, but the islands attract a fair passage of migrating birds such as wheatears, warblers and flycatchers, and have the highest breeding population in the country of great grey shrikes and stone curlews. Partridges occur in the centre, too.

EAST COAST: ACCESS AND ACCOMMODATION

Sousse

For the **saltpans at Monastir**, take a bus to the airport or a train to SAHLINE and walk; for **Oued Sed**, a bus on the main road north from SOUSSE crosses the river after 20km; and for **Sebkhet Kelbia**, the main road to KAIROUAN passes through DAR EL OUESSEF at its northern end.

For all of these sites, SOUSSE is the obvious base.

Gulf of Gabes

There aren't many internationally important wildlife sites within walking distance of a major town, but the **saltpans of Sfax** are one of them. Walk south down the main street of SFAX, Ave. Habib Bourguiba, and after less than 2km on the Gabes road you'll come across a left turn signed to the fishing port. Walk up that, and the mudflats start on your right just before the port. The entrance to the saltpans is clearly marked Cotusal, and has a gate and a high wire fence. Which brings me to the next point . . .

Sfax: Permission

Although the mudflats are public land, they're not too good (even dangerous) to walk across, as well as being pretty foully polluted with Sfax's industrial and domestic waste. The best way to see the birds is to wander along the banks at the seaward side of the saltpans – but this is private land, and you'll need to get permission first. Ideally write in advance (to The Director, *Cotusal*, Salines de Sfax, SFAX), or, if you can't, ask permission at the gate. The current director, Mr Nourredine Guermazi, is an extremely helpful and sympathetic man, but he will doubtless become less so if birdwatchers start trespassing around the saltpans!

Kerkennah Isles

Ferries run the two hour trip to the **Kerkennah Isles** regularly – several times a day in summer – from the docks in SFAX. From there, a bus runs along the length of the island as far as Remla. Most of the hotels on the island are clustered at SIDI FREJ, just over the causeway, ranging from the cheap and friendly *Cercina* to more modern and expensive hotels. One of them, the *Hotel Grand*, hires out bikes; a worthwhile investment and a good way of seeing the island.

THE STEPPES

The steppes cover a vast area of the centre of the country – from the southern foothills of the Dorsale ridge down to the Chotts. Most are **degraded forests**; it's a sobering thought that Hannibal probably got his elephants from this region! Over the centuries, the wood has been felled and the land grazed by sheep, goats and camels, resulting in a landscape only marginally productive for agriculture.

The **vegetation** is sparse but characteristic: various species of spiny thorn bushes, interspersed with wiry desert grasses and low plants. Botanically, this is *terra incognita*, covered by none of the available field guides. The relatively high population of raptors points to a high population of their prey; desert rats, gerbils and the like for long-legged buzzards, and reptiles and snakes for short-toed eagles.

The steppes, and particularly the low hills and wadis rising up from them, can be rich in some **unusual small birds**. **Larks and wheatears** are the most dominant groups and come in a bewildering variety of species. One or two worth special mention are the crested larks, common here as they are all over the country, looking like a skylark but with a pronounced crest. An especially strange steppes species is the **hoopoe lark**, so called because of its long decurved bill and black and white wings. It begins its song flight with a series of low notes on the ground, slowly ascending in pitch until it leaps up vertically with a final flurry of notes, before spiralling down to start all over again. All the wheatears have characteristic black and white tails, but vary widely from the black wheatear of the mountains to the sandy-coloured desert wheatear. In the rocky hills and wadis, look out for trumpeter finches, a thick-billed pink finch with a weird nasal call, and rock buntings are found up in the rocky hills too.

In **villages** house buntings are common. An attractive bird, like a thin brown sparrow with a grey head, it is treated with some reverence by the local people, and is extremely tame. Rufous bush chats – a chestnut bird with a long tail tipped with black and white – are characteristic birds of this region, too, as are fulvous babblers, looking like scrawny brown elongated thrushes with a decurved bill.

Away from the villages, the **steppes proper** are worth exploring. There are cream-coloured coursers here, a bird related to the pratincoles; they are sandy-coloured and long-legged, with a prominent black and white eyestripe, and they're usually seen running along the ground rather than flying. Of the larks, bar-tailed desert lark is probably the commonest, a small sandy lark with a black tipped tail (but beware the almost identical desert lark!), but you should also see Temminck's horned lark, a striking bird with a black and white head pattern, and, in breeding plumage, two distinct black "horns".

Out in the steppes, you'll also, with patience and luck, begin to see some of the **true desert mammals**. Desert rats are the commonest, but jerboas and gerbils are reasonably common and so are susliks, a sort of short-tailed ground squirrel with an upright "begging" posture. Most of the larger desert antelopes have been reduced to extinction by excessive hunting, but an ambitious reintroduction programme is underway at the National Park of **Bou Hedma**, just south of MAKNASSY. Gazelle, oryx and addax are all being introduced, as well as ostriches, which were only exterminated this century in the south. Bou Hedma, if you can get to it, is also a fantastic place for watching **spring bird migration** across the desert, and the mountain range nearby is worth exploring too.

Specific sites

Wildlife is evenly spread in this semi-desert environment, unlike the north of the country, and there are few "hotspots" to make for. The road from GABES to KEBILI, north of **Djebel Tebaga**, is good, and so is the area of stone desert further north around MAKNASSY and MEZZOUNA.

Look carefully whenever you see accessible mountains or any freshwater; the mountains around the **Seldja gorges** at METLAOUI are especially noted for birds of prey as well as other smaller birds. The National Park at **Bou Hedma** is south of MAKNASSY, but inaccessible by public transport; adventurous travellers who want to make the trip should get a permit from the *Direction des Fôrets* office in Maknassy first.

THE STEPPES: ACCESS AND ACCOMMODATION

Since this is such a large area, it's hard to be specific. In general, there's a trade off between wildlife and convenience. Large towns with hotels will be a long way from good wildlife spots, and remote villages teeming with exciting birds won't have anywhere to stay! Exceptions to this are SBEITLA and the GAFSA/METLAOUI area; both are accessible by public transport and have plenty of cheap hotels. Needless to say, if you can afford to hire a car it would pay dividends.

THE DESERT

Predictably, the **stony desert** or *hammada* that covers much of the southeast of Tunisia has a sparse wildlife population. The sand desert in the southwest has, if anything, even less. Neither habitat owes very much to Mediterranean influence, with the huge Sahara to the south dominating the ecosystem.

Plants are thin on the ground, but the wonder is that they can survive at all. They do this by special adaptation, and they are called *xerophytes* – literally, "dry plants" from the Greek. Their leaves are often reduced to thin straps to reduce water loss via transpiration to a minimum. Otherwise, some familiar groups are present; I came across a desert dandelion *Launaea anthoclada* south of Douz that had a typical dandelion flower, but hardly any leaves – just wiry green stalks. Another strategy that some plants pursue is

Desert
dandelion
Launaea anthoclada

to have swollen leaves which can store water; cacti are best known for this, but many other plants do it too. One common shrub that uses this strategy is *Zygophyllum album*, with small swollen leaves and tiny white flowers.

The small **desert mammals** are almost entirely nocturnal, feeding on the plants and seeds in the cool of the night. The big ears of the jerboas are not just for acute hearing – they may also serve a temperature control function in the same way as an elephant's ears do. On the other hand, desert lizards are active by day – though hard to see well since they have a surprising turn of speed.

Birds fall into two groups – those that concentrate around the oases, and the true desert birds which live out in the inhospitable wastes. In the **oases** themselves, house buntings and sparrows are common; look carefully at the sparrows – a rare species called the **desert sparrow** nests in some of these oases, differing from the ordinary sparrows in that they are a much paler buff colour. Palm doves are common: this is their "home" habitat, and they have spread throughout the rest of Tunisia's towns in much the same way as the collared dove has done in northern Europe. Rubbish tips – there's a large one at DOUZ – are worth exploring for raven and for the very similar brown-necked raven, a true desert bird.

Out **in the desert** and away from the villages and oases, there are many of the steppe birds mentioned above – larks, wheatears, cream-coloured coursers, shrikes and so on. Lurk around any area of oasis water in the early morning and the reward may be a flock of **sandgrouse** coming in to drink. They look nothing like grouse – more like small long-tailed doves – and fly fast in flocks. Four species occur in Tunisia, but you'll be lucky indeed if you see all four; pintailed and black-bellied are the two most likely ones. **Small warblers**, surprisingly, pick up a living in the desert – desert, scrub and Tristram's warblers are three species which all occur in southern Tunisia.

The oases at the western edge of **Chott El Djerid** – TOZEUR and NEFTA – are good bases for the semi-desert birds of the Chott and are crowded with migrating small birds in spring and autumn, especially in April when they provide the first water and food after the long trans-Saharan hop. On the southeast edge of the Chott, DOUZ is a convenient base for getting into the sand dunes to the south. Douz has become something of a tourist centre of late, but although the camel market may be crowded, the dunes remain fairly deserted.

An alternative site for the desert lies south of the cave dwellers of MATMATA, a much visited tourist site. The oasis of TATAHOUINE is as good a base as any, with the full range of desert species; south of Tatahouine the going gets rugged. This was the last region in Tunisia where ostriches were found – they still, perhaps, hang on north of the Sahara in southern Egypt – but a sighting of a large long-legged bird with a black and white neck is likely to be a **Houbara bustard** – uncommon and little studied.

THE DESERT: ACCESS AND ACCOMMODATION

The comments in the previous section apply – if you're relying on public transport, then it can be hard to get to the good wildlife spots at the right time of day. But even without a car, places like DOUZ, TATAHOUINE and TOZEUR are within reasonable striking distance of a representative desert environment, and all are on the bus route and have plenty of accommodation. And, of course, the further off the beaten track, the more likely it is that you'll be offered food and a bed for the night in someone's house.

information and publications

The *Organisation . National de Tourism Tunisien* (*ONTT*) with offices throughout the country, is helpful but usually not well informed about wildlife. The *Direction des Fôrets* is the government department dealing with National Parks and with permits generally. Contact them at 30, rue Alain Savary, Tunis 1002.

Les Amis des Oiseaux is a local bird-watching organisation who are extremely helpful to visiting birders. They can be contacted c/o *INRST*, Unite d'Ornithologie, BP 95, 2050 Hammam Lif.

MAPS

The **Michelin** no. 172 covers Algeria and Tunisia, but includes an awful lot of bare desert.

Kümmerley and Frey publish a 1:1,000,000 road map which is good for general purposes, but the free map produced by the *ONTT* is on the same scale and shows most of the same information.

GUIDES

Tunisia: The Rough Guide (Harrap Columbus; £5.95) has all the practicalities.

BOOKS

There are very few books in English specifically about Tunisian wildlife, though the country is covered by many of the general guides listed at the back of this book. *The Birds of Tunisia* by Peter Thomsen and Peder Jacobsen (Copenhagen, 1979; rare) provides an annotated list of species and a guide to the main sites.

TURKEY

I n its wildlife as in its culture, Turkey is the meeting point of east and west. Although the Mediterranean and Aegean coastlines are similar to those of Greece or France, the hinterland in the south and west is a terrain of spectacularly high mountains leading to high inland plateaux that resemble the steppes of central Asia more than any European landscape.

Thus the true Mediterranean zone around the coast is generally **narrow but long**: from Antakya in the southeast to Istanbul in the northwest is 1800km by boat, and the actual coastline is a good deal longer because of its indentations and crenellations. This strip has been continually degraded over Turkey's 10,000 years of human settlement, and none of the original forest cover remains, although the Turkish forestry authority is now making successful efforts to redress the balance.

Wildlife flourishes in the coastal *maquis* and *garigue* scrub wherever the pressures of building development and grazing domestic stock are not too intense. The **spring flowers** are wonderful, and the **bird population** includes numerous

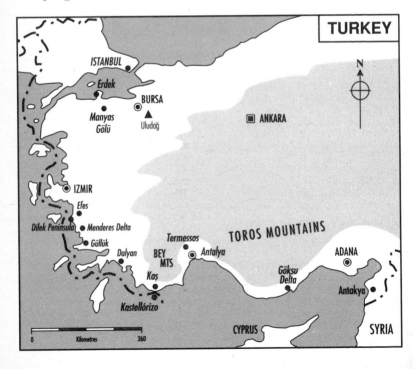

eastern species as well as probably the best concentration of **migrating birds** in Europe. The lakes to the south of the Sea of Marmara are one of the very few places where breeding pelicans can be seen, and Turkey also has one of only two breeding beaches in the Med of the endangered **loggerhead turtle**. There are wildlife attractions in the hills and mountains that lie behind the coast, too – eagles and vultures are frequent, alpine flowers bloom higher up, and even rarer species such as wolves and bears are present, though elusive. Finally, the sea off the southern and western coasts is unpolluted beyond the big towns, and has excellent snorkelling in summer.

Climate and land use

Since Turkey lies at the eastern end of the Med, its **climate** is as much influenced by the Asian continental land mass as by the sea. This means very hot summers and generally cold winters, with the extremes most noticeable in the north and east of the country, where the winters can be very harsh indeed. The south coast, though pleasantly mild in winter, gets up to well over 40°C in July and August; this may be good for reptiles and marine life, but for plants and birds it's less congenial, and wildlife-watching is effectively restricted to the early morning. The **best time to visit** is spring, from mid-March in the south to late May in the north and the hills; peak bird migration moves up the west coast in the last two weeks of April. The returning flights cross the Bosphorus in September, and an autumn visit can also produce late-flowering bulbs; the sea is still warm enough for snorkelling then as well.

WHEN AND WHERE TO GO

It's sensible to avoid the worst of the tourist crowds by visiting in **spring and autumn**, and if you do stay in one of the major resorts, you'll have to be prepared to travel a little. Car hire is expensive, but both long-distance and local **bus services** are exceptionally good; there are rarely problems getting off the beaten track.
The main sites described are:

● **ISTANBUL AND THE SEA OF MARMARA** The northwest has the lake of **Manyas Gölü**, with its outstanding bird life, and the nearby coastal resort of **Erdek**. The mountain of **Uludağ** just above Bursa, is notable for its alpine flowers and mountain birds. **Istanbul** itself is exceptional for migrating birds of prey.

● **AEGEAN COAST** The ancient sites are invariably rich in wildlife: in particular, **Efes and Selçuk**, and two of the sites in the **Büyük Menderes Delta** – Priene and Miletus. Although the coastline is heavily developed, some delightful areas remain: **Güllük** is a representative small town, surrounded by low Mediterranean hills rich in flowers and animals. Finally, the **Dilek Peninsula** is a haven of genuine wilderness right on the edge of the Kuşadası resort area.

● **MEDITERRANEAN COAST** From west to east. The small town of **Dalyan** is close to a large lake and marshes, as well as the ancient site of Kaunos. **Kaş** has good surrounding hillsides and the town of **Antalya** is the best base to explore the Bey mountains and the National Park at **Termessos**. On the other side of the Toros mountains, the **Göksu Delta** near Silifke is renowned for birds, and the gorge just inland has good flowers. Finally, the **Antakya** region on the Syrian border has excellent flowers and another bird migration bottleneck at the Belen Pass.

The **land-use pressures** on the coastal strip are intense but localised. Most of the valleys between the mountains have been drained and reclaimed for their rich alluvial soil, and flocks of sheep and goats reduce much of the hillside vegetation to tightly clipped mounds of spiny shrubs. **Reafforestation** of degraded hillsides is happening in many areas; huge new forests, mostly of pine and some eucalyptus, show that the government has recognised the strategic need for timber. These forests marginally improve the wildlife interest, but don't approach the richness and diversity of the ancient native forests felled long ago.

Building development is more evident on the Turkish coast than anywhere else around the Med, as the country strives to become a major package-tourist goal. Planning regulations restrict the height of new buildings, but the result of this is that the developments cover a larger area and destroy more of the coastal habitats. Resorts such as Kuşadası and Marmaris have spread with extraordinary rapidity along the coast in a ribbon of look-alike concrete villas and hotels. There has to be some doubt as to the size of the tourist market. If the tourists fail to fill the new developments – and Turkey, frankly, is not at its best in the peak summer season – then the whole programme may turn out to have been an expensive and damaging mistake.

ISTANBUL AND THE SEA OF MARMARA

Surprisingly, two of the country's best wildlife sites are close to major towns. **Istanbul** lies on the main migration route up the east of the Med, and the mountain of **Uludağ**, on the other side of the Sea of Marmara, is right next to the industrial centre of Bursa. West of Bursa, the countryside is flat and agricultural, with a series of lakes of which **Manyas Gölü** is the most accessible; the coastal resort of **Erdek** is surrounded by pleasant headlands.

Istanbul

ISTANBUL is hardly an hospitable city for wildlife. Crowded and heavily polluted, it's markedly low on open green space, and therefore not a rewarding place to look for flowers or insects. However, the **birds** are a different story, for the Bosphorus, as the narrowest gap between Asia and Europe, has always been a conduit for migrating large birds. Broad-winged soaring birds – mostly storks and birds of prey – circle to gain height on the Asian side in spring before gliding across to the European side; vice versa in autumn.

In **autumn**, the **Çamlıca hills** just over the Bosphorus behind the suburb of Üsküdar, dominated by the huge radio mast on Büyük Çamlıca, are the place to head for. White storks pass over in thousands in late August, along with similar numbers of honey buzzards. By mid-September, a wider variety of birds of prey are moving through, including common buzzards, the two very similar spotted eagles, harriers and the much smaller Levant sparrowhawk. Lesser numbers of the rare black stork join their white relatives at this time. Binoculars are essential, for on warm clear days the birds pass over at quite a height; they fly lower early and late in the day, and when the weather is windy.

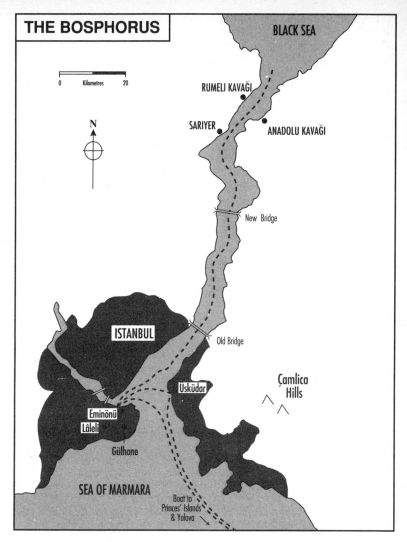

THE BOSPHORUS

BLACK SEA

RUMELI KAVAĞI

SARIYER   ANADOLU KAVAĞI

New Bridge

ISTANBUL   Old Bridge

Çamlıca Hills

Üsküdar

Eminönü

Lâleli

Gülhane

SEA OF MARMARA

Boat to Princes' Islands & Yalova

0   Kilometres   20

N

In **spring**, the passage is less numerous, simply because there are no young birds and many have died over the winter. All the same, good numbers of the same species all pass through, starting in mid-March with the storks and moving on to the bulk of the birds of prey in mid-April. If you watch from **Çamlıca** again, make for the lower **Küçük Çamlıca** which has better bird passage in springtime, and also has a fair representation of spring flowers. But the densest spring flight-path is further north up the Bosphorus, near the huge electricity pylons that cross at Sarayer. Just north of Sarayer, the final European stop of **Rumeli Kavağı** and its opposite number on the Asian side, **Anodolu Kavağı** are both backed by good hilltop vantage points. The flowers are nothing special round here, since most open ground is tightly grazed, but the dense *maquis* holds plenty of small birds including buntings, finches and scrub warblers.

The **Bosphorus** has several gull species as well as the brown and white *yelkouan* race of the Manx shearwater. The shearwaters live up to their name, wheeling around on stiff wings in groups of up to a hundred, almost touching the water with their wing tips.

Even the centre of **Istanbul** has a few bird highlights. For a start, there's a large and easily observed heronry in the plane trees above the zoo in **Gülhane Parkı**. These are **grey herons**, a common enough bird, but great to watch in spring as they mate, display and build their nests; it's bizarre to watch this colony of wild birds nesting directly above enclosures of animals being kept with little thought for animal welfare or public education. **Swifts** are very much a feature of the evening skies in spring and summer, flying in screaming packs around the mosques and minarets. The smaller common swifts are often joined by the much larger Alpine swift, with a white breast and throat separated by a brown band; it's a breathtakingly fast flier. The mosque at **Laleli** is a good place to watch them – conveniently in the middle of the cheap hotels and cut-price clothes shops. Finally, look closely at the small doves you see in town, for Istanbul is the only European site for the **palm dove**, a small dark dove with a necklace of dark spots on a cinammon background.

Uludağ

Its name translating as "Great Mountain", the 2543-metre **ULUDAĞ** towers over the city of BURSA, and, on a clear day, gives phenomenal views over the town down to the distant Sea of Marmara. There are two ways to get up the mountain from Bursa. The easiest is to leap onto the **cable car** (*Teleferik*), which climbs steeply over pine plantations that soon give way to beech, and deposits you some ten minutes later in the **Alpine meadow** at KADIYAYLA, an intermediate stop at around 1000m. The pasture here is heavily grazed, but in spring clumps of violets and grape hyacinths grow, along with a delightful pink primrose *Primula vulgaris var* (variety) *sibthorpii*. Leopardsbane *Duronicum orientalis* also grows here, looking like a large flat dandelion. In the course of the ascent to the highest stop, SARIALAN (1635m), the landscape changes dramatically again, the beech beginning to give way to true **upland forest** of fir *Abies sp.*, with a ground cover of low juniper *Juniperus communis*. Among them grow more violets and grape hyacinths – the latter is *Muscari racemosum*, beloved of British gardeners – and in spring other bulbs add to the scene. In March, two crocus species flower in sheets of colour: the purple *Crocus sieberi* and the yellow *Crocus flavus*, and in April they are joined by the loose-flowered pale blue of *Scilla bifolia*. Tiny flowers of yellow *Gagea* and white star of Bethlehem *Ornithogalum* stud the low grass amongst the juniper.

The **bird life** of the forest can be hard to see, but Kruper's nuthatch is resident (a small grey and white bird, with a splash of chestnut on the breast), and crossbills live in the firs, their weirdly crossed beaks perfectly adapted to extracting the seeds from fir cones. Ravens croak harshly as they fly over the forest, and there's always a chance of one of the larger birds of prey visiting from higher up the mountain. You'll need a lot of luck to see the secretive black woodpecker; the largest woodpecker of the region, it's almost as big as a crow, and entirely black apart from a fiery red crown. Finally, of the abundant tits and finches feeding on the tree seeds, the tiny goldcrest and firecrest are both resident.

The other route to the top takes you up the long twisting road to the **ski resort** near the summit. Here, above the tree line, where the scree slopes are often snow-covered well into early summer, there's a second chance to see the spring-flowering bulbs, which bloom a few weeks later than their counterparts lower down the mountain. May is perhaps the best month, when the flowers are good and the bird breeding season is in full swing. The rare **lammergeier** and the golden eagle both hunt over the mountain, with other birds of prey. Ravens are joined by the red-billed chough and the yellow-billed Alpine chough. Parties of small birds feeding along the slopes may include the badly named shore lark, a plump bird with black and yellow head markings; the male has prominent black "horns" in breeding plumage. Finally, red-fronted serins can sometimes be seen on the scree too, very obvious with a scarlet cap crowning its otherwise dark plumage. The most fruitful mountain-top walk in good weather is along the ridge to the east of the hotel zone, which brings you to the mine workings just below the summit.

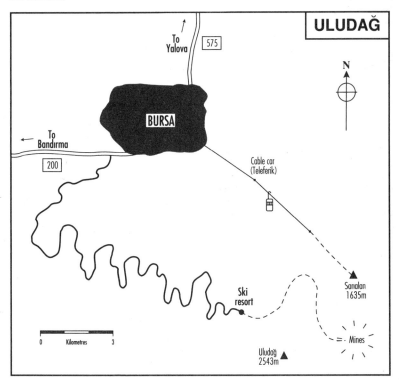

Manyas Gölü

The string of three large lakes along the southern shore of the Sea of Marmara are significant for their breeding and migratory bird populations. **MANYAS GÖLÜ**, the most westerly one, is labelled as **Kuş Gölü** on some maps – fittingly, as this means "bird lake". Although the lake is huge, it's not well served by tracks, but on the northeastern corner there's the National Park at **Kuşcenneti** (Bird Paradise), the smallest of Turkey's National Parks at only half a square kilometre, and an excellent viewing spot. The park consists of a small museum, a short walkway through a poplar plantation, and a high viewing tower looking out over the main breeding colony. Binoculars are essential here, for the birds' needs have priority over the birdwatchers' and the tower is some way from the colony.

In spring and early summer, the **breeding colony** is a constant mass of movement as birds arrive, leave, display and squabble amongst the trees in which they breed. The noise is deafening, the croaks and grunts from the herons above

Spoonbill

combining with the constant calling of marsh frogs from below. Hundreds of pairs of cormorants dominate the upper layers, with lower numbers of their much smaller relative, the pygmy cormorant; grey herons and **spoonbills** occupy the next layer down. The latter bird is very obvious – large and white and flying with an outstretched neck – and this is the most easily visible colony around the Med. Still lower down and in the reed beds below there are smaller species: little egrets, the rare all-black glossy ibis, and night herons, a squat dumpy species that looks all grey in its bouncing flight.

As if this weren't enough, **Dalmatian pelicans** breed here too, and the globally endangered **white pelican** passes through en route to its breeding grounds in northern Greece and eastern Europe. Some sixty pairs of pelicans breed on the platforms built for them in the reed beds, and are clearly visible there and as they soar above the trees on their way to and from the lake.

Although the breeding site is fascinating, don't ignore the foreshore of Eskısığırcı, the small village next to the reserve, for a few hours sitting here can give excellent views of all the birds. The pelicans sit hopefully in the water around the fishing boats, spoonbills and herons stalk the water margins and are joined by **white storks** that breed in the village.

Erdek

Twenty kilometres west of BANDIRMA is the resort of **ERDEK**, on the south side of a little peninsula. Although not an exceptional wildlife site, it does have a good selection of the commoner species and some pleasant walks; it's a well-established resort for the home market, very crowded in summer, but a good place to stay in spring or autumn, and makes a fine alternative base to Bursa for exploring the south Marmara shore.

To the west of the town, after the long line of hotels has ended, cross over the little river by *Ay Camping*, and continue along the as yet undeveloped beach. The **rocky hillside** of olive groves that rises up at the far end is a riot of colour from common flowers in spring. Poppies, marigolds and lupins combine with the brilliant blue of the low-growing dyer's alkanet *Alkanna tinctoria* and the small flat white flowers of one of the *Tordylium* umbellifer species. This is an excellent butterfly spot in the springtime, attracting the common swallowtail *Papilio machaon* and the paler scarce swallowtail *Iphiclides podalirius*, as well as browns, blues, green hairstreaks *Callophrys rubi* and very large numbers of one of the *Pyrgus* skippers. Predictably, the olives and low shrubs are rich in finches and warblers, including the large Orphean warbler. Reptiles include marsh frogs in the river and spur-thighed tortoises *Testudo graeca*, as well as the ubiquitous small *Lacerta* lizards.

In the opposite direction, the **wooded promontory** overlooking the military base to the east of the town is also worth exploring. Follow the road by the shore, and then branch off right along a track just after the ruined disco. The stony slopes here have similar butterflies to the other end of the town, and the flowers include the fleshy yellow *Sedum sediforme* and masses of the bright purple Venus' looking glass *Legousia speculum-veneris*. A close look amongst the shrubs and grass might find blue-winged grasshoppers, possibly *Orthoptera caerulescens*, or a brown praying mantis *Empusa fasciata*. The track continues through a pine plantation – tortoises are easily seen here as they slip and slide around the pine needles – and ends at an **old quarry**. The quarry floor is overgrown with shrubs, including the Judas tree *Cercis siliquastrum*, covered in bright pink flowers in spring. These flowers attract hundreds of insects – bees, hoverflies, the huge glossy purple carpenter bee *Xylocopa violacea*, and shiny green chafer beetles *Cetonia spp*.

The quarry also provides a safe **nesting place** for birds. Ravens and kestrels breed here, as well as smaller cliff-nesting birds such as the blue rock thrush and rock nuthatches. Peregrine falcons have been seen here too. On the way back, the pine-forested side of the hill overlooking the military base is less exciting, although *Anemone pavonina* grows here in colours ranging from pale pink to deep purple, along with the common yellow orchid *Ophrys lutea*.

Inland from Erdek, olive groves cover the bare land, but the **deciduous woodland** on the slopes of the mountain of Kapıdağı, in the centre of the peninsula, is worthy of further exploration for those with energy or a car.

Other sites in the area

ULUABAT GÖLÜ, also known as **Lake Apolyont** after the Roman settlement of Apollonia on its eastern shores, lacks the breeding colonies of Manyas but has higher numbers of wildfowl, especially at migration time. The best vantage point is about 10km down the raised track that leads south from the village of ULUABAT down the west shore of the lake. Another place to watch from is the village of GÖLYAZI, near the ancient site on the northeastern corner of the lake.

The river Koca drains the lake, and comes to the sea north of Karacabey at the **KOCABAŞ DELTA**, where lakes, marshes and flooded forest make an outstanding bird area. The road from KARACABEY to the coast is the best access point. For both of these sites, a car is distinctly handy, and Bursa is probably the best base.

ISTANBUL AND MARMARA: ACCESS AND ACCOMMODATION

Istanbul
For **Çamlıca**, catch the ferry from the Galata bridge across to Üsküdar and get a bus or a *dolmuş* from there. For the **Bosphorus** the easiest – and nicest – way to get there is to take one of the Bosphorus ferries and simply get off where you see a good number of birds going over. Tourist ferries leave twice daily from Eminönü.

Uludağ
Bursa itself is well served by bus, but the best way to get to it from Istanbul is by ferry across the Sea of Marmara to YALOVA, perhaps taking the chance to stop off on the Princes' Islands en route. Regular buses run the trip from Yalova to Bursa, where there are plenty of hotels – cheap and noisy around the bus station, a bit more expensive but still noisy around Heykel (the town centre), and quieter and still more expensive in the spa suburb of Çekirge. The Tourist Information Centre by the Grand Mosque is particularly helpful.

The **cable car** is easily found by taking a short bus or *dolmuş* ride up from Heykel. Getting to the **ski resort** can be more difficult unless you have a car, although technically a *dolmuş* service does run from a small kiosk on the north side of Heykel.

Manyas Gölü
The National Park at **Kuşcenneti** is 3km off the BANDIRMA to BALEKESIR road (route 565), 15km south of Bandirma. Inter-city buses between Bursa and Bandirma will drop you at the turn-off, leaving you to walk the last few kilometres over the railway track and down to the lake. There is a slower and less frequent bus between Bandirma and the village of ESKISIĞIRCI.

For staying in the village itself, *Pansiyon Cennet* has simple but adequate rooms, and provides food as well. It's very quiet and there'll be no other tourists in town, so a knowledge of basic Turkish or at least German comes in handy. It's ideally placed for early morning and evening birdwatching – the best times – and you can even sit on the balcony and watch the pelicans skimming distantly over the water.

Erdek
Access by bus or *dolmuş* from the BANDIRMA bus station is fast and frequent, and there are *pansiyons* and hotels to suit all budgets in Erdek itself.

THE AEGEAN COAST

The Aegean coast is the most heavily developed section of the Turkish coastline, with apartment blocks springing up in many of the choicest areas, both for foreign tourism and as holiday houses for the wealthier residents of Istanbul and Ankara. But there are unspoilt parts, and they are well worth hunting out, as it's a coastline of astonishing beauty.

The many ancient sites are often promising for wildlife, and those of **Ephesus** and the three sites in the **Büyük Menderes Delta** are no exception. The **Dilek Peninsula** has exciting woods and gorges and is protected by national park status, while the fishing port and resort of **Güllük** has a nearby river delta and some flower-rich hillsides.

Ephesus and Selçuk

Ancient **EPHESUS** (EFES) is a good place to look for flowers, since grazing animals are fenced out. Outside the archaeological zone, three plants dominate: the tall white-flowered *Asphodelus microcarpus*, the yellow spikes of *Asphodeline lutea*, and above all the feathery green fronds and tall yellow umbels of the giant fennel *Ferula communis*. These are all distasteful to sheep and goats, and their presence is a sure sign that everything else has been nibbled out. Inside the enclosed site the plant life is far more varied and prolific, although herbicides are sprayed to keep the ruins free of "weeds". The walls escape this treatment, and thus support wild purple-flowered snapdragon *Antirrhinum majus*, cushions of everlasting flowers *Helichrysum sp.*, and a variety of bellflowers *Campanula spp*.

Many **orchids** grow around the site, too, including 8 separate *Ophrys* species. One of the best places to look for them is on the flat land at the top of the site, opposite the Odeon. The species that can be found in spring, growing among the scarlet flowers of *Anemone coronaria*, include the large *Ophrys sphegodes mammosa*, a beautiful species with two-tone pink and green sepals and a shiny blue H-shaped mark on its purple lip. Other species here include *Ophrys speculum, O. lutea* and *O. scolopax*. Daisy-like flowers of camomile *Anthemis sp.* provide the background for these colourful orchids and anemones.

The most noticeable **reptile** – as on most ancient sites in Turkey – is the agama *Agama stellio*, looking rather prehistoric with its spiny grey skin and long banded tail. Tortoises also lumber around. Spring **butterflies** include the scarce swallowtail *Iphiclides podalirius*, Camberwell beauty *Nymphalis antiopa* and eastern festoon *Allancastria cerisyi*. Ephesus is not particularly rich in **birds**, though the jangling song of the corn bunting is frequent, and stonechats are common too. Rock nuthatches forage the crevices for food, and from the top of the main amphitheatre you can look down on the red-rumped swallows as they wheel below.

Although most people arrive at Ephesus at the main gate, there's a pleasant walk from the site back into Selçuk. Leave by the top entrance, walk down the hill past the east gymnasium, and take the first track on the left; this leads through the fields and almond groves, and is often sunken between deep flower-filled banks, especially good for butterflies. Watch out for finches and larks in the fields, and woodchat shrikes perched hungrily on the surrounding bushes. The track comes out opposite a hideous oil depot on the Denizli road out of Selçuk.

Selçuk

In **SELÇUK** itself, **white storks** are a highlight, nesting on chimneys and rooftops all over the town, especially in a long line of nests on the pillars of the ruined Byzantine viaduct by the train station. The storks feed out on the marshes between Selçuk and the sea (the silted former harbour of Efes), where marsh harriers, warblers, penduline tits and even otters can also be seen. Finally, the beach at nearby **Pamucak** is sometimes a stopover point for migrating flamingoes, and the low dunes behind it are home to the ferocious larvae of the ant-lion *Myrmeleon sp.*

White storks

These larvae sit at the bottom of a conical depression in the sand, feeding on unsuspecting ants which fall into the trap and slide down to be eaten, sometimes helped on their way by a bombardment of sand from the predator. The adults fly in summer, looking rather like dragonflies.

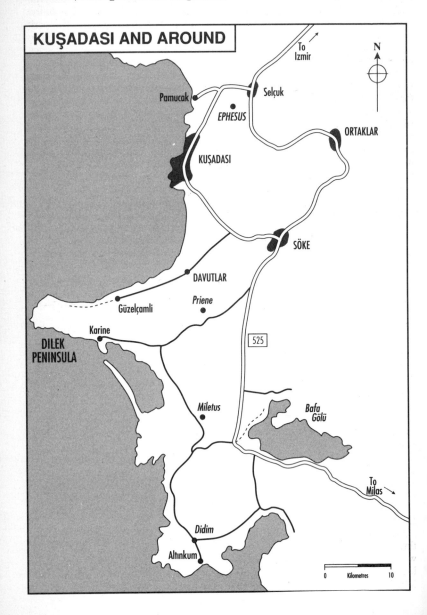

The Dilek Peninsula

The **DILEK YARIMADASI MILLI PARKI** (Dilek Peninsula National Park)
covers a large area of the peninsula that juts out opposite Samos, just south of the
built-up coastline of **Kuşadası**. It's a striking example of the effectiveness of the
Turkish National Park legislation: the wave of concrete breaks against the park
boundary at a resort called Güzelçamlı, whereafter all is peace and quiet. The
logo of this particular park is a prowling leopard, but it's a very long time since
one was seen here – though they still exist in the wilds over in eastern Turkey.

A tarmac road penetrates some 8km into the park along the coast and then
stops; you must explore on foot from there. The basic vegetation is deciduous
forest and planted pines, along with patches of *maquis* scrub, and the land rises to
steep mountains in the middle of the peninsula, intersected by gorges. Tracks
run down off the road to long beaches, behind which, in spring, grow blue
anemones *Anemone pavonina* and blue annual lupins *Lupinus angustifolius*. The
sides of the road are colourfully lined with Judas trees and the dark green bushes
of bean trefoil *Anagyris foetida*, a poisonous foul-smelling shrub with hanging
clusters of yellow pea-like flowers.

On the other side of the road, a track leads up into a large **gorge**, passing
through woodland with Oriental plane trees *Platanus orientalis*, tall cypresses
Cupressus sempervirens, carob trees *Ceratonia siliqua* and pines; underneath,
sweet bay *Laurus nobilis* grows to over 6m, its aromatic leaves interspersed with
creamy flowers in spring. On the ground, the many-petalled blue *Anemone blanda*
flowers in spring, and *Anemone hortensis* can be found higher up. In the autumn,
cyclamens flower under the trees. Orchids include the omnipresent *Ophrys lutea*
and the delicate pale pink *Orchis anatolica*. Wild boar are very much a presence –
their tracks are commonly seen. And **butterflies** are plentiful along the trackside,
including large tortoiseshells *Nymphalis polychloros*, orangetips *Anthocharis
cardamines* and eastern festoons *Allancastria cerisyi*.

The Büyük Menderes Delta

The huge flood plain of the River Menderes has been widely drained for intensive
agriculture, and now the river meanders (its name is the origin of the word)
through cotton fields and drainage channels. Poking up in the middle of it is
MILETUS, an ancient site of great beauty and some wildlife interest.

Behind the ancient theatre, tracks lead to the ruined mosque of Ilyas Bey,
which houses several pairs of **storks** amongst the grass and camomile on its
domed roof – one of the most dramatic nest sites in all Turkey. The graveyard in
front of the mosque is full of the white *Iris florentina*, a fine sight in late April.
Although the rest of the large site is heavily grazed and dominated by asphodels
and thistles, there are orchids to be found, including the woodcock orchid *Ophrys
scolopax orientalis*, with pale pink sepals and a brown lip with cream markings.
Large green lizards *Lacerta spp.* are quite common here, as are tortoises.

Over by the forum, pools are fringed by tamarisk bushes and carpeted with the
tiny white flowers of water crowfoot in spring. The bushes are full of migrating
warblers and other small birds, and penduline tits and reed warblers stay on to
breed. Cretzschmar's bunting, a bird with a very restricted European range, is
found here too, and there's always a chance of a marsh harrier overhead.

Didyma and Priene

Of other ancient sites in the delta, **DIDYMA** is in the middle of a fairly grim town, and is notable only for the lesser kestrels which breed in the ancient walls. **PRIENE**, further to the north, is more interesting, set on the south side of the mountains that form the spine of the Dilek Peninsula, with superb views over the flood plain. Look below for storks, egrets and marsh harriers, and above for birds of prey; the buzzards here are of the eastern race, confusingly similar to the long-legged buzzard. Black kites and Bonelli's eagles can both be seen, perhaps breed-ing on the cliffs above the agora. Wall lizards and agamas, predictably, abound on the ancient walls. The flowers of Priene consist of the usual aspho-dels and giant fennel – which, incidentally, attracts abundant insects to its yellow flowers – and honey-wort *Cerinthe major* forms abundant ground cover, with hanging tubular chocolate and yellow flowers. Several bellflowers *Campanula spp.* grow here, including one with superb large blue flowers. The flat land below the theatre is rich in orchids, including the ploughshare orchid *Serapias sp.*; of the insect-imitating ones, *Ophrys sphegodes* occurs in two forms, along with *O. speculum* and *O. lutea*.

Honeywort
Cerinthe major

Other nearby sites

At the saltpans of **KARINE** – in the north of the delta coast – flamingoes are often seen on migration, along with a variety of waders and seabirds; notable among the latter is the rare Audouin's gull. In winter the delta is used by tens of thousands of ducks, whereas in summer, Eleonora's falcons – which breed on the offshore islands – use the estuary as a hunting ground. Further south, there's more difficult access to the estuary from AKKÖY; the sprawl of ALTINKUM at the extreme south has little to recommend it.

The large lake of **BAFA GÖLÜ**, on the other hand, is well worth stopping for. The easiest access is from the main route 525, which skirts its southern edge; the roadside gives good views of the lake, although it is actually the flowers here which are of most interest. The olive groves by the road are exceptionally rich in spring-flowering orchids and anemones, especially 2km west of the lakeside fish restaurants. Neither of the two anemone species (pink *Anemone hortensis* and red *A. coronaria*) nor the orchids (yellow *Ophrys lutea* and blue-lipped *O. speculum*) is rare, but they grow here in extraordinary profusion – an unforgettable sight.

The **birds** of Bafa Gölu can be seen from the same road, but some exploration is needed for a better view. After the main road leaves the lake at the western edge, there's a left turn to Akköy and Didyma; opposite this is a little teahouse, at the side of which a track runs 2km to a concrete sluice on a drainage ditch; turn right, and follow the ditch down to the lake. Herons, storks and egrets will be fishing amongst the reeds, while gulls, terns, and large flocks of coot and great crested grebe search the open water for fish. There's a chance of rarer birds such as pelicans and the ruddy shelduck. Two scarce **kingfishers** may be seen in this area, too; both considerably larger than the common species, the pied kingfisher is black and white, while the Smyrna kingfisher is blue and brown with a white breast and a huge red bill.

Güllük

Situated on the mouth of the River Değirmen, roughly halfway between MILAS and BODRUM, **GÜLLÜK** offers a range of wildlife and the bonus of the marshy lake at the nearby delta. It's a relatively undeveloped fishing port and resort, although huge housing villages are being constructed on the coast to the south. Get there soon, or out of season.

On the outskirts of the town, on the road to Milas, there's a bauxite holding station, opposite which a **scrub-covered hillside** leads to a flat hilltop. The dense *maquis* has many colourful shrubs in spring: the two common species of bushy rockrose grow here – *Cistus salvifolius*, with densely massed white flowers, and *Cistus incanus*, with big crinkled pink flowers. The blue spikes of French lavender *Lavandula stoechas* are much in evidence, as are the pale blue iris-like flowers of the Barbary nut *Gynandiris sisyrinchium*. At the top and in the surrounding olive groves, the scrub thins out to a more open habitat, where orchids and anemones grow despite the obvious grazing. The red anemone is *Anemone coronaria*, and of the eight or so orchid species *Orchis italica* is the most obvious, with a clustered spike of pale pink flowers. *Barlia robertiana* grows here too – the biggest orchid of the region, it climbs up to 50cm high, with dull green and pink flowers. Tortoises are especially common, and the hilltop is a good place to watch migrating swallows and martins in spring.

Three kilometres further out on the same road is the small village of **KARAKIŞLA**, the easiest point for access to the **river delta**. A track leads from the village to the lake shore, between tamarisk bushes and huge reed beds predictably full of reed warblers and moorhens, while herons and egrets feed here on frogs and the abundant eel population. Little crakes are present too, though they're hard to see. A reasonable view of the water can be had from the low surrounding hills, and may produce ruddy shelduck, pygmy cormorants sitting on the posts, and terns fishing over the water – including black terns and the slightly paler whiskered tern. Marsh harriers hang over the reed beds, and, with luck, even pelicans can be seen on migration.

On the south shore, the most easterly hillside (nearest to Karakişla) has escaped grazing, and is a recommended walk back to the main road and Güllük. The land near the lake edge is rich in blue and red anemones and orchids, including the handsome *Ophrys scolopax orientalis* and *Ophrys sphegodes*. A curious plant here is birthwort *Aristolochia spp.*; a low-growing plant with heart-shaped leaves and a flower shaped like a tenor saxophone, it's the food plant of the caterpillars of the eastern festoon butterfly *Allancastria cerisyi*, which flies here in spring. Among lizard species, agamas can be found on the rocks and large green lizards amongst the bushes. Further up the hillside, the scrub becomes thicker and is home to many warblers; the dominant one is Rüppell's warbler, with its black head and throat and white "moustache". The species is probably commoner on this coast than anywhere else in the world.

Rüppell's warbler

Back in town, look out for lesser kestrels around the school at the top of the hill on the road coming in. Finally, the rocky coastline here has clear water and is perfect for snorkelling in summer or autumn.

Other nearby sites

Although heavily developed, the **BODRUM PENINSULA** has a coastline of great beauty, the unspoilt bits having similar flora to Güllük. Eleonora's falcons can be seen in summer off the western tip of this peninsula, and at Knidos on the end of the **DATÇA PENINSULA**, the next headland to the south. Datça itself is a pleasantly quiet spot to stay, and is close to some good hillsides for flowers; in summer, there's good snorkelling to the south of the town, past the main beach. The boat trip from Datça to Knidos gives good views of the twisted layers of limestone that make up the sea-cliffs, as well as a chance of porpoises, dolphins and flying fish.

The road to Datça leads through **MARMARIS** – not a place to stay for wildlife enthusiasts, but the boat trips round the bay offer reasonable snorkelling in summer. The **Atatürk park**, just to the east of the town, has a large wood of the rare Oriental sweet gum *Liquidamber orientalis*. It looks a bit like a small plane tree, with star-shaped leaves and hanging clusters of round fruits.

AEGEAN COAST: ACCESS AND ACCOMMODATION

Ephesus and Selçuk
Both sites can be easily reached by bus from touristy KUŞADASI – though Selçuk is a far better place to stay. It has excellent and cheap restaurants, a good Saturday market, and numerous friendly *pansiyons*. Bird freaks may want to try the *Pansiyon Barım 1*, just behind the museum, since storks nest on its roof. Get one of the top-floor rooms, and the nest is 5m away at eye height; their bill-clapping displays make a pleasant alarm call in the early morning.

Dilek Peninsula
Buses run the 17km from KUŞADASI and from SOKE to the park. It's quite accessible for a day trip from as far away as SELÇUK, although there are hotels in the resort of GÜZEKCAMLI and the agricultural village of DAVUTLAR.

Menderes Delta
PRIENE, MILETUS and DIDYMA are firmly on the tourist circuit; it's possible to see them all in a day from as far away as SELÇUK or KUŞADASI, although the section between Priene and Didyma is a bit tricky on public transport. For KARINE and the estuary a car is a great help. BAFA GÖLÜ can be explored on foot from the park teahouse, and the southern shore is on regular bus and *dolmuş* routes between SÖKE and MILAS.

Güllük
Direct access is by *dolmuş* from MILAS. Buses to BODRUM and the rest of the peninsula pass along the end of the road to Güllük; hitch or catch a *dolmuş* for the remaining few kilometres. There are plenty of *pansiyons* in Güllük, though you may have to hunt around a bit to find one open out of season.

THE MEDITERRANEAN COAST

The dividing line between Turkey's Mediterranean and Aegean coasts is rather arbitrary – we've chosen to start at **Dalyan**, a site within easy reach of a range of habitats. Along the coast to the east, **Kaş** has good hillsides and the offshore island of **Kastellorizo**. Behind Kaş, the Bey and Toros mountains make the coast even wilder; the **Termessos National Park** is a good example of mountain wood-land, and the **Göksu delta and gorge** is a riverine site backed by the Toros moun-tains. Finally, away on the Syrian border, **Antakya** is the best base for this little-explored region.

Dalyan and around

The small town of **DALYAN** lies right by the huge **LAKE KÖYCEĞIZ** , whose waters attract many wintering wildfowl. Pygmy cormorants are common, as are the white storks that feed on the lake margins and surrounding fields. The reed beds are inhabited by egrets and herons, and migrating spoonbills and glossy ibis call here too. The only feasible way to see much of the lake is by **boat**; tourist boats run from Dalyan, and one can be hired for the day reasonably cheaply.

To walk to the lake edge from the town, head north from the waterfront up the track alongside the *Denizatı* restaurant. From here the river can be reached by cutting across the cotton fields on the left. The **ditches** are full of reptiles and amphibians. Marsh frogs *Rana ridibunda* (usually with a pale green or cream stripe down the middle of the back) leap into the water as they are disturbed, and

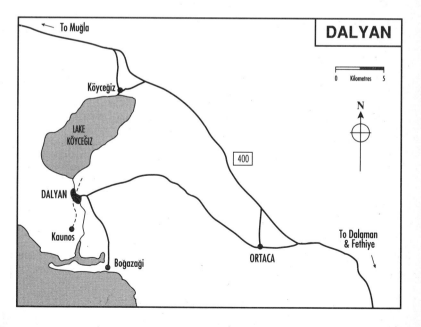

stripe-necked terrapins *Mauremys caspica* make a louder noise as they follow suit. The ditches are home to many water snakes, generally the non-venomous dice snake *Natrix tessallata*. It's essential to walk slowly and quietly along the ditches to get a good view of these animals; walk carelessly, and a chorus of plops and splashes will be your only reward. Tortoises are also very common on the banks, and iridescent green and blue damselflies *Agrion sp.* dance over the ditches in spring. The fields are then crowded with migrating wheatears and wagtails, while the monotonous song of the corn bunting is everywhere.

By the side of the **river** there are yet more terrapins, some up to 30cm long, which is exceptionally large for this species. Search the bottom of the reed stems for large orange and cream **crabs**, which crouch upright, looking as if they would be more at home in a tropical mangrove swamp. Kingfishers are regular, with the familiar small blue one sometimes joined by the much larger Smyrna species.

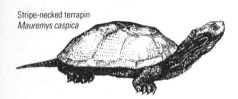

Stripe-necked terrapin
Mauremys caspica

Continuing north, a **rocky hill** rises above the town rubbish dump and gives a reasonable if distant view of the reed beds around the lake; it's a colourful place with spring poppies, marigolds, bellflowers and purple viper's bugloss *Echium sp.*

Kaunos

Two kilometres south of Dalyan, the ancient site of **KAUNOS** is another fine spot for wildlife. From Dalyan, head south along the river past the shops, turn right after the school, and someone will then row you across the river; a track leads south past the site's rock tombs. The banks to the right of the track have been taken over by large colonies of a mining bee *Eucera sp.*. The abundant spring **butterflies** include the yellow *Gonepteryx cleopatra*, as well as eastern festoons and large tortoiseshells. This scrub, just north of Kaunos itself, is rich in small birds, and blackcaps and lesser whitethroats migrate through in large numbers.

Rock nuthatches breed in the walls of the ancient **theatre** at Kaunos, and agamas, as always, dart around the rocks. Anemones brighten up the stone steps, and the yellow-flowered Jerusalem sage *Phlomis fruticosa* grows in abundance on the bare land to the north. Later in the year, *Acanthus spinosus* can be seen, its tall purple and white flowering spikes rising from thistle-like leaves. One particularly striking colour combination on the walls is the large-flowered blue bellflower *Campanula tomentosa* growing alongside the purple-throated bright yellow flowers of henbane *Hyoscamus aureus*.

Kaş

KAŞ, though no longer the sleepy fishing village it was until discovery by tourism in the mid-1980s, retains an air of relaxation and is a comfortable base from which to explore the surrounding hillsides and olive groves. To get onto the slopes, head towards the rock tombs, find the *Pansiyon Zakkum*, and take the track that leads through the scrub. The dense *maquis* shrubs support a full warbler population, with the dominant Rüppell's warbler joined by the attractive subalpine warbler.

THE TURTLES OF DALYAN

The story of the turtles of Dalyan is one of conservation success against considerable odds. In 1986, **Istuzu beach** – which, with Zákinthos in Greece, is the most important Med site for the endangered loggerhead turtle *Caretta caretta* – began to be developed for tourism. Local people living in huts on the beach were evicted, and plans were drawn up for a hotel complex. The lights and noise from this would have frightened the adult turtles – which build 400 nests here each year – and hopelessly disorientated the hatchlings as they make their first journey down to the sea. Fortunately, amongst those cleared from the beach was the remarkable "Captain" June Haimoff, who mobilised international support to save the turtles. Pressure was put on the Turkish government as well as the German financiers, and plans for the hotel were finally dropped in 1988.

This means that the turtles are safer, if not yet completely secure. The beach is a **protected area**, and access during the hours of darkness is prohibited from June, when eggs are laid, to September, when the young hatch out. But there is as yet no money for wardens, and nests are easily trampled in the day by tourists or dug up at night by jackals and wild boar.

A **visit to the beach by day** in June or early July will certainly turn up turtle tracks, showing where they have hauled themselves up the beach to lay eggs. And there's always a chance of seeing an adult swimming offshore in the late afternoon.

At the top of the path, just before a new building complex, cut off right into the rocky *garigue*; this more open habitat is dominated by the bushes of *Euphorbia dendroides*, with gorses and Jerusalem sage growing between. The bare earth is colourfully patched with Virginia stock *Malcolmia sp.*, interspersed by white star of Bethlehem *Ornithogalum sp.* In the rock cracks a few wild gladioli grow, a delicate plant with pink flowers, much more graceful than its blowsy cultivated relatives. Orchids here include the grandly named *Ophrys speculum var. regisfernandii*, a form of *O. speculum* with a slender shining blue lip that makes it look remarkably like a fly.

Ophrys speculum

On the other side of the track, the background to the **olive groves** leading up to the road is formed mainly by pink clovers and yellow vetches, with splashes of scarlet from the pheasant's eye *Adonis annua*, a buttercup with a finely divided leaf. Tiny campanulas and red topped sage *Salvia viridis*, a small annual with purple upper leaves, complete the picture. The whole area literally buzzes with insect life, mostly crickets, grasshoppers and bees, but including the odd praying mantis and carpenter bee as well. Later in the year, thistles and marigolds take over, and the whole area is excellent for butterflies. Hoopoes can sometimes be observed too.

One reason why the wildlife of this hillside is so abundant is that goats are fenced out. Walk east from the town along the coast road, and you'll come across the barrier running behind the *Hotel Linda*. It's a dramatic demonstration of the effects of grazing – to the east the rock is virtually bare, whereas to the west there is luxuriant growth. Nonetheless, even this cropped hillside is a good spot for Sardinian warblers and Cretzschmar's bunting, and rock nuthatches breed here as well.

In Kaş itself, listen out for the **Scops owls** that call monotonously from the trees at the night; trying to see them is a frustrating and difficult experience, since they are small and well camouflaged.

Kastellórizo

The Greek island of **KASTELLÓRIZO** lies just off Kaş. Getting over for the day from Turkey is possible – in 1989 there was a boat running day trips – but involves a considerable amount of form-filling with the customs officials. The island is delightful and the steep hill behind the town is excellent for **flowers**. It's lightly grazed *garigue* habitat, rich in aromatic herbs such as sage and thyme, and dominated by the rounded shrubs of *Euphorbia dendroides*. Barbary nuts raise their iris-like flowers by the trackside, and golden drop *Onosma spp.* hangs its tubular yellow flowers downwards from the cliffs. The silvery bushes of everlasting flowers *Helichrysum sp.* are common, and there's the occasional orchid, mostly the yellow *Ophrys lutea*. Rainfall brings out numerous small brick-red **salamanders**; keep an eye out for Eleonora's falcons in summer, and the extremely rare monk seal has been seen offshore.

Termessos

Just to the north of ANTALYA, the **TERMESSOS NATIONAL PARK** gives a good introduction to the vegetation of the Bey mountains, as well as having a marvellous ancient Psidian site perched on top of a remote valley. At the entrance to the park, **pine forests** dominate the scene, with an undergrowth of oleander *Nerium olender*; the delicate *Orchis anatolica*, pale pink and with a spotted lip, grows here in some numbers. Kruper's nuthatch, one of the special birds of Turkey, can be seen feeding amongst the pines. The **museum** at the entrance has a rather sad collection of stuffed animals, but does give an insight into what can be found in the more remote parts of the Bey mountains – lynx, ibex and even a family of bears still survive.

From the museum, a rough track winds 8km to the ruins at the top. The pine forest gives way to more scrubby Mediterranean *maquis*, with olive *Olea europaea* and the eastern strawberry tree *Arbutus andrachne* prominent; the latter species has a leaf like a rhododendron and a pinkish smooth stem. Tortoises and agamas are common and the few grassy clearings amongst the scrub are rewarding for plants such as the pasque flower *Pulsatilla sp.*, with its bright purple flower and feathery leaves. After this scrubby zone, the top area around the ruins is genuine **mixed woodland**; eastern beech *Fagus orientalis* and Turkey oak *Quercus cerris* form the deciduous canopy, over a layer of smaller oak and *Lentiscus* species. Holm oak *Quercus ilex* and Phoenician juniper make up the evergreen component. In March, look for the hanging cream flowers of *Clematis cirrhosa* on the ruins. In June, the **lady's slipper orchid** *Cyprepedium calceolus*, one of the rarest and most spectacular of the Med orchids, grows sparsely under this mixed woodland – unmistakable with its purple petals and sepals, and swollen yellow lip. Among **birds**, the sombre tit is especially common; the size of the great tit, it has a grey back, pale front and cheeks, and black cap and throat.

The Bey Mountains

Getting into the heart of the **BEY MOUNTAINS** calls for some thought and proper equipment, since this is a harsh environment, rising to over 3000m. However, the road from KORKUTELI to ELMALI and thence down to Kaş winds through some extraordinary mountain scenery, with twisted **woodlands** of oak and juniper. Ignore maps that show a large lake near Elmalı called Kara Gölü – it has long since been drained for agriculture. The hills of the Bey mountains and around Elmalı are home to two eastern birds not found west of the Turkish mountains – **Finsch's wheatear**, a black and white wheatear similar to its other relatives, and the **red-fronted serin**, a small dark finch with a stunning red cap.

The road through Elmalı is on a regular bus route; exploration out from Elmalı is best done on foot or by hitching, although the occasional *dolmuş* appears.

The Göksu Delta and Gorge

The **GÖKSU RIVER** cuts through the Toros mountains before coming to the sea in a **marshy delta** – now partly reclaimed – near the town of SILIFKE, 85km west of MERSIN. The delta is a combination of reed-fringed marshy pools, sandy fields, scrubland and beach, and is an outstanding site for birds. As well as the usual ducks and terns, the pools have breeding populations of **purple gallinules**; resembling a huge moorhen with a bright crimson bill, it's a secretive bird, best seen by intensive observation of the reed beds. Pelicans can be seen on the lagoons, especially on spring and autumn migration, and another special bird is

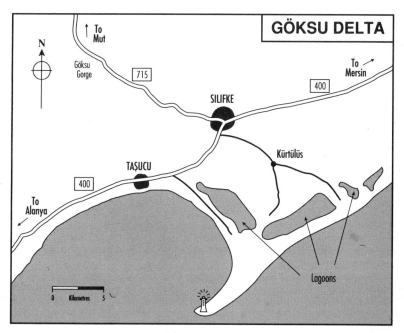

the **marbled teal**, a small dabbling duck with a restrained mottled plumage. Commoner but nonetheless exciting birds include colonies of bee-eaters breeding in the sandy fields, and pratincoles – a short-legged wader – on the bare land.

Two endemic Med bird species are found here: Audouin's gull (around Taşucu harbour, especially in the evenings), and the long-winged and graceful Eleonora's falcon (in summer only). Keen birders will want to watch the reed beds and bushes for the **graceful warbler**, a small long-tailed warbler that is here right on the western edge of its range – most other *Prinia* species are found in Asia and further east. The delta is close to the Gulf of Iskenderun migration bottleneck between Syria and Turkey; there is thus a great passage of storks, pelicans and birds of prey in spring and especially in late August. Five thousand white storks have been seen passing over in one day.

The Gorge

Inland from SILIFKE, the river cuts through the limestone **GÖKSU GORGE**, with the road to MUT and KARAMAN running along the top. This gorge – and especially the most southerly 20km of it – is a fine place for plants. The typical Med scrub of strawberry tree and *Cistus* bushes are accompanied by the scarlet flowers of *Tulipa boetica* in spring, and orchids include the handsome *Ophrys ferrum-equinum*, with a metallic blue mark shaped like a horseshoe on its deep purple lip.

Birds here include gorge specialists such as crag martin and blue rock thrush. There's also a good chance of large raptors such as the Egyptian vulture, the huge griffon vulture, and the short-toed eagle, with more species over the migration periods.

Antakya

ANTAKYA (ancient Antioch) is a large town, tucked in amongst the mountains close to the Syrian border. Although much of the surrounding land is used for arable crops, some is grassland used for common grazing – a strange landscape of erratic limestone rocks, not unlike the *causses* of southern France. The only time to visit this region is in spring, since in summer the temperatures rise to the point where plants and people both wilt away. Around the field margins and road edges, irises, cyclamens and anemones are frequent, along with fritillaries and many orchids. The road from Antakya to ALTINÖZÜ is a good route from which to explore.

Although the delta of the **Orontes River**, which runs through Antakya and thence to the sea, has been greatly reclaimed for agriculture, it's still a rewarding place for wildlife, with abundant storks passing over at migration time, and a vocal amphibian population that includes the eastern spadefoot *Pelobates syriacus*. Stripe-necked terrapins, as always, are a common sight in the ditches and drainage channels.

Further north from Antakya, the **Belen Pass** is a significant bird migration bottleneck, where numbers are at least as high as at the much better-known site at Istanbul. Situated at a height of 740m on the main road between ISKENDERUN and ANTAKYA, the pass is particularly important for storks, spoonbills and pelicans: it has been estimated that the entire population of **white pelicans** breeding in Europe and western Russia fly this route. Any surrounding wetlands are likely to be important as migration staging posts too, especially since the draining of Amik Gölü, a large lake in the middle of the agriculturally rich Amik plain, in the 1960s.

A very rare plant of the pine woods around the Belen Pass is the orchid *Cephalanthera kurdica*, a large red helleborine that flowers in late spring and grows to 70cm; some of the best sites for this species are now occupied by refugee camps, and its future is as uncertain as that of the camps' human inhabitants.

MEDITERRANEAN COAST: ACCESS AND ACCOMMODATION

Dalyan

Dalyan is a short *dolmuş* ride from ORTACA, on the main coastal road between FETHIYE and MUĞLA. Occasionally, boats go there down Lake Köyceğiz from the town of the same name. There are plenty of *pansiyons* and hotels in Dalyan, with more being built every year; the nicest are perhaps those on the river south of the town – though beware of the mosquitoes in summer. The *Göl Motel*, overlooking the waterfront, is popular and good value.

The sandspit of Istuzu beach is reached at the western end by boat down the river, and at the eastern end by a long journey through BOĞAZAĞI.

Kaş

Both access and accommodation are straightforward, since Kaş has ample *pansiyons* and small hotels, and is on the main coastal bus route. There's a pleasant campsite just past the theatre on the road to the peninsula; the situation is lovely, and the surrounding trees and shrubs are good for small birds, although the flowers have mostly been grazed out and replaced by asphodels.

Termessos

ANTALYA is undoubtedly the most convenient base, and buses from there to KORKUTELI run past the Termessos park entrance. Getting up the hill to the ruins is a long and (in summer) extremely hot climb, but the number of tourist cars make hitching relatively simple.

Göksu Delta

The easiest base for the delta is TAŞUCU, one of the ports for the ferry to Turkish Cyprus, and with a range of places to stay from simple *pansiyons* to plush hotels. From Taşucu, walk out on the SILIFKE road and turn right down a track after a fenced-off industrial estate; the track passes some holiday villas, and the first lagoon – Ak Gölü – is on the left. For those with a car, another track leads into the eastern part of the delta from near Silifke via the small village of KURTULUŞ.

Antakya

ANTAKYA and ISKENDERUN are both big towns, with ample accommodation; more remotely, the town of BELEN at the head of the pass itself, and ALTINÖZÜ, southeast of Antakya, both have *pansiyons*. As usual in Turkey, the bus network, even on remote roads, is excellent.

information and publications

In most major towns the tourist office – *Kültür ve Turizm Müdürlüğü* – is an obvious first port of call, though they won't often know much about wildlife. Where there's no tourist office, then a visit to the town hall – *Belediye sarayı* – is sometimes productive and always entertaining.

MAPS

Most maps of Turkey try to cover the whole country, which is so huge that the scale is inevitably very small. A reliable one in this category is the 1:800,000 map from *Lascelles*, widely available in the UK. For trips to the southwest coast, *Bartholomew Clyde* do a good map, at the incomprehensible scale of 1:435,000, which covers the coast between Izmir and Alanya; it's best bought before you go.

Some of the resorts produce their own map of the region, usually available from the Tourist Office. Some are excellent, some are unreliable, and some are downright fanciful. The local **bus station** is often the best place to ask for information about where to go and how to get there.

GUIDES

Turkey: The Rough Guide (Harrap Columbus) is forthcoming in 1991; meanwhile, make do with Diana Darke's *Aegean Turkey* and *Eastern Turkey* (Michael Haag, £7.95 each). Marc Dubin's *Trekking in Turkey* (Lonely Planet, £5.95) is also useful.

BOOKS

Many of the general Mediterranean field guides include Turkey. There's no specific book on Turkish flora, although Polunin and Huxley's *Flowers of the Mediterranean* covers many common species. For birds, make sure you take *The Birds of Britain and Europe* by Heinzel, Fitter and Parslow, which covers the Middle East and North Africa as well as Europe.

Turkey has been much visited by British birders, who tread a well-worn circuit around the country in search of rarities. Keen birders should contact the **Foreign Birdwatching Information Service** (address p.368), and read John Gooders' *Where to watch Birds in Britain and Europe* (Croom Helm, £9.95).

CHAPTER NINE

YUGOSLAVIA

T he view of Yugoslavia that many holidaymakers carry home is one of bare, almost desert-like mountains stretching precipitously down to a brief area of *maquis* vegetation and a blue sea. But the increasingly developed coastline is only one, rather atypical, aspect of the country, about three-quarters of which is covered with range after range of **mountains**, mostly of karst limestone and rich in **plant species**. Unlike the coastal ranges, which were accessible to ships and logged out hundreds of years ago, many inland areas still maintain huge **broadleaf and conifer forests**. There are **alpine meadows**, too, and extensive populations of bears, wolves and other large mammals. And, in contrast to many of the countries described in this book, the truly Mediterranean coastal area is so narrow that the range of **upland habitats** are easily accessible from the coast. Indeed, as developments swallow up more and more of the coast and islands, naturalists have to travel inland up the steep mountain roads to find the best areas of natural and semi-natural habitat.

Highlights of the unspoilt parts of the **coast** include classic *maquis* flowers and birds, good underwater life in pollution-free areas, and a steady stream of migrating birds in spring and autumn. Up in the **mountains** the outstanding feature is that here is a melting pot of three distinct ecological zones – the **Mediterranean**, the **Balkan** and the **Central European**. The dense forests harbour rare birds such as the Ural owl, and some of the woodpeckers, while the extremely rich flora includes many endemic species. All this is set amongst wonderful limestone karst scenery.

Climate and land use

Although the Yugoslav coast is classically Mediterranean, there's much diversity elsewhere, with the mountains, interior basins (and deforestation) creating **local climates**. Geography is also more diverse than might be imagined from a quick glance at a relief map. The country is predominantly mountainous but there is much variation of rock types and vegetation, from the Julian and Karawanken Alps in the north, through several ranges of Dinaric mountains stretching parallel to the coast, to the huge and immensely rugged areas of karst limestone in Montenegro and Macedonia, which are essentially Balkan and contain many relict and endemic species. The **karst** areas are probably the most exciting, both from a natural history perspective and because of the amazing scenery. The mountains are spectacular and there are also high plains, covered with grotesquely shaped rocks which look like virtual moonscapes, and are unlike anything else found in Europe.

Wetlands are the most disappointing habitat. Shortage of agricultural land has meant that, with the exception of a handful of nature reserves, virtually all marshy areas have been encroached upon or destroyed by **drainage**. The pace of change has been fairly quick, so don't put too much faith in wetland areas marked on even fairly new maps; many of them are now full of arable crops.

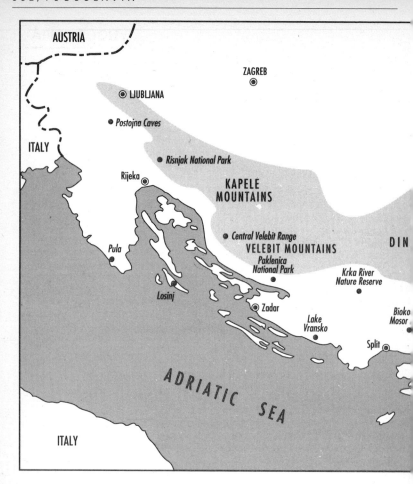

Over most of the country **agriculture and forestry** are the predominant factors influencing wildlife. Apart from lowland drainage, upland areas are often heavily grazed by goats and sheep, and the vegetation is usually impoverished even in existing oak and beech forests. Many of the upland meadows, on the other hand, are harvested for hay, and in consequence maintain a good plant population. Though many forest areas have been maintained, it's said that about three hundred miles of the coastal forests south from Trieste were felled to build Venice. Since then, grazing and, in the past, cultivation on terraces, have both helped impoverish the landscape. More recently, pollution from industry and from sewage has started to seriously affect some areas of the Adriatic coast; this is a particular tragedy because in the past the Adriatic has remained relatively free of the problems facing other Mediterranean coastal areas.

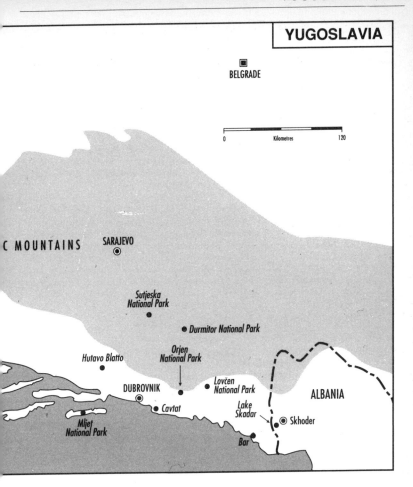

YUGOSLAVIA

BELGRADE

Kilometres
0   120

C MOUNTAINS

SARAJEVO ◎

Sutjeska
National Park ●

● Durmitor National Park

Hutavo Blatto ●

Orjen
National Park

DUBROVNIK ◎   ● Lovčen
              National Park

● Cavtat

Lake
Skadar

● Skhoder

ALBANIA

Mljet
National Park

Bar

WHEN AND WHERE TO GO

The **early spring** is the best time for flowers and birds. The wildlife is good from April onwards, with May probably being the best month. However, many of the upland reserves and sites described may still be under snow at this time. Even for the traveller constrained by more conventional holiday periods, the **uplands** remain floristically rich late into the summer, and alpine meadows are still full of flowers well into August.

The **bus service** is extensive if not always reliable; check times at bus stations. Hire cars are variable too, sometimes very good but occasionally downright dangerous, so check brakes, etc carefully before setting out. Don't forget to watch out for tortoises as you drive.

The following sites have been described:

● **MONTENEGRO** The southernmost coastal state, merging into Albania, is highly mountainous. **Lovcen** is a mountain nature reserve near the coast, while further south **Lake Skadar** is the country's largest and most famous lake, well known for its colonies of pygmy cormorants and Dalmatian pelicans. Further inland, the **Durmitor National Park** has spectacular scenery.

● **BOSNIA-HERCEGOVINA** Grouped for convenience with the middle state is the coastal region around Dubrovnik, technically in Croatia. Highlights include the wonderful forests of the national park at **Sutjeska**; the wooded island of **Mljet**, one of the best offshore visits, and the wetlands of **Hutavo Blato**. The coast near **Cavtat** provides an introduction to coastal *maquis* and marine life.

● **CROATIA** has many of Yugoslavia's finest National Parks and wildlife areas. **Lake Vransko** is an important wetland near the coast. Inland, outstanding upland areas include the **Central Velebit Mountains** and **Paklenica**. Further north, **Risnjak National Park** is a remote area of limestone and upland forest.

● **SLOVENIA** almost falls outside the remit of a book about the Med, but the world famous caves at **Postojna** are so unique that they couldn't be excluded.

MONTENEGRO

Until recently, the coastal area of **Montenegro** was one of the least developed parts of the Adriatic, but tourist centres are now springing up almost as far as the Albanian border. Inland, Montenegro is the most spectacular Yugoslavian state, with huge areas of karst, limestone mountains and large forests. **Lovčen** and **Durmitor** national parks are representative of this upland habitat, while **Lake Skadar** is the country's prime wetland.

Lake Skadar

LAKE SKADAR is the most famous wetland in Yugoslavia for birdwatching. It is also the largest lake in the country, set against a bare, rugged, mountain backdrop – and with a fair proportion of its shoreline in Albania. It is further down the coast than most tourists bother to travel, but nevertheless one of the key sites for any serious naturalist. Although not listed as a protected area in any of the international guides, the lake is surrounded by signs declaring it to be a National Park and presumably enjoys some protected status.

Water birds are the reason that naturalists visit the lake. It is most famous as the breeding site, perhaps the last in the country, of the **Dalmatian pelican**. However, there are numerous other unusual and exciting water birds, including pygmy cormorants, glossy ibises, squacco and purple herons, great white and little egrets and ferruginous ducks. Whiskered terns quarter the shoreline in places, and there are many waterfowl in the winter. Coots and moorhens are abundant along the water's edge and little grebes and black-necked grebes are both much in evidence.

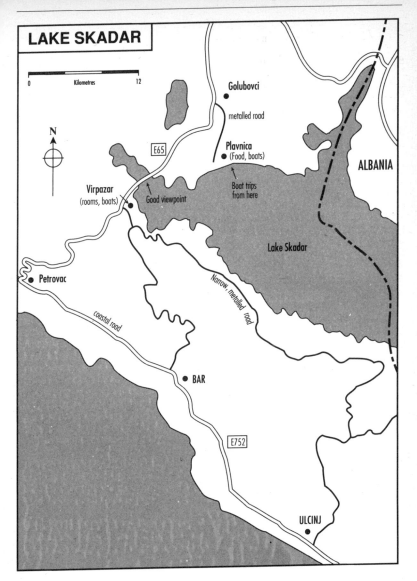

The woods along the shore, and extensive areas of reed swamp, provide good habitat for **small birds**. Amongst warblers recorded are moustached, wood, Savi's and Cetti's. There are also vast numbers of red-rumped swallows in the breeding season, flickering over the water's surface catching mosquitoes. Birds of prey include the common black kite, but also lesser spotted and Bonelli's eagles, hunting from their breeding sites in the **Morača gorge**, just to the north.

Although the bird life is the main attraction for visitors, don't forget that their presence betrays an abundance of food for them, from insects up to the more obvious **reptiles and amphibians**. These are the main prey for the marsh harriers that drift over the lake, and, along with the abundant fish, for the multitude of herons, ibis and egrets. The handsome green toad *Bufo viridis* is very evident, with its beautifully marbled green and cream skin, and so too is the mostly aquatic dice snake *Natrix tessallata*, which wriggles through the water at surprising speed.

Dice snake
Natrix tessallata

Lovćen National Park

LOVCEN NATIONAL PARK is one of the most accessible upland areas on the coast, being under 4km as the crow flies from the small resort of KOTOR. However, to reach it you have to travel 13km and about 1600m up one of the most precipitous and famous roads in this mountainous country. The reward is what everyone agrees is one of the best views in Yugoslavia, looking over the beautiful Gulf of Kotor and surrounded by huge mountains on all other sides. And Lovćen itself is beautiful as well, with a hotel and mountain hut accommodation inside the park, and tracks to follow up to the highest point, where there is a large radio mast. The park is also the site of a mausoleum to Njegoš, the most famous ruler of Montenegro, which itself attracts many visitors.

The park is mountainous and for the most part **forested**. The lower slopes are dominated by hop hornbeam *Ostrya carpinifolia* and the same downy oak *Quercus pubescens* found in the coastal *maquis*. Above about 1000m there is a forest zone of eastern beech *Fagus orientalis*, which has leaves like western beech but branches which slant upwards, giving the impression of a forest of trees standing with their arms in the air. There are many other tree species, including the Montpelier maple *Acer monspessulanum*, turkey oak *Quercus cerris*, whitebeam *Sorbus aria*, mountain ash *Sorbus aucuparia* and hazel *Corylus avellana*, along with numerous pines.

Although the forest has apparently suffered from heavy grazing underneath the trees, there are over 1200 different **plants** recorded, including some endemic to the area such as *Lamium lovenicum*, a local dead nettle species. The mountain meadows are rich with a wide range of plants, some of the most noticeable being the bright blue globe thistle *Echinops ritro*, several species of pinks *Dianthus spp.*, and many bellflowers including the large *Campanula latifolia*. Although early summer is the best time for plants, many are still in flower in August.

Lovćen is the home for several **birds of prey**, including the imperial eagle, buzzard, peregrine and the griffon vulture. The imperial eagle can be distinguished from other large eagles by the white flashes on its shoulders, although these are less obvious in this eastern race than in those found in Spain. The presence of peregrine is more exciting than it might appear as its status in Yugoslavia is not very well known. Alpine swifts scream over the village and jays are common. Rock partridges can be seen on the higher ground.

Less is known about the **mammals**. Beech martens and foxes are common enough in the park, but although wolves and wild cats have been seen, both are fairly rare and difficult to spot. There are apparently no bears in the park.

Durmitor National Park

Even if there were little natural history interest in **DURMITOR**, it would be worth a visit on account of the spectacular karst limestone mountains which cover most of its area. In addition, the park is unusual for southern Yugoslavia in having extensive accommodation, camping and hiking facilities. It is divided into two parts, a mountain massif and a gorge, and is a UN World Heritage Site. Access is easiest from the east, which is quite accessible and developed; from the west, there is just a dirt track leading into the park.

The **massif**, which reaches over 2500m, has a mixture of conifer and broadleaf forest, along with huge areas of upland, Alpine-type meadows, which are still grazed in the summer by sheep and cattle. The **flowers** are exceptional. Even fairly late in the summer, there is a rich, Alpine-type assortment of plants including many endemic or relict species, such as the saxifrage *Saxifraga preuja*, a unique figwort *Verbascum durmitoreum*, and a local trefoil *Trifolium durmitoreum.*. There are a whole range of commoner species, too, as well as these rarities, including *Polygala major*, the largest of the milkworts, *Linum capitatum*, a flax with clusters of bright yellow flowers, and *Gentiana utriculosa*, the small annual gentian.

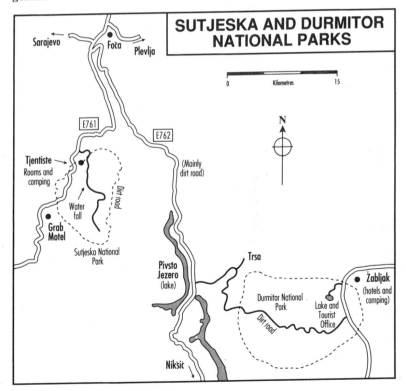

SUTJESKA AND DURMITOR
NATIONAL PARKS

Sarajevo
Foča
Plevlja

0   Kilometres   15

N

E761

E762

Tjentiste
Rooms and
camping

(Mainly
dirt road)

Water
fall

Dirt road

Grab
Motel

Sutjeska National
Park

Pivsto
Jezero
(lake)

Trsa

Žabljak
(hotels and
camping)

Durmitor National
Park

Lake and
Tourist
Office

Dirt road

Niksic

The park was fairly unregulated with respect to hunting until quite recently, so large **mammals and birds** are still scarce, although now hopefully increasing. There are plenty of ravens and hooded crows; the latter taking over from the Western European carrion crow throughout Yugoslavia. There are also a number of birds of prey and game birds, including peregrines and black grouse.

MONTENEGRO: ACCESS AND ACCOMMODATION

Lake Skadar

The nearest big town is TITOGRAD, which is easily reached by bus or car from PETROVAC on the coast, or by train from inland or from the far southern coast at BAR. On Lake Skadar itself, there are three main viewing places. The best plan is perhaps to travel 17km south, through GOLUBOVCI to PLAVNICA, where boats can be hired. A boat trip is one of the best ways to see the lake, although the one we had was fairly disappointing, on a boat with a noisy engine which did not provide much in the way of close views of birds.

An alternative is to approach the park from further south and overlook the lake from the causeway between Titograd and Petrovac. More boats can be hired at VIRPAZAR on the western edge of the lake, just south of the causeway. And, most spectacular, although not necessarily the best for birds, is to drive right along the southern edge of the lake, through some spectacular forests of sweet chestnut, to within a mile of the Albanian border, before the road swings away down to the coast at ULCINJ. However, this option is only open for those with their own car – or to extremely fit cyclists!

Accommodation is easily found in TITOGRAD, although it's not a very interesting place to stay, to put it mildly. There is a restaurant at PLAVNICA, but no rooms, and a couple of guesthouses at VIRPAZAR. The southern shore of the lake is very sparsely populated.

Lovčen

The park can be reached by bus from Kotor to CETINJE, along one of the most precipitous bus routes in the country. The bus usually travels along the main road (not *very* main!) which skirts to the north of the park, although it is possible to walk into the park from here. Alternatively, make your way up through the centre of the park itself, where there is a smaller road and a settlement with one hotel and a bar.

Durmitor

The park is further inland than most of the sites in this chapter, about 100km north of NIKŠIĆ. Easiest access is by bus or car to ŽABLJAK, which is a small, but growing resort village at the edge of the park, where there are camping facilities and many hotels and rooms. There's also a visitor information centre here, at the end of a path which leads from Žabljak down to the Black Lake, with a restaurant, souvenir shop and a place to buy good, but quite expensive, maps of the area. This is the starting point for many of the paths which criss-cross the reserve.

An alternative route into the park, though again only really an option for those with a car, is to drive south along the E762 from FOČA and take a steep, winding road into the park from the west. This is wilder and more attractive, but the road is not in particularly good condition; even the main road, shown in red on most maps, is still unmetalled for much of the route, so travelling is slow. This way in makes sense for people coming from Sutjeska Park (see Bosnia-Hercegovina).

BOSNIA-HERCEGOVINA

This landscape of Bosnia-Hercogovina is characterised by rugged mountain ranges and areas of high plateaux, such as that around the largely Muslim town of Mostarem. Between this upland region and the sea extends some of the country's least developed coastal areas, their isolation guaranteed (so far) by the coastal highway's slightly inland route. The coast around **Cavtat** is a typical example of coastal *maquis* vegetation and attendant birdlife, and underwater marine life; there are a few undrained wetlands including the reserve of **Hutavo Blatto**; inland, the national parks at **Sutjeska** and **Orjen** have upland forests and wild mountains; and, finally, the island reserve of **Mljet** is definitely worth a visit.

Cavtat

Although the whole coastline adjoining the Bosnian republic is of interest to naturalists, the north has been badly affected by deforestation and the effects of the coast road. The town of **CAVTAT** – just south of DUBROVNIK – is a good centre, not yet wholly dominated by tourism, and with miles of undeveloped (and not easily accessible) coastline to the south. This is a good place to get to know the **Balkan maquis** and to spend time looking at Yugoslavia's superb **marine life**.

Driving or walking south from Cavtat takes you through a particularly impressive area of **poplar forest**, one of the most characteristic vegetation types of the southern Yugoslavian coast. The coastal area itself has an interesting selection of **passerine birds**, especially in the summer, although as always they are most active early or late in the day. Look out particularly for the colourful green and yellow **bee-eater** and the bright blue **roller**, best spotted on telegraph wires beside the road or, in the case of the roller, indulging in the spectacular tumbling display flight which explains its name. The lesser grey shrike is still common in Yugoslavia and is fairly easy to spot

Bee-eater

because it perches in places where it can overlook a large area, and watch out for the red-backed shrike, too. There are relatively few species of **warbler** in the *maquis* as compared to wetland areas or forests, although the Sardinian, barred, orphean, sub-alpine and olivaceous warblers can all be found breeding in places. Apparently olive tree warblers also extend north at least as far as Dubrovnic, but they are not common.

Birds of prey likely to be seen along this coast include the ubiquitous kestrel and the lanner falcon – whose status is not known particularly well. During the spring and autumn, migration can be watched along the coast, including parties of grey and purple herons, little egrets, squacco and night herons, red-footed falcons, collared flycatchers and, sometimes, Mediterranean gulls.

Despite the damage done by the wildlife trade, there are still quite a few **tortoises** to be seen in Yugoslavia, although they are never particularly easy to spot unless they move. Unfortunately, the easiest way to see them is when they

MARINE LIFE ON THE CAVTAT COAST

Virtually any rocky shore area of the Adriatic is worth exploring for marine life, other than highly polluted harbours and estuaries. CAVTAT is an especially good example – and has the bonus of being a place where you can walk around the small peninsula and swim off rocks without too many people around.

The **Adriatic seashore life** is quite different from that found in northern Europe. The virtual **lack of tides** means that rock pools and intertidal areas don't really exist in the same way. This means that you have to go into the sea itself; a mask is essential, a snorkel desirable, and flippers a bonus. Diving down, there's a sudden change in temperature after a few feet, and this cooler water changes the marine life as well.

Immediately noticeable, even from the shore, are two very distinctive species of **algae**. The **peacock's tail** *Padina pavonia* has a white and brown striped fan a few inches across, and the **mermaid's cup** looks like a tiny white toadstool. Both are abundant in shallow water and around clean harbours. There is also a bewildering array of red algae and, especially in polluted water or where freshwater streams flow into the sea, the sea lettuce *Ulva lactua*.

Amongst the most obvious **marine animals** is the **black sea urchin** *Arbacia lixula*, which is usually common on any rocky area of shore. There are also a range of other sea urchins in deeper water, along with their relatives, brittle stars and starfish. And some of the **marine worms** are spectacular, even in quite shallow water, building calcareous tubes several inches high, pointing upwards and with the beautiful fan of the worm itself visible so long as it is not alarmed, when it will retreat convulsively into its tube.

Molluscs are abundant, including the only European species of the tropical *Conus* shells. Like many *Conus*, this one is poisonous and can sometimes be fatal; I swam around with one in my hand for some time once without realising this, but obviously picked up a good natured specimen ! The large and brightly coloured **top shells** are common, along with such Mediterranean specialities as keyhole limpets, which are small limpets with a notch on the top of the shell, abalones, and many bivalves. On the seabed, a range of **sea slugs** browse away at the algae and general detritus, including some very large sea hares *Aplysia spp*, so called because they are brown and have two tentacles which look a bits like long ears; in the Med they can grow up to 20cm or more in length.

One of the most unusual species on the seabed is the **sea cucumber**. The most common sort is usually about 25cm long, dark brown and with a slightly spiky skin. It lies around on the seabed looking like a slightly obscene sausage and, if provoked, spews its stomach out as a form of aggression (it later grows a new one). The **fish** are spectacular as well, great shoals swimming all around in the best waters and visible from any shoreline or harbourside.

From the shore

A couple of tips for the shorebound. **Lights** on the water at night attract a whole range of animals, including fish and the black sea urchins; an evening walk along the seafront at Cavtat might well reveal shoals of fish and literally dozens of urchins in the pool of light created by a harbourside street lamp. And areas where **rubbish** has been dumped in the water, which unfortunately are all too common, provide food for many scavenging creatures like the octopus and squid. You almost certainly won't spot these superbly camouflaged creatures unless they move, so be prepared to settle down for a few minutes in a likely looking spot and watch for a slow creeping or the blink of the octopus's baleful orange eye.

are suicidally crossing the road. There are many species of lizards as well, including the spectacular green lizards *Lacerta viridis* and *L. trilineata*.

The **maquis vegetation** is well worth a careful look. Throughout most of the Yugoslavian coastal area, *maquis* is the result of degradation of the original forest. Although it appears very similar to that found throughout the Mediterranean, and contains many of the same species, the Balkan *maquis* is easily recognised as a distinctive habitat. South of Cavtat there are extensive

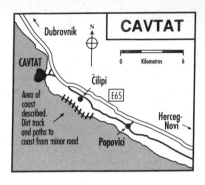

areas of scrub containing, amongst others, the strawberry tree, *Arbutus unedo*; the laurel *Laurus nobilis*; *Phillyrea latifolia*, another small evergreen shrub; the downy or white oak *Quercus pubescens*; Kermes oak *Quercus coccifera* with its spiny leaves; large stands of the prickly juniper, *Juniperus oxycedrus*; and, sounding a long way from home, the Spanish broom *Spartium junceum*. Below these a lower layer is dominated by the heather *Erica manipuliflora*, which is much taller than northern European species. Many of the bushes are heavily armed with spikes and thorns, so forcing a passage off the path isn't easy.

Neretva Valley and Hutavo Blatto

The **NERETVA VALLEY AND DELTA**, to the west of DUBROVNIK, is one of Yugoslavia's most important areas for migratory and wintering birds. Heading south past the small village of BACINA, the coast road descends into the Neretva valley taking in several small lakes connected to the sea at KARDELJEVO. These pools are flanked by reedbeds, marshland and highly productive farmland, providing ideal conditions for waterfowl; and they are relatively easily accessible from the road to birdwatchers.

The **wetlands** of the Neretva valley are too open and disturbed now to be a major bird breeding area, but they still come into their own during **migration**, when some 235 bird species have been recorded. These include rare, spectacular water birds such as the **great white egret**, the size of the familiar grey heron but pure white apart from its black bill and legs. Pygmy cormorants, something of an eastern speciality, occur too, along with spoonbills – always a thrill to see. Many wader species pass through, including ones on the westerly edge of their range such as the marsh sandpiper which breeds on the Russian steppes. Although many birds, such as the purple heron, are on their long migration to and from southern Africa, large numbers stay on over the winter. In cold weather they are joined by ducks and geese, including the rather uncommon bean goose.

There are also about 500 species of **flowering plants** recorded from the area, along with many species of lichens, mosses etc. Many of these may have disappeared under the drainage schemes, although there are still large areas of reed-swamp remaining. These are rich in small and very elusive birds such as crakes and rails; the high insect population supports many breeding warblers nesting amongst the reed stems. Prominent amongst them is the great reed warbler, with its loud and penetrating song; another vocal bird is Cetti's warbler which prefers to breed in the willow scrub that fringes the reedbeds.

Birds of prey are frequently seen over the valley and the lakes. Short-toed eagles are perhaps the commonest, easily identified by their almost pure white underparts and their habit of hovering as they search for snakes. But larger and rarer species have been seen, including both Egyptian and the much larger griffon vultures. The fish population of the lakes and marshes attracts a few white-tailed eagles, a very large and squarely built bird which feeds mostly on fish and carrion; only the adult shows the characteristic white tail.

Hutavo Blato
Not surprisingly, the area has come under intense pressure for drainage and conversion to farmland. Nowhere is this more so than **HUTAVO BLATO**, a nature reserve 5km north of the town of METKOVIĆ. Although the wetland area is only a shadow of its former self, it remains an important and exciting reserve, and well worth visiting for the spring or autumn migrations.

Sutjeska National Park

The main reason for coming to the **SUTJESKA NATIONAL PARK** is to visit the **Forest of Perucica**, one of the best known and richest virgin areas in Europe, with over 150 tree species. Perucica forms a strict nature reserve within the park itself, and attracts many visitors because of a magnificent waterfall (to be seen from a small path leading off halfway up the main reserve track).

The **trees** themselves, though, are an outstanding attraction. The forest is immensely dense and productive, and it is claimed that the best parts have over 1000 cubic metres of timber per hectare. There are 143 known deciduous species and 12 conifers, and the trees are markedly zoned with altitude, with broad leaves gradually giving way to evergreen. Amongst the most notable are the eastern beech/silver birch *Fagus orientalis/Betula pendula* community which dominates the lower slopes, the spruce *Picea excelsa*, which is found further up, and the dwarf

Hop hornbeam
Ostrya carpinifolia

mountain pine *Pinus mugo*, which extend almost to the summit. Other common trees include the manna ash *Fagus ornus* and the hop hornbeam *Ostrya carpinifolia*, which, as its name suggests, looks similar to an ordinary hornbeam but with fruits looking like hops. For enthusiasts, there are rarities including the Tartarian maple, *Acer tataricum*; *Spirea chamaedryfolia*, a rose family shrub; and *Petteria ramentacea*, a legume shrub confined to a few areas of southern Yugoslavia.

Partly because of the magnificent forest, and also because hunting has been more successfully controlled in the area, this is a good place to come and try to spot **large mammals** such as wolves, bears and chamois. This said, although they are present they're certainly not easy to see, and most visitors will remain disappointed, as we were. The **bird life** is more visible, with a wide range of finches and tits amongst the trees, as well as the occasional owl and woodpecker wherever the trees are old enough to have holes for their nest sites. **Honey buzzards** cruise overhead, their short heads and thin bills well adapted for plundering the nests of bees and wasps – they feed on the larvae rather than the honey their name suggests. They're easily distinguished from the common buzzard when overhead by their rather long tail which has two dark bands. The huge **capercaillie** stalks the forest floor; a game bird the size of a turkey, it can be disconcerting to meet one since they defend their breeding territory quite aggressively.

Mljet National Park

The National Park of **MLJET** is a wooded island sanctuary with a rich Mediterranean flora which somehow escaped the clearfelling of the mainland. The park covers the northwest end of the island, embracing the connected bays of **Veliko** and **Malo Jezero**. It's a peaceful and beautiful haven after the tumult and commercial tourist developments of the Adriatic Highway. The park – more of a managed reserve – hides several discreetly located cafés and restaurants as well as places to stay. Even if it is only for a day, Mljet is definitely worth a visit.

The **wooded areas** comprise two distinct forest communities of oak and pine. Holm oak *Quercus ilex* and manna ash *Fraxinus ornus* are common on the more shady northern slopes, and Aleppo pine *Pinus halapensis* is found throughout the island and dominates the southerly facing aspects. They now form some of the finest remaining stands in Yugoslavia. Typical Mediterranean *maquis* and *garrigue* vegetation fill in much of the remaining crags and open ground. Shrubs include the prickly juniper *Juniperus oxycedrus*, mastic tree *Pistachia lentiscus*, stawberry tree *Arbutus unedo*, and germander tree *Teucrium fruticans*. Climbing amongst them are the fragrant clematis *Clematis flammula*, honeysuckle *Lonicera implexa* and black byrony *Tamus communis*.

Several species of **butterfly** are common including the Cleopatra *Gonepteryx cleopatra* and the southern white admiral *Limenitis reducta*. **Reptiles** incluude the Turkish gecko *Hemidactylus turcicus*, the sharp-snouted rock lizard *Lacerta oxycephala*, a typical small lacertid lizard with distinctly blue underparts, and Dahl's whip snake *Coluber najadum*, a very slender non-poisonous snake with

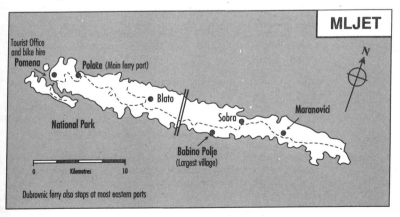

characteristic dark spots on the side of its neck. It is said that vipers were considered such a problem on Mljet (Saint Paul was apparently bitten by one when his ship went aground on his way to Rome) that a colony of mongooses were imported at the turn of the century. These have now become a pest at the expense of other animals.

The waters in and around the island are clear and marine life is plentiful. The **monk seal** used to live and breed around the island, though there have been no sightings of this rare animal for many years.

BOSNIA-HERCEGOVINA: ACCESS AND ACCOMMODATION

Cavtat

Cavtat is about 20km south of DUBROVNIK and slightly north of Dubrovnik airport; there are frequent buses. The best way down to the coast is 12km south of the town along a back road; this is easily reached by walking down one of the side roads if you catch a bus down the main route E65. Alternatively just walk along the bathing beach south of Cavtat and keep going.

Cavtat has a campsite and numerous boarding houses and hotels.

Hutavo Blato

Heading north along the SARAJEVO road from Metković, take a right turn to SUITAVA a few kilometres after DRACEVO and past the signposted turning to the reserve. You arrive at a higher level than the surrounding fenland and lake which provides a good perspective of the wetland reserve. A dyke runs at right angles to the road which can be reached across a stream. When you are parallel to the end of the dyke drop down off the road and pick up the footpath which takes you across a footbridge to the dyke. The dyke, which provides a good vantage point for bird-watching, extends the length of the eastern side of the lake.

There are only one or two hotels in METKOVIĆ and these tend to be relatively expensive. The tourist office denied knowledge of rooms, but they are probably available if you ask around. As Metković is almost entirely avoided by tourists it is an interesting place to spend an evening, especially as a large river flows through the town, supporting a wildlife of its own.

Sutjeska

The main DUBROVNIK–SARAJEVO road runs through the Sutjeska valley, passing through the western edge of the park. The most obvious centre is the village of TJENTISTE, also on this road and at the park's edge. There is also a motel at GRAB, just south of the park. Although access to the park itself is relatively easy for those without a car, it is by no means clear if you are allowed inside the forest reserve itself on foot. Drivers have to pass a checkpoint and leave a passport or driving licence, and have to be out by 7pm in the summer.

Note that for people with a car, it makes sense to visit Sutjeska in the same trip as Durmitor (see Montenegro).

Mljet

A ferry makes the round trip between TRSTENIK, a small village tucked into the side of the Peljesec Peninsula, to POLAČE, a small harbour in the park itself. Admission tickets and maps of the island are available here. There are also ferries starting from DUBROVNIK, although it is difficult to make a day trip from there – and the ferry starts back again at 4am!

CROATIA

Croatia includes both the northern coastal regions, including the cities of Split and Zadar, and the extensive inland area bordering Hungary. It has the most (and best known) National Parks in the country. Highlights include the strange **Lake Vransko**; **Paklenica National Park** on the Dalmatian coast; and the inland mountains of the **Central Velebit** range and the **Risnjak National Park**.

Lake Vransko

LAKE VRANSKO, northeast of BIOGRAD, is Croatia's largest lake; it extends for about 13km parallel to the sea to which it is connected by **underground channels**, giving the lake a brackish nature. The lake is a key fishing site with European eel, grey mullet, and sole living in the lake, and it is located on the main migratory flightpath, playing host to grey, purple, squacco and night herons, to many waders and to birds of prey.

The lake's tranquillity and rich bird life provide welcome relief from the tourist developments sprawling between ZADAR and ŠIBENIK. Unfortunately the lake is itself now the focus for new tourist developments and agriculture. The western part is almost entirely reclaimed at the expense of important breeding grounds.

Central Velebit Range

The spectacular karst **VELEBIT MOUNTAINS** provide a marked contrast to the scorched coastal plains alongside the Adriatic. Behind the coastal plain, between SENJ and KARLOBAG, lie vast tracts of almost primeval beech, pine and fir forest covering mountains up to 1700m. These have been minimally affected by human interference, and are rarely visited by tourists. The reason for both lies in the range's inaccessibility. However, for those prepared for either some trekking, or rough car hire driving, the experience well repays the effort.

A **good route** is to turn off the coast road by the garage just north of KARLOBAG, towards GOSPIĆ; this road winds up to the **Stara Vrata Pass** at 928m. A short tunnel breeches the watershed and makes the transition from coastal strip to subalpine scenery, broadleafed woodland and pine forest. The road passes through pine and beech forests onto flat meadow and pasture land. At GOSPIC head left in the direction of Otocac and Perusac. At PERUSAC, turn left in the centre of the village (if you come to the level crossing, you have gone too far); this leads to meadowland and across **Lake Kruscica**, a fertile area humming with dragonflies and birds and rich in flowers. The lake offers an opportunity for a refreshing swim; then head off for Klanac.

At KLANAC take a right turn by the church (there's a silver crucifix by the roadside) to head west, back into the mountains and deep forest. At the small hamlet of VELIKA PLANA, the metalled road ends and the forest track begins. This winds along for 25km before arriving at a rare clearing with the small lumberjack community of STIROVACA. Double back to the right and after 2km there's the choice of a rough track back down to the coast at JABLANAC, or a further 30km to the logging village of KRASNO by newly metalled roads, built, no doubt, for logging purposes. The first main building you see after leaving the forest is Kransko's bar, hotel and restaurant. It's a good place to stay, with live Croatian music most nights and a colourful mixture of loggers and occasional tourists.

In the mountains, dense beech, fir and patches of spruce forest leave little light for anything else to grow, though the area is rich in bulbous plants. The flowering season falls between February and May, and there's a wonderful and bewildering array of **crocuses** and their relatives. The tiny yellow flowers of *Sternbergia colchiflora* and the pink or white *Colchicum hungaricum* appear in spring while *Colchicum visianii* flowers in autumn. The pale lavender *Crocus dalmaticus* and the deep purple *Crocus reticulatus* both appear at lower altitudes in spring. *Crocus vernus* prefers the top of the Velebit range in deeper soils around trees. **Endemic plants** include *Campanula velebitica*, *Saxifraga velebitica*, *Aubretia croatica* and the blue columbine *Aquilegia kitaibelii*.

Paklenica National Park

PAKLENICA, surprisingly the only National Park on the Dalmatian Coast, lies at the south of the Velebit mountain range. It is easy of access from the coastal plain, but entrance is restricted to avoid over-exploitation, a situation which has preserved both the park's beauty and its diverse plant and animal life.

Approaching Paklenica, the transition from baked coastal plain and *garrigue* vegetation to **beech-clad valleys** and rocky **limestone peaks** is impressive. Climbing up through the narrow gorge entrance, whose limestone and dolomite rocks rear 400m into the air (a haunt of multi-coloured Italian and German rock climbers), you pass through woodlands of white oak *Quercus pubescens*, manna ash *Fraxinus ornus*, oriental hornbeam *Carpinus orientalis*, and finally extensive beech *Fagus sylvatica*. There are two notable bellflowers in these rocks and cliffs: *Campanula fenestrellata*, with blue goblet-shaped flowers, and *Campanula waldsteiniana*. **Endemic species** include yet another bellflower *Campanula velebitica*, along with *Saxifraga velebitica* and *Aubretia croatia*.

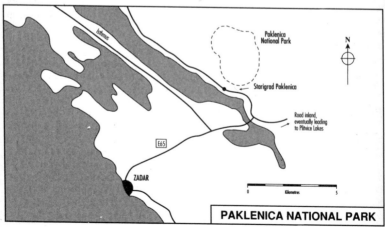

PAKLENICA NATIONAL PARK

Exposed areas of the park reveal vertical ravines, funnels and other karst features. There are many **caves**, of which MANITA PEĆ and JAMA VODARICA are the finest. The most beautiful **pine forests** are located around MOCILA.

Birds of prey are common and include golden eagle and eagle owl, a permanent community of griffon vultures (living in Mala Paklenica), and several species of falcon. The rock nuthatch, blue rock thrush, black redstart, wallcreeper and several species of warbler are all to be seen in the park. The brown bear is extremely rare, but fox, wild boar, roe deer and weasel are all relatively numerous.

Risnjak National Park

RISNJAK stands at the westerly end of the Dinaric mountains, about 30km inland from the port of RIJEKA. It's the first reserve of interest travelling south from Italy or the Istrian peninsula, and comprises mountainous country of karst limestone, with large forest areas and upland meadows. Large areas of the forest have never been exploited, and have strict nature reserve status.

From the village of CRNI LUG there is a marked forest track to MARKOV BRLOG close to Mount Rijeka. This track passes through the dominant forests of beech and fir and transitional woods of oriental hornbeam and hop hornbeam *Ostrya carpinifolia*, before finally ending up in thickets of dwarf mountain pine *Pinus mugo* and a characteristically alpine form of beech forest.

One of the most striking karst features is the 200m-deep funnel on Mount Risnjak, itself the highest peak in the park at 1528m. Known as the **Viljska Ponikva**, the funnel creates a temperature inversion which in turn gives rise to an inversion of vegetation zones. Hence there are beech forest species at the top of the funnel and higher ridges, and dwarf mountain pine on the lower slopes – a remarkable reversal of the normal zonation. Above the tree line, the **alpine pasture** has colourful and scarce plants such as the alpenrose *Rhododendron ferrugineum*, a bushy shrub with bright pink flowers, black vanilla orchid *Nigritella nigra*, the orange lily *Lilium bulbiferum* and a blue gentian *Gentiana symphyandra*. Around thirty different plant communities have been described in the park.

Highlights among the **bird species** include an extraordinary array of woodpeckers, including most of the European species, and both red-breasted and collared flycatchers; honey buzzards are a common predator. There's also a faint chance of a glimpse of the rare and local **Ural owl**, right at the southern edge of its range; almost the size of an eagle owl, it often hunts by day, feeding off animals as big as the red squirrel.

Biokovo and Mosor ranges

Betwen SPLIT and the Neretva Gorge lie the the small mountain ranges of MOSOR and BIOKOVO. They run parallel to the coast, rising sharply from the sea to 1700m, and the Adriatic Highway here clings precipitously to sheer limestone cliffs. The areas are worth exploration for their unusual vegetation and correspondingly good habitats for birds.

The cold, dry *bora*, a remorseless northeasterly wind which bears down over the mountains and onto the coastal strip, has a profound effect on the local vegetation, giving the remaining *maquis* a bizarre **Balkan** flavour. Typical Mediterranean *maquis* and *garrigue* vegetation is found in the more sheltered pockets of warmer microclimates, while hardy Balkan species survive the more exposed and rocky areas. Typical Balkan plants to be found include the blue-violet campanula-like *Edrainthus pumilo*, a dwarf version of the endemic *E. dalmaticus*. Others here for the searching are the rock cranesbill *Geranium macrorrhizum*, a local and large-flowered chickweed *Cerastium grandiflorum*, one of the mountain thymes *Thymus striatus*, and the broom *Genista radiata* with yellow flowers on almost bare green stems.

Plitvice

The **PLITVICE LAKES** form Yugoslavia's most famous National Park, visited by over a million people every year, many of them driving from Germany, Austria and Italy. The tourist industry here is highly organised with buses depositing visitors at meticulously prepared walkways and scheduled boat services setting off from various points. Nonetheless, this remains a United Nations World Heritage Site, and combines nature conservation with tourism. The main feature of the park (and the reason for all the visitors) is a series of sixteen forest lakes linked together by **waterfalls**. To explore the whole park, you will need a couple of days – one for the southern system, which starts below Lake Proscán, the highest of the lakes; the other for the quieter, northern system, where the lakes narrow up towards the Plitvice Falls.

Away from the lakes there are fine beech and fir forests, including some **virgin forest areas**, which are strictly protected, and upland **alpine meadows**. Wild boar are plentiful and there are reported to be about fifty **brown bears** present – although, as always, these are not at all easy to spot.

Krka River Nature Reserve

KRKA RIVER NATURE RESERVE is again visited mainly for its rivers and waterfalls. Filling a 75-kilometre stretch of the Krka valley are a series of lakes, lengths of deep gorge and waterfalls – the most famous site being the Skradinski Buk, a quietly impressive cascade, 500m wide, spilling through pools of languid reeds. Beyond are the less dramatic Roski Slapovi falls, at 26 metres just over half the height of the Skradinski.

Around the falls there's a fair amount of tourist development – restaurants, cafés, souvenir shops and a taxi boat service shuttling visitors upstream to the monastery island of Visovac. But this heavy tourist pressure has not ruined the valley. The reserve encompasses extensive areas of beech, holm oak and oriental hornbeam forest, preserved in a natural state, and within these forests a rich, but still largely unidentified, flora thrives. **Birds** found in the park include the Egyptian vulture and the lesser kestrel, the latter nesting colonially, often in towns. Mammals include the foxes, pine martens, polecats and otters, though the last is very rare.

CROATIA: ACCESS AND ACCOMMODATION

Lake Vransko

Heading north from BIOGRAD, leave the road between CRVNA LUKA and PAKOSTANE in the direction of VRANA. At the head of the lake, just before a small bridge and white pumping station, a rough man made promontory extends about 300m into the lake amid reed beds and marsh vegetation. Locals use this to launch fishing dinghies and it provides an ideal location for birdwatching.

The eastern edge of the lake is exclusively agricultural, though access can be gained along a rough track at the northwest end of the lake. This cuts across fertile, and in some cases private, farmland, so keep to the tracks.

Central Velebit Range

Access is not easy without a car. The route outlined is easiest approached from KARLOBAG on the coast road. KARLOBAG and GOSPIĆ have rooms and hotels.

Paklenica

The entrance to the park is just south of STARIGRAD-PAKLENICA. The road is paved from the coast, past the small village of MARASOVICI, to a car park and park entrance. There is a very small entrance fee. Once here, further access is by foot or (increasingly popular) mountain bike.

Most visitors to the park go only as far as the hostel at RAMICI-PARICI, about two hours' walk from the park entrance. The hostel is a friendly centre, run by the Paklenica Mountaineers Society; it serves good basic food.

Risnjak

The best introduction to the park is along the road to CRNI LUG, a small village on the east side of the park. By car, take the road signposted to ČABAR and GEROVO, two kilometres west of DELNICE on the main ZAGREB–RIJEKA road. Some local buses also go here – check at the main bus station in Rijeka for details.

The most southerly point of the park touches the main RIJEKA–ZAGREB road at GORENJE JELENJE. Local and national buses stop here and you can simply walk into the park along a forest track. After half an hour the track forks right to MOUNT RISNJAK (about 12km) and left to PLATAK (about 10km). Both Platak and Mount Risnjak have small hostels – the best bases for exploring. There are no detailed maps of the park but tracks are generally well signposted.

Biokovo and Mosor Ranges

Access to the ranges is difficult without a car. The valleys running parallel to the coast can be penetrated only along steep winding roads and tracks from OMIŠ, and at MAKARSKA or PODGORA. The road from Omiš is particularly spectacular.

Plitvice Lakes

The lakes are around 40km from SENJ, from which there are regular buses. These put you down at carefully numbered walkways and quays for boat trips. There are hotels and private rooms around Entrance 2 (the main entrance), plus a tourist office and bike hire. The closest campsite is *Korana*, 1km from Entrance 1.

Krka River Nature Reserve

Access is from ŠIBENIK. There is a campsite in the park, and many footpaths, which visitors are legally obliged to keep to.

SLOVENIA

Slovenia is really outside the scope of this book, being for the most part well away from the Mediterranean coast. However, the cave systems in the limestone hills are so famous (and unique) that a brief description is included below.

Postojna Caves

Going to the **POSTOJNA CAVES** is such a patent tourist trip that many self-respecting naturalists may be put off by the razzamatazz. Don't be. The caves are amongst the most amazing natural features in Yugoslavia and they have several unique species of animals as well.

There are, in fact, dozens of individual caves amidst Postojna's 27-kilometre system, but it's the 16.5-km long Postojna Cave that is the focus for visitors, who are shuttled by train along the initial sections before swooping down into the cavernous central chambers. Other nearby caves, including Pivka and Planina, are apparently less commercialised, whilst remaining spectacular.

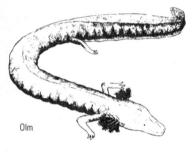

Olm

The most important focus for the naturalist is the **olm** *Proteus anguinus*, a cave dwelling amphibian which has been living at Postojna – and other cave systems along the Adriatic coast – for aeons. It lives permanently in its larval state, never maturing to become an adult and lose its external feathery gills in the way that most other amphibians do – a process of arrested development is called **neoteny**. It sometimes reaches a length of 30cm, is usually white with pink gills, and is virtually blind, since eyes aren't much use in its dark underground home. Finding wild specimens is said to be very difficult, but there are captive olms to be seen in the caves.

Other specialised cave dwellers are found in the system as well. There are several species of **crustaceans**, including some relatives of the common pond slater, *Aselius cavernicolus* and *A. carniolicus*. There is also a cave harvestman *Nelima troglodytes*, along with cave-dwelling spiders and moths. Despite the commercialisation of some areas, many of the caves have never been explored, and biologists believe that other unique life forms could come to light.

SLOVENIA: ACCESS AND ACCOMMODATION

Postojna Caves

The caves are at POSTOJNA on the main rail route between LJUBLJANA and Trieste, and Postojna is also connected by regular buses (which stop nearer the caves) from Ljubljana. They can be visited easily as a day trip from Ljubljana, though the tourist office at POSTOJNA can arrange rooms or hotels, and there's also a local campsite.

information and publications

The best initial sources of information are the Tourist Offices in most towns, found under a variety of names of which *Turist Biro* is the most common. The bigger National Parks such as Durmitor have information centres too, and a letter or visit to the Yugoslav National Tourist Office in your home country is worthwhile before you leave (UK address: 143 Regent Street, London W1; ☎071/734 5243). Most conservation groups are centrally based; one of the most active is *The Association for the Conservation of Nature in Yugoslavia* (Molerova ul. 35, Belgrade).

MAPS

Many Yugoslav maps are wildly optimistic about the state of roads, so that a red major road can sometimes be no better or worse than the most minor track, ie unmetalled and full of ruts. The roads are being improved in the inland areas, but beware of taking the map-maker's interpretation too literally! Also, many of the wetlands shown on even quite up-to-date maps are simply not there any more.

Having said that, there are a number of good maps on the market. One of the clearest is the *Roger Lascelles* map of the Yugoslavian coast. Another good buy is the ever-reliable **Kummerley and Frey**, which covers Yugoslavia in two parts at a scale of 1:500,000. Detailed **walking maps** are available for some areas, and particularly for some National Parks as indicated in the text, but coverage is incomplete.

GUIDES

Yugoslavia: The Rough Guide (Harrap Columbus, £5.95) has all the practicalities.

BOOKS

There are few specific books about Yugoslavian wildlife in English. Among wider range field guides, *The Wild Flowers of Greece and the Balkans* by Oleg Polunin is a key text; it describes many of the National Parks and other areas within Yugoslavia, as well as providing descriptions of many plants. Particularly useful are the double-page line drawings of plants likely to be found in specific habitats, which makes getting hold of the commonest species in a given area much easier.

For all other groups – birds, butterflies, amphibians and so on – consult the standard field guides listed in the general bibliography.

PART THREE

THE
CONTEXTS

HISTORICAL
FRAMEWORK

Human history is something of a footnote in wildlife terms. To look at the factors that influence the plants and animals of the Mediterranean it is necessary to start nearly a million times further back than the ancient Egyptians.

ORIGINS OF LIFE

The **earth formed** some 4600 million years ago. For almost the first half of its history it was a lifeless planet – the sea a soup of chemicals, the atmosphere thin and devoid of oxygen, the land rocky and full of volcanoes. Slowly, though, perhaps under the influence of the ultraviolet light that would have bathed the planet, and the electrical storms that filled the sky, the chemicals in the sea interacted to form more complex molecules of sugars and amino acids; these in turn combined to produce deoxyribonucleic acid (DNA).

DNA had the crucial twin abilities to carry genetic information coded in its own structure, and to replicate itself. With its appearance, life had begun – albeit in very simple forms akin to bacteria. Scientists have found bacteria-like fossils in rocks which have been dated to around 3000 million years ago.

Although things moved rather slowly for the next two billion years or so, one crucial step occurred. Some of the simple single-celled organisms developed the ability to manufacture their own food, rather than feeding on the soup of organic chemicals. This process is called **photosynthesis**, and the organisms that did it first were **algae** – the ancestors of all modern plants. One of the by-products of photosynthesis is oxygen, and so these early algae slowly began to change the atmosphere of the planet into one that could, eventually, support air-breathing life.

The oxygen also did something else – it created, high in the atmosphere, a screen called the **ozone layer** which shields the earth from harmful ultraviolet radiation. The creation of this ozone layer undoubtedly took hundreds of millions of years. (We have taken just 50 years of releasing chlorine into the atmosphere, largely from a group of aerosol propellants, chlorofluorocarbons, to produce the large hole discovered over Antarctica in 1986.)

At the same time as the algae were evolving, some of the bacteria were becoming more complex, and turning into the sort of single-celled animals, **protozoans**, that can still be found in the sea or in freshwater – *Amoeba* is the best known. The foundations of the **plant and animal kingdoms** had been laid down.

Around 1000 million years ago, the protozoans developed further by grouping themselves together into multi-celled animals; the **sponges** were the first, swiftly (on this time scale at least) followed by other marine animals such as **corals**, **sea anemones**, **jellyfish**, and the like.

Life continued to evolve in the sea for the next 500 million years, until the next great leap forward – the colonisation of the land. The first

THE TIMESCALE	
	million years ago
Formation of the planet	4600
First living things (bacteria)	3000
First complex animals (sponges)	1000
First marine vertebrates (sea squirts)	550
First land plants (mosses)	450
First land animals (millipedes)	400
First land vertebrates (amphibians)	350
First reptiles	280
First mammals	225
First birds	180
First human ancestors (*Homo erectus*)	2
First humans (*Homo sapiens*)	0.05

land plants — primitive ancestors of the mosses — started growing on the edges of the sea about 450 million years ago, and then transformed the land by clothing it in green from a variety of **mosses** and **ferns**; there were no flowers, for flowering plants were not to evolve until a mere 100 million years ago.

At the same time as the green plants were moving onto land, some of the **marine animals** were doing the same. The first seem to have been the **arthropods**, the group of jointed animals that includes modern **insects** and **crustaceans**; the ones which crawled out of the water some 400 million years ago were rather like modern woodlice, millipedes and worms — although with no competition from other animals, they grew rather larger than today's descendants. One primitive millipede grew to two metres long.

For a long time, these non-flowering plants and invertebrate animals had the land to themselves, but meantime animals in the sea were becoming ever more complex; one group, primitive **fishes**, developed a **backbone**, and the **amphibians** that came out from the water 350 million years ago are their descendants.

With the existence of both vertebrate and invertebrate life on land and in water, the stage was set for yet **further diversification**. Insects came from the invertebrate side, evolving into an extraordinary variety of species in parallel with the evolution of the plants on which they mostly feed. Reptiles, birds and mammals evolved from amphibians.

What, you may reasonably ask, has this incomprehensibly ancient history to do with the wildlife that the average visitor might see around the Med? The answer is that the wildlife of the Med, like anywhere else on the planet, is a **living testimony to evolution**. It's rather like a wall that has been painted and repainted many times, and then has been weathered; the early layers of life — sponges or scorpions, spiders and mosses — show through the later layers of birds, mammals and flowering plants. Thrushes and blackbirds — mere newcomers at less than 40 million years old — feed on snails and spiders that have been around for ten times as long. But evolution and competition between species are not the only factors that influence what animals and plants happen to be in a particular place at a particular time — **geology** and **climate** play equally important roles.

GEOLOGY

The **surface of the earth** is also like the much-painted wall mentioned in the last section; not only has it been painted over as successive layers of rock have been laid down, but it has been bent and deformed by earth movements, baked by the sun, blasted by the wind and submerged underwater at various times. The rocks and soil in any one place are like a lump of multicoloured Plasticene of different ages and mineral compositions. These underlying rocks form the parent material of the soil, and the soil type has vast influence on the type of wildlife to be seen, so some knowledge of geology helps to understand the jigsaw of ecology.

For a start, it's not as if the Med has always been the same shape or even in the same place on the planet. Pressures from deep within the earth's surface cause **continental drift**, a process that has only recently been understood and still more recently accepted. In essence, land masses are constantly and very slowly drifting over the earth's surface: apparently, the American continent is moving away from Europe at about the same rate as your fingernails grow. Some 450 million years ago, when the first plants were colonising the land, there were probably three continents, looking nothing at all like the surface of the earth today. One hundred million years ago, they were all fused into one land mass called Pangaea, which drifted apart to form the continents we know today. For a long time Africa was an island, separated from Europe and Asia by the **Tethys Sea**; about 20 million years ago it bumped into Asia, forming the land bridge which is now the Middle East, and perhaps 10 million years ago north Africa connected with Spain, forming what is now the Med as a landlocked remnant of the Tethys.

This **inland sea** must have had a wildly fluctuating water level and salinity; the hot sun would have evaporated it, rivers partially replenished it, and at various times earth movements and sea level changes would have caused the Atlantic to break through the gap at the Straits of Gibraltar to reflood it. Thick layers of salt found in the Med seabed show that at times it must have completely **dried out**; seemingly, the last time it was completely dry was just over 5 million years ago, when a movement in the earth's crust caused the **Straits of Gibraltar** to sink, and a gigantic waterfall poured across from the Atlantic. It's been a sea ever since – but of course will not remain so for ever.

All these changes in water level meant that **land bridges** occurred between different islands at different times; coincide those with the evolution of different species, and you begin to get some idea of why some species occur in one place but not another. Mobile animals like birds can colonise freely, of course, but other groups are relatively stuck in one place, marooned from close relatives as the sea level changes or continents drift apart. One Med amphibian – the **cave salamanders** – have their only living relatives in north America, a striking example of populations that became separated as the single mega-continent of Pangaea broke up and drifted apart.

Not only did the collision of the drifting continents affect the distribution of plants and animals, it also created **mountains**, folded up by the sheer pressure as Africa and Europe locked together. The **Alps** and **Pyrenees** were formed this way, and are called **new-fold mountains** because they were formed relatively recently. That's the reason they are the highest mountains around the Med – they are too young to have been substantially eroded away. (The highest mountains in the world, the Himalayas, were formed in the same way by another recent continental drift collision – when India ceased to float in the Indian Ocean and bumped into the coast of southern Asia.)

The **rocks** that surround the Med are mostly **sedimentary** – that is, rocks that have been laid down as undersea deposits during periods when the land has been underwater. These rocks are of different types depending on the parent material – sand, not surprisingly, forms **sandstone**; finer clays and silts form **mudstone**; and the most characteristic rock of the Med, **limestone**, is largely made from the finely ground-up shells of marine animals. In many places around the Med these sedimentary rocks have been exposed on cliff faces and river banks, and you can see clearly the many layers of the different deposits, bent and twisted as they have been heaved upwards by the pressure of colliding continents and other earth movements.

These **sedimentary rocks** are relatively new, laid down well within the last 100 million years. Underlying them, and in places breaking through, are older rocks, usually exposed as eroded mountain chains. Some of these are sedimentary in origin, but have been at some point buried deep in the earth's crust and therefore changed by extreme temperature and pressure to different and harder material. Called **metamorphic rocks**, and composed of marble, gneiss and schist, these are essentially the solid crystalline core of the continents. The French **Massif Central** and the **Rhodopi Mountains** (which form the Greece–Bulgaria border) are two examples of old metamorphic rock exposures.

Finally, **igneous rocks** break through in some places; these rocks, such as basalt and granite, have been formed deep within the earth's crust and either subsequently uplifted – **granite**, or exuded from volcanoes – **basalt**. Each rock type has a different mineral composition, and this means that it will break up on the surface to produce a different soil type – leading to different plants and animals.

The **soil** is thin around much of the Med, a product of erosion caused by steep hillsides and by deforestation. Only in the **river valleys and deltas** are there deep rich deposits of soil – and most of these have now been taken over for intensive agriculture, as in the Po Valley of Italy, the Medjerda of Tunisia or the Rhône Delta in France. Most of the **wildlife refuges**, therefore, are away from the fertile land and on the thinner soils of the hillsides and mountains, which are less intensively cultivated and so are richer in animals and plants.

CLIMATE

The Mediterranean climate, with its hot dry summers and cool damp winters, is an extremely unusual one, duplicated only in other subtropical zones on the west of continental landmasses. (The only places with a similar climate are southwest Australia, California, the Cape of Good Hope and a small patch of central western Chile.) The Med is easily the most extensive of these areas, owing its climate to the existence of the sea itself; without the sea, the Med climatic zone would be restricted to the southwestern coasts of the Iberian peninsula.

Three main winds have a profound effect on the Med climate. **Atlantic moist winds** come from the west, usually in the winter months in the familiar pattern of a series of depressions, bringing rain wherever they are intercepted by high mountains such as the Atlas of north Africa or the Pyrenees. Understandably, therefore, the western end of the Med is much wetter than the eastern end, with Gibraltar experiencing twice the annual rainfall of Athens. The Sahara, with its almost permanent high pressure system, dominates the south, creating **warm Saharan winds**, at their most extreme in north Africa. The third important influence is the central European landmass, which becomes very cold in winter. **Northerly cold winds** start from this region in winter and spring, called by different local names of which the French *mistral* is the best known. This wind can make for surprisingly chilly days even as late as May, and limits the northern extension of some Mediterranean plant species. However, as the European landmass hots up over summer and autumn, northerly winds become warmer; the *meltemi* of Greece and Turkey feels almost as warm as the Saharan winds.

Coastal countries, in general, have less extreme summer and winter temperatures than landlocked countries at the centre of continents. This is because the sea is constantly circulating and maintaining a fairly even temperature, whereas the land has no mechanism for transferring heat from hot areas to cold areas. Therefore, the eastern end of the Med, being more landlocked, has hotter summers and cooler winters than the western end. Athens, for instance, has an average January temperature of 9.3°C and an average August one of 27.5°C, a difference of 18.2°C. The comparable figures for the Algarve in southern Portugal are 12°C and 24°C, a difference of only 12°C. Since every plant has its own particular tolerances of heat and cold, these differences have a big effect on plant growth and distribution, and hence on the occurrence of the animals that feed on them.

The **climatic history** of the Med, of course, has varied widely from desert to sub-Arctic conditions. Before the continents took up their present positions, they drifted around the surface of the planet, experiencing all sorts of weather; to make matters even more complex, the poles of the earth have been constantly changing as well, leading to long-term changes in sunshine levels, and the sun itself goes through shorter term changes in activity. More recently, well after the final flooding of the Med and the establishment of the sea as we know it, the planet went through a period of global cooling – the **Ice Ages**.

The Ice Ages began some 300,000 years ago and ended (or at least temporarily ceased) only 10,000 years ago. Although the great ice sheets that extended from the north only reached southern England and central Germany, there were local icecaps in the Alps and the Pyrenees, sending glaciers grinding out over Spain, France and northern Italy. The fact that the south of Spain and Greece were not covered by ice is a major reason for the extreme richness and variety of flowering plants found there. Another effect of the ice was to take up water from the oceans, thereby reducing the sea level. It seems that land bridges appeared at the height of the Ice Age between Corsica and Sardinia, Majorca and Minorca, and other islands too – for the last time, animals were able to cross and intermingle, colonising new areas and perhaps wiping out competing species.

All of these climatic changes happened **very slowly**, allowing animals to adapt, retreat or expand their ranges. The planet seems now to be in a slow period of global cooling, but in the last fifty years effects of **human impact** have become evident for the first time – and on a potentially dramatic scale. The legacy of the industrial revolution was the availability of fossil fuels for power consumption, and burning them releases carbon dioxide into the atmosphere. Carbon dioxide allows sunlight to pass through it, but is impervious to the longer wave infrared light which is reflected back from the earth's surface; this heat is therefore trapped within the atmosphere – the **greenhouse effect** – and most scientists agree that a global warming of between 1°C and 3°C is likely by the end of the next century.

This may not seem much, but it is likely to cause great changes, not least a rise in sea levels as ice from the polar icecaps melts. Many of today's beaches may be some way underwater within a couple of generations, along with the coastal marshes of the

Camargue and the Coto Doñana – and most of Venice. A general rise in temperature could also mean changes in land use and agriculture, along with plant distribution, animal populations and bird migration routes. But nothing is certain. There is even a chance that a large scale global warming could cause ocean currents to reverse their flow. If the Gulf stream reversed, then it might mean that the Med would become colder rather than warmer. Human influences on the Med, therefore, will be profound in future just as they have been profound in the past.

HUMAN INFLUENCE

Exactly when humans became **recognisably human** is a matter of some debate, and every time a new fossil find is made, things change around and new theories come into vogue. The popular idea of a nice straight linear chain leading from the apes to modern humans is likely to be illfounded – the picture is probably much more complicated, with different human ancestors living side by side for long periods; perhaps crossbreeding was as important as genetic mutation in the human evolutionary process. It seems – at present, at least – that the founder of the human family *Hominidae* was a species called *Australopithecus*, which split off from the great apes between 5 and 15 million years ago. From this evolved the first "modern man" *Homo erectus*, probably in Africa around two million years ago.

Homo erectus was a successful animal, living in caves and feeding by hunting animals and gathering wild plants, and spread from Africa through to much of the planet; fossilised remains have been found in Java, China and central Europe. It seems certain that a million years ago, primitive – **Neanderthal** – people like *Homo erectus* were living on the shores of the Med. It appears that they had a sophisticated culture. Mostly living in caves, they used fire, made complex stone tools, ritually buried their dead, and lived off the food of the forest in a harmonious and sustainable way; possibly they worshipped the cave bear, to judge by the number of bear skulls found in their caves.

Towards the end of the Ice Ages, around 30,000 years ago, the Neanderthalers disappeared from the fossil record, and their place was taken by our own species, **Homo sapiens**. Quite how the transfer of dominance from

one species to the other took place is unknown – perhaps the Neanderthalers were wiped out by disease, or unable to adapt to the warming climate (they had, after all, been living on the edge of the ice for the last 250,000 years), or perhaps the newcomers were more successful and simply killed them off or interbred with them and assimilated them.

With the arrival of *Homo sapiens*, human beings were well and truly established around the Med, and their caves and paintings are particularly concentrated in southern France and northern Spain. They lived a life similar to the Neanderthalers throughout the early Stone Age – the **Palaeolithic** – and through to the late Stone Age or Neolithic, but with one important difference. Perhaps because of the development of language and communication, they were more successful – and they became more **effective hunters**.

Whereas the Neanderthalers walked lightly on the earth, Palaeolithic and Neolithic peoples were at least partially responsible for the extinction of a range of species that disappeared at the end of the last glaciation – **cave bears**, **great elks**, **cave lions** and so on. Some of these animals, it is true, had evolved to live in cold climates and were perhaps unable to adapt to the new warmth – but some were doubtless further reduced by hunting pressure. Human impact on the environment had begun to be noticeable.

Despite this, the people in the caves around the Med 10,000 years ago were still basically hunter-gatherers, scarcely modifying the habitats in which they lived. At the same time, in the eastern Med, a hugely important step was taking place – the development of **settled agriculture** through the twin discoveries of arable crops and domestic animals. Food supply became instantly more reliable, and longevity and the birth survival rate both seem to have leapt, leading to dramatic population increase. People no longer needed to live in small groups, each with a large hunting territory which could sustainably support them – **towns** were for the first time a possibility. The earliest towns, at places like Jericho, Uruk in Syria or Catal Hoyuk in Turkey, were all founded just less than 10,000 years ago. The last of them, between Konya and Antalya in southern Turkey, is reputed to be the oldest known, dated at 7500 BC. All these towns would have been in extremely fertile land, for although the climate may have been broadly similar then to now, the ice had only recently retreated from northern Europe, and the Middle East would have been a far greener and more forested place than it is today.

In fact, the whole of the Med basin would have been a green and fertile land. Most of it was **forest** – **cedar** in north Africa and southern Spain, **pines** and **evergreen oaks** elsewhere. Neolithic people spread out from the early towns to found civilisations in Egypt, Crete, Greece and Italy – and these set about destroying the green Eden at a rate and on a scale unprecedented in the planet's history. The marks left by the Neanderthals were few – some tantalising bones in caves; even the cave-dwellers of France and Spain only left us a legacy of bones and some beautiful cave paintings. But the Neolithic people and early civilisation left much more – pyramids, temples and literature to show how advanced they had become in building and writing, and hectares of **desert and degraded scrub** to show how efficient they had become at habitat destruction. It's a gloomy and depressing picture, and although much of the Med forests were destroyed by the time of Christ, one that has not changed much since. What David Attenborough rightly calls the "relics of Eden" are still under threat, as modern technology enables us to change the remotest parts of the Med basin.

The changing **religions** of the Med also illustrate this growth in human domination. Early religions mostly worshipped Nature in one form or another – the ancient Egyptians, for instance, worshipped the earth goddess Nut and the sun god Ra above all others, and Minoans worshipped the bull. Even in those religions, however, an inherent belief in human superiority can be seen, a belief that came into full and explicit flowering in the Hebrew Old Testament. The **creation myth** of the Book of Genesis, accepted as common ground by both Christians and Muslims, the two dominant religions of the Med for the last 2000 years, gives full licence to the **exploitation of the environment** that we live in:

"And God blessed them, and God said unto them, Be fruitful, and multiply, and replenish the earth, and subdue it: and have dominion over the fish of the sea, and over the fowl of the air, and over every living thing that moveth over the earth."

Genesis I.28

This mandate has been followed to the letter. Population has vastly increased, and the earth has been "subdued" over the last few thousand years – a mere blink in the history of life – to the extent that almost every habitat around the Med shows the scars of **human interference**. Voices have always been raised against habitat destruction; as long ago as 500 BC, Plato, in a passage from the *Critias*, was complaining of soil erosion on the hills of Attica because of deforestation. The deserts of north Africa, the badlands of southern Spain, the scrubby hillsides of *maquis* and *garrigue* that surround the Med – all were once forests, rich in wildlife, holding and protecting the underlying soil from erosion by wind and rain.

There is, however, a wonderful thing amidst this depressing story – a rich and exciting wildlife still flourishes despite everything that we can fling at it. Of course, it is fragile and threatened; of course there are places where pollution, modern agriculture or insensitive building have effectively driven out all but the most adaptable species; but nonetheless it is there to seen and marvelled at. This book aims to describe it, explain it, and highlight where it can best be seen, in the hope that the destruction of the past 10,000 years can be checked or even reversed.

WILDLIFE ISSUES

The Mediterranean and its widlife is under threat on a variety of fronts – from pollution, deforestation, draining of wetlands, hunting and trapping, even smuggling of its flora. Below, representatives of various campaigning organisations for the region outline the problems – and possible solutions.

POLLUTION: GREENPEACE OBJECTIVES IN THE MED

Xavier Pastor of Greenpeace, Spain, explains the organisation's concerns over pollution in the Mediterranean.

Since 1986, the defence of the Mediterranean, one of the world's most threatened marine ecosystems, has been one of the most ambitious campaigns tackled by Greenpeace. The motivation behind this campaign is a conviction that the situation is not yet irreversible and that technical and scientific progress can provide Mediterranean societies and governments with solutions which will help them put a stop to the growing deterioration of this sea and ultimately reverse the process. It is possible to restore the quality of the water, and it is equally possible to bring the exploitation of its rural resources and fish stocks back to reasonable, sustainable levels.

Through the campaign, Greenpeace also wishes to help safeguard the survival of rare species – such as the monk seal, sea turtles and Mediterranean cetaceans. We are trying to conserve the last fragments of coastline in their natural state, and we insist that it is imperative to eliminate any type of nuclear threat from this traditionally conflict-prone area.

A PROGRESSIVE PHENOMENON

For thousands of years, Mediterranean peoples have used the seas off their towns and cities to discharge waste water and even, on occasion, their refuse. Until midway through this century, the impact of this effluent seemed to be absorbed by the Mediterranean without undue problems. Until that time, the population was small compared to present levels. The major migrations from inland areas towards the coasts had not yet taken place and the tourist centres were yet to be developed. No big industrial and petrochemical plants had yet been built, and the waste produced consisted basically of degradable organic products of natural origin.

Over the past forty years, the situation has changed radically. Today, 350 million people living in countries bordering the Mediterranean discharge waste produced by their urban and industrial activities directly into the sea, the rivers that flow into it or the aquifers from which drinking water then has to be obtained. They are joined every year by 100 million tourists who increase the pressure on the ecosystem in a multiplicity of ways.

It is not just the number of people discharging waste that has changed. The rise in standard of living and consumption in Mediterranean countries, and changes in lifestyles have also led to a spectacular increase in the volume of waste water per inhabitant. The quality of the effluent is also different. Together with natural and biodegradable products, growing amounts of synthetic, toxic, bioaccumulative and persistent compounds are discharged today, against which living organisms lack adequate defences and for which they do not have adequate elimination mechanisms.

Today, according to data collected by the United Nations Environment Programme (*UNEP*) through its Mediterranean Action Plan (*MAP*), 85 percent of urban effluent is discharged directly into the sea without any previous treatment. The presence of pathogenic microorganisms can cause hepatitis, cholera and paratyphoid infections among bathers and consumers of shellfish and other seafoods. At the same time, two million tonnes of crude oil are discharged into the Mediterranean by tankers in the course of the loading, unloading and tank-cleaning operations.

From the coast and through rivers, 120,000 tonnes of mineral oils, 12,000 tonnes of phenols, 60,000 tonnes of detergents, 100 tonnes of mercury, 3,800 tonnes of lead and 3,600 tonnes of phosphorus as well as other environmentally harmful substances enter the Mediterranean every year.

SOLUTIONS WITHIN OUR GRASP

This situation is not inevitable. The treatment of urban effluent has been highly perfected and suitable methods exist for any size of community. Purification plants for medium-sized and large towns can ensure 100 percent purification of domestic effluent. If the sewage network is kept separate from industrial discharges, this water can be reused for agricultural or urban irrigation or to restore salt-laden aquifers. For small communities, there are biological purification techniques using lagoon systems and other methods. Adequate undersea outlets, properly maintained and discharging at a suitable distance from the coast and at a sufficient depth may be an acceptable system for communities of several thousands of inhabitants.

Due recognition must be given to the efforts being made by some Mediterranean states to purify their urban effluent. In some cases the quality of the water has begun to improve – purely from this point of view – in the last few years. Nevertheless, it will take at least a decade before the plans are sufficiently advanced and operational to produce a clearly noticeable effect. Such progress is coming up against obstacles which will have to be overcome. Along with the usual problems of maintaining purification plants, it is vital to ensure that their design is not immediately overtaken by the scale of the requirements. At the same time, the population explosion taking place in the countries of North Africa and the Eastern Mediterranean may mean that any progress made in some parts of the Mediterranean will be dramatically overshadowed by a drastic worsening in areas which, until today, were not among the worst affected. Only international aid to the countries in this critical state and an adequate policy of population control in the developing countries can prevent this situation from slipping irrevocably out of control.

The situation of industrial waste has taken a parallel course. In the 50s, 60s and 70s, a series of multinational or national industrial and petrochemical plants sprang up along the Mediterranean coastline, taking advantage of low labour costs, the need for development in the countries around its shores and the virtual absence of environmental protection legislation. These have had a tremendous impact on both the coastal environment and the living organisms which have accumulated halogenated organic compounds and heavy metals.

In this case too, there are viable and realistic solutions which depend solely on the willingness of governments to force companies to remedy the damage they have done to the collective environment. There are manufacturing processes which eliminate or drastically reduce the production of toxic wastes and which should be adopted as standard. For the proportion of waste which cannot be totally eliminated, purification or closed circuit recycling processes should be set up to reduce discharges into the sea or rivers to nil.

OILS AND PESTICIDES

The problem of oil discharge into the sea has been alleviated to some extent with the growing application of the Marpol International Convention for the Prevention of Pollution from Ships. Crude oil slicks and pitch balls are still very common in the Mediterranean, but there has been a reduction over the past few years. Nevertheless, there is still a long way to go before all Mediterranean ports possess the mandatory ballast-water reception facility in proper working order and all ships sailing this sea comply strictly with the rules which prohibit or strictly control discharges.

Every year tens of thousands of tonnes of pesticides are carried into the Mediterranean by overflowing rivers. Products such as DDT, whose manufacture, sale and use are prohibited in many countries, continue to be used in many parts of this region. The progress of biological methods for prevention of infestation, and the study and use of alternative pesticides with lesser ecological impact, are imperative if we are not to arrive at extreme situations in which bioaccumulation threatens the viability of animal and plant populations and jeopardises human health.

OVER-FISHING

Many of the Mediterranean's natural resources are being severely overexploited. The case of fish stocks is a classic example. The sea has traditionally been a source of food and economic activity for the inhabitants of the countries around it. However, in the past three decades, the situation has changed from one of balanced and sustainable exploitation in most cases to one of very serious depletion of many of the stocks. This has obviously been a result of a heavy increase in fishing activity and the fact that breaches of the legislation which attempts to regulate the exploitation of fishing grounds have gone unpunished.

The wooden vessels which tourists still see in a romantic light as small traditional fishing boats have been equipped for several years now with powerful engines and equipment, efficient echolocation and depth scanning apparatus and extremely unselective nets. The oversized fleets of most Mediterranean countries perpetrate all manner of abusive fishing practices: they fish far above legal depths, use nets with non-regulation mesh and catch fish much too small to enable the exploited populations to be maintained at a sustainable level. The use of dynamite for fishing is common practice in some countries. Moreover, a growing number of "sports" vessels use professional fishing techniques, and divers using compressed air cylinders capture all kinds of crustaceans, molluscs and regular size fish to be found at depths of less than 50m.

Furthermore, it is not only Mediterranean fishermen who work this sea. Recently, the crew of the Greenpeace vessel "Sirius" discovered a fleet of a dozen or so large Japanese fishing boats operating with flags of convenience in international waters to catch spawning tunny during their annual migration to their breeding grounds around the Balearic Islands.

All these factors are compounded by increased pollution on the coastal fringe and destruction of the vital banks of seagrass (*Posidonia oceania*). The depletion of fish stocks – and of corallines, which are suffering a similar fate – has been at a worrying level for several years now. The fleets continue to operate simply because tourist demand for fish enables prices in the markets and restaurants to rise indefinitely as catches diminish. For some years, most of the fish consumed by people living in Mediterranean countries has had to be imported from Atlantic fisheries.

Fish biologists have been recommending solutions to overexploitation for many years. The establishment of – and compliance with – controls on fishing which will allow stocks to recover before it is too late would make possible a return to sustained maximum catches, greatly to the benefit of all concerned – fishermen and the ecosystem alike. All that is required is, yet again, political will and the proper establishment of supervisory and disciplinary services at sea, in markets and in the restaurant trade.

DESTRUCTION OF HABITATS AND EXTINCTION OF RARE SPECIES

Once the coasts of Spain, France and Italy became covered with concrete in the form of hotels, urban development and marinas, the eyes of the tourist industry turned towards other areas such as Greece, Turkey, Yugoslavia and North Africa, which had not yet suffered such assaults.

Apart from the serious aesthetic, environmental and sociological damage caused by this phenomenon, massive use of the shore for industrial or tourist purposes is robbing the Mediterranean of the last surviving representatives of species which lived in this sea for thousands of years before man, and, in only a few decades, placed them in serious danger of extinction.

For instance, monk seals and sea turtles no longer have suitable habitats in which to live and reproduce and are being driven out from their last refuges in Greece and Turkey in spite of a few recent, timid efforts by the governments of those countries. While their habitats are being destroyed, seals, turtles and dolphins also fall victim to fishermen who capture them either deliberately or accidentally.

In spite of innumerable promises, and although a growing number of governmental and non-governmental organisations are concerning themselves with the seals, turtles and marine mammals of the Mediterranean, their numbers are falling as a result of incompetence and a lack of determination on the part of the authorities in many countries. The only hope for the survival of these creatures is the establishment of strictly managed nature reserves in their few remaining refuges – the economic cost involved being borne internationally – and the effective imposition of severe penalties for anyone harming these species or their habitats.

THE NUCLEAR THREAT

The Mediterranean lives in the shadow of the nuclear menace, through the presence of seventy nuclear power stations on the coasts and besides the rivers of the states around its shores, and constant manoeuvres in this strife-prone sea by four of the world's five nuclear-armed fleets. The USA and the USSR between them have over five hundred nuclear warheads permanently installed in ships sailing the Mediterranean, many of them also propelled by atomic reactors which are much less safe than the power stations built on land.

The Mediterranean states can and must replace their nuclear power stations and promote the production of electricity by a variety of traditional and alternative nonpolluting methods using renewable resources. By leaving the Mediterranean, the nuclear fleets can help to make it a true sea of peace, a less polluted place where the harmonious coexistence of man and nature is a positive reality.

Further details/UK membership: Greenpeace, 30–31 Islington Green, London N1 8XE.

MIGRATORY BIRDS: STOP THE MASSACRE

Dorothy Bashford outlines the plight of migratory birds in the Med under threat from trapping and hunting.

Imagine a September Sunday afternoon in the Mediterranean holiday island of Malta. There are not many trees to be found on the rocky landscape, but the large wooded area of Buskett Gardens should provide a welcome roosting place for birds of prey on their migration south to Africa for the winter. Buskett is, after all, a bird "sanctuary", protected by law for the benefit of birdlife. However, there are hunters strolling around in the woods, carrying guns. They will ensure that no bird that attempts to rest there will leave to continue its journey in the morning. The honey buzzards, kestrels and marsh harriers will have been blasted out of the sky as they attempted to find a safe roosting-place.

Let us now look at Cyprus – perhaps things will be better there. It is early morning and all seems to be peaceful. There is no volley of gunfire to be heard, but nevertheless, hunters have been here, too. In the bushes on the hillside they have hidden many long sticks covered in a sticky glue called bird-lime. Unsuspecting birds, like robins and blackcaps, alight on the twigs and are held fast, and no amount of frenzied fluttering will free them. It may be several hours before the trapper returns to collect them.

These are just two examples of what is happening to our birds in the Mediterranean region. Every year literally *hundreds of millions* of birds are killed. The reason is mainly for fun.

The methods vary; mist-nets are used in Cyprus and Italy, and the numbers of wings and feet left dangling in the nets tells how carefully the birds are removed; in Portugal, spring-traps on the ground, baited with tethered flying ants, catch robins by the legs, and caged decoy-birds which sing to attract flocks of finches are used for clap-netting in Malta, France and Spain. Indiscriminate killing methods like these are illegal in countries which belong to the EC, but enforcement of the law is almost non-existent.

What is being done to counteract these massive threats to birds? The International Council for Bird Preservation has long recognised the need for international cooperation to work on the problem, and has set up a special Migratory Birds Programme to deal with it. This Programme is supported in turn by fund-raising committees in several northern European countries. "Stop the Massacre" is the slogan used by the British committee whose task is to publicise the problem and raise money for projects.

The RSPCA is a founder member of the British committee, which is also supported by the Anglo-Italian Society for the Protection of Animals, the Fauna and Flora Preservation Society, the Greek Animal Welfare Fund, the International Fund for Animal Welfare, the People's Trust for Endangered Species, the Royal Society for the Protection of Birds, the Society for the Protection of Animals in North Africa, the World Society for the Protection of Animals and the World Wide Fund for Nature.

Representatives from all these organisations meet about twice a year to allocate funds that have been raised. There is so much that needs to be done, but in recent years some outstanding successes have been realised. In France, for example, the French Bird Protection

Society (LPO) asked for help in mounting a campaign against the illegal shooting of turtle doves in southwest France. Following a major demonstration in the region in 1985, the Ministry of the Environment declared spring shooting illegal. Since then, hunters have been prosecuted and fined, and there has been a noticeable decrease in their numbers. However, the number of turtle doves migrating through the region has also dropped, and the LPO will continue its work in the area and also start action to prevent similar large scale shooting by French hunters in Morocco.

In autumn 1987, the Cyprus Anti-Liming Committee asked for our help to print and deliver postcards, bearing a message of protest against bird-liming, to the President of Cyprus and the High Commissioner in London. These cards were also distributed to conservationists and bird protection societies in Europe, and many thousands of cards were posted, leaving the Cyprus Government in no doubt as to the strength of feeling on this issue. Earlier this year, the Cyprus Government took a great step forward in ratifying the Berne Convention on the conservation of European Wildlife and Natural Habitats, but subsequently moved several steps back by opening a spring shooting season. The situation must be carefully watched.

The Malta Ornithological Society (MOS) celebrated its 25th anniversary in 1987. Over the years, the Fund has supported several projects to help this Society, whose membership has now risen to nearly 1000 (600 of whom form the very active MOS-Youth). The Society has so far been entirely run by volunteers but is just about to employ its first full-time paid member of staff. Recognising the vital role this person will play in the growth of the activities of MOS, the Stop the Massacre Fund is to make a substantial contribution. The MOS has many imaginative educational projects in operation and has just opened an education centre. We know that our support for them will be a wonderful investment in the future of bird protection in Malta.

Further information: Dorothy Bashford (Secretary), Stop the Massacre Campaign, c/o The Lodge, Sandy, Bedfordshire SG19 2DL.

THE BLACK MARKET FOR FLOWERS

Sara Oldfield looks at the trade in plants and bulbs – from Turkey in particular – which fill north European nurseries at the expense of decline or possibly even extinction at home.

Smuggling and black markets may seem a far cry from local garden centres or specialist plant nurseries, but there is increasing evidence of widespread illegal trade in rare and protected plants. Smuggling, in the majority of cases, may be too strong a term – as there has been little need for concealment or espionage to obtain legally protected plants or sale in this country. The situation is now changing, however, as more countries adhere to trade control and genuine efforts are made by horticulturalists to propagate rare species.

The list of wild plants which still occur commonly in trade is surprising. Exotic orchids, of course, conjure up visions of intrepid explorers searching for the elusive rarity worth thousands of pounds, and the lure of the exotic certainly prevails, with wild, tropical orchids of the genera *Cattleya*, *Paphiopedilum* and *Vanda* dug up for trade and imported into Britain. But most of the large, colourful orchid blooms on sale in Britain are hybrids, which are routinely produced by nurseries throughout the world. This trade in relatively humble European orchids, such as the lady's slipper, is of equal concern to the exotics – and it is quite unnecessary, as propagation techniques exist to satisfy the demand.

Cacti are often described as the poor man's orchids, and they, too, have been uprooted for trade around the world. Nowadays, as with orchids, most varieties are produced in bulk from seed and cuttings, but, nevertheless, it remains cheaper to dig up the rare and slow growing species which some determined enthusiasts desire. This also applies to many of the succulents which occur naturally in the Old and New World; species of *Euphorbia*, *Aloe*, *Haworthia*, *Pachypodium* and *Agave* are just a few which are eagerly sought by collectors.

Garden bulbs have a much wider market than either orhids or succulent plants, and here the scale of the trade in wild plants is staggering. Not all the species involved are rare or threatened with extinction but when species such as the snowdrop *Galanthus elwesii* are dug up by the million in Turkey there must be concern about the long term effects. Approximately forty million bulbs of the genus *Galanthus* were exported from Turkey in 1984. Other wild bulbs in trade include anemone, eranthis, muscari, scilla and miniature species of narcissus. And the list does not end there. Insectivorous plants, water plants, alpines, bromeliads, cycads and ferns are all subject to varying degrees of exploitation for trade.

With the horticultural trade so well established in Britain and the development of sophisticated propagation techniques, one might well ask why there is a need to import wild plants at all? It is, of course, economics, rather than any concern for conservation, which usually dictates the species chosen for mass production. Also, there is with some collectors an unexplained desire for the "genuine" article. Fortunately, some nurseries are motivated by conservation as well as profit and realise that quality, home-grown plants in the long run make better sense.

Legislation governing the import and export of wild plants has been in force in Britain for ten years. The Endangered Species Act of 1976 is the means by which Britain has implemented the Convention on International Trade in Endangered Species of Wild Fauna and Flora (*CITES*). The plants which are covered by the Convention are those which are internationally recognised as threatened by trade. All orchids, cacti and cyclamen are covered, together with a list of other species which is amended as more information becomes available. There is no doubt that protection should be extended to cover a wider range of bulbs in order to halt their decline in the wild.

Over ninety countries have now ratified *CITES*. Under provisions of the Convention, countries are required to license imports and exports of a wide range of species which are commercially exploited in the wild; these are listed in the appendices to the Convention. Trade in wild, collected specimens of certain endangered species is therefore practically banned altogether. In practice, enforcement of the controls for plants has been weak throughout the world as efforts have generally been concentrated on controlling the animal trade. Numerous ploys have been used to evade the plant controls, most commonly by claiming that wild plants have been nursery-raised from seeds or cuttings. More importantly, certain key countries in the rare plant trade have remained outside the Convention altogether.

In the Mediterranean, Turkey is one such country yet to sign *CITES*. Until recently, it exported millions of cyclamen tubers of rare and common species alike. Despite a number of seizures of major consignments by customs, Britain appeared powerless to stem the flow, primarily because of the involvement of the Netherlands – a major centre of the international plant trade. Dug up in Turkey, most of the tubers, along with wild bulbs of anemone, scilla, eranthis and galanthus, were then planted out to overwinter in the Dutch bulb fields; those that survived were re-exported to Britain the following year. The Netherlands had no conservation controls on trade in rare plants until it was obliged to enforce the EC *CITES* regulations. In response to this, Turkey agreed to stop exports of its endemic cyclamens. As yet, Turkey's other rare bulbs have no protection. Now that the Netherlands is having to regulate its international trade in plants, the extent of illegal imports is becoming clearer. Consignments of foreign species are checked before they enter the Dutch auction system or go on sale in specialist nurseries. There have been several prosecutions of nurseries – most for illegal import of orchid and cyclamen species.

The time, however, has come for nurseries to be questioned about the origins of their plants, and for them to adopt a more positive approach to conservation. And perhaps most important of all, the level of consumers' awareness needs to be raised. If readers are tempted to buy any plants labelled "rare, new into the country", do check whether they have been imported legally. Also, please refrain from buying any European orchids. With the range of seed of rare plants now available, and a more enlightened nursery trade, there is no excuse for the commercial collection of rare plants and no excuse for buying them.

Reprinted with permission from "Natural World", the RSNC magazine.

BOOKS

To identify everything you come across around the Med would require a battery of reference books. But most of the basic field guides are fairly small, and the addition of one or two can usefully supplement the very general information in this book. This list is of guides that cover more than one country; books on individual countries have been covered in the country chapters.

FIELD GUIDES

A good field guide should be portable, well illustrated, and honest about how comprehensive it is. Collins have virtually cornered the market, except on plants and birds; their books are always reliable and easy to use; treat most others with caution.

BIRDS

Bruun, Svensson and Delu *The Hamlyn Guide to the Birds of Britain and Europe* (Hamlyn, £19.95). This re-issue of one of the most reliable field guides includes three cassettes of birdsong, making it good value, especially for novice birders. A knowledge of what birds sound like is just as useful in identification as what they look like.

John Gooders *Field Guide to the Birds of Britain and Europe* (Kingfisher, £10.95). A relatively weighty but very comprehensive field guide, excluding Turkey and north Africa, but beautifully illustrated; each species has its own page. Excellent for the backpack or the car – possibly less use in the pocket.

Heinzel, Fitter and Parslow *The Birds of Britain and Europe with North Africa and the Middle East* (Collins, £7.95). The only field guide to cover the entire Med region – and one of the best standard works.

Christopher Perrins *Collins New Generation Guide to the Birds of Britain and Europe* (Collins, £6.95). Doesn't cover north Africa or Turkey, and the pictures are too small; its advantage is that it includes a great deal of useful stuff on bird ecology.

Peterson, Mountfort and Hollom *A Field Guide to the Birds of Britain and Europe* (Collins, £9.95). The original bird guide, published in 1954. Peterson's drawings are still outstanding, and the text good – though harder to use than other guides with the text opposite the pictures.

PLANTS

Oleg Polunin and Anthony Huxley *Flowers of the Mediterranean* (OUP, £9.95). The only book to cope with the flowers of the whole region; invariably selective, it has good photographs, is easily portable, and is by far the best general introduction to the Med flora.

Oleg Polunin *Flowers of Greece and the Balkans* (OUP, £12.95), and **Oleg Polunin and Brian Smythies** *Flowers of Southwest Europe* (OUP, £9.95). Both of these books are heavier than the previous one (in every sense), but have thankfully been recently published in paperback. They're both brilliant, but not for beginners; the first covers Greece and Yugoslavia, as well as countries further east, and the second covers the Iberian peninsula and southwest France.

Christopher Grey-Wilson and Marjorie Blamey *The Alpine flowers of Britain and Europe* (Collins, £6.95). Small, portable and excellent, but only covers the central and western Med, with nothing east of the Velebit mountains of Yugoslavia or south of Rome.

Paul and Jenne Davies and Anthony Huxley *Wild Orchids of Britain and Europe* (Chatto & Windus, £9.95). Marvellous for orchid freaks, covering Europe and the eastern Med round to Israel, though not north Africa. The best book on these fascinating plants.

INSECTS

Michael Chinery *Collins Guide to the Insects of Britain and Western Europe* (Collins, £7.95). One of the few readable and portable introductions to insects, this guide is the best there is. It actually excludes most of the Med, though this doesn't really matter since for most groups identification down to species is unlikely. Don't confuse this guide with Chinery's earlier book *Insects of Britain and Northern Europe* (Collins £9.95), which is more of a textbook and has less coverage of the Med.

Lionel Higgins and Norman Riley *A Field Guide to the Butterflies of Britain and Europe* (Collins, £8.95). The standard field guide, reliable and beautifully illustrated, but perhaps too detailed for casual naturalists. Chinery's book (above) includes enough about butterflies for identification down to genus.

REPTILES AND AMPHIBIANS

Arnold, Burton and Ovenden *A Field Guide to the Reptiles and Amphibians of Britain and Europe* (Collins, £8.95). The only good field guide, though it excludes Turkey and north Africa.

MAMMALS

Corbet and Ovenden *The Mammals of Britain and Europe* (Collins, £7.95). Again, the only good field guide, though it excludes Turkey and north Africa. For the latter, you're stuck with **Theodor Haltenorth and Helmut Diller** *A Field Guide to the Mammals of Africa* (Collins, £9.95), of which the vast majority naturally refers to species found south of the Sahara.

MARINE

A.C. Campbell *The Hamlyn Guide to the Flora and Fauna of the Mediterranean sea* (Hamlyn/ Country Life). Sadly, this has been out of print for the last few years – it's the only good field guide to the underwater life of the Med.

OTHER BOOKS

David Attenborough *The First Eden* (Collins/ BBC, £6.99). An excellent history of the Med, concentrating more on human impact on wild-

life and habitats than on the wildlife itself. Very worthwhile background.

John Gooders *Where to Watch Birds in Britain and Europe* (Christopher Helm, £9.95). A classic sourcebook for dedicated birders, listing sites throughout Europe, including Turkey and north Africa. High on species, low on ecology.

Michael Shepherd *Ornitholidays Guides.* (Available from *Ornitholidays*, 1–3 Victoria Drive, Bognor Regis, Sussex.) A series of booklets, primarily about birds and covering selected areas, published by one of the leading bird tour companies. Med titles include the Camargue, northern Turkey, northern Greece, southern Spain, Majorca and southern Morocco.

Jean Henri Fabre Almost anything by the great French entomologist of the last century makes good background reading.

REPORTS

Foreign Birdwatching Reports and Information Service. A brilliant scheme, run by Steve Whitehouse (5 Stenway Close, Blasckpole, Worcester WR4 PXL; ☎0905 54541). Amateur birdwatchers send in reports of their foreign trips, which are then available for a nominal sum to everyone. Invaluable for serious birders – write off for a catalogue.

BUYING BOOKS AND MAPS

Most booksellers stock field guides. If you have problems, *The Natural History Book Service* (2 Wills Road, Totnes, Devon; ☎0803 865913) has a comprehensive, efficient **mail order service**, and produces a mouthwatering catalogue.

For **maps**, *Stanfords* (12 Long Acre, London WC2; ☎071/836 1321) and *Robertson McCarta* (122 Kings Cross Road, London WC1; ☎071/278 8278) are two long-established mail order and specialist shops. I have been impressed by the speed and friendliness of the mail order service run by *The Map Shop* (15 High St, Upton-on-Severn, Worcs; ☎06846 3146).

SCIENTIFIC NAMES

BIRDS

Accentor, Alpine	*Prunella collaris*
Avocet	*Recurvirostra avosetta*
Babbler, fulvous	*Turdoides squamiceps*
Bee-eater	*Merops apiaster*
blue cheeked	*Merops superciliosus*
Bittern	*Botaurus stellaris*
little	*Ixobrychus minutus*
Blackbird	*Turdus merula*
Blackcap	*Sylvia atricapilla*
Bluethroat	*Luscinia svecica*
Bulbul, common	*Pycnototus barbatus*
Bunting, black-headed	*Emberiza melanocephela*
cinereous	*Emberiza cineracea*
cirl	*Emberiza cirlus*
corn	*Emberiza calandra*
Cretzschmar's	*Emberiza caesia*
house	*Emberiza striolata*
ortolan	*Emberiza hortulana*
reed	*Emberiza schoeniclus*
rock	*Emberiza cia*
Bush chat, rufous	*Cercotrichas galactotes*
Bustard, Arabian	*Ardeotis arabs*
great	*Otis tarda*
Houbara	*Chalmydotis undulata*
little	*Otis tetrax*
Buzzard	*Buteo buteo*
honey	*Pernis apivorus*
long-legged	*Buteo rufinus*
Capercaillie	*Tetrao urogallus*
Chaffinch	*Fringilla coelebs*
Chiffchaff	*Phylloscopus collybita*
Chough	*Pyrrhocorax pyrrhocorax*
Alpine	*Pyrrhocorax graculus*
Chukar	*Alectoris chukar*
Coot	*Fulica atra*
crested	*Fulica cristata*
Cormorant	*Phalacrocorax carbo*
pygmy	*Phalacrocorax pygmeus*
Courser, cream-coloured	*Cursorius cursor*
Crake, Baillon's	*Porzana pusilla*
little	*Porzana parva*
Crane	*Grus grus*
Crossbill	*Loxia curvirostra*
Crow, carrion/hooded	*Corvus corone*
Cuckoo	*Clamator canorus*
great spotted	*Clamator glandarius*
Curlew	*Numenius arquata*
slender-billed	*Numenius tenuirostris*
stone	*Burhinus oedicnemus*
Dipper	*Cinclus cinclus*
Diver, red-throated	*Gavia stellata*
Dove, collared	*Streptopelia decaocto*
palm	*Streptopelia senegalensis*
rock	*Columba livia*
turtle	*Streptopelia turtur*
Duck, ferruginous	*Aythya nyroca*
tufted	*Aythya fuligula*
white-headed	*Oxyura leucocephala*
Dunlin	*Calidris alpina*
Eagle, Bonelli's	*Hieraeatus fasciatus*
booted	*Hieraeatus pennatus*
golden	*Aquila chrysaetos*
imperial	*Aquila heliaca*
lesser spotted	*Aquila pomarina*
short-toed	*Circaetus gallicus*
spotted	*Aquila clanga*
white-tailed	*Haliaeatus albicilla*
Egret, cattle	*Bubulcus ibis*
little	*Egretta garzetta*
Falcon, Barbary	*Falco peregrinoides*
Eleonora's	*Falco eleonorae*
lanner	*Falco biarnicus*
red footed	*Falco vespertinus*
peregrine	*Falco peregrinus*
Finch, citril	*Serinus citrinella*
crimson-winged	*Rhodopechys sanguinea*
snow	*Montifringilla nivalis*
trumpeter	*Rhodopechys githaginea*
Firecrest	*Regulus ignicapillus*
Flamingo	*Phoenicopterus ruber*
Flycatcher, pied	*Ficedula hypoleuca*
spotted	*Muscicapa striata*
Gadwall	*Anas strepera*
Gallinule, purple	*Porphyrio porphyrio*
Gannet	*Sula bassana*
Garganey	*Anas querquedula*
Godwit, bar-tailed	*Limosa lapponica*
black-tailed	*Limosa limosa*
Goldcrest	*Regulus regulus*
Goose, bean	*Anser fabalis*
greylag	*Anser anser*
red-breasted	*Branta ruficollis*
white-fronted	*Anser albifrons*
Goshawk	*Accipiter gentilis*
Grebe, black-necked	*Podiceps nigricollis*
great-crested	*Podiceps cristatus*
little	*Tachybaptus ruficollis*

Greenshank	*Tringa nebularia*	Mallard	*Anas platyrhynchos*
Grouse, black	*Tetrao tetrix*	Martin, crag	*Hirundo rupestris*
Guillemot	*Uria aalge*	sand	*Riparia riparia*
Gull, Audouin's	*Larus audouinii*	Merganser, red-	*Mergus serrator*
black-headed	*Larus ridibundus*	breasted	
common	*Larus canus*	Moorhen	*Gallinula chloropsis*
herring	*Larus argentatus*		
lesser black-backed	*Larus fuscus*	Nightingale	*Luscinia megarhynchos*
Mediterranean	*Larus melanocephalus*	Nightjar	*Caprimulgus europaeus*
Sabine's	*Larus sabini*	Egyptian	*Caprimulgus aegyptius*
slender-billed	*Larus genei*	red-necked	*Caprimulgus ruficollis*
		Nutcracker	*Nucifraga*
Harrier, hen	*Circus cyaneus*		*caryocatactes*
marsh	*Circus aeruginosus*	Nuthatch, Algerian	*Sitta ledanti*
Montagu's	*Circus pygargus*	Corsican	*Sitta whiteheadi*
Hawfinch	*Coccothraustes*	Kruper's	*Sitta kruperi*
	coccothraustes	rock	*Sitta neumayer*
Hedgesparrow	*Prunella modularis*		
Hemipode, Andalusian	*Turnix sylvatica*	Oriole, golden	*Oriolus oriolus*
Heron, great white	*Egretta alba*	Osprey	*Pandion haliaetus*
grey	*Ardea cinerea*	Ostrich	*Struthio camelus*
night	*Nycticorax nycticorax*	Owl, African marsh	*Asio capensis*
purple	*Ardea purpurea*	barn	*Tyto alba*
squacco	*Ardeola ralloides*	eagle	*Bubo bubo*
Hobby	*Falco subbuteo*	little	*Athene noctua*
Hoopoe	*Upapa epops*	Scops	*Otus scops*
		short-eared	*Asio flammeus*
Ibis, bald	*Geronticus eremita*	tawny	*Strix aluco*
glossy	*Plegadis falcinellus*	Ural	*Strix uralensis*
Jay	*Garrulus garrulus*	Partridge, Barbary	*Alectoris barbara*
		red-legged	*Alectoris rufa*
Kestrel	*Falco tinnunculus*	Pelican, Dalmatian	*Pelecanus crispus*
lesser	*Falco naumanni*	white	*Pelecanus onocrotalus*
Kingfisher	*Alcedo atthis*	Petrel, Leach's	*Oceanodroma*
pied	*Ceryle rudis*		*leucorrhoa*
Smyrna	*Halcyon smyrnensis*	Madeiran	*Oceanodroma castro*
Kite, black	*Milvus migrans*	storm	*Hydrobates pelagicus*
black-shouldered	*Elanus caeruleus*	Wilson's	*Oceanites oceanicus*
red	*Milvus milvus*	Pheasant	*Phasianus colchicus*
		Pigeon, wood	*Columba palumbus*
Lammergeir	*Gypaetus barbatus*	Pintail	*Anas acuta*
Lapwing	*Vanellus vanellus*	Pipit, tawny	*Anthus campestris*
Lark, bar-tailed desert	*Ammomanes cincturus*	Plover, golden	*Pluvialis apricaria*
calandra	*Melanocorypha*	grey	*Pluvialis squatarola*
	calandra	Kentish	*Charadrius alexandrinus*
crested	*Galerida cristata*	little ringed	*Charadrius dubius*
hoopoe	*Alaemon alaudipes*	ringed	*Charadrius hiaticula*
shore	*Eremophila alpestris*	sociable	*Vanellus gregarius*
short-toed	*Calandrella cinerea*	spur-winged	*Vanellus spinosus*
sky	*Alauda arvensis*	Pochard	*Aythya ferina*
Temminck's horned	*Eremophila bilopha*	red-crested	*Netta rufina*
Thekla	*Galerida theklae*	Pratincole, collared	*Glareola pratincola*
thick-billed	*Rhamphocorys clot-bey*	Ptarmigan	*Lagopus mutus*
Linnet	*Acanthis cannabina*		
		Quail	*Coturnix coturnix*
Magpie, azure-winged	*Cyanopica cyanus*		

Rail, water	*Rallus aquaticus*	white	*Ciconia ciconia*
Raven	*Corvus corax*	Swallow	*Hirundo rustica*
brown-necked	*Corvus ruficollis*	red-rumped	*Hirundo daurica*
Redshank	*Tringa totanus*	Swan, mute	*Cygnus olor*
spotted	*Tringa erythropus*	whooper	*Cygnus cygnus*
Redstart	*Phoenicurus phoenicurus*	Swift	*Apus apus*
black	*Phoenicurus ochruros*	Alpine	*Apus melba*
Moussier's	*Phoenicurus erythrogaster*	little	*Apus affinis*
Roller	*Coracius garrulus*	pallid	*Apus pallidus*
Ruff	*Philomachus pugnax*		
		Teal	*Anas crecca*
Sandgrouse, black-bellied	*Pterocles orientalis*	marbled	*Anas angustirostris*
		Tern, black	*Chlidonias niger*
pin-tailed	*Pterocles alchata*	Caspian	*Sterna caspia*
spotted	*Pterocles senegallus*	common	*Sterna hirundo*
Sandpiper, broad-billed	*Limicola falcinellus*	gull-billed	*Gelochelidon nilotica*
		little	*Sterna albifrons*
common	*Tringa hypoleucos*	Sandwich	*Sterna sandvicensis*
green	*Tringa ochropus*	whiskered	*Chlidonias hybrida*
marsh	*Tringa stagnatalis*	white-winged black	*Chlidonias leucopterus*
Terek	*Tringa cinereus*	Thrush, blue rock	*Monticola solitarius*
Serin	*Serinus serinus*	rock	*Monticola saxatilis*
red-fronted	*Serinus pusillus*	song	*Turdus philomelos*
Shag	*Phalocrocorax aristotelis*	Tit, bearded	*Panurus biarmicus*
Shearwater, Cory's	*Calonectris diomedea*	blue	*Parus caeruleus*
Manx	*Puffinus puffinus*	coal	*Parus ater*
sooty	*Puffinus griseus*	crested	*Parus cristatus*
Shelduck	*Tadorna tadorna*	great	*Parus major*
ruddy	*Tadorna ferruginea*	penduline	*Remiz pendulinus*
Shoveler	*Anas clypeata*	sombre	*Parus lugubris*
Shrike, black-headed	*Tchagra senegala*	Treecreeper	*Certhia familiaris*
bush		short-toed	*Certhis brachydactyla*
great grey	*Lanius excubitor*	Turnstone	*Arenaria interpres*
lesser grey	*Lanius minor*		
masked	*Lanius nubicus*	Vulture, black	*Aegypius monachus*
red-backed	*Lanius collurio*	Egyptian	*Neophron percnopterus*
woodchat	*Lanius senator*	griffon	*Gyps fulvus*
Siskin	*Carduelis spinus*		
Skua, Arctic	*Stercorarius parasiticus*	Wagtail, grey	*Motacilla cinerea*
Snipe	*Gallinago gallinago*	white	*Motacilla alba*
Sparrow, desert	*Passer simplex*	yellow	*Motacilla flava*
house	*Passer domesticus*	Wallcreeper	*Tichodroma muraria*
rock	*Petronia petronia*	Warbler, Bonelli's	*Phylloscopus bonelli*
Spanish	*Passer hispaniolensis*	Cetti's	*Cettia cetti*
Sparrowhawk	*Accipiter nisus*	Dartford	*Sylvia undata*
Levant	*Accipiter brevipes*	desert	*Sylvia nana*
Spoonbill	*Platalea leucorodia*	fan-tailed	*Cisticola juncidis*
Starling	*Sturnus vulgaris*	graceful	*Prinia gracilis*
spotless	*Sturnus unicolor*	great reed	*Acrocephalus arundinaceus*
Stilt, black-winged	*Himantopus himantopus*	Marmara's	*Sylvia sarda*
Stint, little	*Calidris minuta*	melodious	*Hippolais polyglotta*
Temminck's	*Calidris temminckii*	moustached	*Acrocephalus melanopogon*
Stonechat	*Saxicola torquata*		
Stork, black	*Ciconia nigra*	olivaceous	*Hippolais pallida*

olive tree	*Hippolais olivetorum*	Isabelline	*Oenanthe isabellina*
Orphean	*Sylvia hortensis*	mourning	*Oenanthe lugens*
reed	*Acrocephalus scirpaceus*	red-rumped	*Oenanthe moesta*
Ruppell's	*Sylvia ruppelli*	Whinchat	*Saxicola rubetra*
Sardinian	*Sylvia melanocephala*	Whitethroat	*Sylvia communis*
Savi's	*Locustella luscinioides*	lesser	*Sylvia curruca*
sedge	*Acrocephalus schoenobaenus*	Wigeon	*Anas penelope*
spectacled	*Sylvia conspicillata*	Woodcock	*Scolopax rusticola*
subalpine	*Sylvia cantillans*	Woodlark	*Lullula arborea*
Tristram's	*Sylvia deserticola*	Woodpecker, black	*Dryocopus martius*
willow	*Phylloscopus trochilus*	great spotted	*Dendrocopos major*
Waxbill	*Estrilda astrild*	green	*Picus viridis*
Wheatear	*Oenanthe oenanthe*	lesser spotted	*Dendrocopos minor*
black	*Oenanthe leucura*	white-backed	*Dendrocopos leucotos*
black-eared	*Oenanthe hispanica*	Wren	*Troglodytes troglodytes*
Finsch's	*Oenanthe finschii*	Wryneck	*Jynx torquilla*

MAMMALS

Addax	*Addax nasomaculatus*	Lynx	*Felilynx*
Ape, Barbary	*Macaca sylvanus*	Marmot, Alpine	*Marmota marmota*
		Marten, beech	*Martes foina*
Badger	*Meles meles*	pine	*Martes martes*
Bat, Egyptian fruit	*Rousettus aegyptiacus*	Mink, American	*Mustela vison*
Bear, brown	*Ursus arctos*	Mole	*Talpa europaea*
Beaver, Canadian	*Castor fiber*	Roman	*Talpa romana*
European	*Castor candensis*	Mongoose, Egyptian	*Herpestes ichneumon*
Boar, wild	*Sus scrofa*	Mouflon	*Ovis musimon*
Buffalo, water	*Bubalus bubalis*		
		Otter	*Lutra lutra*
Cat, wild	*Felis sylvestris*	Oryx	*Oryx gazella*
Chamois	*Rupicapra rupicapra*		
		Polecat	*Mustela putorius*
Deer, fallow	*Cervus dama*	Porcupine, crested	*Hystrix cristata*
red	*Cervus elaphus*	Porpoise	*Phocoena phocoena*
roe	*Capreolus capreolus*		
Desman, Pyrenean	*Galemys pyrenaicus*	Rabbit	*Oryctolagus cuniculus*
Dolphin, bottlenosed	*Tursiops truncatus*		
common	*Delphinus delphi*	Seal, monk	*Monachus monachus*
Dormouse, fat	*Glis glis*	Shrew, pygmy	*Suncus etruscus*
		white-toothed	
Fox, fennec	*Fennecus zerda*	water	*Neomys fodiens*
red	*Vulpes vulpes*	Squirrel, red	*Sciurus vulgaris*
		ground	*Atlantoxerus getulus*
Gazelle, Edmi	*Gazella gazella*	Stoat	*Mustela erminea*
Genet	*Genetta genetta*	Suslik, European	*Spermophilus citellus*
Goat, wild	*Capra aegagrus*		
Gundi	*Ctenodactylus gundi*	Vole, snow	*Microtus nivalis*
		water	*Arvicola sapidus*
Hare, brown	*Lepus canensis*		
Hedgehog, desert	*Erinaceus algirus*	Weasel	*Mustela nivalis*
eastern	*Erinaceus concolor*	Whale, fin	*Balaenoptera physalis*
western	*Erinaceus europaeus*	minke	*Balaenoptera*
			acutorostrata
Ibex, Alpine	*Capra ibex*	sperm	*Physeter catodon*
Spanish	*Capra pyrenaica*	Wolf	*Canis lupus*
Jackal, common	*Canis aureus*		

PLACE INDEX

ITALY

MOROCCO